Marketing Research Essentials

Eighth Edition

Marketing Research Essentials

Eighth Edition

Carl McDaniel, Jr.
University of Texas
at Arlington

Roger Gates
DSS Research

WILEY

VICE PRESIDENT & EXECUTIVE PUBLISHER	George Hoffman
SENIOR ACQUISITIONS EDITOR	Franny Kelly
PROJECT EDITOR	Brian Baker
EDITORIAL ASSISTANT	Melissa Solarz
ASSOCIATE DIRECTOR OF MARKETING	Amy Scholz
MARKETING MANAGER	Kelly Simmons
SENIOR MARKETING ASSISTANT	Ashley Tomeck
DESIGN DIRECTOR	Harry Nolan
SENIOR DESIGNER	Madelyn Lesure
SENIOR PRODUCTION EDITOR	Sujin Hong
PRODUCTION MANAGEMENT SERVICES	Furino Production
SENIOR PHOTO EDITOR	Sheena Goldstein
SENIOR PRODUCT DESIGNER	Allison Morris
COVER PHOTOS	*Globe:* © Angela Waye/iStockphoto
	Title Panel: © Shirley Kaiser/iStockphoto

This book was set in Adobe Garamond by MPS Limited, and printed and bound by RRD Von Hoffmann. The cover was printed by RRD Von Hoffmann.

This book is printed on acid free paper. ∞

Founded in 1807, John Wiley & Sons, Inc. has been a valued source of knowledge and understanding for more than 200 years, helping people around the world meet their needs and fulfill their aspirations. Our company is built on a foundation of principles that include reposibility to the communities we serve and where we live and work. In 2008, we launched a Corporate Citizenship Initiative, a global effort to address the environment, social, economic, and ethical challenges we face in our business. Among the issues we are addressing are carbon impact, papter specifications and procurement, ethical conduct within our business and among our vendors, and community and charitable support. For more information, please visit our website: www.wiley.com/go/citizenship.

ISBN: 978-1-118-24932-1

Printed in the United States of America

10 9 8 7 6 5 4 3 2

CONTENTS IN BRIEF

CONTENTS

PREFACE

Welcome to Our World of Marketing Research

Our worldview is that of marketing research. We are here every day not as observers but as participants. Roger Gates, one of our coauthors, is president of DSS Research, one of America's largest healthcare marketing research firms. You can learn more at *www.dssresearch.com*. Carl McDaniel was a cofounder of a marketing research company that is vibrant today. He also was a cofounder of the master of science in marketing research program at the University of Texas at Arlington. Along with Roger Gates and several others, Carl created the MSMR Advisory Board. The advisory board consists of leaders and shakers in the marketing research industry. You are holding the only text written by marketing research insiders. We are not spectators viewing marketing research from afar. That would be like writing about football while witnessing the game from the stands rather than as a player on the field. Unlike authors of other research texts, we are on the field. **Welcome to the real world of marketing research**.

As a Global Leading Marketing Research Text, We Practice What We Preach

Marketing research is a managerial tool used to better understand customers, potential customers, and the marketplace. To stay on top, we must deliver a text that meets ever-changing needs. Recently, John Wiley & Sons commissioned a virtual focus group that helped us more efficiently plan this 8th edition. We are grateful to The Grandview Group for conducting the research and to the following participants for their excellent feedback: Joseph Ballenger (Stephen F. Austin State University), Joseph Cangelosi (University of Central Arkansas), Curt Dommeyer (California State University, Northridge), MaxwellHsu (University of Wisconsin), Bill Johnson (Nova Southeastern University), Ben Ong (California State University, Fullerton), Carolyn Predmore (Manhattan College), and Kabir Sen (Lamar University). Their suggestions have made this market-leading textbook even better.

What's New? Cutting–Edge Trends and Methodology in Every Chapter

We have learned through our research that chapter-opening vignettes are not necessary. They have been dropped from this edition. We also learned that you find our real end-of-chapter cases useful and interesting to read, so we have updated them and added a new, real-world case in each chapter.

New Content by Chapter

Chapter 1—"The Role of Marketing Research in Management Decision Making" New section on social media and user-generated content. New discussion of basic research. New examples throughout.

Chapter 2—"Problem Definition, Exploratory Research, and the Research Process" New box titled, "Where Do I Send the RFP?" New examples throughout.

Chapter 3—"Secondary Data and Databases"
Major new sections on behavioral targeting and the privacy battle.

Chapter 4—"Qualitative Research"
New discussion of the client's role in focus group research. New section on focus group trends. New material on focus group participants.

Chapter 5—"Traditional Survey Research"
New discussion on predictive dialing. New material on cell phone interviewing.

Chapter 6—"Online Marketing Research"
Updated online statistics. Updated and added sources of secondary data online. New material on researchers' use of blogs. New material on online individual depth interviewing.

Chapter 7—"Primary Data Collection: Observation"
Greatly expanded material on ethnographic research. Discussion on ethnography and focus groups. New material on mystery shopping. New discussion on observation using an MRI. New material on eye tracking. New section on gender- and age-recognition systems. Update on people meters. New section on the Symphony IRI Consumer Network. Major new discussion on Internet tracking. New discussion on Internet scraping. New section on comScore.

Chapter 8—"Primary Data Collection: Experimentation and Test Markets"
New box titled "Data Use: The Insidious Top-box and Its Effect on Measuring Line Share." New discussion of test marketing. New box titled "Quick Scans of Product-Specific Test Markets."

Chapter 9—"The Concept of Measurement and Attitude Scales"
New examples througout. New material on the measurement process.

Chapter 10—"Questionnaire Design"
New box titled "It's All about the Objectives." New section on laddering. New material on probing. New material on interview instructions. New section on using Facebook as a survey research platform.

Chapter 11—"Basic Sampling Issues"

New material on address-based sampling. New examples throughout.

Chapter 12—"Sample Size Determination"

New material on sample size and sample size tables. New discussion on sample size in qualitative research.

Chapter 13—"Data Processing, Data Analysis, and Statistical Testing"

New material on interview validation. New discussion on data analysis software.

Chapter 14—"More Powerful Statistical Methods"

New material on explaining correction results.

Chapter 15—"Communicating Results and Managing Marketing Research."

New box titled, "Lost in Translation: Challenges Researchers Face in Communicating Their Results to Clients." New box titled, "Doing High-Quality Work—On Time." New material on challenges researchers face in communicating their results to clients. New material on presentations on the Internet.

Outstanding Resources for All Teaching Needs

Classroom-Tested Instructor's Manual

We have done everything possible to facilitate your teaching marketing research with a comprehensive instructor's manual. Each chapter contains the following:

- *Suggested lesson plans.* Suggestions are given on how to decide the chapter material, based on the frequency and duration of your class period.
- *Chapter scan.* A quick synopsis highlights the core material in each chapter.
- *Learning objectives.* The list of learning objectives found in the test is repeated here.
- *General chapter outline.* The main headers provide a quick snapshot of all the content areas within the chapter.
- *List of key terms.* The key terms introduced to the students in the text are repeated here.
- *Detailed chapter outline.* This outline fleshes out the general outline given previously. It also indicates where ancillary materials fit into the discussion: PowerPoint slides, exhibits from the text, learning objectives, and review questions. Boxed features are also included in this outline.
- *Summary explaining learning objectives.* An explanation of how the learning objectives are satisfied by chapter material is the basis of the Instructor's Manual summary.
- *Answers to pedagogy.* Suggested answers and approaches to the critical thinking questions, the Internet activities, the cases, the cross-functional questions, and the ethical dilemmas are offered at the end of each chapter or part.

Instructors can access the electronic files on the Instructor Companion Site.

Comprehensive PowerPoint Package

We have created a comprehensive, fully interactive PowerPoint presentation with roughly 400 slides in the package. You can tailor your visual presentation to include the material you choose to cover in class. This PowerPoint presentation gives you the ability to completely integrate your classroom lecture with a powerful visual statement of chapter material. Keep students engaged and stimulate classroom discussion! The entire collection of slides is available for download from our Web site.

Classroom-Tested Comprehensive Test Bank

Our test bank is comprehensive and thoroughly classroom tested. The questions range from definitions of key terms to basic problem-solving questions to creative-thinking problems. This new and improved test bank includes approximately 60 questions per chapter, consisting of multiple-choice, true/false, and essay questions. Regardless of the type and level of knowledge you wish to test, we have the right questions for your students. A computerized version of this newly created test bank is also available on the book's companion Web site so that you can customize your quizzes and exams. Instructions can access the electronic files on the Instructor's Companion Site.

Focus Group Video and Lecture Launches

Additional *Real Research* is offered through a focus group video conducted by another one of our research partners, Jerry Thomas, president of Decision Analyst (*www.decisionanalyst.com*). Decision Analyst, Incorporated is a large international marketing research firm. The focus group subject is an online dating data case. We also offer several interviews featuring Jerry Thomas and author Carl McDaniel, discussing key topics in marketing research. For more information on this 45-minute video, available on DVD, please contact your local Wiley representative.

New Marketing Research Video Series

Brand new interview-style video clips of top marketing research companies. Each video, six to eight minutes in length, presents interviews with key personnel to discuss how they apply the major concepts of marketing research to their business. The Wiley Marketing Research Video Series can be accessed on the Student and Instructor's Companion sites.

Acknowledgments

This book could not have been written and published without the generous expert assistance of many people. A big thanks goes to Pam Rimer for typing Carl McDaniel's portion of the manuscript and to Jan Schneider for all the assistance she provided to Roger Gates on this edition.

Our deepest gratitude goes to the team at John Wiley & Sons for continuing the trend of excellence established by this text. Thank you to Franny Kelly (Senior Acquisitions Editor), Brian Baker (Project Editor), and Melissa Solarz (Editorial Assistant).

The Role of Marketing Research in Management Decision Making

CHAPTER 1

LEARNING OBJECTIVES

→ **1.** To review the marketing concept and the marketing mix.

→ **2.** To comprehend the marketing environment within which managers must make decisions.

→ **3.** To define marketing research.

→ **4.** To understand the importance of marketing research in shaping marketing decisions.

→ **5.** To learn when marketing research should and should not be conducted.

→ **6.** To learn how the Internet is changing marketing research.

→ **7.** To understand the history of marketing research.

Welcome to the fascinating world of marketing research! How does marketing research help managers reach their goals? How did the field of marketing research evolve? We will explore these topic in this chapter.

The Nature of Marketing

> **→ marketing**
> The process of planning and executing the conception, pricing, promotion, and distribution of ideas, goods, and services to create exchanges that satisfy individual and organizational objectives.

Marketing is the activity, set of institutions, and processes for creating, communicating, delivering, and exchanging offerings that have value for customers, clients, partners, and society at large.[1] Good customer relationships often result in exchanges; that is, a good or service is exchanged for money. The potential for exchange exists when there are at least two parties and each has something of potential value to the other. When the two parties can communicate and deliver the desired goods or services, exchange can take place. How do marketing managers attempt to stimulate exchange? They follow the "right" principle. They attempt to get the right goods or services to the right people at the right place at the right time at the right price, using the right promotion techniques. The "right" principle describes how marketing managers control the many factors that ultimately determine marketing success. To make the "right" decisions, management must have timely decision-making information. Marketing research is a primary channel for providing that information.

The Marketing Concept

> **→ marketing concept**
> A business philosophy based on consumer orientation, goal orientation, and systems orientation.

To efficiently accomplish their goals, firms today have adopted the **marketing concept**, which requires (1) a consumer orientation, (2) a goal orientation, and (3) a systems orientation. A **consumer orientation** means that firms strive to identify the people (or firms) most likely to buy their product (the target market) and to produce a good or offer a service that will meet the needs of target customers most effectively in the face of competition. The second tenet of the marketing concept is **goal orientation**; that is, a firm must be consumer-oriented only to the extent that it also accomplishes corporate goals. The goals of profit-making firms usually center on financial criteria, such as a 15 percent return on investment.

> **→ consumer orientation**
> The identification of and focus on the people or firms most likely to buy a product and the production of a good or service that will meet their needs most effectively.

The third component of the marketing concept is a **systems orientation**. A system is an organized whole—or a group of diverse units that form an integrated whole—functioning or operating in unison. It is one thing for a firm to say it is consumer oriented and another actually to *be* consumer oriented. First, systems must be established to find out what consumers want and to identify market opportunities. As you will see later, identifying target market needs and finding market opportunities are the tasks of marketing research. Next, this information must be fed back to the firm. Without feedback from the marketplace, a firm is not truly consumer oriented.

> **→ goal orientation**
> A focus on the accomplishment of corporate goals; a limit set on consumer orientation.

The Opportunistic Nature of Marketing Research

> **→ systems orientation**
> The creation of systems to monitor the external environment and deliver the desired marketing mix to the target market.

Marketing research is an excellent tool for discovering opportunities in the marketplace. Marketing research recently discovered that when it comes to selecting cosmetics, consumers look for brands they trust and brands that make makeup—both buying it and applying it—natural and easy. Seventy percent of the respondents claim that they use makeup. They favor Cover Girl over any other brand. Out of 60 cosmetic brands, Cover Girl was cited by 14 percent as their favorite, placing it on top. Clinique was second on the list, with 10 percent of the mentions, and Maybelline (L'Oreal) and Mary Kay tied for third, with 8 percent each.

When the consumers were asked what they loved most about their favorite makeup line, they chose brand trust over all the other factors; the actual product attributes mattered much less. More than two-thirds said they love their makeup because they trust the brand, while only one-third cited loving it "because it feels wonderful." Factors like "uses humane testing/is environmentally safe" were not weighted strongly and emerged toward the bottom of the list.

Cover Girl led the other brands in most of the attributes consumers care about most, scoring highest in categories such as great value, brand trust, wears well throughout the day, and easy, no-mess application.

A common sentiment that emerged in the survey is that makeup wearers want a natural and authentic look rather than something ultramodern.

Among those still buying new products, tween girls (ages 8–12) have upped their product usage, while teens (ages 13–17) and young women (18–24) reported declines in their usage of beauty products.

Significantly more influential to tweens than TV and even their friends, these girls say that they "look to their parents and siblings to see what they are using to help decide what to buy and use."[2]

So marketing research has identified the market leaders, determined why specific brands are popular, learned the "look" that makeup wearers are seeking, ascertained which market segments for new products are growing and which are in decline, and, for the growth segment (tweens), who influences their purchase decisions. Insights such as these will help a cosmetic marketing manager create a more powerful and effective marketing mix.

External Marketing Environment

Over time, the **marketing mix** must be altered because of changes in the environment in which consumers and businesses exist, work, compete, and make purchasing decisions. Some new consumers and businesses will become part of the target market, while others will drop out of the market; those who remain may have different tastes, needs, incomes, lifestyles, and purchase habits than the original target consumers.

> **marketing mix**
> The unique blend of product/service, pricing, promotion, and distribution strategies designed to meet the needs of a specific target market.

Although managers can control the marketing mix, they cannot control elements in the external environment that continually mold and reshape the target market. Unless management understands the external environment, the firm cannot intelligently plan its future, and organizations are often unaware of the forces that influence their future.

Marketing research is a key means for understanding the environment. Knowledge of the environment helps a firm not only to alter its present marketing mix, but also to identify new opportunities. For example, when Ann Arbor, Michigan–based Domino's Pizza introduced its pizza delivery in Japan, a major change in Japanese consumers' behavior was needed as well. Domino's managed to rise to the challenge successfully. If Domino's had merely tested the acceptability of the service it delivered in other parts of the world, it never would have entered Japan. Japanese consumers typically don't eat tomato-based food, and Asians tend to have allergies to milk products. Home delivery was not widely accepted, housewives were reluctant to give up cooking, houses were small, and finding customers in the labyrinthine streets of Tokyo seemed impossible. A market for pizza didn't exist, nor was there any sign of hope for creating one.

Instead of trying to sell its existing product and service to the market, Domino's used its marketing research about customers to design a new product and service offering for Japan. It introduced toppings such as fish and sushi. To sustain its 30-minute delivery, Domino's developed a complex address database and small scooters to navigate the narrow streets in Tokyo. Through this research process, this pizza-delivery service that no one asked for became a big hit in Japan.[3]

Marketing Research and Decision Making

Marketing research plays two key roles in the marketing system. First, as part of the marketing intelligence feedback process, marketing research provides decision makers with data on the effectiveness of the current marketing mix and offers insights into necessary changes. Second, marketing research is the primary tool for exploring new opportunities in the marketplace. Segmentation research and new product research help identify the most lucrative opportunities for a firm.

Marketing Research Defined

Now that you have an understanding of how marketing research fits into the overall marketing system, we can proceed with a formal definition of the term, as stated by the American Marketing Association:

Marketing research is the function that links the consumer, customer, and public to the marketer through information—information used to identify and define marketing opportunities and problems; generate, refine, and evaluate marketing actions; monitor marketing performance; and improve understanding of marketing as a process. Marketing research specifies the information required to address these issues, designs the method for collecting information, manages and implements the data collection process, analyzes the results, and communicates the findings and their implications.

→ **marketing research**
The planning, collection, and analysis of data relevant to marketing decision making and the communication of the results of this analysis to management.

We prefer another definition: **Marketing research** is the planning, collection, and analysis of data relevant to marketing decision making and the communication of the results of this analysis to management.

The Importance of Marketing Research to Management

Marketing research can be viewed as playing three functional roles: descriptive, diagnostic, and predictive. Its **descriptive function** includes gathering and presenting statements of fact. What is the historic sales trend in the industry? What are consumers' attitudes and beliefs toward a product? Opening a pack of bacon is a messy job. Bacon lovers have to reach into the package, and if they pull out only a few slices, there's no easy way to store the remainder. Oscar Mayer marketing researchers heard plenty from consumers about what they disliked about its former bacon packaging. So marketers figured the best solution would be a packaging innovation that eliminated the chore of placing the opened pack in a resealable plastic bag or wrapping it in plastic or foil. This unwanted task was done so that the last piece of bacon would be as fresh as the first.

→ **descriptive function**
The gathering and presentation of statements of fact.

Oscar Mayer Center Cut Bacon was introduced in a new "Stay-Fresh Reclosable Tray." The flip-top lid allows easy access to the bacon inside. The top snaps closed, making it readily resealable. The flat tray makes for simplified storage in the refrigerator.

→ **diagnostic function**
The explanation of data or actions.

The second role of research is the **diagnostic function**, wherein data and/or actions are explained. For example, what was the impact on sales when the Oscar Mayer package design was changed? How can product/service offerings be altered to better serve customers and potential customers? Since kids eat over 5 billion ounces of ketchup each year, Heinz decided that the heavy users (kids) should have a lot to say (via marketing research) about how to make ketchup fun. Heinz listened and watched children using ketchup, which resulted in a new bottle design and name selection. The true ketchup connoisseurs helped create Heinz EZ Squirt ketchup!

The final role of research is the **predictive function**. How can the firm best take advantage of opportunities as they arise in the ever-changing marketplace? Kraft Foods noticed that consumers were flocking to "low-carb" diets. The company used marketing research to determine whether this was a fad or a long-term trend. Determining that "low carb" was more than a fad, it entered into an alliance with Arthur Agatston, the creator of the South Beach Diet. The result was certain Kraft products being labeled "South Beach Diet Recommended." Further marketing research led to a broad line of products under the "South Beach Diet" brand. Products include cereal, meal replacement and cereal bars, refrigerated sandwich wraps, frozen entrees, and frozen pizza.

> ➤ **predictive function**
> Specification of how to use descriptive and diagnostic research to predict the results of a planned marketing decision.

The Unrelenting Drive for Quality and Customer Satisfaction Quality and customer satisfaction have become the key competitive weapons as America emerges from the worst recession since the 1930s. American automobile manufacturers have been among the most battered in recent years. Now, the watchwords are quality and customer service. As one auto executive puts it:

If you go back to even a very short time ago, our whole idea of a customer was that we would wholesale a car to a dealer, the dealer would then sell the car to the customers, and we hoped we never heard from the customer—because if we did, it meant something was wrong. Today, we want to establish a dialogue with the customer throughout the entire ownership experience. We want to talk to and toumers are every step of the way. We want to be a consumer-products and services company that just happens to be in the automotive business.[4]

Where does marketing research come into play? The J. D. Power Awards rank cars based on the level of customer satisfaction. This, in turn, drives sales of specific companies and models. Lexus has always done well in a number of quality and customer satisfaction studies. This has helped increase sales of the IS, LS, and RX models. At some Lexus dealers, you can get a manicure and a massage while having your oil changed. Automobile manufacturers use marketing research to aid designers, determine what new features to add to specific models, and learn how their cars stack up with those of the competition.

Quality that means little to customers usually doesn't produce a payoff in improved sales, profits, or market share; it represents wasted effort and expense. Today, the new mantra is **return on quality**, which means that (1) the quality being delivered is the quality desired by the target market and (2) the added quality must have a positive impact on profitability. For example, banking giant Bank of America measures every improvement in service quality, from adding more tellers to offering new products, in terms of added profitability.

> ➤ **return on quality**
> A management objective based on the principles that (1) the quality being delivered is at a level desired by the target market and (2) the level of quality must have a positive impact on profitability.

The passion to drive down costs can destroy the delicate balance between efficiency and service. For example, a University of Michigan annual marketing research survey, the American Customer Satisfaction index, revealed that Home Depot slipped to dead last among major U.S. retailers.[5] Cost cutting, including replacing many full-time workers with part-timers and reducing the profit-sharing pool for all workers, created a customer service disaster. As a result, same-store sales at Home Depot lagged far behind the much better-liked Lowe's. New management has now placed a priority on customer service, and sales are improving.

The Paramount Importance of Keeping Existing Customers An inextricable link exists between customer satisfaction and customer loyalty. Long-term relationships don't just happen; they are grounded in the delivery of service and value. Customer retention pays big dividends for firms. Powered by repeat sales and referrals, revenues and market share grow. Costs fall because firms spend less funds and energy attempting to replace defectors. Steady customers are easy to serve because they understand the modus operandi and make fewer demands on employees' time. A firm's ability to retain customers also drives job satisfaction and pride, which leads to higher employee retention. In turn, long-term employees acquire additional knowledge that increases productivity.

A Bain & Company study estimates that a 5 percent decrease in the customer defection rate can boost profits by 25 to 95 percent.[6] Another study found that the customer retention rate has a major impact on the value of a firm.[7]

The ability to retain customers is based on an intimate understanding of their needs. This knowledge comes primarily from marketing research. For example, British Airways recast its first-class transatlantic service based on detailed marketing research. Most airlines stress top-of-the-line service in their transatlantic first-class cabins. However, British Air research found that most first-class passengers simply want to sleep. British Air now gives premium flyers the option of dinner on the ground, before takeoff, in the first-class lounge. Then, once on board, they can slip into British Air pajamas, put their heads on real pillows, slip under blankets, and enjoy an interruption-free flight. On arrival at their destination, first-class passengers can have breakfast, use comfortable dressing rooms and showers, and even have their clothes pressed before they set off. These changes in British Air's first-class service were driven strictly by marketing research.

Understanding the Ever-Changing Marketplace

Marketing research also helps managers to understand trends in the marketplace and to take advantage of opportunities. Marketing research has been practiced for as long as marketing has existed. The early Phoenicians carried out market demand studies as they traded in the various ports on the Mediterranean Sea. Marco Polo's diary indicates that he was performing a marketing research function as he traveled to China. There is evidence that the Spanish systematically conducted marketing surveys as they explored the New World, and examples exist of marketing research conducted during the Renaissance.

Social Media and User-Generated Content

In the past few years, the world of promotion has been turned upside down. Previously, marketers created a message and then one, or a series, of traditional media, TV, print, radio, and billboards to deliver that message to a target market. Now, we have more people than ever participating in blogs, forums, online communities, product/service reviews— think

Asking the right questions in marketing research can be as important as getting good answers. UPS found that customers wanted more interaction with their UPS drivers. Go to *http://www.ups.com* to find out how UPS uses marketing research to better serve its customers.

© David R. Frazier Photolibrary, Inc./Alamy

Trip Advisor—and social media sites that created user-generated content (UGC). The opinions expressed in the venues are unsolicited; are typically honest, candid, and passionate; and can be extremely thoughtful. Social media such as Twitter, Facebook, and LinkedIn generate millions of comments each day about products and services. About 20 percent of all tweets are about brands.[8]

Marketing researchers are tapping into these huge streams of data to determine what people think about their products and services as well as these of the competition. Researchers are building profiles of persons online and using these data to target their promotional efforts. Other researchers tap online communities to build new products and services.

Indications are that the stream of UGC and social media users will continue to grow. For example, 56 percent of social media users need to check Facebook at least once a day, and 12 percent check in every couple hours. Forty-eight percent said that they check their Facebook or Twitter pages before bed, during the night, or as soon as they wake up. After going to bed, persons under 25 were much more likely to check their social media during the night.[9]

The skyrocketing growth of UGC and social media has already brought numerous changes to the marketplace and to the field of marketing research. We will be touching on these changes throughout the book, including the emotionally charged issue of Internet privacy.

The Proactive Role of Marketing Research

Understanding the nature of the marketing system is a necessity for a successful marketing orientation. By having a thorough knowledge of factors that have an impact on the target market and the marketing mix, management can be proactive rather than reactive. Proactive management alters the marketing mix to fit newly emerging patterns in economic, social, and competitive environments, whereas reactive management waits for change to have a major impact on the firm before deciding to take action. It is the difference between viewing the turbulent marketing environment as a threat (a reactive stance) and as an opportunity (a proactive stance). Apple, for example, has been very proactive about bringing cutting-edge technology products to the marketplace. This, in turn, has generated huge profits for the company.

A proactive manager not only examines emerging markets but also seeks, through strategic planning, to develop a long-run **marketing strategy** for the firm. A marketing strategy guides the long-term use of the firm's resources based on the firm's existing and projected internal capabilities and on projected changes in the external environment. A good strategic plan is based on good marketing research. It helps the firm meet long-term profit and market share goals.

> **marketing strategy**
> A plan to guide the long-term use of a firm's resources based on its existing and projected internal capabilities and on projected changes in the external environment.

Applied Research versus Basic Research

Virtually all marketing research is conducted to better understand the market, to find out why a strategy failed, or to reduce uncertainty in management decision making. All research conducted for these purposes is called **applied research**. For example, should the price of DiGiorno frozen pizza be raised 40 cents? What name should Toyota select for a new sedan? Which commercial has a higher level of recall: A or B? On the other hand, **basic**, or **pure**, **research** attempts to expand the frontiers of knowledge; it is not aimed at a specific pragmatic problem. Basic research is conducted to validate an existing theory or learn more about a concept or phenomenon. For example, basic marketing research might test a hypothesis about high-involvement decision making or consumer information processing. In the long run, basic research helps us understand more about the world in which we live. The findings of basic research usually cannot be implemented by managers in the short run. Most basic marketing research is now conducted in universities; the findings are reported in such publications as *The Journal of Marketing Research* and *The Journal of Marketing*. In contrast, most research undertaken by businesses is applied research because it must be cost-effective and of demonstrable value to the decision maker.

Although basic research is still important at some firms, particularly high tech, the notion of time-to-market has changed. That is, the basic research can be fairly long term but must have a focus on ultimately solving real-world problems. Companies conducting basic research include Microsoft, IBM, Xerox, and Hewlett-Packard. H-P's research arm, for example, has been doing work in areas such as nanotechnology and computer

> **applied research**
> Research aimed at solving a specific, pragmatic problem—such as better understanding of the marketplace, determination of why a strategy or tactic failed, or reduction of uncertainty in management decision making.

> **basic, or pure, research**
> Research aimed at expanding the frontiers of knowledge rather than solving a specific, pragmatic problem.

algorithms that could more efficiently sift the Internet for huge amounts of public data to predict business trends.

Prith Banerjee, director of HPLabs, said that about two-thirds of the labs' projects are relatively short-term initiatives that are intended to produce results within about five years. The remaining one-third is basic research that may not pan out for a decade or more.[10]

Nature of Applied Research

> **programmatic research**
> Research conducted to develop marketing options through market segmentation, market opportunity analyses, or consumer attitude and product usage studies.

> **selective research**
> Research used to test decision alternatives.

> **evaluative research**
> Research done to assess program performance.

Marketing research studies can be classified into three broad categories: programmatic, selective, and evaluative. **Programmatic research** is conducted to develop marketing options through market segmentation, market opportunity analysis, or consumer attitude and product usage studies. **Selective research** is used to test decision alternatives. Some examples are testing concepts for new products, advertising copy testing, and test marketing. **Evaluative research** is done to assess program performance; it includes tracking advertising recall, doing organizational image studies, and examining customer attitudes on a firm's quality of service.

Programmatic research arises from management's need to obtain a market overview periodically. For example, product management may be concerned that the existing market information base is inadequate or outdated for present decision making, or marketing plans may call for the introduction of new products, ad campaigns, or packaging. Whatever the specific situation, current information is needed to develop viable marketing options. Typical programmatic research questions include the following:

- Has its target market changed? How?
- Does the market exhibit any new segmentation opportunities?
- Do some segments appear to be more likely candidates than others for the firm's marketing efforts?
- What new product or service opportunities lie in the various segments?

Selective research typically is conducted after several viable options have been identified by programmatic research. If no one alternative is clearly superior, product management usually will wish to test several alternatives. However, selective research may be required at any stage of the marketing process, such as when advertising copy is being developed, various product formulations are being evaluated, or an entire marketing program is being assessed, as in test marketing.

The need for evaluative research arises when the effectiveness and efficiency of marketing programs must be evaluated. Evaluative research may be integrated into programmatic research when program changes or entirely new options are demanded because of present performance.

"I don't *know* what I'm doing—this is pure research!"
Rex F. May

The Decision to Conduct Marketing Research

A manager who is faced with several alternative solutions to a particular problem should not instinctively call for applied marketing research. In fact, the first decision to be made is whether to conduct marketing research at all. In a number of situations, it is best not to conduct research:

- *Resources are lacking.* There are two situations in which a lack of resources should preclude marketing research. First, an organization may lack the funds to do the research properly. If a project calls for a sample of 800 respondents but the budget allows for only 50 interviews, the quality of the information would be highly suspect. Second, funds may be available to do the research properly but insufficient to implement any decisions resulting from the research. Small organizations in particular sometimes lack the resources to create an effective marketing mix. In one case, for example, the director of a performing arts guild was in complete agreement with the recommendations that resulted from a marketing research project. However, 2 years after the project was completed, nothing had been done because the money was not available.

- *Research results would not be useful.* Some types of marketing research studies measure lifestyle and personality factors of steady and potential customers. Assume that a study finds that introverted men with a poor self-concept but a high need for achievement are most likely to patronize a discount brokerage service. The management of Charles Schwab's discount brokerage service might be hard-pressed to use this information.

- *The opportunity has passed.* Marketing research should not be undertaken if the opportunity for successful entry into a market has already passed. If the product is in the late maturity or decline stage of the product life cycle (such as cassette recorders or black-and-white television sets), it would be foolish to do research on new product entry. The same may be true for markets rapidly approaching saturation, such as super-premium ice cream (Häagen-Dazs, Ben & Jerry's). For products already in the market, however, research is needed to modify the products as consumer tastes, competition, and other factors change.

- *The decision already has been made.* In the real world of management decision making and company politics, marketing research has sometimes been used improperly. Several years ago, a large marketing research study was conducted for a bank with over $800 million in deposits. The purpose of the research project was to guide top management in mapping a strategic direction for the bank during the next 5 years. After reading the research report, the president said, "I fully agree with your recommendations because that was what I was going to do anyway! I'm going to use your study tomorrow when I present my strategic plan to the board of directors." The researcher then asked, "What if my recommendations had been counter to your decision?" The bank president laughed and said, "They would have never known that I had conducted a marketing research study!" Not only was the project a waste of money, but it also raised a number of ethical questions in the researcher's mind.

- *Managers cannot agree on what they need to know to make a decision.* Although it may seem obvious that research should not be undertaken until objectives are specified, it sometimes happens. Preliminary or exploratory studies are commonly done to better understand the nature of the problem, but a large, major research project should not be. It is faulty logic to say, "Well, let's just go ahead and do the study and then we will better understand the problem and know what steps to take." The wrong phenomena

© Pictorium /Alamy

The super-premium ice cream market is reaching saturation. At this point, it might not be wise to enter this market. However, marketing research is necessary to keep products already in the market ahead of the competition.

might be studied, or key elements needed for management decision making may not be included.

▪ *Decision-making information already exists.* Some companies have been conducting research in certain markets for many years. They understand the characteristics of their target customers and what they like and dislike about existing products. Under these circumstances, further research would be redundant and a waste of money. Procter & Gamble, for example, has extensive knowledge of the coffee market. After it conducted initial taste tests, P&G went into national distribution with Folger's Instant Coffee without further research. The Sara Lee Corporation did the same thing with its frozen croissants, as did Quaker Oats with Chewy Granola Bars. This tactic, however, does not always work. P&G thought it understood the pain reliever market thoroughly, so it bypassed marketing research for Encaprin, encapsulated aspirin. The product failed because it lacked a distinct competitive advantage over existing products, and it was withdrawn from the market.

▪ *The costs of conducting research outweigh the benefits.* Rarely does a manager have such tremendous confidence in her or his judgment that additional information relative to a pending decision would not be accepted if it were available and free. However, the manager might have sufficient confidence to be unwilling to pay very much for it or wait long to receive it. Willingness to acquire additional decision-making information depends on a manager's perception of its quality, price, and timing. The manager would be willing to pay more for perfect information (that is, data that leave no doubt as to which alternative to follow) than for information that leaves uncertainty as to what to do. Therefore, research should be undertaken only when the expected value of the information is greater than the cost of obtaining it.

Two important determinants of potential benefits are profit margins and market size. Generally speaking, new products with large profit margins are going to have greater potential benefit than products with smaller profit margins, assuming that both items have the same sales potential. Also, new product opportunities in large markets are going to offer greater potential benefits than those in smaller markets if competitive intensity is the same in both markets (see Exhibit 1.1).

EXHIBIT 1.1	Deciding Whether to Conduct Marketing Research	
Market Size	**Small Profit Margin**	**Large Profit Margin**
Small	Costs likely to be greater than benefits (e.g., eyeglass replacement screw, tire valve extension). DON'T CONDUCT MARKETING RESEARCH.	Benefits possibly greater than cost (e.g., ultra-expensive Lamborghini-type sportswear, larger specialized industrial equipment like computer-aided metal stamping machines). PERHAPS CONDUCT MARKETING RESEARCH. LEARN ALL YOU CAN FROM EXISTING INFORMATION PRIOR TO MAKING DECISION TO CONDUCT RESEARCH.
Large	Benefits likely to be greater than costs (e.g., Stouffer's frozen entrees, Crest's whitener strips). PERHAPS CONDUCT MARKETING RESEARCH. LEARN ALL YOU CAN FROM EXISTING INFORMATION PRIOR TO MAKING DECISION TO CONDUCT RESEARCH.	Benefits most likely to be greater than costs (e.g., medical equipment like CAT scanners, Toshiba's 3D television). CONDUCT MARKETING RESEARCH.

SUMMARY

Marketing is an organizational function and a set of processes for creating, communicating, and delivering value to customers and for managing customer relationships in ways that benefit the organization and its stockholders. Marketing managers attempt to get the right goods or services to the right people at the right place at the right time at the right price, using the right promotion technique. This may be accomplished by following the marketing concept, which is based on consumer orientation, goal orientation, and systems orientation.

A marketing manager must work within an internal environment of an organization and understand the external environment over which he or she has little, if any, control. The primary variables over which a marketing manager has control are distribution, price, promotion, and product/service decisions. The unique combination of these four variables is called the *marketing mix*.

Marketing research plays a key part in providing information managers need to shape the marketing mix. Marketing research has grown in importance because of management's focus on customer satisfaction and retention. It is also a key tool in proactive management. Marketing research should be undertaken only when the perceived benefits are greater than the costs.

A marketing research study can be described as programmatic, selective, or evaluative. Programmatic research is done to develop marketing options through market segmentation, market opportunity analysis, or consumer attitude and product usage studies. Selective research is used to test decisional alternatives. Evaluative research is done to assess program performance.

KEY TERMS & DEFINITIONS

marketing The process of planning and executing the conception, pricing, promotion, and distribution of ideas, goods, and services to create exchanges that satisfy individual and organizational objectives.

marketing concept A business philosophy based on consumer orientation, goal orientation, and systems orientation.

consumer orientation The identification of and focus on the people or firms most likely to buy a product and the production of a good or service that will meet their needs most effectively.

goal orientation A focus on the accomplishment of corporate goals; a limit set on consumer orientation.

systems orientation The creation of systems to monitor the external environment and deliver the desired marketing mix to the target market.

marketing mix The unique blend of product/service, pricing, promotion, and distribution strategies designed to meet the needs of a specific target market.

marketing research The planning, collection, and analysis of data relevant to marketing decision making and the communication of the results of this analysis to management.

descriptive function The gathering and presentation of statements of fact.

diagnostic function The explanation of data or actions.

predictive function Specification of how to use descriptive and diagnostic research to predict the results of a planned marketing decision.

return on quality A management objective based on the principles that (1) the quality being delivered is at a level desired by the target market and (2) that level of quality must have a positive impact on profitability.

marketing strategy A plan to guide the long-term use of a firm's resources based on its existing and projected internal capabilities and on projected changes in the external environment.

applied research Research aimed at solving a specific, pragmatic problem—such as

better understanding of the marketplace, determination of why a strategy or tactic failed, or reduction of uncertainty in management decision making.

basic, or pure, research Research aimed at expanding the frontiers of knowledge rather than solving a specific, pragmatic problem.

programmatic research Research conducted to develop marketing options through market segmentation, market opportunity analyses, or consumer attitude and product usage studies.

selective research Research used to test decision alternatives.

evaluative research Research done to assess program performance.

QUESTIONS FOR REVIEW & CRITICAL THINKING

1. The role of marketing is to create exchanges. What role might marketing research play in facilitating the exchange process?

2. Marketing research traditionally has been associated with manufacturers of consumer goods. Today, an increasing number of organizations, both for-profit and nonprofit, are using marketing research. Why do you think this trend exists? Give some examples.

3. Explain the relationship between marketing research and the marketing concept.

4. Comment on the following statement by the owner of a restaurant in a downtown area: "I see customers every day whom I know on a first-name basis. I understand their likes and dislikes. If I put something on the menu and it doesn't sell, I know that they didn't like it. I also read the magazine *Modern Restaurants* to keep up with industry trends. This is all the marketing research I need to do."

5. Why is marketing research important to marketing executives? Give several reasons.

6. What differences might you note among marketing research conducted for (a) a retailer, (b) a consumer goods manufacturer, (c) an industrial goods manufacturer, and (d) a charitable organization?

7. Comment on the following: Ralph Moran is planning to invest $1.5 million in a new restaurant in Saint Louis. When he applied for a construction financing loan, the bank officer asked whether he had conducted any research. Ralph replied, "I checked on research, and a marketing research company wanted $20,000 to do

the work. I decided that with all the other expenses of opening a new business, research was a luxury that I could do without."

8. What is meant by "return on quality"? Why do you think that the concept evolved? Give an example.

9. Describe three situations in which marketing research should not be undertaken. Explain why this is true.

10. Give an example of (a) the descriptive role of marketing research, (b) the diagnostic role of marketing research, and (c) the predictive function of marketing research.

11. Using the Internet and a Web browser, visit a search engine such as Google or Yahoo! and type, "marketing research." From the thousands of options you are offered, pick a Web site that you find interesting and report on its content to the class.

12. [*Team exercise*] Divide the class into groups of four. Each team should visit a large organization (for-profit or nonprofit) and conduct an interview with a top marketing executive to discover how this firm is using marketing research. Each team then should report its findings in class.

13. How is the Internet changing the field of marketing research?

REAL-LIFE RESEARCH • 1.1

Give Me a Coupon That I Can Use Online!

While consumers certainly enjoy coupons, what do retailers stand to gain? Turns out, plenty. The study suggests that coupons have a significant impact on retailers' bottom lines, in addition to the obvious consumer benefit, as couponers are likely to spend more, have higher satisfaction, and return to the retailer where the coupon was used, according to Online Shopper Intelligence, a study from Boston research company Compete.

More than half of the consumers who used a coupon code during their last online purchase said that if they had not received the discount, they would not have bought the item(s)—57 percent said no, 43 percent yes—and more online shoppers are using coupons now than ever. One-third of online shoppers reported that they generally use coupon sites while shopping online, and 35 million consumers visited coupon sites monthly. Coupons have a high return on investment, as the small discount consumers receive encourages them to spend money. When asked how much they spent on their most recent online purchase, consumers who use a coupon spent almost twice as much as consumers who did not use a coupon ($216 with a coupon versus $122 without).

Offering coupons can be an effective way for retailers to build goodwill with consumers and increase customer satisfaction. When asked about their overall shopping experience, consumers who used a coupon expressed higher satisfaction than did those who did not. Ninety-two percent of coupon shoppers were extremely or very satisfied, versus 88 percent of noncouponers. Consumers who used a coupon also said they are more likely to buy from the retailer again when compared to those who did not use a coupon. Ninety-one percent of consumers with coupons reported being extremely or very likely to shop again at the retailer where the coupon was redeemed versus 86 percent of consumers without coupons.[11]

Questions

1. How might a firm like Home Depot use this information? Would Amazon.com use the same couponing strategy as Home Depot?

2. Do you think that Home Depot might need more research before it develops a couponing strategy? If so, what does it need to know?

3. Do you think it is necessary for online retailers to conduct marketing research? Why?`

APPENDIX 1-A
CAREERS IN MARKETING RESEARCH

Marketing research offers a variety of career paths, depending upon one's education level, interests, and personality. Most jobs are to be found with either research suppliers (firms that conduct research for clients) or research users (corporations that depend on marketing research for decision-making guidance). A limited number of marketing research positions are also available with advertising agencies, nonprofit organizations, associations, and various branches of government.

Positions with research suppliers (or research firms) tend to be concentrated in a few large cities—for example, New York, Chicago, Los Angeles, San Francisco, and Dallas. Although research suppliers are found throughout the country, a majority of the larger firms (and entry-level jobs) are found in these cities. Research users (corporations, organizations, etc.), on the other hand, tend to be more widely scattered and found in communities of various size—for example, General Mills in Minneapolis; Tyson in Springdale, Arkansas.

Women have long been accepted as equals in the marketing research industry, and some of the larger research firms were founded by women. At the college entry-level position of junior analyst, women are twice as prevalent as men! Obviously, young women increasingly are recognizing the opportunities that await them in the exciting field of marketing research.

There was a time when a decision to go into marketing research represented a lifetime career commitment. Once you were a marketing researcher, there was a good chance you would always be a marketing researcher. Today this inflexibility is not so prevalent. Now it is more common to see people transfer into and out of the marketing research department as part of a career in marketing.

Exhibit 1-A.1 presents a comparative summary of career positions within the research industry. Not all companies have all positions, but you will find people with these titles across the industry. The table also lists the minimum experience and education typical for each position.

EXHIBIT 1-A.1	Career Opportunities in Marketing Research: General Duties and Qualifications		
Positions	**Level of Responsibility**	**Minimum Experience**	**Minimum Education**
Director or vice president	Department administration	10+ years	Graduate degree
Assistant director	Projects administration	5+ years	Graduate degree
Senior analyst	Project supervision	3–5 years	College degree (may require graduate degree)
Analyst	Project analysis and expediting	2–4 years	College degree (may require graduate degree)
Statistician	Statistical analysis	0 years	College degree (may require graduate degree)
Clerical	Office management	3–5 years	Vocational
Junior analyst	Project assistance	0 years	College degree
Field director	Data collection supervisor	3–5+ years	High school diploma
Librarian	Library management	0 years	College degree
Interviewer	Questionnaire administration	0 years	Some high school
Tabulator	Simple tabulation, filing, and organizing	0 years	Some high school

Positions within Supplier Organizations

Research suppliers offer a majority of the entry-level career positions in the marketing research field. Many of the newer firms are entrepreneurial in nature and headed by a founder or partners. In smaller companies, the founder-owner not only manages the company but typically is involved in selling and conducting research projects. Owners of larger supplier organizations perform basically the same functions as top managers in other large corporations, such as creating strategic plans and developing broad corporate polices. It is also common in large supplier organizations to have managers that specialize in either a specific industry or type of research—for example, manager of healthcare research, manager of financial research, or political polling. Firms also may have a director of qualitative research or a director of multivariate studies. A list of jobs found in supplier firms follows:

Statistician. A person holding this position is viewed as an internal expert on statistical techniques, sampling methods, and statistical software programs such as SPSS, SAS, or R-Language. Normally, a master's degree or even a PhD is required.

Tabulation programmer. A person holding this position uses tabulation software such as SPSS to create cross-tabulations of survey data. Tabulation programmers are often involved in data cleaning and data management functions, and they may need knowledge of database systems. Normally a bachelor's degree is required.

Senior analyst. A senior analyst is usually found in larger firms. The individual typically works with an account executive to plan a research project and then supervises several analysts who execute the projects. Senior analysts work with a minimal level of supervision themselves. They often work with analysts in developing questionnaires and may help in analyzing difficult data sets. The final report is usually written by an analyst but reviewed, with comments, by the senior analyst and/or account executive. This position is usually given budgetary control over projects and responsibility for meeting time schedules.

Analyst. The analyst usually handles the bulk of the work required for executing research projects. An analyst normally reports to a senior analyst. He or she assists in questionnaire preparation, pretests, then does data analysis, and, finally, writes the preliminary report. Much of the secondary data work is performed by the analyst.

Junior analyst. This is typically an entry-level position for a person with a degree. A junior analyst works under close supervision on rather mundane tasks; for example, editing and coding questionnaires, performing basic statistical analysis, conducting secondary data searches, and writing rough draft reports on simple projects.

Project director. The project director actively manages the flow of research projects, works out schedules, performs quality assurance checks, and provides information and directions to subcontractors and operations. Sometimes the project director is also involved in questionnaire design development of a tabulation plan, and report preparation.

Account executive. An account executive is responsible for making sales to client firms and keeping client organizations satisfied enough to continue funneling work to the research supplier. An account executive works on a day-to-day basis with clients and serves as liaison between the client and the research organization. Account managers must understand each client's problems and know what research techniques should be employed to provide the right data. He or she must be able to explain to the client what research techniques are needed in a nontechnical manner. Moreover, the account executive must be able to sell the firm's services and abilities over competing suppliers. Account executives work hand in hand with research analysts to develop the research methodology to solve the client's problems. This position often requires an MBA or another master's degree.

Senior executive (vice president, senior vice president, executive vice president). Typically, this executive oversees several departments or teams of account executives and also has business development responsibilities in addition to managerial responsibilities. These executives are responsible for the hiring, training, and development of account executives, analysts, and project directors; in addition, they spend much of their time in high-level meetings with major clients.

Field work director. Most market research firms do not have their own interviewers. Instead, they rely on market research field services throughout the United States to conduct the actual interviews. Field services are the production line of the market research industry. They hire, train, and supervise interviewers within a specific geographic area. A field work director is responsible for obtaining completed interviews in the proper geographic area, using the specified sampling instructions, within a specified budget and on time. Field work directors keep in close touch with field services thoughout the United States. They know which field services have the best interviewers and can maintain time schedules. After a study has been fielded, the field service director obtains daily reports from the field service. Typical data reported include the number of completed interviews; the number of refusals; interviewing hours, travel time, and mileage; and problems, if any.

Director of operations. Larger research firms will have a large operations function with a number of departments (data preparation, sampling, data entry, tabulation, questionnarie programming, control center, and so on). The director oversees these departments, schedules projects, ensures quality assurance, hires and trains staff, and makes sure that research projects are properly executed.

Positions within Research Departments and Advertising Agencies

Many manufactures, retailers, and other organizations have marketing research departments, although the fashion these days is to call these "consumer insights" departments. These companies, like Kraft, Wal-Mart, Frito-Lay, Sears, and Procter & Gamble, have research groups of varying sizes and responsibilities. Some research departments act like internal research companies, while other research departments function as internal consultants but subcontract all the work to research suppliers. Corporate research departments often have internal teams headed by directors or managers. Some research departments are organized by brand, while others are organized by research technique specialization. In some companies, competitive intelligence is a separate function, and in others it is a part of the research department. Also, in some companies, strategic planning is a subgroup within the research function, while in others it is a separate department. Organizational structure varies from company to company. Descriptions of some positions follow:

Research director. The research director (sometimes vice president of research or even senior vice president) is responsible for the entire research program of the company. The director may conduct strategic research for top management or accept work from new product managers, brand managers, or other internal clients. In some cases, the director may initiate proposals for studies but typically just responds to requests. He or she has full responsibility for the market research budget and, since resources are limited, may have to set priorities regarding projects undertaken. The director hires the professional staff and exercises general supervision of the research department. He or she normally presents the findings of strategic research projects to top management. This position often requires a master's degree and, in some companies, a PhD. The director is often viewed as the top technical expert in the department as well.

Assistant research director. This position is normally found only in large, full-scale research departments. The person is second in command and reports to the research director. Senior analysts, statisticians, database analysts, syndicated data analysts, secondary data analysts and data processing specialists usually report to the assistant director, who performs many of the same functions as the director.

Research Directors and Others in Limited-Function Research Departments

Most research departments in corporations or advertising agencies are limited in their functions. Therefore, they do not conduct the research or analyze the data. Instead, they formulate requests for research proposals, analyze the proposals, award contracts to research suppliers, and evaluate the supplier's work. Internally, they work with brand managers and new product specialists in formulating research problems and interpreting and implementing the recommendations of the research reports provided by the suppliers.

The research director and assistant director (if any) function in a manner as described earlier. Analysts formulate and evaluate proposals and the work of research suppliers. They also help implement the recommendations. With the exception of a secretary, there is usually no other personnel in a limited-function research department.

Some of the most effective departments in corporate settings and advertising agencies are organized by *brand* or *business unit,* rather than by *function* or *method.* Researchers who are assigned to specific brands are expected to have a working knowledge of many different research processess and approaches. This broad knowledge, as well as daily involvement with a given brand or business unit, creates greater value for the organization as a whole. This person essentially becomes an integral part of a brand or account team, affording him or her a greater understanding of the business issues. In turn, research-based recommendations are often more relevant and actionable.

The Rewards of Marketing Research

Marketing researchers typically find their work interesting and fulfilling. Researchers normally gain recognition for a job well done. Most firms offer fact-track promotion opportunities for outstanding employees. Many researchers find it relatively easy to switch companies to obtain a brighter future. Compensation for client-side marketing researchers (those working for manufacturers, service businesses, government, and advertising agencies) is shown in Exhibit 1-A.2.

EXHIBIT 1-A.2	Client-Side Researchers Compensation		
Job Title	Base	Bonus	Total
Senior Vice President or Vice President	$152,841	$27,341	$180,182
Market Research Director/Senior Director	$127,229	$20,187	$147,416
Market Research Manager	$92,612	$9,144	$101,756
Account Executive/Manager	$69,000	$4,500	$73,500
Customer Insights Manager	$93,612	$7,621	$101,241
Director of Marketing	$108,611	$6,889	$115,500
Brand Manager or Product Manager	$85,286	$3,857	$89,143
Project Manager	$76,520	$11,440	$87,960
Senior Research Analyst	$77,916	$5,133	$83,048
Research Analyst	$54,923	$3,631	$58,554
Statistician	$65,750	$3,750	$69,500
Research Assistant	$42,000	$667	$42,667
Sales/Account Representative	$67,500	$38,333	$105,833

Source: Joseph Rydholm, "Stable Earnings, Wandering Eye?" *Quirk's Marketing Research Review,* July 2010, p. 30.

APPENDIX 1-B
MARKETING RESEARCH ETHICS

→ **ethics**
Moral principles or values,
generally governing the
conduct of an individual or
a group.

The two most important factors for research clients in their relationships with research departments/suppliers are client confidentiality and honesty. Each is a question of ethics. **Ethics** are moral principles or values generally governing the conduct of an individual or group. Ethical behavior is not, however, a one-way relationship. Clients, suppliers, and field services must also act in an ethical manner.

Ethical questions range from practical, narrowly defined issues, such as a researcher's obligation to be honest with its customers, to broader social and philosophical questions, such as a company's responsibility to preserve the environment and protect employee rights. Many ethical conflicts develop from conflicts between the differing interests of company owners and their workers, customers, and surrounding community. Managers must balance the ideal against the practical—the need to produce a reasonable profit for the company's shareholders with honesty in business practices, and larger environmental and social issues.

Ethical Theories

People usually base their individual choice of ethical theory on their life experiences. The following are some of the ethical theories that apply to business and marketing research.[1]

Deontology

The deontological theory states that people should adhere to their obligations and duties when analyzing an ethical dilemma. This means that a person will follow his or her obligations to another individual or society because upholding one's duty is what is considered ethically correct. For instance, a deontologist will always keep his promises to a friend and will follow the law. A person who follows this theory will produce very consistent decisions since they will be based on the individual's set duties. Note that this theory is not necessarily concerned with the welfare of others. Say, for example, a research supplier has decided that it's his ethical duty (and very practical!) to always be on time to meetings with clients. Today he is running late. How is he supposed to drive? Is the deontologist supposed to speed, breaking his duty to society to uphold the law, or is the deontologist supposed to arrive at his meeting late, breaking his duty to be on time? This scenario of conflicting obligations does not lead us to a clear ethically correct resolution, nor does it protect the welfare of others from the deontologist's decision.

Utilitarianism

The utilitarian ethical theory is founded on the ability to predict the consequences of an action. To a utilitarian, the choice that yields the greatest benefit to the most people is the choice that is ethically correct. One benefit of this ethical theory is that the utilitarian can compare similar predicted solutions and use a point system to determine which choice is most beneficial for the most people. This point system provides a logical and rational argument for each decision and allows a person to use it on a case-by-case context.

There are two types of utilitarianism: act utilitarianism and rule utilitarianism. *Act utilitarianism* adheres exactly to the definition of utilitarianism as described in the above section. In act utilitarianism, a person performs the acts that benefit the most people, regardless of personal feelings or the societal constraints such as laws. *Rule utilitarianism*, however, takes into account the law and is concerned with fairness. A rule utilitarian seeks to benefit the most people but through the fairest and most just means available. Therefore, added benefits of rule utilitarianism are that it values justice and doing good at the same time.

As is true of all ethical theories, however, both act and rule utilitarianism contain numerous flaws. Inherent in both are the flaws associated with predicting the future. Although people can use their life experiences to attempt to predict outcomes, no human being can be certain that his predictions will be true. This uncertainty can lead to unexpected results, making the utilitarian look unethical as time passes because his choice did not benefit the most people as he predicted.

Another assumption that a utilitarian must make is that he has the ability to compare the various types of consequences against each other on a similar scale. However, comparing material gains such as money against intangible gains such as happiness is impossible since their qualities differ so greatly.

Casuist

The casuist ethical theory compares a current ethical dilemma with examples of similar ethical dilemmas and their outcomes. This allows one to determine the severity of the situation and to create the best possible solution according to others' experiences. Usually, one will find examples that represent the extremes of the situation so that a compromise can be reached that will hopefully include the wisdom gained from the previous situations.

One drawback to this ethical theory is that there may not be a set of similar examples for a given ethical dilemma. Perhaps that which is controversial and ethically questionable is new and unexpected. Along the same line of thinking, this theory assumes that the results of the current ethical dilemma will be similar to results in the examples. This may not be necessarily true and would greatly hinder the effectiveness of applying this ethical theory.

Understanding ethical theories will help us better decide how certain unethical practices in marketing research should be resolved. Exhibit 1-B.1 details some of the unethical practices most common among the various groups involved in marketing research.

Research Supplier Ethics

Unethical research supplier practices range from low-ball pricing to violating client confidentiality.

Low-Ball Pricing

A research supplier should quote a firm price based on a specific incidence rate (percentage of the respondents in the sample that will qualify to complete the survey) and

EXHIBIT 1-B.1	Unethical Practices in Marketing Research	
Research Suppliers	**Research Clients**	**Field Services**
Low-ball pricing	Issuing bid requests when a supplier has been predetermined	
Allowing subjectivity in research	Soliciting free advice and methodology via bid requests	Using professional respondents
Abusing respondents		Not validating data
Selling unnecessary research	Making false promises	
Violating client confidentiality	Issuing unauthorized requests for proposal	
Black box branding		

→ **low-ball pricing**
Quoting an unrealistically low price to secure a firm's business and then using some means to substantially raise the price.

questionnaire length (time to complete). If either of the latter two items changes, then the client should expect a change in the contract price. Low-ball pricing in any form is unethical. In essence, **low-ball pricing** is quoting an unrealistically low price to secure a firm's business and then using some means to substantially raise the price. For example, quoting a price based on an unrealistically high incidence rate is a form of low-ball pricing. Offering to conduct a focus group at $6,000 a group and, after the client commits, saying, "The respondents' fees for participating in the group discussion are, of course, extra" is a form of low-balling.

Allowing Subjectivity in Research

Research suppliers must avoid using biased samples, misusing statistics, ignoring relevant data, and creating a research design with the goal of supporting a predetermined objective. One area of research today is so-called advocacy studies. These studies are commissioned by companies or industries for public relations purposes or to advocate or prove a position. For example, Burger King once used positive responses to the following question in an advocacy study in an attempt to justify the claim that its method of cooking hamburgers was preferred over that of McDonald's: "Do you prefer your hamburgers flame-broiled or fried?" When another researcher rephrased the question—"Do you prefer a hamburger that is grilled on a hot stainless-steel grill or cooked by passing the meat through an open gas flame?"—the results were reversed: McDonald's was preferred to Burger King.

Kiwi Brands, a shoe polish company, commissioned a study on the correlation between ambition and shiny shoes. The study found that 97 percent of self-described ambitious young men believe polished shoes are important. In many cases, advocacy studies simply use samples that are not representative of the population. For example, a news release for a diet products company trumpeted: "There's good news for the 65 million Americans currently on a diet." A company study had shown that people who lose weight can keep it off; the sample consisted of 20 graduates of the company's program, who also endorsed its products in commercials.

When studies are released to the news media, the methodology should be readily available to news reporters. Typically, this information is withheld, often on the ground that the material is proprietary. A survey done for Carolina Manufacturer's Service, a coupon redemption company, found that "a broad cross-section of Americans find coupons to be true incentives for purchasing products." The description of the methodology was available only at a price: $2,000.

Abusing Respondents

Respondent abuse can take several forms. Perhaps the most common is lengthy interviews. This problem stems in part from the "as long as you're asking questions" mentality of many product managers. It is not uncommon for clients to request additional "nice to know" questions, or even exploratory questions on an entirely separate project. This leads to lengthy questionnaires, 30-minute telephone or Internet interviews, and 40-minute mall-intercept interviews. As a result of long interviews and telephone sales pitches, more and more Americans are refusing to participate in survey research. The refusal rate for telephone surveys now averages 60-plus percent, an increase of 10 percent over 10 years. Forty-nine percent of the people who do participate say the surveys are "too personal."

Predictive dialers are tremendous productivity tools for survey research telephone call centers. They remove much of the idle time an interviewer would otherwise spend manually dialing numbers and recording call dispositions, such as no-answer and busy signals.

Jack Starr/PhotoLink/Getty Images, Inc.

When studies are released to the news media, the methodology should be readily available to news reporters. A survey done for a coupon redemption company found that "a broad cross-section of Americans find coupons to be true incentives for purchasing products." The description of the methodology, however, was available only for a price of $2,000.

By definition, predictive dialers dial phone numbers ahead of available interviewers, predicting when an interviewer will become available. Adjusting the pacing manually sets the aggressiveness of this dial-ahead capability. Obviously, there is strong motivation for call-center managers to increase the pacing and minimize the time an interviewer spends between calls. However, this action has undesirable consequences because some respondents are contacted before an interviewer is available. In most cases, the dialer than places the respondent on hold or disconnects the call. Both actions decrease respondent goodwill.[2]

Interest in a product or service is often discerned during the interviewing process, and the researcher knows the interviewees' potential purchasing power from their answers to income and other pertinent financial questions. Although the introduction phase of the questionnaire usually promises confidentiality, some researchers have sold names and addresses of potential customers to firms seeking sales leads. Individuals willing to participate in the survey research process have a right to have their privacy protected.

The state of New York sued Student Marketing Group for selling information on a broad scale to direct marketers. The survey filled out by students included age, gender, religious affiliation, career interests, and grade point average. The company said that it was gathering the data to provide to universities to help the students gain admission and financial aid. Direct marketers used the information to sell credit cards, magazines, videos, cosmetics, and other products.[3]

Selling Unnecessary Research

A research supplier dealing with a client who has little or no familiarity with marketing research often has the opportunity to "trade the client up." For example, if a project called for four focus groups and an online survey of approximately 350 consumers, the research supplier might sell eight groups and 1,000 Internet interviews, with a 400-interview telephone follow-up in six months.

It is perfectly acceptable to offer a prospective client several research designs with several alternative prices when and if the situation warrants alternative designs. The supplier should point out the pros and cons of each method, along with sample confidence intervals. The client, in consultation with the supplier, then can decide objectively which design best suits the company's needs.

Violating Client Confidentiality

Information about a client's general business activities or the results of a client's project should not be disclosed to a third party. The supplier should not even disclose the name of a client unless permission is received in advance.

The thorniest issue in confidentiality is determining where "background knowledge" stops and conflict arises as a result of work with a previous client. One researcher put it this way:

I get involved in a number of proprietary studies. The problem that often arises is that some studies end up covering similar subject matter as previous studies. Our code of ethics states that you cannot use data from one project in a related project for a competitor. However, since I often know some information about an area, I end up compromising my original client. Even though upper management formally states that it should not be done, they also expect it to be done to cut down on expenses. This conflict of interest situation is difficult to deal with. At least in my firm, I don't see a resolution to the issue. It is not a onetime situation, but rather a process that perpetuates itself. To make individuals redo portions of studies which have recently been done is ludicrous, and to forgo potential new business is almost impossible from a financial perspective.[4]

Black Box Branding

Marketing research suppliers have discovered branding. Synovate has more than 25 branded product offerings, including Brand Vision and M2M. Maritz Research offers Loyalty Maximizer, and Harris Interactive has TRBC, a scale bias correction algorithm. Go to virtually any large marketing research firm's Web site, and you'll see a vast array of branded research products for everything from market segmentation to customer value analysis—all topped off with a diminutive [SM], [TM], or[®].

A common denominator across some of these products is that they are proprietary, which means the firms won't disclose exactly how they work. That's why they're also known pejoratively as black boxes. A black box method is proprietary—a company is able to protect its product development investment. And if customers perceive added value in the approach, suppliers can charge a premium price to boot. (Black boxes and brand names are not synonymous. Almost all proprietary methods have a clever brand name, but there are also brand names attached to research methods that are not proprietary.)

At least two factors have given rise to this branding frenzy. First, competitive pressures force organizations to seek new ways to differentiate their product offerings from those of their competitors. Second, many large research companies are publicly held, and publicly held companies are under constant pressure to increase sales and profits each quarter. One way to do this is to charge a premium price for services. If a company has a proprietary method for doing a marketing segmentation study, presumably it can charge more for this approach than can another firm using publicly available software such as SPSS or SAS.

Clients have no objective way of determining whether the results of a proprietary method would vary significantly from those of more standard approaches, and neither have we. Go to five different companies that have five different black boxes for choice modeling, for example. Each company claims its method is superior, yet it's impossible to assess, from a psychometric perspective, which possesses the highest level of validity.

Of course, no one is forcing clients to purchase a black box method, and they can always contact other organizations that have used a supplier's proprietary method to assess its effectiveness. Often clients will obtain multiple bids on a project so that they can select from a variety of approaches to help them answer their research questions.[5]

Client Ethics

Like research suppliers, clients (or users) also have a number of ethical do's and don'ts. Some of the most common client problems are requesting bids when a supplier has been predetermined, requesting bids to obtain free advice and methodology, making false promises, and issuing unauthorized RFPs.

Requesting Bids When a Supplier Has Been Predetermined

It is not uncommon for a client to prefer one research supplier over another. Such a preference may be due to a good working relationship, cost considerations, ability to make deadlines, friendship, or quality of the research staff. Having a preference per se is not unethical. It is unethical, however, to predetermine which supplier will receive a contract and yet ask for proposals from other suppliers to satisfy corporate requirements. Requiring time, effort, and money from firms that have no opportunity to win the contract is very unfair. Why more than a single RFP? Some corporations require more than one bid.

Requesting Bids to Obtain Free Advice and Methodology

Client companies seeking bargain-basement prices have been known to solicit detailed proposals, including complete methodology and a sample questionnaire, from a number of suppliers. After "picking the brains" of the suppliers, the client assembles a questionnaire and then contracts directly with field services to gather the data. A variation of this tactic is to go to the cheapest supplier with the client's own proposal, derived by taking the best ideas from the other proposals. The client then attempts to get the supplier to conduct the more elaborate study at the lower price.

Making False Promises

Another technique used by unethical clients to lower their research costs is to hold out a nonexistent carrot. For example, a client might say, "I don't want to promise anything, but we are planning a major stream of research in this area, and if you will give us a good price on this first study, we will make it up to you on the next one." Unfortunately, the next one never comes—or if it does, the same line is used on another unsuspecting supplier.

Requesting Proposals without Authorization

In each of the following situations, a client representative sought proposals without first receiving the authority to allocate the funds to implement them:

1. A client representative decided to ask for proposals and *then* go to management to find out whether she could get the funds to carry them out.

2. A highly regarded employee made a proposal to management on the need for marketing research in a given area. Although managers were not too enthused about the idea, they told the researcher to seek bids so as not to dampen his interest or miss a potentially (but, in their view, highly unlikely) good idea.

3. A client representative and her management had different ideas on what the problem was and how it should be solved. The research supplier was not informed of

the management view, and even though the proposal met the representative's requirements, management rejected it out of hand.

4. Without consulting with the sales department, a client representative asked for a proposal on analyzing present sales performance. Through fear of negative feedback, corporate politics, or lack of understanding of marketing research, the sales department blocked implementation of the proposal.

Field Service Ethics

Marketing research field services are the production arm of the research industry requiring telephone or face-to-face interviews. They are the critical link between the respondent and the research supplier. It is imperative that they properly record information and carefully follow sampling plans. Otherwise, even the best research design will produce invalid information (garbage in, garbage out). Maintaining high ethical standards will aid a field service in procuring good raw data for the research firm.

Using Professional Respondents

The problem of professional respondents arises most often in the recruitment of focus group participants. Virtually all field services maintain a database of people willing to participate in qualitative discussion groups, along with a list of their demographic characteristics. Maintaining such a list is good business and quite ethical. When qualifications for group participants are easy (for example, pet owners, persons who drive SUVs), there is little temptation to use professional respondents. However, when a supplier wants, for example, persons who are heavy users of Oxydol detergent or who own a Russian Blue cat, it is not unheard of for a group recruiter to call a professional respondent and say, "I can get you into a group tomorrow with a $75 respondent fee, and all you need to say is that you own a Russian Blue cat."

In an attempt to weed out professional respondents, a research supplier may specify that the participant must not have been a member of a qualitative discussion group within the past six months. However, dishonest field services will simply tell the professional respondent to deny having participated in a group within the past six months.

Data Collection Code of Ethics

The Marketing Research Association (MRA) is an association to which many field services belong. The organization is dedicated to promoting excellence in data collection. To this end, it recently enacted the following code of ethics:

Companies Engaged in Data Collection . . .

1. will treat the respondent with respect and not influence a respondent's opinion or attitude on any issue through direct or indirect attempts, including the framing of questions.

2. will conduct themselves in a professional manner and ensure privacy and confidentiality.

3. will ensure that all formulas used during bidding and reporting during the data collection process conform with the MRA/Council of American Survey Research Organizations (CASRO) Incidence Guidelines.

4. will make factually correct statements to secure cooperation and will honor promises made during the interview to respondents, whether verbal or written.

5. will give respondents the opportunity to refuse to participate in the research when there is a possibility they may be identifiable even without the use of their name or address (e.g., because of the size of the population being sampled).

6. will not use information to identify respondents without the permission of the respondent except to those who check the data or are involved in processing the data. If such permission is given, the interviewer must record it, or a respondent must do so, during all Internet studies, at the time the permission is secured.

7. will adhere to and follow these principles when conducting online research:

   ▨ Respondents' rights to anonymity *must* be safeguarded.

   ▨ Unsolicited e-mail *must not* be sent to those requesting not to receive any further e-mail.

   ▨ Researchers interviewing minors *must* adhere to the Children's Online Privacy Protection Act (COPPA).

   ▨ Before collecting, using, or disclosing personal information from a child, the researcher must obtain verifiable parental consent from the child's parent. *Refer to MRA Internet Ethics Guidelines "Use of the Internet for Conducting Opinion and Marketing Research" for more educational information. www.mra-net .org/codes/internet_ethics_guidelines.PDF.*

8. for Internet research, will not use any data in any way contrary to the provider's published privacy statement without permission from the respondent.

9. will respect the respondent's right to withdraw or refuse to cooperate at any stage of the study and will not use any procedure or technique to coerce or imply that cooperation is obligatory.

10. will obtain and document respondent consent when it is known that the personally identifiable information of the respondent may be passed by audio, video, or Interactive Voice Response to a third party for legal or other purposes.

11. will obtain permission and document consent of a parent, legal guardian, or responsible guardian before interviewing children 13 years of age or younger. Prior to obtaining permission, the interviewer should divulge the subject matter, length of interview, and other special tasks that may be required of the respondent.

12. will ensure that all interviewers comply with any laws or regulations that may be applicable when contacting or communicating to any minor (18 years old or younger) regardless of the technology or methodology utilized.

13. will not reveal any information that could be used to identify clients without their written authorization.

14. will ensure that companies, their employees, and subcontractors involved in the data collection process adhere to reasonable precautions so that multiple surveys are not conducted at the same time with a specific respondent without explicit permission from the sponsoring company or companies.

15. will consider all research materials provided by the client or generated as a result of materials provided by the client to be the property of the client. These materials will not be disseminated or disposed of without the verbal or written permission of the client.

16. will, as time and availability permit, give their client the opportunity to monitor studies in progress to ensure research quality.

17. will not represent a nonresearch activity to be opinion and marketing research, such as:

    ▨ the compilation of lists, registers, or data banks of names and addresses for any nonresearch purposes (e.g., canvassing or fund raising).

- industrial, commercial, or any other form of espionage.
- the acquisition of information for use by credit rating services or similar organizations.
- sales or promotional approaches to the respondent.
- the collection of debts.[6]

Respondents' Rights

Respondents in a marketing research project typically give their time and opinions and receive little or nothing in return. These individuals, however, do have certain rights that should be upheld by all marketing researchers. All potential participants in a research project have the right to choose, the right to safety, the right to be informed, and the right to privacy.

Right to Choose

Everyone has the right to determine whether or not to participate in a marketing research project. Some people, such as poorly educated individuals or children, may not fully appreciate this privilege. A person who would like to terminate an interview or experiment may give short, incomplete answers or even false data.

The fact that a person has consented to be part of an experiment or to answer a questionnaire does not give the researcher carte blanche to do whatever she or he wants. The researcher still has an obligation to the respondent. For example, if a person participating in a taste test involving a test product and several existing products prefers the test product, the researcher does not have the right to use the respondent's name and address in a promotion piece, saying that "Ms. Jones prefers new Sudsies to Brand X."

Right to Safety

Research participants have the right to safety from physical or psychological harm. While it is unusual for a respondent to be exposed to physical harm, there have been cases of persons becoming ill during food taste tests. Also, on a more subtle level, researchers rarely warn respondents that a test product contains, say, a high level of salt. An unwitting respondent with hypertension could be placed in physical danger if the test ran several weeks.

It is much more common for a respondent to be placed in a psychologically damaging situation. Individuals might experience stress when an interviewer presses them to participate in a study. Others might experience stress when they cannot answer questions or are given a time limit to complete a task (for example, "You have five minutes to browse through this magazine, and then I will ask you a series of questions").

Right to Be Informed

Research participants have the right to be informed of all aspects of a research task. Knowing what is involved, how long it will take, and what will be done with the data, a person can make an intelligent choice as to whether to participate in the project.

Often, it is necessary to disguise the name of the research sponsor to avoid biasing the respondent. For example, it is poor research practice to say, "We are conducting a survey for Pepsi; which brand of soft drink do you consume most often?" In cases in which disguising the sponsor is required, a debriefing should take place following the completion of the interview. The debriefing should cover the study's purpose, the sponsor, what happens next with the data, and any other pertinent information. A debriefing can reduce respondent stress and build goodwill for the research industry. Unfortunately, taking the time to debrief a respondent is a cost that most companies are unwilling to incur.

In some business and academic research, the researcher may offer to provide the respondent with a copy of the research results as an incentive to obtain his or her participation in the project. When a commitment has been made to disseminate the findings to survey respondents, it should be fulfilled. On more than one occasion, we have participated in academic surveys where the carrot of research results was offered but never delivered.

Right to Privacy

All consumers have the right to privacy. All major research organizations, including the MRA (discussed above), CASRO, the Internet Marketing Research Association (IMRO), the American Marketing Association (AMA), and the Advertising Research Foundation (ARF), have privacy codes. For example, with online research, lists of potential respondents must have one of two characteristics. Potential respondents must have either a prior opt-in for contact or they must have an existing business relationship with the sender through which an e-mail contact would not be considered a random, unsolicited e-mail (spam).

Consumer privacy can be defined in terms of two dimensions of control. The first dimension includes control of unwanted telephone, mail, e-mail, or personal intrusion in the consumer's environment, and the second concerns control of information about the consumer. Consumer privacy can be viewed in the context of any interaction, profit or nonprofit, between marketer and consumer, including (but not limited to) credit and cash sales, consumer inquiries, and marketer-initiated surveys. The very nature of the marketing research business requires interviewers to invade an individual's privacy. An interviewer calls or approaches strangers, requests a portion of their limited free time, and asks them to answer personal questions—sometimes *very* personal questions. Perhaps the greatest privacy issue for consumers today is the role of marketing databases (see Chapter 3).

A number of laws have been passed in recent years dealing with various aspects of privacy as it relates to the marketing research industry. Diane Bowers, president of the CASRO, poses the following questions to marketing researchers:

Did you know. . . .
> *You may be violating the law if you interview customers of financial institutions who have not consented to that research? (Federal regulations require opt-out; some states require opt-in.)*
> *You may be violating the law if patients you interview for health care research have not consented to that research? (Federal regulations require opt-in.)*
> *You may be violating the law if telephone customers you interview for telecommunications research have not consented to that research? (Federal regulations require opt-out.)*
> *You may be violating the law if you exchange personal data about respondents with someone in Europe without complying with the U.S. Safe Harbor and the EU Directive on Data Protection? (U.S. Safe Harbor principles must be verifiably adhered to, or contractually met, or you must be EU-certified.)*
> *You may be violating the law if you disclose personal information about respondents to a subcontractor, including interviewers and data processors? (Privacy laws require binding confidentiality agreements before any "onward transfer" of such information.)*

*You are violating the law if you fail to comply with any material aspect of your online privacy statement or offline privacy policy? (The FTC, for example, has the ability to impose fines of up to several thousands of dollars **per day** for such violations.)*

You are legally and professionally liable for the privacy and confidentiality of your research respondents and the integrity of your research?[7]

Ethics and Professionalism

Digital Vision/Getty Images

Today's business ethics are actually a subset of the values held by society as a whole. The values that underlie marketing decisions have been acquired through family, educational, and religious institutions, and social movements (for example, women's rights, environmental protection). A marketing researcher with a mature set of ethical values accepts personal responsibility for decisions that affect the community. Considerations include the following:

■ Employees' needs and desires and the long-range best interests of the organization

■ The long-range goodwill and best interests of people who are directly affected by company activities (a bonus: good publicity for the firm)

■ The societal values and conditions that provide the basis for the social structure in which the company exists

High standards of ethics and professionalism go hand in hand. Good ethics provide a solid foundation for professionalism, and striving for a lofty level of professionalism requires ethical behavior on the part of researchers.

Fostering Professionalism

A profession and membership in it are objectively determined; professionalism is evaluated on more personal and subjective levels.

Because of the specialized knowledge and expertise they possess, members of a profession have influence and power over those for whom they provide a particular service. The tools of a doctor or lawyer cannot easily be obtained and sold in the marketplace; these professions guard their knowledge and control who has access to it. Although marketing researchers and marketers wield power and influence over their customers and even society, the marketing industry does not have a credentialing process or high entry barriers. The argument can be made that the marketers who most need to think, believe, and behave with professionalism are those in marketing research.

The distinction between a profession and professionalism is important: a **profession** and membership in it are objectively determined (for example, by medical board exams), whereas **professionalism** is evaluated on more personal and subjective levels. A study designed to measure the level of professionalism in marketing research found that researchers had autonomy in their jobs, were permitted to exercise judgment, and were recognized for their level of expertise and ability to work independently. These characteristics are marks of professionalism. However, most researchers did not readily identify the contribution

➜ **profession**
An organization whose membership is determined by objective standards, such as an examination.

that marketing makes to society, nor did most firms tend to reward researchers' participation in professional organizations. These characteristics do not indicate a high level of professionalism.

Several steps have been taken recently to improve the level of professionalism in the marketing research industry. For example, CASRO has sponsored symposia dealing with ethical issues in survey research. CASRO also has created a code of ethics that has been widely disseminated to research professionals. The CASRO board has worked with groups such as the Marketing Research Association to provide input to legislatures considering antimarketing research legislation.

> **professionalism**
> A quality said to be possessed by a worker with a high level of expertise, the freedom to exercise judgment, and the ability to work independently.

Researcher Certification

Today, it is far too easy to begin practicing marketing research. We have seen several "fast talkers" convince unwary clients that they are qualified researchers. Unfortunately, relying on poor information to make major decisions has resulted in loss of market share, reduction in profits, and, in some cases, bankruptcy.

Certification has generated a great deal of debate among members of the marketing research industry. It should be noted that certification is not licensing. *Licensing* is a mandatory procedure administered by a governmental body that allows one to practice a profession. *Certification* is a voluntary program administered by a nongovernmental body that provides a credential for differentiation in the marketplace. The issue of certification is sensitive because it directly affects marketing researchers' ability to practice their profession freely.

The MRA has launched a Professional Researcher Certification program. The objectives, according to the MRA, are "to encourage high standards within the profession in order to raise competency, establish an objective measure of an individual's knowledge and proficiency, and to encourage continued professional development."[8] The program allows for certification as a research user, supplier, or data collector. The process requires a series of continuing education credits and then passing an exam. Researchers can be grandfathered into certification if they meet the MRA's standards for a specific research job. The grandfathering period ended on February 28, 2007.

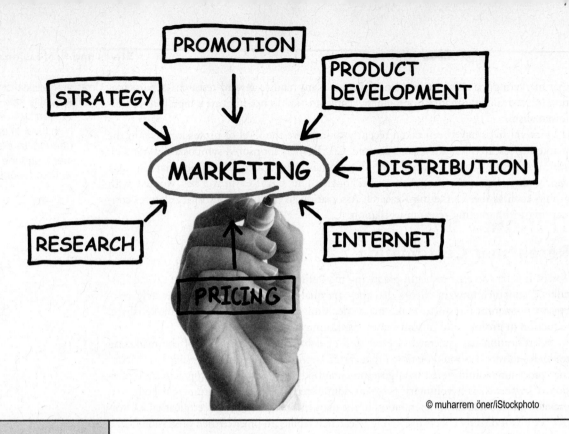

CHAPTER 2

Problem Definition, Exploratory Research, and the Research Process

LEARNING OBJECTIVES

→ 1. To understand the problem definition process.

→ 2. To learn the steps involved in the marketing research process.

→ 3. To understand the components of a research request.

→ 4. To learn the advantages and disadvantages of survey, observation, and experiment research techniques.

→ 5. To become familiar with how the marketing research process is initiated.

Conducting marketing research involves a series of logical steps, beginning with problem definition and research objectives. What are the steps in the marketing research process? How is the research process initiated? These are the issues we will address in this chapter.

Critical Importance of Correctly Defining the Problem

Correctly defining the problem is the crucial first step in the marketing research process. If the research problem is defined incorrectly, the research objectives will also be wrong, and the entire marketing research process will be a waste of time and money. A large consumer packaged goods company wanted to conduct a study among a brand's heavy users in order to understand the brand's equity. More specifically, it wanted to expand that equity into new products. The brand had very low penetration, so the company needed new products to meet the upcoming fiscal year's volume goal of double-digit growth. Notice the absence of tying research learning—understanding the brand's equity—to the business objective.

The brand had a small base from which to grow, so simply investigating the brand's equity among its most loyal users wouldn't help decision makers reach a double-digit growth rate. Upon reflection, the business objective focused on identifying marketing levers that would increase brand penetration—and thus growth. Accordingly, the research objectives transformed into understanding barriers to current brand purchase and identifying bridges that would motivate category users to buy the brand.

Study results showed that the brand chiefly suffered from awareness problems. Both brand and category users liked the product, but didn't use it as often as others in the category because they simply forgot about the brand. Reminders—in the form of advertising, incentives, and new products—became the levers that could improve brand penetration and growth. Conducting an equity study among heavy users clearly wouldn't have caught this.[1]

The process for defining the problem is shown in Exhibit 2.1. Note that the ultimate goal is to develop clear, concise, and meaningful marketing research objectives. Researching such objectives will yield precise decision-making information for managers.

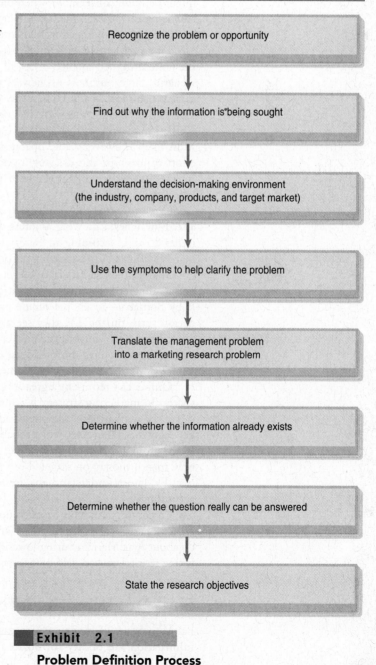

Recognize the problem or opportunity

Find out why the information is being sought

Understand the decision-making environment
(the industry, company, products, and target market)

Use the symptoms to help clarify the problem

Translate the management problem
into a marketing research problem

Determine whether the information already exists

Determine whether the question really can be answered

State the research objectives

Exhibit 2.1

Problem Definition Process

Recognize the Problem or Opportunity

The marketing research process begins with the recognition of a marketing problem or opportunity. As changes occur in the firm's external environment, marketing managers are faced with the questions "Should we change the existing marketing mix?" and, if so, "How?" Marketing research may be used to evaluate products and services, promotion, distribution, and pricing alternatives. In addition, it may be used to find and evaluate new opportunities, in a process called **opportunity identification**.

→ **opportunity identification**
Using marketing research to find and evaluate new opportunities.

Let's look at an example of opportunity identification. By 2015 there will likely be a major shift in online video. Perhaps half of all videos will be viewed online. This estimate might be quite conservative when one considers the historical adoption of other related technologies. For example, DVD players were in 70 percent of American TV households by 2004—only 6 years after their commercial introduction.[2]

There are several different ways the transition could play out, but the outcome is the same: Internet-enabled TVs will find their way into most American homes. In one scenario, large numbers of viewers will learn to use the built-in Internet capabilities available in most new TVs in a way that complements their consumption of broadcast video. Alternatively, the aggressive new breed of video providers, such as Apple TV and Netflix, may win over American consumers with their promises of on-demand video. Most likely, however, cable operators and alternative delivery systems, in a concerted effort to preempt this onslaught and retain their subscription businesses, will rapidly replace today's set-top boxes with units that combine broadcast, DVR, and online video in a single box.

One reason for this production is that Generation Y, born between 1979 and 1994, already watches a growing amount of video online. In 2010, 29 percent of consumers under 25 did, according to Research Now. But over the next 5 years, this group will mature and make up a growing portion of U.S. households.[3]

Second, the user interface on set-top boxes will vastly improve by automatically recommending content and making it easier for all viewers—including the less tech-savvy Baby Boomers—to choose online video over broadcast. Imagine the scenario: When a person turns on the TV, they see a welcome screen that includes an option to watch, immediately, on demand, the next episode of their favorite show. Or they could spend a half an hour trolling the broadcast channels in hopes of finding something they like. Which one's the more likely outcome?

Online can represent a great opportunity to Netflix and even Dish Network, but a successful marketing strategy is required to be successful. This requires an understanding of the marketplace, the rate of adoption of online video, online video watcher market segments (Gen Yers will probably use it differently from Baby Boomers), and so forth. From a different perspective, a major advertiser, like Procter & Gamble, which now spends mostly on targeted online ads and traditional media like radio and broadcast TV, must understand the trend toward online video and adjust its media mix accordingly.

Of course, marketing research doesn't always deal with opportunities. Managers may want to know, for example, "Why are we losing marketing share?" or "What should we do about Ajax Manufacturing lowering its prices by 10 percent?" In these instances, marketing researchers can help managers solve problems.

Find Out Why the Information Is Being Sought

Large amounts of money, effort, and time are wasted because requests for marketing information are poorly formulated or misunderstood. For example, managers may not have a clear idea of what they want or may not phrase their questions properly. Therefore, marketing researchers often find the following activities helpful:

- Discuss what the information will be used for and what decisions might be made as a result of the research. Work through detailed examples to help clarify the issue.
- Try to get the client or manager to prioritize their questions. This helps sort out central questions from those of incidental interest.
- Rephrase the questions in several slightly different forms and discuss the differences.
- Create sample data and ask if such data would help answer the questions. Simulate the decision process.
- Remember that the more clear-cut you think the questions are and the more quickly you come to feel that the questions are straightforward, the more you should doubt that you have understood the real need.

Understand the Decision-Making Environment with Exploratory Research

Once researchers understand the motivation for conducting the research, often they need additional background information to fully comprehend the problem. This may mean simply talking to brand managers or new product managers, reading company reports, visiting production facilities and retail stores, and perhaps talking with suppliers. If the industry has a trade association, researchers might peruse its Web site for information published by the association. The better the marketing researcher understands the decision-making environment, including the industry, the firm, its products or services, and the target market, the more likely it is that the problem will be defined correctly. This step may be referred to as conducting a **situation analysis**.

Sometimes informed discussions with managers and suppliers and on-site visits aren't enough. **Exploratory research** may be conducted to obtain greater understanding of a concept or to help crystallize the definition of a problem. It is also used to identify important variables to be studied. Exploratory research is preliminary research, not the definitive research used to determine a course of action.

Exploratory research can take several forms: pilot studies, experience surveys, secondary data analysis, pilot studies case analysis, and focus groups. **Pilot studies** are surveys using a limited number of respondents and often employing less rigorous sampling techniques than are employed in large, quantitative studies.

Experience Surveys Analysis
A second form of exploratory research is experience surveys. **Experience surveys** involve talking with knowledgeable individuals, both inside and outside the organization, who may provide insights into the problem. Rarely do experience surveys include a formal questionnaire. Instead, the researcher may simply have a list of topics to be discussed. The survey, then, is much like an informal discussion. For example, if Jet Blue is redesigning the interior of its aircraft, it may use experience surveys to speak with interior designers, frequent flyers, flight attendants, and pilots.

Secondary Data Analysis
Secondary data analysis is another form of exploratory research. Because secondary data analysis is covered extensively in Chapter 3, we will touch on it only lightly here. *Secondary data* are data that have been gathered for some purpose other than the one at hand. Today, marketing researchers can use the Internet to access countless sources of secondary data quickly and at minimal

→ **situation analysis**
Studying the decision-making environment within which marketing research will take place.

→ **exploratory research**
Preliminary research conducted to increase understanding of a concept, to clarify the exact nature of the problem to be solved, or to identify important variables to be studied.

→ **pilot studies**
Surveys using a limited number of respondents and often employing less rigorous sampling techniques than are employed in large, quantitative studies.

→ **experience surveys**
Discussions with knowledgeable individuals, both inside and outside an organization, who may provide insights into the problem.

expense. There are few subjects that have not been analyzed at one time or another. With a bit of luck, the marketing researcher can use secondary data to help precisely define the problem.

Case Analysis   Case analysis represents the fourth form of exploratory research. The purpose of **case analysis** is to review information from a few other situations that are similar to the present research problem. For example, electric utilities across America are scrambling to adopt the marketing concept and to become customer oriented; these utilities are conducting market segmentation research, customer satisfaction studies, and customer loyalty surveys. To better understand the deregulation of the electric utility industry, marketing researchers are examining case studies on the deregulation of the airline industry. Researchers, however, must always take care to determine the relevancy of any case study to the present research problem.

Focus Groups   Focus groups are in-depth discussions, usually consisting of 8 to 12 participants, which are led by a moderator and are generally limited to one particular concept, idea, or theme. The general idea is to have what one person says generate thoughts and comments by others, therefore creating group dynamics. That is, the interplay of responses will yield more information than if the same number of persons had contributed in individual interviews. Focus groups are the primary topic of discussion in Chapter 4, so they will be lightly covered here. We mention them now because they are probably the most popular form of exploratory research.

Using Intranets for Exploratory Research   Computers and mobile devices can be very powerful tools, for doing exploratory research. In very large organizations with intranets, a researcher has the capability of determining whether needed or relevant information is available somewhere inside the organization. The corporate marketing research department at Texas Instruments (TI), for example, has developed a powerful intranet application that permits TI managers worldwide to search for past research studies and those currently in progress on the basis of key words. They have immediate online access to a brief description of each study and can send e-mail seeking permission to view the full text of reports on old projects. Permission can be granted electronically via e-mail by the owner of the report (the person who paid for it), and the full text can be accessed online.

   While intranets provide easy access to internal data, the Internet is an invaluable resource for searching tens of millions of external sources for the information needed. At the exploratory stage, a researcher might use any one or several of the online search engines to find information needed. This type of search not only is much faster than a traditional library search but also provides access to an incredible array of information that is not available in any library. The researcher can perform an Internet search and point out or download the desired information in a matter of hours rather than the days or weeks a standard library search might require. Finally, the researcher can identify a range of discussion or special-interest groups on the Internet that may be relevant to a research project.

Completing Exploratory Research   The end of exploratory study comes when the marketing researchers are convinced that they have found the major dimensions of the problem. They may have defined a set of questions that can be used as specific guides to a detailed research design. Or they may have developed a number of potential ideas about possible causes of a specific problem of importance to management. They may also have determined that certain other factors are such remote possibilities that they can be

➜ **case analysis**
Reviewing information from situations that are similar to the current one.

safely ignored in any further study. Finally, the researchers may end exploration because they feel that further research is not needed or is not presently possible due to time, money, or other constraints.

Use the Symptoms to Clarify the Problem

Marketing researchers must be careful to distinguish between symptoms and the real problem. A symptom is a phenomenon that occurs because of the existence of something else. For example, managers often talk about the problem of poor sales, declining profits, increased customer complaints, or defecting customers. Each of these is a symptom of a deeper problem. That is, something is causing a company's customers to leave. Is it lower prices offered by the competition? Or is it better service? Focusing on the symptoms and not the true problem is often referred to as the *iceberg principle*. Approximately 10 percent of an iceberg rises out of the ocean; the remaining 90 percent is below the surface. Preoccupied with the obstacle they can see, managers may fail to comprehend and confront the deeper problem, which remains submerged.

Ensuring that the true problem has been defined is not always easy. Managers and marketing researchers must use creativity and good judgment. Cutting through to the heart of a problem is a bit like peeling an onion—you must take off one layer at a time. One approach to eliminating symptoms is to ask "What caused this to occur?" When the researcher can no longer answer this question, the real problem is at hand. For example, when a St. Louis manufacturer of pumps faced a 7 percent decline in sales from the previous year, managers asked, "What caused this?" A look at sales across the product line showed that sales were up or about the same on all items except large, heavy-duty submersible pumps, whose sales were down almost 60 percent. They then asked, "What caused this?" Sales of the pump in the eastern and central divisions were about the same as in the previous year. However, in the western region, sales were zero! Once again, they asked, "What caused this?" Further investigation revealed that a Japanese manufacturer was dumping a similar submersible pump in Western markets at about 50 percent of the St. Louis manufacturer's wholesale price. This was the true problem. The manufacturer lobbied the Justice Department to fine the Japanese company and to issue a cease-and-desist order.

Whenever possible, top management should be involved in defining the problem. This topic is discussed in the Practicing Marketing Research box that appears on page 65.

Translate the Management Problem into a Marketing Research Problem

Once the true management decision problem has been identified, it must be converted into a marketing research problem. A **marketing research problem** specifies what information is needed to solve the problem and how that information can be obtained efficiently and effectively. The **marketing research objective**, then, is the goal statement, defining the specific information needed to solve the marketing research problem. Managers must combine this information with their own experience and other related information to make a proper decision.

In contrast to the marketing research problem, the **management decision problem** is action oriented. Management decision problems tend to be much broader in scope and far more general than marketing research problems, which must be narrowly defined and specific if the research effort is to be successful. Sometimes several research studies must be conducted to solve a broad management decision problem.

> **marketing research problem**
> A statement specifying the type of information needed by the decision maker to help solve the management decision problem and how that information can be obtained efficiently and effectively.

> **marketing research objective**
> A goal statement, defining the specific information needed to solve the marketing research problem.

> **management decision problem**
> A statement specifying the type of managerial action required to solve the problem.

Determine Whether the Information Already Exists

It often seems easier and more interesting to develop new information than to delve through old reports and data files to see whether the required information already exists. There is a tendency to assume that current data are superior to data collected in the past, as current data appear to be a "fix on today's situation." And because researchers have more control over the format and comprehensiveness of fresh data, they promise to be easier to work with. Yet, using existing data can save managers time and money if such data can answer the research question.

Research objectives must be as specific and unambiguous as possible. Remember that the entire research effort (in terms of time and money) is geared toward achieving the objectives. When the marketing researcher meets with a committee to learn the goals of a particular project, committee members may not fully agree on what is needed. We have learned from experience to go back to a committee (or the individual in charge) with a written list of research objectives. The researcher should then ask the manager, "If we accomplish the objectives on this list, will you have enough information to make informed decisions about the problem?" If the reply is yes, the manager should be asked to sign off on the objectives. The researcher should then give the manager a copy and keep a copy for the research files. Putting the agreed-on objectives in writing prevents the manager from saying later, "Hey, this is not the information I wanted." In a busy and hectic corporate environment, such misunderstandings happen more frequently than one might imagine.

Avoiding the Nice-to-Know Syndrome

Even after conducting exploratory research, managers often tend to discuss research objectives in terms of broad areas of ignorance. They say, in effect, "Here are some things I don't know." A Starbucks executive might wonder: "You know, we already sell fresh-baked goods in our stores . . . I wonder if people would buy frozen Starbucks pastries and rolls in supermarkets? Maybe I'll ask this question on our out-of-home advertising media study." Unfortunately, this scenario usually leads to disappointment. There is nothing wrong with interesting findings, but they must also be *actionable*. That is, the findings must provide decision-making information. Accomplishment of a research objective has to do more than reduce management's level of ignorance. Unless all the research is exploratory, it should lead to a decision. Perhaps the best way to assure that research is actionable is to determine how the research results will be implemented. Asking a single question about purchase intent of Starbucks frozen baked goods in a grocery store is not actionable. So much more would have to be known—for example, type of goods, price points, packaging design, and so forth. Numerous taste tests would also have to be conducted.

Determine Whether the Question Can Be Answered

When marketing researchers promise more than they can deliver, they hurt the credibility of marketing research. It is extremely important for researchers to avoid being impelled—either by overeagerness to please or by managerial a machismo—into an effort that they know has a limited probability of success. In most cases, you can discern in advance the likelihood of success by identifying the following:

- Instances in which you know for certain that information of the type required exists or can be readily obtained.
- Situations in which you are fairly sure, based on similar prior experiences, that the information can be gathered.
- Cases in which you know that you are trying something quite new and there is a real risk of drawing a complete blank.

PRACTICING MARKETING RESEARCH

Importance of Top Management's Definition of the Management Problem

Researchers report that they receive incomplete, and even incorrect, answers if the person who commissions a study is not the ultimate decision maker. In one case, the commissioning agent (a midlevel manager) said the research was being conducted to learn about the market. In reality, the senior decision maker wanted to know whether version A or B would gain a bigger share of the market. The research did a great job of exploring the boundaries of the market, defining customer segments and their needs, and identifying likely competitors. But the senior decision maker found the research largely irrelevant because it did not tell him whether to go with version A or B.

While senior decision makers may say they are too busy to talk or insist on delegating the task to someone junior, researchers who have stood firm and insisted on talking to the senior person report the effort is worth it. "First, I asked to meet the [CEO] to discuss the firm's mission and strategy and how the research would help him make better decisions. When that wasn't an option, I wrote up a one-page description of the situation and the research objectives and asked to have the CEO approve it before I designed the research. When he didn't have time to look at it, I said I couldn't waste the firm's resources by starting without clear goals. *Then* I got his full attention. We met and, believe me, the CEO's needs were quite different from what I had been told. I was really glad I had insisted. If I'd waited until the research was done, I'd never have gotten his attention, and the research would have been largely irrelevant."[4]

Questions

1. Should top management always be involved in defining a management problem?

2. What tactics might marketing researchers use to get top management involved in problem definition?

State the Research Objectives

The culmination of the problem definition process is a statement of the research objectives. These objectives are stated in terms of the precise information necessary to address the marketing research problem/opportunity. Well-formulated objectives serve as a road map in pursuing the research project. They also serve as a standard that later will enable managers to evaluate the quality and value of the work by asking "Were the objectives met?" and "Do the recommendations flow logically from the objectives and the research findings?"

Research Objectives as Hypotheses   Often researchers state a research objective in the form of a hypothesis. A **hypothesis** is a conjectural statement about a relationship between two or more variables that can be tested with empirical data; it is considered to be plausible, given the available information. A good hypothesis will contain clear implications for testing stated relationships. For example, based on exploratory research, a researcher might hypothesize that a doubling of expenditures for billboards in cities of 300,000 or more population will increase the sales of Starbucks summer drinks by 15 percent. Alternatively, a second hypothesis might be that spending $30,000 for vehicle wraps in cities of 300,000 or more will have no significant impact on the sales of Starbucks summer drinks.

> → **hypothesis**
> A conjectural statement about a relationship between two or more variables that can be tested with empirical data.

The Marketing Research Process

We have just discussed the first step in the marketing research process: identifying the problem/opportunity and stating the marketing research objectives. The other steps in the process are creating the research design, choosing the method of research, selecting the sampling procedure, collecting the data, analyzing the data, writing and presenting the report, and following up on any recommendations that were made as a result of the report (see Exhibit 2.2). The overview of the process in this section forms the foundation for the remainder of the text. The following chapters examine specific aspects of the marketing research process.

Creating the Research Design

→ **research design**
The plan to be followed to answer the marketing research objectives.

The **research design** is a plan for addressing the research objectives or hypotheses. In essence, the researcher develops a structure or framework to answer a specific research problem/opportunity. There is no single best research design. Instead, different designs offer an array of choices, each with certain advantages and disadvantages. Ultimately, trade-offs are typically involved. A common trade-off is between research costs and the quality of the decision-making information provided. Generally speaking, the more precise and error-free the information obtained, the higher the cost. Another common trade-off is between time constraints and the type of research design selected. Overall, a researcher must attempt to provide management with the best information possible, subject to the various constraints under which he or she must operate. The researcher's first task is to decide whether the research will be descriptive or causal.

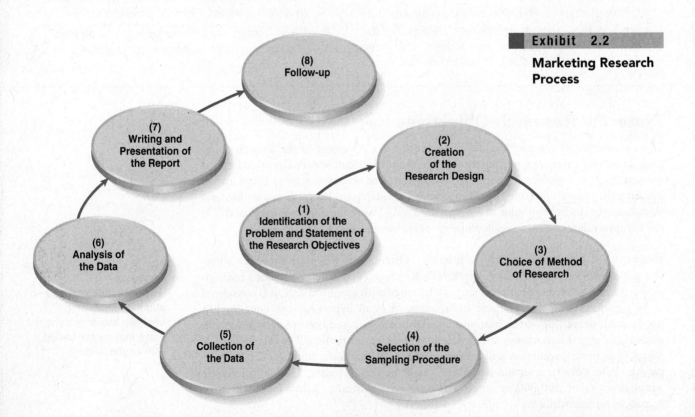

Exhibit 2.2

Marketing Research Process

Descriptive Studies   **Descriptive studies** are conducted to answer who, what, when, where, and how questions. Implicit in descriptive research is the fact that management already knows or understands the underlying relationships among the variables in the problem. A **variable** is simply a symbol or concept that can assume any one of a set of values.

A descriptive study for Starbucks might include demographic and lifestyle characteristics of typical, light, and heavy patronizers of Starbucks stores, purchasers of Starbucks baked goods, purchasers of Starbucks sandwiches, and buyers of coffee to take home. Other questions might determine drive time from work or home to the nearest Starbucks and whether purchasers pay by cash or credit.

Descriptive research can tell us that two variables, such as advertising and sales, seem to be somehow associated, but it cannot provide convincing evidence that high levels of advertising cause high sales. Because descriptive research can shed light on associations or relationships, it helps the researcher select variables for a causal study.

Causal Studies   In **causal studies**, the researcher investigates whether the value of one variable causes or determines the value of another variable, in an attempt to establish linkage between them. Experiments (see Chapter 7) often are used to measure causality. A **dependent variable** is a symbol or concept expected to be explained or affected by an independent variable. In contrast, an **independent variable** is a variable that the market researcher can, to some extent, manipulate, change, or alter. An independent variable in a research project is a presumed cause of or influence on the dependent variable, the presumed effect. For example, Starbucks may like to know whether the level of advertising (independent variable) determines the level of sales (dependent variable).

A causal study for Starbucks might involve changing one independent variable (for example, the number of direct mailings offering a 10 percent discount on a 1-pound bag of coffee over a 6-month period to target customers) and then observing the effect on coffee sales. Here, there is an appropriate causal order of events, or **temporal sequence**; the effect follows closely the hypothesized cause. Temporal sequence is one criterion that must be met for causality.

A second criterion for causality is **concomitant variation**—the degree to which a presumed cause (direct-mail promotion) and a presumed effect (coffee sales) occur together or vary together. If direct-mail promotions are a cause of increased coffee sales, then when the number of direct-mail promotions is increased, coffee sales should go up, and when the number of promotions is decreased, sales should fall. If, however, an increase in direct-mail promotions does not result in an increase in coffee sales, the researcher must conclude that the hypothesis about the relationship between direct-mail promotions and coffee sales is not supported.

An ideal situation would be one in which sales of coffee increased markedly every time Starbucks increased its e-mail promotions (up to a saturation level). But, alas, we live in a world where such perfection is rarely achieved. One additional saturation e-mail might bring a small increase in sales and the next e-mail a larger increment, or vice versa. And during the next 6-month period, an increase in e-mail promotions might produce no increase or even a decline in sales.

Remember, even perfect concomitant variation would not prove that A causes B. All the researcher could say is that the association makes the hypothesis more likely.

An important issue in studying causality is recognizing the possibility of **spurious association**, in which other variables are actually causing changes in the dependent variable. In an ideal situation, the researcher would demonstrate a total absence of other causal factors. However, in the real world of marketing research, it is very difficult to identify and control all other potential causal factors. Think for a moment of all the variables that could cause sales of 1-pound bags of coffee to increase or decrease—for example, prices, newspaper and television advertising, coupons, discounts, and weather.

descriptive studies
Research studies that answer the questions who, what, when, where, and how.

variable
A symbol or concept that can assume any one of a set of values.

causal studies
Research studies that examine whether the value of one variable causes or determines the value of another variable.

dependent variable
A symbol or concept expected to be explained or influenced by the independent variable.

independent variable
A symbol or concept over which the researcher has some control and that is hypothesized to cause or influence the dependent variable.

temporal sequence
An appropriate causal order of events.

concomitant variation
The degree to which a presumed cause and a presumed effect occur or vary together.

spurious association
A relationship between a presumed cause and a presumed effect that occurs as a result of an unexamined variable or set of variables.

The researcher may be able to lower spurious associations by trying to hold constant these other factors. Alternatively, the researcher may look at changes in sales in similar socioeconomic areas.

Choosing a Basic Method of Research

A research design, either descriptive or causal, is chosen based on a project's objectives. The next step is to select a means of gathering data. There are three basic research methods: (1) survey, (2) observation, and (3) experiment. Survey research is often descriptive in nature but can be causal. Observation research is typically descriptive, and experiment research is almost always causal.

© Peter Arnold, Inc./Alamy Limited

Scanning bar code information is a means of observation research that is widely used today.

→ **survey research**
Research in which an interviewer (except in mail and Internet surveys) interacts with respondents to obtain facts, opinions, and attitudes.

→ **observation research**
Typically, descriptive research that monitors respondents' actions without direct interaction.

→ **experiments**
Research to measure causality, in which the researcher changes one or more independent variables and observes the effect of the changes on the dependent variable.

Surveys **Survey research** involves an interviewer (except in mail and Internet surveys) who interacts with respondents to obtain facts, opinions, and attitudes. A questionnaire is used to ensure an orderly and structured approach to data gathering. Face-to-face interviews may take place in the respondent's home, a shopping mall, or a place of business.

Observations **Observation research** is examining patterns of behavior as opposed to asking consumers why they do what they do. This may involve people watching consumers or the use of a variety of machines. Kimberly-Clark, the maker of Huggies, Kleenex, and other household staples, outfits consumers with mini video cameras mounted to visors and linked to a recording device. Paid participants wear the somewhat strange-looking eye gear, known internally as the Consumer Vision System (CVS), while doing chores or shopping.

Under the system, K-C discovered that mothers who used Huggies Baby Wash, a bathing lotion, had trouble holding the bottle and needed two hands to open and dispense its contents. "[Moms] almost always have to have one hand on the baby at one time," said Becky Walter, K-C director-innovation, design and testing.[5]

K-C redesigned the product with a grippable bottle and a large lid that could easily be lifted with a thumb. The result was a significant increase in market share. Observation research is discussed in detail in Chapter 6.

Experiments **Experiments** are the third method researchers use to gather data. Experiment research is distinguished by the researcher's changing one or more independent variables—price, package, design, shelf space, advertising theme, or advertising expenditures—and observing the effects of those changes on a dependent variable (usually sales). The objective of experiments is to measure causality. The best experiments are those in which all factors other than the ones being manipulated are held constant. This enables the researcher to infer with confidence that changes in sales, for example, are caused by changes in the amount of money spent on advertising.

Holding all other factors constant in the external environment is a monumental and costly, if not impossible, task. Factors such as competitors' actions, weather, and economic conditions in various markets are beyond the control of the researcher. One way researchers attempt to control factors that might influence the dependent variable is to use a laboratory experiment—that is, an experiment conducted in a test facility rather than in the natural environment. Researchers sometimes create simulated supermarket environments, give consumers scrip (play money), and then ask them to shop as they normally would for groceries. By varying package design or color over several time periods, for example, the researcher can determine which package is most likely to stimulate sales. Although laboratory techniques can provide valuable information, it is important to recognize that the consumer is not in a natural environment; how people act in a test facility may differ from how they act in an actual shopping situation. Experiments are discussed in detail in Chapter 7.

Selecting the Sampling Procedure

A sample is a subset from a larger population. Although the basic nature of a sample is specified in the research design, selecting the sampling procedure is a separate step in the research process. Several questions must be answered before a sampling procedure is selected. First, the population or universe of interest must be defined. This is the group from which the sample will be drawn. It should include all the people whose opinions, behaviors, preferences, attitudes, and so on will yield information needed to answer the research problem—for example, all persons who eat Mexican food at least once every 60 days.

After the population has been defined, the next question is whether to use a probability sample or a nonprobability sample. A **probability sample** is a sample for which every element in the population has a known nonzero probability of being selected. Such samples allow the researcher to estimate how much sampling error is present in a given study. All samples that cannot be considered probability samples are nonprobability samples. **Nonprobability samples** are those in which the chances of selection for the various elements in the population are unknown. Researchers cannot statistically calculate the reliability of a nonprobability sample; that is, they cannot determine the degree of sampling error that can be expected. Sampling is the topic of Chapter 13.

> **probability sample**
> A subset of a population where every element in the population has a known nonzero chance of being selected.

> **nonprobability sample**
> A subset of a population in which the chances of selection for the various elements in the population are unknown.

Collecting the Data

Most survey-based data are now collected on the Internet. Interviewer-based data collection is done by marketing research field services. Field service firms throughout the country specialize in collecting data through personal and telephone interviewing on a subcontract basis. A typical interviewer-based research study involves data collection in several cities and requires working with a comparable number of field service firms. To ensure that all subcontractors do everything exactly the same way, detailed field instructions should be developed for every job. Nothing should be left to chance; in particular, no interpretations of procedures should be left to the subcontractors.

In addition to doing interviewing, field service firms often provide group research facilities, mall intercept locations, test product storage, and kitchen facilities for preparing test food products. They may also conduct retail audits (counting the amount of product sold from retail shelves).

Analyzing the Data

After the data have been collected, the next step in the research process is data analysis. The purpose of this analysis is to interpret and draw conclusions from the mass of collected data. The marketing researcher may use a variety of techniques, beginning with simple frequency analysis and culminating in complex multivariate techniques. Data analysis will be discussed later in the text.

Writing and Presenting the Report

After data analysis is completed, the researcher must prepare the report and communicate the conclusions and recommendations to management. This is a key step in the process because a marketing researcher who wants project conclusions acted on must convince the manager that the results are credible and justified by the data collected.

The researcher usually will be required to present both written and oral reports on a project. The nature of the audience must be kept in mind when these reports are being prepared and presented. The oral report should begin with a clear statement of the research objectives, followed by an outline of the methodology. A summary of major findings should come next. The report should end with a presentation of conclusions and recommendations for management. In today's fast-paced world of marketing research, long, elaborately written reports are virtually a thing of the past. Decision makers today typically want only a copy of the PowerPoint presentation.

Judging the Quality of a Report
Because most people who enter marketing become research users rather than research suppliers, it is important to know what to look for in a research report. The ability to evaluate a research report is crucial. As with many other items we purchase, the quality of a research report is not always readily apparent. Nor does paying a high price for a project necessarily guarantee superior quality. The basis for measuring a report's quality lies in the research proposal. Does the report meet the objectives established in the proposal? Has the methodology outlined in the proposal been followed? Are the conclusions based on logical deductions from the data analysis? Do the recommendations seem prudent, given the conclusions?

Using the Internet to Disseminate Reports
It is becoming increasingly commonplace for research suppliers and clients to publish reports directly to the Web. Most companies, such as Texas Instruments, locate this material not in public areas on the Web but on corporate intranets or in password-protected locations on Web sites. Publishing reports on the Web has a number of advantages:

1. The reports become immediately accessible to managers and other authorized and interested parties worldwide.
2. The reports can incorporate full multimedia presentation, including text, graphs, various types of animation, audio comments, and video clips.
3. The reports are fully searchable. Suppose a manager is interested in any material relating to advertising. Instead of manually scanning a long and detailed report for such mentions, he or she can search the report for comments relating to advertising.

Following Up

After a company has spent a considerable amount of effort and money on marketing research and the preparation of a report, it is important that the findings be used. Management should determine whether the recommendations were followed and, if not, why not. As you will learn in the next section, one way to increase the likelihood that research conducted by a corporate marketing department will be used is to minimize conflict between that department and other departments within the company.

Managing the Research Process

The Research Request

Before conducting a research project, a company such as Microsoft® might require approval of a formal research request. Moderate- and large-size retailers, manufacturers, and nonprofit organizations often use the **research request** as a basis for determining which projects will be funded. Typically, in large organizations there are far more requests by managers for marketing research information than there is money available to conduct such research. Requiring a research request is a formalized approach to allocating scarce research dollars.

It is very important for a brand manager, a new product specialist, or whoever is in need of research information to clearly state in the formal research request why the desired information is critical to the organization. Otherwise, the person with approval authority may fail to see why the expenditure is necessary.

In smaller organizations, the communication link between brand managers and marketing researchers is much closer. Their day-to-day contact often removes the need for a formal research request. Instead, decisions to fund research are made on an ad hoc basis by the marketing manager or the director of marketing research.

Completion and approval of the request represent a disciplined approach to identifying research problems and obtaining funding to solve them. The degree of effort expended at this step in the research process will be reflected in the quality of the information provided to the decision maker because a well-conceived research request will guide the design, data-gathering, analysis, and reporting processes toward a highly focused objective. The sections of a formal research request are as follows:

> → **research request**
> An internal document used by large organizations that describes a potential research project, its benefits to the organization, and estimated costs; it must be formally approved before a research project can begin.

1. *Action.* The decision maker should describe the action to be taken on the basis of the research. This will help the decision maker focus on what information should be obtained and guide the researcher in creating the research design and in analyzing the results.

2. *Origin.* The decision maker should state the events that led to a need for a decision. This will help the researcher understand more deeply the nature of the management decision problem.

3. *Information.* The decision maker should list the questions that she or he needs to have answered to take action. Carefully considering the questions will improve the efficiency of the research.

4. *Use.* This section should explain how each piece of information will be used to help make the actual decision. By giving logical reasons for each part of the research, it will ensure that the questions make sense in light of the action to be taken.

5. *Target groups and subgroups.* By describing those from whom information must be gathered to address the research problem, this section will help the researcher design the sample procedure for the research project.

6. *Logistics.* Time and budget constraints always affect the research technique chosen for a project. For this reason, approximations of the amount of money available and the amount of time left before results are needed must be included as a part of the research request.

7. *Comments.* Any other comments relevant to the research project must be stated so that, once again, the researcher can fully understand the nature of the problem.

Request for Proposal

→ **request for proposal (RFP)**
A solicitation sent to marketing research suppliers inviting them to submit a formal proposal, including a bid.

A research request is an internal document used by management to determine which projects to fund. A **request for proposal (RFP)** is a solicitation sent to marketing research suppliers inviting them to submit a formal proposal, including a bid. The RFP is the lifeblood of a research supplier. Receiving it is the initial step in getting new business and, therefore, revenue.

A typical RFP provides background data on why a study is to be conducted, outlines the research objectives, describes a methodology, and suggests a time frame. In some RFPs, the supplier is asked to recommend a methodology or even help develop the research objectives. Most RFPs also ask for (1) a detailed cost breakdown, (2) the supplier's experience in relevant areas, and (3) references. Usually, a due date for the proposal will be specified.

Maryanne Spillane McInturf, director of marketing and communications at Boston College's Carroll School of Management and Linda M. Stevenson, president of Lucidity Works, a Rochester, New York–based provider of search, retrieval, and report generation software, discusses where to send the RFP after it is completed in the Practicing Marketing Research box.

Suppliers must exercise care in preparing their proposals in response to the RFP. More than one client has said, "We find the quality of the proposals indicative of the quality of work produced by the firm." Thus, a research supplier that doesn't have the necessary time to adequately prepare a proposal should simply not submit a bid.

PRACTICING
MARKETING RESEARCH

Where Do I Send the RFP?

For most companies, it's best to pinpoint suppliers through extensive research or professional referrals, Linda Stevenson says. "I like to go through the networking route," she says. "I can pick up the phone and say, 'Who would you use for this project?'"

Maryanne Spillane McInturf recommends honing in on a very select group of suppliers to target. "Start with a manageable number of firms you want to approach," she says. "It can get overwhelming if you do a dozen." By pinpointing five or six suppliers who offer the specific services you're looking for or have completed similar projects in the past, "you're not wasting their time, and they're not wasting your time," she says.

"I try to get the company that's doing the written proposal to also come in and do a presentation, if it's possible," Spillane McInturf says. The more information the supplier has from you and the more information you have from your supplier, the better the match—and the results—can be.[6]

Questions

1. Each year Quirks publishes the *Researcher Source Book*, which lists suppliers by state, alphabetically. Each listing describes the specialties of the firm. Would this be a good starting point for finding suppliers to include in an RFP mailing list?

2. Do you think that the best way to get the lowest price for a project is to send out as many RFPs as possible?

The Marketing Research Proposal

When marketing research suppliers receive an RFP, they respond to the potential client with a research proposal. The **research proposal** is a document that presents the research objectives, research design, time line, and cost of a project. We have included an actual proposal (disguised) prepared by two project managers at Decision Analyst (a large international marketing research firm) in Appendix 2-A. Most research proposals today are short (3 to 5 pages) and are transmitted back to the potential client as an e-mail attachment. A proposal for the federal government can run 50 pages or longer. The federal proposal will include a number of standard forms mandated by the government.

➜ **research proposal**
A document developed, usually in response to an RFP, that presents the research objectives, research design, time line, and cost of a project.

Most proposals contain the following elements:

I. Title Page

This includes the title of the project from the RFP, the names of the preparers of the proposal, and contact information; who the proposal is being prepared for; and the date.

II. Statement of the Research Objectives

These are often stated in the RFP. If not, they must be determined as described earlier in the chapter.

III. Study Design

This presents a statement of how the data will be gathered and who will be sampled and the sample size.

IV. Areas of Questioning

This is not found in all proposals, but in our experience we have found it to be very helpful. It is a tentative list of survey topics based on the research objectives.

V. Data Analysis

This states which techniques will be used to analyze the data.

VI. Personnel Involved

This provides a complete list of all supervisory and analytical personnel who will be involved in the project and a short vita of each. Each person's responsibility is also outlined. This element is typically not included when the client and supplier have an ongoing relationship. It is mandatory in most government work.

VII. Specifications and Assumptions

Most RFPs are relatively short and don't spell out every detail. In order to make certain that the supplier and potential client are on the same page, it is a good idea to list the specifications and assumptions that were made when creating the proposal (see Appendix 2-A).

Exhibit 2.3 details the benefits of a good proposal to both the client and the supplier.

VIII. Services

This section spells out exactly what the research supplier will do (see Appendix 2-A). For example, who is designing the questionnaire? Is it the client, the supplier, or is it a joint effort? Again, the purpose is to make sure that the client and the research supplier operate from the same set of expectations.

EXHIBIT 2.3	**Benefits of a Good Proposal**
Client	**Supplier**
Serves as a road map for the project:	Serves as a road map for the project:
<ul><li>specifies research methodology</li><li>specifies time line</li><li>specifies deliverables</li><li>specifies projected costs</li><li>allows for planning-team member involvement and resource allocation</li></ul>	<ul><li>identifies specific responsibilities of the vendor</li><li>identifies the role the client has in fielding the research</li><li>allows for planning-team member involvement and resource allocation</li></ul>
Ensures that competing vendors carefully consider:	Serves as a valuable tool for managing client expectations, especially when the client:
<ul><li>project specifications</li><li>research design/methodology</li><li>project cost</li></ul>	<ul><li>contributes to delays or revises project time line</li><li>mandates changes to project scope</li><li>requests additional or alternative deliverables</li><li>cancels the project</li></ul>
Ensures that the selected vendor has an explicit understanding of business decisions the research will affect	Provides an objective method for clients to examine vendor qualifications
Prompts the client to consider unique capabilities that individual firms offer, which might contribute to project success	

Source: Matthew Singer, "Writer's Lock," *Marketing Research* (Fall 2006), p. 38.

IX. Cost

This specifies the cost and payment schedule.

X. Timing

This states when various phases of the project will be completed and provides a final completion date.

Preparing proposals may be the most important function a research supplier performs inasmuch as proposals and their acceptance or rejection determine the revenue of the firm. If a research firm's proposals are not accepted, the company will have no funds and will ultimately go out of business! Moreover, if the price that is quoted is too low, the researcher may get the job but lose money. If the price is too high, the proposal may be outstanding, but the researcher will lose the work to a competitor.

What to Look for in a Marketing Research Supplier

Market Directions, a Kansas City marketing research firm, asked marketing research clients around the United States to rate the importance of several statements about research companies and research departments. Replies were received from a wide range of industries, resulting in the following top 10 list of desirable qualities in marketing researchers:

1. Maintains client confidentiality.
2. Is honest.

3. Is punctual.
4. Is flexible.
5. Delivers against project specifications.
6. Provides high-quality output.
7. Is responsive to the client's needs.
8. Has high-quality control standards.
9. Is customer oriented in interactions with client.
10. Keeps the client informed throughout a project.[7]

The two most important qualities, confidentiality and honesty, are ethical issues; the remaining factors relate to managing the research function and maintaining good communications.

Good communications are a necessity. Four of the qualities on the top 10 list—flexibility, responsiveness to clients' needs, customer orientation, and keeping the client informed—are about good communications. A successful marketing research organization requires good communications both within the research company and with clients.

How important is communication? Consider this: Managers spend at least 80 percent of every working day in direct communication with others. In other words, 48 minutes of every hour are spent in meetings, on the telephone, or talking informally. The other 20 percent of a typical manager's time is spent doing desk work, most of which is communication in the form of reading and writing.[8] Communications permeate every aspect of managing the marketing research function.

What Motivates Decision Makers to Use Research Information?

When research managers communicate effectively, generate quality data, control costs, and deliver information on time, they increase the probability that decision makers will use the research information they provide. Yet academic research shows that political factors and preconceptions can also influence whether research information is used. Specifically, the determinants of whether or not a manager uses research data are (1) conformity to prior expectations, (2) clarity of presentation, (3) research quality, (4) political acceptability within the firm, and (5) lack of challenge to the status quo.[9] Managers and researchers both agree that technical quality is the most important determinant of research use. However, managers are less likely to use research that does not conform to preconceived notions or is not politically acceptable. This does not mean, of course, that researchers should alter their findings to meet management's preconceived notions.

Marketing managers in industrial firms tend to use research findings more than do their counterparts in consumer goods organizations.[10] This tendency among industrial managers is attributed to a greater exploratory objective in information collection, a greater degree of formalization of organizational structure, and a lesser degree of surprise in the information collected.

SUMMARY

The process for correctly defining the research problem consists of a series of steps: (1) recognize the problem or opportunity, (2) find out why the information is being sought, (3) understand the decision-making environment, (4) use the symptoms to help clarify the problem, (5) translate the management problem into a marketing research problem, (6) determine whether the information already exists, (7) determine whether the question can really be answered, and (8) state the research objectives. If the problem is not defined correctly, the remainder of the research project will be a waste of time and money.

The steps in the market research process are as follows:

1. Identification of the problem/opportunity and statement of the marketing research objectives
2. Creation of the research design
3. Choice of the method of research
4. Selection of the sampling procedure
5. Collection of data
6. Analysis of data
7. Preparation and presentation of the research report
8. Follow-up

In specifying a research design, the researcher must determine whether the research will be descriptive or causal. Descriptive studies are conducted to answer who, what, when, where, and how questions. Causal studies are those in which the researcher investigates whether one variable (independent) causes or influences another variable (dependent). The next step in creating a research design is to select a research method: survey, observation, or experiment. Survey research involves an interviewer (except in mail and Internet surveys) interacting with a respondent to obtain facts, opinions, and attitudes. Observation research, in contrast, monitors respondents' actions and does not rely on direct interaction with people. An experiment is distinguished by the fact that the researcher changes one or more variables and observes the effects of those changes on another variable (usually sales). The objective of most experiments is to measure causality.

A sample is a subset of a larger population. A probability sample is a sample for which every element in the population has a known nonzero probability of being selected. All samples that cannot be considered probability samples are nonprobability samples. Any sample in which the chances of selection for the various elements in the population are unknown can be considered a nonprobability sample.

In larger organizations, it is common to have a research request prepared after the statement of research objectives. The research request generally describes the action to be taken on the basis of the research, the reason for the need for the information, the questions management wants to have answered, how the information will be used, the target groups from whom information must be gathered, the amount of time and money available to complete the project, and any other information pertinent to the request. The request for proposal (RFP) is the document used by clients to solicit proposals from marketing research suppliers.

Marketing research proposals are developed in response to an RFP. In some cases, the proposals are created based on an informal request such as in a telephone conversation between a client and research supplier. The research proposal gives the research objectives, research design, time line, and cost. Research proposals are the tool that generates revenue for the research firm.

Good communications are the foundation of research management and the basis for getting decision makers to use research information. The information communicated to a decision maker depends on the type of research being conducted.

KEY TERMS & DEFINITIONS

opportunity identification Using marketing research to find and evaluate new opportunities.

situation analysis Studying the decision-making environment within which marketing research will take place.

exploratory research Preliminary research conducted to increase understanding of a concept, to clarify the exact nature of the problem to be solved, or to identify important variables to be studied.

pilot studies Surveys using a limited number of respondents and often employing less rigorous sampling techniques than are employed in large, quantitative studies.

experience surveys Discussions with knowledgeable individuals, both inside and outside an organization, who may provide insights into the problem.

case analysis Reviewing information from situations that are similar to the current one.

marketing research problem A statement specifying the type of information needed by the decision maker to help solve the management decision problem and how that information can be obtained efficiently and effectively.

marketing research objective A goal statement, defining the specific information needed to solve the marketing research problem.

management decision problem A statement specifying the type of managerial action required to solve the problem.

hypothesis A conjectural statement about a relationship between two or more variables that can be tested with empirical data.

research design The plan to be followed to answer the marketing research objectives.

descriptive studies Research studies that answer the questions who, what, when, where, and how.

variable A symbol or concept that can assume any one of a set of values.

causal studies Research studies that examine whether the value of one variable causes or determines the value of another variable.

dependent variable A symbol or concept expected to be explained or influenced by the independent variable.

independent variable A symbol or concept over which the researcher has some control and that is hypothesized to cause or influence the dependent variable.

temporal sequence An appropriate causal order of events.

concomitant variation The degree to which a presumed cause and a presumed effect occur or vary together.

spurious association A relationship between a presumed cause and a presumed effect that occurs as a result of an unexamined variable or set of variables.

survey research Research in which an interviewer (except in mail and Internet surveys) interacts with respondents to obtain facts, opinions, and attitudes.

observation research Typically, descriptive research that monitors respondents' actions without direct interaction.

experiments Research to measure causality, in which the researcher changes one or more independent variables and observes the effect of the changes on the dependent variable.

probability sample A subset of a population where every element in the population has a known nonzero chance of being selected.

nonprobability sample A subset of a population in which the chances of selection for the various elements in the population are unknown.

research request An internal document used by large organizations that describes a potential research project, its benefits to the organization, and estimated costs; it must be formally approved before a research project can begin.

request for proposal (RFP) A solicitation sent to marketing research suppliers inviting them to submit a formal proposal, including a bid.

research proposal A document developed, usually in response to an RFP, that states the research objectives, research design, time line, and cost.

QUESTIONS FOR REVIEW & CRITICAL THINKING

1. The definition of the research problem is one of the critical steps in the research process. Why? Who should be involved in this process?

2. What role does exploratory research play in the marketing research process? How does exploratory research differ from other forms of marketing research?

3. Give some examples of symptoms of problems and then suggest some underlying real problems.

4. Give several examples of situations in which it would be better to take a census of the population than to take a sample.

5. Critique the following methodologies and suggest more appropriate alternatives:

   a. A supermarket is interested in determining its image. Cashiers drop a short questionnaire into the grocery bag of each customer prior to bagging the groceries.

   b. To assess the extent of its trade area, a shopping mall stations interviewers in the parking lot every Monday and Friday evening. After people park their cars, interviewers walk up to them and ask them for their zip codes.

   c. To assess the potential for new horror movies starring alien robots, a major studio invites people to call a 900 number and vote yes if they would like to see such movies or no if they would not. Each caller is billed a $2 charge.

6. You have been charged with determining how to attract more business majors to your school. Outline the steps you would take, including sampling procedures, to accomplish this task.

7. What can researchers do to increase the chances that decision makers will use the marketing research information they generate?

8. Explain the critical role of the research proposal.

9. [*Team exercise*] Divide the class into teams of four or five. Half of the teams should prepare short RFPs on the following topics:

   a. Food on campus
   b. Role of fraternities and sororities on campus
   c. Entertainment in your city
   d. Your university Web site
   e. Role of student internships in education
   f. Online purchasing of school supplies
   g. Purchasing music on the Internet

   The RFPs should state clearly and precisely the research objectives and other pertinent information. The remaining teams should create proposals in response to the RFPs.

WORKING THE NET

1. Go to the Internet and search on "intranet and the future." Report your findings to the class.

2. Describe how putting research reports on the Web can benefit managers.

3. Go to a search engine and type "writing RFPs." Explain what kind of help is available to prepare RFPs.

REAL-LIFE RESEARCH • 2.1

Cessna Aircraft

Cessna Aircraft is one of the largest manufacturers of small, private-business airplanes in the United States. It is always looking for new market opportunities, which may involve cultivating existing segments or developing and exploiting new ones. Recent research by Cessna revealed that although a very small percentage of the total adult population enrolls in private pilot-training programs, about half of the individuals who enter a training program complete it. And the number of people with pilot's licenses is increasing. Eventually, about one out of five people with a private pilot's license buys a private airplane. Thus, pilot training is an important part of the total market for Cessna and its competitors.

A small percentage of pilots are women. Similarly, a small percentage of the students in training programs are women; this figure has shown only a slight increase in recent years. Moreover, there are very few women instructors in pilot-training programs. A substantial number of women have the necessary skills, time, and income to enroll in and complete the basic training program. Cessna is interested in learning why more women don't enter the program and how the program and/or promotional materials could appeal to and motivate more women to consider or inquire about such programs.

There may be several specific market segments worthy of examination. These include wives of pilots, businesswomen, women who have the income and desire to travel for pleasure, and young women who seek future employment as corporate aircraft pilots. Cessna realizes that the limiting factor may be low levels of interest or motivation and perhaps attitudes toward the desirability of women pilots. But opportunities for women are increasing in many different fields. Cessna therefore believes that a vital market may exist that is not being fully exploited.

Questions

1. What is the management decision problem?
2. Define the marketing research problem(s).
3. Develop the marketing research objectives.
4. Explain how a marketing researcher should use the problem definition process to answer the above questions.

APPENDIX 2-A
A MARKETING RESEARCH PROPOSAL

Decision Analyst, Inc.
Proposal to Conduct
a Brand Equity Study

Confidential

Prepared for:
Fun City Gaming, Inc.

Prepared by:
Kathi McKenzie & Sally Danforth
January 2012

Background

Fun City Gaming, Inc., currently operates a multilevel dockside riverboat casino and a land-based pavilion with three restaurants and a hotel, all located on the Arlen River. The casino offers 1,500 slot machines and 70 table games, and it is the "flagship" of the Fun City franchise. The Fun City Casino has four primary competitors currently operating in the area, all within a roughly 30-mile radius of the Fun City. The Fun City Casino ranks second in revenue but first in profit among these competitors. In addition to these competitors, additional competition will be provided by the planned "River Wild" casino, which will likely begin construction in about a year. This casino will be located in St. George, minutes from the Fun City Casino.

Fun City is currently undergoing a large redevelopment, involving construction of a completely new gaming vessel, significant upgrades to the pavilion, addition of new restaurants, and a new parking garage. The gaming vessel will feature 2,500 slot machines, 84 table games, high-limit gaming areas, and upgraded décor. The new Fun City will offer superior features to the current product as well as to primary competitors.

In order to be financially feasible, this project must increase business from current customers as well as attract customers from competitive casinos, some of whom may have to travel past competitive casinos to arrive at Fun City. In addition, the new offering should be especially attractive to premium casino players.

Objectives

The overall objective of this study would be to help management position the new Fun City offering. Key questions to be addressed include:

- What should be the positioning of the new casino?
- Should the Fun City name be used, or should it be rebranded?
- If rebranded, what name should be used?

Study Design

This study would be conducted using a targeted telephone survey among 800 gamblers within a 100-mile radius of the Fun City Casino location. Specifically, we will survey 400 within the Arlen Valley portion of this area and 400 in the area eastward, where the majority of current/future competition lies. Respondents will be screened based on past 12-month casino usage.

Areas of Questioning

Decision Analyst would work closely with Fun City Gaming in developing the questionnaire. Assuming that we have three to four potential positionings to test, tentative survey topics would include:

- Current casino usage and gambling behavior.
- Awareness and overall rating for the Fun City name, as well as names of key competitors and other names owned by Fun City Gaming which might be used for the new casino.
- Rating of the Fun City and key competitors on several (8 to 10) image attributes.

- Exposure to brief description of the "new" (redeveloped) casino. Each respondent would be exposed to the description with *one* of the potential positionings. This will result in a readable sample size for each positioning.
- Overall rating and rating on key image attributes for the "new" casino.
- Rating of the Fun City name and other potential names on overall appeal and fit with this description.
- Projected use of new casino; effect on gambling habits and share of casino visits.

Data will be analyzed both by area of residence and by gambling value (high/medium/low value gamblers).

Data Analysis

Factor analysis will be conducted, and the factors that are most related to the overall rating of the casino will be identified. On the basis of these factors, a perceptual map will be created to show visually the relationship between the current Fun City and competitive brands, based on brand image. The image projected by the new casino description will also be shown on this map, and a gap analysis conducted to highlight possible differences in image projected by each of the three to four positionings.

Personnel Involved

This project will be supervised by Kathi McKenzie and Sally DanGorth. Kathi will be the overall supervisor, and Sally will be responsible for the data analysis and presentation. (*Note: A short bio of each person would normally be attached.*)

Specifications/Assumptions

The cost estimate is based on the following assumptions:

- Number of completed interviews = 800
- Average interview length = 20 minutes
- Average completion rate = 0.62 Complete per hour
- Assumed incidence = 25%
- No open-ended questions
- Type of sample: targeted random digit
- Up to two banners of statistical tables in Word format
- Factor analysis, two perceptual maps (total sample and high-value gambler), and gap analysis
- Report
- Personal presentation, if desired

Services

Decision Analyst, Inc., would:

- Develop the questionnaire, in conjunction with Fun City Gaming management
- Generate sample within the target area

- Program the survey
- Manage and administer the project
- Monitor and oversee all telephone interviewing
- Process data, specify cross-tabulations, and compile statistical tables
- Analyze the data and prepare presentation-style report, if desired.

Cost

The cost to conduct this study, as described, would be $61,900, plus or minimum a 10 percent contingency fee, which would be spent only with specific prior approval of Fun City Gaming. This cost estimate does not include the cost of any travel outside of the Dallas–Fort Worth area. Any overnight deliveries or travel expenses would be billed at cost at the end of the study.

Decision Analyst would closely monitor data collection. If the actual data collection experience differed from the stated specifications and assumptions, we would notify you immediately to discuss the options available.

Timing

After approval of the final questionnaire, the project would require approximately five to six weeks, as outlined below:

Survey programming and quality control	3–4 days
Data collection	3 weeks
Final data tabulations	3 days
Final report	1–2 weeks

Secondary Data and Databases

CHAPTER 3

LEARNING OBJECTIVES

→ **1.** To understand how a firm creates an internal database.

→ **2.** To learn about the advantages of creating a database from Web site visitors.

→ **3.** To become familiar with data mining.

→ **4.** To understand the advantages and disadvantages of using secondary data.

→ **5.** To understand the role of the Internet in obtaining secondary data.

→ **6.** To learn about types of information management systems.

W̶hat is secondary data, and what are the advantages and disadvantages of secondary data? How is data mining used by managers to extract insights from databases? Most importantly, how do managers manage the huge flow of information they have available? You will learn the answers to these questions in this chapter.

The Nature of Secondary Data

→ **secondary data**
Data that have been previously gathered.

→ **primary data**
New data gathered to help solve the problem under investigation.

Secondary data consist of information that has already been gathered and might be relevant to the problem at hand. **Primary data**, in contrast, are survey, observation, and experiment data collected to solve the particular problem under investigation. It is highly unlikely that any marketing research problem is entirely unique or has never occurred before. It is also probable that someone else has investigated the problem or one similar to it in the past. Therefore, secondary data can be a cost-effective and efficient means of obtaining information for marketing research. There are two basic sources of secondary data: the company itself (internal databases, like Bud Net) and other organizations or persons (external databases).

Secondary information originating within the company includes annual reports, reports to stockholders, sales data, customer profiles, purchase patterns, product testing results (perhaps made available to the news media), and house periodicals composed by company personnel for communication to employees, customers, or others. Often all this information is incorporated into a company's internal database.

Outside sources of secondary information include innumerable government (federal, state, and local) departments and agencies that compile and publish summaries of business data, as well as trade and industry associations, business periodicals, and other news media that regularly publish studies and articles on the economy, specific industries, and even individual companies. When economic considerations or priorities within the organization preclude publication of summaries of the information from these sources, unpublished summaries may be found in internal reports, memos, or special-purpose analyses with limited circulation. Most of these sources can be found on the Internet.

Advantages of Secondary Data

Marketing researchers use secondary information because it can be obtained at a fraction of the cost, time, and inconvenience associated with primary data collection. Additional advantages of using secondary information include the following:

▪ *Secondary data may help to clarify or redefine the problem during the exploratory research process* (see Chapter 2). Consider the experience of a local YMCA. Concerned about a stagnant level of membership and a lack of participation in traditional YMCA programs, it decided to survey members and nonmembers. Secondary data revealed that there had been a tremendous influx of young single persons into the target market, while the number of "traditional families" had remained constant. The problem was redefined to examine how the YMCA could attract a significant share of the young single adult market while maintaining its traditional family base.

▪ *Secondary data may actually provide a solution to the problem.* It is highly unlikely that the problem is unique; there is always the possibility that someone else has addressed the identical problem or a very similar one. Thus, the precise information desired may have been collected, but not for the same purpose.

Many states publish a directory of manufacturers (typically available online) that contains information on companies: location, markets, product lines, number of plants, names of key personnel, number of employees, and sales levels. When a consulting company specializing in long-range strategic planning for members of the

PRACTICING
MARKETING RESEARCH

Does What You Need To Know Already Exist?

Would you pull off the road to fill your gas tank if you could already see that the needle was showing full? Probably not. However, we have found that many companies are essentially doing just that by executing surveys to gather data on questions for which they already have the answers.

A major hotel chain found that it successfully delivered clean bathrooms 99.6 percent of the time. To monitor their continued success, rather than survey 10,000 people to get back 1,000 surveys 4 weeks later, of which 4 would have bathroom complaints, the chain chose to put a sticker in the bathroom and on the room desk highlighting the guest services hotline. Customers' call rates would let the chain know if quality had slipped.

In another situation, a bank was surveying customers on their satisfaction with the uptime of the ATMs. However, the bank already had internal IT metrics that measured ATM uptime to four decimal places.

In summary, make sure the data do not already exist. We have found that departments often operate in silos, unaware of the research being done or data being collected by their co-workers. Sharing existing research and internal metrics not only gives immediate access to actionable data but does so without incurring the costs of conducting surveys.[1]

Questions

1. What can companies do to make sure that the data do not already exist?
2. How can an intranet help avoid duplicate research?

---

semiconductor industry needed a regional profile of its potential clients, it used individual state directories to compile the profile; no primary data collection was necessary. John Goodman and David Beinhacker of TARP, an Arlington, Virginia, marketing research firm, note in the above Practicing Marketing Research box that secondary data may help companies save a lot of money by not conducting unnecessary surveys.

Secondary data may provide primary data research method alternatives. Each primary data research endeavor is custom-designed for the situation at hand; consequently, the marketing researcher should always be open to sources that suggest research alternatives. For example, when we started work on a research project for a large southwestern city's convention and visitor's bureau, we obtained a research report prepared by *Meeting and Convention Planners* magazine. In designing our questionnaire, we used a series of scales from the magazine's questionnaire. Not only were the scales well designed, but results from our study could be compared with the magazine's data.

Secondary data may alert the marketing researcher to potential problems and/or difficulties. In addition to alternatives, secondary information may divulge potential dangers. Unpopular collection methods, sample selection difficulties, or respondent hostility may be uncovered. For example, examination of a study of anesthesiologists by a researcher planning to conduct a study of their satisfaction with certain drugs discovered a high refusal rate in a telephone survey. The researcher had planned to use a telephone study but instead switched to a mail questionnaire with a response incentive.

■ *Secondary data may provide necessary background information and build credibility for the research report.* Secondary information often yields a wealth of background data for planning a research project. It may offer a profile of potential buyers versus non-buyers, industry data, desirable new product features, language used by purchasers to describe the industry, and the advantages and disadvantages of existing products. Language used by target consumers can aid in phrasing questions that will be meaningful to respondents. Sometimes background data can satisfy some of the research objectives, eliminating the need to ask certain questions; shorter questionnaires typically have higher completion rates. And secondary data can enrich research findings by providing additional insights into what the data mean or by corroborating current findings. Finally, secondary data can serve as a reference base for subsequent research projects.

■ *Secondary data may provide the sample frame.* If a company, such as UPS, wants to track its levels of customer satisfaction each quarter, the names of customers must come from its database. Thus, the customer list is the sample frame, and the sample frame is the list or device from which a sample is drawn.

Limitations of Secondary Data

Despite the many advantages of secondary data, they also pose some dangers. The main disadvantages of secondary information are lack of availability, lack of relevance, inaccuracy, and insufficiency.

Lack of Availability   For some research questions, there are simply no available data. Suppose Kraft General Foods wants to evaluate the taste, texture, and color of three new gourmet brownie mixes. No secondary data exist that can answer these questions; consumers must try each mix and then evaluate it. If McDonald's wants to evaluate its image in Phoenix, Arizona, it must gather primary data. If BMW wants to know, the reaction of college students to a new two-seater sports car design, it must show prototypes to the students and evaluate their opinions. Of course, secondary data may have played a major role in the engineer's design plan for the car.

Lack of Relevance   It is not uncommon for secondary data to be expressed in units or measures that cannot be used by the researcher. For example, Joan Dermott, a retailer of oriental rugs, determined that the primary customers for her rugs were families with a total household income of $40,000 to $80,000. Higher-income consumers tended to purchase pricier rugs than those Dermott carried. When she was trying to decide whether to open a store in another Florida city, she could not find useful income data. One source offered class breakdowns of $30,000 to $50,000, $50,000 to $70,000, $70,000 to $90,000, and so forth. Another secondary source broke down incomes into less than $15,000, $15,000 to $30,000, and more than $30,000. Even if the given income brackets had met Joan's needs, she would have faced another problem: outdated information. One study had been conducted in 1995 and the other in 2001. In Florida's dynamic markets, the percentages probably were no longer relevant. This is often the case with U.S. Census data, which are nearly a year old before they become available.

Inaccuracy   Users of secondary data should always assess the accuracy of the data. There are a number of potential sources of error when a researcher gathers, codes, analyzes, and presents data. Any report that does not mention possible sources and ranges of error should be suspect.

Using secondary data does not relieve a researcher from attempting to assess the accuracy of those data. A few guidelines for determining the accuracy of secondary data are as follows:

1. *Who gathered the data?* The source of the secondary data is a key to their accuracy. Federal agencies, most state agencies, and large commercial marketing research firms generally can be counted on to have conducted their research as professionally as possible. Marketing researchers should always be on guard when examining data in which a hidden agenda might be reflected. A chamber of commerce, for instance, is always going to put its best foot forward. Similarly, trade associations often advocate one position over another.

2. *What was the purpose of the study?* Data are always collected for some reason. Understanding the motivation for the research can provide clues to the quality of the data. A chamber of commerce study conducted to provide data that could be used to attract new industry to the area should be scrutinized with a great deal of caution. There have been situations in which advertising agencies have been hired by clients to assess the impact of their own advertising programs. In other words, they have been asked to evaluate the quality of the job they were doing for their clients!

3. *What information was collected?* A researcher should always identify exactly what information was gathered and from whom. For example, in a dog food study, were purchasers of canned, dry, and semimoist food interviewed, or were just one or two types of dog food purchasers surveyed? In a voters' survey, were only Democrats or only Republicans interviewed? Were the respondents registered voters? Was any attempt made to ascertain a respondent's likelihood of voting in the next election? Were self-reported data used to infer actual behavior?

4. *When was the information collected?* A shopping mall study that surveyed shoppers only on weekends would not reflect the opinions of "typical" mall patrons. A telephone survey conducted from 9:00 A.M. to 5:00 P.M. would vastly underrepresent working persons. A survey of Florida visitors conducted during the summer probably would reveal motivations and interests different from those of winter visitors.

5. *How was the information collected?* Were the data collected by mail, telephone, Internet, or personal interview? Each of these techniques offers advantages and disadvantages. What was the refusal rate? Were decision makers or their representatives interviewed? In short, the researcher must attempt to discern the amount of bias injected into the data by the information-gathering process. A mail survey with a 1 percent response rate (that is, only 1 percent of those who received the survey mailed it back) probably contains a lot of self-selection bias.

6. *Is the information consistent with other information?* A lack of consistency between secondary data sets should dictate caution. The researcher should delve into possible causes of the discrepancy. Differences in the sample, time frame, sampling methodology, questionnaire structure, and other factors can lead to variations in studies. If possible, the researcher should assess the validity of the different studies as a basis for determining which, if any, study should be used for decision making.

Insufficiency   A researcher may determine that available data are relevant and accurate but still not sufficient to make a decision or bring closure to a problem. For example, a manager for Wal-Mart may have sufficient secondary data on incomes, family sizes, number of competitors, and growth potential to determine in which of five Iowa towns Wal-Mart wishes to locate its next store. But if no traffic counts exist for the selected town, primary data will have to be gathered to select a specific site for the store.

Internal Databases

For many companies, a computerized database containing information about customers and prospects has become an essential marketing tool. An internal database is simply a collection of related information developed from data within the organization.

Creating an Internal Database

→ **internal database**
A collection of related information developed from data within the organization.

A firm's sales activities can be an excellent source of information for creating an **internal database.** A traditional starting point has been the firm's sales or inquiry processing and tracking system. Typically, such a system is built on salespersons' "call reports." A call report provides a blueprint of a salesperson's daily activities. It details the number of calls made, characteristics of each firm visited, sales activity resulting from the call, and any information picked up from the client regarding competitors, such as price changes, new products or services, credit term modifications, and new product or service features.

Growing Importance of Internal Database Marketing

→ **database marketing**
Marketing that relies on the creation of a large computerized file of customers' and potential customers' profiles and purchase patterns to create a targeted marketing mix.

Perhaps the fastest-growing use of internal databases is **database marketing**. Database marketing relies on the creation of a large computerized file of customers' and potential customers' profiles and purchase patterns to create a targeted marketing mix. A recent study found that 94 percent of the large companies in America have a marketing database.[2]

In the 1950s, network television enabled advertisers to "get the same message to everyone simultaneously." Database marketing can get a customized, individual message to everyone simultaneously through direct mail. This is why database marketing is sometimes called *micromarketing*. Database marketing can create a computerized form of the old-fashioned relationship that people used to have with the corner grocer, butcher, or baker. "A database is sort of a collective memory," says Richard G. Barlow, president of Frequency Marketing, Inc., a Cincinnati-based consulting firm. "It deals with you in the same personalized way as a mom-and-pop grocery store, where they knew customers by name and stocked what they wanted."[3]

The size of some databases is impressive: Ford Motor Company's holds about 50 million names; Kraft General Foods, 30 million; Citicorp, 30 million; and Kimberly Clark, maker of Huggies diapers, 10 million new mothers. American Express can pull from its database all cardholders who made purchases at golf pro shops in the past 6 months, who attended symphony concerts, or who traveled to Europe more than once in the past year, as well as the very few people who did all three.

The San Diego Padres baseball team used database marketing to attract 60,000 new fans and collected about $400,000 in revenues from new season ticket sales. This was accomplished by marrying the database with customer relationship marketing (CRM) software. New, powerful CRM software is helping marketers enhance their recruitment of new customers and also keep current clients.

Aided by technology, sports-specific strategies are helping marketers reconnect with their fans. Even when a team is winning and stadiums are packed, CRM helps identify those fans most likely to buy season tickets or ticket packages in advance by creating databases on fan attendance. A team can then target these prospects for season tickets the following year. Advance ticket sales are extremely valuable to sports teams since they guarantee a certain revenue level for the season.

"Club cards," similar to ATM cards, are at the heart of fan loyalty programs these days. Although programs vary slightly from team to team, the idea is pretty much the same: Each time fans use their card, they rack up attendance points redeemable for promotional coupons or items such as food, drinks, and souvenirs. The more points they compile, the more "rewards" they receive. In return, the teams get a database filled with information on their fans, which could lead to additional revenue streams.[4]

Data Mining

American Express uses a neural network to examine the hundreds of millions of entries in its database that tell how and where individual cardholders transact business. A **neural network** is a computer program that mimics the processes of the human brain and thus is capable of learning from examples to find patterns in data. The result is a set of *purchase propensity scores* for each cardholder. Based on these scores, AmEx matches offers from affiliated merchants to the purchase histories of individual cardholders and encloses these offers with their monthly statements. The benefits are reduced expenses for AmEx and information of higher value for its cardholders; American Express is engaged in data mining.

Data mining is the use of statistical and other advanced software to discover nonobvious patterns hidden in a database. The objective is to identify patterns that marketers can use in creating new strategies and tactics to increase a firm's profitability. Camelot Music Holdings used data mining to identify a group of high-spending, 65-plus customers (members of its frequent shopper club) who were buying lots of classical and jazz music and movies. Further data mining revealed that a large percentage were also buying rap and alternative music; these were grandparents buying for the grandkids. Now, Camelot tells the senior citizens what's hot in rap and alternative music, as well as in traditional music.

Data mining involves searching for interesting patterns and following the data trail wherever it leads. The discovery process often requires sifting through massive quantities of data; electronic point-of-sale transactions, inventory records, and online customer orders matched with demographics can easily use up hundreds of gigabytes of data storage space. Probability sampling, descriptive statistics, and multivariate statistics are all tools of data mining that make the task manageable. (Probability sampling was discussed in Chapter 2; descriptive statistics programs will be covered in Chapters 13 and 14.) Other more advanced data mining tools, such as genetic algorithms and case-based reasoning systems, must be left for an advanced text.

Data mining has many potential uses in marketing. Those with widest application include the following:

- *Customer acquisition.* In the first stage of a two-stage process, direct marketers apply data mining methods to discover customer attributes that predict their responses to special offers and communications such as catalogues. In the second stage, attributes that the model indicates make customers most likely to respond are matched to the attributes appended to rented lists of noncustomers in order to select noncustomer households most likely to respond to a new offer or communication.

- *Customer retention.* In a typical marketing application, data mining identifies those customers who contribute to the company's bottom line but who are likely to leave and go to a competitor. With this information, the company can target the vulnerable customers for special offers and other inducements not available to less vulnerable customers.

- *Customer abandonment.* Some customers cost more than they contribute and should be encouraged to take their business elsewhere. At Federal Express, customers who spend a lot with little service and marketing investment get different treatment

> **neural network**
> A computer program that mimics the processes of the human brain and thus is capable of learning from examples to find patterns in data.

> **data mining**
> The use of statistical and other advanced software to discover nonobvious patterns hidden in a database.

Farmers Group Insurance used data mining to find out that, as long as a sports car wasn't the only vehicle in a household, the accident rate for sports cars wasn't much greater than that for regular cars. This information led to lower insurance rates for sports cars in this category.

© Bill Grove/iStockphoto

from, say, those who spend just as much but cost more to keep. If their shipping volume falters, "good" clients can expect a phone call, which can head off defections before they occur. As for the "bad" clients—those who spend but are expensive to the company—FedEx is turning them into profitable customers, in many cases, by charging higher shipping prices. And the "ugly" clients, those customers who spend little and show few signs of spending more in the future? They can catch the TV ads. "We just don't market to them anymore," says Sharanjit Singh, managing director for marketing analysis at FedEx. "That automatically brings our costs down."[5]

Market basket analysis. By identifying the associations among product purchases in point-of-sale transactions, retailers and direct marketers can spot product affinities and develop focused promotion strategies that work more effectively than traditional one-size-fits-all approaches. The American Express strategy of selectively stuffing offers in monthly statements is an example of how market basket analysis can be employed to increase marketing efficiency.

Behavioral Targeting

→ **behavioral targeting**
The use of online and offline data to understand a consumer's habits, demographics, and social networks in order to increase the effectiveness of online advertising.

Behavioral targeting is the use of online and offline data to understand a consumer's habits, demographics, and social networks in order to increase the effectiveness of online advertising. As the Internet has matured, nontargeted advertising has decreased in efficiency. One study found that only 4 percent of Internet users account for 67 percent of all display ad clicks. Another recent study by DoubleClick reported an average click-through rate of just 0.1 percent. Translated, that means that only 1 out of 1,000 people actually click through the average display ad. Behavioral targeting attempts to change the odds in favor of the advertiser. In fact, recent research confirms that targeted ad click-throughs and conversion rates are significantly higher than nontargeted ads.[6]

EXelate Media, a research firm that collects and sells Web data, announced an alliance with Nielsen, one of America's largest marketing research firms. The deal tied eXelate's data on more than 150 million Internet users to Nielsen's database on 115 million American households to provide more detailed profiles of consumers.

EXelate gathers online consumer data through deals with hundreds of Web sites. The firm determines a consumer's age, sex, ethnicity, marital status, and profession by scouring Web-site registration data. It pinpoints, for example, which consumers in the market to buy a car are fitness buffs, based on their Internet searches and the sites they frequent. It gathers and stores the information using tracking cookies, or small strings of data that are placed on the hard drive of a consumer's computer when that consumer visits a participating site. A more detailed discussion of the tracking process can be found in Chapter 7.

An auto maker, for instance, could use EXelate and Nielsen's databases to target ads promoting a sports car to people who visit auto blogs, search online for sports cars, and fit into a group Nielsen calls the "young digerati." This group includes tech-savvy, affluent consumers who live in trendy apartments or condos, are 25 to 44 years old, make about $88,000 a year, and typically read *The Economist*.[7]

The addition of social networking data has been a huge boost to behavioral targeting. Users of Facebook and other social sites reveal interests, connections, and tastes like never before. In the past, online advertisers have found it very effective to promote to persons who have either bought from them, visited their site, or interacted with an ad. The problem comes in with generating demand among people who may not even know the product. This is where social data comes into play. Companies like Media 6° takes an advertiser's customer data and links it to social user information it licenses from social networking sites. The technology matches a prospect with his or her closest friends. So a remessaging campaign can target the original customer plus his or her friends. Instead of reaching one prospect, the campaign may reach 8 or 10 million prospects. It is the idea that "birds of a feather flock together."[8]

Lotame and 33across are among the other companies aiming to mine social networking data for advertisers. Lotame attempts to use social data to get at influencers. It trolls social networks, blogs, and message boards for users who have created content about specific topics. Then it expands the circle by adding in people who consumed that user-generated content. Finally, it adds people who look like those content creators and consumers.[9] Both EBay and Spring have used 33across to improve their online advertising effectiveness.

The Battle over Privacy

There is a downside to behavioral targeting: invasion of consumer privacy. The researchers say that their data contain no personally identifiable information. In one survey, only 24 percent said that they were comfortable with advertisers using their browsing history to deliver more relevant ads.[10] How much tracking actually goes on? *The Wall Street Journal* picked 50 Web sites that account for about 40 percent of all U.S. page views. The 50 sites installed a total of 3,180 tracking cookies on a test computer used to conduct the study. Only one site, Wikipedia.org, installed none. Twelve sites, including Comcast.net and MSN.com, installed more than 100 tracking tools apiece. Dictionary.com installed 168 tracking tools that didn't let users decline to be tracked and 121 tools that, according to privacy statements, didn't rule out collecting financial or health data.[11]

Congress is considering laws to limit tracking. The Federal Trade Commission is developing privacy guidelines for the industry. If "you were in the Gap, and the sales associate said to you, 'OK, from now on, since you shopped here today, we are going to follow you around the mall and view your consumer transactions,' no person would ever agree to that," Senator George LeMieux of Florida said in a Senate hearing on Internet privacy.[12]

Computer consultant Tom Owad has published the results of an experiment that provided a lesson in just how easy it is to extract sensitive personal data from the Net.

Mr. Owad wrote a simple piece of software that allowed him to download public wish lists that Amazon.com customers post to catalog products that they plan to purchase or would like to receive as gifts. These lists usually include the name of the list's owner and his or her city and state.

Using a couple of standard-issue PCs, Mr. Owad was able to download over 250,000 wish lists over the course of a day. He then searched the data for controversial or politically sensitive books and authors, from Kurt Vonnegut's *Slaughterhouse-Five* to the Koran. He then used Yahoo People Search to identify addresses and phone numbers for many of the list owners.

Mr. Owad ended up with maps of the United States showing the locations of people interested in particular books and ideas, including George Orwell's *1984*. He could just as easily have published a map showing the residences of people interested in books about treating depression or adopting a child. "It used to be," Mr. Owad concluded, "you had to get a warrant to monitor a person or a group of people. Today, it is increasingly easy to monitor ideas. And then track them back to people."

What Mr. Owad did by hand can increasingly be performed automatically, with data mining software that draws from many sites and databases. One of the essential characteristics of the Net is the interconnection of diverse stores of information. The "openness" of databases is what gives the system much of its power and usefulness. But it also makes it easy to discover hidden relationships among far-flung bits of data.[13]

An emerging technique that is upsetting many privacy advocates is called "scraping." Firms offer to harvest online conversations and collect personal details from social networking sites, résumé sites, and online forums, where people might discuss their lives. (Scraping is discussed in more detail in Chapter 7.)

Recently, the Web site PatientsLikeMe.com noticed suspicious activity on its "Mood" discussion board. There, people exchange highly personal stories about their emotional disorders, ranging from bipolar disease to a desire to cut themselves.[14] It was a break-in. A new member of the site, using sophisticated software, was "scraping," or copying, every single message off PatientsLikeMe's private online forums. PatientsLikeMe managed to block and identify the intruder: Nielsen Co., the privately held New York media research firm. Nielsen monitors online "buzz" for clients, including major drug makers, which, Nielsen says, buy data gleaned from the Web to get insight from consumers about their products.

"I felt totally violated," says Bilal Ahmed, a 33-year-old resident of Sydney, Australia, who used PatientsLikeMe to connect with other people suffering from depression.[15] He used a pseudonym on the message boards, but his PatientsLikeMe profile linked to his blog, which contains his real name. After PatientsLikeMe told users about the break-in, Mr. Ahmed deleted all his posts, plus a list of drugs he uses. "It was very disturbing to know that your information is being sold," he says. Nielsen says it no longer scrapes data from private message boards.[16]

Behavioral tracking has become the foundation of the $25 billion plus online advertising industry. Online advertising is why a company like Google can spend millions and millions of dollars on free services like its search engine, Gmail, mapping tools, Google Groups, and more.

A new system designed to police privacy abuses by companies that track consumers' Web-surfing habits for ad targeting will be launched in coming months by groups whose members include heavy users of this type of information—Internet companies such as Yahoo! and Microsoft Corp. and advertising companies such as WPP PLC.

The system is part of a broader push by Madison Avenue and the Internet industry to develop stricter self-regulation, in part to ward off federal regulation of the online advertising industry. A coalition of trade groups, including the Council of Better Business Bureaus and Direct Marketing Association trade group, is leading the effort.[17]

Identity Theft   People have a right to be concerned. Identity theft costs $55 billion annually.[18] One company that has come under fire is ChoicePoint. Since spinning off from the credit bureau Equifax in 1997, it has been buying up databases and data mining operations. Businesses, individuals, even the FBI, now rely on its storehouse. Other customers: Nigerian scammers who apparently used the data to steal people's identities.

The problem was unreliable safeguards. To ensure that only certain businesses had access to its data, ChoicePoint set up certain requirements that potential customers must meet. A man named Olatunji Oluwatosin—and possibly others—used fake names and a Hollywood copy shop fax machine to create fictitious small businesses requesting ChoicePoint service. Before Oluwatosin was caught—after someone at ChoicePoint grew suspicious about one of his applications—he accessed at least 145,000 names. (Oluwatosin pleaded no contest to felony identity theft in California in February 2005; he served a 16-month sentence.)[19] ChoicePoint announced in 2005 that it will no longer sell consumer data that includes driver's license numbers and Social Security numbers.[20]

In many cases, finding Social Security and credit card numbers or medical records on the Internet doesn't require much computer expertise. Such information is accessible to anyone who knows where to look.

A file containing names, Social Security numbers, and home phone numbers of about 1,000 current and former Atlanta Fire Rescue employees was discovered online by city officials.

Social Security and driver's license numbers of hundreds of people associated with Edward Waters College in Jacksonville, Florida, were on the Internet and indexed by search engines.[21]

Eric Johnson, a professor at Dartmouth College's Tuck School of Business, has found files containing names, Social Security numbers, and health insurance numbers belonging to thousands of individuals exposed by so-called peer-to-peer software. The software, such as LimeWire, which allows computers to connect directly to one another, is most often used to trade music and video files but is capable of transmitting any data, including workplace documents and spreadsheets.

By entering basic search terms such as hospital names into the software, Mr. Johnson said he turned up a 1,718-page document containing insurance details and diagnoses leaked by a medical-testing lab. He said he also found spreadsheets from a hospital system that contained contact information and Social Security numbers for more than 20,000 patients. "There's no hacking or anything like that going on," he said. "We were just searching."[22] Mr. Johnson said he contacts the organizations, but even if they remove the peer-to-peer software from employee computers, copies of the shared files may still be available online.

In many cases files containing sensitive personal information are downloaded by known cyber criminals, said Rick Wallace, a researcher at Tiversa Inc., a security company that looks for leaked files on behalf of corporate clients. Tiversa found more than 13 million leaked files that contained information about its customers in one 12-month period.

Governmental Actions   Key laws, one a state law, have been passed to protect consumers from identity theft.

Federal Laws

Gramm-Leach-Bliley Act (Financial Services Modernization Act): Aimed at financial companies. Requires those corporations to tell their customers how they use their personal information and to have policies that prevent fraudulent access to it. Partial compliance has been required since 2001.

Health Insurance Portability and Accountability Act: Aimed at the healthcare industry. Limits disclosure of individuals' medical information and imposes penalties on organizations that violate privacy rules. Compliance has been required for large companies since 2003.

Fair Credit Reporting Act (FCRA): Enforced by the Federal Trade Commission, promotes accuracy in consumer reports, and is meant to ensure the privacy of the information in them.

Children's Online Privacy Protection Act (COPPA): Aims to give parents control over what information is collected from their children online and how such information may be used.

State Laws

California's Notice of Security Breach Law: If any company or agency that has collected the personal information of a California resident discovers that nonencrypted information has been taken by an unauthorized person, the company or agency must tell the resident. Compliance has been required since 2003. (Some 30 other states are considering similar laws.)

Getting Paid to Give Up Your Privacy   A number of marketing research firms are paying people to participate in online surveys, to track their click streams, or to evaluate Web sites. This, of course, is legitimate research. Usually, consumers are willing to give up their right to privacy quite cheaply. A recent Jupiter report said that 82 percent of respondents would give personal information to new shopping sites to enter a $100 sweepstakes.[23] There is also a dark side to getting paid for online surveys. Many Web sites, such as Express Paid Surveys, Get Cash for Surveys, and Opinion Paycheck, promise money for taking surveys. The catch is that you must first pay a membership fee; such fees range from $25 to $37.

Marketing Research Aggregators

> **marketing research aggregator**
> A company that acquires, catalogs, reformats, segments, and resells reports already published by large and small marketing research firms.

The **marketing research aggregator** industry is a $100 million business that is growing about 6 percent a year. Companies in this field acquire, catalog, reformat, segment, and resell reports already published by large and small marketing research firms. Even Amazon.com has added a marketing research aggregation area to its high-profile e-commerce site.

The role of aggregator firms is growing because their databases of research reports are getting bigger and more comprehensive—and more useful—as marketing research firms get more comfortable using resellers as a sales channel. Meanwhile, advances in Web technology are making the databases easier to search and deliveries speedier. And aggregators are slicing and repackaging research reports into narrower, more specialized sections for resale to better serve small- and medium-sized clients who often cannot afford to commission their own studies or buy full reports—essentially nurturing a new target market for the information.

Research aggregators are indirectly tapping new markets for traditional research firms. Selling smaller chunks of data at a lower price point is putting big research firms' results into the hands of small- and medium-sized business clients, who often cannot afford to spend more than a few hundred dollars for a report.

Prior to the emergence of research aggregators, a lot of marketing research was only available as premium-priced subscription services. For example, a $2,800 report from Wintergreen Research, Inc. (based in Lexington, Massachusetts), was recently broken up and sold (on AllNetResearch.com) for $350 per chapter for the report's 17 chapters, significantly boosting the overall revenue generated by the report.

In addition to AllNetResearch.com, other major aggregators are Profound.com, Bitpipe.com, USADATA.com, and MarketResearch.com.

Information Management

Computerized databases, secondary data published or posted on the Internet, and internal databases are important parts of an organization's information system. Intelligent decision making is always predicated on having good information. The problem today is how to manage all the information available. It was sometime after the middle of the 20th century that—for the first time in human history—we began to produce information faster than we could process it. Various innovations—computers, microwave transmissions, television, satellites, and the like—have pushed us from a state of information scarcity to a state of information surplus in a very short time.

The need to make better decisions requires that emphasis move from the problems of data acquisition to the problems of effectively managing and utilizing the vast sea of data available. Everyone who has been faced with a decision recognizes that information is the single most important input influencing the quality of that decision. Information is necessary to define the problem, to determine its scope and magnitude, and to generate and evaluate alternatives. Poor decisions are usually the result of using incorrect information, making invalid assumptions, or inappropriately analyzing the information available.

Today, most managers in large and medium-size organizations and progressive smaller ones are bombarded with information. The concern at firms such as American Airlines, Pfizer, and Citicorp has shifted from the generation of information to the shaping and evaluation of information to make it useful to decision makers.

Decision Support Systems

A **decision support system (DSS)** is designed to support the needs and styles of individual decision makers. In theory, a DSS represents something close to the ultimate in data management. We say "in theory" because, for the most part, the ideal has not been realized in practice. However, there have been some notable exceptions that have provided a glimpse of how a DSS can truly support the decision-making process. Characteristics of a true DSS are as follows:

➤ **decision support system (DSS)**
An interactive, personalized information management system, designed to be initiated and controlled by individual decision makers.

- *Interactive.* The manager gives simple instructions and sees results generated on the spot. The process is under the manager's direct control; no computer programmer is needed, and there is no need to wait for scheduled reports.
- *Flexible.* A DSS can sort, regroup, total, average, and manipulate data in a variety of ways. It will shift gears as the user changes topics, matching information to the problem at hand. For example, the chief executive can see highly aggregated figures, while the marketing analyst can view detailed breakouts.
- *Discovery-oriented.* A DSS helps managers probe for trends, isolate problems, and ask new questions.
- *Easy to learn and use.* Managers need not be particularly knowledgeable about computers. Novice users can elect a standard, or default, method of using the system, bypassing optional features to work with the basic system immediately. The opportunity to gradually learn about the system's possibilities minimizes the frustration that frequently accompanies use of new computer software.

Managers use a DSS to conduct sales analyses, forecast sales, evaluate advertising, analyze product lines, and keep tabs on market trends and competitors' actions. A DSS not only allows managers to ask "what if" questions but enables them to view any given slice of the data.

Here's a hypothetical example of using a DSS provided by a manager of new products:

To evaluate sales of a recently introduced new product, we can "call up" sales by the week, then by the month, breaking them out at [the vice president's] option by, say, customer segments. As he works at his terminal, his inquiries could go in several directions depending on the decision at hand. If his train of thought raises questions about monthly sales last quarter compared to forecasts, he wants his decision support system to follow along and give him answers immediately.

    He might see that his new product's sales were significantly below forecast. Forecasts too optimistic? He compares other products' sales to his forecasts and finds that the targets were very accurate. Something wrong with the product? Maybe his sales department is getting insufficient leads, or is not putting leads to good use? Thinking a minute about how to examine that question, he checks ratios of leads converted to sales, product by product. The results disturb him. Only 5 percent of the new product's leads generate orders compared to the company's 12 percent all-product average. Why? He guesses that the sales force is not supporting the new product vigorously enough. Quantitative information from the DSS perhaps could provide more evidence to back that suspicion. But already having enough quantitative knowledge to satisfy himself, the VP acts on his intuition and experience and decides to have a chat with his sales manager.

SUMMARY

Secondary data are previously gathered information that might be relevant to the problem at hand. They can come from sources internal to the organization or external to it. Primary data are survey, observation, or experiment data collected to solve the particular problem under investigation.

A database is a collection of related data. A traditional type of internal marketing database is founded on customer information. For example, a customer database may have demographic and perhaps psychographic information about existing customers and purchase data such as when the goods and services were bought, the types of merchandise procured, the dollar amount of sales, and any promotional information associated with sales. A database can even be created from recorded conversations. An internal database also may contain competitive intelligence, such as new products offered by competitors and changes in competitors' service policies and prices.

Data mining has dramatically increased users' ability to get insightful information out of databases. It can be used to acquire new customers, retain existing customers, abandon accounts that are not cost-effective, and engage in market-based analyses.

The proliferation of databases on and off the Internet and behavioral targeting have raised consumer and government concerns over privacy. Several laws have been passed to protect our privacy. These include the Gramm-Leach-Bliley Act, the Health Insurance Portability and Accountability Act, the Fair Credit Reporting Act, the Children's Online Privacy Act, and California's Notice of Security Breach Law.

Using secondary data has several advantages. Secondary data may (1) help to clarify or redefine the problem during the exploratory research process, (2) actually provide a solution to the problem, (3) provide primary data research method alternatives, (4) alert the marketing researcher to potential problems and difficulties, and (5) provide necessary background data and build credibility for the research report. The disadvantages of using secondary data include lack of availability, lack of relevance, inaccuracy, and insufficient data.

Decision support systems are designed from an individual decision maker's perspective. A DSS is interactive, flexible, discovery-oriented, and easy to learn; it can offer many benefits to small and large firms alike.

KEY TERMS & DEFINITIONS

secondary data Data that have been previously gathered.

primary data New data gathered to help solve the problem under investigation.

internal database A collection of related information developed from data within the organization.

database marketing Marketing that relies on the creation of a large computerized file of customers' and potential customers' profiles and purchase patterns to create a targeted marketing mix.

neural network A computer program that mimics the processes of the human brain and thus is capable of learning from examples to find patterns in data.

data mining The use of statistical and other advanced software to discover nonobvious patterns hidden in a database.

behavioral targeting The use of online and offline data to understand a consumer's habits, demographics, and social networks in order to increase the effectiveness of online advertising.

marketing research aggregator A company that acquires, catalogs, reformats, segments, and resells reports already published by large and small marketing research firms.

decision support system (DSS) An interactive, personalized information management system, designed to be initiated and controlled by individual decision makers.

QUESTIONS FOR REVIEW & CRITICAL THINKING

1. Why should a company consider creating an internal marketing database? Name some types of information that might be found in such a database and the sources of this information.
2. Why has data mining become so popular with firms such as United Airlines, American Express, and Ford Motor Company?
3. What are some of the keys to ensuring the success of an internal database?
4. Why are secondary data often preferred to primary data?
5. What pitfalls might a researcher encounter in using secondary data?
6. Why has behavioral targeting become so popular with marketers? Why is it controversial?

7. In the absence of company problems, is there any need to conduct marketing research or develop a decision support system?

8. What is a marketing research aggregator? What role does it play in marketing research?

9. [*Team exercise*] Divide the class into groups of four or five. Each team should go to the Internet and look up database marketing. Each team should then report to the class on how a specific company is effectively using databases to improve their marketing efficiency.

WORKING THE NET

1. What makes vendors' Web sites desirable tools for creating an internal database?

2. Go to *www.yankelovich.com*. Explain to the class the nature and scope of the Yankelovich MONITOR. How can marketing researchers use the data from this research?

3. Go to the National Opinion Research Center, at *www.norc.uchicago.edu*, and describe what new reports are available for researchers.

4. You are interested in home-building trends in the United States, as your company, Whirlpool, is a major supplier of kitchen appliances. Go to *www.nahb.com* and describe what types of information at this site might be of interest to Whirlpool.

5. Go to *www.claritas.com*. Describe types of secondary data available at this site.

6. Go to *www.marketresearch.com* and explain what types of reports are available.

7. Go to *www.comscore.com* and explain what they offer their customers.

8. Go to *www.Nielsen.com* and read about BuzzMetrics. Explain how it works and why it is a valuable tool to some marketers.

REAL-LIFE RESEARCH • 3.1

The Changing Face of Motherhood

Today's mothers of newborns are older, better educated, less likely to be white, and less likely to be married than their counterparts were in 1990.

There were more births to teenagers in 1990 than to women ages 35 and older. By 2008 (the latest date for which data are available), things had changed: Fourteen percent of births were to older women and 10 percent were to teens. Across all major race and ethnic groups, the rate of births to women ages 35 and older grew 64 percent between 1990 and 2008.

Another study on fertility attitudes and trends found the following:

• 35 percent of parents cited the reason "It wasn't a decision; it just happened" as very important and 12 percent as somewhat important in the decision to have their first or only child.

- Women (51 percent) were somewhat more likely than men (42 percent) to say that "it just happened" was somewhat or very important.

- Forty six percent said two children was the ideal number for a family; 26 percent said three; 9 percent said four; and 3 percent each said zero, one, or five or more. Among parents of three or more children, 33 percent said two was ideal.

- Nearly two-thirds of Americans (65 percent) said the growing number of single women having babies is bad for society. Only a minority disapproved of more women having babies after age 40 (33 percent), more women undergoing fertility treatment in order to have a baby (28 percent), and more women not ever having children (38 percent).

- Most adults said they knew at least one woman who had a baby while she was not married and one man who fathered a child while he was not married. One-third said they knew a woman who had fertility treatment in order to get pregnant.

There are fewer women in the prime childbearing years now than in 1990, as the youngest Baby Boomers have aged into their mid-40s. But changes in the racial and ethnic makeup of young women—mainly, the growth of the Hispanic population, which has higher birth rates that other groups—have helped keep birth numbers relatively level.

Another influence on births is the nation's growing number of immigrants, who tend to have higher birth rates than the native-born (although those rates have declined in recent years). The share of births to foreign-born mothers—15 percent of U.S. births in 1990—grew as least 60 percent through 2004. Births to foreign-born women in 2004 accounted for the majority of Hispanic (61 percent) and Asian (83 percent) births.

Eighty-two percent of the nation's population growth through 2050 will be accounted for by immigrants who arrived in the United States after 2005 and their descendants, assuming current trends continue. Of the 142 million people added to the population from 2005 to 2050, the projections say, 50 million will be the children or grandchildren of the new immigrants.

The average age for U.S. mothers who had their first baby in 2008 was 25, a year older than the average first-time mother in 1990. Among all women who had a baby in 2008, the average age is 27, up from 26 in 1990. The prime childbearing years remain 29–34—three-quarters of mothers of newborns are in this age range. Birth rates peak among women in their late 20s.

Since 1990, birth rates have risen for all women ages 30 and older. Although in some cases the number of births is small, the rate increases have been sharpest for women in the oldest age groups—47 percent for women ages 35–39 and 80 percent for women ages 40–44, for example.

Dual Factors

The delay in age of motherhood is associated with delay in age of marriage and with growing educational attainment, the report notes. The more education a woman has, the later she tends to marry and have children. Birth rates also have risen for the most educated women—those with at least some college education—while staying relatively stable for women with less education. These dual factors have worked together to increase the education levels of mothers and newborns.

Among mothers under age 50 and fathers under age 60, 82 percent say they plan to have no more children. When those parents, as well as parents beyond the childbearing ages, were asked why they decided to limit the number of children they had, the only reason cited as "very important" by most parents (64 percent) was that they wanted to devote time to the children they already had. A total of 76 percent described this reason as very important or somewhat important. A total of 72 percent said the cost of having another child was very or somewhat important to them in deciding to limit their family size.

Cited by smaller groups of respondents as very or somewhat important were the stress of raising children (49 percent), the wishes of their spouse or partner for no more children (46 percent), their age (42 percent), and their desire to have time for other interests (40 percent).[24]

Questions

1. Is this information primary or secondary data?
2. How might Gerber use this information? Would it need to follow up with primary research?
3. Cite examples of how promotion may need to change to reach new mothers.
4. If Disney World considers adding a new theme area to its Orlando park, what clues might it pull from the above case? Suggest areas of follow-up research.

Qualitative Research

LEARNING OBJECTIVES

→ **1.** To define qualitative research.

→ **2.** To explore the popularity of qualitative research.

→ **3.** To learn about focus groups and their tremendous popularity.

→ **4.** To gain insight into conducting and analyzing a focus group.

→ **5.** To learn about other forms of qualitative research.

What is qualitative research, and what are the advantages and disadvantages of it? Why are focus groups so popular, and what are the trends in focus group research? What other qualitative tools are available to marketing researchers? These areas are covered in this chapter.

The Nature of Qualitative Research

→ **qualitative research**
Research whose findings are not subject to quantification or quantitative analysis.

→ **quantitative research**
Research that uses mathematical analysis.

Qualitative research is a term used loosely to refer to research whose findings are not subject to quantification or quantitative analysis. A quantitative study may determine that a heavy user of a particular brand of tequila is 21 to 35 years of age and has an annual income of $25,000 to $40,000. While **quantitative research** might be used to find statistically significant differences between heavy and light users, qualitative research could be used to examine the attitudes, feelings, and motivations of the heavy user. Advertising agencies planning a campaign for tequila might employ qualitative techniques to learn how heavy users express themselves and what language they use—essentially, how to communicate with them.

The qualitative approach was derived from the work of the mid-18th-century historian Giambattista Vico. Vico wrote that only people can understand people and that they do so through a faculty called *intuitive understanding*. In sociology and other social sciences, the concept of *Verstehen*, or the intuitive experiment, and the use of empathy have been associated with major discoveries (and disputes).

Qualitative Research versus Quantitative Research

Exhibit 4.1 compares qualitative and quantitative research on several levels. Perhaps most significant to managers is the fact that qualitative research typically is characterized by small samples—a trait that has been a focal point for criticism of all qualitative techniques. In essence, many managers are reluctant to base important strategy decisions on small-sample research because it relies so greatly on the subjectivity and interpretation of the researcher. They strongly prefer a large sample, with results analyzed on a computer

EXHIBIT 4.1	Qualitative versus Quantitative Research	
	Qualitative Research	**Quantitative Research**
Types of questions	Probing	Limited probing
Sample size	Small	Large
Amount of information from each respondent	Substantial	Varies
Requirements for administration	Interviewer with special skills	Interviewer with fewer special skills or no interviewer
Type of analysis	Subjective, interpretive	Statistical, summation
Hardware	Sound recorders, projection devices, video recorders, pictures, discussion guides	Questionnaries, computers, printouts, mobile devices
Degree of replicability	Low	High
Researcher training	Psychology, sociology, social psychology, consumer behavior, marketing, marketing research	Statistical, decision models, decision support systems, computer programming, marketing, marketing research
Type of research	Exploratory	Descriptive or causal

and summarized into tables. These managers feel comfortable with marketing research based on large samples and high levels of statistical significance because the data are generated in a rigorous and scientific manner.

Popularity of Qualitative Research

Companies are now spending over $4.3 billion annually on qualitative research.[1] Why does the popularity of qualitative research continue to grow? First, qualitative research is usually much cheaper than quantitative research. Second, there is no better way to understand the in-depth motivations and feelings of consumers. When, in a popular form of qualitative research, product managers unobtrusively observe from behind a one-way mirror, they obtain firsthand experiences with flesh-and-blood consumers. Instead of plodding through a computer printout or consultant's report that requires them to digest reams of numbers, the product manager and other marketing personnel observe consumers' reactions to concepts and hear consumers discuss their own and their competitors' products at length, in their own language. Sitting behind a one-way mirror can be a humbling experience for a new product-development manager when the consumer begins to tear apart product concepts that were months in development in the sterile laboratory environment.

A third reason for the popularity of qualitative research is that it can improve the efficiency of quantitative research. Reckitt Benckiser PLC, the maker of Woolite and Lysol, knew women were not happy with how glasses were cleaned in a dishwasher. Focus groups learned that, over time, glasses washed in a dishwasher tended to become cloudy and stained. The company decided to embark on a major quantitative study to determine the extent of the perceived "staining" problem among households with dishwashers. The quantitative study verified that consumers were indeed unhappy with how their glasses looked after numerous rounds in the dishwasher. They also were willing to pay a reasonable price to find a solution. Reckitt Benckiser recently introduced Finish Glass Protector, a dishwasher detergent that protects glassware from mineral corrosion. Thus qualitative research led to a well-conceived quantitative study that verified demand for the new product.

It is becoming more common for marketing researchers to combine qualitative and quantitative research into a single study or a series of studies. The Finish Glass example showed how qualitative research can be used prior to quantitative research; in other research designs, the two types of research are conducted in the reverse order. For instance, the patterns displayed in quantitative research can be enriched with the addition of qualitative information on the reasons and motivations of consumers. One major insurance company conducted a quantitative study in which respondents were asked to rank the importance of 50 service characteristics. Later, focus groups were conducted in which participants were asked to define and expound on the top 10 characteristics. Most of these characteristics dealt with client–insurance agent interactions. From these focus groups the researchers found that "agent responds quickly" may mean either a virtually instantaneous response or a response within a reasonable time; that is, it means "as soon as is humanly possible for emergencies" and "about 24 hours for routine matters." The researchers noted that had they not conducted focus groups after the quantitative study, they could only have theorized about what "responds quickly" means to customers.

In the final analysis, all marketing research is undertaken to increase the effectiveness of decision making. Qualitative research blends with quantitative measures to provide a more thorough understanding of consumer demand. Qualitative techniques involve open-ended questioning and probing. The resulting data are rich, human, subtle, and often very revealing.

Limitations of Qualitative Research

Qualitative research can and does produce helpful and useful information—yet it is held in disdain by some researchers. One drawback relates to the fact that marketing successes and failures many times are based on small differences in attitudes or opinions about a marketing mix, and qualitative research does not distinguish those small differences as well as large-scale quantitative research does. However, qualitative research is sometimes able to detect problems that escape notice in a quantitative study. For example, a major manufacturer of household cleaners conducted a large quantitative study in an effort to learn why its bathroom cleanser had lackluster sales when in fact its chemical compound was more effective than those used by leading competitors. The quantitative study provided no clear-cut answer. The frustrated product manager then turned to qualitative research, which quickly found that the muted pastel colors on the package did not connote "cleansing strength" to the shopper. In light of this finding and the finding that a number of people were using old toothbrushes to clean between their bathroom tiles, the package was redesigned with brighter, bolder colors and with a brush built into the top.

A second limitation of qualitative studies is that they are not necessarily representative of the population of interest to the researcher. One would be hard-pressed to say that a group of 10 college students was representative of all college students, of college students at a particular university, of business majors at that university, or even of marketing majors! Small sample size and free-flowing discussion can lead qualitative research projects down many paths. Because the subjects of qualitative research are free to talk about what interests them, a dominant individual in a group discussion can lead the group into areas of only tangential interest to the researcher. It takes a highly skilled researcher to get the discussion back on track without stifling the group's interest, enthusiasm, and willingness to speak out.

The Importance of Focus Groups

→ **focus group**
A group of 8 to 12 participants who are led by a moderator in an in-depth discussion on one particular topic or concept.

Focus groups had their beginnings in group therapy used by psychiatrists. Today, a **focus group** consists of 8 to 12 participants who are led by a moderator in an in-depth discussion on one particular topic or concept. The goal of focus group research is to learn and understand what people have to say and why. The emphasis is on getting people to talk at length and in detail about the subject at hand. The intent is to find out how they feel about a product, a concept, an idea, or an organization; how it fits into their lives; and their emotional involvement with it.

Focus groups are much more than merely question-and-answer interviews. A distinction is made between *group dynamics* and *group interviewing*. The interaction associated with **group dynamics** is essential to the success of focus group research; this interaction is the reason for conducting research with a group rather than with individuals. One idea behind focus groups is that a response from one person will become a stimulus for another person, thereby generating an interplay of responses that will yield more information than if the same number of people had contributed independently.

→ **group dynamics**
Interaction among people in a group.

The idea for group dynamics research in marketing came from the field of social psychology, where studies indicated that, unknown to themselves, people of all walks of life and in all occupations would talk more about a topic and do so in greater depth if they were encouraged to act spontaneously instead of reacting to questions. Normally, in group dynamics, direct questions are avoided. In their place are indirect inquiries that stimulate free and spontaneous discussions. The result is a much richer base of information, of a kind impossible to obtain by direct questioning.

Popularity of Focus Groups

The terms *qualitative research* and *focus groups* are often used as synonyms by marketing research practitioners. Popular writing abounds, with examples of researchers referring to qualitative research in one breath and focus groups in the next. Although focus groups are but one aspect of qualitative research, the overwhelming popularity of the technique has virtually overshadowed the use of other qualitative tools.

How popular are focus groups? Most marketing research firms, advertising agencies, and consumer goods manufacturers use them. Today, most of all marketing research expenditures for qualitative research is spent on focus groups. The majority of focus research projects in the United States take place in over 750 focus facilities and are directed by over 1,000 moderators. The most common formats of qualitative research are focus groups and individual depth interviews (IDIs).

Focus group research is a globally accepted form of marketing research. It is estimated that over 550,000 focus groups are conducted worldwide each year. Approximately 255,000 focus group sessions take place in the United States annually.[2]

Conducting Focus Groups

On the following pages, we will consider the process of conducting focus groups, illustrated in Exhibit 4.2. We devote considerable space to this topic because there is much potential for researcher error in conducting focus groups.

Setting Focus groups are usually held in a **focus group facility**. The setting is often a conference room, with a large one-way mirror built into one wall. Microphones are placed in an unobtrusive location (usually the ceiling) to record the discussion. Behind the mirror is the viewing room, which holds chairs and note-taking benches or tables for the clients. The viewing room also houses the recording or videotaping equipment. The photo in Exhibit 4.3 illustrates a focus group in progress.

Some research firms offer a living-room setting as an alternative to the conference room. It is presumed that the informality of a living room (a typical homelike setting) will make the participants more at ease. Another variation is to televise the proceedings to a remote viewing room rather than use a one-way mirror. This approach offers clients

> **focus group facility**
> A research facility consisting of a conference room or living room setting and a separate observation room with a one-way mirror or live audiovisual feed.

Exhibit 4.2

Steps in Conducting a Focus Group

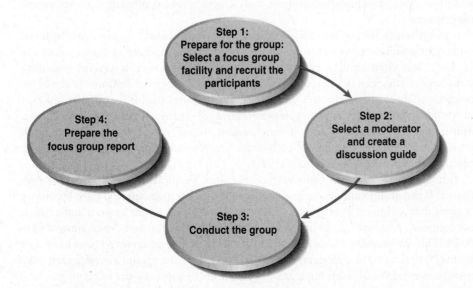

Step 1:
Prepare for the group:
Select a focus group facility and recruit the participants

Step 2:
Select a moderator and create a discussion guide

Step 3:
Conduct the group

Step 4:
Prepare the focus group report

Exhibit 4.3

A Focus Group in Progress

Source: "Screen shot from a video we took of one of our focus group sessions" - moderated by Jerry Thomas of Decision Analyst, Inc.

the advantage of being able to move around and speak in a normal tone of voice without being heard through the wall. On more than one occasion, focus groups have been distracted by a flash seen through the mirror when a client moved too suddenly while watching the group.

Participants　Participants for focus groups are recruited from a variety of sources. Two traditional procedures are mall-intercept interviewing and random telephone screening. (Both methods are described in detail in Chapter 5.) Researchers normally establish criteria for the group participants. For example, if Quaker Oats is researching a new cereal, it might request as participants mothers who have children between 7 and 12 years old and who have served cold cereal, perhaps of a specific brand, in the past 3 weeks.

Focus group recruiters go where the target market is to find qualified respondents. This type of recruiting means going to nursery schools to find moms with kids, health clubs to find people with active lifestyles, the home improvement center to find do-it-yourselfers, supermarkets to find primary food shoppers, and community centers to find senior citizens.

Usually, researchers strive to avoid repeat, or "professional," respondents in focus groups. Professional respondents are viewed by many researchers as actors or, at the very least, less than candid participants. Questions also may be raised regarding the motives of the person who would continually come to group sessions. Is she or he lonely? Does she or he really need the respondent fee that badly? It is highly unlikely that professional respondents are representative of many, if any, target markets. Unfortunately, field services find it much easier to use repeat respondents than to recruit a new group of individuals each time. Sample screening questions to identify repeat respondents are shown in Exhibit 4.4.

Although there is no ideal number of participants, a typical group will contain 8 participants. If the group contains more than 8 people, group members will have little time to express their opinions. Rarely will a group last more than 2 hours; an hour and a half is more common. The first 10 minutes is spent on introductions and an explanation of procedures. This leaves about 80 useful minutes in the session, and up to 25 percent of that time may be taken by the moderator. With 10 people in the group, an average of only 6 minutes per individual is left for actual discussion. If the topic is quite interesting or of a

Exhibit 4.4

Sample Screening Questions for Identifying Professional Focus Group Participants

1. Past Participation Series

Sometimes it is important to talk with people who have participated in previous research because they have experience talking about certain topics. At other times, it is important to talk with people who have never participated in an opinion study. Often we are looking for a mix of different experiences. What type of opinion studies, if any, have you ever participated in? (DO NOT READ LIST.)

	CIRCLE ALL MENTIONS
One-on-one in-person depth interview	1
Group interview with two or more participants	2
Mock jury or trial	3
Product placement test with a follow-up interview	4
Mail interview	5
Internet survey	6
Phone survey	7
Other (SPECIFY)	8
None	9

1A. When was the last time you participated in a

_____ Group interview with two or more participants

_____ (LIST ANOTHER TYPE OF RESEARCH YOU MIGHT CONSIDER INAPPROPRIATE.)

IF WITHIN THE LAST SIX MONTHS, THANK AND TERMINATE.

1B. What were the topics of all of the group interviews in which you have participated?

_____

_____

IF ONE OF THE TOPICS LISTED BELOW IS MENTIONED, THANK AND TERMINATE.

(   ) MP3 Players

(   ) Camera Cell Phones

1C. Are you currently scheduled to participate in any type of market research study?

	CIRCLE	
Yes	1→	(THANK AND TERMINATE)
No	2	→ (CONTINUE)

Source: Merril Shugoll and Nancy Kolkebeck, "You Get What You Ask For," _Quirk's Marketing Research Review,_ December 1999, pp. 61–65. Reprinted by permission.

technical nature, fewer than 8 respondents may be needed. The type of group will also affect the number recruited.

Moderator   Having qualified respondents and a good focus group moderator are the keys to a successful focus group. A **focus group moderator** needs two sets of skills. First, the moderator must be able to conduct a group properly. Second, he or she must have good business skills in order to effectively interact with the client. Key attributes for conducting a focus group include the following:

1. Genuine interest in people, their behavior, emotions, lifestyles, passions, and opinions.

→ **focus group moderator**
A person hired by a client to lead the focus group; this person should have a background in psychology or sociology or, at least, marketing.

2. Acceptance and appreciation for the differences in people, especially those whose lives vary greatly from your own.

3. Good listening skills: the ability both to hear what is being said and to identify what is not being said.

4. Good observation skills: the ability to see in detail what is happening or not happening and to interpret body language.

5. Interest in a wide range of topics and the ability to immerse yourself in the topic and learn the necessary knowledge and language quickly.

6. Good oral and written communication skills: the ability to clearly express yourself and to do so confidently in groups of all types and sizes.

7. Objectivity: the ability to set your personal ideas and feelings aside and remain open to the ideas and feelings of others.

8. Sound knowledge of the basic principles, foundations, and applications of research, marketing, and advertising.

9. Flexibility, ability to live with uncertainty, make fast decisions, and think on your feet (or the part of your anatomy that is seated in the moderator's chair).

10. Good attention to detail and organizational ability.[3]

Rapport makes research work. Rapport means being in a close or sympathetic relationship. A moderator develops a free and easy sense of discourse about anything with respondents. These strangers meet and are helped to a common ground through the ease of rapport. In a comfortable, nonthreatening, lively place, they can talk about anything at all—about sausage, insurance, tires, baked goods, magazines. In research the moderator is the bridge builder, and rapport is the bridge between people's everyday lives and the client's business interest.

In the past few years, there has been an increase in the number of formal moderator training courses offered by advertising agencies, research firms, and manufacturers with large marketing research departments. Most programs are strictly for employees, but a few are open to anyone. Also, there is the Qualitative Research Consultants Association that promotes professionalism in a qualitative research. The association has a quarterly publication, *QRCAViews*, that features ideas and tools for qualitative research. In addition, the organization holds an annual conference dedicated to improving qualitative research. You can learn more at *www.qrca.org*.

Discussion Guide   Regardless of how well trained and personable the moderator is, a successful focus group requires a well-planned discussion guide. A **discussion guide** is a written outline of the topics to be covered during the session. Usually the guide is generated by the moderator based on the research objectives and client information needs. It serves as a checklist to ensure that all salient topics are covered and in the proper sequence. For example, an outline might begin with attitudes and feelings toward eating out, then move to fast foods, and conclude with a discussion of the food and decor of a particular chain. It is important to get the research director and other client observers, such as a brand manager, to agree that the topics listed in the guide are the most important ones to be covered. It is not uncommon for a team approach to be used in generating a discussion guide.

The guide tends to lead the discussion through three stages. In the first stage, rapport is established, the rules of group interactions are explained, and objectives are given. In the second stage, the moderator attempts to provoke intensive discussion. The final stage is used for summarizing significant conclusions and testing the limits of belief and commitment.

Exhibit 4.5 shows an actual discussion guide for diet breads by a Decision Analyst moderator. The groups were held in several cities around the country.

→ **discussion guide**
A written outline of topics to be covered during a focus group discussion.

Exhibit 4.5

Decision Analyst, Inc., Discussion Outline on Diet Breads

I. **Introduction**
   A. Recording/observers
   B. Casual, relaxed, informal
   C. No right or wrong answers
   D. Be honest. Tell the truth
   E. Discussion rules
      - Talk one at a time
      - Don't dominate the discussion
      - Talk in any order
      - Listen to others

II. **General Attitudes toward Bread**
   A. Eating more or less bread now, compared to two years ago? Explore reasons.
   B. Advantages of bread, compared to other foods?
   C. Disadvantages of bread, compared to other foods?
   D. Words/mental images associated with great tasting bread?
   E. Foods bread goes with best? Why?

III. **Usage/Purchase of Bread**
   A. When and where is bread consumed most often?
   B. How does bread usage vary by household member? Why?
   C. Types of bread used most frequently?
   D. Likes/dislikes of each type of bread?
   E. Brands preferred? Why these brands? Vary by family member?

IV. **Bread Consumption When Dieting**
   A. Changes in bread consumption related to dieting? Why?
   B. Types of bread eaten when dieting, if any reasons?
   C. Role of bread in dieting?

V. **Attitudes toward Diet Breads**
   A. Awareness of diet breads/brands?
   B. Experiences with diet breads/brands?
   C. Satisfaction with each brand? Why like or not like? Brand perceptions?
   D. Important factors/product attributes associated with preferred brands?

VI. **The Perfect Diet Bread**
   A. Product characteristics?
      - Taste
      - Texture
      - Color
      - Crust
   B. Nutritional benefits?
   C. Packaging preferences?

VII. **Show and Discuss Advertising Concepts**
   A. Overall reactions to each concept?
   B. Likes/dislikes for each concept?
   C. Main idea for each concept?
   D. Believability?

VIII. **Reactions to Diet Bread Samples**
   A. Overall reactions to each bread?
   B. Reactions to taste?
   C. Reactions to texture and mouth feel?
   D. Reaction to slice shape and thickness?
   E. Reaction to loaf shape and size?
   F. Reaction to color?
   G. Reaction to feel in hand?

www.decisionanalyst.com

Focus Group Length   Many managers today prefer shorter (around an hour) focus groups. Yet the average group today is still about 90 minutes. Although shorter groups may be the trend, there is much to be said for longer focus groups. By a longer group we mean 2 hours or longer. A long group helps managers get more things done in a single session, and it also allows the respondents to get more involved, participate in more time-consuming tasks, and interact more extensively.

The issue of group length is not an isolated one; rather, it is intertwined with a second key factor: the number of questions in the discussion guide. One of the biggest problems with focus groups today, in our opinion, is the tendency to prepare discussion guides that pose far too many questions, which virtually precludes any depth of coverage or any significant group interactions. Managers want to get their money's worth, so it makes sense for them to ask every possible question. The "focus group" turns into a group interrogation or survey but without the controls and statistical power of scientific surveys.

In order to think more explicitly and logically about the number of questions to ask, managers should examine the interactions between the length of the focus group and the size of the discussion guide. As illustrated in Exhibit 4.6, more questions and less time combine to create a research environment that elicits responses that are mere survey-like sound bites. Also, moderators who have to plow through 40 questions in 90 minutes are likely to feel rushed, unable to probe interesting responses, and inclined to be abrupt with long-winded or slow individuals. As we move up and to the right in the table, these pressures and constraints diminish. With fewer questions and more time, respondents can elaborate their answers, moderators can probe more effectively, and the pace becomes more relaxed, natural, and humanistic.[4]

The Client's Role   The client, of course, selects the supplier and sometimes the moderator as well.[5] The client typically selects the markets where the groups will be held and specifies the characteristics of the group respondents. Sometimes the client will hand a finished discussion guide to the moderator, and, in other circumstances, the moderator and the client work together to create a final guide.

The client should go over not only the discussion guide with the moderator but the product or service being discussed as well. For example, a moderator was doing a group on new earpieces, and the client had not shown the moderator how they worked. The moderator was not told that, if you wore glasses, the frames would interfere with putting on the earpieces. When the moderator attempted to demonstrate the earpieces, they would not fit in his hears. Obviously, this created a negative impression among group participants.[6]

EXHIBIT 4.6	Response Time per Question per Respondent		
	Focus Group Length		
Number of Questions	**75 min.**	**90 min.**	**120 min.**
15	:30	:36	:48
20	:23	:27	:36
25	:18	:22	:29
30	:15	:18	:24
35	:13	:15	:21
40	:11	:14	:18

Note: The analysis assumes a group comprising 10 respondents.

Source: Dennis Rook, "Out of Focus Groups," *Marketing Research,* Summer 2003, p. 13.

Focus Group Report Typically, after the final group in a series is completed, there will be a moderator debriefing, sometimes called **instant analysis**. This tradition has both pros and cons. Arguments for instant analysis include the idea that it serves as a forum for combining the knowledge of the marketing specialists who viewed the group with that of the moderator. It gives the client an opportunity to hear and react to the moderator's initial perceptions, and it harnesses the heightened awareness and excitement of the moment to generate new ideas and implications in a brainstorming environment.

The shortcomings include the possibility of biasing future analysis on the part of the moderator with this "hip-shooting commentary," conducted without the benefit of time to reflect on what transpired. Instant analysis will be influenced by recency, selective recall, and other factors associated with limited memory capabilities; it does not allow the moderator to hear all that was said in a less than highly involved and anxious state. There is nothing wrong with a moderator debriefing as long as the moderator explicitly reserves the right to change her or his opinion after reviewing the tapes.

Today, a formal focus group report is typically a PowerPoint presentation. The written report is nothing more than a copy of the PowerPoint slides.

Jacob Brown of In-Depth Research discusses conducting focus groups in the accompanying Global Research box.

> ➤ instant analysis
> Moderator debriefing, offering a forum for brainstorming by the moderator and client observers.

Focus Group Trends

Video Transmissions A very popular trend in focus group research is conducting the groups online. This topic is discussed in detail in Chapter 6. Even when focus groups are conducted in traditional focus group facilities there is a growing tendency for clients to watch the sessions online. The advantage to the client is that they can avoid the time and expense of traveling to a distant city. Over 25 percent of all focus groups conducted in traditional facilities involve video transmissions.

Focus Group Panels Typically, a screening question for participating in a focus group is: "Have you participated in a focus group within the past 6 months?" If the answer is "yes," they are disqualified. The notion is that clients don't want professional respondents but want "fresh participants." A different model now being used by some firms is a focus group panel. The idea is to establish a group of about 8 to 12 qualified respondents who agree to participate in a series of interviews on a given product, service, or topic. Once recruited, the same group of respondents would then agree to meet once a month for approximately a 6-month period.

One advantage of the panel is that a variety of topics can be addressed and then revisited, if necessary. For example, assume that a consumer packaged-goods company is seeking to launch a new line of salad dressings. Its qualitative panel starts out first with the seeds of new ideas for a line of salad dressings. The next session refines those ideas to the point where packaging, graphics and flavor concepts are developed. And before the subsequent session, advertising stimuli boards can be created with positioning statements and potential names generated. This, ultimately, can save clients time and money.

Adding Marketing Professionals as Repondents When a product or service concept warrants it, marketing professionals (for example, advertising executives, new product development managers, marketing officers) are mixed in with typical consumers. These professionals are referred to as "prosumers." British Airways was looking to challenge American Airlines and Virgin Atlantic for dominance of business-class travel on the airlines' transatlantic routes. The qualitative research being conducted with consumers

GLOBAL RESEARCH

Planning Global Focus Groups

Consistency is best achieved by building a well-defined research template that clearly communicates research guidelines but still allows each moderator to adapt the process to fit local culture and individual style. Clearly articulating these ground rules will eliminate much of the ambiguity and reduce opportunities for misunderstanding. Some simple suggestions include the following:

- Start the research in your home country (we'll assume you're a U.S.-based company). That way all the stakeholders have a chance to attend the groups and agree on how the research "should" look before you fan out across the globe.

- Send copies of the U.S. videotapes to each foreign moderator. Remember that you may need to convert the tapes to the appropriate video format for each country and pay to have a translator watch the video with the moderator.

- Have the U.S. moderator schedule conference calls with each moderator to discuss the research process and answer questions—after they have watched the videos.

- If your budget allows it, have the U.S. moderator travel to each country. The U.S. moderator can manage the process locally, give consistent direction to each moderator, and ensure that the research doesn't get off course.

Internationally, most moderators have a more passive moderating style. They generally like a more leisurely pace and a more open group environment. As a result, you may not be able to cover as many topics as you might in the United States, nor will you be able to drill down quite as deeply.

Tips for Some Major Countries

Here are a few facts about conducting research in some of the major markets.

Japan

Scheduling a large number of B2B groups can be a challenge in Japan since you can only do one focus group each night, not two as we do in the United States. Professionals have long commutes, they work late, and they can't leave early or do a lunch group. However, they are willing to come in and do groups or interviews on the weekend. So, if you need to do six groups, think of doing three on Saturday and three on Sunday. But remember that there's a lot of competition for space at facilities on the weekend, so book early.

Germany

When doing any research in Germany, be aware that the privacy laws are probably the most restrictive in the world. Your ability to get names from e-mail lists, publication lists, or other databases can be severely constrained. Even using names from your own company database may be an issue.

France

Paris is famous for strikes, especially among the transportation workers. Check with the recruiter to see if there are any strikes on the horizon. If strikes have been in the news, make sure you schedule enough replacements and expect some delays. If a transportation strike is expected, you can still do the research, but have the recruiter check with each respondent about his or her ability to get to the facility if there is a strike. And make sure your hotel is within walking distance of the facility.

England

There is a wide mix of educational levels among UK businesspeople. Leaving school early is not uncommon in England, and many successful businesspeople have relatively little formal education. If a degree is important, make sure to include it in the screener—don't assume it the way you would in the United States. Conversely, don't require a degree in the screener unless you really feel it's important.

Scandinavia

Companies often overlook the Scandinavian countries when planning European research. But remember: Scandinavia has the best technology infrastructure and the most educated and fluent English-speaking professionals in Europe.[7]

Questions

1. Can focus groups be conducted the same way all over the world?

2. How might culture impact a focus group?

was not getting the research team the kind of insights they were seeking. They decided they would need to shake things up if they were going to achieve any breakthroughs that would help British Airways differentiate its business-class travel experience.

The research team took an unusual step. They set up focus groups that involved the usual target—regular business travelers. But they added product-development and marketing professionals who frequently traveled from New York to London—precisely the kind of professional who would typically be intentionally screened out.

After a joint focus group that included both consumers and these "prosumers," the prosumers group joined British Airways' leadership team for a gloves-off creative session that incorporated what was learned in the focus group, but also took into account the prosumers' understanding of the types of informed, innovative thinking the research team was seeking.

One of those prosumers, a research and development director at Unilever, shared the confidence that when she travels, she likes a seat that fully reclines but does not like to be sleeping in full-recline mode next to strangers or business associates. And she presumed that many women travelers would probably agree with her. From that observation, an idea was born. And now, seats that cradle passengers and pullout privacy panels are designed into almost all international business-travel sections.

"Her professional experience—understanding demographics, knowing that we were looking for breakthrough ideas—and her ability to express her ideas in a useful way to the research team made her a key part of the process," says Christopher Miller, founder of Lancaster, Pennsylvania-based Innovation Focus, Inc. "That creative tension, where respondents speak both personally and as a professional, has become the foundation of this process."[8]

Benefits and Drawbacks of Focus Groups

The benefits and drawbacks of qualitative research in general also apply to focus groups. But focus groups have some unique pros and cons that deserve mention.

Advantages of Focus Groups   The interactions among respondents can stimulate new ideas and thoughts that might not arise during one-on-one interviews. And group pressure can help challenge respondents to keep their thinking realistic. Energetic interactions among respondents also make it likely that observation of a group will provide firsthand consumer information to client observers in a shorter amount of time and in a more interesting way than will individual interviews.

Another advantage focus groups offer is the opportunity to observe customers or prospects from behind a one-way mirror, video feed, or online. In fact, there is growing use of focus groups to expose a broader range of employees to customer comments and views. "We have found that the only way to get people to really understand what customers want is to let them see customers, but there are few people who actually come in contact with customers," says Bonnie Keith, corporate market research manager at Hewlett-Packard. "Right now, we are getting people from our manufacturing and engineering operations to attend and observe focus groups."

Another advantage of focus groups is that they can be executed more quickly than many other research techniques. In addition, findings from groups tend to be easier to understand and to have a compelling immediacy and excitement. "I can get up and show a client all the charts and graphs in the world, but it has nowhere near the impact of showing 8 or 10 customers sitting around a table and saying that the company's service isn't good," says Jean-Anne Mutter, director of marketing research at Ketchum Advertising.

Disadvantages of Focus Groups   Unfortunately, some of the strengths of focus groups also can become disadvantages. For example, the immediacy and apparent understandability of focus group findings can cause managers to be misled instead of informed. Mutter says, "Even though you're only getting a very small slice, a focus group gives you a sense that you really understand the situation." She adds that focus groups can strongly appeal to "people's desire for quick, simple answers to problems, and I see a decreasing willingness to go with complexity and to put forth the effort needed to really think through the complex data that will be yielded by a quantitative study."

Other disadvantages relate to the focus group process. For example, focus group recruiting may be a problem if the type of person recruited responds differently to the issues being discussed than do other target segments. White middle-class individuals, for example, participate in qualitative research in numbers disproportionate to their presence in the marketplace. Also, some focus group facilities create an impersonal feeling, making honest conversation unlikely. Corporate or formal settings with large boardroom tables and unattractive or plain decor may make it difficult for respondents to relax and share their feelings.

The greatest potential for distortion is during the group interview itself. As a participant in the social interaction, the moderator must take care not to behave in ways that prejudice responses. The moderator's style may contribute to bias. For example, an aggressive, confronting style may lead respondents to say whatever they think the moderator wants them to say, to avoid attack. Or "playing dumb" may create the perception that the moderator is insincere or phony and cause respondents to withdraw.

Respondents also can be a problem. Some individuals are simply introverted and do not like to speak out in group settings. Other people may attempt to dominate the discussion. These are people who know it all—or think they do—and answer every question first, without giving others a chance to speak. A dominating participant may succeed in swaying other group members. If a moderator is abrupt with a respondent, it can send the wrong message to other group members—"You'd better be cautious, or I will do the same thing to you." Fortunately, a good moderator can stifle a dominant group member and not the rest of the group. Simple techniques used by moderators include avoiding eye contact with a dominant person; reminding the group that "we want to give everyone a chance to talk;" saying "Let's have someone else go first;" or if someone else is speaking and the dominant person interrupts, looking at the initial speaker and saying, "Sorry, I cannot hear you."

Other Qualitative Methodologies

Most of this chapter has been devoted to focus groups because of their pervasive use in marketing research. However, several other qualitative techniques are also used, albeit on a much more limited basis.

Individual Depth Interviews

Individual depth interviews (IDI) are relatively unstructured one-on-one interviews. The interviewer is thoroughly trained in the skill of probing and eliciting detailed answers to each question. Sometimes psychologists are used as depth interviewers: They may employ nondirective clinical techniques to uncover hidden motivations. IDIs are the second most popular form of qualitative research.

> **individual depth interviews** One-on-one interviews that probe and elicit detailed answers to questions, often using nondirective techniques to uncover hidden motivations.

The direction of a depth interview is guided by the responses of the interviewee. As the interview unfolds, the interviewer thoroughly probes each answer and uses the replies as a basis for further questioning. For example, a depth interview might begin with a discussion of snack foods. The interviewer might follow each answer with "Can you tell me more?" "Would you elaborate on that?" or "Is that all?" The interviewer might then move into the pros and cons of various ingredients, such as corn, wheat, and potatoes. The next phase could delve into the sociability of the snack food. Are Fritos, for example, more commonly eaten alone or in a crowd? Are Wheat Thins usually reserved for parties? When should you serve Ritz crackers?

The advantages of depth interviews over focus groups are as follows:

1. Group pressure is eliminated, so the respondent reveals more honest feelings, not necessarily those considered most acceptable among peers.

2. The personal one-on-one situation gives the respondent the feeling of being the focus of attention—that his or her thoughts and feelings are important and truly wanted.

3. The respondent attains a heightened state of awareness because he or she has constant interaction with the interviewer and there are no group members to hide behind.

4. The longer time devoted to individual respondents encourages the revelation of new information.

5. Respondents can be probed at length to reveal the feelings and motivations that underlie statements.

6. Without the restrictions of cultivating a group process, new directions of questioning can be improvised more easily. Individual interviews allow greater flexibility to explore casual remarks and tangential issues, which may provide critical insights into the main issue.

7. The closeness of the one-on-one relationship allows the interviewer to become more sensitive to nonverbal feedback.

8. A singular viewpoint can be obtained from a respondent without influence from others.

9. The interview can be conducted anywhere, in places other than a focus group facility.

10. Depth interviews may be the only viable technique for situations in which a group approach would require that competitors be placed in the same room. For example, it might be very difficult to do a focus group on systems for preventing bad checks with managers from competing department stores or restaurants.

11. When the research objective is to understand individual decision processes or individual responses to marketing stimuli (for example, Web sites), IDIs are typically the choice. IDIs allow detailed exploration of a single respondent's reactions without contamination. They are particularly valuable when researchers want individual reactions placed in the context of the individual's experiences.

12. If the topic is highly sensitive (for example, serious illnesses), use of IDIs is indicated. Subjects that are highly personal (for example, bankruptcy) or very detailed (for example, divorce decrees) are best probed deeply with IDIs.

The disadvantages of depth interviews relative to focus groups are as follows:

1. The total cost of depth interviews can be more expensive than focus groups, but not on a cost-per-respondent minute.

2. Depth interviews do not generally get the same degree of client involvement as focus groups. It is difficult to convince most client personnel to sit through multiple hours of depth interviews so as to benefit firsthand from the information.

3. Because depth interviews are physically exhausting for the moderator, they do not cover as much ground in one day as do focus groups. Most moderators will not do more than four or five depth interviews in a day, whereas they can involve 20 people in a day in two focus groups.

4. Focus groups are called for when consensus or debate is required to explore disparate views. Groups generate opportunities for point–counterpoint discussion and resolutions.

5. Focus groups give the moderator an ability to leverage the dynamics of the group to obtain reactions that might not be generated in a one-on-one session.[9]

Good depth interviewers, whether psychologists or not, are hard to find and expensive. A second factor that determines the success of depth research is proper interpretation. The unstructured nature of the interview and the clinical nature of the analysis increase the complexity of the task. Small sample sizes, the difficulty of making comparisons, the subjective nature of the researcher's interpretations, and high costs have all contributed to the lack of popularity of depth interviewing. Classic applications of depth interviews include:

- Communication checks (for example, review of print, radio, or TV advertisements or other written materials)
- Sensory evaluations (for example, reactions to varied formulations for deodorants or hand lotions, sniff tests for new perfumes, or taste tests for a new frosting)
- Exploratory research (for example, defining baseline understanding or a product, service, or idea)
- New product development, prototype stage
- Packaging or usage research (for example, when clients want to "mirror" personal experience and obtain key language descriptors)[10]

A variation of the depth interview is called customer care research (CCR). The basic idea is to use depth interviewing to understand the dynamics of the purchase process. The following seven questions are the basis for CCR:

1. What started you on the road to making this purchase?
2. Why did you make this purchase now?
3. What was the hardest part of this process? Was there any point where you got stuck?
4. When and how did you decide the price was acceptable?
5. Is there someone else with whom I should talk to get more of the story behind this purchase?
6. If you've purchased this product before, how does the story of your last purchase differ from this one?
7. At what point did you decide you trusted this organization and this person to work with in your best interests?[11]

Cost of Focus Groups versus IDI In a standard, eight-person, 90-minute focus group, there are nine people (eight participants plus moderator) sharing the floor. On average, therefore, each respondent is allotted 10 minutes of talk time across those 90 minutes (90 minutes divided by nine people).

The cost of a focus group of this type is about $10,000. That number includes everything: recruiter, moderator, participant stipend, food, facility, report write-up, and the cost of getting a few observers to the event. Divide 80 minutes of participant talk time (the moderator doesn't count) into the $10,000 expense, and your cost per respondent minute in this case is $125 ($10,000/80).

If, however, a typical in-depth interview runs 30 minutes and costs between $600 and $800 (including recruiting, interviewing, participant stipend, and reporting), the cost per respondent minute is in the range of $20 to $27. The big difference results from the amount of time the respondent spends talking, which is typically about 20 to 25 of those 30 minutes in an in-depth phone interview.

Thus, when considering the cost per respondent minute, in-depth interviews can provide much greater value.[12] Of course, the quality of both the focus groups and the IDI determines the real value of the research.

Using Hermeneutics Some IDI researchers use a technique called hermeneutic research to achieve their goals. **Hermeneutic research** focuses on interpretation as a basis of understanding the consumer. Interpretation comes about through "conversations" between the researcher and the participant. In hermeneutic research, the researcher answers the participant's questions and, as in the traditional method, the researcher only questions the respondent. There are no predetermined questions, but questions arise spontaneously as the conversation unfolds.

> **hermeneutic research** Research that focuses on interpretation through conversations.

For example, a researcher and a consumer in conversation about why that individual purchased a high-end home theater system may discuss the reasons for making the purchase, such as holding movie parties, enjoying a stay-at-home luxury, or immersing one-self in sporting events. The researcher may interpret "holding movie parties" as a reason for purchase to mean that without the system, the consumer would not hold the parties at all, and so the researcher will return to the consumer for additional information. Upon reviewing the data and talking more, the researcher and consumer determine that why the item was purchased and why it is used (which may or may not be the same) are not as telling as how the product makes its owner feel. In this case, the owner may feel confident as an entertainer, more social, powerful, wealthy, relaxed, or rejuvenated. Talking and probing more about the use of the home theater, the researcher uncovers both new data and new issues to address or consider moving forward.[13]

Writing an IDI report, whether or not hermeneutics are used, is quite different from writing a quantitative report.

Using the Delphi Method   The **Delphi Method** is often used in new product development when firms are looking for creative new ideas to incorporate in products or services. The term *Delphi* has its roots in Greek history. The city of Delphi was a hub of activity, combining culture, religion, and perspective into one highly populated area of information. Delphi was also home to the Oracle of Pythia, a woman believed to offer great insight into the future. The Oracle was a great influence to visitors, who believed this knowledge of the future would help them succeed in life.

Typically, the Delphi Method relies on people who are experts in some area. It may be product development researchers, marketing managers, professional people (MDs, engineers, etc.), magazine editors, executives, priests, and so forth. Obviously, the type of experts used depends on the objectives of the Delphi session. If one is looking for more efficient ways to handle materials management in a warehouse, the experts may simply be the workers in the warehouse.

The Delphi Method involves a number of rounds of data collection. In the classical Delphi procedure, the first round is unstructured, in order to allow individual experts relative freedom to identify and elaborate the pertinent issues from their point of view. These issues are then consolidated by the researcher(s) into a structured questionnaire.

This questionnaire is subsequently used to elicit the opinions and judgments of the panel of experts in a quantitative form. The responses are analyzed and statistically summarized and presented back to the panelists for further consideration. Respondents are then given the opportunity to alter prior opinions on the basis of feedback. The number of rounds varies from two to ten, but seldom goes beyond one or two iterations.

The key characteristics of Delphi are anonymity, iteration, feedback, and aggregation of group responses. The objective is to obtain the most reliable consensus of opinion via a series of intensive questionnaires, interspersed with opinion feedback.

The purpose of anonymity in a Delphi study is to exclude group interaction, which can cause a number of problems, such as group conflict and individual dominance. Delphi relies on a structured, indirect approach to group decision making; that is, participants don't meet, relying instead on statistical aggregation of individual predictions and ideas.

Controlled feedback, developed from the results of a round, is presented back to the panel of experts at the start of the next round. The form of the feedback varies depending on the topic. It may simply be an aggregation of ideas, or, if the group is estimating sales of a proposed new product, then quantitative estimates, for example, medians, may be given. Sometimes the Delphi Method creates scenarios—for example, how can we create a better customer relationship management (CRM) software that will enable us to take market share from the two market leaders? Scenarios can be used to answer two types of questions: (1) Precisely how might some hypothetical situation come about, step by step? and (2) What alternatives exist, for each actor, at each step, for preventing, diverting, or facilitating the process?

The iteration, controlled feedback, and aggregation of group responses aim to produce as many high-quality responses and opinions as possible on a given issue(s) from a panel of experts to enhance decision making. By feeding back responses from the panel to each member in the group, through a series of iterations, experts are able to adjust their estimates on the basis of others' comments.[14]

Projective Tests

Projective techniques are sometimes incorporated into depth interviews. The origins of projective techniques lie in the field of clinical psychology. In essence, the objective of any **projective test** is to delve below surface responses to obtain true feelings, meanings, and motivations. The rationale behind projective tests comes from the knowledge that people are often reluctant or unable to reveal their deepest feelings. In some instances, they are unaware of those feelings because of psychological defense mechanisms.

> ➤ **projective test**
> A technique for tapping respondents' deepest feelings by having them project those feelings into an unstructured situation.

Projective tests are techniques for penetrating a person's defense mechanisms to allow true feelings and attitudes to emerge. Generally, a respondent is presented with an unstructured and nebulous situation and asked to respond. Because the situation is ill-defined and has no true meaning, the respondent must impose her or his own frame of reference. In theory, the respondent "projects" personal feelings into the unstructured situation, bypassing defense mechanisms because the respondent is not referring directly to herself or himself. As the individual talks about something or someone else, her or his inner feelings are revealed.

Why is projection important? Consumers (or doctors, voters, managers, or whomever we are studying) may not tell us everything that influences them. Three obstacles stand in the way:

1. Respondents may be unconscious or unaware of a particular influence.

2. They may be aware of an influence but feel it is too personal or socially undesirable to admit (for example, prestige, image, racial bias).

3. They may be aware that they perceive a product a particular way, but they may not bother to mention this because, in their view, it is not a logical, rational reason for buying or not buying the product. Some doctors, for example, are adamant that what they prescribe has nothing to do with the sound of a drug's name or the attractiveness of the manufacturer's logo, and is based solely on decision-making factors such as research findings, clinical experience, and patient compliance.[15]

Most projective tests are easy to administer and are tabulated like other open-ended questions. They are often used in conjunction with nonprojective open- and closed-ended questions. A projective test may gather "richer," and perhaps more revealing, data than do standard questioning techniques. Projective techniques are used often in image questionnaires and concept tests, and occasionally in advertising pretests. It is also common to apply several projective techniques during a depth interview.

The most common forms of projective techniques used in marketing research are word association tests, sentence and story completion tests, cartoon tests, photo sorts, consumer drawings, storytelling, and third-person techniques. Other techniques, such as psychodrama tests and the Thematic Apperception Test (TAT), have been popular in treating psychological disorders but of less help in marketing research.

Word Association Tests **Word association tests** are among the most practical and effective projective tools for marketing researchers. An interviewer reads a word to a respondent and asks him or her to mention the first thing that comes to mind. Usually, the individual will respond with a synonym or an antonym. The words are read in quick succession to avoid allowing time for defense mechanisms to come into play. If the respondent fails to answer within 3 seconds, some emotional involvement with the word is assumed.

> ➤ **word association test**
> Projective test in which the interviewer says a word and the respondent must mention the first thing that comes to mind.

Word association tests are used to select brand names, advertising campaign themes, and slogans. For example, a cosmetic manufacturer might ask consumers to respond to the following words as potential names for a new perfume: infinity, encounter, flame, desire, precious, erotic. One of these words or a synonym suggested by respondents might then be selected as the brand name.

Analogies

➤ **analogy**
Comparison of two items based on similarities.

Analogies   Slightly different from word associations, **analogies** draw a comparison between two items in terms of their similarities. For example, a researcher investigating consumers' perceptions of Ford automobiles may ask: "I'm going to read you a list of stores, and then I'd like you to tell me which of these is most similar to Ford cars. If possible, try to give the first answer that comes to mind. The stores are Neiman Marcus, Wal-Mart, Macy's, JCPenney, Kmart, Nordstrom, Target, and Lord & Taylor." As a follow-up, the researcher would then ask: "What is it about [Store X] that is most similar to Ford cars? How are the qualities of Ford cars similar to this store?" This line of questioning induces the respondent to talk (indirectly) about his or her perceptions of Ford cars.

The use of analogies in this instance is not to determine which store(s) people associate with Ford cars but rather to get people to talk about their perceptions of Ford cars in ways they might otherwise be unable to do. Because perceptions of stores vary, some respondents may choose Store A, and some may choose Store B. The researcher should be less concerned with identifying the store(s) that respondents tend to select and more concerned with determining the reasons respondents give for the choices they make. Person A may select a different store from Person B, but this is of little significance if these two individuals share similar perceptions of the stores they chose, and hence of the Ford brand.[16]

➤ **personification**
Drawing a comparison between a product and a person.

Personification   A technique similar to analogies, **personification** involves drawing a comparison between a product and a person. To continue with the example from above, the researcher might say, "Think about the Ford brand, and imagine it were a person. Who would this brand be? How would you describe this person? What personality characteristics would this person have? In what ways do you associate this person with the brand?"

During this type of exercise, the researcher should encourage the participant to discuss such things as the person's values, beliefs, goals, lifestyle, appearance, age, occupation, socioeconomic status, hobbies, and interests. All of these can speak volumes about the respondent's attitudes toward the brand and can go significantly beyond the output of standard lines of questioning.[17]

➤ **sentence and story completion test**
A projective test in which respondents complete sentences or stories in their own words.

Sentence and Story Completion Tests   **Sentence and story completion tests** can be used in conjunction with word association tests. The respondent is furnished with an incomplete story or group of sentences and asked to complete it. A few examples of incomplete sentences follow:

1. Best Buy is . . .
2. The people who shop at Best Buy are . . .
3. Best Buy should really . . .
4. I don't understand why Best Buy doesn't . . .

Here's an example of a story completion test:

Sally Jones just moved to Chicago from Los Angeles, where she had been a salesperson for IBM. She is now a district manager for the Chicago area. Her neighbor Rhonda Smith has just come over to Sally's apartment to welcome her to Chicago. A discussion of where to shop ensues. Sally notes, "You know, I've heard some things about Best Buy. . . ." What is Rhonda's reply?

Exhibit 4.7

Cartoon Test

As you can see, story completion tests provide a more structured and detailed scenario for the respondent. Again, the objective is for the interviewees to put themselves in the role of the imaginary person mentioned in the scenario.

Some researchers consider sentence and story completion tests to be the most useful and reliable of all the projective tests. Decision Analyst is now offering both online sentence completion and online word association research to its clients.

Cartoon Tests The typical **cartoon test** consists of two characters with balloons, similar to those seen in comic books; one balloon is filled with dialogue, and the other balloon is blank (see Exhibit 4.7). The respondent is asked to fill in the blank balloon.

Note that the cartoon figures in Exhibit 4.7 are left vague and without expression so that the respondent is not given clues regarding a suggested type of response. The ambiguity is designed to make it easier for the respondent to project his or her feelings into the cartoon situation.

Cartoon tests are extremely versatile and highly projective. They can be used to obtain differential attitudes toward two types of establishments and the congruity or lack of congruity between these establishments and a particular product. They can also be used to measure the strength of an attitude toward a particular product or brand, or to ascertain what function is being performed by a given attitude.

Photo Sorts With **photo sorts**, consumers express their feelings about brands by manipulating a specially developed photo deck depicting different types of people, from business executives to college students. Respondents connect the individuals in the photos with the brands they think they would use.

BBDO Worldwide, one of the country's largest advertising agencies, has developed a trademarked technique called Photosort. A Photosort conducted for General Electric found that consumers thought the brand attracted conservative, older, business types. To change that image, GE adopted the "Bring Good Things to Life" campaign. A Photosort for Visa found the credit card to have a wholesome, female, middle-of-the-road image in customers' minds. The "Everywhere You Want to Be" campaign was devised to interest more high-income men.

➜ **cartoon test**
A projective test in which the respondent fills in the dialogue of one of two characters in a cartoon.

➜ **photo sort**
A projective technique in which a respondent sorts photos of different types of people, identifying those people who she or he feels would use the specified product or service.

Another photo sort technique, called the Pictured Aspirations Technique (PAT), was created by Grey Advertising, a large New York advertising agency. The technique attempts to uncover how a product fits into a consumer's aspirations. Consumers sort a deck of photos according to how well the pictures describe their aspirations. In research done for Playtex's 18-hour bra, this technique revealed that the product was out of sync with the aspirations of potential customers. The respondents chose a set of pictures that depicted "the me they wanted to be" as very energetic, slim, youthful, and vigorous. But the pictures they used to express their sense of the product were a little more old-fashioned, a little stouter, and less vital and energetic looking. Out went the "Good News for Full-Figured Gals" campaign, with Jane Russell as spokesperson, and in came the sexier, more fashionable concept of "Great Curves Deserve 18 Hours."

Consumer Drawings   Researchers sometimes ask consumers to draw what they are feeling or how they perceive an object. **Consumer drawings** can unlock motivations or express perceptions. For example, the McCann-Erickson advertising agency wanted to find out why Raid roach spray outsold Combat insecticide disks in certain markets. In interviews, most users agreed that Combat is a better product because it kills roaches without any effort on the user's part. So the agency asked the heaviest users of roach spray—low-income women from the southern United States—to draw pictures of their prey (see Exhibit 4.8). The goal was to get at their underlying feelings about this dirty job.

→ **consumer drawings**
A projective technique in which respondents draw what they are feeling or how they perceive an object.

Exhibit   4.8

Consumer Drawings That Helped Identify Respondents' Need for Control

Source: Courtesy of McCann-Erickson, New York.

"One night I just couldn't take the horror of these bugs sneaking around in the dark. They are always crawling when you can't see them. I had to do something. I thought wouldn't it be wonderful if when I switch on the light the roaches would shrink up and die like vampires to sunlight. So I did, but they just all scattered. But I was ready with my spray so it wasn't a total loss. I got quite a few . . . continued tomorrow night when nighttime falls."

"A man likes a free meal you cook for him; as long as there is food he will stay."

"I tiptoed quietly into the kitchen, perhaps he wasn't around. I stretched my arm up to turn on the light. I hoped I'd be alone when the light went on. Perhaps he is sitting on the table I thought. You think that's impossible? Nothing is impossible with that guy. He might not even be alone. He'll run when the light goes on I thought. But what's worse is for him to slip out of sight. No, it would be better to confront him before he takes control and 'invites a companion'."

All of the 100 women who participated in the agency's interviews portrayed roaches as men. "A lot of their feelings about the roach were very similar to the feelings that they had about the men in their lives," said Paula Drillman, executive vice president at McCann-Erickson. Many of the women were in common-law relationships. They said that the roach, like the man in their life, "only comes around when he wants food." The act of spraying roaches and seeing them die was satisfying to this frustrated, powerless group. Setting out Combat disks may have been less trouble, but it just didn't give them the same feeling. "These women wanted control," Drillman said. "They used the spray because it allowed them to participate in the kill."

Storytelling As the name implies, **storytelling** requires consumers to tell stories about their experiences. It is a search for subtle insights into consumer behavior.

> **storytelling**
> A projective technique in which respondents are required to tell stories about their experiences, with a company or product, for example; also known as the *metaphor technique.*

Gerald Zaltman, a Harvard Business School professor, has created a metaphor laboratory to facilitate the storytelling process. (A metaphor is a description of one thing in terms that are usually used to describe another; it can be used to represent thoughts that are tacit, implicit, and unspoken.) Zaltman elicits metaphors from consumers by asking them to spend time over several weeks thinking about how they would visually represent their experiences with a company. To help them with the process, he asks them to cut out magazine pictures that somehow convey those experiences. Then, consumers come to his lab and spend several hours telling stories about all of the images they chose and the connections between the images and their experiences with the firm.

One metaphor study was conducted on pantyhose. "Women in focus groups have always said that they wear them because they have to, and they hate it," says Glenda Green, a marketing research manager at DuPont, which supplies the raw material for many pantyhose manufacturers. "We didn't think we had a completely accurate picture of their feelings, but we hadn't come up with a good way to test them."[18] DuPont turned to storytelling for better insights. Someone brought a picture of a spilled ice cream sundae, capturing the rage she feels when she spots a run in her hose. Another arrived with a picture of a beautiful woman with baskets of fruit. Other photos depicted a Mercedes and Queen Elizabeth. "As we kept probing into the emotions behind the choice of these photos, the women finally began admitting that hose made them feel sensual, sexy, and more attractive to men," says Green. "There's no way anyone would admit that in a focus group." Several stocking manufacturers used this information to alter their advertising and package design.

Third-Person Technique Perhaps the easiest projective technique to apply, other than word association, is the **third-person technique**. Rather than directly asking respondents what they think, researchers couch the question in terms of "your neighbor," "most people," or some other third party. Rather than asking a mother why she typically does not fix a nutritionally balanced breakfast for her children, a researcher might ask, "Why don't many people provide their families nutritionally balanced breakfasts?" The third-person technique is often used to avoid questions that might be embarrassing or evoke hostility if posed directly to a respondent.

> **third-person technique**
> A projective technique in which the interviewer learns about respondents' feelings by asking them to answer for a third party, such as "your neighbor" or "most people."

SUMMARY

Qualitative research refers to research whose findings are not subject to quantification or quantitative analysis. It is often used to examine consumer attitudes, feelings, and motivations. Qualitative research, particularly the use of focus groups, continues to grow in popularity for three reasons. First, qualitative research is usually cheaper than quantitative studies. Second, it is an excellent means of understanding the in-depth motivations and feelings of consumers. Third, it can improve the efficiency of quantitative research.

Qualitative research is not without its disadvantages. Sometimes, qualitative research does not distinguish small differences in attitudes or opinions about a marketing mix as well as large-scale quantitative studies do. Also, respondents in qualitative studies are not necessarily representative of the population of interest to the researcher. And the quality of the research may be questionable, given the number of individuals who profess to be experts in the field, yet lack formal training.

Focus groups are the most popular type of qualitative research. A focus group typically consists of 8 to 12 paid participants who are led by a moderator in an in-depth discussion on a particular topic or concept. The goal of the focus group is to learn and understand what people have to say and why. The emphasis is on getting people to talk at length and in detail about the subject at hand. The interaction associated with group dynamics is essential to the success of focus group research. The idea is that a response from one person will become a stimulus for another person, thereby generating an interplay of responses that will yield more information than if the same number of people had contributed independently.

Most focus groups are held in a group facility, which is typically set up in a conference room, with a large one-way mirror built into one wall. Microphones are placed in unobtrusive locations to record the discussion. Behind the mirror is a viewing room. The moderator plays a critical role in the success or failure of the group and is aided in his or her efforts by a well-planned discussion guide.

A number of other qualitative research methodologies are used but on a much more infrequent basis. One such technique is depth interviews. Individual depth interviews are unstructured one-on-one interviews. The interviewer is thoroughly trained in the skill of probing and eliciting detailed answers to each question. He or she often uses nondirective clinical techniques to uncover hidden motivations. Other qualitative techniques are hermeneutics and the Delphi Method. The use of projective techniques represents another form of qualitative research. The objective of any projective test is to delve below the surface responses to obtain true feelings, meanings, or motivations. Some common forms of projective techniques are word association tests, analogies, personification sentence and story completion tests, cartoon tests, photo sorts, consumer drawings, storytelling, and third-person techniques.

KEY TERMS & DEFINITIONS

qualitative research Research whose findings are not subject to quantification or quantitative analysis.

quantitative research Research that uses mathematical analysis.

focus group A group of 8 to 12 participants who are led by a moderator in an in-depth discussion on one particular topic or concept.

group dynamics Interaction among people in a group.

focus group facility A research facility consisting of a conference room or living room setting and a separate observation room with a one-way mirror or live audio-visual feed.

focus group moderator A person hired by a client to lead the focus group; this person should have a background in psychology or sociology or, at least, marketing.

discussion guide A written outline of topics to be covered during a focus group discussion.

instant analysis Moderator debriefing, offering a forum for brainstorming by the moderator and client observers.

individual depth interviews One-on-one interviews that probe and elicit detailed answers to questions, often using nondirective techniques to uncover hidden motivations.

hermeneutic research Research that focuses on interpretation through conversations.

Delphi Method Rounds of individual data collection from knowledgeable people. Results are summarized and returned to the participants for further refinement.

projective test A technique for tapping respondents' deepest feelings by having them project those feelings into an unstructured situation.

word association test Projective test in which the interviewer says a word and the respondent must mention the first thing that comes to mind.

analogy Comparison of two items based on similarities.

personification Drawing a comparison between a product and a person.

sentence and story completion test A projective test in which respondents complete sentences or stories in their own words.

cartoon test A projective test in which the respondent fills in the dialogue of one of two characters in a cartoon.

photo sort A projective technique in which a respondent sorts photos of different types of people, identifying those people who she or he feels would use the specified product or service.

consumer drawings A projective technique in which respondents draw what they are feeling or how they perceive an object.

storytelling A projective technique in which respondents are required to tell stories about their experiences, with a company or product, for example; also known as the *metaphor technique*.

third-person technique A projective technique in which the interviewer learns about respondents' feelings by asking them to answer for a third party, such as "your neighbor" or "most people."

QUESTIONS FOR REVIEW & CRITICAL THINKING

1. What are the major differences between quantitative and qualitative research?
2. What are some of the possible disadvantages of using focus groups?
3. Create a story completion test for downloading music from the Internet.
4. What can a client do to get more out of focus groups?
5. What is the purpose of a projective test? What major factors should be considered in using a projective technique?
6. Divide the class into groups of four and eight. The groups of four will select a topic below (or one suggested by your instructor) and create a discussion guide. One of the four will then serve as the group moderator. One of the groups of eight will serve as participants in the focus group. The groups should last at least 20 minutes and be observed by the remainder of the class. Suggested topics:
   a. New video games
   b. Buying a hybrid gasoline/electric car

    c. Student experiences at the student union

    d. The quality of existing frozen dinners and snacks and new items that would be desired by students

    e. How students spend their entertainment dollars and what additional entertainment opportunities they would like to see offered

7. What are some major issues in conducting international focus groups?

8. Take a consumer drawing test—draw a typical Pepsi drinker and a typical Coke drinker. What do the images suggest about your perceptions of Coke and Pepsi drinkers?

9. Use the metaphor technique to tell a story about going to the supermarket.

WORKING THE NET

Go to *www.researchconnections.com*. Under "Demos," look at the information available at Virtual Focus Facility. Report your findings to the class.

REAL-LIFE RESEARCH • 4.1

Steering Midas in the Right Direction

Midas, Inc., is one of the best-known providers of automotive services, offering brakes, maintenance, tires, exhaust, steering, and suspension repairs at nearly 2,400 franchised, licensed and company-owned Midas shops in 16 countries, including more than 1,600 in the United States and Canada. Although he works for Midas, Inc., Garry Rosenfeldt is the first to admit that some of his company's customers could have the same uneasy feelings about visiting a Midas shop. "As an industry, we are typically not known for warm and fuzzy customer service," says Rosenfeldt, the firm's director of marketing research.

But car owners may soon begin looking at Midas, in a different way. Rosenfeldt has used two large-scale qualitative research projects to help show the company's franchisees how bad things are in the auto service realm and, more importantly, how good things could get if shop managers started adhering to a set of basic service guidelines and behaviors that have not become a fundamental component of a broader retail operating model called the Midas Way. When initial discussions were held about undertaking a project to research and document the state of customer service in the car repair business, Rosenfeldt knew that the edicts to improve service would perhaps be better received internally if they were in the consumers' own words rather than those of Midas's corporate chiefs. "It occurred to me that the best way to get franchisees on board is to have somebody else basically say what they should be doing and hey, wouldn't it be great if that 'somebody else' happened to be real, live customers?"

The best way to accomplish this was to enable consumers to do the talking to video cameras in the privacy of their own homes. For the first project, Rosenfeldt recruited all of the respondents himself. He went to an electronics retailer and bought 150 video cameras and sent them out with instruction packets.

The goal was to learn about the ideal car repair service, not just at a Midas location but anywhere, so respondents had to complete a handful of tasks. For the first assignment, they were asked to look at scores of photos that represented many of the things that would happen in an auto service experience and expres their thoughts—have they experienced the same thing, what did they think about it, and so on.

Next they were asked to make an appointment for some kind of car service—an oil change, new brakes, and the like—at any service provider of their choosing and explain why they chose the shop they did, whether they had been there before, what they expected to happen, and how they expected to be treated. After the service, the consumers gave a wrap-up of how things went, including what was good, what was bad, and what could have been better.

Rosenfeldt edited the hundreds of hours of videotape down to the most important, impactful responses and set about distributing the video to franchisees over the Midas corporate Web portal, on DVDs in the mail, and via various road shows to explore and explain the results to internal audiences.

The franchisees' response? "We found that it was among the best, most effective research projects we've ever done."

The next step was to say, "We heard what you said. Here is what we have done. Is it correct? Are we doing the right thing?" Midas used the initial research to adopt new service protocols. This second phase was conducted by QualVu, an online video-based qualitative research firm. The company recruited respondents and distributed cameras. Both Midas customers and noncustomers were selected. Respondents were asked to have their cars serviced at Midas and report back.

Midas learned that it got the service model correct. "Customers did in fact notice a huge difference in the way the stores operated. Three main components of the Midas service model are greet, explain, and thank. "When you are a shop manager and a customer walks in the door, you need to do three things: greet them, explain what you are doing and thank them," Rosenfeldt says. "It sounds ridiculously simple, but it almost never happens in this industry. We have found that when shops are able to execute those behaviors consistently, our customer satisfaction goes way up and people come back and they purchase more services from me.[19]

Questions

1. We discussed a number of different types of qualitative research in this chapter. What type of research was conducted by Midas?

2. Could these data have been gathered using other forms of qualitative research? If so, which ones?

3. How did this form of research facilitate getting "buy-in" from the franchisees?

4. Should quantitative research play a role in the future for Midas? If so, how?

© Alex/iStockphoto

CHAPTER

Traditional Survey Research

LEARNING OBJECTIVES

→ **1.** To understand the reasons for the popularity of survey research.

→ **2.** To learn about the types of errors in survey research.

→ **3.** To learn about the types of surveys.

→ **4.** To gain insight into the factors that determine the choice of particular survey methods.

Survey research involves using a questionnaire to gather facts, opinions, and attitudes; it is the most popular way to gather primary data. What are the various types of survey research? As noted previously, not everyone is willing to participate in a survey. What kinds of errors does that create? What are the other types of errors encountered in survey research? Why has Internet survey research become so popular, and what are its drawbacks? These questions are answered in this chapter.

Popularity of Survey Research

Some 126 million Americans have been interviewed at some point in their lives. Each year, about 70 million people are interviewed in the United States, which is the equivalent of over 15 minutes per adult per year. Surveys have a high rate of usage in marketing research compared to other means of collecting primary data, for some very good reasons:

- *The need to know why.* In marketing research, there is a critical need to have some idea about why people do or do not do something. For example, why did they buy or not buy a particular brand? What did they like or dislike about it? Who or what influenced them? We do not mean to imply that surveys can prove causation, only that they can be used to develop some idea of the causal forces at work.

- *The need to know how.* At the same time, the marketing researcher often finds it necessary to understand the process consumers go through before taking some action. How did they make the decision? What time period passed? What did they examine or consider? When and where was the decision made? What do they plan to do next?

- *The need to know who.* The marketing researcher also needs to know who the person is, from a demographic or lifestyle perspective. Information on age, income, occupation, marital status, stage in the family life cycle, education, and other factors is necessary for the identification and definition of market segments.

A new survey of marketing research professionals found that the most common source of market research information is survey data, used by 94 percent of companies surveyed. Other sources include syndicated research (78 percent); focus groups (74 percent); company sales data (67 percent); and scanner data (16 percent). Also, 88 percent of corporations use online methods to conduct survey-based market research. Sixty-five percent of those surveyed agree that the speed of online research has helped accelerate the pace of their business. More than half of all online research dollars are spent on projects transitioning from traditional (that is, telephone, mail, mall) research methods.[1]

Types of Errors in Survey Research

When assessing the quality of information obtained from survey research, a manager must determine the accuracy of those results. This requires careful consideration of the research methodology employed in relation to the various types of errors that might result (see Exhibit 5.1).

Sampling Error

Two major types of errors may be encountered in connection with the sampling process. They are random error and systematic error, sometimes referred to as bias.

Surveys often attempt to obtain information from a representative cross section of a target population. The goal is to make inferences about the total population based on the

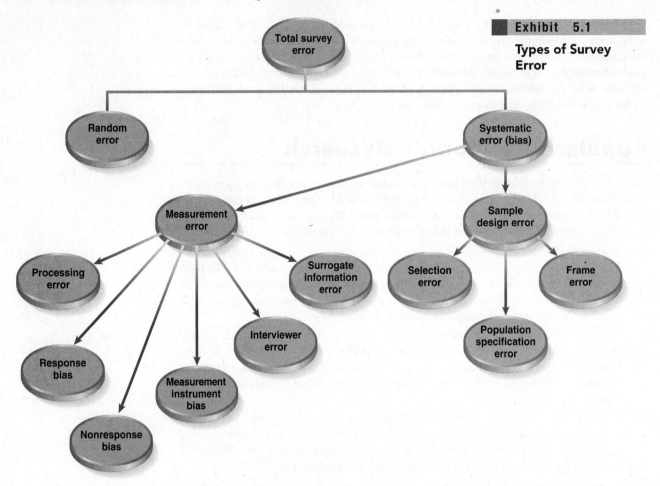

Exhibit 5.1

Types of Survey Error

→ **random error, or random sampling error**
Error that results from chance variation.

→ **chance variation**
The difference between the sample value and the true value of the population mean.

→ **systematic error, or bias**
Error that results from problems or flaws in the execution of the research design; sometimes called *nonsampling error*.

→ **sample design error**
Systematic error that results from an error in the sample design or sampling procedures.

responses given by respondents sampled. Even when all aspects of the sample are investigated properly, the results are still subject to a certain amount of **random error** (or **random sampling error**) because of chance variation. **Chance variation** is the difference between the sample value and the true value of the population mean. This error cannot be eliminated, but it can be reduced by increasing the sample size. It is possible to estimate the range of random error at a particular level of confidence. Random error and the procedures for estimating it are discussed in detail in Chapters 12.

Systematic Error

Systematic error, or **bias**, results from mistakes or problems in the research design or from flaws in the execution of the sample design. Systematic error exists in the results of a sample if those results show a consistent tendency to vary in one direction (consistently higher or consistently lower) from the true value of the population parameter. Systematic error includes all sources of error except those introduced by the random sampling process. Therefore, systematic errors are sometimes called *nonsampling errors*. The nonsampling errors that can systematically influence survey answers can be categorized as *sample design error* and *measurement error*.

Sample Design Error   **Sample design error** is a systematic error that results from a problem in the sample design or sampling procedures. Types of sample design errors include frame errors, population specification errors, and selection errors.

Frame Error

The **sampling frame** is the list of population elements or members from which units to be sampled are selected. **Frame error** results from using an incomplete or inaccurate sampling frame. The problem is that a sample drawn from a list that is subject to frame error may not be a true cross section of the target population. A common source of frame error in marketing research is the use of a published telephone directory as a sampling frame for a telephone survey. Many households are not listed in a current telephone book because they do not want to be listed or are not listed accurately because they have recently moved or changed their telephone number. Research has shown that those people who are listed in telephone directories are systematically different from those who are not listed in certain important ways, such as socioeconomic levels. This means that if a study purporting to represent the opinions of all households in a particular area is based on listings in the current telephone directory, it will be subject to frame error.

Population Specification Error

Population specification error results from an incorrect definition of the population or universe from which the sample is to be selected. For example, suppose a researcher defined the population or universe for a study as people over the age of 35. Later, it was determined that younger individuals should have been included and that the population should have been defined as people 20 years of age or older. If those younger people who were excluded are significantly different in regard to the variables of interest, then the sample results will be biased.

Selection Error

Selection error can occur even when the analyst has a proper sampling frame and has defined the population correctly. **Selection error** occurs when sampling procedures are incomplete or improper or when appropriate selection procedures are not properly followed. For example, door-to-door interviewers might decide to avoid houses that do not look neat and tidy because they think the inhabitants will not be agreeable to doing a survey. If people who live in messy houses are systematically different from those who live in

> **sampling frame**
> The list of population elements or members from which units to be sampled are selected.

> **frame error**
> Error resulting from an inaccurate or incomplete sampling frame.

> **population specification error**
> Error that results from incorrectly defining the population or universe from which a sample is chosen.

> **selection error**
> Error that results from incomplete or improper sample selection procedures or not following appropriate procedures.

A population must be defined before research can begin. Errors can occur if a population is not defined correctly or if selection procedures are not followed properly.

Grant Faint /Getty Images, Inc.

tidy houses, then selection error will be introduced into the results of the survey. Selection error is a serious problem in nonprobability samples, a subject discussed in Chapter 11.

Measurement Error   Measurement error is often a much more serious threat to survey accuracy than is random error. When the results of public opinion polls are given in the media and in professional marketing research reports, an error figure is frequently reported (say, plus or minus 5 percent). The television viewer or the user of a marketing research study is left with the impression that this figure refers to total survey error. Unfortunately, this is not the case. This figure refers only to random sampling error. It does not include sample design error and speaks in no way to the measurement error that may exist in the research results. **Measurement error** occurs when there is variation between the information being sought (true value) and the information actually obtained by the measurement process. Our main concern in this text is with systematic measurement error. Various types of error may be caused by numerous deficiencies in the measurement process. These errors include surrogate information error, interviewer error, measurement instrument bias, processing error, nonresponse bias, and response bias.

Surrogate Information Error

Surrogate information error occurs when there is a discrepancy between the information actually required to solve a problem and the information being sought by the researcher. It relates to general problems in the research design, particularly failure to properly define the problem. A few years ago, Kellogg spent millions developing a line of 17 breakfast cereals that featured ingredients that would help consumers cut down on their cholesterol. The product line was called Ensemble. It failed miserably in the marketplace. Yes, people want to lower their cholesterol, but the real question was whether they would purchase a line of breakfast cereals to accomplish this task. This question was never asked in the research. Also, the name "Ensemble" usually refers to either an orchestra or something you wear. Consumers didn't understand either the product line or the need to consume it.

Interviewer Error

Interviewer error, or interviewer bias, results from the interviewer's influencing a respondent—consciously or unconsciously—to give untrue or inaccurate answers. The dress, age, gender, facial expressions, body language, or tone of voice of the interviewer may influence the answers given by some or all respondents. This type of error is caused by problems in the selection and training of interviewers or by the failure of interviewers to follow instructions. Interviewers must be properly trained and supervised to appear neutral at all times. Another type of interviewer error occurs when deliberate cheating takes place. This can be a particular problem in door-to-door interviewing, where interviewers may be tempted to falsify interviews and get paid for work they did not actually do. The procedures developed by the researcher must include safeguards to ensure that this problem will be detected.

Measurement Instrument Bias

Measurement instrument bias (sometimes called *questionnaire bias*) results from problems with the measurement instrument or questionnaire (see Chapter 10). Examples of such problems include leading questions or elements of the questionnaire design that make recording responses difficult and prone to recording errors. Problems of this type can be avoided by paying careful attention to detail in the questionnaire design phase and by using questionnaire pretests before field interviewing begins.

Processing Error

Processing errors are primarily due to mistakes that occur when information from survey documents is entered into the computer. For example, a document may be scanned incorrectly.

→ **measurement error**
Systematic error that results from a variation between the information being sought and what is actually obtained by the measurement process.

→ **surrogate information error**
Error that results from a discrepancy between the information needed to solve a problem and that sought by the researcher.

→ **interviewer error, or interviewer bias**
Error that results from the interviewer's influencing—consciously or unconsciously—the answers of the respondent.

→ **measurement instrument bias**
Error that results from the design of the questionnaire or measurement instrument; also known as *questionnaire bias.*

→ **processing error**
Error that results from the incorrect transfer of information from a survey document to a computer.

Nonresponse Bias

Ideally, if a sample of 400 people is selected from a particular population, all 400 of those individuals should be interviewed. As a practical matter, this will never happen. Response rates of 5 percent or less are common in mail surveys. The question is "Are those who did respond to the survey systematically differ in some important way from those who did not respond?" Such differences lead to **nonresponse bias**. We recently examined the results of a study conducted among customers of a large savings and loan association. The response rate to the questionnaire, included in customer monthly statements, was slightly under 1 percent. Analysis of the occupations of those who responded revealed that the percentage of retired people among respondents was 20 times higher than in the local metropolitan area. This overrepresentation of retired individuals raised serious doubts about the accuracy of the results.

> **nonresponse bias**
> Error that results from a systematic difference between those who do and those who do not respond to a measurement instrument.

Obviously, the higher the response rate, the less the possible impact of nonresponse because nonrespondents then represent a smaller subset of the overall picture. If the decrease in bias associated with improved response rates is trivial, then allocating resources to obtain higher response rates might be wasteful in studies in which resources could be used for better purposes.

Nonresponse error occurs when the following happens:

- A person cannot be reached at a particular time.
- A potential respondent is reached but cannot or will not participate at that time (for example, the telephone request to participate in a survey comes just as the family is sitting down to dinner).
- A person is reached but refuses to participate in the survey. This is the most serious problem because it may be possible to achieve future participation in the first two circumstances.

The **refusal rate** is the percentage of persons contacted who refused to participate in a survey. Today, the overall refusal rate is approximately 60 percent—up from 52 percent in 1992, according to the Council for Marketing and Opinion Research (CMOR). Most refusals (68 percent) occur before the survey introduction (initial refusals); only one-quarter (26 percent) occur after the introduction is read (qualified refusals). Few (6 percent) terminate once the survey is under way. While most individuals (71 percent) express a willingness to participate in future surveys, this willingness is lukewarm (nearly three times as many are "fairly willing" compared to "very willing").[2] While these percentages are based on a study by the CMOR and are not necessarily reflective of the entire industry, they do reflect the significant increase in the refusal rate.

> **refusal rate**
> The percentage of persons contacted who refused to participate in a survey.

Response Bias

If there is a tendency for people to answer a particular question in a certain way, then there is **response bias**. Response bias can result from deliberate falsification or unconscious misrepresentation.

> **response bias**
> Error that results from the tendency of people to answer a question incorrectly through either deliberate falsification or unconscious misrepresentation.

Deliberate falsification occurs when people purposefully give untrue answers to questions. There are many reasons why people might knowingly misrepresent information in a survey. They may wish to appear intelligent, they may not reveal information that they feel is embarrassing, or they may want to conceal information that they consider to be personal.

For example, in a survey about fast-food buying behavior, the respondents may have a fairly good idea of how many times they visited a fast-food restaurant in the past month. However, they may not remember which fast-food restaurants they visited or how many times they visited each restaurant. Rather than answering "Don't know" in response to a question regarding which restaurants they visited, the respondents may simply guess.

Unconscious misrepresentation occurs when a respondent is legitimately trying to be truthful and accurate but gives an inaccurate response. This type of bias may occur because of question format, question content, or various other reasons.

Strategies for minimizing survey errors are summarized in Exhibit 5.2.

EXHIBIT 5.2	**Types of Errors and Strategies for Minimizing Them**

I. Random error
This error can be reduced only by increasing sample size.

II. Systematic error
This error can be reduced by minimizing sample design and measurement errors.

  A. Sample design error

    Frame error
This error can be minimized by getting the best sampling frame possible and doing preliminary quality control checks to evaluate the accuracy and completeness of the frame.

    Population specification error
This error results from incorrect definition of the population of interest. It can be reduced or minimized only by more careful consideration and definition of the population of interest.

    Selection error
This error results from using incomplete or improper sampling procedures or not following appropriate selection procedures. It can occur even with a good sampling frame and an appropriate specification of the population. It is minimized by developing selection procedures that will ensure randomness and by developing quality control checks to make sure that these procedures are followed in the field.

  B. Measurement error

    Surrogate information error
This error results from seeking and basing decisions on the wrong information. It results from poor design and can be minimized only by paying more careful attention to specification of the types of information required to fulfill the objectives of the research.

    Interviewer error
This error occurs because of interactions between the interviewer and the respondent that affect the responses given. It is minimized by careful interviewer selection and training. In addition, quality control checks should involve unobtrusive monitoring of interviewers to ascertain whether they are following prescribed guidelines.

    Measurement instrument bias
Also referred to as *questionnaire bias*, this error is minimized only by careful questionnaire design and pretesting.

    Processing error
This error can occur in the process of transferring data from questionnaires to the computer. It is minimized by developing and following rigid quality control procedures for transferring data and supporting quality control checks.

    Nonresponse bias
This error results from the fact that those people chosen for the sample who actually respond are systematically different from those who are chosen and do not respond. It is particularly serious in connection with mail surveys. It is minimized by doing everything possible (e.g., shortening the questionnaire, making the questionnaire more respondent friendly, doing callbacks, providing incentives, contacting people when they are most likely to be at home) to encourage those chosen for the sample to respond.

    Response bias
This error occurs when something about a question leads people to answer it in a particular way. It can be minimized by paying special attention to questionnaire design. In particular, questions that are hard to answer, might make the respondent look uninformed, or deal with sensitive issues should be modified (see Chapter 10).

Types of Surveys

Asking people questions is the essence of the survey approach. But what type of survey is best for a given situation? The non-Internet survey alternatives discussed in this chapter are door-to-door interviews, executive interviews, mall-intercept interviews, telephone interviews, self-administered questionnaires, and mail surveys.

Door-to-Door Interviews

→ **door-to-door interviews**
Interviews conducted face-to-face with consumers in their homes.

Door-to-door interviews, in which consumers are interviewed in person in their homes, were at one time thought to be the best survey method. This conclusion was based on a number of factors. First, the door-to-door interview is a personal, face-to-face interaction with all the attendant advantages—immediate feedback from the respondent, the ability to explain complicated tasks, the ability to use special questionnaire techniques that require visual contact to speed up the interview or improve data quality, and the ability to show the respondent product concepts and other stimuli for evaluation. Second, the participant is at ease in a familiar, comfortable, secure environment.

Door-to-door interviews began a steep decline in the early 1970s and have now virtually disappeared altogether from the U.S. marketing research scene. The primary reason is the cost of paying an interviewer's travel time, mileage, and survey time as well as ever-rising refusal rates. The method is still used in some government research. For example, some of the most recent U.S. Census was done door-to-door. Door-to-door interviewing is also used in developing countries.

Executive Interviews

→ **executive interviews**
The industrial equivalent of door-to-door interviewing.

Marketing researchers use **executive interviews** as the industrial equivalent of door-to-door interviews. This type of survey involves interviewing businesspeople at their offices concerning industrial products or services. For example, if Hewlett-Packard wants information about user preferences for features that might be offered in a new line of office printers, it needs to interview prospective user-purchasers of the printers. It would thus be appropriate to locate and interview these people at their offices.

This type of interviewing is expensive. First, individuals involved in the purchasing decision for the product in question must be identified and located. Sometimes lists can be obtained from various sources, but more frequently screening must be conducted over the telephone. A particular company may indeed have individuals of the type being sought, but locating them within a large organization can be expensive and time-consuming. Once a qualified person is located, the next step is to get that person to agree to be interviewed and to set a time for the interview. This is not usually as hard as it might seem because most professionals seem to enjoy talking about topics related to their work.

Finally, an interviewer must go to the particular place at the appointed time. Long waits are frequent; cancellations are common. This type of survey requires highly skilled interviewers because they are frequently interviewing on topics they know little about. Executive interviews have essentially the same advantages and disadvantages as door-to-door interviews. More and more executive interviews are moving online.

Mall-Intercept Interviews

→ **mall-intercept interviews**
Interviews conducted by intercepting mall shoppers (or shoppers in other high-traffic locations) and interviewing them face to face.

Mall-intercept interviews are a popular survey method for conducting personal interviews. This survey approach is relatively simple. Shoppers are intercepted in public areas of shopping malls and either interviewed on the spot or asked to come to a permanent interviewing facility in the mall. Approximately 500 malls throughout the country have permanent survey facilities operated by marketing research firms. An equal or greater number of malls permit marketing researchers to interview on a daily basis. Many malls do not permit marketing research interviewing, however, because they view it as an unnecessary nuisance to shoppers.

Mall surveys are less expensive than door-to-door interviews because respondents come to the interviewer rather than the other way around. Interviewers spend more of their time actually interviewing and less of their time hunting for someone to interview. Also, mall interviewers do not have the substantial travel time and mileage expenses associated with door-to-door interviewing. In addition to low-cost, mall-intercept interviews have many of the advantages associated with door-to-door interviews in that respondents can try test products on the spot.

However, a number of serious disadvantages are associated with mall-intercept interviewing. First, it is virtually impossible to get a sample representative of a large metropolitan area from shoppers at a particular mall. Even though malls may be large, most of them draw shoppers from a relatively small local area. In addition, malls tend to attract certain types of people, based on the stores they contain. Studies also show that some people shop more frequently than others and therefore have a greater chance of being selected. Finally, many people refuse mall interviews. In summary, mall-intercept interviewing cannot produce a good or representative sample except in the rare case in which the population of interest is coincident with or is a subset of the population that shops at a particular mall.

Second, the mall environment is not always viewed as a comfortable place to conduct an interview. Respondents may be ill at ease, in a hurry, or preoccupied by various distractions outside the researcher's control. These factors may adversely affect the quality of the data obtained. Even with all its problems, the popularity of mall-intercept interviews has only slightly declined in recent years.

Telephone Interviews

Until 1990, telephone interviewing was the most popular form of survey research. The advantages of telephone interviewing are compelling. First, telephoning is a relatively inexpensive way to collect survey data. Second, the telephone interview has traditionally produced a high-quality sample. Ninety-five percent of all Americans have some type of phone. *Random-digit sampling*, or *random-digit dialing*, is a frequently used sampling approach. The basic idea is simple: Instead of drawing a sample from the phone book or other directory, researchers use telephone numbers generated via a random-number procedure. This approach ensures that people with unlisted numbers and those who have moved or otherwise changed their telephone numbers since the last published phone book are included in the sample in the correct proportion.

Predictive Dialing   Today, random digit dialing has been merged with sophisticated software to create predictive dialing. One provider of predictive dialing is SPSS, Incorporated, which also provides the statistical software that is provided with each new copy of this test. The company has launched SPSS mrDialer 4.0 with Voice over Internet Protocol (VoIP), a product designed to deliver faster completion of projects, allow lower staff costs, and give market researchers more control over survey projects.

Since VoIP uses broadband connections instead of analog phone lines, SPSS mrDialer 4.0 is intended to support virtual call centers where interviewers are dispersed over a wide geographic space, either in separate offices or working from their homes. MrDialer 4.0 is designed to allow market researchers to centralize control of the call center, operate around the clock, and scale resources without significant cost escalation.

SPSS mrDialer uses predictive dialing algorithms to identify busy, unanswered, or unobtainable numbers. It is also designed to be adaptable to new rules and dialing methodologies that can be updated with a graphical user interface.

SPSS mrDialer 4.0 is designed to offer market researchers the ability to record interviews for quality assurance and capture responses; analyze busy signals and unanswered, modem and fax calls; prioritize recalls to meet a preset appointment time; simultaneously run multiple interviewing projects; deliver real-time reporting of numbers dialed and attempted, along with completed, interviews; and monitor the interview screen and voices from any station.[3]

Cell Phone Interviewing   Today, almost 40 percent of American households can only be reached on a cell phone or smart phone.[4] Remember, in this chapter, we are speaking about traditional telephone interviews—that is, an interviewer asking a series of questions to a respondent. The respondent may answer on a traditional telephone, cell phone, or smart phone. Smart phones, of course, can be used to reply to Web surveys. Mobile Internet surveys are covered in Chapter 6.

Cell phone interviewing enables researchers to access people otherwise unreachable for a telephone interview. Yet, cell phone interviewing tends to substantially drive up costs. Each completed interview can cost double or triple that of a landline interview.[5] Federal law requires interviewers to hand dial cell phone numbers rather than using auto dialers. Researchers also pay $1 to $10 or more to the respondents to cover the cost of the minutes. Also, it takes more calls to achieve a completed interview. People may not answer their cell phone when their usage isn't free, and they may defer a call when driving or in a public place.

A new Federal Communications Commission (FCC) proposal allows automatic dialers but will require "prior written consent" from the respondent. The Market Research Association has complained to the FCC that the new proposal will result in decreased response rates, add to the cost of research, increase the time required to complete studies, and decrease the representativeness of survey and opinion research. The association also claims that the proposed rule will impose serious recordkeeping burdens on researchers and increase risks to security and confidentiality.[6]

Besides the cell phone problems, the telephone survey approach has several inherent disadvantages. First, respondents cannot be shown anything in a traditional telephone interview. This shortcoming ordinarily eliminates the telephone survey as an alternative in situations that require respondents to comment on visual product concepts, advertisements, and the like. Of course, smart phone surveys overcome this problem.

A second disadvantage of the telephone interview is that it limits the quantity and types of information that can be obtained. A respondent's patience wears thin more easily over the phone, and it is easy to hang up the phone. The telephone is also a poor vehicle for conducting a depth interview or a long interview with many open-ended questions.

A third disadvantage of telephone interviewing is associated with the increased use of screening devices. These include answering machines, do-not-call lists, call blocking, caller ID, and distinctive ringing. On the average, for every hour an interviewer spends on the phone, 30 minutes is spent just trying to find a person who will agree to be surveyed. This, of course, drives up the cost of telephone surveys.

Today, nearly all telephone interviews are central-location call center interviews. In some cases, firms are further centralizing the process by conducting completely automated telephone surveys but only from landlines.

Call Center Telephone Interviews

Call center telephone interviews are conducted from a facility set up for that purpose. The reason for the popularity of call center phone interviews is fairly straightforward—in a single word, control. First, the interviewing process can be monitored; most call center telephone interviewing facilities have unobtrusive monitoring equipment that permits supervisors to listen in on interviews as they are being conducted. Interviewers who are not doing the interview properly can be corrected, and those who are incapable of conducting a proper interview can be terminated. One supervisor can monitor from 10 to 20 interviewers. Ordinarily, each interviewer is monitored at least once per shift. Second, completed interviews are edited on the spot as a further quality control check. Interviewers can be immediately informed of any deficiencies in their work. Finally, interviewers' working hours are controlled.

Virtually all research firms have computerized the call center telephone interviewing process. In **computer-assisted telephone interviews (CATI)**, each interviewer is seated in front of a computer terminal or a personal computer. When a qualified respondent

→ **call center telephone interviews**
Interviews conducted by calling respondents from a centrally located marketing research facility.

→ **computer-assisted telephone interviews (CATI)**
Call center telephone interviews in which interviewers enter respondents' answers directly into a computer.

gets on the line, the interviewer starts the interview by pressing a key or series of keys on the keyboard. The questions and multiple-choice answers appear on the screen one at a time. The interviewer reads the question and enters the response, and the computer skips ahead to the appropriate next question. For example, the interviewer might ask whether the respondent has a dog. If the answer is yes, there might be a series of questions regarding what type of dog food the person buys. If the answer is no, those questions would be inappropriate. The computer takes into account the answer to the dog ownership question and skips ahead to the next appropriate question.

In addition, the computer can help customize questionnaires. For example, in the early part of a long interview, a respondent is asked the years, makes, and models of all the cars he or she owns. Later in the interview, questions might be asked about each specific car owned. The question might come up on the interviewer's screen as follows: "You said you own a 2011 GMC truck. Which family member drives this vehicle most often?" Other questions about this vehicle and others owned would appear in similar fashion.

Another advantage of CATI is that computer tabulations can be run at any point in the study. Based on preliminary tabulations, certain questions might be dropped, saving time and money in subsequent interviewing. If, for example, 98.3 percent of those interviewed answer a particular question in the same manner, there is probably no need to continue asking the question. Tabulations may also suggest the need to add questions to the survey. If an unexpected pattern of product use is uncovered in the early stages of interviewing, questions can be added that delve further into this behavior. Finally, management may find the early reporting of survey results useful in preliminary planning and strategy development.

Self-Administered Questionnaires

The self-administered and mail survey methods explained in this section have one thing in common: They differ from the other survey methods discussed in that no interviewer—human or computer—is involved. The major disadvantage of **self-administered questionnaires** is that no one is present to explain things to the respondent and clarify responses to open-ended questions. For example, if someone were asked via an open-ended question why he or she does not buy a particular brand of soft drink, a typical answer might be "because I don't like it." From a managerial perspective, this answer is useless. It provides no information that can be used to alter the marketing mix and thereby make the product more attractive. An interviewer conducting the survey, however, would "probe" for a response—after receiving and recording the useless response, the interviewer would ask the respondent what it was that he or she did not like about the product. The interviewee might then indicate a dislike for the taste. Next, the interviewer would ask what it was about the taste that the person did not like. Here the interviewer might finally get something useful, with the respondent indicating that the product in question was, for example, "too sweet." If many people give a similar response, management might elect to reduce

Spencer Grant /PhotoEdit

Kiosk-based computer interviewing is a relatively new and successful way of capturing data on consumers' recent experiences. Go to *www.intouchsurvey.com* to find out more about the kiosk-based offerings of In-Touch Survey Systems, Inc.

the sweetness of the drink. The point is that, without probing, management would have only the useless first response.

Some have argued that the absence of an interviewer is an advantage in that it eliminates one source of bias. There is no interviewer whose appearance, dress, manner of speaking, or failure to follow instructions may influence respondents' answers to questions.

Self-administered interviews are often used in malls or other central locations where the researcher has access to a captive audience. Airlines, for example, often have programs in which questionnaires are administered during the flight. Passengers are asked to rate various aspects of the airline's services, and the results are used to track passenger perceptions of service over time. Many hotels, restaurants, and other service businesses provide brief questionnaires to patrons to find out how they feel about the quality of service provided (see Exhibit 5.3).

A recent development in the area of direct computer interviewing is kiosk-based computer interviewing. Kiosks are developed with multimedia, touch-screen computers contained in freestanding cabinets. These computers can be programmed to administer complex surveys, show full-color scanned images (products, store layouts), and play sound and video clips. Kiosks have been used successfully at trade shows and conventions and are now being tested in retail environments, where they have many applications. From a research standpoint, kiosk-based interviewing can be used in place of exit interviews to capture data on recent experiences. Kiosks have other definite advantages: This form of interviewing tends to be less expensive, and people tend to give more honest answers than they would to a human interviewer, and internal control is higher because the survey is preprogrammed.[7]

> **self-administered questionnaires**
> Questionnaires filled out by respondents with no interviewer present.

Mail Surveys

Two general types of mail surveys are used in marketing research: ad hoc mail surveys and mail panels. In **ad hoc mail surveys** (sometimes called *one-shot mail surveys*), the researcher selects a sample of names and addresses from an appropriate source and mails questionnaires to the people selected. Ordinarily, there is no prior contact, and the sample is used only for a single project. However, the same questionnaire may be sent to nonrespondents several times to increase the overall response rate. In contrast, **mail panels** operate in the following manner:

1. A sample group is precontacted by letter. In this initial contact, the purpose of the panel is explained, and people are usually offered a gratuity.

2. As part of the initial contact, consumers are asked to fill out a background questionnaire on the number of family members, their ages, education level, income, types of pets, types of vehicles and ages, types of appliances, and so forth.

3. After the initial contact, panel participants are sent questionnaires from time to time. The background data collected on initial contact enable researchers to send questionnaires only to appropriate households. For example, a survey about dog food usage and preferences would be sent only to dog owners.

A mail panel is a type of longitudinal study. A **longitudinal study** is one that questions the same respondents at different points in time. Several companies, including Synovate, NPD Research, and The Gallup Panel, operate large (more than 100,000 households) consumer mail panels.

On first consideration, mail appears to be an attractive way to collect survey data. There are no interviewers to recruit, train, monitor, and pay. The entire study can be sent out and administered from a single location. Hard-to-reach respondents can be readily surveyed. Mail surveys appear to be convenient, efficient, and inexpensive. The promise of anonymity is another benefit. While personal and telephone interviews may indicate

> **ad hoc mail surveys**
> Questionnaires sent to selected names and addresses without prior contact by the researcher; sometimes called *one-shot mail surveys*.

> **mail panels**
> Precontacted and pre-screened participants who are periodically sent questionnaires.

> **longitudinal study**
> A study in which the same respondents are resampled over time.

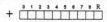

GATWICK EXPRESS
Customer Survey

+ [0 1 2 3 4 5 6 7 8 R]

Self-Administered Questionnaire: Airport Travel
Please fill out the following questionnaire. Check the appropriate boxes and write your answers in the space provided.

1. Where are you flying from? Where are you going? Please list the departure and arrival times of your flights as well as the airline you are flying with.
   - Departure Location: _____
     - Departure Time: _____
     - Airline/Flight Number: _____
   - Arrival Locations _____
     - Arrival Time: _____
     - Airline/Flight Number: _____

2. Which class are you sitting in?
   - First Class ○
   - Coach ○

3. Are your flights direct? If not, where is your layover? How long is your layover?
   _____

4. Where do you live?
   _____

5. What is your age, gender, and yearly household income?
   - Age _____
   - Gender _____
   - Income _____

6. How many adults are in your party? How many children?
   - Adults _____
   - Children _____

7. Why are you flying today? Check all that apply.
   - Business
   - Vacation
   - Visiting friends or relatives ○
   - Other

8. How many times have you flown in the last 12 months?
   _____

9. How did you book your flight?
   - Online
   - Through a travel agency
   - Over the phone

10. How did you first hear about the airline you are flying with today?
    _____

11. Did you consider alternative modes of transportation? If so, which ones? And why did you ultimately choose to fly with the airline you chose?
    _____

12. Please comment on your travel experience today with your particular airline.
    Comments:
    _____

Thank you for completing today's airline travel questionnaire. Enjoy your flight!

that all information collected will be kept confidential, blind mail surveys absolutely guarantee it. This is particularly important to someone who may be asked to provide information of a confidential or personal nature.[8]

Like self-administered questionnaires, mail surveys of both types encounter the problems associated with not having an interviewer present. In particular, no one is there to probe responses to open-ended questions, a real constraint on the types of information that can be sought. The number of questions—and, consequently, the quantity of obtainable information—is usually more limited in mail surveys than in surveys involving interviewers.

EXHIBIT 5.4	Non-Internet Forms of Survey Research
Type of Interview	**Description**
Door-to-door interviews	Interviews are conducted in respondents' homes (rarely used today in the United States).
Executive interviews	Interviews of industrial product users (e.g., engineers, architects, doctors, executives) or decision makers are conducted at their place of business.
Mall-intercept interviews	Interviews with consumers are conducted in a shopping mall or other high-traffic location. Interviews may be done in a public area of the mall, or respondents may be taken to a private test area.
Call center telephone interviews	Interviews are conducted from a telephone facility set up for that purpose. These facilities typically have equipment that permits supervisors to unobtrusively monitor the interviewing while it is taking place. Many of these facilities do national sampling from a single location. An increasing number have computer-assisted interviewing capabilities. At these locations, the interviewer sits in front of a computer terminal with a personal computer. The questionnaire is programmed into the computer, and the interviewer uses the keyboard to directly enter responses.
Self-administered questionnaires	Self-administered questionnaires are most frequently employed at high-traffic locations such as shopping malls or in captive audience situations such as classrooms and airplanes. Respondents are given general information on how to fill out the questionnaire and are expected to fill it out on their own. Kiosk-based point-of-service touch screens provide a way to capture information from individuals in stores, health clinics, and other shopping or service environments.
Ad hoc (one-shot) mail surveys	Questionnaires are mailed to a sample of consumers or industrial users, without prior contact by the researcher. Instructions are included; respondents are asked to fill out the questionnaire and return it via mail. Sometimes a gift or monetary incentive is provided.
Mail panels	Questionnaires are mailed to a sample of individuals who have been precontacted. The panel concept has been explained to them, and they have agreed to participate for some period of time, in exchange for gratuities. Mail panels typically generate much higher response rates than do ad hoc mail surveys.

Ad hoc mail surveys suffer from a high rate of nonresponse and attendant systematic error. Nonresponse in mail surveys is not a problem as long as everyone has an equal probability of not responding. However, numerous studies have shown that certain types of people—such as those with more education, those with high-level occupations, women, those less interested in the topic, and students—have a greater probability of not responding than other types. Response rates in ad hoc mail surveys may run anywhere from less than 5 percent to more than 50 percent, depending on the length of the questionnaire, its content, the group surveyed, the incentives employed, and other factors. Those who operate mail panels claim response rates in the vicinity of 70 percent.

Mail surveying is declining in popularity in commercial marketing research. Today, many research projects that, in the past, would have been conducted by mail are now being moved to the Internet.

Non-Internet survey alternatives discussed in this section are summarized in Exhibit 5.4.

Determination of the Survey Method

A number of factors may affect the choice of a survey method in a given situation. The researcher should choose the survey method that will provide data of the desired types, quality, and quantity at the lowest cost. The major considerations in the selection of a survey method are summarized in Exhibit 5.5.

Sampling Precision

The required level of sampling precision is an important factor in determining which survey method is appropriate in a given situation. Some projects by their very nature require a high level of sampling accuracy, whereas this may not be a critical consideration in other projects.

EXHIBIT 5.5	Factors That Determine the Selection of a Particular Survey Method
Factor	**Comment**
Sampling precision	If the need for accuracy in the study results is not great, less rigorous and less expensive sampling procedures may be appropriate.
Budget	It is important to determine how much money is available for the survey portion of the study.
Need to expose respondent to various stimuli and have respondent perform specialized tasks	Taste tests and prototype usage tests usually require face-to-face contact. Card sorts, certain visual scaling methods, and the like require either face-to-face contact or the Internet.
Quality of data required	It is important to determine how accurate the results of the study need to be.
Length of questionnaire	Long questionnaires are difficult to do by mail, over the phone, or in a mall.
Incidence rate	Are you looking for people who make up 1 percent of the total population or 50 percent of the population? If you are looking for a needle in a haystack, you need an inexpensive way to find it. The Internet is probably the best source.
Degree of structure of questionnaire	Highly unstructured questionnaires may require data collection by personal interview.
Time available to complete survey	There may not be time to wait for responses via snail mail. The Internet is the fastest way to go.

Alden Pellett/AP/Wide World Photos

Taste tests are most often conducted in a controlled environment because of their unique requirements. Can you imagine conducting this type of research through a mail survey?

If sampling accuracy were the only criterion, the appropriate data-collection technique would probably be call center telephone interviewing, an online survey of a sample drawn from a huge Internet panel, or some other form of polling of a sample drawn from customer lists. The appropriate survey method for a project not requiring a high level of sampling accuracy might be the mail approach or some type of mall survey.

The trade-off between the call center telephone survey, Internet panel, and the mail survey methods in regard to sampling precision is one of accuracy versus cost. A call center telephone survey employing a random-digit dialing sampling procedure that includes cell phone and smart phones might produce a better sample than the mail survey method. However, the mail survey will most likely cost less. In some cases, Internet samples will provide both lower cost and greater accuracy.

Budget

Commercial marketing researchers frequently encounter situations in which the budget available for a study has a strong influence on the survey method used. For example, assume that for a particular study the budgetary constraint for interviewing is $10,000 and the sample size required for the necessary accuracy is 1,000. If the cost of administering the questionnaire using the mall-intercept method is $34.50 per interview and the cost of administering it via Internet survey is $1.50 per interview, the choice is fairly clear—assuming that nothing about the survey absolutely requires face-to-face contact.

Requirements for Respondent Reactions

In some studies, a marketing researcher needs to get respondent reactions to various marketing stimuli—perhaps product prototype usage (a new style of PC keyboard) or a taste test. In these cases, the need to get respondent reactions to stimuli normally requires personal contact between interviewer and respondent.

Taste tests typically require food preparation. This preparation must be done under controlled conditions so that the researcher can be certain that each person interviewed is responding to the same stimulus. The only viable survey alternative for tests of this type is the mall-intercept approach or some variant. One variant, for example, is recruiting people to come to properly equipped central locations, such as community centers, to sample products and be interviewed.

Some surveys require face-to-face interviewing because of the need to use special measurement techniques or obtain specialized forms of information. The tasks are so complex that the interviewer must be available to explain the tasks and ascertain whether the respondents understand what is required of them.

Quality of Data

The quality of data required is an important determinant of the survey method. Data quality is measured in terms of validity and reliability. (These two concepts are discussed in detail in Chapter 9.) *Validity* refers to the degree to which a measure reflects the characteristic of interest. In other words, a valid measure provides an accurate reading of whatever the researcher is trying to measure. *Reliability* refers to the consistency with which a measure produces the same results with the same or comparable populations.

Many factors beyond the interviewing method affect data quality. Sampling methods, questionnaire design, specific scaling methods, and interviewer training are a few of them. However, each of the various interviewing methods has certain inherent strengths and weaknesses in terms of data quality. These strengths and weaknesses are summarized in Exhibit 5.6.

The important point here is that the issue of data quality may override other considerations such as cost. For example, although the least expensive way to get responses to a long questionnaire with many open-ended questions might be via a mall-intercept interview, the data obtained by this method might be so biased—because of respondent fatigue, distraction, and carelessness—that the results would be worthless at best and misleading at worst.

The Length of a Questionnaire

The length of a questionnaire—the amount of time it takes the average respondent to complete a survey—is an important determinant of the appropriate survey method to use. If the questionnaire for a particular study takes an hour to complete, the choices of survey method

EXHIBIT 5.6	Strengths and Weaknesses of Selected Data-Collection Methods in Terms of Quality of Data Produced	
Method	**Strengths**	**Weaknesses**
Mall-intercept interview	Interviewer can show, explain, and probe.	Many distractions are inherent in the mall environment; respondent may be in a hurry, not in proper frame of mind to answer survey questions; there is more chance for interviewer bias; nonprobability sampling problems arise.
Call center telephone interview	Supervisor can monitor the interviewing process easily; excellent samples can be obtained; interviewer can explain and probe.	Respondent may be distracted by things going on at their location; problems arise in long interviews and interviews with many open-ended questions. Many refuse to participate.
Self-administered questionnaire	Interviewer and associated biases are eliminated; respondent can complete the questionnaire when convenient; respondent can look up information and work at own pace.	There is no interviewer to show, explain, or probe; sample may be poor because of nonresponse; who actually completes the questionnaire cannot be controlled.
Mail survey	Same strengths as for self-administered method.	Same weaknesses as for self-administered questionnaire; sample quality is better with mail panel.

are extremely limited. Telephone, mall-intercept, and most other types of surveys, with the exception of personal interviews, will not work. People shopping at a mall ordinarily do not have an hour to spend being interviewed. Terminations increase and tempers flare when interviewers must try to keep respondents on the phone for an hour. Response rates plummet when people receive through the mail questionnaires that take an hour or more to complete. The trick is to match the survey technique to the length of the questionnaire.

SurveySpot, SSI's huge Internet panel, asked its panel members what was the ideal survey length. The responses were as follows:[9]

— Less than 2 minutes	2%
— 2 to 5 minutes	21%
— 6 to 10 minutes	44%
— 11 to 15 minutes	21%
— 16 to 25 minutes	3%
— 26 minutes or more	0%
— No ideal length	8%
— Not sure	1%

Incidence Rate

Recall that the incidence rate refers to the percentage of people, households, or businesses in the general population that would qualify as interviewees in a particular study. Search costs, which correlate with the time spent trying to locate qualified respondents, sometimes exceed the costs of interviewing. In situations where the researcher expects incidence rates to be low and search costs high, it is important to select the method or combination of methods that will provide the desired survey results at a reasonable cost.

Doing a low-incidence rate study in a mall would be very expensive. This approach should be taken only if there is some compelling reason for doing so—a long in-depth interview, for example. The lowest-cost survey alternative for the low-incidence study is probably the Internet panel, assuming that this approach meets the other data-collection requirements of the study. One advantage of the Internet panel is that it can be prescreened; people can be asked a number of questions, usually including some on product usage. For example, if panel members were asked during prescreening whether anyone in their household participated in downhill or alpine skiing, the Internet panel operator could—at very low cost—pull out only those households with one or more skiers for a survey of Alpine skiers.

The Structure of a Questionnaire

In addition to the length of a questionnaire, the degree of structure required in a questionnaire may be a factor in determining which survey method is most appropriate for a given study. *Structure* refers to the extent to which the questionnaire follows a set sequence or order, has a predetermined wording of questions, and relies on closed-ended (multiple-choice) questions. A questionnaire that does all these things would be structured; one that deviates from these set patterns would be considered unstructured. A questionnaire with little structure is likely to require a face-to-face interview. Very brief, highly structured questionnaires do not require face-to-face contact between interviewer and respondent. Mail, telephone, self-administered, and online surveys are viable options for studies of this type.

The Time Available to Complete a Survey

If a client needs to have survey results quickly, using the Internet is the best choice. Generally, call center telephone and mall-intercept interviews can also be completed in a timely manner.

SUMMARY

Surveys are popular for several reasons. First, managers need to know why people do or do not do something. Second, managers need to know how decisions are made. Third, managers need to know what kind of person, from a demographic or lifestyle perspective, is making the decision to buy or not to buy a product.

There are two major categories of errors in survey research: random error and systematic error, or bias. Systematic error can be further broken down into measurement error and sample design error. Types of sample design error include selection, population specification, and frame errors. Frame error results from the use of an incomplete or inaccurate sampling frame. Population specification error results from an incorrect definition of the universe or population from which the sample is to be selected. Selection error results from adopting incomplete or improper sampling procedures or not properly following appropriate selection procedures.

The second major category of systematic error is measurement error. Measurement error occurs when there is a discrepancy between the information being sought (true value) and the information actually obtained by the measurement process. Measurement error can be created by a number of factors, including surrogate information error, interviewer error, measurement instrument bias, processing error, nonresponse bias, and response bias. Surrogate information error results from a discrepancy between the information actually required to solve a problem and the information sought by the researcher. Interviewer error occurs when an interviewer influences a respondent to give untrue or inaccurate answers. Measurement instrument bias is caused by problems within the questionnaire itself. Processing error results from mistakes in the transfer of information from survey documents to the computer. Nonresponse bias occurs when a particular individual in a sample cannot be reached or refuses to participate in the survey. Response bias arises when interviewees tend to answer questions in a particular way, whether out of deliberate falsification or unconscious misrepresentation.

There are several types of traditional surveys. Mall-intercept interviews are conducted with shoppers in public areas of shopping malls, either by interviewing them in the mall or by asking them to come to a permanent interviewing facility within the mall. Executive interviews are the industrial equivalent of door-to-door interviews; they involve interviewing professional people at their offices, typically concerning industrial products or services. Call center telephone interviews are conducted from a facility set up for the specific purpose of doing telephone survey research. Computer-assisted telephone interviewing (CATI) is a form of call center interviewing. Each interviewer is seated in front of a computer terminal or personal computer. The computer guides the interviewer and the interviewing process by exhibiting appropriate questions on the computer screen. The data are entered into the computer as the interview takes place. A self-administered questionnaire is filled out by the respondent. The big disadvantage of this approach is that probes cannot be used to clarify responses. Mail surveys can be divided into ad hoc, or one-shot, surveys and mail panels. In ad hoc mail surveys, questionnaires are mailed to potential respondents without prior contact. The sample is used for only a single survey project. In a mail panel, consumers are precontacted by letter and are offered an incentive for participating in the panel for a period of time. If they agree, they fill out a background questionnaire. Then, periodically, panel participants are sent questionnaires.

The factors that determine which survey method to use include the degree of sampling precision required, budget size, whether respondents need to react to various stimuli or to perform specialized tasks, the quality of data required, the length of the questionnaire, the degree of structure of the questionnaire, and the time available to complete the survey.

KEY TERMS & DEFINITIONS

random error, or random sampling error Error that results from chance variation.

chance variation Difference between the sample value and the true value of the population mean.

systematic error, or bias Error that results from problems or flaws in the execution of the research design; sometimes called nonsampling error.

sample design error Systematic error that results from an error in the sample design or sampling procedures.

sampling frame List of population elements or members from which units to be sampled are selected.

frame error Error resulting from an inaccurate or incomplete sampling frame.

population specification error Error that results from incorrectly defining the population or universe from which a sample is chosen.

selection error Error that results from incomplete or improper sample selection procedures or not following appropriate procedures.

measurement error Systematic error that results from a variation between the information being sought and what is actually obtained by the measurement process.

surrogate information error Error that results from a discrepancy between the information needed to solve a problem and that sought by the researcher.

interviewer error, or interviewer bias Error that results from the interviewer's influencing—consciously or unconsciously—the respondent.

measurement instrument bias Error that results from the design of the questionnaire or measurement instrument; also known as questionnaire bias.

processing error Error that results from the incorrect transfer of information from a survey document to a computer.

nonresponse bias Error that results from a systematic difference between those who do and those who do not respond to a measurement instrument.

refusal rate The percentage of persons contacted who refused to participate in a survey.

response bias Error that results from the tendency of people to answer a question incorrectly through either deliberate falsification or unconscious misrepresentation.

door-to-door interviews Interviews conducted face-to-face with consumers in their homes.

executive interviews The industrial equivalent of door-to-door interviewing.

mall-intercept interviews Interviews conducted by intercepting mall shoppers (or shoppers in other high-traffic locations) and interviewing them face-to-face.

call center telephone interviews Interviews conducted by calling respondents from a centrally located marketing research facility.

computer-assisted telephone interviews (CATI) Call center telephone interviews in which interviewers enter respondents' answers directly into a computer.

self-administered questionnaires Questionnaires filled out by respondents with no interviewer present.

ad hoc mail surveys Questionnaires sent to selected names and addresses without prior contact by the researcher; sometimes called one-shot mail surveys.

mail panels Precontacted and prescreened participants who are periodically sent questionnaires.

longitudinal study A study in which the same respondents are resampled over time.

QUESTIONS FOR REVIEW & CRITICAL THINKING

1. The owner of a hardware store in Eureka, California, is interested in determining the demographic characteristics of people who shop at his store versus those of people who shop at competing stores. He also wants to know what his image is relative to the competition. He would like to have the information within three weeks and is working on a limited budget. Which survey method would you recommend? Why?

2. Discuss this statement: "A mall-intercept interview is representative only of people who shop in that particular mall. Therefore, only surveys that relate to shopping patterns of consumers within that mall should be conducted in a mall-intercept interview."

3. A colleague is arguing that the best way to conduct a study of attitudes toward city government in your community is through a mail survey because it is the cheapest method. How would you respond to your colleague? If time were not a critical factor in your decision, would your response change? Why?

4. Discuss the various types of sample design errors and give examples of each.

5. Why is it important to consider measurement error in survey research? Why is this typically not discussed in professional marketing research reports?

6. What types of error might be associated with the following situations?
   a. Conducting a survey about attitudes toward city government, using the telephone directory as a sample frame.
   b. Interviewing respondents only between 8:00 A.M. and 5:00 P.M. on features they would like to see in a new condominium development.
   c. Asking people if they have visited the public library in the past two months.
   d. Asking people how many tubes of toothpaste they used in the past year.
   e. Telling interviewers they can probe using any particular example they wish to make up.

REAL-LIFE RESEARCH • 5.1

Yes, Teens Love Their Mobile Phones!

Cell phone texting has become the preferred channel of basic communication between teens and their friends, and cell calling is a close second. Some 75 percent of 12- to 17-year-olds own cell phones, up from 45 percent in 2004. Those phones have become indispensable tools in teen communication patterns. Fully 72 percent of all teens—or 88 percent of teen cell phone users—are text-messengers. That is a sharp rise from the 51 percent of teens who were texters in 2006. More than half of teens (54 percent) are daily texters.

Among all teens, the frequency of use of texting has now overtaken the frequency of every other common form of interaction with their friends.

Fully two-thirds of teen texters say they are more likely to use their cell phones to text their friends than talk to them by cell phone.

One in three teens sends more than 100 text messages a day, or 3,000 texts a month.

Daily text messaging by teens to friends has increased rapidly since early 2008. Some 38 percent of teens were daily texters in February 2008, and that has risen to 54 percent of teens who use texting in September 2009. Of the 75 percent of teens who own cell phones, 87 percent use text messaging at least occasionally. Among those texters:

- Half of teens send 50 or more text messages a day, or 1,500 texts a month, and one in three send more than 100 texts a day, or more than 3,000 texts a month.
- 15 percent of teens who are texters send more than 200 texts a day, or more than 6,000 texts a month.
- Boys typically send and receive 30 texts a day; girls typically send and receive 80 messages per day.
- Teen texters ages 12–13 typically send and receive 20 texts a day.
- 14- to 17-year-old texters typically send and receive 60 text messages a day.
- Older girls who text are the most active, with 14- to 17-year-old girls typically sending 100 or more messages a day, or more than 3,000 texts a month.
- While many teens are avid texters, a substantial minority are not. One-fifth of teen texters (22 percent) send and receive just 1–10 texts a day, or 30–300 a month.

Calling is still a central function of the cell phone for teens, and for many teens, voice is the primary mode of conversing with parents.

Among cell phone–owning teens, using the phone for calling is a critically important function, especially when it comes to connecting with their parents. But teens make and receive far fewer phone calls than text messages on their cell phones.

Teens typically make or receive 5 calls a day. White teens typically make or receive 4 calls a day, or around 120 calls a month, while African American teens exchange 7 calls a day, or about 210 calls a month, and Hispanic teens typically make and receive 5 calls a day, or about 150 calls a month.

Girls more fully embrace most aspects of cell phone–based communication.

As we see with other communicative technologies and applications, girls are more likely than boys to use both text messaging and voice calling and are likely to do each more frequently.

- Girls typically send and receive 80 texts a day; boys send and receive 30.
- 86 percent of girls text message friends several times a day; 64 percent of boys do the same.
- 59 percent of girls call friends on their cell phone every day; 42 percent of boys call friends daily on their cell phones.

Girls are also more likely than boys to text for social reasons, to text privately, and to text about school work:

- 59 percent of girls text several times a day to "just say hello and chat"; 42 percent of boys do so.

- 84 percent of girls have long text exchanges on personal matters; 67 percent of boys have similar exchanges.
- 76 percent of girls text about school work, while 64 percent of boys text about school work.

Cell phones are not just about calling or texting—with expanding functionality, phones have become multimedia recording devices and pocket-sized Internet-connected computers.

Teens who have multipurpose phones are avid users of those extra features. The most popular are taking and sharing pictures and playing music. Among teen cell phone owners:

- 83 percent use their phones to take pictures.
- 64 percent share pictures with others.
- 60 percent play music on their phones.
- 46 percent play games on their phones.
- 32 percent exchange videos on their phones.
- 31 percent exchange instant messages on their phones.
- 27 percent go online for general purposes on their phones.
- 23 percent access social network sites on their phones.
- 21 percent use e-mail on their phone.
- 11 percent purchase things via their phones.[10]

Questions

1. How might Verizon use this information?
2. This study was conducted by the Pew Research Center. What would you want to ask the Pew researchers about the data and the methods used to collect the data before purchasing the complete report?
3. What are the various survey methods that could have been used to collect this data? What are the advantages and disadvantages of each?

CHAPTER 6

Online Marketing Research

LEARNING OBJECTIVES

1. To understand the online world as it applies to marketing research.

2. To learn about using the Internet to gather secondary data for marketing research.

3. To appreciate Internet search strategies.

4. To understand the popularity and types of online focus groups.

5. To gain insights into survey research on the Internet.

6. To appreciate the importance of panel management in maintaining data quality.

This chapter explores the ever-increasing role of the Internet in secondary data searches, qualitative research, and survey research. Online observation research, another form of research growing at a sizzling pace, is covered in Chapter 7.

The Online World

The world's Internet population will total almost 2 billion users by the time you read this paragraph. That's right, about 30 percent of the world's population is online. In the United States and Canada, over 77 percent of the population is online, spanning every ethnic, socioeconomic, and educational divide. Since the year 2000, while online growth in the United States and Canada has grown by almost 150 percent, the growth in Africa and the Middle East is in excess of 2,000 percent![1] It is no wonder then that most managers accept the idea that online research can, under appropriate conditions, accurately represent U.S. consumers as a whole.[2] Nonadopters of the Internet tend to be older, low-income consumers (aged 65+ and with household incomes less than $30,000).[3] These consumers are not the target market for many companies' goods and services.

The popularity of online research continues to grow, with the vast majority of America's marketing research companies conducting some form of online research.[4] Today, online survey research has replaced computer-assisted telephone interviewing (CATI) as the most popular mode of data collection.[5] Internet data collection is also rated as having the greatest potential for further growth. Having made this observation, we must also report that there is no sign that paper surveys are disappearing as two-thirds of market research companies are still relying on them.[6]

Using the Internet for Secondary Data

Recall from Chapter 3 that secondary data can play a key role early in the marketing research process. It can clarify the problem, perhaps suggest a methodology for approaching the problem, and, if you are really lucky, provide a solution so that the time and cost of primary research are avoided.

Sites of Interest to Marketing Researchers

Exhibit 6.1 details a number of different sites where researchers can go to obtain secondary information, including competitive intelligence. You will note that a rich variety of data are available on many different topics. Although a lot of information is free, some, such as that offered by Claritas International, must be purchased.

Periodical, Newspaper, and Book Databases   Several excellent periodical, newspaper, and book databases are available to researchers. We have also posted these on our Web site, at *www.wiley.com/college/McDaniel*. Some can be directly accessed via the Internet and others through your local library's Web site.

Newsgroups

A primary means of communicating with other professionals and special-interest groups on the Internet is through newsgroups. With an Internet connection and newsreader software, you can visit any newsgroup supported by your service provider. If your service provider does not offer newsgroups or does not carry the group in which you are interested, you can find one of the publicly available newsgroup servers that does carry the group you'd like to read.

EXHIBIT 6.1	Secondary Data Available Online for Marketing Researchers

Organization	URL	Description
American Marketing Association	www.marketingpower.com	Enables users to search all of the AMA's publications by using keywords.
American Fact Finder	www.factfinder.census.gov	Provides ongoing data collected by the Census Bureau.
BLS Consumer Expenditure Surveys	www.bls.gov/cex	Provides information on the buying habits of consumers, including data on their expenditures, income, and credit ratings.
Bureau of Economic Analysis	www.bea.gov	Offers a wide range of economic statistics.
Bureau of Transportation Statistics	www.bts.gov	Serves as a comprehensive source for a wide range of statistics on transportation.
American City Business Journals	www.bizjournals.com	Offers a wealth of articles, reports, news, and data on everything from ratings of America's best small cities to statistics on men's and women's salaries. Current articles and reports, as well as an extensive archive dating back to 1994, provide insight and analysis of key business and economic trends.
Center for International Earth Science Network	www.ciesin.org	Serves as an excellent source of demographic information concerning the United States.
Centers for Disease Control/National Center for Health Statistics	www.cdc.gov/nchs	Maintains data on vital events, health status, lifestyle, exposure to unhealthy influences, onset and diagnosis of illness and disability, and use of health–care, through the National Center for Health Statistics. The NCHS, a subdivision of the Centers for Disease Control and Prevention, is the federal government's principal agency for vital and health statistics.
Clickz.com	www.clickz.com	Provides statistics on Internet research: weekly usage statistics, online populations, browser statistics and more.
The Dismal Scientist	www.dismal.com	Provides timely economic information, with comprehensive data and analyses at the metro, state, and national levels. This authoritative site also has data and analyses of global issues, including situations facing Asia, South America, and Europe. Visitors can rank states and metro areas on more than 100 economic, socioeconomic, and demographic categories.
Easy Analytic Software, Inc./The Right Site	www.easidemographics.com	Offers demographic site reports, or three-ring studies, including current estimates for population and households. Each three-ring study has census estimates for race, ethnicity, age distribution, and income distribution, as well as weather data.
EconData.net	www.econdata.net	Enables users to access a tremendous number of links to government, private, and academic data sources. Check out the list of top 10 data sources at this premier site for researchers interested in economics and demographics.
FreeDemographics	www.freedemographics.com	Offers free demographic market analysis reports.
Harris InfoSource	www.harrisinfo.com	Provides business-to-business data on American manufacturers and key decision makers.
Hoovers	www.hoovers.com	Gives company descriptions and industry information.
Internet Public Library	www.ipl.org/div/aon	Offers a collection of over 1,100 Internet sites providing information about a wide variety of professional and trade associations.
Marketing Research Association	www.mra-net.org	Offers causes and solutions of "declining respondent cooperation" and links to research suppliers.
Mediamark Research/Top-Line Reports	www.mediamark.com/mri/docs/toplinereports.html	Allows marketers and researchers to access demographic data on magazines, cable TV, and 53 different product or service categories. Top-Line Reports breaks down cable TV networks' viewers according to age, sex, and income. Magazines are listed by total audience, circulation, readers per copy, median age, and income.

(continues)

EXHIBIT 6.1	(Continued)	
Organization	**URL**	**Description**
Opinion Research (ORC International)	www.opinionresearch.com	Offers consulting and research services. Their Web site claims expertise in a broad range of industries, including information technology and telecommunications, healthcare, financial services, public services, energy and utilities market research, and more.
Population Reference Bureau	www.prb.org	Source of demographic information on population issues.
Quirks	www.quirks.com	Magazine for market researchers.
Service Intelligence	www.serviceintelligence.com	Has an area devoted to customer stories of unpleasant experiences with airlines, banks, restaurants, and other service businesses. However, "hero" stories are also included.
Social Security Administration	www.socialsecurity.gov/policy	Provides a range of government statistics about social security beneficiaries.
U.S. Census Bureau	www.census.gov	Serves as the source for all federal census data.
U.S. Department of Agriculture/Economic Research Service	www.ers.usda.gov	Offers a wide range of agricultural statistics.
USAData	www.usadata.com	Provides access to consumer lifestyle data on a local, regional, and national basis.
U.S. Government	www.fedstats.gov	Serves as a source for statistics and reports for more than 100 government agencies. Also links to other sources of relevant information. Highly recommended site but you may have to dig a little.
Valuation Resources	www.valuationresources.com	Offers a directory of resources that address subjects such as industry overview, issues, trends, and outlook, industry financial information and financial ratios, and compensation and salary surveys for a wide variety of industries.
Wikipedia	www.wikipedia.org	Functions as the free encyclopedia that anyone can edit.
World Fact Book	www.cia.gov/library/publications/the-world-factbook	Provides detailed information about countries of the world, including political and economic aspects.
WorldOpinion	www.worldopinion.com	Offers thousands of marketing research reports. This is perhaps the premier site for the marketing research industry.

Newsgroups function much like bulletin boards for a particular topic or interest. A newsgroup is established to focus on a particular topic. Readers stop by that newsgroup to read messages left by other people, post responses to others' questions, and send rebuttals to comments with which they disagree. Generally, there is some management of the messages to keep discussions within the topic area and to remove offensive material. However, readers of a newsgroup are free to discuss any issue and communicate with anyone in the world who visits that group. Images and data files can be exchanged in newsgroups, just as they can be exchanged via e-mail.

With over 250,000 newsgroups currently in existence and more being added every day, there is a newsgroup for nearly every hobby, profession, and lifestyle. Most browsers come with newsgroup readers. If you do not already have a newsgroup reader, you can go to one of the search engines and search for a freeware or shareware newsgroup reader. These newsgroup readers function much like e-mail programs.

→ **newsgroup**
An Internet site where people can read and post messages devoted to a specific topic.

Blogs

The traditional definition of a blog, or Web log, was a frequent, chronological publication of personal thoughts and Web links. Now companies are also using blogs to communicate directly with customers and other businesses. More recently market researchers have used blogs to monitor brands, track trends, profile customers, and identify unmet needs. Blogs are growing to be an important tool in the exploratory research stage of many formal survey projects.[7]

Companies also use blogs to talk to customers and to other businesses. Blogging gained popularity with the introduction of automated published systems, most notably at *bloggeratblogger.com*. Marketing researchers are finding blogs to be an important source of information on just about any topic imaginable. Researchers have used them to recruit respondents for surveys. Although blogs can be found on most search engines, several engines such as blogsearchengine.com are dedicated to blog searches.

Internet Search Strategies

There is perhaps no single best way to search the Web, but we recommend a five-step strategy:[8]

Step One: Analyze your topic to decide where to begin.

Step Two: Test run a word or phrase in a search engine such as Google. Consider synonyms or equivalent terms.

Step Three: Learn as you go and vary your approach with what you learn. Don't assume that you know what you want to find. Look at the search results and see what else you might use in addition to what you thought of.

Step Four: Don't get bogged down in any strategy that doesn't work. Consider using a subject directory. A few of the best are the Librarian's Index, *lii.org*; Infomine, *infomine.ucr.edu*; Academic Info, *www.academicinfo.net*; Google Directory, *directory.google.com*; About.com, *www.about.com*; and Yahoo Directory, *dir.yahoo.com*. Many researchers switch back and forth between directories and search engines.

Step Five: If you haven't found what you want, go back to earlier steps better informed.

Evaluating Web Pages   Once you have found what you were looking for, the next step is to evaluate the quality. Things are not always as they seem. For example, recall the Web sites that want you to pay a membership fee to become an online survey respondent. There is a Web site that supposedly ranks Web sites that provide an entrée to earning cash through completing interviews. All of the sites ranked required a membership fee, and no real marketing research firms, such as Greenfield Online or Harris Interactive, were included. Of course, legitimate researchers don't charge a fee to become a panel member. The ranking site was probably created by one of the sites that charge a membership fee. No criteria were given for how the rankings were determined.

Techniques for evaluating Web pages are detailed in Exhibit 6.2.

EXHIBIT 6.2 | **How to Evaluate Web Pages**

1. What can the URL tell you?
Techniques for Web Evaluation:

1. Before you leave the list of search results—before you click and get interested in anything written on the page—glean all you can from the URLs of each page.
2. Then choose pages most likely to be reliable and authentic.

Questions to ask:
Is it somebody's *personal page*?
- Read the URL carefully:
  - Look for a personal name (e.g., jbarker or barker) following a tilde (~), a percent sign (%), or the words "users," "members," or "people."
  - Is the server a commercial *ISP* * or other provider mostly of Web page hosting (like aol.com or geocities.com)

What are the implications?
Personal pages are not necessarily "bad," but you need to investigate the author very carefully. For personal pages, there is no publisher or domain owner vouching for the information in the page.

Look for appropriateness and fit. What kind of information source do you think is most reliable for your topic?

What type of *domain* does it come from?
(educational, nonprofit, commercial, government, etc.)
- Is the domain appropriate for the content?
  - Government sites: look for .gov, .mil, .us, or other country code
  - Educational sites: look for .edu

2. Scan the perimeter of the page, looking for answers to these questions.
Techniques for Web Evaluation:

1. Look for links that say **"About us," "Philosophy," "Background," "Biography," "Who am I,"** etc.
2. If you cannot find any links like these, you can often find this kind of information if you truncate back the URL.

   INSTRUCTIONS for Truncating back a URL: In the top Location Box, delete the end characters of the URL stopping just before each/(leave the slash). Press enter to see if you can see more about the author or the origins/nature of the site providing the page. Continue this process, one slash (/) at a time, until you reach the first single/which is preceded by the domain name portion. This is the page's server, or "publisher."

3. Look for the date "last updated"—usually at the bottom of a Web page. Check the date on all the pages on the site. Do not rely on a date given in browser file properties or page information displays. These dates can be automatically kept current and are useless in critical evaluation.

Questions to ask:
Who wrote the page?
- Look for the name of the author, or the name of the organization, institution, agency, or whatever, who is responsible for the page
  - An e-mail contact is not enough.
- If there is no personal author, look for an agency or organization that claims responsibility for the page.
  - If you cannot find this, locate the publisher by truncating back the URL (see technique above). Does this publisher claim responsibility for the content? Does it explain why the page exists in any way?

What are the implications?
Web pages are all created with a purpose in mind by some person or agency or entity. They do not simply "grow" on the Web like mildew grows in moist corners. You are looking for someone who claims accountability and responsibility for the content. An e-mail address with no additional information about the author is not sufficient for assessing the author's credentials. If this is all you have, try e-mailing the author and asking politely for more information about him or her.

3. Look for indicators of quality information:
Techniques for Web Evaluation:

1. Look for a link called "links," "additional sites," "related links," etc.
2. In the text, if you see little footnote numbers or links that might refer to documentation, take the time to explore them. What kinds of publications or sites are they? reputable? scholarly? Are they real? On the Web (where no publisher is editing most pages), it is possible to create totally fake references.
3. Look at the publisher of the page (first part of the URL). Expect a journal article, newspaper article, and some other publications that are recent to come from the original publisher if the publication is available on the Web. Look at the bottom of such articles for copyright information or permissions to reproduce.

(continues)

EXHIBIT 6.2 (Continued)

Question to ask:
Are sources documented with footnotes or links?
- Where did the author get the information?
  - As in published scholarly/academic journals and books, you should expect documentation.
- If there are links to other pages as sources, are they to reliable sources?
- Do the links work?

What are the implications?
In scholarly/research work, the credibility of most writings is proven through footnote documentation or other means of revealing the sources of information. Saying what you believe without documentation is not much better than just expressing an opinion or a point of view.

4. What do others say?
Techniques for Web Evaluation:
1. Find out what other Web pages link to this page.
   a. Use *alexa.com* URL information:
   Simply paste the URL into alexa.com's search box.
   You will see, depending on the volume of traffic to the page:
   - Traffic rank
   - Subjective reviews
   - "Site statistics" including some page history, sites that link to the page
   - Contact/ownership information for the domain name

5. Does it all add up?
Techniques for Web evaluation:
1. Step back and think about all you have learned about the page. Listen to your gut reaction. Think about why the page was created, the intentions of its author(s).
   If you have doubts, ask your instructor or come to one of the library reference desks and ask for advice.
2. Be sensitive to the possibility that you are the victim of irony, spoof, fraud, or other falsehood.
3. Ask yourself if the Web is truly the best place to find resources for the research you are doing.

Questions to ask:
Why was the page put on the Web?
- Inform, give facts, give data?
- Explain, persuade?
- Sell, entice?
- Share?
- Disclose?

So what? What are the implications?
These are some reasons to think of. The Web is a public place, open to all. You need to be aware of the entire range of human possibilities of intentions behind Web pages.

Source: Copyright 2004 by the Regents of the University of California. All Rights Reserved. Created by Joe Barker, Teaching Library, UC Berkeley.

Creating a Database from a Web Site—A Marketer's Dream[9]

If a person today were opening, say, a wine shop, which of the following would give the owner the best opportunity to build a database—a traditional store or a Web retailer such as wine.com?

A Web merchant like wine.com has access to data about its clients that would make its physical-world counterparts very envious. A customer's conduit to an online store is a two-way electronic link, allowing the online merchant to gather all sorts of information, particularly if that customer has shopped with that merchant before.

Getting the customer's name, address, and purchasing history is only the beginning. A Web merchant can record the customer's actions as he or she moves through the merchant's site, taking note not only of purchases but also of window shopping. The end result is a file that allows the merchant to determine what that customer is most likely to purchase next—and then offer inducements to make it happen.

Meanwhile, back in the physical world, the wine store owner sits behind the register, eyeing the anonymous customer who just went out empty-handed. Had the customer visited the store before? If so, what did he or she buy? Did the customer even see the new Chardonnay that just came in? Unfortunately, the owner was too busy to ask those questions (and the customer would have been offended if the owner had). Maybe the customer will come back—maybe not.

Preview Travel Inc., an online travel agency based in San Francisco, determined that Las Vegas, Orlando, and Cancun were the top three vacation spots among its customers.

The firm quickly purchased key words for the three destinations on several Internet directory sites; when a Web surfer performs a search for any of the three vacation spots, a Preview Travel advertising banner accompanies the list of results. Karen Askey, senior vice president of consumer marketing at Preview Travel, says traditional travel agencies could employ the same promotional tactics, but she doubts they could spot top destinations as quickly. "When you're online, the speed at which you can get that data is basically instantaneous," she says.

Online Qualitative Research

The primary form of online qualitative research is focus groups. These come in two categories in the online world: *traditional*, sometimes referred to as synchronous groups, and *online bulletin boards*, sometimes referred to as asynchronous groups. You will learn that online focus groups can take several forms. Traditional online groups are what the name implies. The goal is to get 8 to 10 participants online at the same time, for a moderator to send questions to the participants, and the participants to provide their comments. Special software from companies such as Itracks (see *www.itracks.com/qual*) provides the environment for these groups. Online bulletin boards are a new form of qualitative research that takes advantage of the online medium. In these groups, questions are posted for participants each day, and they have all day to provide their responses. They usually run for two to three days, sometimes longer. The moderator answers questions from participants throughout the day. Questions for the next day can be modified based on what participants have to say. Probing questions can be sent to individual participants or to all. Supporting software can permit participants to see what others had to say after they respond. An even newer twist on online focus groups are Web communities, which we will also examine in this section. We conclude with a brief look at online individual depth interviewing.

The Popularity of Online Focus Groups

Perhaps the hottest area in qualitative research today is **online focus groups**. Many marketing researchers, such as NFO Interactive, and Harris Black International, believe that Internet focus groups can replace face-to-face focus groups, although they acknowledge that online research has limitations. Others that are moving aggressively into online marketing research, such as Millward Brown International and Digital Marketing Services (DMS), were slower to use online focus groups.

> **online focus groups**
> Focus groups conducted via the Internet.

Advantages of Online Focus Groups Marketers who have used online focus groups, and the marketing researchers conducting them, say that the benefits far outweigh the limitations. Those benefits include much lower costs (about half as much), faster turnaround time, respondents, ability to be geographically separate and be located anywhere, and intangibles such as increased openness on the part of respondents when they do not have a moderator staring them in the face.

"I think [the panelists] were more definite about things they didn't like than they'd be in front of a moderator," said Lisa Crane, vice president of sales and marketing for

Universal Studios Online, which used an online focus group to test a redesigned site it's developing for Captain Morgan Original Spiced Rum, a brand of its parent company, Seagram Company. Rudy Nadilo, president and CEO of Greenfield Online, which conducted the online focus groups for Universal, said they are meant "to complement, not replace" traditional panels.[10] Not only are the costs lower for online focus groups, but there are substantial travel savings for the client as well. Expenditures for round-trip airline tickets to distant cities, meals, hotels, and taxis are avoided. Clients merely log on in their own office, or even at home, to observe the research in progress.

Another advantage of online focus groups lies in access to the hard-to-reach target population. Online, it's possible to reach populations that are traditionally inaccessible because of time or professional constraints—groups such as physicians, lawyers, and senior business executives. Chances are higher that they will be available to participate, too, since they do not need to take time from their busy schedules to visit a focus group facility but, rather, can participate from the privacy of their own homes.

Another advantage claimed for online focus groups is efficient moderator–client interaction. During the traditional focus group, the client observes the discussion from behind a one-way glass; communication with the moderator is impossible without interfering with the discussion. An online focus group, however, offers a remarkable opportunity for two-way interaction between the moderator and the client. This direct interaction, while the moderator conducts the group, has become a necessity in operating a fully effective online focus group discussion and can facilitate the probing of sensitive personal topics.[11] Rather than sneaking into the room with a note scribbled on a piece of paper, the client can address the moderator directly, clearly, and efficiently, without interrupting the group dynamic.

Traditional focus groups always include "natural talkers," who dominate the discussion, despite a good moderator's attempt to equalize participant contributions. Other participants will be less comfortable voicing opinions in a group; they may express themselves more freely when not face to face with their peers. The online focus group has a built-in leveling effect, in the sense that shy participants can express themselves as freely as more outgoing participants. One participant points out why he likes participating in online focus groups, explaining, "I can be honest without the face-to-face peer pressure of focus groups"; another offers, "I get to express my opinion without having to hear someone's reaction."[12] At least in terms of honesty and willingness to offer genuine ideas and opinions, respondents tend to feel more comfortable participating from the privacy of their own homes.

Disadvantages of Online Focus Groups   Critics say that the research community does itself an injustice by calling qualitative research sessions conducted over the Internet "focus groups." Their criticisms include the following.

Group Dynamics

One of the key reasons for using traditional focus groups is to view the interactions among the group participants, as they can provide excellent insights.

In cyberspace, it is difficult, if not impossible, to create any real group dynamics, particularly when the participants are reading from computer screens rather than interacting verbally.

Nonverbal Inputs

Experienced moderators use nonverbal inputs from participants while moderating and analyzing sessions. It is not always possible to duplicate the nonverbal input in an online environment.

Client Involvement

Many organizations use the focus group methodology because it gives clients an opportunity to experience direct interface with consumers in an objective environment. Nothing can replace the impact of watching focus groups from behind a one-way mirror, no matter how good the videotapes, remote broadcast facilities, streaming video, or reports written by moderators.

Exposure to External Stimuli

A key use of focus groups is to present advertising copy, new product concepts, prototypes, or other stimuli to the participants in order to get their reactions. In an online chat situation, it is almost impossible to duplicate the kind of exposure to external stimuli that occurs in the live focus group environment. As a result, the value of the input received online is more questionable than that of input coming from a live environment.

Role and Skill of the Moderator

Most marketing professionals agree that the most important factor in the quality of traditional focus group research is the skill of the moderator. Experienced moderators do more than simply ask questions of participants. A good moderator uses innovative techniques to draw out quiet or shy participants, energize a slow group, and delve a little deeper into the minds of the participants. The techniques available to a moderator sitting at a computer terminal are not the same as face-to-face involvements.

Exhibit 6.3 summarizes the advantages and disadvantages of traditional and online focus groups.

EXHIBIT 6.3	Advantages and Disadvantages of Traditional and Online Focus Groups	
	Traditional Focus Groups	**Online Focus Groups**
Basic costs	More expensive.	Cheaper.
Participants	Participants are locally based because of travel time and expense.	Anyone in the world with a computer and modem can participate.
Time commitment	Approximately 3½-hour time commitment. Busy respondents are less likely to be available.	No driving to facility, approximately 60-minute time commitment. Busy respondents are more likely to be available.
Openness of respondents	Some respondents are intimidated and afraid to speak openly in a face-to-face group setting.	Lack of direct face-to-face contact may lead respondents to express true feelings in writing if no Web cam is available.
Group dynamics	What one person says and does (gestures and expressions) can lead others to react.	None, according to critics.
Nonverbal communication	Body language can be observed.	Body language can only be observed if Web cameras are used.
Transcripts	Transcript is time-consuming and expensive to obtain; often not in complete sentences or thoughts.	Word-for-word transcripts are available almost immediately; usually in complete sentences/ thoughts.
Respondent recruiting	Recruiting certain types of respondents (e.g., physicians, top managers) is difficult.	It is easier to obtain all types of respondents.
Client travel costs	Very expensive when client must go to several cities for one or two days each.	None.
Communication with moderator	Observers can send notes into focus group room.	Observers can communicate privately with moderator on a split screen.
Respondent security	Participants are accurately identified.	It is sometimes more difficult to ascertain who is participating.
Client involvement	Client can observe flesh-and-blood consumers interacting.	Client can observe via Web cameras.
Exposure to external stimuli	Package designs, advertising copy, and product prototypes with demonstrations can be shown to participants.	Ability to show stimuli is somewhat limited.

Using the Web to Find Focus Group Participants   The Internet is proving to be an excellent tool to locate group participants that fit a very specific set of requirements. Researchers are tapping online bulletin boards such as Craigslist, which attracts 5 million visitors each month to its classified advertisements. The site is most useful "when you're trying to find niche users to a small population of users that is hard to find," says Tim Plowman, an anthropologist who works at Cheskin, a marketing consulting firm.

Point Forward, Inc., a Redwood City, California, marketing research firm, has used Craigslist to find people who fit very specific categories, such as people who travel frequently between the United States and Mexico, says Vice President Michael Barry.

A recent Craigslist posting by a different marketing research firm offered $350 to $900 to New York residents willing to give researchers a tour of their liquor cabinets, take them on a liquor-shopping trip, or make a video-based documentary of a social event they were planning.

Screening questions included: "When you are out for drinks or purchasing alcohol in a store, do people tend to ask for your advice on which brands of liquor to buy? If yes, how often does that happen?"[13]

→ **web community**
A carefully selected group of consumers who agree to participate in an ongoing dialogue with a corporation.

Web Community Research[14]   A **Web community** is a carefully selected group of consumers who agree to participate in an ongoing dialogue with a particular corporation. All community interaction takes place on a custom-designed Web site. During the life of the community—which may last anywhere from 6 months to a year or more—community members respond to questions posed by the corporation on a regular basis. These discussions, which typically take the form of qualitative "dialogues," are augmented by the ability of community members to talk to one another about topics that are of interest to them as well.

The popularity and power of Web communities initially came from several key benefits. Web communities:

- Engage customers in a space where they are most comfortable, allowing clients to interact with them on a deeper level.
- Uncover "exciters" and "eureka moments," resulting in customer-derived innovations.
- Establish brand advocates who are emotionally invested in a company's success.
- Offer real-time results, enabling clients to explore ideas that normal time constraints prohibit.
- Create a forum in which natural dialogue allows customers to initiate topics important to them.[15]

In addition, Web communities help companies create a customer-centered organization by putting employees into direct contact with consumers from the comfort of their own desks.

Since communities provide advantages in speed, flexibility, and 24/7 access to consumers, they let the organization be agile in its research decision making and prudent in its spending.

By adding a research focus to the Web community environment, this holistic perspective deepens as the community becomes a way to:

- Map the psyche of consumer segments.
- Brainstorm new ideas.
- Co-create and test new products.
- Observe natural consumer behavior.
- Rally the company around a customer-centered perspective.[16]

Online Individual Depth Interviewing   Depth interview projects can be very expensive when done in person. Although depth interviews can be conducted by phone, they must be recorded and transcribed. A few marketing research firms are experimenting with online individual depth interviews (IDIs). After respondents are recruited, via a secured chat platform, each participant is given a private blog where they can create their online journal for the project. Over a period of days, the respondents are given a series of questions to ponder in their blogs. The result is an immediate perfect transcription.[17] A second phase of the research may feature a telephone, e-mail, or bulletin board in-depth discussion. The discussion topics are derived from the blogs.

Online depth interviews are appropriate when group dynamics are not important to generating responses. Advantages of these time-extended depth interviews include (1) an effective method for interviewing high-level persons like physicians and busy executives, (2) richer content and deeper insights per respondent, and (3) ability to view transcripts at any time and make adjustments in the process by communicating with moderators.[18]

New innovative solutions for qualitative research are described in the following Practicing Marketing Research feature.

PRACTICING MARKETING RESEARCH

Have Technology, Will Investigate: Innovative Online Solutions for Qualitative Research[19]

New technologies offer significant improvements in online research over the original online platforms and provide many different tools marketers can use. When incorporating these online tools, however, a researcher must remember they are only part of the project design. A few options that researchers might consider looking into further are as follows:

Text-message posting to discussion boards

Respondents can post answers to these question via smartphone anytime and from anywhere. This tool is especially effective at getting in-the-moment reactions from respondents. Such responses might encourage reactions from other discussion board respondents as well.

In-situ narrations

Questions are sent to the respondent via e-mail or text, and the respondent leaves a recorded answer on an answering machine. This method also allows the researcher to acquire substantial in-the-moment insights.

Word-and-picture diaries

Respondents answer questions in online diaries that can include photos and videos as well. This method can effectively capture evolving impressions of a product over time.

Wireless Webcams

The Webcam is set up to observe a particular activity the respondent is engaged in (such as using a new convection oven). This offers a more complete account of the experience than a written log would. Researchers must take time, however, to make sure they understand the respondent's environment and that setup of the Webcam is done correctly. Offering the Webcam to the respondent as compensation is a common practice.

"Mark-up" tools

Respondents are shown a print ad, a concept sketch, or another stimulus and then use the interface's editing tools to mark up the item with rough drawings, likes, dislikes, and comments. The moderator can control how much of each other's commentary respondents can see. This is a highly engaging method for getting feedback on ad mock-ups.

Private virtual communities

Respondents create profiles in a private virtual community which the researcher creates around her specific project. Respondents can interact with other community members while engaging with the researcher's study questions. Less suited for shorter projects, virtual communities can provide a means of keeping respondents involved and invested in long-term projects.

Video-editing tools

Video supplements are becoming much easier to include in research reports. Researchers can incorporate prerecorded questions with answer videos from individual respondents or real-time video discussions between a group of respondents and the researcher.

Questions

1. Which innovative method for collecting primary data would you most like to try?
2. Rank the new online tools from most beneficial to least beneficial to a company. Why did you rank the choices as you did?

Online Survey Research

The Internet has forever changed the way we conduct survey research. As noted earlier, a vast majority of U.S. research firms are now conducting online research. In the United States, the online population is now closely tracking the U.S. population in most key demographic areas. Moreover, the number of Internet users around the world continues to explode. As the number of users grows worldwide, characteristics of a country's population and Internet user characteristics tend to meld. The reason for the phenomenal growth of online research is straightforward. The advantages far outweigh the disadvantages.

Advantages of Online Surveys

Most companies today face shorter product life cycles, increased competition, and a rapidly changing business environment. Management decision makers are having to make complex, rapid-fire decisions, and Internet research can help by providing timely information. The specific advantages of online surveys include the following:[20]

- *Rapid deployment and real-time reporting.* Online surveys can be broadcast to thousands of potential respondents simultaneously. Respondents complete surveys and the results are tabulated and posted for corporate clients to view as the returns arrive. Thus, Internet survey results can be in the decision maker's hands in significantly less time than traditional survey results.
- *Reduced costs.* The use of electronic survey methods can cut costs by 25 to 40 percent and provide results in half the time it takes to do traditional telephone surveys.

Data-collection costs account for a large proportion of any traditional marketing research budget. Telephone surveys are labor-intensive efforts incurring training, telecommunications, and management costs. Online surveys eliminate these costs almost completely. Although the costs of traditional survey techniques rise in proportion to the number of interviews desired, electronic solicitations can grow in volume with less increase in project costs.

Ready personalization. Internet surveys can be highly personalized for greater relevance to each respondent's own situation, thus speeding up the response process. Respondents appreciate being asked only pertinent questions, being able to pause and then resume the survey as needed, and having the ability to see previous responses and correct inconsistencies.

High response rates. Busy respondents may be growing increasingly intolerant of "snail mail" or telephone-based surveys. Online surveys take less time to complete than phone interviews do, can be accomplished at the respondent's convenience (after work hours), and are much more stimulating and engaging. Graphics, interactivity, links to incentive sites, and real-time summary reports make the interview more enjoyable. The result: much higher response rates.

Ability to contact the hard-to-reach. Certain groups are among the most difficult to reach (doctors, high-income professionals, CIOs in Global 2000 firms). Most of these groups are well represented online. Internet surveys provide convenient anytime/anywhere access that makes it easy for busy professionals to participate.

Simplified and enhanced panel management. Internet panels are electronic databases, linked via the Internet, that are committed to providing feedback and counsel to research firms and their clients. They may be large or small, syndicated or proprietary, and they may consist of customers, potential customers, partners, or employees. Internet panels can be built and maintained at less cost and time required for traditional panels. Once a panel is created and a questionnaire is finalized, surveys can be deployed, data are collected, and top-level results are reported within days.

A sophisticated database tracks panelist profile data and survey responses, facilitating longitudinal studies and data mining to yield insights into attitudes and behaviors over time and across segments. Response rates are high, typically 20 to 60 percent, because respondents have agreed in advance to participate in the survey. These participants tend to provide more detailed and thoughtful answers than do those in traditional surveys, because they don't have to give demographic and lifestyle information (it's already been captured) and because they become engaged in the panel over time.

External Internet panels simplify life for research suppliers. The availability of huge Internet panels maintained by firms such as Harris Interactive, SSI, Greenfield Online, Research Now, and Decision Analyst makes the sampling process much easier for research companies that utilize these panels. We will discuss these panels in detail later in the chapter. Moreover, the cost to use the panels has dropped as the number of panel suppliers has increased.

Advantages of online research in key global markets, such as Russia, are discussed in the following Global Research feature.

GLOBAL RESEARCH

Research in Russia[21]

Over the past decade, the Russian economy has emerged from the chaos of the 1990s and made dramatic steps toward stability and prosperity. One of the biggest indicators of growth has been the rise in disposable income, which has increased on average by 27 percent each year since 2000. Multinational companies and their marketing departments are taking notice too, especially as growth in many developed markets has slowed.

As Lyudmila Krokhina, a market research director for Wrigley, the candy and gum company, says, "There is an increased importance of market research overall and more decisions are based on consumer feedback." Luckily, Russian consumers are generally open to interacting with researchers and are eager to share their opinions on growing consumer choices. Still, researchers in Russia face several challenges.

One of those challenges is determining an appropriate representative sample of the Russian market. Russia covers a wide span of territories, so a true representative sample should cover all eight regions or, more specifically, all 89 federal districts. The sample would also need to account for typical demographic variables, such as age, gender, and socioeconomic status.

Despite the need for such a broad representative sample, most research focuses on major cities because that's where the majority of disposable income is located. Typically, market entry into Russia begins in Moscow and, increasingly, Saint Petersburg and other large cities. The need for marketing research throughout Russia has grown rapidly over the past decade. The challenge is how to collect data.

Face-to-face interviews are difficult because of the country's size and because telephone surveyors have to navigate the inefficiencies of the government-controlled telecommunications system. Online marketing research is only a recent development as Internet access has grown. Roughly 12 to 17.5 percent of the 142 million Russians have Internet access; however, these numbers are growing quickly at about 27 percent year-over-year. Larger cities like Moscow and Saint Petersburg tend to have higher penetration rates.

Even though online research has several advantages over other collection methods, it also has downsides. Certain demographics tend to be underrepresented in online research. Response rates of people over age 40 tend to be lower, as do those of women. Young, wealthy, educated males are the easiest group of Russians to access. Timing can be another issue for online researchers, as internal debate over the best approach to take with this market can drag out the research process. To make the most of online methods in Russia, researchers can consider converting standard studies into online studies. Conducting parallel studies both online and offline is also a good strategy.

As the Russian market continues to grow, understanding the Russian consumer will become increasingly important to firms looking to operate there as they try to create a sustainable competitive advantage.

Questions

1. How are the challenges facing researchers in Russia similar to those faced by researchers in other developed nations? How do you think they differ?

2. If most of Russia's disposable income is located in major metropolitan areas, why should a researcher concern himself with getting a sample that includes remote, less affluent regions?

Disadvantages of Online Surveys

The most common complaint about the use of online surveys traditionally was that Internet users are not representative of the population as a whole. As mentioned earlier, this comment has largely disappeared in the United States. Harris Interactive and DSS Research have conducted more than 300 surveys using parallel modes (telephone and Internet) and found that the research produced similar results. In all of the studies, it was rare to find a statistically significant difference between the sampling modes.[22] DSS concluded that the Internet panel methodology offered the best alternative for market share measurement and competitive benchmarking objectives based on cost (half the cost of telephone), speed (can be completed in less than half the time of telephone), and accuracy of measurement.

Lee Smith, COO of Insight Express, conducted a side-by-side comparison of online research and mail surveys. He found that online research delivered data of the same quality as using mail surveys in one-eighth the time and at one-eighth the cost.[23] Other research has shown that in most countries where the Internet penetration rate exceeds 20 percent, online surveys tend to yield results similar to those found in traditional methods such as telephone or paper-and-pencil survey research.[24]

A second problem exists when an **unrestricted Internet sample** is set up on the Internet. This means anyone who wishes to complete the questionnaire can do so. It is fully self-selecting and probably representative of no one except Web surfers. The problem gets worse if the same Internet user can access the questionnaire over and over. For example, the first time *InfoWorld*, a computer user magazine, conducted its Readers' Choice survey on the Internet, the results were so skewed by repeat voting for one product that the entire survey was publicly abandoned and the editor had to ask for readers' help to avoid the problem again. All responsible organizations conducting surveys over the Internet easily guard against this problem by providing unique passwords to those individuals they invite to participate. These passwords permit one-time access to the survey.

> → **unrestricted Internet sample** A self-selected sample group consisting of anyone who wishes to complete an Internet survey.

A third problem is that the sample frame needed may not be available on the Internet. Assume that Guido's, a popular Italian restaurant in Dayton, Ohio, wanted to know how its customers perceived the food quality and service compared with that of the big chains, such as Olive Garden. A large Internet panel, such as Greenfield Online, is probably not going to have enough members in Dayton, Ohio, that patronize Guido's to give a representative sample. If Guido's doesn't have customer e-mail addresses, then an Internet sample isn't feasible.

Other problems include a lack of "callback" procedures to clarify open-end responses, potential for questionnaire programming errors, and a lack of bandwidth (some potential respondents can't complete the survey or download photos and video quickly). Some companies may view Internet research as fast and simple, and software to conduct basic surveys is readily available. However, some research companies don't have the technical expertise to conduct Internet research properly.

Methods of Conducting Online Surveys

There are several basic methods for conducting online surveys: Web survey software, survey design Web sites, and Web hosting.

Web Survey Software   Web survey software includes software systems specifically designed for Web questionnaire construction and delivery. In a typical use, the questionnaire is constructed with an easy-to-use edit feature, using a visual interface, and then automatically transmitted to a Web server system. The Web server distributes the questionnaire and files responses in a database. The user can query the server at any time for completion statistics, descriptive statistics on responses, and graphical displays of data. Several popular online survey research software packages are SPSS Quanquest, Inquisite, Sawtooth CiW, Infopoll, Designer, and SurveyGold.

Gaining Survey Completions   Do-it-yourself software, such as SPSS Quanquest, requires that you offer the respondent a good experience if you expect the person to complete the survey. The more engaged respondents are, the better quality insights they will provide. The following tips can help create a better experience for the interviewee:

- As with any other questionnaire, use language that is less "research-ese" and more conversational.
- Be honest and upfront about the time required to complete a study.
- Provide more opportunities for participants to provide open-ended answers and truly express themselves.
- Ensure that all possible answer choices are given; avoid overuse of "other."
- Keep the survey to less than 20 minutes in length and provide participants with progress information as they advance through the survey.
- Consider using graphics when possible or appropriate to make the experience more visually engaging.
- Explore new ways to facilitate interaction between respondents and a researcher.
- Make studies more informative—participants are particularly motivated by acquiring new knowledge and information about a product or topic.
- Offer participants the opportunity to be contacted again to receive updates on projects of products being tested.[25]

Survey Design and Web Hosting Sites   Many Web sites allow the researcher to design a survey online without loading design software. The survey is then administered on the design site's server. Some offer tabulation and analysis packages as well. Popular sites that offer Web hosting are WebSurveyor, Perseus Survey Monkey, Research Now, and Zoomerang.

Commercial Online Panels

→ commercial online panel
A group of individuals who have agreed to receive invitations to do online surveys from a particular panel company, such as eRewards or SSI. The panel company charges organizations doing surveys for access to the panel. Charges are usually so much per survey, depending on survey length and the type of people being sought for the survey. The panel company controls all access to the members of its panel.

Many researchers turn to commercial online panel providers to assist in the process of completing a market research study, often by hosting a survey on their Web site. Commercial online panels are not created for the exclusive use of any one specific company or for any one particular project. Instead, **commercial online panels** are created for the use of multiple projects by many different companies. The companies providing access to the online panels have invested in the pre-recruitment of people who opt to participate in online market research surveys. Some online panels are for use by a specific industry, such as construction, medical, or technology industries, and may have a few thousand panel members, while the large commercial online panels have millions of people who have opted to participate in online surveys of varying topics. When people join most online panels, they answer an extensive profiling questionnaire that records demographic, lifestyle, and psychographic information, typically with hundreds of dimensions. This profiling information enables the panel provider to record detailed information on every panel member. Using this information, the panel provider can then target research efforts to panel members who meet specific criteria.

Panel Management

While online panels are quite effective at reducing costs and field time, the quality of the data is dependent on how well the panel is managed. Several factors influence the quality of an online panel. These include the recruitment methods, respondent participation, panel management practices, and types of incentives offered.

Panel Recruitment The method of recruitment of panel members is critical to the quality of the panel. If the panel is to meet a researcher's needs for a study requiring a general audience of consumers, it is important to evaluate whether the panel's recruitment method draws from a representative audience of consumers. Likewise, if a researcher's project requires business professionals, the panel's recruitment methods should draw from a universe of business professionals. Ideally, a panel should represent a diverse sampling of the population under study. Panel member recruitment methodology is a key distinction among online panels. There are essentially two methods for recruiting for an online panel: open source and by invitation only.

Intercepting people as they surf the Internet through ads is known as open recruitment. **Open online panel recruitment** allows any person who has access to the Internet to "self-select" and enroll in a market research panel. This provides the benefit of building a panel quickly with people who are Internet-savvy and responsive to online advertising.

A key drawback is the lack of control over who is recruited. A panel with open recruitment may sign up millions of Web surfers who share similar characteristics, but may include only people who are responsive to Web ads and/or "seek out" an opportunity to join an online panel by using search engines. This leaves out a large percentage of the general population.

In many cases, open recruitment leads to an overabundance of panel members who participate in many different panels and complete an inordinate amount of surveys. These are known in the industry as "professional survey takers"—people who sign up to take hundreds of surveys in order to enter into sweepstakes drawings or other types of incentives. The primary concerns associated with professional survey takers are that (1) they can give false or misleading information in an attempt to get through a survey quickly without regard to providing well-considered responses; (2) they tend to go through surveys in a perfunctory manner, which shows up in the time they take to complete the survey; and (3) they can make up a disproportionate amount of survey responders, leading to biased and unrepresentative research data. To the detriment of Internet marketing research, some Web sites have been developed to recruit people to sign up for several panels at one time. One study found that more than 30 percent of all online surveys are completed by less than 1 percent of the population. The study also found that professional survey takers respond to an average of 80 surveys over a 90-day period—with some taking several surveys per day.[26] However, it is important to consider that not all online panels are made up of professional survey takers. This is why it is so important to understand the recruitment methods used by an online panel before employing them in the research process.

The other method used for recruiting respondents to an online panel, the by-invitation-only method, was first used by Research Now, one of America's largest commercial online panel providers. **Closed online panel recruitment**, or by invitation only, invites only prevalidated individuals, or individuals who share known characteristics, to enroll in a market research panel. Most often, this is accomplished by inviting customers from large, highly trusted leading brands who collectively have a large, diverse base of customers in a given population (for example, general consumers, business professionals). In recruiting for its consumer panel, for example, Research Now has partnered with large, well-known

→ **open online panel recruitment**
Recruitment in which any person with Internet access can self-select to be in a research panel.

© Daniel Laflor/iStockphoto

A research study may focus on people who meet a specific criterion, such as golfing once a week.

→ **closed online panel recruitment**
Invitation of only prevalidated individuals or those with shared known characteristics to enroll in a research panel.

companies that have large, diverse customer bases. Similarly, in recruiting for its panel of business professionals, they have partnered with major airlines, hotels, and car rental companies. There is some natural overlap in the recruiting since business professionals who travel are also consumers, but Research Now pays close attention to panelist enrollment to ensure there isn't panelist duplication.

The "by-invitation-only" method enables a panel researcher to recruit people with specific demographics into the panel in order to meet a client's needs for a representative sample of the understudy population, or to meet specific needs. For example, in order to recruit affluent panel members, the panel provider may recruit customers from upscale retailers to join the panel. To recruit teenagers, a panel provider may recruit customers of specific clothing retailers that specialize in the teen market. To recruit business decision makers, a panel provider may recruit customers from companies that cater to business-people, such as airlines, hotels, car rental companies, and subscribers to business publications.

Using a by-invitation-only recruitment method gives a panel provider greater control over who is invited to the panel and greatly reduces the likelihood of professional survey takers. One particular area that requires attention with this approach is that the panel composition is dependent on the people who are invited to join the panel and may be biased by customers of a specific recruitment source. Thus, it is important that a by-invitation-only panel have a large number of diverse recruitment sources by working with companies in many different areas to ensure balanced representation in the panel.

Open versus Closed Recruitment

Research Now conducted a study of recruitment methods to compare "open" versus "closed" recruitment. During a 6-month test, Research Now, which recruits exclusively with a closed-loop recruitment approach termed *by invitation only*, enrolled 38,162 panel members into an experimental consumer panel using an open enrollment methodology. They then conducted a parallel tracking experiment that compared closed-sourced panelists to these open-sourced panelists (see Exhibit 6.4).

The experiment revealed that open-sourced panelists are often quite different from closed-sourced panelists. Open-sourced panelists were much more likely to be homemakers, retired people, students, and unemployed. They were also more likely to exhibit the behaviors of professional survey takers, including enrollment in multiple panels, a preference for multiple surveys each week, and a tendency to complete surveys more quickly, indicating a lack of thoughtful participation.

EXHIBIT 6.4	**Open versus Closed Panel ("by-invitation-only") Recruitment Methods**	
	Open Recruitment	**Closed Recruitment**
Working outside of the home	45.6%	77.0%
Homemaker	15.7%	4.4%
Female	73.7%	47.5%
Participate in multiple survey panels	87.3%	39.5%
Participate in five or more panels	55.2%	19.6%
Mean number of online panels joined	5.4	1.4
Mean time to take survey	8 min: 22 sec	9 min: 45 sec

Source: Research Now, 2011.

Respondent Cooperation

Respondent participation is critical to the success of the research process in order to minimize nonresponse bias. Therefore, it is important to understand the panel management practices and incentives employed by an online panel. Response rates for online surveys can vary dramatically, with some populations having average response rates less than 5 percent, others with response rates closer to 30 percent, and sometimes well over 60 percent for prescreened individuals, who have been alerted to expect to receive a survey at a specific time or date. The diminishing response rates observed with telephone interviewing have played a key role in the increased usage of online panels.

Ensuring participation is a function of several factors, including to what extent panel members are engaged in the research process, their experience with surveys and the panel in general, and the topic of the research. Of course, one of the primary drivers of participation is the incentive program.

Generally, online panels use two incentive models: the sweepstakes model and the pay-all model. The sweepstakes model offers survey participants a chance to be entered into a drawing for a prize, often hundreds or thousands of dollars, albeit with extremely low odds of winning. Pay-all incentive models pay each respondent a small incentive for their time and participation each time they take part in a survey.

The choice of incentive model is not trivial. A sound incentive model influences not only survey response rates, but also retention rates for panel members—which becomes very important when there is a need to use profiling information for targeting a specific type of respondent. Panel members who do not feel adequately compensated for their time and effort are much less likely to participate in research studies.

A study conducted by Research Now, using a third-party online panel, compared sweepstakes and pay-all incentive methods. For a 3-minute survey about books and music with 100 percent qualifying incidence, 40,000 people were invited to complete the survey in order to be entered into a sweepstakes drawing of $2,500 for one winner. An additional 4,000 people were invited to complete the same survey in exchange for $2.00 in cash. Both groups were selected randomly and then invited on the same day of the week and at the same time of day (Wednesday afternoon), and both were given 7 days to complete the survey.

The study found that the pay-all model was much more effective than the sweepstakes method (see Exhibit 6.5). People who were offered the pay-all incentive responded more quickly, and the response rate for the pay-all incentive group was 58 percent higher than that of the sweepstakes group (19.3 percent response rate vs. 12.2 percent response rate). While response rate is not the only measure of the quality of an online panel, it is a key metric.

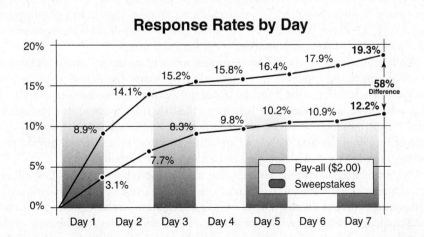

Response Rates by Day

Exhibit 6.5

Pay-All versus Sweepstakes

Source: Research Now, 2007.

Controlling the Panel

In addition to effective panel recruitment and respondent cooperation programs, online panel providers must have effective ongoing management of their panel to ensure a high level of quality. Panels must continually see that that their participants have positive experiences with every research project. Among other components, good panel management includes frequency controls to see that panel members are not surveyed too little or too much. Panel members should be given enough survey opportunities to stay effectively engaged in the research process, but not surveyed too much as to be burdened with survey invitations. Other keys to guaranteeing a positive panel member's experience is providing respondent privacy, safeguarding personal information, and protecting members from bogus research that attempts to use online surveys as a sales channel (this is the practice of "sugging"—selling under the guise of research).

Panel providers are continually recruiting new members to keep up with the growth in demand for online samples, as well as replace any panel members who may drop out. Even with exceptional panel member retention, some panel members will become less active in responding to surveys. In addition, panels will often recruit new members to assist in growing certain hard-to-reach segments and/or balancing the panel to have maximum representation of the overall population. Ensuring a growing supply of engaged, active panel members is a constant goal of every panel provider.

Finally, panel management includes ensuring panel freshness. As panel members change, their profiles must be updated. A single, 25-year-old college student with an annual income of $12,000 from last year may now be a married 26-year-old accountant with a new baby and a household income of $45,000. Updating profiles ensures that panel providers are able to consistently target qualified people for surveys.

When evaluating the quality of an online panel, there are several key drivers that contribute toward a panel's overall methodologies. If a panel does not have well-defined guiding principles to help deliver the highest level of quality, a sample purchaser should beware of the potential negative implications for the quality of the data.

Mobile Internet Research—The Next Step

In 2010 the mobile Web grew 110 percent in the United States and 148 percent worldwide. Forty-seven million Americans or 38 percent of the mobile Internet users access the Internet from their mobile phones daily. With regard to age, 65 percent of users 18–29 go online from their phones versus 43 percent of those aged 30–49. The highest rates of usage of cell phones accessing the Internet are college graduates and persons earning more than $75,000 per year. Despite this rapid growth, mobile Web accounted for only 1.26 percent of total Web consumption in the United States.[27]

While global online penetration continues to increase, mobile phones have quickly become the preferred mode of communication for many consumers. Mobile phones share the characteristics of the four traditional quantitative methodologies—face-to-face, postal, telephone, and online—but benefit particularly from location and immediacy of results. Furthermore, as the infrastructure supporting mobile usage has grown, and global trends of mobile usage and mobile ad spending continue to accelerate, mobile phone-based interviewing is quickly emerging as a fifth research methodology.

One prevailing assumption has been that mobile research methods are only useful for short, simple surveys. Early on, researchers cited the high cost of text messaging, difficulties in getting people to divulge mobile contact information, and data security concerns as critical challenges to using mobile research to a fuller extent. Many of the early obstacles to mobile research have since been overcome, however, and mobile research can actually accommodate a wide variety of question-and-answer features beyond basic SMS messages and wireless application protocol mobile device surveys, including the following:

- Pictures and videos
- Time/date stamps on responses
- GPS locations
- Anonymity for respondents
- Personalized surveys

When combined with the other four methodologies, mobile research can create a variety of new research options, such as point-of-sale customer satisfaction queries, continuous real-time event feedback, brand and advertising tracking and feedback, and live product concept testing—to name a few.

For mobile research to be effective, however, researchers must still apply general principles of good research. For those who do, opportunities are numerous to capitalize on the mobile research revolution and to engage consumers on the cutting edge of communication.[28]

Mobile research offers:

- An alternative way to conduct research with hard-to-reach groups.
- Increased respondent cooperation from all demographic groups.
- Immediate feedback on research questions concerning marketing campaigns, ad testing, and more.
- Cost savings—faster reply to surveys, shorter project completion time.
- Use as a mobile recruiting tool to direct respondents to online surveys.
- Another way of reaching people on the go.[29]

A few disadvantages of mobile Internet surveys are as follows:

- Lightspeed found that the response rate decreased with age due to lower usage of mobile Internet services among older people. Thus, the profile doesn't reflect the average consumer.
- Questionnaires must be short.
- Question types are limited, as is the length of questions.
- Higher incentives must be offered to remove the financial burden of receiving and completing mobile surveys from the respondent.[30]

Mobile Internet technologies provide an exciting new channel for marketing researchers. However, their limitations will mean that traditional online marketing research will be the channel of choice for most survey research.

SUMMARY

Almost 30 percent of the world's population is online. In the United States and Canada the figure is over 77 percent. Over 90 percent of America's research firms are conducting online research. Secondary data can play a key role in the marketing research process. It can clarify a problem, suggest a particular research methodology, or sometimes actually provide a solution to the problem. Exhibit 6.1 offers an extensive list of online sources of secondary data. The Internet has, in many ways, revolutionized the gathering of secondary data. Now, rather than wait for replies from government agencies or other sources, users can find millions of pieces of information on the Internet. Trips to the library may become a thing of the past for many researchers. Search engines and directories contain links to millions of documents throughout the world. Special-interest discussion groups and blogs on the Internet can also be valuable sources of secondary data. A five-step approach to searching the Internet is presented. This is followed by a detailed procedure that explains how to evaluate the quality of Web pages.

Web site databases can produce important insights. A Web merchant can track a person as he or she clicks through a site. The merchant can examine what was looked at and what was bought. The screen the customer will see first on the next visit to the site can be tailored to the customer's past purchase and browsing behavior. Cookies are an important tool for monitoring a user's behavior within a site.

More and more focus groups are being conducted online because online focus groups are fast and cost effective; they also reach populations that are typically inaccessible. However, there are several problems associated with online focus groups. Asynchronous focus groups are time-extended focus groups conducted much like an online chat group. Web community research is where a group of consumers agree to participate in an ongoing dialogue with a company. The discussion may last a year or more, and participants respond to questions that are regularly posted to the community. Insights from the community can be used as a basis for traditional marketing research.

Some firms are experimenting with individual depth interviews online. Each participant creates an online journal based on a series of questions provided by the researcher.

Internet surveys offer rapid deployment and real-time reporting, dramatically reduced costs, ready personalization, high response rates, ability to reach low-incidence respondents, simplified and enhanced panel management, and profitability for survey research firms. The disadvantages are the potential nonrepresentativeness of Internet users, lack of callback procedures to clarify open-ended responses, bandwidth problems, and the fact that the sample frame needed may not be available on the Internet.

Commercial online panels are used for multiple projects by many different companies. While panels reduce cost and field time, the quality of the data requires good panel management. Panel recruitment can be by open source or "by invitation only." The by-invitation-only method is highly preferred for quality purposes. Good panel management requires the blocking of professional survey takers. Typically, Internet panels use either a "pay-all" or a sweepstakes strategy to gain respondent cooperation. Pay-all tends to be much more effective. Mobile Internet technologies will probably be the next platform in Internet survey research.

KEY TERMS & DEFINITIONS

newsgroup An Internet site where people can read and post messages devoted to a specific topic.

online focus groups Focus groups conducted via the Internet.

web community A carefully selected group of consumers who agree to participate in an ongoing dialogue with a corporation.

unrestricted Internet sample A self-selected sample group consisting of anyone who wishes to complete an Internet survey.

commercial online panel A group of individuals who have agreed to receive invitations to do online surveys from a particular panel company, such as eRewards or SSI. The panel company charges organizations doing surveys for access to the panel. Charges are usually so much per survey, depending on survey length and the type of people being sought for the survey. The panel company controls all access to the members of its panel.

open online panel recruitment Recruitment in which any person with Internet access can self-select to be in a research panel.

closed online panel recruitment Invitation of only prevalidated individuals or those with shared known characteristics to enroll in a research panel.

QUESTIONS FOR REVIEW & CRITICAL THINKING

1. Do you think that eventually all marketing research will be done on the Internet? Why or why not?

2. Explain the relationship between blogs and marketing research.

3. How can a researcher evaluate the quality of a Web page?

4. How can a company benefit from building an internal database from its Web site visitors? Is there an advantage that a Web retailer might have over a traditional store?

5. Discuss the advantages and disadvantages of online focus groups.

6. Explain the differences between real-time focus groups and asynchronous focus groups.

7. Do you think that a company such as Caterpillar could benefit from Web community research? Ford? American Airlines?

8. Discuss the popularity of online survey research. Why is it so popular?

9. What are some techniques for increasing survey completion rates?

10. Describe some ways to recruit for online panels.

11. How does one avoid professional survey takers with online panels?

12. Is panel management a critical task for a quality online panel?

WORKING THE NET

Go to Exhibit 6.1 and, using it as a resource, determine the 10 highest-income counties in the United States; where the highest ratio of pickup trucks per capita is found; the oldest median age zip code in America; a list of key decision makers in the U.S. steel industry; a reader profile on *Time* magazine; where most avocados are grown; and this week's Internet usage in the United States.

Compare and contrast the offerings of ***www.surveysampling.com***, ***www.zoomerANg.com***, ***www.researchnow.com***, and ***www.surveymonkey.com***.

REAL-LIFE RESEARCH • 6.1

Good Things Come to Brands That Give

In Kenya, Coca-Cola is helping teach children how to test drinking water for contamination. The company also is providing water-purification systems for some of the country's most poverty-stricken areas.

In India, Starbucks is addressing sanitation-related health problems by donating $1 million to WaterAid. Coca-Cola and Starbucks have taken the initiative to illustrate the good they are doing for the 1.1 billion people who lack access to clean drinking water.

Such efforts are applauded not only from a humanitarian standpoint, but also from a branding perspective. Sixty percent of U.S. adults over age 18 said "knowing a company is mindful of its impact on the environment and society makes me more likely to buy their products and services," according to findings in the Lifestyles of Health & Sustainability (LOHAS) *Consumer Trends Database* by the Natural Marketing Institute in Harleysville, Pennsylvania.

The company surveyed 2,000 adults via the Web to gauge their perceptions of how companies are dealing with social and environmental issues as well as how those perceptions impact their buying decisions.

Fifty-seven percent of consumers said they feel more loyal to companies that are socially responsible, and about half (52 percent) said they were more likely to talk to their friends and families about such mindful corporations.

More than a third (38 percent) said they'd be willing to pay extra for products produced by socially responsible companies, and 35 percent said they were more likely to buy stock in such corporations. "Consumers are more likely to be brand loyal and less likely to be price sensitive," said Steve French, managing partner at the Natural Marketing Institute, which was founded in 1990.

Despite that, the study found that many companies that do good, do a bad job of promoting the fact. "There's a big disconnect between what companies are doing and what consumer perceptions are," said French.[31]

Questions

1. Given the general nature of this survey, would an open panel be an acceptable source for a sample? Why or why not?

2. If a researcher was going to place restrictions on who might participate in this survey, what might those be? Age was already mentioned as a qualifier.

3. Could this survey have been done just as easily by mail? Why or why not?

4. How might a firm like McDonald's or Microsoft use this information?

Primary Data Collection: Observation

CHAPTER 7

LEARNING OBJECTIVES

→ **1.** To develop a basic understanding of observation research.

→ **2.** To learn the approaches to observation research.

→ **3.** To understand the advantages and disadvantages of observation research.

→ **4.** To explore the types of human observation.

→ **5.** To understand the types of machine observation and their advantages and disadvantages.

→ **6.** To explore the tremendous impact of scanner-based research on the marketing research industry.

→ **7.** To learn about observation research on the Internet.

What is observation research, and how is it used in marketing research? What is ethnography, and why is it so popular? Observation research has exploded on the Internet. Why? Why is Internet observation research so controversial? What machines can be used in observation research, and what kind of data do they produce? We will answer these questions in this chapter.

The Nature of Observation Research

→ **observation research**
A systematic process of recording patterns of occurrences or behaviors without normally communicating with the people involved.

Instead of asking people questions, as a survey does, observation research depends on watching what people do. Specifically, **observation research** can be defined as the systematic process of recording patterns of occurrences or behaviors without normally questioning or communicating with the people involved. (Mystery shopping is an exception.) A marketing researcher using the observation technique witnesses and records events as they occur or compiles evidence from records of past events. The observation may involve watching people or watching phenomena, and it may be conducted by human observers or by machines. Exhibit 7.1 gives examples of some common observation situations.

Conditions for Using Observation

Three conditions must be met before observation can be successfully used as a data-collection tool for marketing research:

1. The needed information must be either observable or inferable from behavior that is observable. For example, if a researcher wants to know why an individual purchased a new Toyota Sequoia rather than a Ford, observation research will not provide the answer.

2. The behavior of interest must be repetitive, frequent, or in some manner predictable. Otherwise, the costs of observation may make the approach prohibitively expensive.

3. The behavior of interest must be of relatively short duration. Observation of the entire decision-making process for purchasing a new home, which might take several weeks or months, is not feasible.

Approaches to Observation Research

Researchers can choose from a variety of observation approaches. They are faced with the task of choosing the most effective approach for a particular research problem, from the standpoint of cost and data quality. The dimensions along which observation approaches vary are (1) natural versus contrived situations, (2) open versus disguised observation, (3) human versus machine observers, and (4) direct versus indirect observation.

EXHIBIT 7.1	Observation Situations
Situations	**Example**
People watching people	Observers stationed in supermarkets watch consumers select frozen Mexican dinners, with the purpose of seeing how much comparison shopping people do at the point of purchase.
People watching phenomena	Observers stationed at an intersection count vehicles moving in various directions to establish the need for a traffic light.
Machines watching people	Movie or video cameras record consumers selecting frozen Mexican dinners.
Machines watching phenomena	Traffic-counting machines monitor the flow of vehicles at an intersection.

Natural versus Contrived Situations   Counting how many people use the drive-in window at a particular bank during certain hours is a good example of a completely natural situation. The observer plays no role in the behavior of interest. Those being observed should have no idea that they are under observation. At the other extreme is recruiting people to do their shopping in a simulated supermarket (rows of stocked shelves set up in a field service's mall facility) so that their behavior can be carefully observed. In this case, the recruited people must be given at least some idea that they are participating in a study. The participants might be given grocery carts and told to browse the shelves and pick out items that they might normally use. The researchers might use alternative point-of-purchase displays for several products under study. To test the effectiveness of the various displays, the observers would note how long the shopper paused in front of the test displays and how often the product was actually selected. Today, many firms, such as Frito-Lay and Procter & Gamble, use online simulated environments.

A contrived environment enables the researcher to better control extraneous variables that might have an impact on a person's behavior or the interpretation of that behavior. Use of such an environment also tends to speed up the data-gathering process. The researcher does not have to wait for natural events to occur but instead instructs the participants to perform certain actions. Because more observations can be collected in the same length of time, the result will be either a larger sample or faster collection of the targeted amount of data. The latter should lower the costs of the project.

The primary disadvantage of a contrived setting is that it is artificial, and thus the observed behavior may be different from what would occur in a real-world situation. The more natural the setting, the more likely it is that the behavior will be normal for the individual being observed.

Open versus Disguised Observation   Does the person being observed know that he or she is being observed? It is well known that the presence of an observer may have an influence on the phenomena being observed. Two general mechanisms work to bias the data. First, if people know they are being observed (as in **open observation**), they may behave differently. Second, the appearance and behavior of the observer offer potential for bias similar to that associated with the presence of an interviewer in survey research.

Disguised observation is the process of monitoring people who do not know they are being watched. A common form of disguised observation is observing behavior from behind a one-way mirror. For example, a product manager may observe respondent reactions to alternative package designs from behind a one-way mirror during a focus group discussion.

> **open observation**
> The process of monitoring people who know they are being watched.

> **disguised observation**
> The process of monitoring people who do not know they are being watched.

Human versus Machine Observers   In some situations, it is possible and even desirable to replace human observers with machines—when machines can do the job less expensively, more accurately, or more readily. Traffic-counting devices are probably more accurate, definitely cheaper, and certainly more willing than human observers. It would not be feasible, for example, for Nielsen Company to have human observers in people's homes to record television viewing habits. Movie cameras and audiovisual equipment record behavior much more objectively and in greater detail than human observers ever could. Finally, the electronic scanners found in most retail stores provide more accurate and timely data on product movement than human observers ever could.

Direct versus Indirect Observation   Much of the observation carried out for marketing research is direct observation of current behavior or artifacts. For example, the contents of 100 women's purses in Portland, Oregon and Plano, Texas were examined as part of an observational study. Nearly every participant (99 percent) had something of a financial nature such as a credit or debit card, checkbook, or wallet. Women who were married, college educated, and with high incomes carried the most cards. Ninety-eight percent of the women carried reward and membership cards. Office supplies, like paper and pens, were found in 93 percent of the purses. Other items discovered, in rank order, were beauty and hair care, items, identification, receipts, cell phones and accessories, insurance cards, food and candy, healthcare products, coupons, glasses, photos, trash, nail care products, feminine care products, tissues, hand sanitizers, food/drink supplies such as napkins and toothpicks, oral care products, religious items, weapons, keepsakes, and cameras. Only 8 percent carried a camera.[1]

Pictures can also be used to see what people have done in certain situations. For example, a global study conducted by New York–based GfK NOP created a massive visual database with the goal of better understanding global consumers. Part of that research was photographing people's kitchens, which in many cultures is the "heart of the home." Examples of the kind of understanding the researchers gleaned from the photos are shown in Exhibit 7.2.

Advantages of Observation Research

Watching what people actually do rather than depending on their reports of what they did has one very significant and obvious advantage: Firsthand information is not subject to many of the biasing factors associated with the survey approach. Specifically, the researcher avoids problems associated with the willingness and ability of respondents to answer questions. Also, some forms of data are gathered more quickly and accurately by observation. Letting a scanner record the items in a grocery bag is much more efficient than asking the shopper to enumerate them. Similarly, rather than asking young children which toys they like, major toy manufacturers prefer to invite target groups of children into a large playroom and observe via a one-way mirror which toys are chosen and how long each holds the child's attention.

Disadvantages of Observation Research

The primary disadvantage of observation research is that only behavior and physical personal characteristics usually can be examined. The researcher does not learn about

Exhibit 7.2

Pictures Can Help Understand Global Consumers

© kevin miller/iStockphoto

motives, attitudes, intentions, or feelings. Also, only public behavior is observed; private behavior—such as dressing for work or committee decision making within a company—is beyond the scope of observation research. A second problem is that present observed behavior may not be projectable into the future. The fact that a consumer purchases a certain brand of milk after examining several alternatives does not mean that he or she will continue to do so in the future.

Observation research can be time-consuming and costly if the observed behavior occurs rather infrequently. For example, if observers in a supermarket are waiting to watch the purchase behavior of persons selecting Lava soap, they may have a long wait. And if the choice of consumers to be observed is biased (for example, shoppers who go grocery shopping after 5:00 P.M.), distorted data may be obtained.

Human Observation

As noted in Exhibit 7.1, people can be employed to watch other people or certain phenomena. For example, people can act as mystery shoppers, observers behind one-way mirrors, or recorders of shopper traffic and behavior patterns.

Ethnographic Research

Ethnographic research comes to marketing from the field of anthropology. The popularity of the technique in commercial marketing research is increasing. **Ethnographic research**, or the study of human behavior in its natural context, involves observation of behavior and physical settings. Ethnographers directly observe the population they are studying. As "participant observers," ethnographers can use their intimacy with the people they are studying to gain richer, deeper insights into culture and behavior—in short, what makes people do what they do. Over $400 million is spent annually on ethnographic research.[2] Today, corporations, such as Procter & Gamble and Microsoft, have their own in-house ethnographers. Procter & Gamble conducted ethnographic research in Mexico City among lower-middle-class families. The research led to Downy Single Rinse, a fabric softener that removed a step from the less mechanized laundry process there. Ethnographic studies can cost anywhere from $5,000 to as much as $800,000, depending on how deeply a company wants to delve into its customers' lives.

> ➔ **ethnographic research** Study of human behavior in its natural context, involving observation of behavior and physical setting.

One of the first uses of ethnographic research in an informal manner goes back to the Spanish Civil War in the 1930s. Forrest Mars, Sr., when he wasn't dodging bullets, was observing soldiers coating their chocolate with sugar. The result of this observational or ethnographic research? M&M's, named for Mars and business associate Bruce Murrie.[3]

Advantages of Ethnographic Research   Both focus groups and individual depth interviews rely on retrospection. That is, they ask respondents to recall their behavior and the behavior of others. Human memory, of course, can sometimes be faulty.

In addition, respondents sometimes reply in a socially desirable manner. For example, a man may be reading adult magazines but claim to be reading *Fortune* and *BusinessWeek*.

Ethnographic research offers a number of advantages. These include the following:

- Ethnography is reality based. It can show exactly how consumers live with a product, not just what they say about it or how they remember using it.
- It can reveal unexpressed needs and wants.
- It can discover unexploited consumer benefits.
- It can reveal product problems.

© Niels Poulsen std/Alamy

- It can show how, when, why and where people shop for brands—and how they perceive it compared to competitive products.
- It can show who in the family actually uses a product and perhaps uncover a whole new potential demographic target.
- It takes advantage of consumers' experience with the category and their hands-on creativity as they demonstrate their ideas for new products and product improvements.
- It can test new products in a real context.
- It can reveal advertising execution ideas that derive directly from consumer experience.
- It can help form a better relationship with your consumers, based on an intimate knowledge of their lifestyles.[4]

Because individuals generally acclimate to an observer's presence over time (often quickly), their behavior becomes relatively unbiased by the observer—resulting in a more accurate characterization of behavior.

Although the ethnographic researcher's principal activity is observing behavior, active interviews or discussion with respondents is a key component. Getting respondents' perspectives on actions, through dialogue, is informative. Furthermore, the ethnographic data can be utilized in mixed method studies, for comparing and contrasting it with data from other sources. For example, a research manager could leverage observational data of the sales reps interacting with customers and prospects, and compare it with information from in-depth district and regional sales manager interviews—identifying any disconnects between what's being done and what's expected.

Conducting Ethnographic Research   The first step is to find participants. Afterward, the observation process can begin. A highly skilled ethnographer is typically trained in anthropology. The research begins with systematic observation and inquiry. The ethnographer is trained to examine human culture: symbols, codes, myths, rituals, beliefs, values, rules for social interaction, and conceptual categories and perceptions.

Many so-called ethnographists' interviews occur over a 90-minute period, which is too brief for close environmental observation and questioning. (Three to four hours per ethnographic observation and interview is far more productive.)

In a study on how consumers think about and use home printers, a highly trained ethnographer would ask:

◼ What are the meanings and processes of printing in their most elemental senses, as if the ethnographer had never seen a printer?

◼ Can we understand the symbolism of printing by exploring how respondents classify nonprinted versus printed matter?

◼ Anthropologists use a construct called binary opposition:

Binary Opposition	
Nonprinted Matter	**Printed Matter**
Intangible	Tangible
Fleeting	Lasting
Public	Private

◼ What are the consumer myths, stories, and beliefs about printing versus not printing and about different brands of printers?

◼ How do printing rituals serve as rites of passage that transform consumers from one state of being into another?

◼ Are people who print and save hard copies different in a "tribal" way from people who see printing as antiquated and wasteful?

◼ Are there social or business situations that demand or deny printing choices and, if so, why?

These questions and observations would undoubtedly enrich new-product development and marketing communications, helping shape product design, brand positioning, and advertising content.[5] In contrast to the above, ethnography-lite would consist of limited observations (under an hour) and a few individual depth interviews. This form of research is often conducted by persons without advanced training in anthropology or sociology. Unfortunately, a number of studies are conducted in this manner, which often yield very few insights.

The next step is to analyze and interpret all of the data collected to find themes and patterns of meaning. This is no simple task. Hours and hours of audio and video must be transcribed and re-studied. Even for the well-trained and experienced ethnographer, the amount of data can at times be overwhelming. But through careful and thorough analysis of the data, themes and categories emerge and applicable findings become clear. Ethnographers usually create frameworks to help companies think about their consumers and understand what it all means.

Triangulation—the process of checking findings against what other people say and against similar research already conducted—is a way to verify the accuracy of collected data. While traditional ethnography stops with the description of the group studies, this is not sufficient for businesses. They need actionable guidelines, recommendations, and an outline of strategy. The findings must be presented in a fashion that will enable companies to create innovative and successful solutions.

For managers at Cambridge SoundWorks, it was a perplexing problem: In retail outlets across the country, men stood wide-eyed when sales reps showed off the company's hi-fi, "blow-your-hair-back" stereo speakers. So why didn't such unabashed enthusiasm for the product translate into larger—and bigger-ticket—sales?

To find out, the Andover, Massachusetts, manufacturer and retailer of stereo equipment hired research firm Design Continuum, in West Newton, Massachusetts, to follow a dozen prospective customers over the course of 2 weeks. The researchers' conclusion: The high-end speaker market suffered from something referred to as "the spouse acceptance factor." While men adored the big black boxes, women hated their unsightly appearance. Concerned about the way the speakers would "look" in the living room, women would talk their husbands out of buying a cool but hideous and expensive piece of stereo equipment. Even those who had purchased the product had trouble showing it off: Men would attempt to display the loudspeakers as trophies in living rooms, while women would hide them behind plants, vases, and chairs. "Women would come into the store, look at the speakers and say, 'that thing is ugly,'" says Ellen Di Resta, principal at Design Continuum. "The men would lose the argument and leave the store without a stereo. The solution was to give the target market what men and women *both* wanted: a great sound system that looks like furniture so you don't have to hide it."

Armed with this knowledge, Cambridge SoundWorks unveiled a new line. The furniture-like Newton Series of speakers and home theater systems comes in an array of colors and finishes. The result: The Newton Series is the fastest-growing and best-selling product line in the firm's 14-year history.

Jim Stengel, Procter & Gamble's chief marketing officer, notes, "I'm a big observational guy." So he has urged the P&G marketers to spend lots of time with consumers in their homes, watching the ways they wash their clothes, clean their floors, and diaper their babies, and asking them about their habits and frustrations. Back in 2000, the typical brand marketer spent less than 4 hours a month with consumers. Says Stengel: "It's at least triple that now."[6]

Ethnography and Focus Groups
Of course, both ethnography and focus groups are forms of qualitative research. Yet most research clients see the two techniques playing different roles in the overall research process. Sometimes both methodologies are used on the same project:

■ Ethnography for strategic understanding, exploratory research at the beginning of the creative/innovation process.

■ Focus groups/IDIs for tactical issues—reactions to stimuli (ads, visuals, concepts, etc.), often ones that have been developed in the first phase. In a sense, these methods have been repositioned in some clients' minds.

I think of focus groups to get narrow things. If I have eight concepts, [I want to know] what's working better than another, what language is working better, etc. When I'm trying to get something deeper and something I didn't know how to ask, I would use one-on-ones. If I have the choice and the time—there's time and money associated with ethnography—I'd opt for ethnography hands-down every time. (pharmaceutical client)

Focus groups still have their place for consensus-building and culling down ideas. For innovation, I do think ethnography has an advantage. (consultant)

It's rare that we do a study that doesn't have both ethnography and focus groups. They both have their purposes. We try [ideas] out in the focus groups based on earlier insights and ideas drawn from the ethnography. Focus groups yield time and efficiency that can lead to tighter and more effective surveys." (financial services client)[7]

Jerry Thomas, CEO of Decision Analyst, discusses online ethnography in the accompanying Practicing Marketing Research box.

PRACTICING MARKETING RESEARCH

Taking Ethnography Online

Online ethnography begins by pulling a sample that is representative of the target market, typically from an online panel. One of the advantages here is that panel members are accustomed to surveys and therefore are more likely to participate than the average man or woman on the street. Moreover, since no one is visiting their homes or offices, a higher share of potential subjects will agree to participate, which creates a more representative sample.

Beyond the sampling advantages, another benefit of this approach is that the online environment promotes a sense of anonymity and safety, which encourages a high level of self-disclosure. In the online environment, participants feel comfortable expressing their feelings. With guidance from experienced moderators, respondents can explore and describe all the behaviors, routines, thoughts, feelings, and experiences they believe are most relevant to their purchasing decisions.

The respondents' normal routines are not disrupted. They can provide their detailed responses at a convenient time and over a span of several days (or sometimes weeks). This expanse of time also gives the respondents an opportunity to reflect on the questions posed and to give detailed descriptions of their thoughts, feelings, and experiences.

So, how does online ethnography work? How is it conducted? The exact design of the project and its execution depend on the product or service category and the objectives of the research.

As a general rule, some or all of the following steps are involved:

- *Respondents might be asked to keep diaries* (either online or offline) to record their behaviors, routines, thoughts, and observations related to the purposes of the study.
- *Participants might be asked to take digital pictures* related to the focus of the study (it could be photos of their refrigerators, pantries, backyards, or bedrooms). And with the spread of digital cameras (even cell phones now have digital cameras), digital photos are relatively easy for most people to take and send (with the moderator subsequently uploading the pictures for discussion).
- *One member of the household could be asked to take photos or videos* of other members of the household at certain times or to record specific behaviors, events, and so on.
- *Participants' stories or explanations typically accompany the photos,* telling us what is in the picture, who is in the picture, what is happening, and perhaps even what it means to the respondent.
- *Projective techniques can be employed* as well (for example, respondents might search and select online photos or be instructed to take photos that represent the personality of a brand, or that bring to mind memories of the brand).

Typically, the digital photos or videos are sent to the moderator via e-mail for review and uploading to the online depth interview. The diaries and photos are studied by the analyst and then used as stimulus in conducting the follow-up online depth interviews. These are typically described as "time-extended" depth interviews since the project unfolds over a period of several days (5 to 10 days, but longer time periods are possible). In fact, the term *time-extended* should be used to describe the whole online ethnography process. Indeed, this is one of the major advantages of the method: the respondent's concentration on a topic for a period of several days sensitizes her to the subject and reveals her own feelings and motives related to the topic.

Example of an Online Ethnography Project

Decision Analyst conducted an online ethnographic project on health and beauty products among women and men from the United States, the United Kingdom, and France. All participants were medium to heavy users of skin-care products.

Study Methodology

- Respondents were asked to take *digital pictures of their skin-care products and other health and beauty products* in their normal storage place. They were also asked to add stories of "what's in the pictures" to accompany the pictures.

- To record *daily diary entries* of their morning/evening routines when using health and beauty products.

- *To provide detailed descriptions* of their experiences from a regular shopping occasion for health and beauty products.

- To keep a *log of advertising* they noticed related to health and beauty.

Follow-up *depth interviews* focused on the following types of questions: How do you define beauty? What motivates your interest in skin beauty? How would you feel if your favorite skin-care lotion should vanish from the marketplace? How much time do you spend daily caring for your skin? What are your favorite brands, and why?

Comments and Pictures from One Participant, Sally, in Chicago

Obviously my medicine cabinet is filled with a variety of products at various price points. I admit that I like to try the high-end brands, but I'm on a budget and also take advantage of the less pricey products one finds at drugstores and stores like Body Shop. So that's why Crème de la Mer is elbowing for room with Olay, and Kinerase is cheek-and-jowl with Ponds.

Once all of the photos, diaries, stories, and interview transcripts are finished, the next step is the analysis, which is the most time-consuming and brain-intensive part of the process. There are no shortcuts. The analyst must comb and re-comb through all of the raw data (photos, videos, diaries, transcripts) and try to understand what it all means. Certainly, some understanding of cultural anthropology is helpful to the analyst, as is some knowledge of psychology, sociology, economics, history, and so on. The most important background, however, is knowledge of the target industry, the product category, and previous experience with marketing and marketing research related to the product or service. If all of these knowledge sets can be integrated, the analysis is apt to be much better than an analysis based on a single academic discipline.[8]

Questions

1. Which do you think reveals the most insights—traditional ethnography or online ethnography?

2. Which is most difficult to conduct?

3. Would you rather participate in an online or traditional ethnographic study?

Mystery Shoppers

> **mystery shoppers**
> People who pose as consumers and shop at a company's own stores or those of its competitors to collect data about customer–employee interactions and to gather observational data; they may also compare prices, displays, and the like.

Mystery shoppers are used to gather observational data about a store (for example, are the shelves neatly stocked?) and to collect data about customer–employee interactions. In the latter case, of course, there is communication between the mystery shopper and the employee. The mystery shopper may ask, "How much is this item?" "Do you have this in blue?" or "Can you deliver this by Friday?" The interaction is not an interview, and communication occurs only so that the mystery shopper can observe the actions and comments of the employee. Mystery shopping is, therefore, classified as an observational marketing research method, even though communication is often involved. It is estimated that 70 percent of America's national retailers use the technique: Wal-Mart, McDonald's, Starbucks, Blockbuster, Jiffy Lube, Rite Aid, PF Chang's restaurants, and Whole Foods Markets are some of the big-name clients that rely on mystery shoppers.

"The No. 1 thing we're trying to do is reinforce a company's training," explains David Rich, president of ICC/Decision Services, which deploys mystery shoppers for such clients as Levi's and Godiva.[9] Mystery shopping gives managers nearly instant feedback on whether their workers are smiling when they ought to, making customers feel at ease, or inviting them to get fries with that. Many companies tie bonuses to performance on mystery inspections, giving employees an incentive to be nice.

The mystery shopping concept has four basic levels, which differ in the depth and type of information collected:

■ *Level 1.* The mystery shopper conducts a mystery telephone call. Here, the mystery shopper calls the client location and evaluates the level of service received over the phone, following a scripted conversation.

■ *Level 2.* The mystery shopper visits an establishment and makes a quick purchase; little or no customer–employee interaction is required. For example, in a Level 2 mystery shop, a mystery shopper purchases an item (for example, gas, a hamburger, or a lottery ticket) and evaluates the transaction and image of the facility.

■ *Level 3.* The mystery shopper visits an establishment and, using a script or scenario, initiates a conversation with a service and/or sales representative. Level 3 mystery shopping usually does not involve an actual purchase. Examples include discussing different cellular telephone packages with a sales representative, reviewing services provided during an oil change, and so forth.

■ *Level 4.* The mystery shopper performs a visit that requires excellent communication skills and knowledge of the product. Discussing a home loan, the process for purchasing a new car, or visiting apartment complexes serve as examples. The "hotel spy" in the Practicing Market Research box in page 164 is another example of a Level 4 mystery shopper.

Mystery shopping can have one or several objectives. As mentioned earlier, a common objective is measuring employee training. Other objectives are:

■ Enabling an organization to monitor compliance with product/service delivery standards and specifications.

■ Enabling marketers to examine the gap between promises made through advertising/sales promotion and actual service delivery.

■ Helping monitor the impact of training and performance improvement initiatives on compliance with or conformance to product/service delivery specifications.

■ Identifying differences in the customer experience across different times of day, locations, product/service types, and other potential sources of variation in product/service quality.[10]

One-Way Mirror Observations

The discussion of focus groups in Chapter 4 noted that focus group facilities almost always provide **one-way mirror observation**, which allows clients to observe the group discussion as it unfolds. New product development managers, for example, can note consumers' reactions to various package prototypes as they are demonstrated by the moderator. (One researcher spent 200 hours watching mothers change diapers to gather information for the redesign of disposable diapers.) In addition, the clients can observe the degree of emotion exhibited by the consumer as he or she speaks. One-way mirrors are also sometimes used by child psychologists and toy designers to observe children at play. At the Fisher-Price Play Lab, some 3,500 children per year pass through. It is set up like a preschool classroom. On the other side of the glass is a narrow carpeted room with

→ **one-way mirror observation**
The practice of watching behaviors or activities from behind a one-way mirror.

PRACTICING
MARKETING RESEARCH

Undercover with a Hotel Spy

J. C. Schaefer unscrews a light bulb from a bedside lamp in the posh Windsor Court Hotel in New Orleans and begins violently whacking it against the bedspread. He shakes the light bulb to make sure the filament inside is broken and then carefully screws it back into the lamp.

Mr. Schaefer isn't your average hotel guest. In fact, he isn't even J. C. Schaefer. His real name is David Richey, and he's a hotel spy who uses a variety of aliases to check out luxury hotels all over the world. Over 2 days, he'll employ an extensive bag of tricks to see if the Windsor Court—rated as the top hotel in the world in a *Condé Nast Traveler* magazine poll—is as good as its reputation. The "burnt-out light bulb" test is one of the toughest. Only 11 percent of hotels tested by Mr. Richey's Chevy Chase, Maryland, firm, Richey International, detect the burnt-out bulb on the housekeeping staff's first pass.

The Windsor Court is a member of Preferred Hotels & Resorts Worldwide, a group of 120 independent luxury hotels that share a common reservations system. Preferred requires that all its hotels meet at least 80 percent of its standards in a test conducted annually by Richey International.

After checking in, Mr. Richey heads off to lunch while his room is being prepared. The Windsor Court has a five-star dining room, but the mystery shopper decides to eat at the hotel bar, the Polo Club Lounge. Mr. Richey orders crab cakes from the menu, then orders french fries to see if the bar readily accommodates off-menu orders. It does.

The food is good, and the service is friendly. But the waiters get marked down for not making eye contact and for not busing away the ketchup after the meal is done. "They're nice guys," Mr. Richey says, "But they're not real polished."

A little after 2 P.M. Mr. Richey walks into a sprawling $295-a-night suite at the Windsor Court. He pulls out a disposable camera and begins taking pictures. Overall, the room gets high marks for cleanliness and creature comforts. But Mr. Richey spots scuff marks on the baseboard and a snag in one of the curtains.

Then it's on to the bathroom. "Forty percent of hotels have hair in either the sink, the tub or on the floor," Mr. Richey announces as he begins his inspection. This room, it turns out, does not.

Before leaving for dinner, Mr. Richey sets up a test to see how well the housekeeping staff will pick up the room when they turn down the covers on the bed later that evening. He leaves some magazines askew in the magazine rack, puts a cup of pistachio shells on the table, and disables the light bulb.

After dinner, Mr. Richey heads downstairs for another test. "I have changed my travel plans and will be going to New York tomorrow," Mr. Richey informs the concierge. "Can you make reservations for me?" "Unfortunately we can't do that," the concierge replies. "You either have to do it yourself or call a travel agent." Mr. Richey, as always, takes the news calmly. "That was awful," he says later. "I'm sure the general manager will be horrified." Back in the room, Mr. Richey finds a neatly turned-down bed. However, the housekeeper hasn't done a very good job of tidying the room. And the defective light bulb hasn't been replaced. Mr. Richey takes copious photos. It's 10 P.M., but Mr. Richey will be up for another couple of hours preparing his report.[11]

Questions

1. Do you think that mystery shopping is beneficial to the Windsor Court? Why?

2. Do you think that Mr. Richey's observations would be meaningful to Motel 6? Why?

about 10 chairs and two video cameras. Nearly all Fisher-Price toys are taken for a spin in the Play Lab at some point in their development.

Machine Observation

The observation methods discussed so far have involved people observing things or consumers. Now we turn our attention to observation by machines, including traffic counters, physiological measurement devices, opinion and behavior management devices, and scanners.

Traffic Counters

Among the most common and popular machines in observation research are **traffic counters**. As the name implies, traffic counters measure vehicular flow over a particular stretch of roadway. Outdoor advertisers rely on traffic counts to determine the number of exposures per day to a specific billboard. Retailers use the information to ascertain where to locate a particular type of store. Convenience stores, for example, require a moderately high-traffic volume to reach target levels of profitability.

> **traffic counters**
> Machines used to measure vehicular flow over a particular stretch of roadway.

Physiological Measurement Devices

When an individual is aroused or feels inner tension or alertness, his or her condition is referred to as *activation*. Activation is stimulated via a subcortical unit called the *reticular activation system (RAS)*, located in the human brain stem. The sight of a product or advertisement, for example, can activate the RAS. When the arousal processes in the RAS are directly provoked, the processing of information increases. Researchers have used a number of devices to measure the level of a person's activation.

Electroencephalograph An **electroencephalograph (EEG) machine** is a machine that measures electric pulses on the scalp and generates a record of electrical activity in the brain. Although electroencephalography probably is the most versatile and sensitive procedure for detecting arousal, it involves expensive equipment, a laboratory environment, and complex data analysis requiring special software programs. Using EEG technology developed by NASA to monitor astronauts' alertness levels, Capita Corporation has begun measuring respondents' reactions to advertisements. Capita uses a headset that reads electrical signals coming from a subject's scalp five times per second, as the person interacts with media such as a television program, a commercial, a Web page, or a banner ad. These brain waves are converted into a scrolling graph synchronized with the visual stimuli on the screen, giving the marketer a play-by-play view of which segments excite the viewer and which ones don't.

> **electroencephalograph (EEG) machine**
> A machine that measures electrical pulses on the scalp and generates a record of electrical activity in the brain.

Recently, Capita, with the help of U.S. Interactive, an Internet services company that tracks Web ads, tested the system's reliability. Capita monitored the brain waves of 48 respondents as they confronted four banner ads with strong click-through rates and four ads with low rates. In three of four tests, Capita's measure correctly identified the "strong" banners.[12]

A UCLA academic study used a magnetic resonance imaging (MRI) machine instead of an EEG Machine to study advertising effectiveness. The researchers found that some participants had increased activity in the medical prefrontal cortex region of the brain while viewing a public service announcement on the importance of using sunscreen. This brain region is located in the front of the brain between the eyebrows. It is associated with self-reflection thinking about what we like and dislike and also motivations and desires. Those with increased brain activity were much more likely to increase their use of sunscreen than those without increased brain activity.[13]

The ability to accurately translate the data is what troubles one cable network executive. "An ad might get someone to perspire or their eyes to dilate or their brain waves to peak, but the resounding issue is, what does that really tell you?" he says. "Just because the needles are moving does not mean that it will affect their behavior, get them to purchase something, or improve their brand awareness."[14]

Galvanic Skin Response   **Galvanic skin response (GSR)**, also known as *electrodermal response*, is a change in the electric resistance of the skin associated with activation responses. A small electric current of constant intensity is sent into the skin through electrodes attached to the palmar side of the fingers. The changes in voltage observed between the electrodes indicate the level of stimulation. Because the equipment is portable and not expensive, measuring GSR is the most popular way to assess emotional reaction to a stimulus. GSR is used primarily to measure stimulus response to advertisements but is sometimes used in packaging research.

Inner Response, Incorporated, uses GSR to evaluate commercials. In tests of an Eastman Kodak Company digital photo processing ad, Inner Response determined that viewers' interest levels built slowly in the opening scenes, rose when a snapshot of an attractive young woman was shown, but spiked highest when a picture appeared of a smiling, pigtailed girl. Knowing which scenes had the highest impact helped Kodak in making changes in the spot's content and cutting its length.[15]

Eye Tracking   There has been a surge in the use of eye-tracking research as the equipment has gotten more sophisticated. Tobii Technology has introduced glasses that look and feel like modern eyewear and allows subjects to walk around freely in a real-world environment. They can browse in stores, use a computer, try out a new product, or read an advertisement.[16] Companies including Unilever, Kimberly-Clark, Con Agra, Heinz, and Kellogg use eye-tracking research. Tobii creates virtual store shelves for Procter & Gamble to test the pulling power of new package designs. A sample of eye tracking on a virtual store shelf is shown in Exhibit 7.3.

Much eye-tracking research is being conducted to improve Web sites and is it providing insights into user interaction with a screen between clicks. This research yields valuable information on which features are the most eye-catching, which features cause confusion, and which ones are ignored altogether. In the realm of Web site usability and online advertising, here are some of the major lessons learned from eye-tracking research:

1. Ads in the top and left portions of a homepage receive the most eye fixations. Ads in the right column are treated by users as an afterthought area. Ads at the bottom of the page are typically only seen by a small percentage of people.

2. Close proximity to popular editorial content helps ads get noticed. When an ad is separated from editorial matter either by white space or a rule, the ad receives fewer fixations than when there is no such barrier.

3. Of all types of ads tested, text ads are viewed most intently. On average, text ads are viewed for about 7 seconds, and the best display-type ads are only looked at for 1 to 2 seconds.

4. When it comes to ads, size matters. Bigger ads have a better chance of being seen. Small ads on the right side of homepages are viewed about a third of the time.

→ galvanic skin response (GSR)
A change in the electric resistance of the skin associated with activation responses; also called *electrodermal response*.

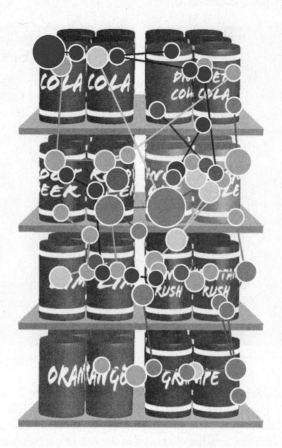

Exhibit 7.3

Eye Tracking at Work

Source: Elaine Wong, "Eye Tracking Sees Growth in Hyper-Competitive Market," *Brand Week,* June 7, 2010, p. 8.

Small ads on the rest of the page rarely attract attention, but this may not equate to the relative costs of these different advertising formats.

5. Larger images hold the eye longer than smaller images. Interestingly enough, people often click on photos, even if clicking doesn't take them anywhere or lead to any significant information.

6. Clean, clear faces in images attract more eye fixations on homepages.

7. People are more likely to recall facts, names, and places correctly when they were presented with that information in a text format. New, unfamiliar, conceptual information is more accurately recalled when participants receive it in a multimedia graphic format.

8. Shorter paragraphs perform better than longer ones and generally receive twice as much eye fixation as those with longer paragraphs.

9. On a Web site, eyes most often fixate first in the upper left of the page, then hover in that area before going left to right. Only after perusing the top portion of the page for some time do eyes explore further down the page.[17]

Facial Action Coding Service (FACS) Researchers at the University of California at San Francisco identified the 43 muscle movements responsible for all human facial expression (see Exhibit 7.4). They spent seven years categorizing roughly 3,000 combinations of such movements and the emotions they convey—the "eyelid tightener" expresses anger, for instance, and the "nasolabial fold deepener" manifests sadness. The system has proved to be highly accurate; the FBI and CIA reportedly use the FACS method to determine the emotions of suspects during interrogations.[18]

© Cameron Whitman/iStockphoto   © Cameron Whitman/iStockphoto

Sensory Logic, a Saint Paul, Minnesota, research firm, uses FACS to get to the "truth." The firm's clients include Target, Nextel, General Motors, and Eli Lilly, according to Dan Hill, the firm's president (see *www.sensorylogic.com*). To measure initial gut reactions to a commercial or ad, Hill first attaches electrodes to the side of a subject's mouth (monitoring the zygomatic muscle, for smiles), above the eyebrow (corrugator muscle, for frowns), and on two fingers (for sweat). He says the facial muscle movements reflect appeal, whereas perspiration translates into what he calls "impact"—emotional power. After Hill takes initial readings, he removes the electrodes and he videotapes an interview with each subject. Later, his FACS-trained team reviews the video, second by second, cataloguing emotions.

Even some of Hill's happy customers say that face reading has limitations. For one thing, not everyone believes that pitches have to aim for the heart. "A lot of the advertising we do is a more rational sell," a General Motors researcher says, "so emotional research doesn't apply."[19]

Gender and Age Recognition Systems   NEC Electronics of Japan has developed technology to recognize gender and approximate age of consumers. It has married this system with digital signs that can be placed in malls, airports, and other heavily trafficked public areas. Mall retailers, for example, can tailor their message to a person as they walk by. The system can also count the number of persons who walked past the flat-panel digital signs during any specific time period. The program uses an algorithm that draws on a database on thousands of faces as a reference. It looks at distinguishing points of the face, from the shape of the ears and eyes to hair color, to determine the age. The database expands as more people walk past the camera, allowing the program to make better judgment calls with time.

NEC also has installed the recognition system in vending machines in Japan. When a person stands in front of a vending machine, the system reads the consumer's profile. It then recommends snacks and drinks that fit the person's profile.

Consumers, meanwhile, may object to getting their faces scanned, without their knowledge. Likewise, retailers may not want to involve themselves in what some may perceive as a violation of privacy. To date, the systems have not been installed in the United States.[20]

Patented People Reader, The Pretesting Company

The People Reader, an opinion and behavior measurement device developed by the PreTesting Company, unobtrusively records reading material and readers' eye activity to determine readers' habits as well as the stopping power and brand-name recall associated with different-sized ads. Go to *www.pretesting.com* to learn about the products and services this company offers.

People Reader   The PreTesting Company has invented a device called the **People Reader**, which looks like a lamp. When respondents sit in front of it, they are not aware that it is simultaneously recording both their reading material and the activity of their eyes. The self-contained unit is totally automatic and can record any respondent—with or without glasses—without the use of attachments, chin rests, helmets, or special optics. It allows respondents to read any size magazine or newspaper and lets them spend as much time as they want reading and rereading the publication. Through use of the People Reader and specially designed hidden cameras, the PreTesting Company has been able to document both reading habits and the results of different-sized ads in terms of stopping power and brand-name recall. The company's research has found the following:

➤ **People Reader**
A machine that simultaneously records a respondent's reading material and eye reactions.

- Nearly 40 percent of all readers either start from the back of a magazine or "fan" a magazine for interesting articles and ads. Fewer than half the readers start from the very first page of a magazine.

- Rarely does a double-page ad provide more than 15 percent additional top-of-mind awareness than a single-page ad. Usually, the benefits of a double-page spread are additional involvement and communication, not top-of-mind awareness.

- In the typical magazine, nearly 35 percent of each ad receive less than 2 seconds' worth of voluntary examination.

- The strongest involvement power recorded for ads has been three or more successive single-page ads on the right-hand side of a magazine.

- Because most ads "hide" the name of the advertisers and do not show a close-up view of the product package, brand-name confusion is greater than 50 percent on many products such as cosmetics and clothing.

- A strong ad that is above average in stopping power and communication will work regardless of which section in the magazine it is placed. It will also work well in any type of ad or editorial environment. However, an ad that is below average in stopping power and involvement will be seriously affected by the surrounding environment.[21]

Television Audience Measurement and the Portable People Meter

For the past decade or so, watching television in America has been defined by the families recruited by Nielsen Media Research who have agreed to have an electronic meter attached to their televisions or to record in a diary what shows they watch. Traditional "people meters" are electronic TV set-top boxes (STBs) that continually record which channel is tuned in. Today, the trend is away from traditional people meters to direct measurement from STBs. These are the boxes installed by the likes of DirectTV, Dish Network, and cable companies to enable you to watch television programs. As the technology develops, researchers will be able to tap second-by-second viewing habits of millions of households. In contrast, Nielsen's national people meter panel consists of only 18,000 people.

Despite the advantage of a huge sample in STB audience measurement, there are many technological and methodological challenges. STBs were never designed to collect and process viewing data. Not only are the internal workings of the cable boxes different system to system, but there are also multiple generations deployed within each system. That leads to a long list of issues that need to be addressed, not the least of which is figuring out if the TV set attached to the box is on or off. According to Nielsen, 10 percent of STBs never get turned off over any month-long period; about 30 percent of boxes remain on for 24 hours on any given day.[22] Even if the TV is on, the question becomes, "who, if anyone, is watching it?" Also, the only demographic data currently available would be at the household level.

Recently Nielsen entered into an agreement with Charter Communications that gives Nielsen access to viewing information from 330,000 homes in the Los Angeles area. One of its first clients was the National Geographic Channel. Early on, the channel found that viewers were changing the channel 10 to 20 seconds before the show would break for ads. National Geographic made a number of changes, including how the show uses story recaps and teasers (about what is coming next). These changes boosted viewership of the channel's commercials.[23]

The Portable People Meter Arbitron has counted radio listeners—and, at various times, television viewers—since the late 1940s. It has harnessed new technology to measure audiences. Participants wear or carry a plastic box that looks like a pager, 3 inches by 2 inches by ½ inch, whose circuitry is roughly as complex as that of a cell phone. The device is called the **portable people meter (PPM)**.

Participants clip the PPM to their belts, or put it in a pocket and wear it throughout their waking hours. Before going to bed, they dock the PPM in a cradle so that overnight it can automatically send its data to a computer center in Maryland, where marketing researchers can download and review the information. Arbitron gathers information from approximately 70,000 consumers in 48 markets. The PPM detects radio, television, smart phone viewing, and even cinema advertising. The technology can measure audiences for out-of-home (OOH) TV viewing: watching a sports program at a friend's home, viewing a news network in an airport, or seeing a health show at the gym or doctor's office.

Arbitron has found that many younger consumers multitask. For example, in the last Winter Olympics, many people watching the Olympics on NBC were also online at NBC's Winter Olympics Web site. Other viewers tended to switch back and forth between the two.[24]

→ **portable people meter (PPM)**
A device worn by people that measures the radio and TV programming to which the participant is exposed during the day.

Symphony IRI Consumer Network

The Symphony IRI Consumer Network is a continuous household purchase panel that receives purchasing data from the National Consumer Panel (NCP), a joint venture between Symphony IRI and the Nielsen Companies. Households are recruited to the

NCP and given incentives to record all of their UPC-based purchases, with a hand-held in-home scanning device.

The data available from the panel include the following:

- Average amount of product purchased by each household during a specific period.
- Total projected category or product volume sold in the specific period.
- Projected number of households that purchased the category or product within the specific period.
- The average number of shopping trips when the product was purchased.
- The average volume sold for the product per purchase occasion.[25]

Observation Research on the Internet

At the time this text was published, the courts had ruled that tracking across Web sites was legal, comparing the practice to allowing someone to listen in on a phone conversation as long as one person involved in the call authorized it. As a result, online tracking has become the foundation of the $25 billion online advertising industry. The industry claims that tracking tools help subsidize content, allowing many Web sites to be free to users.[26]

Internet tracking is fundamentally another form of observation research. A cookie is a piece of text stored by a user's Web browser. It can be used for authentication, storing site preferences, shopping cart contents, and other useful functions. Cookies can also be used for tracking the Internet user's Web browsing habits. A "flash cookie" is a cookie placed on a computer via Adobe System's popular Flash program. Using Flash is the most common way to show video online.

Online tracking has come a long way since the now-defunct Netscape created the first cookies. For example, Lotame Solutions, Inc., a New York company, uses sophisticated software called a "beacon" to capture what people are typing on a Web site—their comments on monies, say, or their interest in parenting and pregnancy. Lotame packages that data into profiles about individuals, without determining a person's name and sells the profiles to companies seeking customers.

Perhaps the most controversial monitoring comes from "third-party cookies." They work like this: The first time a site is visited, it installs a tracking file, which assigns the computer a unique ID number. Later, when the user visits another site affiliated with the same tracking company, it can take note of where that user was before and where he is now. This way, over time the company can build a robust profile.

The new technologies are transforming the Internet economy. Advertisers once primarily bought ads on specific Web pages—a car ad on a car site. Now, advertisers are paying a premium to follow people around the Internet, wherever they go, with highly specific marketing messages.

Blue Kai, a collector of Internet user data, recently followed a Web surfer as he browsed for electronics on eBay, searched for cruises, and checked out snowboards. It also tracked when a Web surfer researched Chevrolet sport utility vehicles on auto site Autobytel and priced flights to Durham, North Carolina, at travel site Expedia.

After collecting that kind of information, Blue Kai groups Web visits into categories of consumers. It then immediately auctions off the data from some of the sites to marketers and Internet companies, which in turn use it for consumer research and ad personalization. Blue Kai regularly records information on more than 160 million unique monthly visitors shopping on retail, travel, and auto Web sites.[27]

Blue Kai and other trackers sell their information at data exchanges, which are like stock exchanges for online information. Web sites then put ad space up for auction, and ad agencies, armed with demographic and behavioral data about the people who visit those sites, bid to place ads for their client's campaigns. Google, Yahoo!, Microsoft, and others run ad auctions.

How popular is online tracking? The *Wall Street Journal* examined the 50 most popular U.S. Web sites, which account for about 40 percent of the Web pages viewed by Americans. It then analyzed the tracking files and programs these sites downloaded onto a test computer.

As a group, the top 50 sites placed 3,180 tracking files in total on the *Journal*'s test computer. Nearly a third of these were innocuous, deployed to remember the password to a favorite site or tally most-popular articles. But over two-thirds—2,224—were installed by 131 companies, many of which are Internet tracking companies.[28] One tracking company not only tracks people online but also stores their names in its databases. This enables the company to merge online behavior with sources such as voter registration, real estate records, shopping histories, and social networking activities to build a very detailed profile of individual consumers. Rapleaf, a tracking software company, says that it never discloses people's names to clients for online advertising.[29] If you want to find out if there is tracking software on your computer, go to *www.ghostery.com*.

comScore

comScore approaches Internet tracking using a different methodology. The firm has created a panel of over 2 million Internet users who have given comScore permission to capture their browsing and purchase behavior. Panel members receive gift certificates or other compensation.[30] comScore provides audience data that many advertisers use for making online advertising purchase decisions. Small Web sites like Digg and Yelp claim that comScore undercounts their audience size. CNBC says that their audience number is also incorrect. CNBC argues that their audience is relatively wealthy. As a result, they are less motivated to join a panel when offered gift certificates or petty cash incentives. Despite the problems, comScore is still the leader in online audience measurement.[31]

Scraping

During July 2010, users spent 1,181,194,905 hours on Facebook.[32] Some portion of this time was spent saying good and bad things about companies and brands. During the same month, Twitter averaged 65 million tweets per day.[33] In addition to social media and Twitter, community groups, product and service reviews, discussion boards, and bloggers also comment about specific products and services. User-generated content (UGC) is typically honest and candid and can also be very thoughtful and passionate. Marketers need to understand what is being said about their offerings and then adapt the marketing mix accordingly. The sheer volume of online conversations is overwhelming, and marketers look for tools to help focus their efforts. One popular solution is to "scrape" the Web and use text analytic tools to automate the analysis (see Chapter 3). How does scraping work? The researcher selects a number of search terms, much like a search engine, and then the tool crawls the Web in search of UGC relating to these search terms. All positive hits are then aggregated in a database, Next, a text analytic tool counts how frequently a product, feature, brand, and so on, is mentioned and makes an attitudinal assessment (for example, positive, neutral, negative) for each statement.[34]

Context is essential to understand meaning. It is also extremely difficult to automate since contextual clues are constantly evolving alongside language and are often very subtle (e.g., discerning Apple the company from apple the food). While text analytic and Web-scraping tools are improving in their ability to understand context, it is certain that any Web-scraped database still includes many irrelevant search results and excludes some relevant ones.[35]

Here are some examples that highlight the contextual confusion issue. Most of today's text analytic tools would classify the following statement as a negative comment about the Toyota Scion: "With the supercharger included on my Scion, it is one bad machine"—not being able to recognize the slang use of the word *bad* to actually mean *good*. Similarly, most of the technology would classify the following statement as being positive for Scion: "I loved my Scion; then I had to replace the transmission twice in the past two years."[36]

Observation Research and Virtual Shopping

Advances in computer technology have enabled researchers to simulate an actual retail store environment on a computer screen. Depending on the type of simulation, a shopper can "pick up" a package by touching its image on the monitor and rotate it to examine all sides. Like buying on most online retailers, the shopper touches the shopping cart to add an item to the basket. During the shopping process, the computer unobtrusively records the amount of time the consumer spends shopping in each product category, the time the consumer spends examining each side of a package, the quantity of product the consumer purchases, and the order in which items are purchased.

Computer-simulated environments like this one offer a number of advantages over older research methods. First, unlike focus groups, concept tests, and other laboratory approaches, the virtual store duplicates the distracting clutter of an actual market. Consumers can shop in an environment with a realistic level of complexity and variety. Second, researchers can set up and alter the tests very quickly. Once images of the product are scanned into the computer, the researcher can make changes in the assortment of brands, product packaging, pricing, promotions, and shelf space within minutes. Data collection is also fast and error-free because the information generated by the purchase is automatically tabulated and stored by the computer. Third, production costs are low because displays are created electronically. Once the hardware and software are in place, the cost of a test is largely a function of the number of respondents, who generally are given a small incentive to participate. Fourth, the simulation has a high degree of flexibility. It can be used to test entirely new marketing concepts or to fine-tune existing programs. The simulation also makes it possible to eliminate much of the noise that exists in field experiments.[37]

Kimberly-Clark has refined the virtual shopping experience even more. Located in Appleton, Wisconsin, the firm's virtual testing lab has a woman standing in a room surrounded by three screens showing a store aisle, a retina-tracking device recording her every glance.

Asked by a Kimberly-Clark researcher to find a "big box" of Huggies Natural Fit diapers in size three, the woman pushed forward on a handle like that of a shopping cart, and the video simulated her progress down the aisle. Spotting Huggies' red packages, she turned the handle to the right to face a dizzying array of diapers. After pushing a button to get a kneeling view of the shelves, she reached forward and tapped the screen to put the box she wanted in her virtual cart.

Kimberly-Clark hopes these virtual shopping aisles will provide better understanding of consumer behavior and make the testing of new products faster, more convenient, and more precise.[38]

Kimberly-Clark's lab also features a U-shaped floor-to-ceiling screen that re-creates in vivid detail interiors of the big retailers that sell the company's products—a tool that the company will use in presentations to executives in bids to win shelf space. A separate area is reserved for real replicas of store interiors, which can be customized to match the flooring, light fixtures, and shelves of retailers such as Target Corp. and Wal-Mart Stores, Inc.

Kimberly-Clark says its studio allows researchers and designers to get a fast read on new product designs and displays without having to stage real-life tests in the early stages of development. Doing the research in a windowless basement, rather than an actual test market, also avoids tipping off competitors early in the development process.

"We're trying to test ideas faster, cheaper, and better," says Ramin Eivaz, a vice president at Kimberly-Clark focusing on strategy. Formerly, new product testing typically took 8 months to 2 years. Now, that time is cut in half, he says. Projects that test well with the virtual-reality tools will be fast-tracked to real-store trials, Mr. Eivaz says.[39]

"It no longer works to show up on a retailer's doorstep with your new product and say, 'Isn't this pretty?'" Mr. Eivaz says. "We need to be an indispensable partner to our retailers and show we can do more for them."[40]

SUMMARY

Observation research is the systematic process of recording patterns of occurrences or behaviors without questioning or normally communicating with the people involved. For observation to be used successfully, the needed information must be observable and the behavior of interest must be repetitive, frequent, or in some manner predictable. The behavior of interest also should be of a relatively short duration. There are four dimensions along which observation approaches vary: (1) natural versus contrived situations, (2) open versus disguised observation, (3) human versus machine observers, and (4) direct versus indirect observation.

The biggest advantage of observation research is that researchers can see what people actually do rather than having to rely on what they say they did, thereby avoiding many biasing factors. Also, some forms of data are more quickly and accurately gathered by observation. The primary disadvantage of this type of research is that the researcher learns nothing about motives, attitudes, intentions, or feelings.

People watching people or objects can take the form of ethnographic research, mystery shopping, one-way mirror observations (for example, child psychologists might watch children play with toys), and shopper pattern and behavior studies.

Machine observation may involve traffic counters, physiological measurement devices, opinion and behavior measurement devices, or scanners. Symphony IRI employs hand-held scanners with its National Consumer Panel to scan all household purchases with UPC codes. This data is then used to measure consumer shopping patterns and sales by product category and brand.

Observation research on the Internet originally focused on tracking the surfing patterns of Internet users. Firms track consumer online behavior via cookies, flash cookies, and beacons. Beacons are the most intrusive because they can capture what people are typing on a Web site. Some firms are blending online data with offline information to build detailed consumer profiles. The objective is to increase the efficiency of targeted online advertising. Advertisers used to buy online advertising based on the Web site's content. Today, they buy based on the profiles of a person's Web activity, demographics, and psychographics.

Virtual shopping using advanced computer technology to create a simulated shopping environment is a rapidly growing form of observation research. It reduces the cost and time it takes to bring new products to the market.

KEY TERMS & DEFINITIONS

observation research A systematic process of recording patterns of occurrences or behaviors without normally communicating with the people involved.

open observation The process of monitoring people who know they are being watched.

disguised observation The process of monitoring people who do not know they are being watched.

ethnographic research Study of human behavior in its natural context, involving observation of behavior and physical setting.

mystery shoppers People who pose as consumers and shop at a company's own stores or those of its competitors to collect data about customer–employee interactions and to gather observational data; they may also compare prices, displays, and the like.

one-way mirror observation The practice of watching behaviors or activities from behind a one-way mirror.

traffic counters Machines used to measure vehicular flow over a particular stretch of roadway.

electroencephalograph (EEG) machine A machine that measures electrical pulses on the scalp and generates a record of electrical activity in the brain.

galvanic skin response (GSR) A change in the electric resistance of the skin associated with activation responses; also called *electrodermal response*.

People Reader A machine that simultaneously records a respondent's reading material and eye reactions.

portable people meter A device worn by people that measures the radio and TV programming to which the participant is exposed during the day.

QUESTIONS FOR REVIEW & CRITICAL THINKING

1. You are charged with the responsibility of determining whether men are brand conscious when shopping for racquetball equipment. Outline an observation research procedure for making that determination.

2. Fisher-Price has asked you to develop a research procedure for determining which of its prototype toys is most appealing to 4- and 5-year-olds. Suggest a methodology for making this determination.

3. What are the biggest drawbacks of observation research?

4. Compare the advantages and disadvantages of observation research with those of survey research.

5. It has been said that "people buy things not for what they will do but for what they mean." Discuss this statement in relation to observation research.

6. You are a manufacturer of a premium brand of ice cream. You want to know more about your market share, competitors' pricing, and the types of outlets where your product is selling best. What kind of observation research data would you purchase? Why?

7. How might a mystery shopper be valuable to the following organizations?
   a. JetBlue Airlines
   b. Macy's department store
   c. H&R Block

8. Use ethnographic research to evaluate the dining experience at your student center. What did you learn?

9. Do you think that tracking beacons should be outlawed? Why or why not?

10. Describe how tracking research can benefit an online retailer.

11. Do you think that virtual shopping will replace other forms of marketing research? Why or why not?

12. Divide the class into teams of five. Each team should select a different retailer (services are okay for mystery shopping). Two members of the team should prepare a list of 10 to 15 questions to be answered. A sample of questions for an Eye Care Clinic is shown below. The remaining three members of the team should become mystery shoppers with the goal of answering the questions created by the team. After the shopping is complete, the team should combine their findings and make a report to the class. *(Team Exercise)*

Sample Mystery Shopping Questions for an Eye Care Clinic

a. Was the phone answered within three rings?
b. How long did you have to wait for an appointment?
c. Were you given clear directions to the office?
d. Did you receive a new patient packet in the mail?
e. Were signs directing you to the office clear and visible?
f. Did the receptionist greet you when you entered the office?
g. How long did you wait before being taken into a room for the pre-exam?
h. Did all staff members have name tags on?
i. Was the facility clean?
j. Were your eyes dilated before you saw the doctor?
k. Were exam procedures explained clearly?
l. Were you given an opportunity to ask the doctor questions?
m. Were your questions answered promptly and respectfully?
n. Were you directed to the optical shop after your exam?
o. Were your glasses/contacts ready when promised?

WORKING THE NET

1. Go to *www.symphonyiri.com* and *www.nielsen.com* and report what types of observation research are being conducted by the two research firms.

2. Go to *www.doubleclick.com* and read its latest research findings. Make an oral presentation to your class.

3. Go to *www.mysteryshop.org* to learn more about mystery shopping.

REAL-LIFE RESEARCH • 7.1

Stovetops and Laptops

Every year On-Site Research conducts a cross-country ethnographic study called Cyber Census. Members of the research team drive an RV across 20 states to track a core group of 150 Americans and their use of and interaction with Web-based and other technology.

The interviews are designed to allow the researchers to embed themselves in the consumer's real life, from a few hours to days spent living with the study participant. Researchers also conduct a full exploration of the consumer's online life via a surf-along, which lets them experience their cyber lives.

The research shows that people are increasingly looking for a space in the home, most often the kitchen or family room, where they can interact with people and media in both physical and cyberspace. They want a highly interactive room that lets them socialize in physical space while using their hand-held devices and computers to access their virtual environments.

This trend has manifested in a number of ways: In some homes, dining rooms are rarely used for dining, computers are migrating out of the home office, and technology of all types has moved to the family kitchen.

These observations led the researchers to the acronym HIVE (highly interactive + virtual environment) and the associated term *hiving*, which is our way of characterizing this trend. People report hiving for many reasons, but the most common reason is that they don't want to be isolated from others. The home office/den filled with technology may give you the ability to communicate with others online, but it does little to connect you with the actual people in the home. Consumers report "catching grief" from spouses because they spend too much time on the computer away from the family, especially during dinner time. Parents are concerned about monitoring their children while they use the computer for homework and other activities. And parents of older children really worry about all the time their teens spend alone on the computer and hand-held devices.

Another factor driving hiving is Americans' addiction to multitasking. Multitasking in the HIVE is what the HIVE is all about. In a well-equipped HIVE, you can make dinner, talk on your phone via Bluetooth, help your kids on the computer do their homework, charge your hand-held devices, download and sync your media, check your e-mail, watch television, check your stocks, pay bills and still feel that you are a part of the social activity in the home. The laptop has become as common as the toaster oven in the kitchen. And electric cords and chargers clutter countertops, making a different kind of spaghetti.[41]

Questions

1. How might this type of research benefit GE, Viking, or Jenn-Air?
2. Should qualitative research be undertaken before any actual strategies are developed? Why?
3. What other types of research could have been used to gather this information?
4. This research was conducted in less than half of the states. Might this bias the survey findings? If so, how?

© Andrzei Podsiad/iStockphoto

CHAPTER 8

Primary Data Collection: Experimentation and Test Markets

LEARNING OBJECTIVES

→ **1.** To understand the nature of experiments.

→ **2.** To gain insight into requirements for proving causation.

→ **3.** To learn about the experimental setting.

→ **4.** To examine experimental validity.

→ **5.** To learn the limitations of experimentation in marketing research.

→ **6.** To compare types of experimental designs.

→ **7.** To gain insight into test marketing.

In this chapter, we cover issues related to the use of experiments for data collection in marketing research. Field experiments, laboratory experiments, and test markets are the major experimental approaches covered. We also present the factors you have to show to prove that one thing caused another (not easy) as well as different types of designs and sources of error in experiments.

What Is an Experiment?

Research based on experimentation is fundamentally different from research based on surveys or observation.[1] In the case of both survey and observation research, the researcher is, in essence, a passive assembler of data. The researcher asks people questions or observes what they do. In experimental research, the situation is very different: The researcher becomes an active participant in the process.

In concept, an **experiment** is straightforward. The researcher changes or manipulates one thing (called an *experimental, treatment, independent,* or *explanatory variable*) to observe the effect on something else (referred to as a *dependent variable*). In marketing experiments, the dependent variable is frequently some measure of sales, such as total sales or market share; experimental variables are typically marketing mix variables, such as price, amount or type of advertising, and changes in product features.

> ➤ **experiment**
> A research approach in which one variable is manipulated and the effect on another variable is observed.

Demonstrating Causation

Experimental research is often referred to as **causal** (not casual) **research** because it is a type of research that has the potential to demonstrate that a change in one variable *causes* some predictable change in another variable. To demonstrate causation (that A likely caused B), one must be able to show three things:

1. Concomitant variation (correlation)
2. Appropriate time order of occurrence
3. Elimination of other possible causal factors

> ➤ **causal research**
> Research designed to determine whether a change in one variable likely caused an observed change in another.

Please note that we are using the terms *causation* and *causality* in the scientific sense.[2] The scientific view of causation is quite different from the popular view, which often implies that there is a single cause of an event. For example, when someone says in everyday conversation that X is the cause of some observed change in Y, he or she generally means that X is the only cause of the observed change in Y. But the scientific view holds that X is only one of a number of possible determining conditions that caused the observed change in Y.

In addition, the everyday view of causality implies a completely deterministic relationship, while the scientific view implies a probabilistic relationship. The popular view is that if X is the cause of Y, then X must always lead to Y. The scientific view holds that X can be a cause of Y if the presence of X makes the occurrence of Y more probable or likely.

Finally, the scientific view holds that one can never definitively prove that X is a cause of Y but only infer that a relationship exists. In other words, causal relationships are always inferred and never demonstrated conclusively beyond a shadow of a doubt. Three types of evidence—concomitant variation, appropriate time order of occurrence, and elimination of other possible causal factors—are used to infer causal relationships.

Concomitant Variation

→ **concomitant variation**
The statistical relationship between two variables.

To provide evidence that a change in A caused a particular change in B, one must first show that there is **concomitant variation**, or correlation, between A and B; in other words, A and B must vary together in some predictable fashion. This might be a *positive* or an *inverse* relationship. Two variables that might be related in a positive manner are advertising and sales. They would be positively related if sales increased by some predictable amount when advertising increased by a certain amount. Two variables that might be related in an inverse manner are price and sales. They would be inversely (negatively) related if sales increased when price decreased and decreased when price increased.

However, concomitant variation by itself does not prove causation. Simply because two variables happen to vary together in some predictable fashion does not prove that one causes the other. For example, suppose you found a high degree of correlation between sales of a product in the United States and the GDP (gross domestic product) of Germany. This might be true simply because both variables happened to be increasing at a similar rate. Further examination and consideration might show that there is no true link between the two variables. To infer causation, you must be able to show correlation— but correlation alone is not proof of causation.

Appropriate Time Order of Occurrence

→ **appropriate time order of occurrence**
Change in an independent variable occurred before an observed change in the dependent variable.

The second requirement for demonstrating that a causal relationship likely exists between two variables is showing that there is an **appropriate time order of occurrence**. To demonstrate that A caused B, one must be able to show that A occurred before B occurred. For example, to demonstrate that a price change had an effect on sales, you must be able to show that the price change occurred before the change in sales was observed. However, showing that A and B vary concomitantly and that A occurred before B still does not provide evidence strong enough to permit one to conclude that A is the likely cause of an observed change in B.

Elimination of Other Possible Causal Factors

→ **elimination of other possible causal factors**
Hard to prove that something else did not cause change in B.

The most difficult thing to demonstrate in marketing experiments is that the change in B was not caused by some factor other than A. For example, suppose a company increased its advertising expenditures and observed an increase in the sales of its product. Correlation and appropriate time order of occurrence are present. But has a likely causal relationship been demonstrated? The answer is "no." It is possible that the observed change in sales is due to some factor other than the increase in advertising. For example, at the same time advertising expenditures were increased, a major competitor may have decreased advertising expenditures, or increased price, or pulled out of the market. Even if the competitive environment did not change, one or a combination of other factors may have influenced sales. For example, the economy in the area might have received a major boost for some reason that has nothing to do with the experiment. For any of these reasons, or many others, the observed increase in sales might have been caused by some factor or combination of factors other than or in addition to the increase in advertising expenditures. Much of the discussion in this chapter is related to designing experiments in order to **eliminate or adjust for the effects of other possible causal factors**.

Experimental Setting

Experiments can be conducted in a laboratory or a field setting.[3] Most experiments in the physical sciences are conducted in a laboratory setting; many marketing experiments are field experiments.

Laboratory Experiments

Laboratory experiments provide a number of important advantages.[4] The major advantage of conducting experiments in a laboratory is the ability to control extraneous causal factors—temperature, light, humidity, and so on—and focus on the effect of a change in *A* on *B*. In the lab, the researcher can effectively deal with the third element of proving causation (elimination of other possible causal factors) and focus on the first two elements (concomitant variation and appropriate time order of occurrence). This additional control strengthens the researcher's ability to infer that an observed change in the dependent variable was caused by a change in the experimental, or treatment, variable. As a result, laboratory experiments are viewed as having greater internal validity (discussed in greater detail in the next section). On the other hand, the controlled and possibly sterile environment of the laboratory may not be a good analog of the marketplace. For this reason, the findings of laboratory experiments sometimes do not hold up when transferred to the marketplace. Therefore, laboratory experiments are seen as having greater problems with external validity (see the next section). However, laboratory experiments are probably being used to a greater extent in marketing research today than in the past because of their many advantages. Laboratory experiments have an important place in marketing, as illustrated in the following Practicing Marketing Research feature.

➔ **laboratory experiments**
Experiments conducted in a controlled setting.

PRACTICING MARKETING RESEARCH

What's It Like to Be Old?[5]

Traditionally, many industries have neglected actively marketing to the 65 and over age demographic, preferring to focus on young, more culturally attractive demographics. Some institutions, however, like the Oregon Health & Science University, the Massachusetts Institute of Technology's AgeLab, and Stanford, are taking a different approach to this demographic: Design products and services for the elderly that promote wellness, autonomy, and social engagement.

Organizations like these are taking innovative approaches to the research and testing parts of their work as well. For instance, the AgeLab developed the Age Gain Now Empathy System (AGNES), a modified jumpsuit designed to help wearers better understand the basic challenges that many elderly people experience daily. Tension cords stretch from a pelvic harness to the arms, legs, and a helmet on the head, constricting limb and joint movement and cramping the neck and spine. Shoes with uneven padded soles disrupt balance. Extra

thick gloves limit manual dexterity. Yellow tinted goggles cloud vision. AgeLab uses tools like AGNES to provide insight into the wants and needs of elderly people and to test new products to see how they can be designed to better serve this market.

One of the biggest takeaways from AgeLab has been simply that elderly people don't like being marketed to as if they are elderly. Products like big-button phones that scream "You're old!" don't go over well. Through its testing programs, AgeLab's goal is to find ways of making products that appeal to a broader demographic but address specific needs of the elderly. For example, a hands-free parallel parking system, which AgeLab is testing for Ford Motor, could greatly benefit older drivers who have trouble turning their necks to look back but could also appeal to any driver who loves smart tech.

As researchers and testers strive to create products enabling health, wellness, independence, and connectivity for seniors, some organizations are even redefining concepts as basic as the traditional testing laboratory. The real-estate developer Pacific Retirement Services and the Oregon Center for Aging & Technology (Orcatech) have teamed up to create the Mirabella, a $130 million luxury high-rise retirement community in downtown Portland. Residents have been encouraged to take part in a "living laboratory" program. Wireless motion sensors track residents' mobility and send the data to Orcatech for monitoring. The monitoring system is undergoing tests itself in the "lab" that is the Mirabella, as Orcatech researchers look to find out how to effectively monitor residents' health status in real time and respond to problems like falls and social withdrawal more quickly—or even prevent them entirely.

The Mirabella also offers a real-life testing ground for other products being studied at Orcatech, like electronic pillboxes and social networking programs for residents. The original design of the building itself even underwent feedback-based changes in response to potential residents asking for space in the garage to stow their kayaks. Like most traditional testing programs, however, the Mirabella is not cheap.

The monitoring system costs $1,000 per resident to set up, and $2,600 per year for technical and research support.

Although prospects look promising right now, many of these methods have yet to prove themselves. Still, as the 65-and-older population continues to grow, one thing is for sure: Researchers must innovate both in products and in the testing methods themselves if they want to tap the potential of this market.

Questions

1. The Mirabella is being used as a kind of test market. How do you think this program affects the way products and services are test-marketed there?

2. Experiments like those discussed here are typically costly. Do you think those costs are worth it, or do you think researchers might be better off finding a cheaper method entirely?

Field Experiments

→ **field experiments**
Tests conducted outside the laboratory in an actual environment, such as a marketplace.

Field experiments are conducted outside the laboratory in an actual market environment. Test markets, discussed later in this chapter, are a frequently used type of field experiment. Field experiments solve the problem of the realism of the environment but open up a whole new set of problems. The major problem is that in the field the researcher cannot control all the spurious factors that might influence the dependent variable, such as the actions of competitors, the weather, the economy, societal trends, and the political climate. Therefore, field experiments have more problems related to internal validity, whereas lab experiments have more problems related to external validity.

Experimental Validity

Validity is defined as the degree to which an experiment actually measures what the researcher was trying to measure (see Chapter 9). The validity of a measure depends on the extent to which the measure is free from both systematic and random error. Two specific kinds of validity are relevant to experimentation: internal validity and external validity.

→ **internal validity**
The extent to which competing explanations for the experimental results observed can be ruled out.

Internal validity refers to the extent to which competing explanations for the experimental results observed can be ruled out. If the researcher can show that the experimental, or treatment, variable actually produced the differences observed in the dependent variable, then the experiment can be said to be internally valid. This kind of validity requires evidence demonstrating that variation in the dependent variable was caused by exposure to the treatment variable and not other possible causal factors.

External validity refers to the extent to which the causal relationships measured in an experiment can be generalized to outside persons, settings, and times.[6] The issue here is how representative the subjects and the setting used in the experiment are of other populations and settings to which the researcher would like to project the results. As noted earlier, field experiments offer a higher degree of external validity and a lower degree of internal validity than do laboratory experiments.

> → **external validity**
> The extent to which causal relationships measured in an experiment can be generalized to outside persons, settings, and times.

Experimental Notation

In our discussion of experiments, we will use a standard system of notation, described as follows:

▪ X is used to indicate the exposure of an individual or a group to an experimental treatment. The experimental treatment is the factor whose effects we want to measure and compare. Experimental treatments may be factors such as different prices, package designs, point-of-purchase displays, advertising approaches, or product forms.

▪ O (for observation) is used to refer to the process of taking measurements on the test units. *Test units* are individuals, groups of individuals, or entities whose response to the experimental treatments is being tested. Test units might include individual consumers, groups of consumers, retail stores, total markets, or other entities that might be the targets of a firm's marketing program.

▪ Different time periods are represented by the horizontal arrangement of the X's and O's. For example,

$$O_1 \ X \ O_2$$

would describe an experiment in which a preliminary measurement O_1 was taken of one or more test units, then one or more test units were exposed to the experimental variable X, and then a measurement O_2 of the test units was taken. The X's and O's can be arranged vertically to show simultaneous exposure and measurement of different test units. For example, the following design involves two different groups of test units:

$$X_1 \ O_1$$
$$X_2 \ O_2$$

The two groups of test units received different experimental treatments at the same time (X_1 and X_2), and then the two groups were measured simultaneously (O_1 and O_2).[7]

Extraneous Variables

In interpreting experimental results, the researcher would like to be able to conclude that the observed response is due to the effect of the experimental variable. However, many things stand in the way of the ability to reach this conclusion. In anticipation of possible problems in interpretation, the researcher needs to design the experiment so as to eliminate as many extraneous factors as possible as causes of the observed effect.

Examples of Extraneous Variables

Examples of extraneous factors or variables that pose a threat to experimental validity are history, maturation, instrument variation, selection bias, mortality, testing effects, and regression to the mean.[8]

→ **history**
The intervention, between the beginning and end of an experiment, of outside variables or events that might change the dependent variable.

History **History** refers to the intervention, between the beginning and end of the experiment, of any variable or event—other than those manipulated by the researcher (experimental variables)—that might affect the value of the dependent variable. Early tests of Prego spaghetti sauce by the Campbell Soup Company provide an example of a possible problem with extraneous variables. Campbell executives claim that Ragu, a competing brand, greatly increased its advertising levels and use of cents-off deals during their Prego tests. They believe that this increased marketing activity was designed to get shoppers to stock up on Ragu and make it impossible for Campbell to get an accurate reading of potential sales for its Prego product.

→ **maturation**
Changes in subjects occurring during the experiment that are not related to the experiment but that may affect subjects' response to the treatment factor.

Maturation **Maturation** refers to changes in subjects during the course of the experiment that are a function of time; it includes getting older, hungrier, more tired, and the like. Throughout the course of an experiment, the responses of people to a treatment variable may change because of these maturation factors and not because of the treatment variable. The likelihood that maturation will be a serious problem in a particular experiment depends on the length of the experiment. The longer the experiment runs, the more likely it is that maturation will present problems for interpreting the results.

→ **instrument variation**
Changes in measurement instruments (e.g., interviewers or observers) that might affect measurements.

Instrument Variation **Instrument variation** refers to any changes in measurement instruments that might explain differences in the measurements taken. It is a serious problem in marketing experiments where people are used as interviewers or observers to measure the dependent variable. If measurements on the same subject are taken by different interviewers or observers at different points in time, differences between measurements may reflect variations in the way the interviewing or observation was done by different interviewers or observers. On the other hand, if the same interviewer or observer is used to take measurements on the same subject over time, differences may reflect the fact that the particular observer or interviewer has become less interested and is doing a sloppier job.

→ **selection bias**
Systematic differences between the test group and the control group due to a biased selection process.

Selection Bias The threat to validity posed by **selection bias** is encountered in situations where the experimental or test group is systematically different from the population to which the researcher would like to project the experimental results or from the control group. In projecting the results to a population that is systematically different from the test group, the researcher may get results very different from those we got in the test because of differences in the makeup of the two groups. Similarly, an observed difference between a test group and an untreated control group (not exposed to the experimental variable) may be due to differences between the two groups and not to the effect of the experimental variable. Researchers can ensure equality of groups through either randomization or matching. *Randomization* involves assigning subjects to test groups and control groups at random. *Matching* involves what the name suggests—making sure that there is a one-to-one match between people or other units in the test and control groups in regard to key characteristics (for example, age). Specific matching procedures are discussed later in this chapter.

→ **mortality**
Loss of test units or subjects during the course of an experiment, which may result in nonrepresentativeness.

Mortality **Mortality** refers to the loss of test units during the course of an experiment. It is a problem because there is no easy way to know whether the lost units would have responded to the treatment variable in the same way as those units that remained throughout the entire experiment. An experimental group that was representative of the population or that matched a control group may become nonrepresentative because of the systematic loss of subjects with certain characteristics. For example, in a study of music preferences of the population, if nearly all the subjects under age 25 were lost during the course of the experiment, then the researcher would likely get a biased picture of music preferences at the end of the experiment. In this case, the results would lack external validity.

Testing Effects   **Testing effects** result from the fact that the process of experimentation may produce its own effect on the responses observed. For example, measuring attitude toward a product before exposing subjects to an ad may act as a treatment variable, influencing perception of the ad. Testing effects come in two forms:

> **testing effect**
> An effect that is a by-product of the research process itself.

- *Main testing effects* are the possible effects of earlier observations on later observations. For example, students taking the GMAT for the second time tend to do better than those taking the test for the first time, even though the students have no information about the items they actually missed on the first test. This effect also can be reactive in the sense that responses to the first administration of an attitude test have some actual effect on subjects' attitudes that is reflected in subsequent applications of the same test.

- *Interactive testing effect* is the effect of a prior measurement on a subject's response to a later measurement. For example, if subjects are asked about their awareness of advertising for various products (pre-exposure measurement) and then exposed to advertising for one or more of these products (treatment variable), postmeasurements would likely reflect the joint effect of the pre-exposure and the treatment condition.

Regression to the Mean   **Regression to the mean** refers to the observed tendency of subjects with extreme behavior to move toward the average for that behavior during the course of an experiment. Test units may exhibit extreme behavior because of chance, or they may have been specifically chosen because of their extreme behavior. The researcher might, for example, have chosen people for an experimental group because they were extremely heavy users of a particular product or service. In such situations, their tendency to move toward the average behavior may be interpreted as having been caused by the treatment variable when in fact it has nothing to do with the treatment variable.

> **regression to the mean**
> The tendency of subjects with extreme behavior to move toward the average for that behavior during the course of an experiment.

Controlling Extraneous Variables

Causal factors that threaten validity must be controlled in some manner to establish a clear picture of the effect of the manipulated variable on the dependent variable. Extraneous causal factors are ordinarily referred to as *confounding variables* because they confound the treatment condition, making it impossible to determine whether changes in the dependent variable are due solely to the treatment conditions.

Four basic approaches are used to control extraneous factors: randomization, physical control, design control, and statistical control.

Randomization is carried out by randomly assigning subjects to treatment conditions so that extraneous causal factors related to subject characteristics can reasonably be assumed to be represented equally in each treatment condition, thus canceling out extraneous effects.

> **randomization**
> Random assignment of subjects to treatment conditions to ensure equal representation of subject characteristics.

Physical control of extraneous causal factors may involve somehow holding constant the value or level of the extraneous variable throughout the experiment. Another approach to physical control is matching respondents in regard to important personal characteristics (for example, age, income, lifestyle) before assigning them to different treatment conditions. The goal is to make sure there are no important differences between characteristics of respondents in the test and control groups.

> **physical control**
> Holding constant the value or level of extraneous variables throughout the course of an experiment.

Design control is the control of extraneous factors by means of specific types of experimental designs developed for this purpose. Such designs are discussed later in this chapter.

> **design control**
> Use of the experimental design to control extraneous causal factors.

PRACTICING MARKETING RESEARCH

Data Use: The Insidious Top-box and Its Effects on Measuring Line Share[9]

Consumers have limited budgets and consumption capacities, so when companies want to make changes to a product line, managers want to know how those changes would affect the choices people make within the category. To find out, marketers often use the "top-box" measurement tool of purchase intent. A survey using top-box presents a given product that respondents will rate on a scale typically ranging from "definitely will buy" to "definitely will not buy." A clear response would seem to provide the information a manager would need.

Even though the response from the survey participant is clear, the answer for the company is not. One potential line extension may rate higher in a top-box scenario, but the top-box comparison offers no indication of whether the higher-rated option will steal share from competitors or pull from other products in the line. Top-box is also known for producing inflated results. Again, this is because it measures desire, not actual choice. It often fails to make distinctions within a broad spectrum of desire, and, as shown in Figure 1, is less able to produce results that clearly demonstrate perceived differences among various product concepts.

Marketers would benefit from using alternative methods, such as conjoint analyses and discrete choice, that measure choice, not simply model it. Researchers should create equivalent test groups from the sample, establishing a control group using a full set of relevant competing products, including those they currently offer, and systematically introduce the test product altering a single different variable for each other test group. This is essentially an application of the scientific method. This approach allows experimenters to manipulate any variable within the test sample or element within the marketing mix. Experimenters can even compare different strategies, such as a product adaptation versus a line extension.

For the marketer who is concerned with growing business and acquiring relevant information on product interaction and line share, rethinking the tools used to gather this data is a worthwhile exercise.

Questions

1. Do you think top-box measurement would be more accurate if only one option were presented rather than multiple options? Why or why not?

2. Do you think any marketing research method can accurately predict action rather than simply assess desire?

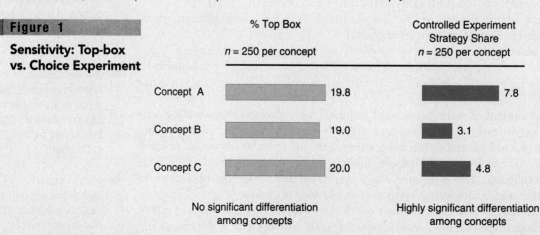

Figure 1

Sensitivity: Top-box vs. Choice Experiment

	% Top Box n = 250 per concept	Controlled Experiment Strategy Share n = 250 per concept
Concept A	19.8	7.8
Concept B	19.0	3.1
Concept C	20.0	4.8
	No significant differentiation among concepts	Highly significant differentiation among concepts

Finally, **statistical control** can be used to account for extraneous causal factors if these factors can be identified and measured throughout the course of the experiment. Procedures such as analysis of covariance can adjust for the effects of a confounded variable on the dependent variable by statistically adjusting the value of the dependent variable for each treatment condition.

> **statistical control**
> Adjusting for the effects of confounded variables by statistically adjusting the value of the dependent variable for each treatment condition.

Experimental Design, Treatment, and Effects

In an **experimental design**, the researcher has control over and manipulates one or more independent variables. In the experiments we discuss, typically only one independent variable is manipulated. Nonexperimental designs, which involve no manipulation, are often referred to as ex post facto (after the fact) research—an effect is observed, and then some attempt is made to attribute this effect to some causal factor.

> **experimental design**
> A test in which the researcher has control over and manipulates one or more independent variables.

An experimental design includes four factors:

1. The *treatment,* or experimental, *variable* (independent variable) that is manipulated
2. The *subjects* who participate in the experiment
3. A *dependent variable* that is measured
4. Some *plan or procedure* for dealing with extraneous causal factors

The **treatment variable** is the independent variable that is manipulated. *Manipulation* refers to a process in which the researcher sets the levels of the independent variable to test a particular causal relationship. To test the relationship between price (independent variable) and sales of a product (dependent variable), a researcher might expose subjects to three different levels of price and record the level of purchases at each price level. As the variable that is manipulated, price is the single treatment variable, with three treatment conditions or levels.

> **treatment variable**
> An independent variable that is manipulated in an experiment.

An experiment may include a test, or treatment, group, and a control group. A *control group* is a group in which the independent variable is not changed during the course of the experiment. A *test group* is a group that is exposed to manipulation (change) of the independent variable.

The term **experimental effect** refers to the effect of the treatment variable on the dependent variable. The goal is to determine the effect of each treatment condition (level of treatment variable) on the dependent variable. For example, suppose that three different markets are selected to test three different prices, or treatment conditions. Each price is tested in each market for 3 months. In Market 1, a price 2 percent lower than existing prices for the product is tested; in Market 2, a price 4 percent lower is tested; and in Market 3, a price 6 percent lower is tested. At the end of the 3-month test, sales in Market 1 are observed to have increased by less than 1 percent over sales for the preceding 3-month period. In Market 2, sales increased by 3 percent; and in Market 3, sales increased by 5 percent. The change in sales observed in each market is the experimental effect.

> **experimental effect**
> The effect of the treatment variable on the dependent variable.

Limitations of Experimental Research

As the preceding discussion shows, experiments are an extremely powerful form of research—the only type of research that can truly explore the existence and nature of causal relationships between variables of interest. Given these obvious advantages over other research designs for primary data collection, you might ask why experimental research is not used more often. There are many reasons, including the cost of experiments, the issue of security, and problems associated with implementing experiments.

The High Cost of Experiments

To some degree, when making comparisons of the costs of experiments with the costs of surveys or observation-based research, we are comparing apples to oranges. Experiments can be very costly in both money and time. In many cases, managers may anticipate that the costs of doing an experiment would exceed the value of the information gained. Consider, for example, the costs of testing three alternative advertising campaigns in three different geographic areas. Three different campaigns must be produced; airtime must be purchased in all three markets; the timing in all three markets must be carefully coordinated; some system must be put into place to measure sales before, during, and after the test campaigns have run; measurements of other extraneous variables must be made; extensive analysis of the results must be performed; and a variety of other tasks must be completed in order to execute the experiment. All of this will cost a bare minimum of $1 million for a low-profile product and as much as tens of millions for a high-profile brand.

Security Issues

Conducting a field experiment in a test market involves exposing a marketing plan or some key element of a marketing plan in the actual marketplace. Undoubtedly, competitors will find out what is being considered well in advance of full-scale market introduction. This advance notice gives competitors an opportunity to decide whether and how to respond. In any case, the element of surprise is lost. In some instances, competitors have actually "stolen" concepts that were being tested in the marketplace and gone into national distribution before the company testing the product or strategy element completed the test marketing.

Implementation Problems

Problems that may hamper the implementation of an experiment include difficulty gaining cooperation within the organization, contamination problems, differences between test markets and the total population, and the lack of an appropriate group of people or geographic area for a control group.

It can be extremely difficult to obtain cooperation within the organization to execute certain types of experiments. For example, a regional marketing manager might be very reluctant to permit her market area to be used as a test market for a reduced level of advertising or a higher price. Quite naturally, her concern would be that the experiment might lower sales for the area.

Contamination occurs when buyers from outside the test area come into the area to purchase the product being tested, thereby distorting the results of the experiment. Outside buyers might live on the fringes of the test market area and receive TV advertisements—intended only for those in the test area—that offer a lower price, a special rebate, or some other incentive to buy a product. Their purchases will indicate that the particular sales-stimulating factor being tested is more effective than actually is the case.

In some cases, test markets may be so different, and the behavior of consumers in those markets so different, that a relatively small experimental effect is difficult to detect. This problem can be dealt with by careful matching of test markets and other similar strategies designed to ensure a high degree of equivalency of test units.

Finally, in some situations, no appropriate geographic area or group of people may be available to serve as a control group. This may be the case in a test of industrial products, whose very small number of purchasers are concentrated geographically. An attempt

→ **contamination**
Inclusion in a test of a group of respondents who are not normally there; for example, buyers from outside the test market who see an advertisement intended only for those in the test area and enter the area to purchase the product being tested.

to test a new product among a subset of such purchasers would almost certainly be doomed to failure.

Selected Experimental Designs

This section presents examples of pre-experimental, true experimental, and quasi-experimental designs.[10] In outlining these experimental designs, we will use the system of notation introduced earlier.

Pre-Experimental Designs

Pre-experimental designs are research designs that do not include basic elements required in a true experimental design. Because of their simplicity, they may make sense in certain situations, but they may be difficult to interpret. Studies using **pre-experimental designs** generally are difficult to interpret because such designs offer little or no control over the influence of extraneous factors. As a result, these studies often are not much better than descriptive studies when it comes to making causal inferences. With these designs, the researcher has little control over aspects of exposure to the treatment variable (such as to whom and when) and measurements. However, these designs frequently are used in commercial test marketing because they are simple and inexpensive. They are useful for suggesting new hypotheses but do not offer strong tests of existing hypotheses. The reasons for this will be clear after you review the discussion of pre-experimental designs that follows.

> **pre-experimental designs**
> Designs that offer little or no control over extraneous factors.

One-Shot Case Study Design The **one-shot case study design** involves exposing test units (people or test markets) to the treatment variable for some period of time and then taking a measurement of the dependent variable. Using standard notation, the design is shown as follows:

> **one-shot case study design**
> A pre-experimental design with no pretest observations, no control group, and an after measurement only.

$$X\ O_1$$

There are two basic weaknesses in this design. No pretest observations are made of the test units that will receive the treatment, and no control group of test units that did not receive the treatment is observed. As a result of these deficiencies, the design does not deal with the effects of any of the extraneous variables discussed previously. Therefore, the design lacks internal validity and, most likely, external validity as well. This design is useful for suggesting causal hypotheses but does not provide a strong test of such hypotheses. Many test markets for new products (not previously on the market) are based on this design because it is simpler and less costly.

One-Group Pretest–Posttest Design The **one-group pretest–posttest design** is the design employed most frequently for testing changes in established products or marketing strategies. The fact that the product was on the market before the change provides the basis for the pretest measurement (O_1). The design is shown symbolically as follows:

> **one-group pretest–posttest design**
> A pre-experimental design with pre- and postmeasurements but no control group.

$$O_1\ X\ O_2$$

Pretest observations are made of a single group of subjects or a single test unit (O_1) that then receives the treatment. Finally, a posttest observation is made (O_2). The treatment effect is estimated by $O_2 - O_1$.

History is a threat to the internal validity of this design because an observed change in the dependent variable might be caused by an event that took place outside the experiment between the pretest and posttest measurements. In laboratory experiments, this threat can be controlled by insulating respondents from outside influences. Unfortunately, this type of control is impossible in field experiments.

Maturation is another threat to this type of design. An observed effect might be caused by the fact that subjects have grown older, smarter, more experienced, or the like between the pretest and the posttest.

This design has only one pretest observation. As a result, the researcher knows nothing of the pretest trend in the dependent variable. The posttest score may be higher because of an increasing trend of the dependent variable in a situation where this effect is not the treatment of interest.

True Experimental Designs

> **true experimental design**
> Research using an experimental group and a control group, to which test units are randomly assigned.

In a **true experimental design**, the experimenter randomly assigns treatments to randomly selected test units. In our notation system, the random assignment of test units to treatments is denoted by (R). Randomization is an important mechanism that makes the results of true experimental designs more valid than the results of pre-experimental designs. True experimental designs are superior because randomization takes care of many extraneous variables. The principal reason for choosing randomized experiments over other types of research designs is that they clarify causal inference.[11] Two true experimental designs are discussed in this section: before and after with control group design and after-only with control group design.

> **before and after with control group design**
> A true experimental design that involves random assignment of subjects or test units to experimental and control groups and pre- and postmeasurements of both groups.

Before and after with Control Group Design
The **before and after with control group design** can be presented symbolically as follows:

$$\text{Experimental Group:} \quad (R) \quad O_1 \quad X \quad O_2$$
$$\text{Control Group:} \quad (R) \quad O_3 \quad \quad O_4$$

Because the test units in this design are randomly assigned to the experimental and control groups, the two groups can be considered equivalent. Therefore, they are likely to be subject to the same extraneous causal factors, except for the treatment of interest in the experimental group. For this reason, the difference between the pre- and postmeasurements of the control group $(O_4 - O_3)$ should provide a good estimate of the effect of all the extraneous influences experienced by each group. The true impact of the treatment variable X can be known only when the extraneous influences are removed from the difference between the pre- and postmeasurements of the experimental group. Thus, the true impact of X is estimated by $(O_2 - O_1) - (O_4 - O_3)$. This design generally controls for all but two major threats to validity: mortality and history.

Mortality is a problem if units drop out during the study and these units differ systematically from the ones that remain. This results in a selection bias because the experimental and control groups are composed of different subjects at the posttest than at the pretest. History will be a problem in those situations where factors other than the treatment variable affect the experimental group but not the control group, or vice versa. Examples of this design and the after-only with control group design are provided in Exhibit 8.1.

> **after-only with control group design**
> A true experimental design that involves random assignment of subjects or test units to experimental and control groups, but no premeasurement of the dependent variable.

After-Only with Control Group Design
The **after-only with control group design** differs from the static-group comparison design (the pre-experimental design with nonequivalent groups) in regard to the assignment of the test units. In the static-group comparison design, test units are not randomly assigned to treatment groups. As a result, it is possible for the groups to differ in regard to the dependent variable before

---

EXHIBIT 8.1 **Examples of True Experimental Designs**

Situation: California Tan wants to measure the sales effect of a point-of-purchase display. The firm is considering two true experimental designs.

After-Only with Control Group Design	Before and After with Control Group Design

After-Only with Control Group Design

Basic design:

Experimental Group: (R) X O_1
Control Group: (R) O_2

Sample: Random sample of stores that sell their products. Stores are randomly assigned to test and control groups. Groups can be considered equivalent.

Treatment (X): Placing the point-of-purchase display in stores in the experimental group for 1 month.

Measurements (O_1, O_2): Actual sales of company's brand during the period that the point-of-purchase displays are in test stores.

Comments:

Because of random assignment of stores to groups, the test group and control group can be considered equivalent.

Measure of the treatment effect of X is $O_1 - O_2$. If $O_1 = 125,000$ units and $O_2 = 113,000$ units, then treatment effect = 12,000 units.

Before and After with Control Group Design

Basic design:

Experimental Group: (R) O_1 X O_2
Control Group: (R) O_3 O_4

Sample: Same as after-only design.

Treatment (X): Same as after-only design.

Measurements $(O_1$ to $O_4)$:

O_1 and O_2 are pre- and postmeasurements for the experimental group;

O_3 and O_4 are the same for the control group.

Results:

$O_1 = 113,000$ units
$O_2 = 125,000$ units
$O_3 = 111,000$ units
$O_4 = 118,000$ units

Comments:

Random assignment to groups means that the groups can be considered equivalent.

Because groups are equivalent, it is reasonable to assume that they will be equally affected by the same extraneous factors.

The difference between pre- and postmeasurements for the control group $(O_4 - O_3)$ provides a good estimate of the effects of all extraneous factors on both groups. Based on these results, $O_4 - O_3 = 7,000$ units. The estimated treatment effect is $(O_2 - O_1) - (O_4 - O_3) = (125,000 - 113,000) - (118,000 - 111,000) = 5,000$ units.

---

presentation of the treatment. The after-only with control group design deals with this shortcoming; it can be shown symbolically as follows:

Experimental Group: (R) X O_1
Control Group: (R) O_2

Notice that the test units are randomly (R) assigned to experimental and control groups. This random assignment should produce experimental and control groups that are approximately equal in regard to the dependent variable before presentation of the treatment to the experimental group. It can reasonably be assumed that test unit mortality (one of the threats to internal validity) will affect each group in the same way.

Considering this design in the context of the sun tan lotion example described in Exhibit 8.1 we can see a number of problems. Events other than the treatment variable may have occurred during the experimental period in one or a few stores in the experimental group. If a particular store in the experimental group ran a sale on certain other products and, as a result, had a larger than average number of customers in the store, sun tan lotion sales might have increased because of the heavier traffic. Events such as these, which are store-specific (history), may distort the overall treatment effect. Also, there is a possibility that a few stores may drop out during the experiment (mortality threat), resulting in selection bias because the stores in the experimental group will be different at the posttest.

Quasi-Experiments

When designing a true experiment, the researcher often must create artificial environments to control independent and extraneous variables. Because of this artificiality, questions are raised about the external validity of the experimental findings. Quasi-experimental designs have been developed to deal with this problem. They generally are more feasible in field settings than are true experiments.

In **quasi-experiments**, the researcher lacks complete control over the scheduling of treatments or must assign respondents to treatments in a *nonrandom* fashion. These designs frequently are used in marketing research studies because cost and field constraints often do not permit the researcher to exert direct control over the scheduling of treatments and the randomization of respondents. Examples of quasi-experiments are interrupted time-series designs and multiple time-series designs.

> **quasi-experiments**
> Studies in which the researchers lack complete control over the scheduling of treatments or must assign respondents to treatments in a nonrandom manner.

> **interrupted time-series design**
> Research in which repeated measurement of an effect "interrupts" previous data patterns.

Interrupted Time-Series Designs **Interrupted time-series designs** involve repeated measurement of an effect both before and after a treatment is introduced that "interrupts" previous data patterns. Interrupted time-series experimental designs can be shown symbolically as follows:

$$O_1 \quad O_2 \quad O_3 \quad O_4 \quad X \quad O_5 \quad O_6 \quad O_7 \quad O_8$$

A common example of this type of design in marketing research involves the use of consumer purchase panels. A researcher might use such a panel to make periodic measurements of consumer purchase activity (the O's), introducing a new promotional campaign (the X) and examining the panel data for an effect. The researcher has control over the timing of the promotional campaign but cannot be sure when the panel members were exposed to the campaign or whether they were exposed at all.

This design is very similar to the one-group pretest–posttest design:

$$O_1 \quad X \quad O_2$$

However, time-series experimental designs have greater interpretability than the one-group pretest–posttest design because the many measurements allow more understanding of extraneous variables. If, for example, sales of a product were on the rise and a new promotional campaign were introduced, the true effect of this campaign could not be estimated if a pretest–posttest design were used. However, the rising trend in sales would be obvious if a number of pretest and posttest observations had been made. Time-series designs help determine the underlying trend of the dependent variable and provide better interpretability in regard to the treatment effect.

The interrupted time-series design has two fundamental weaknesses. The primary weakness is the experimenter's inability to control history. Although maintaining a careful log of all possibly relevant external happenings can reduce this problem, the researcher has no way of determining the appropriate number and timing of pretest and posttest observations.

The other weakness of this design comes from the possibility of interactive effects of testing and evaluation apprehension resulting from the repeated measurements taken on test units. For example, panel members may become "expert" shoppers or simply become more conscious of their shopping habits. Under these circumstances, it may be inappropriate to make generalizations to other populations.

> **multiple time-series design**
> An interrupted time-series design with a control group.

Multiple Time-Series Designs If a control group can be added to an interrupted time-series design, then researchers can be more certain in their interpretation of the treatment effect. This design, called the **multiple time-series design**, can be shown symbolically as follows:

Experimental Group:	O_1	O_2	O_3	O_4	O_5	O_6
Control Group:	O_1	O_2	O_3	O_4	O_5	O_6

The researcher must take care in selecting the control group. For example, if an advertiser were testing a new advertising campaign in a test city, that city would constitute the experimental group and another city that was not exposed to the new campaign would be chosen as the control group. It is important that the test and control cities be roughly equivalent in regard to characteristics related to the sale of the product (for example, competitive brands available).

Test Markets

The development of products and services goes through a sequence of rather predictable steps, beginning with idea generation, screening of ideas, concept testing, business analysis, prototype development, test marketing, and commercialization. Probably the least predictable of the development steps is test marketing. Marketers may or may not rest market a product or service depending on its expected rate of diffusion, the degree to which it is different from existing competitive offerings, and a host of other factors. It is a crucial step since it represents the last step before the company's offering is commercialized.

Test marketing is a common form of experimentation used by marketing researchers. The term **test market** is used rather loosely to refer to any research that involves testing a new product or change in an existing marketing strategy (for example, product, price, place promotion) in a single market, group of markets, or region of the country through the use of experimental or quasi-experimental designs.[12]

> **test market**
> Real-world testing of a new product or some element of the marketing mix using an experimental or quasi-experimental design.

New product introductions play a key role in a firm's financial success or failure. The conventional wisdom in the corporate world is that new products will have to be more profitable in the future than they were in the past because of higher levels of competition and a faster pace of change. Estimates of new-product failure rates vary all over the place and range to more than 90 percent.

As you probably already recognize, test market studies have the goal of helping marketing managers make better decisions about new products and additions or changes to existing products or marketing strategies. A test market study does this by providing a real-world test for evaluating products and marketing programs. Marketing managers use test markets to evaluate proposed national programs with many separate elements on a smaller, less costly scale. The basic idea is to determine whether the estimated profits from rolling the product out on a national basis justify the potential risks. Test market studies are designed to provide information in regard to the following issues:

- Estimates of market share and volume.
- The effects that the new product will have on sales of similar products (if any) already marketed by the company. This is referred to as the *cannibalization rate*.
- Characteristics of consumers who buy the product. Demographic data will almost surely be collected, and lifestyle, psychographic, and other types of classification data may also be collected. This information is useful in helping the firm refine the marketing strategy for the product. For example, knowing the demographic characteristics of likely purchasers will help in developing a media plan that will effectively and efficiently reach target customers. Knowing the psychographic and lifestyle characteristics of target customers will provide valuable insights into how to position the product and the types of promotional messages that will appeal to them.
- The behavior of competitors during the test. This may provide some indication of what competitors will do if the product is introduced nationally.

Types of Test Markets

The vast majority of test markets can be categorized into four types—traditional, scanner or electronic, controlled, and simulated.[13] The *traditional or standard test market*

© Courtney Keating/iStockphoto

Lifestyle data are often collected to find out about the characteristics of possible consumers. This information helps a firm refine the marketing strategy for its product. What might lifestyle data reveal about consumers who would purchase this iPhone?

involves testing the product and other elements of the marketing mix through a firm's regular channels of distribution. Traditional test markets take a relatively long time (6 months or more), are costly, and immediately tip one's hand to the competition. Some have argued that the traditional test market provides the best read on how a product and the associated marketing mix will actually do if introduced because it provides the best analog of the real marketplace. However, some of the other options, discussed in this section, may provide very good estimates at a fraction of the cost, more quickly and without giving the competition advance warning regarding what a company is planning to do.

Scanner or electronic test markets are markets where scanner panel research firms have panels of consumers who carry scannable cards for use in buying particular products, especially those sold through grocery stores. These panels permit us to analyze the characteristics of those consumers who buy and those who don't buy the test products. Purchase/nonpurchase by individual panel participants can be related to their detailed demographic data, past purchase history, and, in some cases, media viewing habits. Firms offering scanner panels include ACNielsen and Information Resources. This approach offers speed, lower cost, and some degree of security regarding the marketing strategy or changes in strategy we are considering. The major criticism of this approach to test marketing relates to what some argue is its unrepresentative sampling: Those who agree to participate in these panels may not be representative of the broader populations of consumers in these and other markets.

Controlled test markets are managed by research suppliers who ensure that the product is distributed through the agreed upon types and numbers of distributors. Research suppliers who offer controlled test markets, such as Nielsen, pay distributors to provide the required amount of shelf space for test products. Research suppliers carefully monitor sales of the product in these controlled test markets. They enable companies to get their products into test markets more quickly, often supply more realistic levels of distribution, and provide better monitoring of product movement.

STMs (simulated test markets) are just what the name implies—simulations of the types of test markets noted above. They can normally be conducted more quickly than the other two approaches, at a lower cost, and produce results that are, in most cases, highly predictive of what will actually happen. In these simulated test markets, a more limited amount of information is used in conjunction with mathematical models that include estimates of the effects of different marketing variables that can be adjusted to fit the situation. A number of different companies, including Nielsen (Bases), Harris Interactive (Litmus), and Synovate (MarkeTest), offer these services and each one has special features. However, they all share the following elements:

- A sample of consumers is selected based on the expected or known characteristics of the target consumer for the test product.
- Consumers sampled are recruited to come to a central location testing facility to view commercials for the test product and competitive products.
- Consumers are then given the opportunity to purchase the test product in the actual marketplace or in a simulated store environment.
- Purchasers are contacted after they have had time to use the product. They are asked how likely they are to repurchase and for their evaluations of the product.
- The above information is used with the proprietary model of the STM company to generate estimates of sales volume, market share, and other key market metrics.[14]

Costs of Test Marketing

Test marketing is expensive. A simple two-market test can cost a bare minimum of $1 million and probably much more. A long-running, more complex test can cost in the tens of millions of dollars. These estimates refer only to direct costs, which may include the following:

- Production of commercials
- Payments to an advertising agency for services
- Media time, charged at a higher rate because of low volume
- Syndicated research information
- Customized research information and associated data analysis
- Point-of-purchase materials
- Coupons and sampling
- Higher trade allowances to obtain distribution[15]

Many *indirect costs* are also associated with test marketing, including the following:

- Cost of management time spent on the test market
- Diversion of sales activity from existing products
- Possible negative impact of a test market failure on other products with the same family brand
- Possible negative trade reactions to products if the firm develops a reputation for not doing well
- Cost of letting competitors know what the firm is doing, thereby allowing them to develop a better strategy or beat the firm to the national market[16]

Test markets are expensive, and, as a result, they should be used only as the last step in a research process that has shown the new product or strategy has potential. In some situations, it may be cheaper to go ahead and launch the product, even if it fails.

The Decision to Conduct Test Marketing

From the preceding discussion, you can see that test markets offer at least two important benefits to the firm conducting the test.[17]

- First and foremost, the test market provides a vehicle by which the firm can obtain a good estimate of a product's sales potential under realistic market conditions. A researcher can develop estimates of the product's national market share on the basis of these test results and use this figure to develop estimates of future financial performance for the product.

- Second, the test should identify weaknesses of the product and the proposed marketing strategy for the product and give management an opportunity to correct any weaknesses. It is much easier and less expensive to correct these problems at the test market stage than after the product has gone into national distribution.

These benefits must be weighed against a number of costs and other negatives associated with test markets.[18] The financial costs of test markets are not insignificant. And test markets give competitors an early indication of what the firm is planning to do. They thus share the opportunity to make adjustments in their marketing strategy; or, if the idea is simple and not legally protected, they may be able to copy the idea and move into national distribution faster than the original firm can.

Four major factors should be taken into account in determining whether to conduct a test market:

1. Weigh the cost and risk of failure against the probability of success and associated profits. If estimated costs are high and you are uncertain about the likelihood of success, then you should lean toward doing a test market. On the other hand, if both expected costs and the risk of product failure are low, then an immediate national rollout without a test market may be the appropriate strategy.

2. Consider the likelihood and speed with which competitors can copy your product and introduce it on a national basis. If the product can be easily copied, then it may be appropriate to introduce the product without a test market.

3. Consider the investment required to produce the product for the test market versus the investment required to produce the product in the quantities necessary for a national rollout. In cases where the difference in investment required is very small, it may make sense to introduce the product nationally without a test market. However, in cases where a very large difference exists between the investment required to produce the product for test market and that required for a national rollout, conducting a test market before making a decision to introduce the product nationally makes good sense.

4. Consider how much damage an unsuccessful new product launch would inflict on the firm's reputation. Failure may hurt the firm's reputation with other members of the channel of distribution (retailers) and impede the firm's ability to gain their cooperation in future product launches.

Steps in a Test Market Study

Once the decision has been made to conduct test marketing, a number of steps must be carried out if we are to achieve a satisfactory result.

Step One: Define the Objective As always with these kinds of lists, the first step in the process is to define the objectives of the test. Typical test market objectives include the following:

- Develop share and volume estimates.
- Determine the characteristics of people who are purchasing the product.
- Determine the frequency and purpose of purchase.
- Determine where (retail outlets) purchases are made.
- Measure the effect of sales of the new product on sales of similar existing products in the line.

Step Two: Select a Basic Approach After specifying the objectives of the test market exercise, the next step is to decide on the appropriate type of test market, given the stated objectives.

Earlier in the chapter, we discussed the characteristics, advantages, and disadvantages of four types of test markets:

- Traditional or standard test market
- Scanner or electronic test market
- Controlled test market
- STM

The decision regarding which type of test market to use in a given situation depends on how much time you have, how much budget you have, and how important it is to keep the competition in the dark about what you are planning to do.

Step Three: Develop Detailed Test Procedures   After the objectives and a basic approach for the test have been developed, the researcher must develop a detailed plan for conducting the test. Manufacturing and distribution decisions must be made to ensure that adequate product is available and that it is available in most stores of the type that sell that particular product class. In addition, the detailed marketing plan to be used for the test must be specified. The basic positioning approach must be selected, the actual commercials must be developed, a pricing strategy must be chosen, a media plan must be developed, and various promotional activities must be specified.

Step Four: Select Test Markets   The selection of markets for the test is an important decision. A number of factors must be taken into account in making this decision.
    First, there are the overall standards:[19]

- There should be a minimum of two test markets, in addition to a control market, for an existing national brand or a minimum of three markets for testing a new brand.

- The markets selected should be geographically dispersed; if the brand is a regional brand, the markets should cover several dispersed markets within that region.

- Markets should be demographically representative of the United States, unless, for instance, a pronounced ethnic skew is desirable for a specific brand.

- Depending on the product purchase cycle, the test should be run for at least 6 months, up to 12 months, before the results can be considered reliably projectable. If the product is purchased infrequently, it is advisable to run the test for even longer than a year.

- The market must have a variety of media outlets, including at least four television stations, cable penetration no more than 10 percent above or below the U.S. average, at least four radio stations, a dominant local newspaper with daily and Sunday editions, a Sunday supplement with a syndicated edition, or a local supplement of similar quality.

© Jeremy Edwards/iStockphoto

© Jonathan Larsen/iStockphoto

Selecting markets for a test is an important decision. Significant regional differences should be considered in choosing cities as test markets. To find some readily apparent regional differences between Seattle and Miami, visit *www.ci.seattle.wa.us* and *www.miami.com*.

■ There should be a dominant newspaper in the market or a dominant newspaper in each city the market encompasses.

■ The market should be as reflective as possible of the U.S. population or regional population if that is more appropriate for the particular test.

Step Five: Execute the Plan Once the plan is in place, the researcher can begin execution. At this point, a key decision has to be made: how long should the test run? The average test runs for 6 to 12 months. However, shorter and longer tests are not uncommon. The test must run long enough for an adequate number of repeat purchase cycles to be observed in order to provide a measure of the "staying power" of a new product or marketing program. The shorter the average period is, the shorter the test needs to be. Cigarettes, soft drinks, and packaged goods are purchased every few days, whereas such products as shaving cream and toothpaste are purchased only every few months. The latter products would require a longer test. Whatever the product type, the test must be continued until the repeat purchase rate stabilizes. The percentage of people making repeat purchases tends to drop for some period of time before reaching a relatively constant level. Repeat purchase rate is critical to the process of estimating ultimate sales of the product. If the test is ended too soon, sales will be overestimated.

Two other considerations in determining the length of the test relate to the expected speed of competitor reaction and the costs of running the test. If there is reason to expect that competitors will react quickly to the test marketing (introduce their own versions of the new product), then the test should be as short as possible. Minimizing the length of the test reduces the amount of time competitors have to react. Finally, the value of additional information to be gained from the test must be balanced against the cost of continuing to run the test. At some point, the value of additional information will be outweighed by its cost.

General Mills used the "rolling rollout" when it introduced MultiGrain Cheerios to the public. Visit *www.generalmills.com* to find out what new products the company may be introducing.

Justin Sullivan/Getty Images, Inc.

PRACTICING MARKETING RESEARCH

Quick Scans of Product-Specific Test Markets

Some locations seem to specialize in favorable conditions for selected test market trials, such as for high-end beer, premium vodkas, or Brazilian steakhouses.

Miller Brewing Company of Milwaukee, Wisconsin, decided to test market three kinds of low-calorie, craft-style light beers in only four cities starting in 2008: Minneapolis, Minnesota; Charlotte, North Carolina; San Diego, California; and Baltimore, Maryland. Their goal was to establish a new category for light craft-style beers and to capitalize on three noticeable trends in the beer industry: the shift toward lighter beers (fewer calories and carbohydrates), more variety, and the so-called premiumization—high-end, quality-perceived offerings. It's a solid idea because craft beer sales for 2006 were up 17.8 percent, and those four cities have the right combination of demographics to warrant the test market.[20]

Fuller's, a London brewery founded in 1711, selected Denver, Colorado, as the premium United States locale to test market its high-end London Pride beer. Why Denver? The area is home to a hefty quantity of beer drinkers who prefer the high-end brews and presumably won't mind spending $8 for a London Pride six-pack. People there, research has found, are "friendly" to premium or craft-style beers. Even better, craft beer commands a 10 percent market share in Colorado, putting it third in the nation. Fuller's marketing approach included radio ads that trolled for the golf and outdoors-focused types who are more the "microbrew set," the company said.[21] Anheuser-Busch is test-running its Purus vodka, distilled in Italy and fetching $35 a bottle retail, in Boston, New York, Washington, and Annapolis. Why there? The company wants to attract the "modern luxury connoisseur" to their organic wheat-based Purus, and they want to test-position it in those cities' most exclusive lounges and restaurants as well as in a handful of specialty groceries and liquor stores. Again, there's evidence of sober thinking behind the approach: U.S. sales of upper-end or ultra-premium vodkas more than doubled between 2003 and 2006. Typical consumers? Young drinkers, aged 21 to 30, who care more about image than price.[22]

What U.S. city did International Restaurant Concepts of Lakewood, Colorado, select to test market its Tucanos Brazilian Grill steakhouse? Provo, Utah. At first glance, Provo's demographics would seem against it: Of its 100,000 residents, 87 percent are white and only 10 percent Hispanic, so where's the market for Tucanos's *churrascaria*? It turns out that because Provo is the home of Brigham Young University and runs a missionary training center for the Church of the Latter-Day Saints, many of the thousands of Mormon students sent out in the field have been posted to Brazil. In addition, the university population comprises many international students—all of which generates an ethnically diverse and language-rich community and good test market.[23]

Questions

1. What characteristics do the cities of Minneapolis, Charlotte, San Diego, and Baltimore possess that make them good markets for introducing premium-level beers?

2. How would you tailor a test market experimentation for Brazilian cuisine in a Mormon-saturated region whose members, nonetheless, are well-traveled and versed in Brazilian foods?

Step Six: Analyze the Test Results   The data produced by an experiment should be evaluated throughout the test period. However, after completion of the experiment, a more careful and thorough evaluation of the data must be performed. This analysis focuses on four areas:

■   *Purchase data.* The purchase data are often the most important data produced by an experiment. The levels of initial purchase (trial) throughout the course of the experiment provide an indication of how well the advertising and promotion program worked. The repeat rate (percentage of initial triers who made second and subsequent purchases) provides an indication of how well the product met the expectations created through advertising and promotion. Of course, the trial and repeat purchase results provide the basis for estimating sales and market share if the product was distributed nationally.

■   *Awareness data.* How effective were the media expenditures and media plan in creating awareness of the product? Do consumers know how much the product costs? Do they know its key features?

■   *Competitive response.* Ideally, the responses of competitors should be monitored during the period of the test market. For example, competitors may try to distort test results by offering special promotions, price deals, and quantity discounts. Their actions may provide some indication of what they will do if the product moves into national distribution and some basis for estimating the effect of these actions on their part.

■   *Source of sales.* If the product is a new entry in an existing product category, it is important to determine where sales are coming from. In other words, which brands did the people who purchased the test product previously purchase? This information provides a true indication of real competitors. If the firm has an existing brand in the market, it also indicates to what extent the new product will take business from existing brands and from the competition.

Based on the evaluation, a decision will be made to improve the marketing program or the product, drop the product, or move the product into national or regional distribution.

Other Types of Product Tests

In addition to traditional test marketing and STMs, there are other means by which companies can gauge a product's potential. One alternative is a *rolling rollout*, which usually follows a pretest. A product is launched in a certain region rather than in one or two cities. Within a matter of days, scanner data can provide information on how the product is doing. The product can then be launched in additional regions; ads and promotions can be adjusted along the way to a national introduction. General Mills has used this approach for products such as MultiGrain Cheerios.

Another alternative is to try a product out in a foreign market before rolling it out globally. Specifically, one or a few countries can serve as a test market for a continent or even the world. This *lead country strategy* has been used by Colgate-Palmolive Company. In 1991, the company launched Palmolive Optims shampoo and conditioner in the Philippines, Australia, Mexico, and Hong Kong. Later, the products were rolled out in Europe, Asia, Latin America, and Africa.

Some marketers think that classic test marketing will make a comeback. It may be that, for totally new products, more thorough testing will be necessary, whereas for other types of product introductions, such as line extensions, an alternative approach is more appropriate.

SUMMARY

Experimental research provides evidence of whether a change in an independent variable causes some predictable change in a dependent variable. To show that a change in A likely caused an observed change in B, one must show three things: concomitant variation, appropriate time order of occurrence, and the elimination of other possible causal factors. Experiments can be conducted in a laboratory or a field setting. The major advantage of conducting experiments in a laboratory is that the researcher can control extraneous factors. However, in marketing research, laboratory settings often do not appropriately replicate the marketplace. Experiments conducted in the actual marketplace are called field experiments. The major difficulty with field experiments is that the researcher cannot control all the other factors that might influence the dependent variable.

In experimentation, we are concerned with internal and external validity. Internal validity refers to the extent to which competing explanations of the experimental results observed can be ruled out. External validity refers to the extent to which causal relationships measured in an experiment can be generalized to other settings. Extraneous variables are other independent variables that may affect the dependent variable and thus stand in the way of the ability to conclude that an observed change in the dependent variable was due to the effect of the experimental, or treatment, variable. Extraneous factors include history, maturation, instrument variation, selection bias, mortality, testing effects, and regression to the mean. Four basic approaches are used to control extraneous factors: randomization, physical control, design control, and statistical control.

In an experimental design, the researcher has control over and manipulates one or more independent variables. Nonexperimental designs, which involve no manipulation, are referred to as ex post facto research. An experimental design includes four elements: the treatment, subjects, a dependent variable that is measured, and a plan or procedure for dealing with extraneous causal factors. An experimental effect is the effect of the treatment variable on the dependent variable.

Experiments have an obvious advantage in that they are the only type of research that can demonstrate the existence and nature of causal relationships between variables of interest. Yet the amount of actual experimentation done in marketing research is limited because of the high cost of experiments, security issues, and implementation problems. There is evidence to suggest that the use of experiments in marketing research is growing.

Pre-experimental designs offer little or no control over the influence of extraneous factors and are thus generally difficult to interpret. Examples include the one-shot case study design and the one-group pretest–posttest design. In a true experimental design, the researcher is able to eliminate all extraneous variables as competitive hypotheses to the treatment. Examples of true experimental designs are the before and after with control group design and the after-only with control group design.

In quasi-experiments, the researcher has control over data-collection procedures but lacks complete control over the scheduling of treatments. The treatment groups in a quasi-experiment normally are formed by assigning respondents to treatments in a non-random fashion. Examples of quasi-experimental designs are the interrupted time-series design and the multiple time-series design.

Test marketing involves testing a new product or some element of the marketing mix by using experimental or quasi-experimental designs. Test markets are field experiments and they are extremely expensive to conduct. The steps in conducting a test market study include defining the objectives for the study, selecting a basic approach to be used, developing detailed procedures for the test, selecting markets for the test, executing the plan, and analyzing the test results.

KEY TERMS & DEFINITIONS

experiment A research approach in which one variable is manipulated and the effect on another variable is observed.

causal research Research designed to determine whether a change in one variable likely caused an observed change in another.

concomitant variation The statistical relationship between two variables.

appropriate time order of occurrence Change in an independent variable occurring before an observed change in the dependent variable.

elimination of other possible causal factors Hard to prove that something else did not cause change in *B*.

laboratory experiments Experiments conducted in a controlled setting.

field experiments Tests conducted outside the laboratory in an actual environment, such as a marketplace.

internal validity The extent to which competing explanations for the experimental results observed can be ruled out.

external validity The extent to which causal relationships measured in an experiment can be generalized to outside persons, settings, and times.

history The intervention, between the beginning and end of an experiment, of outside variables or events that might change the dependent variable.

maturation Changes in subjects occurring during the experiment that are not related to the experiment but that may affect subjects' response to the treatment factor.

instrument variation Changes in measurement instruments (e.g., interviewers or observers) that might affect measurements.

selection bias Systematic differences between the test group and the control group due to a biased selection process.

mortality Loss of test units or subjects during the course of an experiment, which may result in nonrepresentativeness.

testing effect An effect that is a by-product of the research process itself.

regression to the mean The tendency of subjects with extreme behavior to move toward the average for that behavior during the course of an experiment.

randomization Random assignment of subjects to treatment conditions to ensure equal representation of subject characteristics.

physical control Holding constant the value or level of extraneous variables throughout the course of an experiment.

design control Use of the experimental de-sign to control extraneous causal factors.

statistical control Adjusting for the effects of confounded variables by statistically adjusting the value of the dependent variable for each treatment condition.

experimental design A test in which the researcher has control over and manipulates one or more independent variables.

treatment variable An independent variable that is manipulated in an experiment.

experimental effect The effect of the treatment variable on the dependent variable.

contamination Inclusion in a test of a group of respondents who are not normally there—for example, buyers from outside the test market who see an advertisement intended only for those in the test area and who enter the area to purchase the product being tested.

pre-experimental designs Designs that offer little or no control over extraneous factors.

one-shot case study design A pre-experimental design with no pretest observations, no control group, and an after measurement only.

one-group pretest–posttest design A pre-experimental design with pre- and postmeasurements but no control group.

true experimental design Research using an experimental group and a control group, to which test units are randomly assigned.

before and after with control group design A true experimental design that involves random assignment of subjects or test units to experimental and control groups and pre- and postmeasurements of both groups.

after-only with control group design A true experimental design that involves random assignment of subjects or test units to experimental and control groups, but no pre-measurement of the dependent variable.

quasi-experiments Studies in which the researchers lack complete control over the scheduling of treatments or must assign respondents to treatments in a nonrandom manner.

interrupted time-series design Research in which repeated measurements of an effect "interrupts" previous data patterns.

multiple time-series design An interrupted time-series design with a control group.

test market Real-world testing of a new product or some element of the marketing mix using an experimental or quasi-experimental design.

QUESTIONS FOR REVIEW & CRITICAL THINKING

1. Divide the class into as many as six groups, as appropriate. Each group will have the task of recommending a test market design and addressing the associated questions for one of the following scenarios.

(Team Exercise)

- Design a test of a new pricing strategy for orange juice concentrate. The brand is an established brand, and we are only interested in testing the effect of a 5 percent price increase and a 5 percent decrease. All other elements of the marketing mix will remain the same.

- A soft-drink company has determined in taste tests that consumers prefer the taste of their diet product when sweetened with Splenda® in comparison to Equal®. Now they are interested in determining how the new sweetener will play in the marketplace. Design a test market that will achieve this goal.

- A national pizza chain wants to test the effect on sales of four different discount coupons. Design a test that will do this in a way that gives a clear read. Your focus should be on the effect on sales volume. Financial analysis after the test results are in will address the revenue and profit impact.

- A national value-priced hotel chain needs to understand the business impact of including a free buffet-style breakfast to guests. Design and justify a test that will do this.

- A credit card company needs to test its strategy for attracting college students to its card. It is going to continue using booths in student unions and other high-traffic campus locations. It has been offering free CDs from a list to those who sign up for its card, but since other card companies are using this approach, the company wants to try some alternatives. It is considering free MP3 downloads from iTunes and t-shirts featuring popular music groups. Design a test that will tell the company which option to choose if its goal is to increase signups by the largest amount.

2. Tico Taco, a national chain of Mexican fast-food restaurants, has developed the "Super Sonic Taco," which is the largest taco in the market and sells for $1.19. Tico Taco has identified its target customers for this new product as men under 30 who are not concerned about health issues, such as fat content or calories. It wants to test the product in at least four regional markets before making a decision to introduce it nationally. What criteria would you use to select test cities for this new product? Which cities would you recommend using? Why would you recommend those cities?

3. Of the primary data-collection techniques available to the researcher (survey, observation, experiment), why is the experiment the only one that can provide conclusive evidence of causal relationships? Of the various types of experiments, which type or types provide the best evidence of causation or noncausation?

4. What are some important independent variables that must be dealt with in an experiment to test consumer reactions to a pilot for a new TV series? Explain why those variables are important.

5. Managers of the student center at your university or college are considering three alternative brands of frozen pizza to be offered on the menu. They want to offer only one of the three and want to find out which brand students prefer. Design an experiment to determine which brand of pizza the students prefer.

6. Night students at the university or college are much older than day students. Introduce an explicit control for day versus night students in the preceding experiment.

7. Why are quasi-experiments much more popular in marketing research than true experiments?

8. How does history differ from maturation? What specific actions might you take to deal with each in an experiment?

9. A manufacturer of microwave ovens has designed an improved model that will reduce energy costs and cook food evenly throughout. However, this new model will increase the product's price by 30 percent because of extra components and engineering design changes. It decides to test market the new oven in a market area with an extremely high household income level. In addition, the producer offers a discount coupon to facilitate product sales. The company wants to determine what effect the new model will have on sales of its microwave ovens. Do you see any potential problems with a sales forecast based on the results of the test market sales? What would you do differently?

10. Discuss various methods by which extraneous causal factors can be controlled.

11. Discuss the alternatives to traditional test marketing. Explain their advantages and disadvantages.

WORKING THE NET

1. Visit *www.questionpro.com/akira/showLibrary.do?categoryID=16&mode=1* to take a psychographics profile with 269 focused questions distributed into 15 categories. What kind of consumer are you? How would you design a test market to attract a customer like yourself?

2. Consult *www.city-data.com* Research city demographics for Cedar Rapids, Iowa; Eau Claire, Wisconsin; and Grand Junction, Colorado, to evaluate why *Advertising Age* (2005) ranked them among the top seven most popular test market sites in the United States for matching the average American demographic profile.

REAL-LIFE RESEARCH • 8.1

Texas Red Soft Drinks

Texas Red is the oldest soft-drink company in Texas. During the 1980s, the company went through bankruptcy because of its inability to compete with the big national soft-drink brands. In 2003, a group of investors purchased the brand name from the bankruptcy court and reincarnated it with distribution primarily through specialty grocery stores and selected theme restaurants. The company is currently available in 267 grocery stores and 123 restaurants across Texas.

The "new" Texas Red has experienced solid growth and financial performance over its almost 8-year history. However, the competitive environment remains tough with the big national brands at one end of the spectrum and other specialty soft-drink producers at the other end. It is critical that Texas Red spend its limited marketing budget in the most efficient manner to drive business to its retail and restaurant locations.

In recent months, the management team at Texas Red has been divided in regard to the best marketing strategy for the company. One contingent wants to pursue a strategy based on a low price relative to other specialty soft drinks. The other group wants to focus on enhancing awareness and image of the brand with a focus on its long history in the state of Texas and the unique aspects and high quality of its products. The difference of opinion between the two factions has become heated and somewhat divisive. Furthermore, time is running out to get their marketing strategy in place for the coming year.

Toby Newbern, director of marketing, knows that it is important to make the right decision and to break the deadlock quickly so that the company can move on with its plans and business development activities. He wants to design a test that will settle the issue once and for all in a scientific manner. Texas Star has always focused on an upscale demographic target. Toby's research plan calls for testing the price-oriented campaign in one market and the image-oriented campaign in another. The impact on sales in the respective markets will indicate the effectiveness of the two approaches. He faces a number of decisions. First, he needs to choose the markets for the test. Second, there is the question of how long to run the test. Finally, it is necessary to sort out what happens in the two test markets from the general trend for Texas Red.

Questions

1. Is the test market approach the best way to tackle this problem, all things considered? Are there other viable options and, if so, what are the options?

2. Which of the experimental designs discussed in the chapter would be most feasible for this project? Why that design?

3. How many markets should be used for the test? What should be the characteristics of these markets?

4. What sort of evidence, from the test, would definitively break the deadlock between the two groups with different visions as the company?

Image Source/Getty Images, Inc.

CHAPTER

The Concept of Measurement and Attitude Scales

LEARNING OBJECTIVES

1. To understand the concept of measurement.

2. To learn about the measurement process and how to develop a good measurement scale.

3. To understand the four levels of scales and their typical usage.

4. To explore the concepts of reliability and validity.

5. To become familiar with the concept of scaling.

6. To learn about the various types of attitude scales.

7. To examine some basic considerations in selecting a type of scale.

What is the nature of measurement? What steps are involved? What are the three levels of measurement? What are the notions of validity and reliability? Why are they so critically important to the concept of measurement? How can attitudes be measured? What factors should be considered in creating an attitude scale? These are the topics of this chapter.

The Measurement Process

Measurement is the process of assigning numbers or labels to persons, objects, or events, in accordance with specific rules for representing quantities or qualities of attributes. Measurement, then, is a procedure used to assign numbers that reflect the amount of an attribute possessed by a person, object, or event. Note that it is not the person, object, or event that is being measured, but rather its attributes. A researcher, for example, does not measure a consumer per se but rather measures that consumer's attitudes, income, brand loyalty, age, and other relevant factors.

The concept of rules is key to measurement. A **rule** is a guide, a method, or a command that tells a researcher what to do. For example, a rule of measurement might state, "Assign the numbers 1 through 5 to people according to their disposition to do household chores. If they are extremely willing to do any and all household chores, assign them a 1. If they are not willing to do any household chores, assign them a 5." The numbers 2, 3, and 4 would be assigned based on the *degree* of their willingness to do chores, as it relates to the absolute end points of 1 and 5.

A problem often encountered with rules is a lack of clarity or specificity. Some things are easy to measure because rules are easy to create and follow. The measurement of gender, for example, is quite simple, as the researcher has concrete criteria to apply in assigning a 1 for a male and a 2 for a female. Unfortunately, many characteristics of interest to a marketing researcher—such as brand loyalty, purchase intent, and total family income—are much harder to measure because of the difficulty of devising rules to assess the true value of these consumer attributes. The steps a researcher should take to measure a phenomenon appear in Exhibit 9.1.

→ **measurement**
The process of assigning numbers or labels to persons, objects, or events, in accordance with specific rules for representing quantities or qualities of attributes.

→ **rule**
A guide, method, or command that tells a researcher what to do.

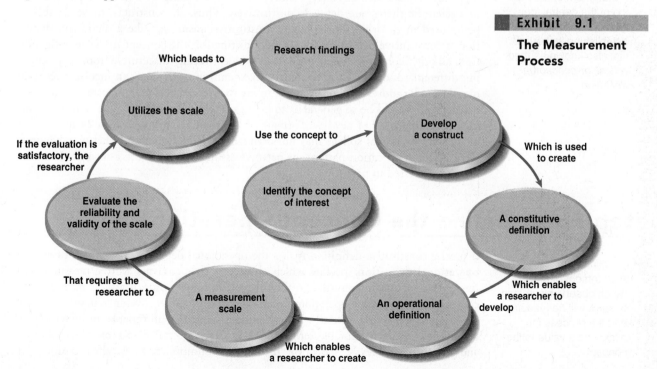

Exhibit 9.1

The Measurement Process

Which leads to — Research findings

Utilizes the scale

If the evaluation is satisfactory, the researcher

Evaluate the reliability and validity of the scale

Use the concept to

Identify the concept of interest

Develop a construct

Which is used to create

A constitutive definition

That requires the researcher to

A measurement scale

An operational definition

Which enables a researcher to develop

Which enables a researcher to create

Step One: Identify the Concept of Interest

The measurement process begins with identification of the concept of interest. A *concept* is an abstract idea generalized from particular facts. It is a category of thought used to group sense data together "as if they were all the same." All perceptions regarding a stop light at the intersection of South and Main streets form a category of thought, though a relatively narrow one. Perceptions of all stoplights, regardless of location, would be a broader concept, or category of thought.

Step Two: Develop a Construct

→ **constructs**
Specific types of concepts that exist at higher levels of abstraction.

Constructs are specific types of concepts that exist at higher levels of abstraction than do everyday concepts. Constructs are invented for theoretical use and thus are likely to cut across various preexisting categories of thought. The value of specific constructs depends on how useful they are in explaining, predicting, and controlling phenomena, just as the value of everyday concepts depends on how helpful they are in everyday affairs. Generally, constructs are not directly observable. Instead, they are inferred by some indirect method from results such as findings on a questionnaire. Examples of marketing constructs include brand loyalty, high-involvement purchasing, social class, personality, and channel power. Constructs aid researchers by simplifying and integrating the complex phenomena found in the marketing environment.

Step Three: Define the Concept Constitutively

→ **constitutive definition**
A statement of the meaning of the central idea or concept under study, establishing its boundaries; also known as *theoretical*, or *conceptual*, *definition*.

The third step in the measurement process is to define the concept constitutively. A **constitutive** (or *theoretical*, or *conceptual*) **definition** is a statement of the meaning of the central idea or concept under study, establishing its boundaries. Constructs of a scientific theory are defined constitutively. Thus, all constructs, to be capable of being used in theories, must possess constitutive meaning. Like a dictionary definition, a constitutive definition should fully distinguish the concept under investigation from all other concepts, making the study concept readily discernible from very similar but different concepts. A vague constitutive definition can cause an incorrect research question to be addressed. For instance, to say that researchers are interested in studying marital roles would be so general as to be meaningless. To say that they want to examine the marital roles of newlyweds (married less than 12 months) from 24 to 28 years of age with 4 years of college may not even suffice. While one researcher may be interested in communication patterns as partners assume certain roles, a second researcher may be interested in parenting roles.

Step Four: Define the Concept Operationally

→ **operational definition**
A statement of precisely which observable characteristics will be measured and the process for assigning a value to the concept.

A precise constitutive definition makes the operational definition task much easier. An **operational definition** specifies which observable characteristics will be measured and the process for assigning a value to the concept. In other words, it assigns meaning to a construct in terms of the operations necessary to measure it in any concrete situation.

Because it is overly restrictive in marketing to insist that all variables be operationally defined in directly measurable terms, many variables are stated in more abstract terms and measured indirectly, based on theoretical assumptions about their nature. For example, it is impossible to measure an attitude directly because an attitude is an abstract concept that refers to things inside a person's mind. It is possible, nonetheless, to give a clear theoretical definition of an attitude as an enduring organization of motivational, emotional, perceptual, and cognitive processes with respect to some aspect of the environment. On the basis of this definition, instruments have been developed for measuring attitudes indirectly, by asking questions about how a person feels, what the person believes, and how the person intends to behave.

In summary, an operational definition serves as a bridge between a theoretical concept and real-world events or factors. Constructs such as "attitude" and "high-involvement purchasing" are abstractions that cannot be observed. Operational definitions transform such constructs into observable events. In other words, they define or give meaning to a construct by spelling out what the researcher must do to measure it. There are many different potential operational definitions for any single concept, regardless of how exact the constitutive definition may be. The researcher must choose the operational definition that fits most appropriately with the objectives of the research.

An example of a constitutive definition, a corresponding operational definition, and a resultant measurement scale are shown in Exhibit 9.2. The operational definition of role ambiguity was developed by two marketing professors for use with salespeople and customer service personnel. The theoretical notion is that role ambiguity leads to job stress and impedes a worker's ability to improve performance and obtain job-based rewards, leading to job dissatisfaction.

Construct equivalence deals with how people see, understand, and develop measurements of a particular phenomenon. The problem confronting a global marketing researcher is that, because of sociocultural, economic, and political differences, construct

EXHIBIT 9.2	Constitutive and Operational Definitions of Role Ambiguity
Constitutive definition	Role ambiguity is a direct function of the discrepancy between the information available to the person and that which is required for adequate performance of a role. It is the difference between a person's actual state of knowledge and the knowledge that provides adequate satisfaction of that person's personal needs and values.
Operational definition	Role ambiguity is the amount of uncertainty (ranging from very uncertain to very certain on a 5-point scale) an individual feels regarding job-role responsibilities and expectations from other employees and customers.
Measurement scale	The measurement scale consists of 45 items, with each item assessed by a 5-point scale with category labels 1 = very certain, 2 = certain, 3 = neutral, 4 = uncertain, and 5 = very uncertain. Samples of the 45 items follow: • How much freedom of action I am expected to have • How I am expected to handle nonroutine activities on the job • The sheer amount of work I am expected to do • To what extent my boss is open to hearing my point of view • How satisfied my boss is with me • How managers in other departments expect me to interact with them • What managers in other departments think about the job I perform • How I am expected to interact with my customers • How I should behave (with customers) while on the job • If I am expected to lie a little to win customer confidence • If I am expected to hide my company's foul-ups from my customers • About how much time my family feels I should spend on the job • To what extent my family expects me to share my job-related problems • How my co-workers expect me to behave while on the job • How much information my co-workers expect me to convey to my boss

Source: Adapted from Jagdip Singh and Gary K. Rhoads, "Boundary Role Ambiguity in Marketing-Oriented Positions: A Multidimensional, Multi-faceted Operationalization," *Journal of Marketing Research*, August 1991, pp. 328–338. Reprinted by permission of the American Marketing Association.

perspectives may be neither identical nor equivalent. The examples provided in the Global Research feature on page 212 highlight the construct equivalence problem faced by global marketing researchers.

Step Five: Develop a Measurement Scale

→ **scale**
A set of symbols or numbers so constructed that the symbols or numbers can be assigned by a rule to the individuals (or their behaviors or attitudes) to whom the scale is applied.

Exhibit 9.2 includes a scale that ranges from "very certain" to "very uncertain." A **scale** is a set of symbols or numbers so constructed that the symbols or numbers can be assigned by a rule to the individuals (or their behaviors or attitudes) to whom the scale is applied. The assignment on the scale is indicated by the individual's possession of whatever the scale is supposed to measure. Thus, a salesperson who feels he knows exactly how he is supposed to interact with customers would mark *very certain* for that item on the scale in Exhibit 9.2.

Creating a measurement scale begins with determining the level of measurement that is desirable or possible. Exhibit 9.3 describes the four basic levels of measurement: nominal, ordinal, interval, and ratio.

The Nominal Level of Measurement

→ **nominal scales**
Scales that partition data into mutually exclusive and collectively exhaustive categories.

Nominal scales are among those most commonly used in marketing research. A nominal scale partitions data into categories that are mutually exclusive and collectively exhaustive, implying that every bit of data will fit into one and only one category and that all data will fit somewhere on the scale. The term *nominal* means "name-like," indicating that the numbers assigned to objects or phenomena are naming or classifying them but have no true number value; that is, the numbers cannot be ordered, added, or divided. The numbers are simply labels or identification numbers and nothing else. Examples of two nominal scales follow:

EXHIBIT 9.3	The Four Basic Levels of Measurement			
Level	**Basic Empirical Description***	**Operations**	**Typical Usage**	**Typical Descriptive Statistics**
Nominal	Uses numerals to identify objects, individuals, events, or groups*	Determination of equality/inequality	Classification (male/ female; buyer/ nonbuyer)	Frequency counts, percentages/modes
Ordinal	In addition to identification, provides information about the relative amount of some characteristic possessed by an event, object, etc.	Determination of greater or lesser	Rankings/ratings (preferences for hotels, banks, etc.; social class; ratings of foods based on fat content, cholesterol)	Median (mean and variance metric)
Interval	Possesses all the properties of nominal and ordinal scales plus equal intervals between consecutive points	Determination of equality of intervals	Preferred measure of complex concepts/ constructs (temperature scale, air pressure scale, level of knowledge about brands)	Mean/variance
Ratio	Incorporates all the properties of nominal, ordinal, and interval scales plus an absolute zero point	Determination of equality of ratios	Preferred measure when precision instruments are available (sales, number of on-time arrivals, age)	Geometric mean/ harmonic mean

*Because higher levels of measurement contain all the properties of lower levels, higher-level scales can be converted into lower-level ones (i.e., ratio to interval or ordinal or nominal, or interval to ordinal or nominal, or ordinal to nominal).
Source: Adapted from S. S. Stevens, "On the Theory of Scales of Measurement," *Science*, June 7, 1946, pp. 677–680.

| Gender: | (1) Male | (2) Female | |
| Geographic area: | (1) Urban | (2) Rural | (3) Suburban |

The only quantifications in numerical scales are the number and percentage of objects in each category—for example, 50 males (48.5 percent) and 53 females (51.5 percent). Computing a mean of 2.4 for geographic area would be meaningless; only the mode, the value that appears most often, would be appropriate.

The Ordinal Level of Measurement

Ordinal scales have the labeling characteristics of nominal scales plus an ability to order data. Ordinal measurement is possible when the transitivity postulate can be applied. (A *postulate* is an assumption that is an essential prerequisite to carrying out an operation or line of thinking.) The *transitivity postulate* is described by the notion that "if *a* is greater than *b*, and *b* is greater than *c*, then *a* is greater than *c*." Other terms that can be substituted for *is greater than* are *is preferred to*, *is stronger than*, and *precedes*. An example of an ordinal scale follows:

> **ordinal scales**
> Scales that maintain the labeling characteristics of nominal scales and have the ability to order data.

Please rank the following online dating services from 1 to 5, with 1 being the most preferred and 5 the least preferred.

www.spark.com   _____
www.eharmony.com   _____
www.match.com   _____
www.greatexpectations.com   _____
www.friendfinder.com   _____

Ordinal numbers are used strictly to indicate rank order. The numbers do not indicate absolute quantities, nor do they imply that the intervals between the numbers are equal. For example, a person ranking fax machines might like HP only slightly more than Canon and view Sharp as totally unacceptable. Such information would not be obtained from an ordinal scale.

Because ranking is the objective of an ordinal scale, any rule prescribing a series of numbers that preserves the ordered relationship is satisfactory. In other words, Spark could have been assigned a value of 30; eHarmony, 40; Match, 27; GreatExpectations, 32; and FriendFinder, 42. Or any other series of numbers could have been used, as long as the basic ordering was preserved. In the case just cited, FriendFinder is 1, eHarmony 2, GreatExpectations 3, Spark 4, and Match 5. Common arithmetic operations such as addition and multiplication cannot be used with ordinal scales. The appropriate measure of central tendency is the mode or the median. A percentile or quartile measure is used for measuring dispersion.

A controversial (yet rather common) use of ordinal scales is to rate various characteristics. In this case, the researcher assigns numbers to reflect the relative ratings of a series of statements, then uses these numbers to interpret relative distance. Recall that the marketing researchers examining role ambiguity used a scale ranging from *very certain* to *very uncertain*. The following values were assigned:

(1)	(2)	(3)	(4)	(5)
Very Certain	**Certain**	**Neutral**	**Uncertain**	**Very Uncertain**

If a researcher can justify the assumption that the intervals are equal within the scale, then the more powerful parametric statistical tests can be applied. Indeed, some measurement scholars argue that equal intervals should be normally assumed.

GLOBAL RESEARCH

Construct Equivalence Problems Often Occur in Global Marketing Research

Construct equivalence problems in global marketing research may relate to functional equivalence, conceptual equivalence, or definitional equivalence. Some examples of each type of problem follow.

Functional Equivalence

In England, Germany, and Scandinavia, beer is generally perceived as an alcoholic beverage. In Mediterranean lands, however, beer is considered akin to soft drinks. Therefore, a study of the competitive status of beer in northern Europe would have to build in questions on wine and liquor. In Italy, Spain, or Greece, the comparison would have to be with soft drinks.

In Italy, it's common for children to have a bar of chocolate between two slices of bread as a snack. In France, bar chocolate is often used in cooking. But a German housewife would be revolted by either practice.

Conceptual Equivalence

A researcher using the concepts "out-group" and "in-group" would be dealing with very different groups in the United States and Greece. In the United States, the in-group includes people from one's own country, and the out-group includes foreigners. In Greece, the out-group includes countrymen with whom one is not closely associated. (When Athenians were asked to help fellow Greeks and foreigners mail letters, the Greeks received worse treatment than did the foreigners.)

Personality traits such as aggressiveness or assertiveness may not be relevant in all countries or cultures. The concept may be absent from the culture and language, or it may have an entirely different meaning.

As a final example, Japanese and Western concepts of decision making differ considerably. Whereas the Westerner sees decision making as a discrete event, the Japanese cannot make that distinction.

Definitional Equivalence

In France, fragrance is measured on a hot–cold continuum. In the United States and the United Kingdom, hot and cold are not attributes assigned to fragrances. That is, an attribute used to categorize product classes may vary from one country or culture to another.

Perceptions of beer, as cited under functional equivalence, also provide an example of problems in achieving definitional equivalence. In the United Kingdom, beer would be classified as an alcoholic drink. In Mediterranean cultures, it would be classified as a soft drink.[1]

Questions

1. Why is construct equivalence important in global research?

2. Do you think that a researcher should worry about construct equivalence between the United States and Canada?

The best procedure would seem to be to treat ordinal measurements as though they were interval measurements but to be constantly alert to the possibility of gross inequality of intervals. As much as possible about the characteristics of the measuring tools should be learned. Much useful information has been obtained by this approach, with resulting scientific advances in psychology, sociology, and education. In short, it is unlikely that researchers will be led seriously astray by heeding this advice, if they are careful in applying it.[2]

The Interval Level of Measurement

Interval scales contain all the features of ordinal scales with the added dimension that the intervals between the points on the scale are equal. The concept of temperature is based on equal intervals. Marketing researchers often prefer interval scales over ordinal scales because they can measure how much of a trait one consumer has (or does not have) over another. An interval scale enables a researcher to discuss differences separating two objects. The scale possesses properties of order and difference but with an arbitrary zero point. Examples are the Fahrenheit and Celsius scales; the freezing point of water is zero on one scale and 32 degrees on the other.

The arbitrary zero point of interval scales restricts the statements that a researcher can make about the scale points. One can say that 80°F is hotter than 32°F or that 64°F is 16° cooler than 80°F. However, one cannot say that 64°F is twice as warm as 32°F. Why? Because the zero point on the Fahrenheit scale is arbitrary. To understand this point, consider the transformation of the two Fahrenheit temperatures to Celsius using the formula Celsius 3 ($F-32$)(5/9); 32°F equals 0°C, and 64°F equals 17.8°C. The statement we made about the Fahrenheit temperatures (64° is twice as warm as 32°) does not hold for Celsius. The same would be true of rankings of online dating services on an interval scale. If Match had received a 20 and GreatExpectations a 10, we cannot say that Match is liked twice as much as GreatExpectations, because a point defining the absence of liking has not been identified and assigned a value of zero on the scale.

Interval scales are amenable to computation of an arithmetic mean, standard deviation, and correlation coefficients. The more powerful parametric statistical tests such as t tests and F tests can be applied. In addition, researchers can take a more conservative approach and use nonparametric tests if they have concern about the equal intervals assumption.

The Ratio Level of Measurement

Ratio scales have all the characteristics of the scales previously discussed as well as a meaningful absolute zero or origin. Because there is universal agreement as to the location of the zero point, comparisons among the magnitudes of ratio-scaled values are acceptable. Thus, a ratio scale reflects the actual amount of a variable. Physical characteristics of a respondent such as age, weight, and height are examples of ratio-scaled variables. Other ratio scales are based on area, distance, money values, return rates, population counts, and lapsed periods of time.

Because some objects have none of the property being measured, a ratio scale originates at a zero point with absolute empirical meaning. For example, an investment (albeit a poor one) can have no rate of return, or a census tract in New Mexico could be devoid of any persons. An absolute zero implies that all arithmetic operations are possible, including multiplication and division. Numbers on the scale indicate the actual amounts of the property being measured. A large bag of McDonald's french fries weighs 8 ounces, and a regular bag at Burger King weighs 4 ounces; thus, a large McDonald's bag of fries weighs twice as much as a regular Burger King bag of fries.

Step Six: Evaluate the Reliability and Validity of the Measurement

An ideal marketing research study would provide information that is accurate, precise, lucid, and timely. Accurate data imply accurate measurement, or $M = A$, where M refers

➔ **interval scales**
Scales that have the characteristics of ordinal scales, plus equal intervals between points to show relative amounts; they may include an arbitrary zero point.

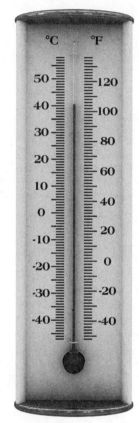

© rzelich/iStockphoto

Commonly used temperature scales are based on equal intervals and an arbitrary zero point. Marketing researchers often prefer interval scales because they can measure how much more of a trait one consumer has than another.

→ **ratio scales**
Scales that have the characteristics of interval scales, plus a meaningful zero point so that magnitudes can be compared arithmetically.

to measurement and *A* stands for complete accuracy. In marketing research, this ideal is rarely, if ever, achieved. Instead,

$$M = A + E$$
where E = errors

Errors can be either random or systematic, as noted in Chapter 5. Systematic error results in a constant bias in the measurements caused by faults in the measurement instrument or process. For example, if a faulty ruler (on which 1 inch is actually 1.5 inches) is used in Pillsbury's test kitchens to measure the height of chocolate cakes baked with alternative recipes, all cakes will be recorded at less than their actual height. *Random error* also influences the measurements but not systematically. Thus, random error is transient in nature. A person may not answer a question truthfully because he is in a bad mood that day.

Two scores on a measurement scale can differ for a number of reasons.[3] Only the first of the following eight reasons does not involve error. A researcher must determine whether any of the remaining seven sources of measurement differences are producing random or systematic error:

1. *A true difference in the characteristic being measured.* A perfect measurement difference is solely the result of actual differences. For example, John rates McDonald's service as 1 (excellent) and Sandy rates its service as 4 (average), and the variation is due only to actual attitude differences.

2. *Differences due to stable characteristics of individual respondents*, such as personality, values, and intelligence. Sandy has an aggressive, rather critical personality, and she gives no one and nothing the benefit of the doubt. She actually was quite pleased with the service she received at McDonald's, but she expects such service and so gave it an average rating.

3. *Differences due to short-term personal factors*, such as temporary mood swings, health problems, time constraints, or fatigue. Earlier on the day of the study, John had won $400 in a "Name That Tune" contest on a local radio station. He stopped by McDonald's for a burger after he picked up his winning check. His reply on the service quality questionnaire might have been quite different if he had been interviewed the previous day.

4. *Differences caused by situational factors*, such as distractions or others present in the interview situation. Sandy was giving her replies while trying to watch her 4-year-old nephew, who was running amok on the McDonald's playground; John had his new fiancée along when he was interviewed. Replies of both people might have been different if they had been interviewed at home while no other friend or relative was present.

5. *Differences resulting from variations in administering the survey.* Interviewers can ask questions with different voice inflections, causing response variation. And because of such factors as rapport with the interviewee, manner of dress, sex, or race, different interviewers can cause responses to vary. Interviewer bias can be as subtle as a nodding of the head. One interviewer who tended to nod unconsciously was found to bias some respondents. They thought that the interviewer was agreeing with them when he was, in fact, saying, "Okay, I'm recording what you say—tell me more."

6. *Differences due to the sampling of items included in the questionnaire.* When researchers attempt to measure the quality of service at McDonald's, the scales and other questions used represent only a portion of the items that could have been used.

Andre Jenny Stock Connection Worldwide/NewsCom

Two scores on a measurement scale can differ for a number of reasons. McDonald's may score higher on one person's survey than on another person's because of real differences in perceptions of the service or because of a variety of random or systematic errors. The reliability and validity of the type of measurement should always be checked.

The scales created by the researchers reflect their interpretation of the construct (service quality) and the way it is measured. If the researchers had used different words or if items had been added or removed, the scale values reported by John and Sandy might have been different.

7. *Differences due to a lack of clarity in the measurement instrument.* A question may be ambiguous, complex, or incorrectly interpreted. A survey that asked "How far do you live from McDonald's?" and then gave choices "(1) less than 5 minutes, (2) 5 to 10 minutes," and so forth, would be ambiguous; someone walking would undoubtedly take longer to get to the restaurant than a person driving a car or riding a bike.

8. *Differences due to mechanical or instrument factors.* Blurred questionnaires, lack of space to fully record answers, missing pages in a questionnaire, incorrect computer keystrokes, or a balky pen can result in differences in responses.

Reliability

A measurement scale that provides consistent results over time is reliable. If a ruler consistently measures a chocolate cake as 9 inches high, then the ruler is said to be reliable. Reliable scales, gauges, and other measurement devices can be used with confidence and with the knowledge that transient and situational factors are not interfering with the measurement process. Reliable instruments provide stable measures at different times under different conditions. A key question regarding reliability is "If we measure some phenomenon over and over again with the same measurement device, will we get the same or highly similar results?" An affirmative answer means that the device is reliable.

Thus, **reliability** is the degree to which measures are free from random error and, therefore, provide consistent data. The less error there is, the more reliable the observation is, so a measurement that is free of error is a correct measure. A reliable measurement, then, does not change when the concept being measured remains constant in value. However, if the concept being measured does change in value, the reliable measure

→ **reliability**
The degree to which measures are free from random error and, therefore, provide consistent data.

will indicate that change. How can a measuring instrument be unreliable? If your weight stays constant at 150 pounds but repeated measurements on your bathroom scale show your weight to fluctuate, the scale's lack of reliability may be due to a weak spring.

There are three ways to assess reliability: test–retest, the use of equivalent forms, and internal consistency.

→ test–retest reliability
The ability of the same instrument to produce consistent results when used a second time under conditions as similar as possible to the original conditions.

Test–Retest Reliability   **Test–retest reliability** is obtained by repeating the measurement with the same instrument, approximating the original conditions as closely as possible. The theory behind test–retest is that if random variations are present, they will be revealed by differences in the scores between the two tests. **Stability** means that very few differences in scores are found between the first and second administrations of the test; the measuring instrument is said to be stable. For example, assume that a 30-item department store image measurement scale was administered to the same group of shoppers at two different times. If the correlation between the two measurements was high, the reliability would be assumed to be high.

→ stability
Lack of change in results from test to retest.

There are several problems with test–retest reliability. First, it may be very difficult to locate and gain the cooperation of respondents for a second testing. Second, the first measurement may alter a person's response on the second measurement. Third, environmental or personal factors may change, causing the second measurement to change.

Equivalent Form Reliability   The difficulties encountered with the test–retest approach can be avoided by creating equivalent forms of a measurement instrument. For example, assume that the researcher is interested in identifying inner-directed versus outer-directed lifestyles. Two questionnaires can be created containing measures of inner-directed behavior (see Exhibit 9.4) and measures of outer-directed behavior. These measures should receive about the same emphasis on each questionnaire. Thus, although the questions used to ascertain the lifestyles are different on the two questionnaires, the number of

EXHIBIT 9.4	**Statements Used to Measure Inner-Directed Lifestyles**

I often don't get the credit I deserve for things I do well.
I try to get my own way regardless of others.
My greatest achievements are ahead of me.
I have a number of ideas that someday I would like to put into a book.
I am quick to accept new ideas.
I often think about how I look and what impression I am making on others.
I am a competitive person.
I feel upset when I hear that people are criticizing or blaming me.
I'd like to be a celebrity.
I get a real thrill out of doing dangerous things.
I feel that almost nothing in life can substitute for great achievement.
It's important for me to be noticed.
I keep in close touch with my friends.
I spend a good deal of time trying to decide how I feel about things.
I often think I can feel my way into the innermost being of another person.
I feel that ideals are powerful motivating forces in people.
I think someone can be a good person without believing in God.
The Eastern religions are more appealing to me than Christianity.
I feel satisfied with my life.
I enjoy getting involved in new and unusual situations.
Overall, I'd say I'm happy.
I feel I understand where my life is going.
I like to think I'm different from other people.
I adopt a commonsense attitude toward life.

questions used to measure each lifestyle should be approximately equal. The recommended interval for administering the second equivalent form is 2 weeks, although in some cases the two forms are given one after the other or simultaneously. **Equivalent form reliability** is determined by measuring the correlation of the scores on the two instruments.

There are two problems with equivalent forms that should be noted. First, it is very difficult, and perhaps impossible, to create two totally equivalent forms. Second, if equivalence can be achieved, it may not be worth the time, trouble, and expense involved. The theory behind the equivalent form approach to reliability assessment is the same as that of the test–retest approach. The primary difference between the test–retest and the equivalent form methods is the testing instrument itself. Test–retest uses the same instrument, whereas the equivalent form approach uses a different, but highly similar, measuring instrument.

> **equivalent form reliability**
> The ability of two very similar forms of an instrument to produce closely correlated results.

Internal Consistency Reliability   **Internal consistency reliability** assesses the ability to produce similar results when different samples are used to measure a phenomenon during the same time period. The theory of internal consistency rests on the concept of equivalence. *Equivalence* is concerned with how much error may be introduced by using different samples of items to measure a phenomenon; it focuses on variations at one point in time among samples of items. A researcher can test for item equivalence by assessing the homogeneity of a set of items. The total set of items used to measure a phenomenon, such as inner-directed lifestyles, is divided into two halves; the total scores of the two halves are then correlated. Use of the **split-half technique** typically calls for scale items to be randomly assigned to one half or the other. The problem with this method is that the estimate of the coefficient of reliability is totally dependent on how the items were split. Different splits result in different correlations when, ideally, they should not.

> **internal consistency reliability**
> The ability of an instrument to produce similar results when used on different samples during the same time period to measure a phenomenon.

> **split-half technique**
> A method of assessing the reliability of a scale by dividing the total set of measurement items in half and correlating the results.

To overcome this problem, many researchers now use the *Cronbach alpha technique*, which involves computing mean reliability coefficient estimates for all possible ways of splitting a set of items in half. A lack of correlation of an item with other items in the scale is evidence that the item does not belong in the scale and should be omitted. One limitation of the Cronbach alpha is that the scale items require equal intervals. If this criterion cannot be met, another test called the KR-20 can be used. The *KR-20 technique* is applicable for all dichotomous or nominally scaled items.

Validity

Recall that the second characteristic of a good measurement device is validity. **Validity** addresses the issue of whether what the researcher was trying to measure was actually measured. When Pontiac brought out the Aztek, research indicated that the car would sell between 50,000 and 70,000 units annually, despite the controversial styling. After selling only 27,000 cars per year, the model was discontinued in 2005. Unfortunately, the research measuring instrument was not valid. The validity of a measure refers to the extent to which the measurement instrument and procedure are free from both systematic and random error. Thus, a measuring device is valid only if differences in scores reflect true differences on the characteristic being measured rather than systematic or random error. You should recognize that a necessary precondition for validity is that the measuring instrument be reliable. An instrument that is not reliable will not yield consistent results when measuring the same phenomenon over time.

> **validity**
> The degree to which what a researcher was trying to measure was actually measured.

A scale or other measuring device is basically worthless to a researcher if it lacks validity because it is not measuring what it is supposed to. On the surface, this seems like a rather simple notion, yet validity often is based on subtle distinctions. Assume that your teacher gives an exam that he has constructed to measure marketing research knowledge, and the test consists strictly of applying a number of formulas to simple case problems. A friend receives a low score on the test and protests to the teacher that she "really understands marketing research." Her position, in essence, is that the test was not valid. She maintains that, rather than measuring knowledge of marketing research, the test measured memorization of formulas and the ability to use simple math to find solutions. The teacher could repeat the exam only to find that student scores still fell in the same order. Does this mean that the protesting student was incorrect? Not necessarily; the teacher may be systematically measuring the ability to memorize rather than a true understanding of marketing research.

Unlike the teacher attempting to measure marketing research knowledge, a brand manager is interested in successful prediction. The manager, for example, wants to know if a purchase intent scale successfully predicts trial purchase of a new product. Thus, validity can be examined from a number of different perspectives, including face, content, criterion-related, and construct validity (see Exhibit 9.5).

face validity
The degree to which a measurement seems to measure what it is supposed to measure.

Face Validity

Face validity is the weakest form of validity. It is concerned with the degree to which a measurement seems to measure what it is supposed to measure. It is a judgment call by the researcher, made as the questions are designed. Thus, as each question is scrutinized, there is an implicit assessment of its face validity. Revisions enhance the face validity of the question until it passes the researcher's subjective evaluation. Alternatively, *face validity* can refer to the subjective agreement of researchers, experts, or people familiar with the market, product, or industry that a scale logically appears to be accurately reflecting what it is supposed to measure.[4] A straightforward question such as "What is your age?" followed by a series of age categories generally is agreed to have face validity. Most scales used in marketing research attempt to measure attitudes or behavioral intentions, which are much more elusive.

content validity
Representativeness, or sampling adequacy, of the content of a measurement instrument.

Content Validity

Content validity is the representativeness, or sampling adequacy, of the content of the measurement instrument. In other words, does the scale provide adequate coverage of the topic under study? Say that McDonald's has hired you to measure its image among adults 18 to 30 years of age who eat fast-food hamburgers at least once a month. You devise the following scale:

Modern building	1	2	3	4	5	Old-fashioned building
Beautiful landscaping	1	2	3	4	5	Poor landscaping
Clean parking lots	1	2	3	4	5	Dirty parking lots
Attractive signs	1	2	3	4	5	Unattractive signs

EXHIBIT 9.5	Assessing the Validity of a Measurement Instrument
Face validity	The degree to which a measurement instrument seems to measure what it is supposed to, as judged by researchers.
Content validity	The degree to which measurement items represent the universe of the concept under study.
Criterion-related validity	The degree to which a measurement instrument can predict a variable that is designated a criterion.
	a. Predictive validity: The extent to which a future level of a criterion variable can be predicted by a current measurement on a scale.
	b. Concurrent validity: The extent to which a criterion variable measured at the same point in time as the variable of interest can be predicted by the measurement instrument.
Construct validity	The degree to which a measurement instrument confirms a hypothesis created from a theory based on the concepts under study.
	a. Convergent validity: The degree of association among different measurement instruments that purport to measure the same concept.
	b. Discriminant validity: A measure of the lack of association among constructs that are supposed to be different.

A McDonald's executive would quickly take issue with this scale, claiming that a person could evaluate McDonald's on this scale and never have eaten a McDonald's hamburger. In fact, the evaluation could be made simply by driving past a McDonald's. The executive could further argue that the scale lacks content validity because many important components of image—such as the quality of the food, cleanliness of the eating area and restrooms, and promptness and courtesy of service—were omitted.

The determination of content validity is not always a simple matter. It is very difficult, and perhaps impossible, to identify all the facets of the image of McDonald's. Content validity ultimately becomes a judgmental matter. One could approach content validity by first carefully defining precisely what is to be measured. Second, an exhaustive literature search and focus groups could be conducted to identify all possible items for inclusion on the scale. Third, a panel of experts could be asked their opinions on whether an item should be included. Finally, the scale could be pretested and an open-ended question asked that might identify other items to be included. For example, after a more refined image scale for McDonald's has been administered, a follow-up question could be "Do you have any other thoughts about McDonald's that you would like to express?" Answers to this pretest question might provide clues for other image dimensions not previously considered.

Criterion-Related Validity

Criterion-related validity examines the ability of a measuring instrument to predict a variable that is designated a criterion. Suppose that we wish to devise a test to identify marketing researchers who are exceptional at moderating focus groups. We begin by having impartial marketing research experts identify from a directory of researchers those they judge to be best at moderating focus groups. We then construct 300 items to which all the group moderators are asked to reply yes or no, such as "I believe it is important to compel shy group participants to speak out" and "I like to interact with small groups of people." We then go through the responses and select the items that the "best" focus group moderators answered one way and the rest of the moderators answered the other way. Assume that this process produces 84 items, which we put together to form what we shall call the Test of Effectiveness in Focus Group

> **criterion-related validity**
> The degree to which a measurement instrument can predict a variable that is designated a criterion.

MARK COWAN/UPI/Landov LLC

A politician is interested in what issues those likely to vote perceive as important. The predictive validity of the politician's measures may determine whether or not he or she is elected.

Moderating (TEFGM). We feel that this test will identify good focus group moderators. The criterion of interest here is the ability to conduct a good focus group. We might explore further the criterion-related validity of TEFGM by administering it to another group of moderators, each of whom has been designated as either "best" or "not as good." Then we could determine how well the test identifies the section to which each marketing researcher is assigned. Thus, criterion-related validity is concerned with detecting the presence or absence of one or more criteria considered to represent constructs of interest.

Two subcategories of criterion-related validity are predictive validity and concurrent validity. **Predictive validity** is the extent to which a future level of a criterion variable can be predicted by a current measurement on a scale. A voter-motivation scale, for example, is used to predict the likelihood that a person will vote in the next election. A savvy politician is not interested in what the community as a whole perceives as important problems but only in what persons who are likely to vote perceive as important problems. These are the issues that the politician would address in speeches and advertising. Another example of predictive validity is the extent to which a purchase intent scale for a new Pepperidge Farm pastry predicts actual trial of the product.

Concurrent validity is concerned with the relationship between the predictor variable and the criterion variable, both of which are assessed at the same point in time—for example, the ability of a home pregnancy test to accurately determine whether a woman is pregnant right now. Such a test with low concurrent validity could cause a lot of undue stress.

Construct Validity Construct validity, though not often consciously addressed by many marketing researchers on a day-to-day basis, is extremely important to marketing scientists. Assessing construct validity involves understanding the theoretical foundations underlying the obtained measurements. A measure has **construct validity** if it behaves according to the theory behind the prediction. Purchase behavior can be observed directly; someone either buys product A or does not. Yet scientists have developed constructs on lifestyle, involvement, attitude, and personality that help explain why someone does or does not purchase something. These constructs are largely unobservable. Researchers can observe behavior related to the constructs—that is, the purchase of a product. However, they cannot observe the constructs themselves—such as an attitude. Constructs help scientists communicate and build theories to explain phenomena.[5]

You might think of construct validity as a "labeling" issue. When you measure a notion (construct) called "high involvement," is that what you are really measuring? Viewed in a slightly different manner, when a researcher claims construct validity, he or she essentially has a theory of how phenomena, people, and measures relate to each other (and other theoretical terms). In other words, the researcher offers us a theoretical pattern. When the researcher claims construct validity, he or she is claiming that the observed pattern in a research project corresponds to the theoretical pattern. In this instance, how the researcher thought the world works is how it works.

Although construct validity is presented here with various other types of validity, it really stands above all others. Why? Because construct validity relates back to the very essence of what you are trying to measure. If your research lacks construct validity, little else matters.[6]

Two statistical measures of construct validity are convergent and discriminant validity. **Convergent validity** reflects the degree of correlation among different measures that purport to measure the same construct. **Discriminant validity** reveals the lack of—or low—correlation among constructs that are supposed to be different. Assume that we

predictive validity
The degree to which a future level of a criterion variable can be forecast by a current measurement scale.

concurrent validity
The degree to which another variable, measured at the same point in time as the variable of interest, can be predicted by the measurement instrument.

construct validity
The degree to which a measurement instrument represents and logically connects, via the underlying theory, the observed phenomenon to the construct.

convergent validity
The degree of correlation among different measurement instruments that purport to measure the same construct.

discriminant validity
A measure of the lack of association among constructs that are supposed to be different.

develop a multi-item scale that measures the propensity to shop at discount stores. Our theory suggests that this propensity is caused by four personality variables: high level of self-confidence, low need for status, low need for distinctiveness, and high level of adaptability. Furthermore, our theory suggests that propensity to shop at discount stores is not related to brand loyalty or high-level aggressiveness.

Evidence of construct validity exists if our scale does the following:

■ Correlates highly with other measures of propensity to shop at discount stores, such as reported stores patronized and social class (convergent validity).

■ Has a low correlation with the unrelated constructs of brand loyalty and a high level of aggressiveness (discriminant validity).

All the types of validity discussed here are somewhat interrelated in both theory and practice. Predictive validity is obviously very important on a scale to predict whether a person will shop at a discount store. A researcher developing a discount store patronage scale probably would first attempt to understand the constructs that provide the basis for prediction. The researcher would put forth a theory about discount store patronage—that, of course, is the foundation of construct validity. Next, the researcher would be concerned with which specific items to include on the discount store patronage scale and whether these items relate to the full range of the construct. Thus, the researcher would ascertain the degree of content validity. The issue of criterion-related validity could be addressed in a pretest by measuring scores on the discount store patronage scale and actual store patronage.

Reliability and Validity—A Concluding Comment

The concepts of reliability and validity are illustrated in Exhibit 9.6. Situation 1 shows holes all over the target, which could be caused by the use of an old rifle, being a poor shot, or many other factors. This complete lack of consistency means there is no reliability. Because the instrument lacks reliability, thus creating huge errors, it cannot be valid. Measurement reliability is a necessary condition for validity.

Situation 2 denotes a very tight pattern (consistency), but the pattern is far removed from the bull's-eye. This illustrates that an instrument can have a high level of reliability (little variance) but lack validity. The instrument is consistent, but it does not measure what it is supposed to measure. The shooter has a steady eye, but the sights are not adjusted properly. Situation 3 shows the reliability and validity that researchers strive to achieve in a measurement instrument; it is on target with what the researcher is attempting to measure.

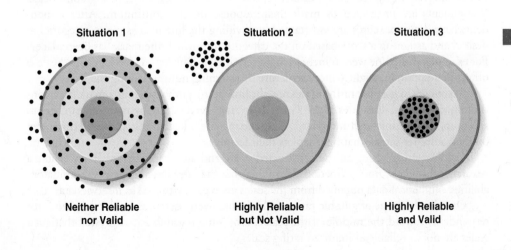

Situation 1

Neither Reliable
nor Valid

Situation 2

Highly Reliable
but Not Valid

Situation 3

Highly Reliable
and Valid

Exhibit 9.6

Illustrations of Possible Reliability and Validity Situations in Measurement

Scaling Defined

→ **scaling**
Procedures for assigning numbers (or other symbols) to properties of an object in order to impart some numerical characteristics to the properties in question.

→ **unidimensional scale**
A scale designed to measure only one attribute of a concept, respondent, or object.

→ **multidimensional scale**
A scale designed to measure several dimensions of a concept, respondent, or object.

The term **scaling** refers to procedures for attempting to determine quantitative measures of subjective and sometimes abstract concepts. It is defined as a procedure for assigning numbers (or other symbols) to properties of an object in order to impart some numerical characteristics to the properties in question. Actually, numbers are assigned to *indicants* of the properties of objects. The rise and fall of mercury in a glass tube (a thermometer) is an indicant of temperature variations.

A scale is a measurement tool. Scales are either unidimensional or multidimensional. **Unidimensional scales** are designed to measure only one attribute of a concept, respondent, or object. Thus, a unidimensional scale measuring consumers' price sensitivity might include several items to measure price sensitivity, but combined into a single measure; all interviewees' attitudes are then placed along a linear continuum, called *degree of price sensitivity*. **Multidimensional scales** are based on the premise that a concept, respondent, or object might be better described using several dimensions. For example, target customers for Jaguar automobiles may be defined in three dimensions: level of wealth, degree of price sensitivity, and appreciation of fine motor cars.

Attitude Measurement Scales

Measurement of attitudes relies on less precise scales than those found in the physical sciences and hence is much more difficult. Because an attitude is a construct that exists in the mind of the consumer, it is not directly observable—unlike, for example, weight in the physical sciences. In many cases, attitudes are measured at the nominal or ordinal level. Some more sophisticated scales enable the marketing researcher to measure at the interval level. One must be careful not to attribute the more powerful properties of an interval scale to the lower-level nominal or ordinal scales.

Graphic Rating Scales

→ **graphic rating scale**
A measurement scale that includes a graphic continuum, anchored by two extremes.

Graphic rating scales offer respondents a graphic continuum, typically anchored by two extremes. Exhibit 9.7 depicts three types of graphic rating scales that might be used to evaluate La-Z-Boy recliners. Scale A represents the simplest form of a graphic scale. Respondents are instructed to mark their response on the continuum. After respondents have done so, scores are ascertained by dividing the line into as many categories as desired and assigning a score based on the category into which the mark has been placed. For example, if the line were 6 inches long, every inch might represent a category. Scale B offers the respondent slightly more structure by assigning numbers along the scale.

Responses to graphic rating scales are not limited to simply placing a mark on a continuum, as scale C illustrates. Scale C has been used successfully by many researchers to speed up self-administered interviews. Respondents are asked to touch the thermometer on the computer screen that best depicts their feelings.

Graphic rating scales can be constructed easily and are simple to use. They enable a researcher to discern fine distinctions, assuming that the rater has adequate discriminatory abilities. Numerical data obtained from the scales are typically treated as interval data.

One disadvantage of graphic rating scales is that overly extreme anchors tend to force respondents toward the middle of the scale. Also, some research has suggested that such scales are not as reliable as itemized rating scales.

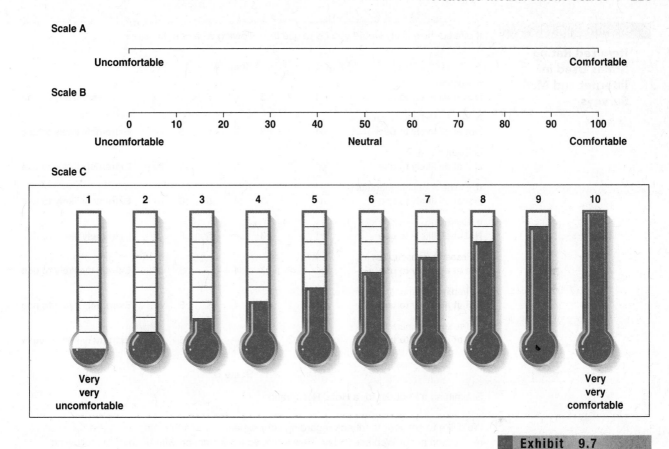

Scale A

Uncomfortable — Comfortable

Scale B

0 10 20 30 40 50 60 70 80 90 100

Uncomfortable — Neutral — Comfortable

Scale C

1 2 3 4 5 6 7 8 9 10

Very very uncomfortable — Very very comfortable

Exhibit 9.7

Three Types of Graphic Rating Scales

Itemized Rating Scales

Itemized rating scales are similar to graphic rating scales, except that respondents must select from a limited number of ordered categories rather than placing a mark on a continuous scale. (Purists would argue that scale C in Exhibit 9.7 is an itemized rating scale.) Exhibit 9.8 shows some examples of itemized rating scales taken from nationwide marketing research surveys. Starting items are rotated on each questionnaire to eliminate the order bias that might arise from starting with the same item each time.

Scale A was used by a dot-com company in determining what features and services it should add to its Web site. Scale B was used in measuring satisfaction with an online travel site. Scale C was used by an e-commerce music retailer to better understand how people select a music Web site. Scale D was also an Internet survey, conducted by a producer of customer relationship management software.

Although itemized rating scales do not allow for the fine distinctions that can be achieved in a graphic rating scale, they are easy to construct and administer. And the definitive categories found in itemized rating scales usually produce more reliable ratings.

When a researcher, for some reason, is interested in the most extreme position views, he or she may elect to use a two-stage format. Research has shown that a two-stage format can provide better data quality in detecting extreme views than a single-stage itemized rating scale. Following is an example of the two-stage approach.[7]

> → **itemized rating scale**
> A measurement scale in which the respondent selects an answer from a limited number of ordered categories.

Exhibit 9.8

Itemized Rating Scales Used in Internet and Mall Surveys

If offered, how likely would you be to use the following areas on this site?

Scale A

a. Auctions
Not at all likely to use   o1   o2   o3   o4   o5   o6   o7   **Extremely likely to use**

b. Fee-based education tools
Not at all likely to use   o1   o2   o3   o4   o5   o6   o7   **Extremely likely to use**

c. Event registration
Not at all likely to use   o1   o2   o3   o4   o5   o6   o7   **Extremely likely to use**

d. Online shopping markets
Not at all likely to use   o1   o2   o3   o4   o5   o6   o7   **Extremely likely to use**

e. Recruiting
Not at all likely to use   o1   o2   o3   o4   o5   o6   o7   **Extremely likely to use**

f. Research subscription
Not at all likely to use   o1   o2   o3   o4   o5   o6   o7   **Extremely likely to use**

g. Trading community
Not at all likely to use   o1   o2   o3   o4   o5   o6   o7   **Extremely likely to use**

h. Training/seminars
Not at all likely to use   o1   o2   o3   o4   o5   o6   o7   **Extremely likely to use**

Scale B

Submitting a Request for a Hotel Reservation

We'd like to get your feedback regarding your experience in submitting a request for a hotel reservation at our Web site today. Please rate your satisfaction with each of the following aspects of *fasthotels.com* based on **your experience this visit**.

	Very Satisfied				Very Dissatisfied
	1	2	3	4	5
Ability to access the offer page	o	o	o	o	o
Ability to locate hotel information	o	o	o	o	o
Ability to locate city information	o	o	o	o	o
Clarity of how the bonus program works	o	o	o	o	o
Clarity of the purchase agreement	o	o	o	o	o

Please rate the extent to which you are satisfied that *Fasthotels.com* **has communicated** each of the following to you during this visit:

	Very Satisfied				Very Dissatisfied
	1	2	3	4	5
Your hotel reservation is/will be nonchangeable	o	o	o	o	o
Your hotel reservation is/will be nonrefundable	o	o	o	o	o

How **satisfied** would you say you were with **this visit** to *Fasthotels.com*?
O   Very satisfied
O   Satisfied
O   Somewhat satisfied
O   Neither satisfied nor dissatisfied
O   Somewhat dissatisfied
O   Dissatisfied
O   Very dissatisfied

Scale C

What factors influence your choice of music Web sites? (Rate the importance of each item.)

Exhibit 9.8

Itemized Rating Scales Used in Internet and Mall Surveys (Continued)

	Not at All Important				Very Important
Customer benefits or rewards for shopping	o	o	o	o	o
Customer service or delivery options	o	o	o	o	o
Ease of use of Web site	o	o	o	o	o
Low prices	o	o	o	o	o
Real-time audio sampling of CDs	o	o	o	o	o
Reviews and artist information	o	o	o	o	o

Scale D

How interested would you be in obtaining additional information about this customer relationship management solution for your business?

o Extremely interested   o Somewhat interested   o Not at all interested
o Very interested   o Not very interested

How likely is it that your business will invest in this type of customer relationship management solution within the next 12 months?

o Extremely likely   o Somewhat likely   o Not at all likely
o Very likely   o Not very likely

Traditional One-Stage Format

"How effective do you believe Senator Foghorn is in having your money stay in the community?"

Very effective	Somewhat effective	Somewhat ineffective	Very ineffective	Don't know
4	3	2	1	0

Two-Stage Format

"How effective do you believe Senator Foghorn is in having your money stay in the community?"

How *effective?*	Would that be very or *somewhat?*
☐ Effective	☐ Very
☐ Ineffective	☐ Somewhat
☐ No opinion	

Rank-Order Scales

Itemized and graphic scales are considered to be **noncomparative scales** because the respondent makes a judgment without reference to another object, concept, or person. **Rank-order scales**, on the other hand, are **comparative scales** because the respondent is asked to compare two or more items and rank each item. Rank-order scales are widely used in marketing research for several reasons. They are easy to use and give ordinal measurements of the items evaluated. Instructions are easy to understand, and the process typically moves at a steady pace. Some researchers claim that rank-order scales force

noncomparative scale
A measurement scale in which judgment is made without reference to another object, concept, or person.

rank-order scale
A measurement scale in which the respondent compares two or more items and ranks them.

comparative scale
A measurement scale in which one object, concept, or person is compared with another on a scale.

Exhibit 9.9

Series of Rank-Order Scales Used to Evaluate Eye Shadows and Car Resale Values

Eye Shadow Scales

Please rank the following eye shadows, with 1 being the brand that best meets the characteristic being evaluated and 6 the worst brand on the characteristic being evaluated. The six brands are listed on card C. (HAND RESPONDENT CARD C.) Let's begin with the idea of having high-quality compacts or containers. Which brand would rank as having the highest quality compacts or containers? Which is second? (RECORD BELOW.)

	Q.48. Having High-Quality Container	Q.49. Having High-Quality Applicator	Q.50. Having High-Quality Eye Shadow
Avon	_____	_____	_____
Cover Girl	_____	_____	_____
Estee Lauder	_____	_____	_____
L'Oreal	_____	_____	_____
Natural Wonder	_____	_____	_____
Revlon	_____	_____	_____

Card C

Avon	Cover Girl	Estee Lauder
L'Oreal	Natural Wonder	Revlon

Car Resale Value Scale

Based on your personal experience or what you have seen, heard or read, please rank the following car brands according to the resale value percentage—that is, the brand that enables you to recover the largest dollar amount (percentage) of your original purchase price of the vehicle.

Place a "1" next to the brand that has the highest resale value percentage, a "2" next to the brand that has the next highest resale value percentage, and so forth. Remember, no two cars can have the same ranking.

_____	Chevrolet
_____	Toyota
_____	BMW
_____	Ford

respondents to evaluate concepts in a realistic manner. Exhibit 9.9 illustrates a series of rank-order scales taken from a study on eye shadows. Exhibit 9.9 shows an online scale on automobile resale value percentage.

Rank-order scales possess several disadvantages. If all of the alternatives in a respondent's choice set are not included, the results could be misleading. For example, a respondent's first choice on all dimensions in the eye shadow study might have been Wet'n'Wild, which was not included. A second problem is that the concept being ranked may be completely outside a person's choice set, thus producing meaningless data. Perhaps a respondent doesn't use eye shadow and feels that the product isn't appropriate for any woman. Another limitation is that the scale gives the researcher only ordinal data. Nothing is learned about how far apart the items stand or how intensely the respondent feels about the ranking of an item. Finally, the researcher does not know why the respondent ranked the items as he or she did.

Paired Comparisons

→ **paired comparison scale**
A measurement scale that asks the respondent to pick one of two objects in a set, based on some stated criteria.

A paired comparison scale asks a respondent to pick one of two objects from a set, based on some stated criteria. The respondent, therefore, makes a series of paired judgments between objects. Exhibit 9.10 shows a paired comparison scale used in a national

Exhibit 9.10

Paired Comparison Scale for Sun Care Products

Here are some characteristics used to describe sun care products in general. Please tell me which characteristic in each pair is more important to you when selecting a sun care product.

a. Tans evenly	b. Tans without burning
a. Prevents burning	b. Protects against burning and tanning
a. Good value for the money	b. Goes on evenly
a. Not greasy	b. Does not stain clothing
a. Tans without burning	b. Prevents burning
a. Protects against burning and tanning	b. Good value for the money
a. Goes on evenly	b. Tans evenly
a. Prevents burning	b. Not greasy

study for sun care products. Only part of the scale is shown; the data-collection procedure typically requires the respondent to compare all possible pairs of objects.

Paired comparisons overcome several problems of traditional rank-order scales. First, it is easier for people to select one item from a set of two than to rank a large set of data. Second, the problem of order bias is overcome; there is no pattern in the ordering of items or questions to create a source of bias. On the negative side, because all possible pairs are evaluated, the number of paired comparisons increases geometrically as the number of objects to be evaluated increases arithmetically. Thus, the number of objects to be evaluated should remain fairly small to prevent interviewee fatigue.

Constant Sum Scales

To avoid long lists of paired items, marketing researchers use **constant sum scales** more often than paired comparisons. Constant sum scales require the respondent to divide a given number of points, typically 100, among two or more attributes based on their importance to him or her. Respondents must value each item relative to all other items. The number of points allocated to each alternative indicates the ranking assigned to it by the respondent, as well as the relative magnitude of each alternative as perceived by the respondent. A constant sum scale used in a national study of tennis sportswear is shown in Exhibit 9.11. Another advantage of the constant sum scale over a rank-order or paired comparison scale is that if the respondent perceives two characteristics to have equal value, he or she can so indicate.

A major disadvantage of this scale is that the respondent may have difficulty allocating the points to total 100 if there are a lot of characteristics or items. Most researchers feel that 10 items is the upper limit on a constant sum scale.

→ **constant sum scale**
A measurement scale that asks the respondent to divide a given number of points, typically 100, among two or more attributes, based on their importance to him or her.

Semantic Differential Scales

The semantic differential scale was developed by Charles Osgood, George Suci, and Percy Tannenbaum.[8] The focus of their original research was on the measurement of meaning of an object to a person. The object might be a savings and loan association and the meaning its image among a certain group of people.

The construction of a **semantic differential scale** begins with determination of a concept to be rated, such as the image of a company, brand, or store. The researcher selects dichotomous (opposite) pairs of words or phrases that could be used to describe the concept. Respondents then rate the concept on a scale (usually 1 to 7). The mean of the responses for each pair of adjectives is computed, and the means are plotted as a profile or image.

→ **semantic differential scale**
A measurement scale that examines the strengths and weaknesses of a concept by having the respondent rank it between dichotomous pairs of words or phrases that could be used to describe it; the means of the responses are then plotted as a profile or image.

Exhibit 9.11

Constant Sum Scale Used in Tennis Sportswear Study

Below are seven characteristics of women's tennis sportswear. Please allocate 100 points among the characteristics such that the allocation represents the importance of each characteristic to you. The more points that you assign to a characteristic, the more important it is. If the characteristic is totally unimportant, you should not allocate any points to it. When you've finished, please double-check to make sure that your total adds to 100.

Characteristics of Tennis Sportswear	Number of Points
Is comfortable to wear	_____
Is durable	_____
Is made by well-known brand or sports manufacturers	_____
Is made in the United States	_____
Has up-to-date styling	_____
Gives freedom of movement	_____
Is a good value for the money	_____
	100 points

Exhibit 9.12 is an actual profile of an Arizona savings and loan association as perceived by noncustomers with family incomes of $80,000 and above. A quick glance shows that the firm is viewed as somewhat old-fashioned, with rather plain facilities. It is viewed as well established, reliable, successful, and probably very nice to deal with. The institution has parking problems and perhaps entry and egress difficulties. Its advertising is viewed as dismal.

The semantic differential is a quick and efficient means of examining the strengths and weaknesses of a product or company image versus those of the competition. More importantly, however, the semantic differential has been shown to be sufficiently reliable and valid for decision making and prediction in marketing and the behavioral sciences.[9] Also, the semantic differential has proved to be statistically robust (generalizable from one group of subjects to another) when applied to corporate image research.[10] This makes possible the measurement and comparison of images held by interviewees with diverse backgrounds.

Although these advantages have led many researchers to use the semantic differential scale as an image measurement tool, it is not without disadvantages. First, the semantic differential scale suffers from a lack of standardization. It is a highly generalized technique that must be adapted for each research problem. There is no single set of standard scales; hence, the development of customized scales becomes an integral part of the research.

The number of divisions on the semantic differential scale also presents a problem. If too few divisions are used, the scale is crude and lacks meaning; if too many are used, the scale goes beyond the ability of most people to discriminate. Researchers have found the 7-point scale to be the most satisfactory.

Another disadvantage of the semantic differential is the *halo effect*. The rating of a specific image component may be dominated by the interviewee's overall impression of the concept being rated. Bias may be significant if the image is hazy in the respondent's mind. To partially counteract the halo effect, the researcher should randomly reverse scale adjectives so that all the "good" ones are not placed on one side of the scale and the "bad" ones on the other. This forces the interviewee to evaluate the adjectives before responding. After the data have been gathered, all the positive adjectives are placed on one side and the negative ones on the other to facilitate analysis.

Stapel Scales

The **Stapel scale** is a modification of the semantic differential. A single adjective is placed in the center of the scale, which typically is a 10-point scale ranging from +5 to –5.

→ **Stapel scale**
A measurement scale that requires the respondent to rate, on a scale ranging from +5 to –5, how closely and in what direction a descriptor adjective fits a given concept.

Adjective 1	Mean of Each Adjective Pair							Adjective 2
	1	2	3	4	5	6	7	
Modern	*	*	*	*	*	*	*	Old-fashioned
Aggressive	*	*	*	*	*	*	*	Defensive.
Friendly	*	*	*	*	*	*	*	Unfriendly
Well established	*	*	*	*	*	*	*	Not well established
Attractive exterior	*	*	*	*	*	*	*	Unattractive exterior
Reliable	*	*	*	*	*	*	*	Unreliable
Appeals to small companies	*	*	*	*	*	*	*	Appeals to big companies
Makes you feel at home	*	*	*	*	*	*	*	Makes you feel uneasy
Helpful services	*	*	*	*	*	*	*	Indifferent to customers
Nice to deal with	*	*	*	*	*	*	*	Hard to deal with
No parking or transportation problems	*	*	*	*	*	*	*	Parking or transportation problems
My kind of people	*	*	*	*	*	*	*	Not my kind of people
Successful	*	*	*	*	*	*	*	Unsuccessful
Ads attract a lot of attention	*	*	*	*	*	*	*	Haven't noticed ads
Interesting ads	*	*	*	*	*	*	*	Uninteresting ads
Influential ads	*	*	*	*	*	*	*	Not influential

Exhibit 9.12

Semantic Differential Profile of an Arizona Savings and Loan Association

The technique is designed to measure both the direction and the intensity of attitudes simultaneously. (The semantic differential scale, on the other hand, reflects how closely the descriptor adjective fits the concept being evaluated.) An example of a Stapel scale is shown in Exhibit 9.13.

The primary advantage of the Stapel scale is that it enables the researcher to avoid the arduous task of creating bipolar adjective pairs. The scale may also permit finer discrimination in measuring attitudes. A drawback is that descriptor adjectives can be phrased in a positive, neutral, or negative vein, and the choice of phrasing has been shown to affect the scale results and the person's ability to respond.[11] The Stapel scale has never had much popularity in commercial research and is used less frequently than the semantic differential scale.

Likert Scales

The **Likert scale** is another scale that avoids the problem of developing pairs of dichotomous adjectives. The scale consists of a series of statements expressing either a favorable or an unfavorable attitude toward the concept under study. The respondent is asked to indicate the level of her or his agreement or disagreement with each statement by assigning it a numerical score. The scores are then totaled to measure the respondent's attitude.

Exhibit 9.14 shows two Likert scales for an Internet game site targeted toward teenagers. Scale A measures attitudes toward the registration process; scale B evaluates users' attitudes toward advertising on the Web site.

With the Likert scale, the respondent is required to consider only one statement at a time, with the scale running from one extreme to the other. A series of statements (attitudes) can be examined, yet there is only a single set of uniform replies for the respondent to choose from.

➤ Likert scale
A measurement scale in which the respondent specifies a level of agreement or disagreement with statements expressing either a favorable or an unfavorable attitude toward the concept under study.

Exhibit 9.13		

Stapel Scale Used to Measure a Retailer's Web Site

	Cheap Prices	Easy to Navigate
	+5	+5
	+4	+4
	+3	+3
	+2	+2
	+1	+1
	Cheap Prices	Easy to Navigate
	−1	−1
	−2	−2
	−3	−3
	−4	−4
	−5	−5

Select a "plus" number for words you think describe the Web site accurately. The more accurately you think the word describes the Web site, the larger the "plus" number you should choose. Select a "minus" number for words you think do not describe the Web site accurately. The less accurately you think the word describes the Web site, the larger the "minus" number you should choose. Therefore, you can select any number from 15 for words you think are very accurate all the way to −5 for words you think are very inaccurate.

© aurumarcus/iStockphoto

People's attitudes toward activities like snowboarding can be measured using Likert scales.

Rensis Likert created this scale to measure a person's attitude toward concepts (for example, unions), activities (for example, swimming), and so forth. He recommended the following steps in building the scale:

1. The researcher identifies the concept or activity to be scaled.

2. The researcher assembles a large number of statements (75 to 100) concerning the public's sentiments toward the concept or activity.

3. Each test item is classified by the researcher as generally "favorable" or "unfavorable" with regard to the attitude under study. No attempt is made to scale the items; however, a pretest is conducted that involves the full set of statements and a limited sample of respondents.

4. In the pretest, the respondent indicates agreement (or not) with *every* item, checking one of the following direction-intensity descriptors:
   a. Strongly agree
   b. Agree
   c. Undecided
   d. Disagree
   e. Strongly disagree

5. Each response is given a numerical weight (for example, 5, 4, 3, 2, 1).

6. The individual's *total attitude score* is represented by the algebraic summation of weights associated with the items checked. In the scoring process, weights are assigned so that the direction of attitude—favorable to unfavorable—is consistent over items. For example, if 5 were assigned to "strongly agree" for favorable items, 5 should be assigned to "strongly disagree" for unfavorable items.

7. After seeing the results of the pretest, the researcher selects only those items that appear to discriminate well between high and low *total* scorers. This may be done by first finding the highest and lowest quartiles of subjects on the basis of *total* score and then comparing the mean differences on each *specific* item for these high and low groups (excluding the middle 50 percent of subjects).

8. The 20 to 25 items finally selected are those that have discriminated "best" (that is, exhibited the greatest differences in mean values) between high and low total scorers in the pretest.

9. Steps 3 through 5 are then repeated in the main study.

Exhibit 9.14

Likert Scales Used by an Internet Game Site

Scale A

How did you feel about the registration process when you became a new user?

	Strongly disagree	Somewhat disagree	Neutral	Somewhat agree	Strongly agree
The registration was simple.	O	O	O	O	O
The registration questions were "nonthreatening."	O	O	O	O	O
Registration here will protect my privacy.	O	O	O	O	O
The registration did not take a long time to complete.	O	O	O	O	O
The registration informed me about the site.	O	O	O	O	O

Scale B

How do you feel about the following statements?

	Strongly disagree	Somewhat disagree	Neutral	Somewhat agree	Strongly agree
Allowing companies to advertise on the Internet allows me to access free services.	O	O	O	O	O
I do not support advertising on this site even though it provides me with free entertainment.	O	O	O	O	O
There is extremely too much advertising on the Internet.	O	O	O	O	O
There is extremely too much advertising on this site.	O	O	O	O	O
It's easy for me to ignore the advertising on this site and just play the game.	O	O	O	O	O

Likert created the scale so that a researcher could look at a summed score and tell whether a person's attitude toward a concept was positive or negative. For example, the maximum favorable score on a 20-item scale would be 100; therefore, a person scoring 92 would be presumed to have a favorable attitude. Of course, two people could both score 92 and yet have rated various statements differently. Thus, specific components of their overall attitude could differ markedly. For example, if respondent A strongly agreed (5) that a particular bank had good parking and strongly disagreed (1) that its loan programs were the best in town and respondent B had the exact opposite attitude, both would have summed scores of 6.

In the world of marketing research, Likert-like scales are very popular. They are quick and easy to construct and can be administered by telephone or via the Internet. Commercial researchers rarely follow the textbook-like process just outlined. Instead, the scale usually is developed jointly by a client project manager and a researcher. Many times, the scale is created following a focus group.

Purchase Intent Scales

➤ **purchase intent scale**
A scale used to measure a respondent's intention to buy or not buy a product.

Perhaps the single scale used most often in marketing research is the **purchase intent scale**. The ultimate issue for marketing managers is, will they buy the product or not? If so, what percentage of the market can I expect to obtain? The purchase intent question normally is asked for all new products and services and product and service modifications by manufacturers, retailers, and even nonprofit organizations.[12]

During new-product development, the purchase intent question is first asked during concept testing to get a rough idea of demand. The manager wants to quickly eliminate potential turkeys, take a careful look at those products for which purchase intent is moderate, and push forward the products that seem to have star potential. At this stage, investment is minimal and product modification or concept repositioning is an easy task. As the product moves through development, the product itself, promotion strategy, price levels, and distribution channels become more concrete and focused. Purchase intent is evaluated at each stage of development and demand estimates are refined. The crucial go–no go decision for national or regional rollout typically comes after test marketing. Immediately before test marketing, commercial researchers have another critical stage of evaluation. Here, the final or near-final version of the product is placed in consumers' homes in test cities around the country. After a period of in-home use (usually 2 to 6 weeks), a follow-up survey is conducted among participants to find out their likes and dislikes, how the product compares with what they use now, and what they would pay for it. The critical question near the end of the questionnaire is purchase intent.

Question 21 in Exhibit 9.15 is a purchase intent question taken from a follow-up study on in-home placement of a fly trap. The trap consisted of two 3-inch disks held about one-quarter inch apart by three plastic pillars; it looked somewhat like a large, thin yo-yo. The trap contained a pheromone to attract the flies and a glue that would remain sticky for 6 months. Supposedly, the flies flew in but never out. Centered on the back side of one of the disks was an adhesive tab so that the disk could be attached to a kitchen window. The concept was to eliminate flies in the kitchen area without resorting to a pesticide. Question 22 was designed to aid in positioning the product, and question 23 traditionally was used by the manufacturer as a double-check on purchase intent. If 60 percent of the respondents claimed that they definitely would buy the product and 90 percent said they definitely would not recommend the product to their friends, the researcher would question the validity of the purchase intent.

The purchase intent scale has been found to be a good predictor of consumer choice of frequently purchased and durable consumer products.[13] The scale is very easy to construct, and consumers are simply asked to make a subjective judgment of their likelihood of buying a new product. From past experience in the product category, a marketing manager can translate consumer responses on the scale to estimates of purchase probability. Obviously, everyone who "definitely will buy" the product will not do so; in fact, a few who state that they definitely will not buy actually will buy the product. The manufacturer of the fly trap is a major producer of both pesticide and nonpesticide pest control products. Assume that, based on historical follow-up studies, the manufacturer has

21. If a set of three traps sold for approximately $3.00 and was available in the stores where you normally shop, would you:

	(51)
definitely buy the set of traps	1
probably buy	2
probably not buy	3
definitely not buy	4

22. Would you use the traps (a) instead of or (b) in addition to existing products?

	(52)
instead of	1
in addition to	2

23. Would you recommend this product to your friends?

	(53)
definitely	1
probably	2
probably not	3
definitely not	4

Exhibit 9.15

Purchase Intent Scale and Related Questions for In-Home Product Placement of Fly Traps

learned the following about purchase intent of nonpesticide home-use pest-control products:

- 63 percent of the "definitely will buy" actually purchase within 12 months.
- 28 percent of the "probably will buy" actually purchase within 12 months.
- 12 percent of the "probably will not buy" actually purchase within 12 months.
- 3 percent of the "definitely will not buy" actually purchase within 12 months.

Suppose that the fly trap study resulted in the following:

- 40 percent—definitely will buy
- 20 percent—probably will buy
- 30 percent—probably will not buy
- 10 percent—definitely will not buy

Assuming that the sample is representative of the target market,

$$(0.4)(63\%) + (0.2)(28\%) + (0.3)(12\%) + (0.1)(3\%)$$
$$= 35.7\% \text{ market share}$$

Most marketing managers would be deliriously happy about such a high market share prediction for a new product. Unfortunately, because of consumer confusion, the product was killed after the in-home placement despite the high prediction.

It is not uncommon for marketing research firms to conduct studies containing a purchase intent scale in cases where the client does not have historical data to use as a basis for weighing the results. A reasonable but conservative estimate would be 70 percent of the "definitely will buy," 35 percent of the "probably will buy," 10 percent of the "probably will not buy," and zero of the "definitely will not buy."[14] Higher weights are common in the industrial market.

Some companies use the purchase intent scale to make go–no go decisions in product development without reference to market share. Typically, managers simply add the "definitely will buy" and "probably will buy" percentages and compare that total to a predetermined go–no go threshold. Combining "definitely" and "probably" is referred to as a top-two box score. One consumer goods manufacturer, for example, requires a box score of 80 percent or higher at the concept testing stage and 65 percent for a product to move from in-home placement tests to test marketing.

Considerations in Selecting a Scale

Most nonimage studies include a purchase intent scale. But many other questions arise in selecting a scale. Considerations include the nature of the construct being measured, type of scale, balanced versus nonbalanced scale, number of scale categories, and forced versus nonforced choice.

The Nature of the Construct Being Measured

A basic check of the appropriateness of a scale is confirmation that it is drawn directly from the overall objective of the research study. The scope of the research objectives has a fundamental effect on the manner in which scales are used for survey measurement.

Type of Scale

Most commercial researchers lean toward scales that can be administered over the telephone or via the Internet, to save interviewing expense. Ease of administration and development also are important considerations. For example, a rank-order scale can be created quickly, whereas developing a semantic differential (rating) scale is often a long and tedious process. The client's decision-making needs are always of paramount importance. Can the decision be made using ordinal data, or must the researcher provide interval information? Researchers also must consider the respondents, who usually prefer nominal and ordinal scales because of their simplicity. Ultimately, the choice of which type of scale to use will depend on the problem at hand and the questions that must be answered. It is not uncommon to find several types of scales in one research study. For example, an image study for a grocery chain might have a ranking scale of competing chains and a semantic differential to examine components of the chain's image.

Marketing researchers sometimes borrow scales directly from other studies or Internet sites. Many online survey sites have libraries of scales available. (See *surveymonkey.com*, *custominsight.com*, *surveysystem.com*, and *express.perseus.com*.) There are also several scale handbooks that facilitate the appropriate measures and encourage researchers to standardize on previously developed and validated measures.[15] This makes the research stream more cumulative. Marketing researchers often find that these borrowed scales work just fine. Sometimes, however, they don't work very well.

A marketing researcher should fully understand the nature of the construct that was measured, the scope of the measurement, and the content and phrasing of the scale items for relevance to a new population before borrowing a scale. In sum, the caveat is "borrow with caution."[16]

Balanced versus Nonbalanced Scale

> **balanced scale**
> A measurement scale that has the same number of positive and negative categories.

> **nonbalanced scale**
> A measurement scale that is weighted toward one end or the other of the scale.

A **balanced scale** has the same number of positive and negative categories; a **nonbalanced scale** is weighted toward one end or the other. If the researcher expects a wide range of opinions, then a balanced scale probably is in order. If past research or a preliminary study has determined that most opinions are positive, then using a scale with more positive gradients than negative ones will enable the researcher to ascertain the degree of positiveness toward the concept being researched. We have conducted a series of studies for the YMCA and know that its overall image is positive. Thus, we used the following categories to track the YMCA's image: (1) outstanding, (2) very good, (3) good, (4) fair, (5) poor.

Number of Scale Categories

The number of categories to be included in a scale is another issue that must be resolved by the marketing researcher. If the number of categories is too small—for example, good, fair, poor—the scale is crude and lacks richness. A 3-category scale does not reveal the intensity of feeling that, say, a 10-category scale offers. Yet, a 10-category scale may go beyond a person's ability to accurately discriminate among categories. Research has shown that rating scales with either 5 or 7 points are the most reliable.[17]

With an even number of scale categories, there is no neutral point. Without a neutral point, respondents are forced to indicate some degree of positive or negative feelings on an issue. Persons who are truly neutral are not allowed to express their neutrality. On the other hand, some marketing researchers say that putting a neutral point on a scale gives the respondent an easy way out, allowing the person with no really strong opinion to avoid concentrating on his or her actual feelings. Of course, it is rather unusual for any individual to be highly emotional about a new flavor of salad dressing, a package design, or a test commercial for a pickup truck!

Stan Behal/YMCA OF GREATER TORONTO//NewsCom

Forced versus Nonforced Choice

As mentioned in the discussion of semantic differential scales, if a neutral category is included it typically will attract those who are neutral and those who lack adequate knowledge to answer the question. Some researchers have resolved this issue by adding a "Don't know" response as an additional category. For example, a semantic differential might be set up as follows:

Friendly	1	2	3	4	5	6	7	**Unfriendly**	Don't Know
Unexciting	1	2	3	4	5	6	7	**Exciting**	Don't Know

A "Don't know" option, however, can be an easy out for the lazy respondent.

If it has a neutral point, a scale without a "Don't know" option does not force a respondent to give a positive or negative opinion. A scale without a neutral point or a "Don't know" option forces even those persons with no information about an object to state an opinion. The argument for forced choice is that the respondent has to concentrate on his or her feelings. The arguments against forced choice are that inaccurate data are recorded and that some respondents may refuse to answer the question. A questionnaire that continues to require respondents to provide an opinion when, in fact, they lack the necessary information to do so can create ill will and result in early termination of the interview.

Past research has indicated that the YMCA has an overall positive image. This means that a nonbalanced scale with more positive gradients than negative can be used in future research about the YMCA. Go to *www.ymca.com* to see how the YMCA is using research to reach new customers.

SUMMARY

Measurement consists of using rules to assign numbers or labels to objects in such a way as to represent quantities or qualities of attributes. A measurement rule is a guide, a method, or a command that tells a researcher what to do. Accurate measurement requires rules that are both clear and specific.

The measurement process comprises the following steps: (1) identify the concept of interest, (2) develop a construct, (3) define the concept constitutively, (4) define the concept operationally, (5) develop a measurement scale, and (6) evaluate the reliability and validity of the scale. A constitutive definition is a statement of the meaning of the central concept under study, establishing its boundaries. An operational definition specifies which observable characteristics will be measured and the process for assigning a value to the concept.

There are four basic levels of measurement: nominal, ordinal, interval, and ratio. A nominal scale partitions data into categories that are mutually exclusive and collectively exhaustive. The numbers assigned to objects or phenomena have no true numerical meaning; they are simply labels. Ordinal scales have the labeling characteristics of nominal scales plus an ability to order data. Interval scales contain all the features of ordinal scales with the added dimension that the intervals between the points on the scale are equal. Interval scales enable the researcher to discuss differences separating two objects. They are amenable to computation of an arithmetic mean, standard deviation, and correlation coefficients. Ratio scales have all the characteristics of previously discussed scales as well as a meaningful absolute zero or origin, thus permitting comparison of the absolute magnitude of the numbers and reflecting the actual amount of the variable.

Measurement data consist of accurate information and errors. Systematic error results in a constant bias in the measurements. Random error also influences the measurements but is not systematic; it is transient in nature. Reliability is the degree to which measures are free from random error and therefore provide consistent data. There are three ways to assess reliability: test–retest, internal consistency, and use of equivalent forms. Validity addresses whether the attempt at measurement was successful. The validity of a measure refers to the extent to which the measurement device or process is free from both systematic and random error. Types of validity include face, content, criterion-related, and construct validity.

The term *scaling* refers to procedures for attempting to determine quantitative measures of subjective and sometimes abstract concepts. It is defined as a procedure for assigning numbers or other symbols to properties of an object in order to impart some numerical characteristics to the properties in question. Scales are either unidimensional or multidimensional. A unidimensional scale is designed to measure only one attribute of a concept, respondent, or object. Multidimensional scaling is based on the premise that a concept, respondent, or object might be better described using several dimensions.

One type of scale is called a graphic rating scale. Respondents are presented with a graphic continuum, typically anchored by two extremes. Itemized rating scales are similar to graphic rating scales except that respondents must select from a limited number of categories rather than placing a mark on a continuous scale. A rank-order scale is a comparative scale because respondents are asked to compare two or more items with each other. Paired comparison scales ask the respondent to pick one of two objects from a set, based on some stated criteria. Constant sum scales require the respondent to divide a given number of points, typically 100, among two or more attributes, based on their importance to him or her. Respondents must value each item relative to all other items. The number of points allocated to each alternative indicates the ranking assigned to it by the respondent.

The semantic differential scale was developed to measure the meaning of an object to a person. The construction of a semantic differential scale begins with determination of a concept to be rated, such as a brand image; then the researcher selects dichotomous pairs of words or phrases that could be used to describe the concept. Respondents next rate the concept on a scale, usually 1 to 7. The mean of the responses is computed for each pair of adjectives, and the means are plotted as a profile or image. In the Stapel scale, a single adjective is placed in the center of the scale. Typically, a Stapel scale is designed to simultaneously measure both the direction and the intensity of attitudes. The Likert scale is another scale that avoids the problem of developing pairs of dichotomous adjectives. The scale consists of a series of statements expressing either a favorable or an unfavorable attitude toward the concept under study. The respondent is asked to indicate the level of his or her agreement or disagreement with each statement by assigning it a numerical score. Scores are then totaled to measure the respondent's attitude.

The scale that is used most often and perhaps is most important to marketing researchers is the purchase intent scale. This scale is used to measure a respondent's intention to buy or not buy a product. The purchase intent question usually asks a person to state whether he would definitely buy, probably buy, probably not buy, or definitely not buy the product under study. The purchase intent scale has been found to be a good predictor of consumer choice of frequently purchased consumer durable goods.

Several factors should be considered in selecting a particular scale for a study. The first is the type of scale to use: rating, ranking, sorting, or purchase intent. Next, consideration must be given to the use of a balanced scale versus a nonbalanced scale. The number of categories also must be determined. A related factor is whether to use an odd or even number of categories. Finally, the researcher must consider whether to use forced or nonforced choice sets.

KEY TERMS & DEFINITIONS

measurement The process of assigning numbers or labels to persons, objects, or events, in accordance with specific rules for representing quantities or qualities of attributes.

rule A guide, method, or command that tells a researcher what to do.

constructs Specific types of concepts that exist at higher levels of abstraction.

constitutive definition A statement of the meaning of the central idea or concept under study, establishing its boundaries; also known as *theoretical*, or *conceptual*, *definition*.

operational definition A statement of precisely which observable characteristics will be measured and the process for assigning a value to the concept.

scale A set of symbols or numbers so constructed that the symbols or numbers can be assigned by a rule to the individuals (or their behaviors or attitudes) to whom the scale is applied.

nominal scales Scales that partition data into mutually exclusive and collectively exhaustive categories.

ordinal scales Scales that maintain the labeling characteristics of nominal scales and have the ability to order data.

interval scales Scales that have the characteristics of ordinal scales, plus equal intervals between points to show relative amounts; they may include an arbitrary zero point.

ratio scales Scales that have the characteristics of interval scales, plus a meaningful zero point so that magnitudes can be compared arithmetically.

reliability The degree to which measures are free from random error and, therefore, provide consistent data.

test–retest reliability The ability of the same instrument to produce consistent results when used a second time under conditions as similar as possible to the original conditions.

stability Lack of change in results from test to retest.

equivalent form reliability The ability of two very similar forms of an instrument to produce closely correlated results.

internal consistency reliability The ability of an instrument to produce similar results when used on different samples during the same time period to measure a phenomenon.

split-half technique A method of assessing the reliability of a scale by dividing the total set of measurement items in half and correlating the results.

validity The degree to which what a researcher was trying to measure was actually measured.

face validity The degree to which a measurement seems to measure what it is supposed to measure.

content validity Representativeness, or sampling adequacy, of the content of a measurement instrument.

criterion-related validity The degree to which a measurement instrument can predict a variable that is designated a criterion.

predictive validity The degree to which a future level of a criterion variable can be forecast by a current measurement scale.

concurrent validity The degree to which another variable, measured at the same point in time as the variable of interest, can be predicted by the measurement instrument.

construct validity The degree to which a measurement instrument represents and logically connects, via the underlying theory, the observed phenomenon to the construct.

convergent validity The degree of correlation among different measurement instruments that purport to measure the same construct.

discriminant validity A measure of the lack of association among constructs that are supposed to be different.

scaling Procedures for assigning numbers (or other symbols) to properties of an object in order to impart some numerical characteristics to the properties in question.

unidimensional scale A scale designed to measure only one attribute of a concept, respondent, or object.

multidimensional scale A scale designed to measure several dimensions of a concept, respondent, or object.

graphic rating scale A measurement scale that includes a graphic continuum, anchored by two extremes.

itemized rating scale A measurement scale in which the respondent selects an answer from a limited number of ordered categories.

noncomparative scale A measurement scale in which judgment is made without reference to another object, concept, or person.

rank-order scale A measurement scale in which the respondent compares two or more items and ranks them.

comparative scale A measurement scale in which one object, concept, or person is compared with another on a scale.

paired comparison scale A measurement scale that asks the respondent to pick one of two objects in a set, based on some stated criteria.

constant sum scale A measurement scale that asks the respondent to divide a given number of points, typically 100, among two or more attributes, based on their importance to him or her.

semantic differential scale A measurement scale that examines the strengths and weaknesses of a concept by having the respondent rank it between dichotomous pairs of words or phrases that could be used to describe it; the means of the responses are then plotted as a profile or image.

Stapel scale A measurement scale that requires the respondent to rate, on a scale ranging from +5 to −5, how closely and in what direction a descriptor adjective fits a given concept.

Likert scale A measurement scale in which the respondent specifies a level of agreement or disagreement with statements expressing either a favorable or an unfavorable attitude toward the concept under study.

purchase intent scale A scale used to measure a respondent's intention to buy or not buy a product.

balanced scale A measurement scale that has the same number of positive and negative categories.

nonbalanced scale A measurement scale that is weighted toward one end or the other of the scale.

QUESTIONS FOR REVIEW & CRITICAL THINKING

(Team Activity)

1. What is measurement?
2. Differentiate among the four types of measurement scales and discuss the types of information obtained from each.
3. How does reliability differ from validity? Give examples of each.
4. Give an example of a scale that would be reliable but not valid. Also give an example of a scale that would be valid but not reliable.
5. What are three methods of assessing reliability?
6. What are three methods of assessing validity?
7. Divide the class into teams of four or five. Each team should use the Internet to find the results of a survey with data. Each team should then determine the face validity and content validity of the research. Also, each team should suggest a method for assessing reliability of the survey.
8. Discuss some of the considerations in selecting a rating, ranking, or purchase intent scale.
9. What are some of the arguments for and against having a neutral point on a scale?
10. Compare and contrast the semantic differential scale, Stapel scale, and Likert scale. Under what conditions would a researcher use each one?
11. The local department store in your home town has been besieged by competition from the large national chains. What are some ways that target customers' attitudes toward the store could be changed?
12. Develop a Likert scale to evaluate the parks and recreation department in your city.
13. Develop a purchase intent scale for students eating at the university's cafeteria. How might the reliability and validity of this scale be measured? Why do you think purchase intent scales are so popular in commercial marketing research?

14. When might a researcher use a graphic rating scale rather than an itemized rating scale?

15. What is the difference between a rating and a ranking? Which is best for attitude measurement? Why?

16. Develop a rank-order scale for soda preferences of college students. What are the advantages and disadvantages of this type of scale?

17. (*Team Exercise*) Divide the class into teams. Each team should create five adjective pairs of phrases that could be used in a semantic differential to measure the image of your college or university. The instructor will then aggregate the suggestions into a single semantic differential. Each team member should then conduct five interviews with students not in the class. The data can then be analyzed later in the term when statistical analysis is covered.

WORKING THE NET

1. Go to a Web search engine and look up "validity and reliability." Describe to the class the new insights you gain into these important concepts.

2. SBI (Strategic Business Insights) is a spinoff of the Stanford Research Institute. One of its most popular products is called VALS (Values and Life Style Survey). SBI uses VALS to segment the marketplace on the basis of personality traits that drive consumer behavior. VALS is used in all phases of the marketing mix. The survey categorizes consumers into one of eight personality types. GEOVALS applies the power of VALS to local marketing efforts by identifying the concentration of the VALS consumer group residing within a specific block group or zip code.

   Go to *www.strategicbusinessinsights.com* and click on the VALS SURVEY link. Next, click on "Take the survey."

   a. Explain the theory behind the creation of VALS.

   b. Do you agree with your VALS classification? Learn more by going to "The VALS Types" link.

   c. What kind of scale was used in the survey? Could other types of scales have been used?

   d. Explain how a marketer could use GEOVALS.

REAL-LIFE RESEARCH • 9.1

Case Backhoe Enters the Global Market

Many types of construction equipment are necessary for modern construction techniques. The most versatile and most often purchased of these is the loader backhoe.

How do engineers identify design advancements for the backhoe to keep the product line fresh and responsive to market needs? How do they make sure the design advancements are appropriate for the varied needs of a global marketplace? And how does marketing research pave the way for success in global construction equipment markets?

Corporate mergers, acquisitions, and joint ventures have brought Case together with other famous names in construction and agricultural equipment: New Holland, Kobelco, Hitachi, and Fiat—each brand a market success on its own. Recently these successful brands were given a new corporate identity in the form of CNH Global, which sells equipment in nearly every country in the world.

A frequent result of corporate mergers and acquisitions is that the newly merged corporation has multiple products competing in the same market. CNH Global is no exception. In particular, CNH Global has three strong brands competing in the global loader backhoe market.

As CNH Global plans for the future, the three loader backhoes will be differentiated in ways that create unique benefits for the customers of each brand while preserving the historic strengths of each brand. Engineering and marketing want advanced models of each brand to generate market share growth.

To design the next series of loader backhoe models, engineers were facing several key questions:

- How do loader backhoe operators view the various brands?
- What are the performance differences of each brand—whether grounded in real engineering design or perceived performance?
- What changes should be made in designing models for each of the CNH Global brands of loader backhoes to both bypass competition and differentiate the CNH brands?
- For answers to these questions, the global engineering team turned to marketing research.

Rigorous Field Tests

The first step was qualitative research, but traditional interviews or focus groups would not suffice. CNH chose field tests of each of five leading brands as the best way to level the playing field for brand experience and made the field tests grueling so that any real performance differences would be detected by equipment operators.

Following each test, operators rated the brand on an extensive list of performance attributes, and then were asked to give reasons for their ratings. Operators used their notes on "reasons" later in the day during in-depth discussions led by a moderator from the research supplier.

Scale Surprises

The field tests were also used to customize and pretest scales for later use in the quantitative stage of the marketing research. The intent was to develop scales that reflect the way operators think about loader backhoe performance. Researchers who routinely use symmetrical 7- or 9-point scales will be surprised by the findings.

Operators clearly identified four levels of satisfaction with loader backhoe performance attributes. They did not find four levels of dissatisfaction. So the symmetrical satisfaction scale often used in marketing research was not appropriate for the quantitative research.

They also found that use of the word *extremely*, as in "extremely satisfied," was inappropriate. While operators frequently said that more than one brand would be very effective for their job needs, they did not perceive anything "extremely" and never used a scale point with that adjective. So if a 7-point scale with the anchor points "extremely satisfied" and "extremely dissatisfied" had been used, as is often the practice in marketing research, it really would have been a 5-point scale from the operator's perspective.

CNH eventually determined that the scale that most effectively reflected the way operators think about their loader backhoes has four levels of satisfaction, a neutral point, and one level of dissatisfaction—a 6-point asymmetrical scale.

A scale with more levels would have introduced "noise" into the responses. Similarly, insisting that there be an equal number of levels of both satisfaction and dissatisfaction would have masked subtle differences in operator responses.

Global Implications

The results had a huge impact on advancing the engineering design of CNH loader backhoes. Operators indicated clear differences in performance among the brands. These findings are being used not only to better differentiate CNH brands from competitor brands but also to differentiate among the CNH brands.[18]

Questions

1. In addition to satisfaction-itemized rating scales, what other scales could have been used in the CNH marketing research?

2. Do you think that the decision to use an asymmetrical satisfaction scale was the right choice? Why or why not?

3. This study was conducted in many countries. Can scales be interpreted in the same manner around the world? For example, is a 2.1 the same in China as it is in Costa Rica?

4. Should purchase intent have been part of this questionnaire? Why or why not?

Winston Davidian/Getty Images, Inc.

Questionnaire Design

CHAPTER 10

LEARNING OBJECTIVES

→ **1.** To understand the role of the questionnaire in the data-collection process.

→ **2.** To become familiar with the criteria for a good questionnaire.

→ **3.** To learn the process for questionnaire design.

→ **4.** To become knowledgeable about the three basic forms of questions.

→ **5.** To learn the necessary procedures for successful implementation of a survey.

→ **6.** To understand how software and the Internet are influencing questionnaire design.

→ **7.** To understand the impact of the questionnaire on data-collection costs.

At a high level, questionnaire design is more art than science. However, when dealing with questionnaire specifics, such as how to ask certain types of questions, there is plenty of science in the form of methodological research that has been conducted by academics and marketing research professionals. In this chapter, we will provide both overall guidance regarding questionnaire design and best practices for handling specific issues based on the findings of methodological research studies.

The Role of a Questionnaire

> **questionnaire**
> A set of questions designed to generate the data necessary to accomplish the objectives of a research project; also called an *interview schedule* or a *survey instrument*.

Every form of survey research relies on the use of a questionnaire, the common thread in almost all data-collection methods. A **questionnaire** is a set of questions designed to generate the data necessary to accomplish the objectives of the research project; it is a formalized schedule for collecting information from respondents. You have most likely seen or even filled out a questionnaire recently. Creating a good questionnaire requires both hard work and imagination.

A questionnaire standardizes the wording and sequencing of questions and imposes uniformity on the data-gathering process. Every respondent sees or hears the same words; every interviewer asks identical questions. Without such standardization, interviewers could ask whatever they wanted, and researchers would be left wondering whether respondents' answers were a consequence of interviewer influence or interpretation; a valid basis for comparing respondents' answers would not exist. The jumbled mass of data would be unmanageable from a tabulation standpoint. In a very real sense, then, the questionnaire is a control device, but it is a unique one, as you will see.

The questionnaire (sometimes referred to as an *interview schedule* or a *survey instrument*) plays a critical role in the data-collection process. An elaborate sampling plan, well-trained interviewers, proper statistical analysis techniques, and good editing and coding are all for naught if the questionnaire is poorly designed. Improper design can lead to incomplete information, inaccurate data, and, of course, higher costs. The questionnaire is the production line of marketing research. It is here that the product, be it good or bad, is created. The questionnaire is the tool that creates the basic product (respondent information).

Exhibit 10.1 illustrates the pivotal role of the questionnaire. It is positioned between survey objectives (drawn from the manager's problem) and respondent information. In this position, it must translate the objectives into specific questions to solicit the required information from respondents.

Assume that Swatch is considering the development of a child's wristwatch. The timepiece would have a plastic casing with printed circuits inside. Swatch's engineering staff believes that it can come up with a watch that will withstand the potential abuse from the normal activities of a child between 8 and 13 years old. Preliminary marketing research is called for to determine the acceptability of the watch to the target market. One objective is to determine children's reactions to the watch. The marketing researchers must translate the objectives into language understandable to child

Exhibit 10.1

The Questionnaire's Pivotal Role in the Research Process

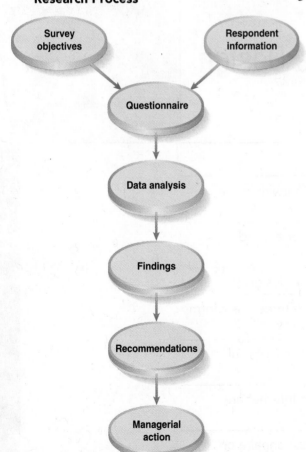

respondents, as an 8-year-old child probably won't be able to respond to questions that use such terms as *acceptability*, *efficiency*, and *likelihood of purchase*.

This example illustrates the pivotal role of the questionnaire: It must translate the survey objectives into a form understandable to respondents and "pull" the requisite information from them. At the same time, it must recover their responses in a form that can be easily tabulated and translated into findings and recommendations that will satisfy a manager's information requirements. Questionnaires also play a key role in survey costs, which will be discussed in detail later in the chapter.

The Questionnaire Design Process

Designing a questionnaire involves a series of logical steps, as shown in Exhibit 10.2. The steps may vary slightly when performed by different researchers, but all researchers tend to follow the same general sequence. Committees and lines of authority can complicate the process, so it is wise to clear each step with the individual who has the ultimate authority for the project. This is particularly true for the first step: determining survey objectives, resources, and constraints. Many work hours have been wasted because a researcher developed a questionnaire to answer one type of question, and the "real" decision maker wanted something entirely different. It also should be noted that the design process itself—specifically, question wording and format—can raise additional

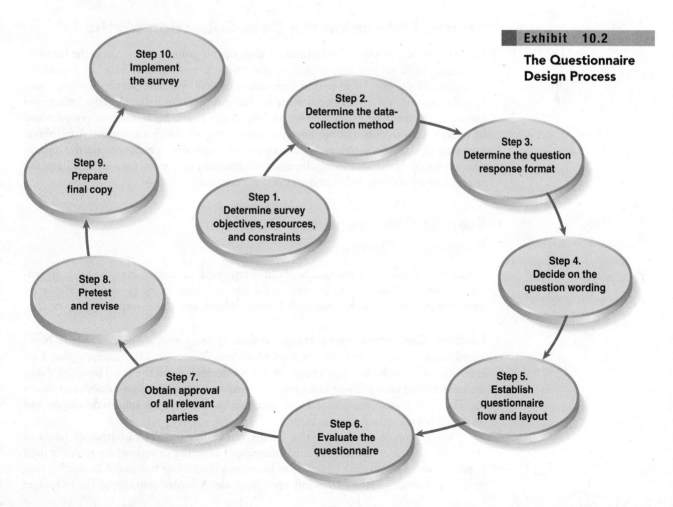

Exhibit 10.2

The Questionnaire Design Process

Step 1. Determine survey objectives, resources, and constraints

Step 2. Determine the data-collection method

Step 3. Determine the question response format

Step 4. Decide on the question wording

Step 5. Establish questionnaire flow and layout

Step 6. Evaluate the questionnaire

Step 7. Obtain approval of all relevant parties

Step 8. Pretest and revise

Step 9. Prepare final copy

Step 10. Implement the survey

issues or unanswered questions. This, in turn, can send the researcher back to step one for a clearer description of the information sought.

Step 1: Determine Survey Objectives, Resources, and Constraints

The research process often begins when a marketing manager, brand manager, or new-product development specialist has a need for decision-making information that is not available. In some firms, it is the manager's responsibility to evaluate all secondary sources to make certain that the needed information has not already been gathered. In other companies, the manager leaves all research activities, primary and secondary, to the research department.

Although a brand manager may initiate the research request, everyone affected by the project—including the assistant brand manager, the group product manager, and even the marketing manager—should provide input into exactly what data are needed. **Survey objectives** (which outline the decision-making information required) should be spelled out as clearly and precisely as possible. If this step is completed carefully and thoroughly, the rest of the process will follow more smoothly and efficiently.

Neil Kalt, president of Neil Kalt and Associates, talks about the importance of research objectives and the questionnaire. He also offers several tips on questionnaire design in the accompanying Practicing Marketing Research box.

> → **survey objectives**
> An outline of the decision-making information sought through a questionnaire.

Step 2: Determine the Data-Collection Method

Given the variety of ways in which survey data can be gathered, such as via the Internet, telephone, mail, or self-administration, the research method will have an impact on questionnaire design. An in-person interview in a mall will have constraints (such as a time limitation) not encountered with an Internet questionnaire. A self-administered questionnaire must be explicit and is usually rather short; because no interviewer will be present, respondents will not have the opportunity to clarify a question. A telephone interview may require a rich verbal description of a concept to make certain the respondent understands the idea being discussed. In contrast, an Internet survey can show the respondent a picture or video or demonstrate a concept.

Step 3: Determine the Question Response Format

Once the data-collection method has been determined, a decision must be made regarding the types of questions to be used in the survey. Three major types of questions are used in marketing research: open-ended, closed-ended, and scaled-response questions.

Ladders Can Sometimes Help   Infiniti recently won a "Best of What's New" award from *Popular Science* for its Around-View Monitor (AVM). Cameras placed on every side of the vehivle reflect objects or other vehicles around the car. The AVM shows the surrounding environment in a composite bird's-eye perspective on a dashboard monitor. The AVM system was one of 25 advanced technology features Infiniti developers had on the table four years before its launch.

The decision to implement this feature came after literally hundreds of hours of employing a research technique called laddering. Laddering interviews are typically used to provide an in-depth understanding of how consumers relate to a brand by delving into hidden, preconscious factors that influence purchase. A desired outcome of the technique

PRACTICING MARKETING RESEARCH

It's All about the Objectives

Every questionnaire has two overriding goals. The first is to keep respondents on-task—to hold their attention as they move through the questionnaire, keep them focused, and get them to answer each question honestly. The second is to generate data that fully addresses the study's objectives.

Achieving the second goal is the key. The sole purpose of achieving the first goal is to make achieving the second possible. How do you achieve both goals? By forging a questionnaire that is well thought out; that is clearly, logically, and succinctly written; that is constructed with the study's objectives in mind; that is always user-friendly; and that, if the stars align, has moments of ingenuity and imagination. The considerations that follow are intended to provide you with the tools and insights to construct questionnaires that satisfy these criteria:

1. **A study's objectives are its first and most important consideration.** They drive the research design, the construction of the questionnaire, and the analysis and interpretation of the data. Which is why this bears repeating: when constructing a questionnaire, the key question is always, "Will this questionnaire generate data that fully addresses the objectives of this study?" Keep asking yourself this question as you construct the questionnaire.

2. **Each question should be clearly written, in plain English, free of jargon, and without ambiguity.** Any question that falls short of this requirement may lessen the validity of the questionnaire. Unfortunately, writing clearly is easier said than done. A key reason is the gap that usually exists between the clarity with which we think we write and the clarity with which we actually write. We can do several things to narrow, and possibly close, this gap:

   - Be aware that it exists. It'll make you think more critically as you write, and it'll get you to review what you've written with a more discerning eye.

   - Ask at least one person whose judgment about the written word you trust to look at your questionnaire and, as warranted, suggest changes.

   - Personally administer your questionnaire to a few people. If you ask, they'll tell you whether the questions are easy to understand.

3. **Try to write questions the way you speak, in a conversational style.** It should make it easier for respondents to understand the questions and answer them, and it may help to keep them interested. One way to get an idea of how close you've come is to read it aloud and listen carefully to how it sounds— you want it to sound as if you're conversing with someone rather than reading aloud to them. Another way is to try it out on a few people and ask how easily it reads.

4. **Every questionnaire should have a logical flow to it and should make intuitive sense as the respondent moves from one question to the next.** One technique is to order them in a way that's consistent with how most people would approach the subject at hand. For example, if you're asking about a particular product, you might begin with questions about awareness, then move to questions about expectations, then to a purchase decision, then to reactions to the product, and finally to the likelihood of purchasing the product again. When you ask people how easily the questionnaire reads, ask them about its flow as well.

5. **The cost of wearing out your welcome is almost always high.** You're asking people to give you one of their more precious possessions—their time. If they feel that you're asking for too much, they may either stop in midstream and walk away or begin to answer quickly and with little or no thought, which is an ugly compromise between feeling obligated to complete the questionnaire and not wanting to give it any more time and effort.

Accordingly, the time it takes to complete a questionnaire should always be reasonable. A key determinant is the respondents' level of involvement in the category. For example, you can probably get away with a longer questionnaire when you're interviewing people who ride motorcycles and asking questions about Harley-Davidsons than you can when you're asking people about toothpaste.

Another key determinant is how easy, or difficult, it is to get through the questionnaire. If there are no bumps in the road, no thorny patches, nothing to annoy or frustrate respondents, then a 15-minute questionnaire should be just fine. However, if there are questions that are less than clear, questions that involve rating and raking an overly long list of attributes, repetitive questions, and questions that don't make sense, then 15 minutes is going to seem like forever and respondents will react accordingly.[1]

Questions

1. Is there a problem with specifying the research objectives after the questionnaire has been designed? Why?

2. Why is questionnaire length an important issue in questionnaire design?

is often information that supports brand identity development and provides emotionally based direction to drive strategy (see Exhibit 10.3).[2]

Ladders can be developed using qualitative research and then examined in more detail in qualitative research. The ladder can be used as a guide for designing the survey questions. In Infiniti's case, laddering was the tool used to prioritize its technology

A Ladder for the Infiniti Around-View Monitor

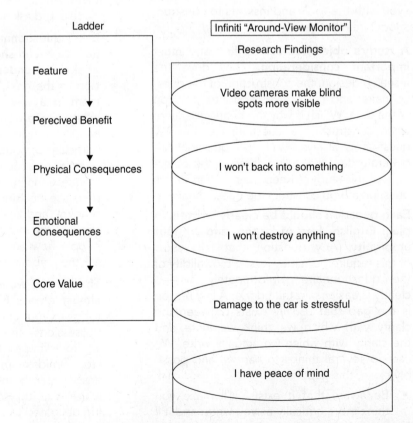

Ladder

Feature
↓
Perecived Benefit
↓
Physical Consequences
↓
Emotional Consequences
↓
Core Value

Infiniti "Around-View Monitor"

Research Findings

Video cameras make blind spots more visible

I won't back into something

I won't destroy anything

Damage to the car is stressful

I have peace of mind

Source: Adapted from Matt Schroder, "Laddering Showed Infiniti How Drivers Viewed Its Around-View Monitor Technology" *Quick's Marketing Research Review,* October 2009, p. 26.

rollouts over several years. In this project, the goal was to identify the core value of individual technology features with the already known core values of the Infiniti brand.

Laddering, of course, is only useful when the tool lines up with the research objectives. Not all research objectives are attempting to uncover core values. In the Infiniti example, you can easily see how the research objectives led to laddering which, in turn, guided questionnaire development. An example of a ladder for a business-to-business survey is shown in Exhibit 10.4. Ladders can also be built for other research objectives and therefore serve as guidelines for questionnaire development.

Open-Ended Questions   **Open-ended questions** are those to which the respondent replies in her or his own words. In other words, the researcher does not limit the response choices.

> → **open-ended question**
> A question to which the respondent replies in her or his own words.

Open-ended questions offer several advantages to the researcher. They enable respondents to give their general reactions to questions like the following:

1. What advantages, if any, do you think ordering from an e-retailer company offers compared with buying from local retail outlets? (*Probe:* What else?)

2. Why do you have one or more of your rugs or carpets professionally cleaned rather than cleaning them yourself or having someone else in the household clean them?

3. What do you think is most in need of improvement here at the airport?

4. What is there about the color of _____ [product] that makes you like it the best? (*Probe:* What color is that?)

5. Why do you say that brand [the one you use most often] is better?

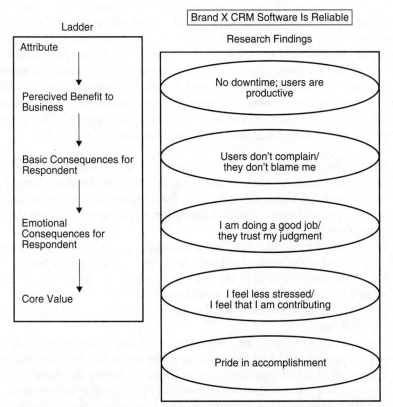

Exhibit 10.4

A Business Ladder for Customer Relationship Management (CRM) Software

Source: Adapted from Bernadette DeLamar, "Get to the Point," *Quirk's Marketing Research Review,* March 2010, p. 53.

Each of the preceding questions was taken from a different nationwide survey covering five products and services. Note that open-ended questions 2 and 4 are part of a skip pattern. Before being asked question 2, the respondent has already indicated that he or she uses a professional carpet cleaning service and does not depend on members of the household.

Open-ended responses have the advantage of providing the researcher with a rich array of information. The respondent's answers are based on his or her personal frame of reference and described in real-world terminology rather than laboratory or marketing jargon. Often, this is helpful in designing promotion themes and campaigns; it enables copywriters to use the consumer's language. This rich array of information can also be captured in computer-assisted interviews and Internet surveys.

The inspection of open-ended responses also can serve as a means of interpreting closed-ended questions. Analysis often sheds additional light on the motivations or attitudes behind closed-ended response patterns. It is one thing to know that color ranks second in importance out of five product attributes—but it might be much more valuable to know why color is important. For example, a recent study of mobile home park residents identified a great deal of dissatisfaction with the trash pick-up service, but further inspection of the open-ended responses uncovered the reason: Neighbors' dogs were allowed to run free and were overturning the receptacles.

Similarly, open-ended questions may suggest additional alternatives not listed in a closed-ended response format. For example, a previously unrecognized advantage of using an e-retail company might be uncovered in responses to question 1. A closed-ended question on the same subject would not have this advantage.

One manufacturer for which the authors consult always ends product placement questionnaires with the following: "Is there anything else that you would like to tell us about the product that you have tried during the past three weeks?" This probe seeks any final tidbit of information that might provide additional insight for the researcher.

Open-ended questions are not without their problems. Editing and coding can consume great amounts of time and money if done manually. Editing open-ended responses requires collapsing the many response alternatives into some reasonable number. If too many categories are used, data patterns and response frequencies may be difficult to interpret. Even if a proper number of categories is used, editors may still have to interpret what the interviewer has recorded and force the data into a category. If the categories are too broad, the data may be too general and important meaning may be lost.

Probing   Often, open-ended questions require probing. Probing means that an interviewer encourages the respondent to elaborate or continue the discussion.[3] Powerful probes will advance a discussion quickly away from top-of-mind responses and seat-of-the-pants answers—and access deeper information, allowing insight into the baseline thinking that drives behavior.

Probes fall into three distinct areas: proactive, reactive, and spontaneous. The last one is also called a "natural probe," since it just pops up instantly in the mind of a researcher who knows that deeper insights need to be expressed. For example, a respondent says: "I get upset when the line is too long at checkout." A natural probe has to be: "What upsets you?"

By contrast, a proactive probe is one that can be planned ahead of time, and it might look like the following:

The original question might be: "What were some key factors of importance to you when buying your last car?" And the proactive probe might be: "In reviewing those key factors in your mind, which one stands out as critical to buying decisions?" A proactive probing series can be planned ahead of time to lead the discussion to fertile areas for discussion, aimed at reaching the study purpose. And from time to time, a family of proactive probes might have a visitor from the "natural" probe family as well.

EXHIBIT 10.5	The Nuances of Probing

Probing Element	Examples
Comprehension or interpretation	– What does the term *outpatient* mean to you? – How do you refer to yourself—as a patient or as an outpatient?
Paraphrasing	– Can you repeat the question I just asked you in your own words?
Confidence or judgment	– How sure are you that your health insurance covers drug as well as alcohol treatment?
Recall	– How many times did you brush your teeth yesterday? – Follow-up probe: What were the reasons for each brushing? – How many times did you go to the bank to make a deposit in person in June? – Follow-up probes: Is June typical or not? If so, in what ways; if not, what are the reasons?
Assessing "self talk"	– You hesitated before answering... what was going on in your head in the pause?
Accessing "values/beliefs"	– What makes you think that cancer is America's most serious health problem?

Source: Naomi Henderson, *Marketing Research*, Winter 2007, p. 38.

Reactive probes are almost like "natural probes," except that they are more "knee jerk" in character. The most common ones are: "What makes you say that?" Or: "What is the basis for that belief on your part?" Those kinds of probes question the baseline thinking of a respondent, rather than relying on a report of behavior. A few examples of probes are as follows:

Request for elaboration: "Tell me more about that." Give me an example of. . . ."

Request for word association: "What do you mean by . . . .? "What does the term _____ mean to you?"

Request for clarification: "How does that differ from. . . .?" "In what circumstances do you. . . .?"

Request for comparison: "How is _____ similar to _____?" Which costs more, X or Y?"

Request for classification: "Where does _____ fit?" "What else is in the category of _____?"

 "Silent" probe: This is a nonverbal probe and is characterized by such actions as raised eyebrows or hand gestures such as moving the right hand in a rolling motion that signifies "Tell me more."[4]

Other examples of probing are shown in Exhibit 10.5.

Precoding open-ended questions can partially overcome these problems. Assume that this question was to be asked in a food study: "What, if anything, do you normally add to a taco that you have prepared at home, besides meat?" Coding categories for this open-ended question might be as follows:

Response	Code
Avocado	1
Cheese (Monterey jack, cheddar)	2
Guacamole	3
Lettuce	4
Mexican hot sauce	5

(continued)

Response	Code
Olives (black or green)	6
Onions (red or white)	7
Peppers (red or green)	8
Pimento	9
Sour cream	0
Other	X

These answers would be listed on the questionnaire, and a space would be provided to write in any nonconforming reply in the "Other" category. In a telephone interview, the question would still qualify as open-ended because the respondents would not see the categories and the interviewer would be instructed not to divulge them. Precoding necessitates that the researcher have sufficient familiarity with previous studies of a similar nature to anticipate respondents' answers. Otherwise, a pretest with a fairly large sample is needed.

Open-ended questions may be biased toward the articulate interviewee. A person with elaborate opinions and the ability to express them may have much greater input than a shy, inarticulate, or withdrawn respondent. Yet, both might be equally likely prospective consumers of a product.

Suppose an editor confronted the following responses to the taco question: "I usually add a green, avocado-tasting hot sauce." "I cut up a mixture of lettuce and spinach." "I'm a vegetarian; I don't use meat at all. My taco is filled only with guacamole." How should the editor code these?

A basic problem with open-ended questions lies in the interpretation-processing area. A two-phase judgment must be made. First, the researcher must decide on an appropriate set of categories, and then each response must be evaluated to determine into which category it falls.

If a food study on tacos asked, "What, if anything besides meat, do you normally add to a taco you have prepared at home?" coding categories would need to be determined to categorize answers to this open-ended question.

Thomas Firak Photography/Getty Images, Inc.

A final difficulty with open-ended questions is their inappropriateness on some self-administered questionnaires. With no interviewer there to probe, respondents may give a shallow, incomplete, or unclear answer. On a self-administered questionnaire without precoded choices, answers to the taco question might read "I use a little bit of everything" or "I use the same things they use in restaurants." These answers would have virtually no value to a researcher.

Closed-Ended Questions   A **closed-ended question** requires the respondent to make a selection from a list of responses. The primary advantage of closed-ended questions is simply the avoidance of many of the problems associated with open-ended questions. Reading response alternatives may jog a person's memory and generate a more realistic response. Interviewer bias is eliminated because the interviewer is simply clicking a box, circling a category, recording a number, or punching a key. Because the option of expounding on a topic is not given to a respondent, there is no bias toward the articulate. Finally, coding and data entry can be done automatically with questionnaire software programs.

> **closed-ended question**
> A question that requires the respondent to choose from a list of answers.

It is important to realize the difference between a precoded open-ended question and a multiple-choice question. A precoded open-ended question allows the respondent to answer in a freewheeling format; the interviewer simply checks coded answers as they are given. Probing is used, but a list is never read. If the answer given is not one of the precoded ones, it is written verbatim in the "Other" column. In contrast, a closed-ended question requires that a list of alternatives be read by the respondent or interviewer.

Traditionally, marketing researchers have separated closed-ended questions into two types: **dichotomous questions**, with a two-item response option, and **multiple-choice** (or multichotomous) **questions**, with a multi-item response option.

> **dichotomous question**
> A closed-ended question that asks the respondents to choose between two answers.

> **multiple-choice question**
> A closed-ended question that asks the respondent to choose among several answers; also called *multichotomous questions*.

Dichotomous Questions   In a dichotomous question, the two response categories are sometimes implicit. For instance, the implicit response options to the question "Did you buy gasoline for your automobile in the last week?" are "Yes" and "No." Even if the respondent says, "I rented a car last week, and they filled it up for me. Does that count?" the question would still be classified as dichotomous. A few examples of dichotomous questions follow:

1. Did you heat the Danish roll before serving it?
   Yes   1
   No   2

2. The federal government doesn't care what people like me think.
   Agree   1
   Disagree   2

3. Do you think that inflation will be greater or less than it was last year?
   Greater than   1
   Less than   2

Because the respondent is limited to two fixed alternatives, dichotomous questions are easy to administer and tabulate and usually evoke a rapid response. Many times, a neutral response option is added to dichotomous questions; if it is omitted, interviewers may jot down "DK" for "Don't know" or "NR" for "No response."

The "don't know" response has raised some concerns as telephone surveys have migrated to the Internet.

Dichotomous questions are prone to a large amount of measurement error. Because alternatives are polarized, the wide range of possible choices between the poles is omitted. Thus, appropriate wording is critical to obtaining accurate responses. Questions phrased in a positive form may well result in opposite answers from questions expressed in a negative form. For example, responses may depend on whether "Greater than" or "Less than" is listed first. These problems can be overcome by using a split ballot technique: One-half of the questionnaires have "Greater than" listed first, and the other half have "Less than" first. This procedure helps reduce potential order bias.

Another problem with the dichotomous question is that responses frequently fail to communicate any intensity of feeling on the part of the respondent. In some cases, like the gasoline purchasing example, the matter of intensity does not apply. But in some instances, strong feelings about an issue may be lost in the dichotomous response form. If the gasoline purchasing interview continued with the question "Would you purchase gasoline priced $1.00 per gallon above current prices if you were guaranteed twice the miles per gallon?" responses would likely range in intensity from "No; absolutely not" to "You bet!"

Multiple-Choice Questions   With multiple-choice questions, replies do not have to be coded as they do with open-ended questions, but the amount of information provided is more limited. The respondent is asked to give one alternative that correctly expresses his or her opinion or, in some instances, to indicate all alternatives that apply. Some examples of multiple-choice questions follow:

1. I'd like you to think back to the last footwear of any kind that you bought. I'll read you a list of descriptions and would like for you to tell me into which category it falls.

Dress and/or formal	1	Specialized athletic shoes	4
Casual	2	Boots	5
Canvas-trainer-gym shoes	3		

2. Please check the age group to which you belong.

A. Under 17	1	D. 35–49 years	4
B. 17–24 years	2	E. 50–64 years	5
C. 25–34 years	3	F. 65 and over	6

3. In the last 3 months, have you used Noxzema Skin Cream . . . (CHECK ALL THAT APPLY)

as a facial wash?	1
for moisturizing the skin?	2
for treating blemishes?	3
for cleansing the skin?	4
for treating dry skin?	5
for softening skin?	6
for sunburn?	7
for making the facial skin smooth?	8

Question 1, from a mall intercept interview, may not cover all possible alternatives and, thus, may not capture a true response. Where, for example, would an interviewer record work shoes? The same thing can be said for question 3. Not only are all possible alternatives not included, but respondents cannot elaborate or qualify their answers. The problem could be easily overcome by adding an "Any other use?" alternative to the question.

The multiple-choice question has two additional disadvantages. First, the researcher must spend time generating the list of possible responses. This phase may require brainstorming or intensive analysis of focus group tapes or secondary data. Second, the researcher must settle on a range of possible answers. If the list is too long, the respondent may become confused or lose interest. A related problem with any list is *position bias*. Respondents typically will choose either the first or the last alternative, all other things being equal. When Internet questionnaire software and CATI systems are used, however, position bias is eliminated by automatically rotating response order.

Scaled-Response Questions The last response format to be considered is **scaled-response questions**, which are closed-ended questions where the response choices are designed to capture intensity of feeling. Consider the following questions:

1. Now that you have used the product, would you say that you would buy it or not? (CHECK ONE)
   Yes, would buy it
   No, would not buy it

2. Now that you have used the product, would you say that you . . .
   (CHECK ONE)
   definitely would buy it?
   probably would buy it?
   might or might not buy it?
   probably would not buy it?
   definitely would not buy it?

→ **scaled-response question**
A closed-ended question in which the response choices are designed to capture the intensity of the respondent's feeling.

The first question fails to capture intensity. It determines the direction ("Yes" versus "No"), but it cannot compare with the second question in completeness or sensitivity of response. The latter also has the advantage of being ordinal in nature.

A primary advantage of using scaled-response questions is that scaling permits measurement of the intensity of respondents' answers. Also, many scaled-response forms incorporate numbers that can be used directly as codes. Finally, the marketing researcher can use much more powerful statistical tools with some scaled-response questions (see Chapter 14).

Sometimes scaling questions simply do not help in accomplishing the research objectives. For example, consider a 10-point scale that asks, "Please rate the timeliness of reports on the following 1- to 10-point scale." How would a researcher interpret a 6, 7, or 8? A simple way to accomplish the research objective is to ask, "Were you satisfied with the timeliness of the reports you received?" (yes or no). This data will provide a clear answer to the objective.

Step 4: Decide on the Question Wording

Once the marketing researcher has decided on the specific types of questions and the response formats, the next task is the actual writing of the questions. Wording specific questions can require a significant investment of the researcher's time unless questionnaire software or a survey Web site like Vovici or Zoomerang is used. Four general guidelines about the wording of questions are useful to bear in mind: (1) The wording must be clear, (2) the wording must not bias the respondent, (3) the respondent must be able to answer the questions, and (4) the respondent must be willing to answer the questions.

Make Sure the Wording Is Clear Once the researcher has decided that a question is absolutely necessary, the question must be stated so that it means the same thing to all respondents. Ambiguous terminology—for example, "Do you live within 5 minutes of here?" or "Where do you usually shop for clothes?"—should be avoided. The respondent's answer to the first question will depend on such factors as mode of transportation (maybe the respondent walks), driving speed, and perceptions of elapsed time. (The interviewer would do better to display a map with certain areas delineated and ask whether the respondent lives within the area outlined.) The second question depends on the type of clothing being purchased and the meaning of the word *Where*.

→ **clarity in wording**
Clarity achieved by avoiding ambiguous terminology, using reasonable, vernacular language adjusted to the target group, and asking only one question at a time.

Clarity also calls for the use of reasonable terminology. A questionnaire is not a vocabulary test. Jargon should be avoided, and verbiage should be geared to the target audience. The question "What is the level of efficacy of your preponderant dishwashing liquid?" probably would be greeted by a lot of blank stares. It would be much simpler to ask "Are you (1) very satisfied, (2) somewhat satisfied, or (3) not satisfied with your current brand of dishwashing liquid?" Words with precise meanings, universal usage, and minimal connotative confusion should be selected. When respondents are uncertain about what a question means, the incidence of "No response" answers increases.

A further complication in wording questions is the need to tailor the language to the target respondent group, whether it is lawyers or construction laborers. This advice may seem painfully obvious, but there are instances in which failure to relate to respondents' frames of reference has been disastrous. A case in point is the use of the word *bottles* (or *cans*) in this question: "How many bottles of beer do you drink in a normal week?" Because in some states beer is sold in 32-, 12-, 8-, 7-, 6-, and even 4-ounce bottles, a "heavy" drinker (defined as someone who consumes eight bottles of beer per week) may drink as little as 32 ounces, while a "light" drinker (defined as someone who consumes up to three bottles) may actually drink as much as 96 ounces.

Clarity can be improved by stating the purpose of the survey at the beginning of the interview. To put the questions in the proper perspective, the respondent needs to understand the nature of the study and what is expected of him or her but not necessarily who is sponsoring the project.

Sometimes questions are asked with categories that are not mutually exclusive. For example:

What is your total yearly household income before taxes?

1. Under $40,000
2. $40,000–$60,000
3. $60,000–$80,000
4. Over $80,000

So if a respondent's family income is $60,000, does he or she pick answer 2 or 3?
Here is a question with conflicting meaning:[5]
Please indicate the product you use most often. Check all that apply.

1. Cell phone
2. Toaster
3. Microwave
4. Vacuum cleaner

In this question, "use most often" and "check all that apply" are conflicting instructions.

Researchers must also be careful in determining when to allow multiple responses. The following question on an Internet survey allowed only one answer but should have been "check all that apply:"[6]

What time of the day do you like to check your e-mail?

▨ Morning
▨ Midday
▨ Evening
▨ Night
▨ Check e-mail once per week or less
▨ Do not use e-mail

Researchers must allow all valid responses. The example below is quite obvious, but in some cases, response categories are much more subtle:

What is your favorite color?

- Red
- Green
- Blue

To achieve clarity in wording, the researcher should avoid asking two questions in one, sometimes called a *double-barreled question*. For example, "How did you like the taste and texture of the coffee cake?" should be broken into two questions, one concerning taste and the other texture. Each question should address only one aspect of evaluation.

Avoid Biasing the Respondent

Questions such as "Do you often shop at lower-class stores like Super Shop?" and "Have you purchased any high-quality Black & Decker tools in the past 6 months?" show an obvious bias. Leading questions, such as "Weren't you pleased with the good service you received last night at the Holiday Inn?" is also quite obviously biased. However, bias may be much more subtle than that illustrated in these examples.

Sponsor identification early in the interviewing process can distort answers. An opening statement such as "We are conducting a study on the quality of banking for Northeast National Bank and would like to ask you a few questions" should be avoided. Similarly, it will not take long, for example, for a person to recognize that the survey is being conducted for Miller beer if, after the third question, every question is related to this product.

respondent biasing
Leading questions that give away the research goal or sponsor identity.

Consider the Respondent's Ability to Answer the Questions

In some cases, a respondent may never have acquired the information needed to answer the question. For example, a husband may not know which brand of sewing thread is preferred by his wife, and respondents will know nothing about a brand or store that they have never encountered. A question worded so as to imply that the respondent should be able to answer it will often elicit a reply that is nothing more than a wild guess. This creates measurement error since uninformed opinions are being recorded.

Another problem is forgetfulness. For example, you probably cannot remember the answers to all these questions: What was the name of the last movie you saw in a theater? Who were the stars? Did you have popcorn? How many ounces were in the container? What price did you pay for the popcorn? Did you purchase any other snack items? Why or why not? The same is true for the typical respondent. Yet a brand manager for Mars, Incorporated, wants to know what brand of candy you purchased last, what alternative brands you considered, and what factors led you to the brand selected. Because brand managers want answers to these questions, market researchers ask them. This, in turn, creates measurement error. Often respondents will give the name of a well-known brand, like Milky Way or Hershey. In other cases, respondents will mention a brand that they often purchase, but it may not be the last brand purchased.

respondent's question-answering ability
Factors affecting this ability include lack of required information, forgetfulness, or incomplete recall ability.

To avoid the problem of a respondent's inability to recall, the researcher should keep the referenced time periods relatively short. For example, if the respondent says "Yes" to the question "Did you purchase a candy bar within the past 7 days?" then brand and purchase motivation questions can be asked. A poor question for Dish Network customers might be "How many movies have you rented in the past year to view at home on Dish Network?" might be replaced with the following:

a. How many movies have you rented in the past month to view on Dish Network?

b. Would you say that, in the last month, you rented more movies, fewer movies, or about the average number of movies you rent per month? (IF "MORE" or "LESS," ASK THE FOLLOWING QUESTION)

c. What would you say is the typical number of movies you rent per month?

Here are two questions from actual marketing research studies. The first is from a mail survey and the second from a telephone survey. Question 1: In the past 3 months, how much have you spent on movies you saw advertised in the newspaper? Most people haven't a clue as to how much they have spent on movies in the last 3 months unless it is "nothing." And they certainly don't recall which of the movies were advertised where. Also, what if the respondent bought tickets for the whole family? Question 2: Of your last 10 drinks of scotch, how many were at home? At a friend's? At a restaurant? At a bar or tavern? A light scotch drinker may have consumed 10 drinks over a period of not less than 2 years! Maybe he carries around a scotch intake logbook, but it's doubtful.

The above questions are bad, but the questions below, from a real mail panel survey, were written by either a careless questionnaire designer or one who lives quite differently from most of us. Question: How many times in an average day do you apply your usual underarm product? One to two times per day? Three to four times per day? Five to six times per day? More than six times per day? Question: How many times in an average day do you shower/bathe? One time per day? Two times per day? Three times per day? Four times per day? Five or more times per day? Good grooming is important, but perhaps these questions are over the line.

→ **respondent's willingness to answer**
Embarrassing, sensitive, or threatening questions or questions divergent from respondent's self-image may cause them to refuse to answer.

Consider the Respondent's Willingness to Answer the Question

A respondent may have a very good memory, yet not be willing to give a truthful reply. If an event is perceived as embarrassing, sensitive in nature, threatening, or divergent from the respondent's self-image, it is likely either not to be reported at all or to be distorted in a socially desirable direction.

Embarrassing questions that deal with topics such as borrowing money, personal hygiene, sexual activities, and criminal records must be phrased carefully to minimize measurement error. One technique is to ask the question in the third person—for example, "Do you think that most people charge more on their credit cards than they should? Why?" By generalizing the question to "most people," the researcher may be able to learn more about individual respondents' attitudes toward credit and debt.

Another method for soliciting embarrassing information is for the interviewer to state, prior to asking the question, that the behavior or attitude is not unusual—for example, "Millions of Americans suffer from hemorrhoids; do you or any member of your family suffer from this problem?" This technique, called *using counterbiasing statements*, makes embarrassing topics less intimidating for respondents to discuss.

Step 5: Establish Questionnaire Flow and Layout

After the questions have been properly formulated, the next step is to sequence them and develop a layout for the questionnaire. Questionnaires are not constructed haphazardly; there is a logic to the positioning of each section (see Exhibit 10.6). Experienced marketing researchers are well aware that good questionnaire development is the key to obtaining a completed interview. A well-organized questionnaire usually elicits answers that are more carefully thought out and detailed. Researcher wisdom has led to the following general guidelines concerning questionnaire flow.

Use Screening Questions to Identify Qualified Respondents
Most marketing research employs some type of quota sampling. Only qualified respondents are interviewed, and specific minimum numbers (quotas) of various types of qualified respondents may be sought. For example, a food products study generally has quotas of users of specific brands, a magazine study screens for readers, and a cosmetic study screens for brand awareness.

EXHIBIT 10.6	How a Questionnaire Should Be Organized		
Location	**Type**	**Examples**	**Rationale**
Screeners	Qualifying questions	"Have you been snow skiing in the past 12 months?" "Do you own a pair of skis?"	The goal is to identify target respondents.
First few questions	Warm-ups	"What brand of skis do you own?" "How many years have you owned them?"	Easy-to-answer questions show the respondent that the survey is simple.
First third of questions	Transitions	"What features do you like best about the skis?"	Questions related to research objectives require slightly more effort.
Second third	Difficult and complicated questions	"Following are 10 characteristics of snow skis. Please rate your skis on each characteristic, using the scale below."	The respondent has committed to completing the questionnaire.
Last third	Classifying and demographic questions	"What is the highest level of education you have attained?"	The respondent may leave some "personal" questions blank, but they are at the end of the survey.

Hello. I'm from Data Facts Research. We are conducting a survey among men, and I'd like to ask you a few questions.

1. Do you or does any member of your family work for an advertising agency, a marketing research firm, or a company that manufactures or sells shaving products?

   (TERMINATE)   Yes ( )
   (CONTINUE WITH Q. 2)   No ( )

2. How old are you? Are you . . . (READ LIST)

   (TERMINATE)   Under 15 yrs. old? ( )
   (CHECK QUOTA CONTROL FORM—IF QUOTA GROUP FOR
   WHICH THE RESPONDENT QUALIFIES *IS NOT* FILLED,   15 to 34 yrs. old? ( )
   CONTINUE, IF QUOTA GROUP *IS* FILLED, THEN TERMINATE.)   Over 34 yrs. old? ( )

3. The last time you shaved, did you use an electric razor or a razor that uses blades?

   (TERMINATE)   Electric Razor ( )
   (CONTINUE WITH Q. 4)   Blade Razor ( )

4. How many times have you shaved in the past 7 days?
   (IF LESS THAN THREE TIMES, TERMINATE. IF THREE OR MORE
   TIMES, CONTINUE WITH THE MAIN QUESTIONNAIRE.)

Exhibit 10.7

Screening Questionnaire That Seeks Men 15 Years of Age and Older Who Shave at Least Three Times a Week with a Blade Razor

Screeners (screening questions) may appear on the questionnaire, or a screening questionnaire may be filled out for everyone who is interviewed. Any demographics obtained provide a basis against which to compare persons who qualify for the full study. A long screening questionnaire can significantly increase the cost of the study, as more information must be obtained from every contact with a respondent. But it may provide important data on the nature of nonusers, nontriers, and persons unaware of the product or service being researched. Short screening questionnaires, such as the one presented in Exhibit 10.7, quickly eliminate unqualified persons and enable the interviewer to move immediately to the next potential respondent.

Most importantly, screeners provide a basis for estimating the costs of a survey. A survey in which all persons are qualified to be interviewed is going to be much cheaper to conduct than one with a 5 percent incidence rate. Many surveys are placed with field services mall surveys at a flat rate per completed questionnaire. The rate is based on a

➤ **screeners**
Questions used to identify appropriate respondents.

stated average interview time and incidence rate. Screeners are used to determine whether, in fact, the incidence rate holds true in a particular city. If it does not, the flat rate is adjusted accordingly.

Begin with a Question That Gets the Respondent's Interest

After introductory comments and screens to find a qualified respondent, the initial questions should be simple, interesting, and nonthreatening. To open a questionnaire with an income or age question could be disastrous. These are often considered threatening and immediately put the respondent on the defensive. The initial question should be easy to answer without much forethought.

Ask General Questions First

Once the interview progresses beyond the opening warm-up questions, the questionnaire should proceed in a logical fashion. First, general questions are asked to get the person thinking about a concept, company, or type of product; then the questionnaire moves to the specifics. For example, a questionnaire on shampoo might begin with "Have you purchased a hair spray, hair conditioner, or hair shampoo within the past 6 weeks?" Then it would ask about the frequency of shampooing, brands purchased in the past 3 months, satisfaction and dissatisfaction with brands purchased, repurchase intent, characteristics of an "ideal" shampoo, respondent's hair characteristics, and finally demographics.

Ask Questions That Require "Work" in the Middle

Initially, the respondent will be only vaguely interested in and understanding of the nature of the survey. As the interest-building questions appear, momentum and commitment to the interview will build. When the interview shifts to questions with scaled-response formats, the respondent must be motivated to understand the response categories and options. Alternatively, questions might necessitate some recall or opinion formation on the part of the respondent. Established interest and commitment must sustain the respondent in this part of the interview.

➤ **prompters**
Short encouraging statements to rebuild respondent interest.

Insert "Prompters" at Strategic Points

Good interviewers can sense when a respondent's interest and motivation sag and will attempt to build them back up. However, it is always worthwhile for the questionnaire designer to insert **prompters** or short encouragements at strategic locations in the questionnaire. These may be simple statements such as "There are only a few more questions to go" or "This next section will be easier." Encouraging words may also be inserted as part of an introduction to a section: "Now that you have helped us with those comments, we would like to ask a few more questions."

Position Sensitive, Threatening, and Demographic Questions at the End

As mentioned earlier, the objectives of a study sometimes necessitate questions on topics about which respondents may feel uneasy. These topics should be covered near the end of the questionnaire to ensure that most of the questions are answered before the respondent becomes defensive or breaks off the interview. Another argument for placing sensitive questions toward the end is that by the time these questions are asked, interviewees have been conditioned to respond. In other words, the respondent has settled into a pattern of seeing or hearing a question and giving an answer.

Put Instructions in Capital Letters

To avoid confusion and to clarify what is a question and what is an instruction, all instructions for self-administered questionnaires should be in capital letters—for example, "IF 'YES' TO QUESTION 13, SKIP TO QUESTION 17." Capitalizing helps bring the instructions to the interviewer's or respondent's attention. Of course, this is done automatically on computer-based surveys.

Use a Proper Introduction and Closing Every questionnaire must have an introduction and closing. The Council for Marketing and Opinion Research (CMOR) has developed a model survey introduction and closing based on research findings from a number of different studies. CMOR recommends the following:[7]

Model Introduction/Opening

- In order to gain the trust of the respondent, the interviewer should provide his or her first name or agreed upon contact name. Providing a last name is optional but is recommended for business-to-business studies or surveys involving professionals such as those in the medical field.
- Provide the name of the company that the interviewer represents and the name of the client/sponsor of the research whenever possible.
- Explain the nature of the study topic/subject matter in general terms.
- State, as early in the interview as possible, that no selling will be involved as a result of the call.
- The respondent should be told in the introduction the approximate length of the survey.
- It is recommended as standard practice to obtain two-party consent to monitoring/recording; that is, both the respondent and the interviewer should be informed that the call might be monitored/recorded for quality control purposes.
- Reinforce the fact that the respondent's time is appreciated/valued.
- Invite the respondent to participate in the survey, determine if the interview time is convenient, and, if not, offer an alternative callback time and date to complete the survey.

Hello, my name is _____ and I'm calling from (company). Today/Tonight we are calling to gather opinions regarding (general subject), and are not selling anything. This study will take approximately (length) and may be monitored (and recorded) for quality purposes. We would appreciate your time. May I include your opinions?

Model Closing

- At the conclusion of the survey, thank the respondent for his or her time.
- Express the desired intention that the respondent had a positive survey experience and will be willing to participate in future market research projects.
- Remind the respondent that his or her opinions do count.

Thank you for your time and cooperation. I hope this experience was a pleasant one and you will participate in other marketing research projects in the future. Please remember that your opinion counts! Have a good day/evening.

Alternative: Participate in collecting respondent satisfaction data to improve survey quality.

Thank you very much for taking part in this survey. Because consumers like you are such a valued part of what we do, I'd like you to think about the survey you just participated in. On a scale from 1 to 10 where 10 means "it was a good use of my time," and 1 means "it was not a good use of my time," which number between 1 and 10 best describes how you feel about your experience today? That's all the questions I have. Please remember that your opinion counts! Have a good day/evening!

Step 6: Evaluate the Questionnaire

Once a rough draft of the questionnaire has been designed, the marketing researcher is obligated to take a step back and critically evaluate it. This phase may seem redundant, given the careful thought that went into each question. But recall the crucial role played by the questionnaire. At this point in the questionnaire development, the following issues should be considered: (1) Is the question necessary? (2) Is the questionnaire too long? (3) Will the questions provide the information needed to accomplish the research objectives?

Is the Question Necessary?

> **necessary questions**
> Questions that pertain directly to the stated survey objectives or are screeners, interest generators, or required transitions.

Perhaps the most important criterion for this phase of questionnaire development is the necessity for a given question. Sometimes researchers and brand managers want to ask questions because "they were on the last survey we did like this" or because "it would be nice to know." Excessive numbers of demographic questions are very common. Asking for education data, numbers of children in multiple age categories, and extensive demographics on the spouse simply is not warranted by the nature of many studies.

Each question must serve a purpose. Unless it is a screener, an interest generator, or a required transition, it must be directly and explicitly related to the stated objectives of the particular survey. Any question that fails to satisfy at least one of these criteria should be omitted.

Is the Questionnaire Too Long?

At this point, the researcher should role-play the survey, with volunteers acting as respondents. Although there is no magic number of interactions, the length of time it takes to complete the questionnaire should be averaged over a minimum of five trials. Any questionnaire to be administered in a mall or over the telephone should be a candidate for cutting if it averages longer than 20 minutes. Sometimes mall-intercept interviews can run slightly longer if an incentive is provided to the respondent. Most Internet surveys should take less than 15 minutes to complete.

Common incentives are movie tickets, pen and pencil sets, and cash or checks. The use of incentives often actually lowers survey costs because response rates increase and terminations during the interview decrease. If checks are given out instead of cash, the canceled checks can be used to create a list of survey participants for follow-up purposes.

A technique that can reduce the length of questionnaires is called a split-questionnaire design. It can be used when the questionnaire is long and the sample size is large. The questionnaire is split into one core component (such as demographics, usage patterns, and psychographics) and a number of subcomponents. Respondents complete the core component plus a randomly assigned subcomponent.

Will the Questions Provide the Information Needed to Accomplish the Research Objectives?

The researcher must make certain that the questionnaire contains sufficient numbers and types of questions to meet the decision-making needs of management. A suggested procedure is to carefully review the written objectives for the research project and then write each question number next to the objective that the particular question will address. For example, question 1 applies to objective 3, question 2 to objective 2, and so forth. If a question cannot be tied to an objective, the researcher should determine whether the list of objectives is complete. If the list is complete, the question should be omitted. If the researcher finds an objective with no questions listed beside it, appropriate questions should be added. Tips for writing a good questionnaire are provided in the Practicing Marketing Research feature on page 263.

Step 7: Obtain Approval of All Relevant Parties

> **approval by managers**
> Managerial review approval after questionnaire drafting to prevent false starts and expensive later redrafts.

After the first draft of the questionnaire has been completed, copies should be distributed to all parties who have direct authority over the project. Practically speaking, managers may step in at any time in the design process with new information, requests, or concerns. When this happens, revisions are often necessary. It is still important to get final approval of the first draft even if managers have already intervened in the development process.

Managerial approval commits management to obtaining a body of information via a specific instrument (questionnaire). If the question is not asked, the data will not be gathered. Thus, questionnaire approval tacitly reaffirms what decision-making information is needed and how it will be obtained. For example, assume that a new product questionnaire asks about shape, material, end use, and packaging. By approving the form, the new-product development manager is implying, "I know what color the product will be" or "It is not important to determine color at this time."

Step 8: Pretest and Revise

When final managerial approval has been obtained, the questionnaire must be pretested. No survey should be conducted without a pretest. Moreover, a pretest does not mean that one researcher is administering the questionnaire to another researcher. Ideally, a pretest is administered to target respondents for the study. In a **pretest**, researchers look for misinterpretations by respondents, lack of continuity, poor skip patterns, additional alternatives for precoded and closed-ended questions, and general respondent reaction to the interview. The pretest should be conducted in the same mode as the final interview— that is, if the study is to be an Internet survey, then the pretest should be, too.

➡ **pretest**
A trial run of a questionnaire.

Step 9: Prepare Final Questionnaire Copy

Even the final copy phase does not allow the researcher to relax. Precise instructions must be created when an interviewer is involved—for example, where to interview, target

---

PRACTICING
MARKETING RESEARCH

Tips for Writing a Good Questionnaire

If you have ever sent what you thought was a "final" questionnaire to a marketing research supplier, only to have it returned to you full of wording changes, deletions, and other editorial comments, you're not alone. Writing a questionnaire does not, at first glance, appear to be a very difficult task: just figure out what you want to know, and write questions to obtain that information. But although writing questions is easy, writing good questions is not. Here are some do's and don'ts when writing questions.

1. *Avoid abbreviations, slang, or uncommon words that your audience might not understand.* For example: What is your opinion of PPOs? It is quite possible that not everyone knows that PPO stands for preferred provider organization. If the question targets the general public, the researcher might run into problems. On the other hand, if the question is for physicians or hospital administrators, then the acronym PPO is probably acceptable.

2. *Be specific.* The problem with vague questions is that they generate vague answers. For example: What is your household income? As respondents come up with numerous interpretations to this question, they will give all kinds of answers—income before taxes, income after taxes, and so on. Another example: How often did you attend sporting events during the past year? (1) Never, (2) Rarely, (3) Occasionally,

(4) Regularly. Again, this question is open for interpretation. People will interpret "sporting event" and the answer list differently—does "regularly" mean weekly, monthly, or what?

3. *On the other hand, don't overdo it.* When questions are too precise, people cannot answer them. They will either refuse or guess. For example: How many books did you read [last year]? You need to give them some ranges: (1) None, (2) 1–10, (3) 11–25, (4) 26–50, (5) More than 50.

4. *Make sure your questions are easy to answer.* Questions that are too demanding will also lead to refusals or guesses. For example: Please rank the following 20 items in order of importance to you when you are shopping for a new car. You're asking respondents to do a fair amount of calculating. Don't ask people to rank 20 items; have them pick the top 5.

4. *Don't assume too much.* This is a fairly common error, in which the question writer infers something about people's knowledge, attitudes, or behavior. For example: Do you tend to agree or disagree with the president's position on gun control? This question assumes that the respondent is aware that the president has a position on gun control and knows what that position is. To avoid this error, the writer must be prepared to do some educating. For example: "The president has recently stated his position on gun control. Are you aware that he has taken a stand on this issue?" If the answer is yes, then continue with: "Please describe in your own words what you understand his position on gun control to be." And, finally, "Do you tend to agree or disagree with his stand?"

6. *Watch out for double questions and questions with double negatives.* Combining questions or using a double negative leads to ambiguous questions and answers. For example: "Do you favor the legalization of marijuana for use in private homes but not in public places?" If this question precisely describes the respondent's position, then a "yes" answer is easily interpreted. But a "no" could mean the respondent favors use in public places but not in private homes, or opposes both, or favors both. Similarly, here is an example of a question with a double negative: "Should the police chief not be directly responsible to the mayor?" The question is ambiguous; almost any answer will be even more so.

7. *Check for bias.* A biased question can influence people to respond in a manner that does not accurately reflect their positions. There are several ways in which questions can be prejudiced. One is to imply that respondents should have engaged in a certain behavior. For example: "The movie, *XYZ*, was seen by more people than any other movie this year. Have you seen this movie?" So as not to appear "different," respondents may say yes even though they haven't seen the movie. The question should be: "Have you seen the movie *XYZ*?" Another way to bias a question is to have unbalanced answer choices. For example: "Currently our country spends XX billion dollars a year on foreign aid. Do you feel this amount should be (1) increased, (2) stay the same, (3) decreased a little, (4) decreased somewhat, (5) decreased a great deal?" This set of responses encourages respondents to select a "decrease" option, since there are three of these and only one increase option.

Pretesting: The Survey before the Survey

All the rewriting and editing in the world won't guarantee success. However, pretesting is the least expensive way to make sure your questionnaire research project is a success. The primary purpose of a pretest is to make certain that the questionnaire gives the respondent clear, understandable questions that will evoke clear, understandable answers.[8]

After completion of the pretest, any necessary changes should be made. Managerial approval should then be re-obtained before going forward. If the original pretest results in extensive design and question alterations, a second pretest is in order.

respondents, and when to show respondents test items like alternative product designs. In a mail survey, compliance and subsequent response rates may be affected positively by a professional-looking questionnaire. For telephone interviews, the copy is typically read from a computer screen. Survey software for online interviews often lets the designer choose backgrounds, formats, and so forth.

Step 10: Implement the Survey

Completion of the questionnaire establishes the basis for obtaining the desired decision-making information from the marketplace. Most mall and telephone research interviewing is conducted by field service firms. It is the firm's job to complete the interviews and send them back to the researcher. In essence, field services are the in-person interviewers, the production line of the marketing research industry. A series of forms and procedures must be issued with the questionnaire to make certain that the field service firm gathers the data correctly, efficiently, and at a reasonable cost. Depending on the data-collection method, these may include supervisor's instructions, interviewer's instructions, screeners, call record sheets, and visual aids.

Supervisor's Instructions   As mentioned earlier, mall, focus group, and some other types of research are handled by field services. This necessitates supervisor's instructions. **Supervisor's instructions** inform the field services firm of the nature of the study, start and completion dates, quotas, reporting times, equipment and facility requirements, sampling instructions, number of interviewers required, and validation procedures. In addition, detailed instructions are required for any taste test that involves food preparation. Quantities typically are measured and cooked using rigorous measurement techniques and devices.

> **supervisor's instructions**
> Written directions to a field service firm on how to conduct a survey.

A vital part of any study handled by a field service, supervisor's instructions establish the parameters for conducting the research. Without clear instructions, the interview may be conducted 10 different ways in 10 different cities. A sample page from a set of supervisor's instructions is shown in Exhibit 10.8.

Field Management Companies

Conducting fieldwork is much easier today than it was in years past. The stereotypical "kitchen table" field service firm is passing into history. In its place are companies that specialize in field management. **Field management companies**, such as QFact, On-Line Communications, and Direct Resource, generally provide questionnaire formatting, screener writing, development of instructional and peripheral materials, shipping services, field auditing, and all coordination of data collection, coding, and tab services required for the project. On completion of a study, they typically submit a single, comprehensive invoice for the project. Generally lean on staff, these companies provide the services clients need without attempting to compete with the design and analytical capabilities of full-service companies and ad agency research staffs.

> **field management companies**
> Firms that provide support services such as questionnaire formatting, screener writing, and coordination of data collection.

A number of full-service companies and qualitative professionals have discovered that using field management companies can be cost-effective; it can increase productivity by allowing them to take on more projects while using fewer of their internal resources. Several qualitative researchers have developed ongoing relationships with field management companies, whose personnel function as extensions of the consultant's staff, setting up projects and freeing up the researcher to conduct groups, write reports, and consult with clients.

Exhibit 10.8	**Purpose**	To determine from diet soft-drink users their ability to discriminate among three samples of Diet Dr Pepper and give opinions and preferences between two of the samples
Sample Page of Supervisor's Instructions for a Diet Soft Drink Taste Test	**Staff**	3–4 experienced interviewers per shift
	Location	One busy shopping center in a middle to upper-middle socioeconomic area. The center's busiest hours are to be worked by a double shift of interviewers.
		In the center, 3–4 private interviewing stations are to be set up, and a refrigerator and good counterspace made available for product storage and preparation.
	Quota	192 completed interviews broken down as follows:
		A minimum of 70 Diet Dr Pepper users
		A maximum of 122 other diet brand users
	Project materials	For this study, you are supplied the following:
		250 Screening Questionnaires
		192 Study Questionnaires
		4 Card A's
	Product/preparation	For this study, our client shipped to your refrigerated facility 26 cases of soft-drink product. Each case contains 24 10-oz. bottles—312 coded with an *F* on the cap, 312 with an *S*.
		Each day, you are to obtain from the refrigerated facility approximately 2–4 cases of product—1–2 of each code. Product must be transported in coolers and kept refrigerated at the location. It should remain at approximately 42°F.
		In the center, you are to take one-half of the product coded *F* and place the #23 stickers on the bottles. The other half of the *F* product should receive #46 stickers.
		The same should be done for product *S*—one-half should be coded #34, the other half #68. A supervisor should do this task before interviewing begins. Interviewers will select product by *code number*. Code number stickers are enclosed for this effort.
		Each respondent will be initially testing three product samples as designated on the questionnaire. Interviewers will come to the kitchen, select the three designated bottles, open and pour 4 oz. of each product into its corresponding coded cup. The interviewer should cap and *refrigerate* leftover product when finished pouring and take only the 3 *cups* of product on a tray to respondent.

Of course, like any other segment of the research industry, field management has its limitations. By definition, field management companies generally do not have design and analytical capabilities. This means that their clients may, on occasion, need to seek other providers to meet their full-service needs. In addition, because this is a relatively new segment of the industry, experience, services, and standards vary tremendously from firm to firm. It's advisable to carefully screen prospective companies and check references. These limitations notwithstanding, field management companies provide a way for researchers to increase their productivity in a cost-effective manner, while maintaining the quality of the information on which their company's decisions and commitments are based.

The Impact of the Internet on Questionnaire Development

As with most other aspects of marketing research, the Internet has affected questionnaire development and use in several ways. For example, a marketing research company can now create a questionnaire and send it as an e-mail attachment to management for comments and approval; once approved, it can be placed on the client's server to be used as an Internet survey. Or researchers can simply use an Internet company like Vovici, Inquisite, WebSurveyor, SSI Web, or many others to create a survey on the Internet.

Perseus, for example, is a leading Internet self-service questionnaire-building site. It allows marketing researchers to create online surveys quickly and then view real-time results anytime and anywhere, using remote access. The advantage is that the marketing research client has no questionnaire software to install, and no programming or administration is required. All operations are automated and performed through the Vovici Web site. This includes survey design, respondent invitation, data collection, analysis, and results reporting.

Software for Questionnaire Development

Sawtooth Software offers some of the most widely used analytical and questionnaire development software in the world. The systems are both powerful and easy to use. SSI's online interviewing product is called SSI Web. Exhibit 10.9 illustrates the kinds of questions that can be used with SSI Web. Some of the capabilities of SSI Web are:

- Easy-to-use, template-based authoring on the researcher's own PC
- Randomization of pages, questions, and response options
- Data piping
- Constructed (dynamic) lists:

  One of the most powerful aspects of SSI Web is the ability to create custom lists of response options. These lists are defined by rules you specify and are customized to each respondent, based on the respondent's answers. The following example demonstrates how a constructed list might be used:

  Which cities have you visited?

  ☒ Seattle
  ☐ Portland ⟶
  ☒ San Diego
  ☒ Denver
  ☐ Dallas

  Out of all the cities that you visited, which is your favorite?

  ○ Seattle
  ○ San Diego
  ○ Denver

- **Automatic question response verification**
  Questions must be answered before moving to the next question.

- **Powerful skip logic**
  SSI Web makes it easy to add skip logic (branching) within your survey. Skips can be executed with the page loads (pre-skips) or after it has been submitted (post-skips).

Exhibit 10.9

Types of Questions That Can Be Used with SSI Web

Single Select Response (radio) question type

If you had the opportunity to visit one of the following cities, which one would you choose?
○ Seattle
○ Hong Kong
○ Miami
○ Paris

Multiple Select Response (checkbox)—question

Please select all of the activities you enjoy:
☐ Shopping   ☐ Walking
☐ Bowling   ☐ Skiing
☐ Swimming   ☐ Golfing
☐ Kayaking   ☐ Other (please specify)
☐ Bird Watching   ☐ None of these

Single Select Response (combo box) question type

Which is your favorite holiday?

[↓]

(Holidays are listed in drop-down box.)

The Numeric question type. A response from 0 to 100 is required.
How old are you?   ☐

Open-end (multiple-line) question type
In the box below tell us about where you grew up.

[   ]

Grid question type. This grid has select questions (radio buttons)
specified for the rows.

Please tell us how likely you are to participate in each activity over the next 3 months.

	Not Likely		Somewhat Likely		Very Likely
Shopping	○	○	○	○	○
Bowling	○	○	○	○	○
Swimming	○	○	○	○	○
Kayaking	○	○	○	○	○
Bird Watching	○	○	○	○	○

Grid question type. This example shows the flexibility in grids by
demonstrating how different question types can be
set for each row.

Please answer the following questions about the electronic products displayed below.

Which items do you own?   ☐   ☐   ☐   ☐
Which is your favorite?   ○   ○   ○   ○
How much would you pay for each? $ $ $ $

Ranking question type

Please rank the top three activities that you enjoy.
☐ Shopping
☐ Bowling
☐ Swimming
☐ Kayaking
☐ Bird Watching

Constant Sum question type

Given a budget of $3,000, please specify how much you would spend for each holiday.
☐ Easter
☐ 4th of July
☐ Halloween
☐ Thanksgiving
☐ Christmas
☐ New Years
☐ Total (Total is automatically computed each time numbers are entered into a holiday box.)

Free Format question type. The Free Format question type
allows researchers to specify their own HTML
to create custom questions.

Personal Information

First Name: _____

Last Name: _____

Street Address: _____

_____

City: _____ **State:** _____ **Zip:** _____ - _____

Gender: ○ **Male** ○ **Female**

Interests: ☐ **Walking**

☐ **Running**

☐ **Hiking**

☐ **Swimming**

☐ **Eating**

Source: Sawtooth Software, Inc.

That means respondents can receive pages that only include the subset of questions that apply to them, and respondents can skip pages that are not relevant:

- Quota control
- Foreign language character support
- Questionnaire preview and testing on local PC
- Ability to create your own custom questions with HTML and "free format" question type
- Power users may insert HTML, JavaScript, or Perl
- Respondent restart (without cookies)
- Similar look across different browsers, including Mac and legacy browsers
- Automatic respondent password generation, or import from text file

■ Link to/from other online interviewing systems and Web sites

■ Online administrative module for real-time reports, download, and data management

■ Exports to common formats (including Excel, SPSS), with label[9]

Facebook As a Survey Research Platform   In late 2010, Facebook launched Facebook Questions. It allows users to post surveys and questions about subjects of their choice, soliciting their friends—or the entire Facebook population—for information and opinions. As this text went to print, the service had gone through beta testing and will be further developed with the test group's feedback in mind.

Whether Facebook Questions will serve as a casual form of research or a more recreational "What song is it that goes X?" or "Which shoes look better with this belt?" remains to be seen, but company and brand Facebook pages will also have the ability to gauge how consumers feel about new products or potential launches and also establish a forum where users and brand fans can be heard right from the comfort of their own Facebook profiles.

Facebook Questions will appear on the user's profile and will also appear in the user's friends' News Feed, so answers are anticipated to be personalized and especially relevant to the poster. Photos can also be added if the user is trying to identify something, such as a type of flower in their garden.

The "social" aspect of Facebook Questions comes in the form of question suggestions and the helpful/unhelpful checkbox. Whenever polls or questions have been answered, users can post them to their own or their friends' profiles, and if a user sees a question for which a friend might have an answer, the user can "suggest" that question for a friend. Facebook Questions will also have a feature similar to ones seen on Digg, Amazon.com, and Yahoo! Answers, where the users' viewing or responding to the question can (anonymously) mark whether they found a respondent's answer helpful or unhelpful. The most helpful answers will rise to the top. Users are also able to "follow" questions, so that a notification will be sent when another user responds to the question.[10]

In the global market of today, a product may be tested in many countries at the same time. The need for questionnaires in several different languages has grown considerably in the past decade.

YOSHIKATSU TSUNO/AFP/Getty Images, Inc.

Today's global marketers offer a variety of products to their customers throughout the world. Many times, a new-product concept is tested simultaneously in a number of different countries, requiring questionnaires in a variety of languages.

Costs, Profitability, and Questionnaires

A discussion of questionnaires would not be complete without mentioning their impact on costs and profitability. Marketing research suppliers typically bid against one another for a client's project. A supplier who overestimates costs will usually lose the job to a lower-cost competitor. In all survey research, the questionnaire and incidence rate (see Chapter 5) are the core determinants of a project's estimated costs. When one of America's largest research suppliers examined costs and bids for all of its projects conducted by central-location telephone interviewing, it found that it had overestimated project costs 44 percent of the time during a recent 18-month period. The resulting overbidding had translated into millions of dollars of lost sales opportunities.

To avoid overbidding, managers must have a better understanding of questionnaire costs. In one central-location telephone study with a 50 percent incidence rate and calls lasting an average of 15 minutes, MARC, a large international marketing research firm, found that only 30 percent of the data-collection costs involved asking the questions. Seventy percent of the data-collection costs were incurred trying to reach qualified respondents.[11]

Exhibit 10.10 depicts the numerous roadblocks an interviewer can encounter trying to get a completed interview. Each roadblock adds to the costs. MARC, for example, has found that simply adding a security screener to a questionnaire can increase the cost of interviewing by as much as 7 percent.

Another major source of extra cost in survey research is premature termination of interviews. People terminate interviews for four major reasons: the subject matter, redundant or difficult-to-understand questions, questionnaire length, and changing the subject during an interview. People like to talk about some subjects and not others. For example, the subject of gum is no problem, but bringing up mouthwash results in many terminations.

> → **questionnaire costs and profitability**
> Factors affecting costs and profits, including overestimating, overbidding, incidence rate, roadblocks to completed interviews, and premature interview terminations.

EXHIBIT 10.10	Difficulties in Finding a Qualified Respondent in a Central-Location Telephone Interview

1. Failed Attempts
   - Busy
   - No answer
   - Answering machine
   - Business number
   - Phone/language problem
   - Discontinued line

2. Cooperation Problems
   - Respondent not at home
   - Respondent refused to be interviewed

3. Screener Determines Respondent Not Eligible
   - Failed security test (works for marketing research firm, advertising agency, or the client)
   - Doesn't use the product
   - Demographic disqualification (wrong gender, age, etc.)
   - Quota filled (For example, survey has a quota of 500 users of Tide and 500 users of other clothes washing powders. Interviewer already has 500 Tide users; the current respondent uses Tide.)

4. Respondent Terminated during Interview

Actual Respondent Termination Patterns for Interviews in Three Different Product Categories

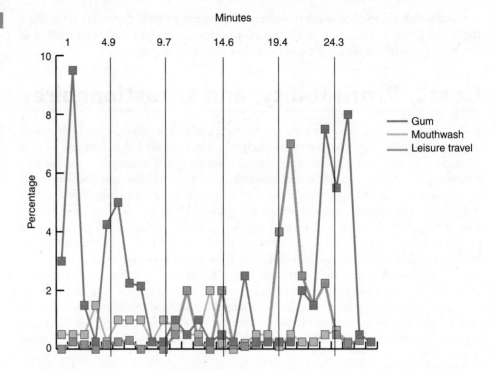

Exhibit 10.11 reveals that a 203-minute interview on gum results in few terminations (actual data). However, many people terminate a mouthwash interview within 3 minutes or in the 19- to 22-minute range. Terminations of a leisure travel interview don't become a serious problem until the interview reaches 20 minutes in length. Terminations usually mean that the interview must be redone and all the time spent interviewing the respondent was wasted. However, preliminary research has found that callbacks on terminated interviews can sometimes result in a completed interview.[12] (The same research on callbacks to persons who originally refused to be surveyed was not productive.)

Once managers understand the actual costs of data collection, they should be in a better position to bid on jobs with a high degree of cost accuracy. Better information should result in less overbidding and therefore more contracts.

SUMMARY

The questionnaire plays a critical role in the data-collection process. The criteria for a good questionnaire may be categorized as follows: (1) providing the necessary decision-making information, (2) fitting the respondent, and (3) meeting editing, coding, and data processing requirements.

The process of developing a questionnaire is a sequential one:

Step 1. Determine survey objectives, resources, and constraints.

Step 2. Determine the data-collection method.

Step 3. Determine the question response format.

Step 4. Decide on the question wording.

Step 5. Establish questionnaire flow and layout.

Step 6. Evaluate the questionnaire.

Step 7. Obtain approval of all relevant parties.

Step 8. Pretest and revise.

Step 9. Prepare final questionnaire copy.

Step 10. Implement the survey.

Three different types of questions—open-ended, closed-ended, and scaled-response questions—each have advantages and disadvantages. In establishing the wording and positioning of questions within the questionnaire, the researcher must try to ensure that the wording is clear and does not bias the respondent and that the respondent will be able and willing to answer the questions.

During the implementation of survey research, procedures must be followed to ensure that the data are gathered correctly, efficiently, and at a reasonable cost. These include preparing supervisor's instructions, interviewer's instructions, screeners, call record sheets, and visual aids. Many research organizations are now turning to field management companies to actually conduct the interviews.

Questionnaire software and the Internet are having a major impact on survey design. Vovici Web surveyor, SSI Web, and others enable researchers to go to the Web site and create online surveys.

The role of the questionnaire in survey research costs can be a decisive one. If a research firm overestimates data-collection costs, chances are that it will lose the project to another supplier. Most data-collection costs are associated not with conducting the actual interview, but with finding a qualified respondent. A respondent's propensity to terminate an interview, which can be costly, is often based on the nature of the topic discussed.

KEY TERMS & DEFINITIONS

questionnaire A set of questions designed to generate the data necessary to accomplish the objectives of a research project; also called an *interview schedule* or a *survey instrument*.

survey objectives An outline of the decision-making information sought through a questionnaire.

open-ended question A question to which the respondent replies in her or his own words.

closed-ended question A question that requires the respondent to choose from a list of answers.

dichotomous question A closed-ended question that asks the respondent to choose between two answers.

multiple-choice question A closed-ended question that asks the respondent to choose among several answers; also called *multichotomous questions*.

scaled-response question A closed-ended question in which the response choices are designed to capture the intensity of the respondent's feeling.

clarity in wording Clarity achieved by avoiding ambiguous terminology, using reasonable, vernacular language adjusted to the target group, and asking only one question at a time.

respondent biasing Leading questions that give away the research goal or sponsor identity.

respondent's question-answering ability Factors affecting this ability include lack of required information, forgetfulness, or incomplete recall ability.

respondent's willingness to answer Embarrassing, sensitive, or threatening questions or questions divergent from respondent's self-image may cause them to refuse to answer.

screeners Questions used to identify appropriate respondents.

prompters Short encouraging statements to rebuild respondent interest.

necessary questions Questions that pertain directly to the stated survey objectives or are screeners, interest generators, or required transitions.

approval by managers Managerial review and approval after questionnaire drafting to prevent false starts and expensive later redrafts.

pretest A trial run of a questionnaire.

supervisor's instructions Written directions to a field service firm on how to conduct a survey.

field management companies Firms that provide support services such as questionnaire formatting, screener writing, and coordination of data collection.

questionnaire costs and profitability Factors affecting costs and profits, including overestimating, overbidding, incidence rate, roadblocks to completed interviews, and premature interview terminations.

QUESTIONS FOR REVIEW & CRITICAL THINKING

1. Explain the role of the questionnaire in the research process.
2. How do respondents influence the design of a questionnaire? Give some examples (for example, questionnaires designed for engineers, baseball players, army generals, and migrant farmworkers).
3. Discuss the advantages and disadvantages of open-ended questions and closed-ended questions.
4. Assume that you are developing a questionnaire about a new sandwich for McDonald's. Use this situation to outline the procedure for designing a questionnaire.
5. Give examples of poor questionnaire wording, and explain what is wrong with each question.
6. Once a questionnaire has been developed, what other factors need to be considered before the questionnaire is put into the hands of interviewers?
7. Why is pretesting a questionnaire important? Are there some situations in which pretesting is not necessary?
8. Design three open-ended and three closed-ended questions to measure consumers' attitudes toward BMW automobiles.
9. What's wrong with the following questions?
    a. How do you like the flavor of this high-quality Maxwell House coffee?
    b. What do you think of the taste and texture of this Sara Lee coffee cake?
    c. We are conducting a study for Bulova watches. What do you think of the quality of Bulova watches?
10. What do you see as the major advantages of using a field management company? What are the drawbacks?

11. Discuss the advantages and disadvantages of Web-based questionnaires.

12. (*Team Activity*): Divide the class into groups of four or five. Next, match the groups evenly into supplier and client teams. The instructor will then pair a client team with a supplier team. Each client team should pick some aspect of the university such as student housing, student transportation, sports, sororities, fraternities, food on campus, or some other aspect of student life. Next, the client team should create four management objectives for their topic and construct a questionnaire to meet the management objectives. In addition, the questionnaire should include the following demographics: age, gender, major, and others determined by your instructor. Once the client team approves the questionnaire, both the client and supplier team members should complete 10 interviews each. The results should then be presented to the class. *Note:* This data can be formatted into SPSS for more detailed analysis later in the text.

WORKING THE NET

1. Visit ***www.vovici.com*** and take a series of free online surveys and evaluate the programs, questions, approach, assumptions, and results. *Note:* Vovici was formerly known as Perseus.

2. Log on to ***www.surveymonkey.com*** and ***www.inquisite.com*** and consider how suitable, or not, their online polling software would be for conducting market research for new customers for iPhone.

3. See what it's like to be at the receiving end of an online survey; take one or two surveys at ***www.greenfield.com*** and click on "Take a Survey."

REAL-LIFE RESEARCH • 10.1

Enticing Americans to Buy New Products

In conjunction with the Better Homes and Gardens Best New Product Awards, Toronto-based BrandSpark International surveyed more than 50,000 U.S. consumers on topics such as "recessionary shopping behavior, healthy eating, future spending priorities, private labels versus premium brands, organic and natural foods, environmental accountability, and money-saving strategies.

"We can see the impact of the recent recession on attitudes towards the environment and health—with both losing ground in terms of importance," said Robert Levy, president and CEO of BrandSpark International and founder of the Best New Products Awards, in the press release. "People have made a big shift to eat at home more and as a result are spending more time and money in the grocery store. Finding new products that really deliver is more important than ever, especially with shoppers demanding greater value for money."

The BrandSpark American Shopper Study included questions about individual product appeal, intent to repurchase, consumer confidence level, and expected future spending habits, among other topics.

A few of the winning best new products were: Health and Beauty: Olay Professional Pro-X Wrinkle Protocol. Best in food and beverage category: Yoplaits Smoothie. Best in household care category: Cascade Complete All-in-1 Action Pacs. A complete list can be found at *www.bestnewproductawards.biz.*

What are the top five purchase drivers for consumers?

In the food and beverage category

1. Taste
2. Price
3. Fresh
4. Looks appetizing
5. Smells good

In health and beauty

1. Price
2. Proven effective
3. Simple to use
4. Trusted brand
5. Allergy-tested

In household products

1. Cleans thoroughly
2. Price
3. Effective
4. Delivers as promised
5. Works the first time

The survey also gathered opinions on two other much-discussed topics: green marketing and organic foods. "Over the past number of years, we have seen environmental accountability grow to be a major concern for American consumers," said Levy. Seventy-seven percent of Americans still feel that companies are exploiting green claims for marketing purposes. Packaging remains a top environmental concern for consumers, with 75 percent believing that manufacturers still have a long way to go to reduce the amount of packaging. Fifty-two percent of Americans feel it's important that a new product is better for the environment.

While interest in organic foods continues, consumers also place a value on foods that are free of artificial flavors or colors. Half of the consumers surveyed believe "It is important that a new product is made from all-natural ingredients" and 37 percent believe "It is more important to me that a product is natural than organic."

Levy attributed part of this to consumer skepticism. Among the consumers who didn't purchase organic products, 39 percent said they "don't trust that all products labeled as organic are actually organic" and "are confused by what the term organic actually guarantees." "It appears that further consumer education is required in the natural versus organic debate," said Levy.[13]

Questions

1. What types of survey research could have been used to gather this data? Which one would you have recommended? Why?

2. Carefully ready through the case and then list the various types of questions that may have been used to gather the data.

3. Create a questionnaire that could provide the information discussed in the case.

© StockLib/iStockphoto

Basic Sampling Issues

CHAPTER 11

LEARNING OBJECTIVES

→ 1. To understand the concept of sampling.

→ 2. To learn the steps in developing a sampling plan.

→ 3. To understand the concepts of sampling error and nonsampling error.

→ 4. To understand the differences between probability samples and nonprobability samples.

→ 5. To understand sampling implications of surveying over the Internet.

The Concept of Sampling

sampling
The process of obtaining information from a subset of a larger group.

Sampling refers to the process of obtaining information from a subset (a sample) of a larger group (the universe or population). A user of marketing research then takes the results from the sample and makes estimates of the characteristics of the larger group. The motivation for sampling is to be able to make these estimates more quickly and at a lower cost than would be possible by any other means. It has been shown time and again that sampling a small percentage of a population can result in very accurate estimates. An example that you are probably familiar with is polling in connection with a presidential election. Most major polls use samples of 1,000 to 1,500 people to make predictions regarding the voting behavior of tens of millions of people and their predictions have proven to be remarkably accurate.

The key to making accurate predictions about the characteristics or behavior of a large population on the basis of a relatively small sample lies in the way in which individuals are selected for the sample. It is critical that they be selected in a scientific manner, which ensures that the sample is representative—that it is a true miniature of the population. All of the major types of people who make up the population of interest should be represented in the sample in the same proportions in which they are found in the larger population. This sounds simple, and as a concept, it is simple. However, achieving this goal in sampling from a human population is not easy.

Population

population
An entire group of people about whom information is needed; also called *universe* or *population of interest*.

In discussions of sampling, the terms *population* and *universe* are often used interchangeably.[1] In this textbook, we will use the term *population*. The **population**, or *population of interest*, is the entire group of people about whom the researcher needs to obtain information. One of the first steps in the sampling process is defining the population of interest. This often involves defining the target market for the product or service in question.

Consider a product concept test for a new nonprescription cold symptom-relief product, such as Contac. You might take the position that the population of interest includes everyone, because everyone suffers from colds from time to time. Although this is true, not everyone buys a nonprescription cold symptom-relief product when he or she gets a cold. In this case, the first task in the screening process would be to determine whether people have purchased or used one or more of a number of competing brands during some time period. Only those who had purchased or used one of these brands would be included in the population of interest.

Defining the population of interest is a key step in the sampling process. There are no specific rules to follow in defining the population of interest. What the researcher must do is apply logic and judgment in addressing the basic issue: Whose opinions are needed in order to satisfy the objectives of the research? Often, the definition of the population is based on the characteristics of current or target customers.

Sample versus Census

census
A collection of data obtained from or about every member of the population of interest.

sample
A subset of all the members of a population of interest.

In a **census**, data are obtained from or about every member of the population of interest. Censuses are seldom employed in marketing research, as populations of interest to marketers normally include many thousands or even millions of individuals. The cost and time required to collect data from a population of this magnitude are so great that censuses are usually out of the question. It has been demonstrated repeatedly that a relatively small but carefully chosen sample can very accurately reflect the characteristics of the population from which it is drawn. A **sample** is a subset of all the members of a population. Information is obtained from or about a sample and used to make estimates about various characteristics of the total population. Ideally, the sample from or about which information is obtained is a representative cross section of the total population.

Note that the popular belief that a census provides more accurate results than a sample is not necessarily true. In a census of a human population, there are many impediments to actually obtaining information from every member of the population. The researcher may not be able to obtain a complete and accurate list of the entire population, or certain members of the population may refuse to provide information. Because of these barriers, the ideal census is seldom attainable, even with very small populations. You may have read or heard about these types of problems in connection with recent U.S. Census results 2000 and 2010.[2]

Developing a Sampling Plan

The process of developing an operational sampling plan can be summarized by the seven steps shown in Exhibit 11.1. These steps are defining the population, choosing a data-collection method, identifying a sampling frame, selecting a sampling method, determining sample size, developing operational procedures, and executing the sampling plan.

Step 1: Define the Population of Interest

The basic issue in developing a sampling plan is to specify the characteristics of those individuals or things (for example, customers, companies, stores) from whom or about whom information is needed to meet the research objectives. The population of interest is often specified in terms of geographic area, demographic characteristics, product or service usage characteristics, and/or awareness measures (see Exhibit 11.2). In surveys, the question of whether a particular individual does or does not belong to the population of interest is often dealt with by means of screening questions. Even with a list of the population and a sample from that list, researchers still need screening questions to qualify potential respondents. Exhibit 11.3 provides a sample sequence of screening questions.

Exhibit 11.1

Developing a Sampling Plan

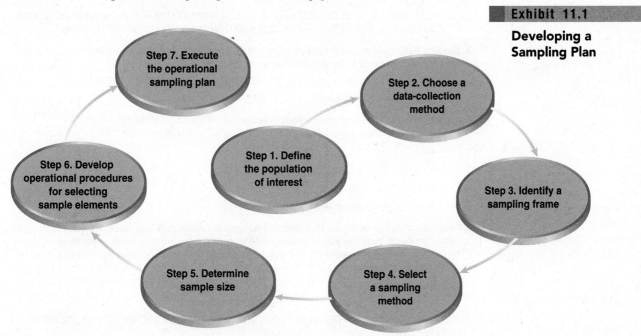

EXHIBIT 11.2	Some Bases for Defining the Population of Interest

Geographic area — What geographic area is to be sampled? This is usually a question of the client's scope of operation. The area could be a city, a county, a metropolitan area, a state, a group of states, the entire United States, or a number of countries.

Demographics — Given the objectives of the research and the target market for the product, whose opinions, reactions, and so on are relevant? For example, does the sampling plan require information from women over 18, women 18–34, or women 18–34 with household incomes over $35,000 per year who work and who have preschool children?

Usage — In addition to geographic area and/or demographics, the population of interest frequently is defined in terms of some product or service use requirement. This is usually stated in terms of use versus nonuse or use of some quantity of the product or service over a specified period of time. The following examples of use screening questions illustrate the point:

- Do you drink five or more cans, bottles, or glasses of diet soft drinks in a typical week?
- Have you traveled to Europe for vacation or business purposes in the past two years?
- Have you or has anyone in your immediate family been in a hospital for an overnight or extended stay in the past two years?

Awareness — The researcher may be interested in surveying those individuals who are aware of the company's advertising, to explore what the advertising communicated about the characteristics of the product or service.

Exhibit 11.3	

Example of Screening Question Sequence to Determine Population Membership

Hello. I'm _____ with _____ Research. We're conducting a survey about products used in the home. May I ask you a few questions?

1. Have you been interviewed about any products or advertising in the past 3 months?

| Yes | (TERMINATE AND TALLY) |
| No | (CONTINUE) |

2. Which of the following hair care products, if any, have you used in the past month? (HAND PRODUCT CARD TO RESPONDENT; CIRCLE ALL MENTIONS)

    1 Regular shampoo

    2 Dandruff shampoo

    3 Creme rinse/instant conditioner

    4 "Intensive" conditioner

(INSTRUCTIONS: IF "4" IS CIRCLED—SKIP TO Q. 4 AND CONTINUE FOR "INTENSIVE" QUOTA; IF "3" IS CIRCLED BUT NOT "4"—ASK Q. 3 AND CONTINUE FOR "INSTANT" QUOTA)

3. You said that you have used a creme rinse/instant conditioner in the past month. Have you used either a creme rinse or an instant conditioner in the past week?

| Yes (used in the past week) | (CONTINUE FOR "INSTANT" QUOTA) |
| No (not used in past week) | (TERMINATE AND TALLY) |

4. Into which of the following groups does your age fall? (READ LIST, CIRCLE AGE)

X	Under 18	(CHECK AGE QUOTAS)
1	18–24	
2	25–34	
3	35–44	
X	45 or over	

5. Previous surveys have shown that people who work in certain jobs may have different reactions to certain products. Now, do you or does any member of your immediate family work for an advertising agency, a marketing research firm, a public relations firm, or a company that manufactures or sells personal care products?

| Yes | (TERMINATE AND TALLY) |
| No | (CONTINUE) |

(IF RESPONDENT QUALIFIES, INVITE HIM OR HER TO PARTICIPATE AND COMPLETE NAME GRID BELOW)

In addition to defining who will be included in the population of interest, researchers should also define the characteristics of individuals who should be excluded. For example, most commercial marketing research surveys exclude some individuals for so-called security reasons. Very frequently, one of the first questions on a survey asks whether the respondent or anyone in the respondent's immediate family works in marketing research, advertising, or the product or service area at issue in the survey (see, for example, question 5 in Exhibit 11.3). If the individual answers "Yes" to this question, the interview is terminated. This type of question is called a *security question* because those who work in the industries in question are viewed as security risks. They may be competitors or work for competitors, and managers do not want to give them any indication of what their company may be planning to do.

There may be other reasons to exclude individuals. For example, the Dr Pepper Company might wish to do a survey among individuals who drink five or more cans, bottles, or glasses of soft drink in a typical week but do not drink Dr Pepper, because the company is interested in developing a better understanding of heavy soft-drink users who do not drink its product. Therefore, researchers would exclude those who drank one or more cans, bottles, or glasses of Dr Pepper in the past week.

Step 2: Choose a Data-Collection Method

The selection of a data-collection method has implications for the sampling process:

■ Mail surveys suffer from biases associated with low response rates (which are discussed in greater detail later in this chapter).

■ Telephone surveys have a less significant problem with nonresponse, but suffer from call screening technologies used by potential respondents and the fact that some people have mobile phones only.

■ Internet surveys have problems with professional respondents and the fact that the panel or e-mail lists used often do not provide appropriate representation of the population of interest.

Step 3: Identify a Sampling Frame

The third step in the process is to identify the **sampling frame**, which is a list of the members or elements of the population from which units to be sampled are to be selected. Identifying the sampling frame may simply mean specifying a procedure for generating such a list. In the ideal situation, the list of population members is complete and accurate. Unfortunately, there usually is no such list. For example, the population for a study may be defined as those individuals who have spent 2 or more hours on the Internet in the past week; there can be no complete listing of these individuals. In such instances, the sampling frame specifies a procedure that will produce a representative sample with the desired characteristics. Thus, there seldom is a perfect correspondence between the sampling frame and the population of interest.

For example, a telephone book might be used as the sample frame for a telephone survey sample in which the population of interest was all households in a particular city. However, the telephone book does not include households that do not have telephones and those with unlisted numbers. It is well established that those with listed telephone numbers are significantly different from those with unlisted numbers in regard to a number of important characteristics. Subscribers who voluntarily unlist their phone numbers are more likely to be renters, live in the central city, have recently moved, have larger families, have younger children, and have lower incomes than their counterparts with listed numbers.[3]

> → **sampling frame**
> A list of population elements from which units to be sampled can be selected or a specified procedure for generating such a list.

There are also significant differences between the two groups in terms of purchase, owner-ship, and use of certain products.

Unlisted numbers are more prevalent in the western United States, in metropolitan areas, among nonwhites, and among those in the 18 to 34 age group. These findings have been confirmed in a number of studies.[4] The extent of the problem is suggested by the data in Exhibit 11.4. The implications are clear: If representative samples are to be obtained in telephone surveys, researchers should use procedures that will produce sam-ples including appropriate proportions of households with unlisted numbers.

One possibility is **random-digit dialing**, which generates lists of telephone numbers at random. This procedure can become fairly complex. Fortunately, companies such as Survey Sampling offer random-digit samples at a very attractive price. Details on the way such companies draw their samples can be found at *www.surveysampling.com/products_samples. php*. Developing an appropriate sampling frame is often one of the most challenging prob-lems facing the researcher.[5]

→ **random-digit dialing**
A method of generating lists of telephone num-bers at random.

Step 4: Select a Sampling Method

The fourth step in developing a sampling plan is selection of a sampling method, which will depend on the objectives of the study, the financial resources available, time limita-tions, and the nature of the problem under investigation. The major alternative sampling methods can be grouped under two headings: probability sampling methods and non-probability sampling methods.

Probability samples are selected in such a way that every element of the population has a known, nonzero likelihood of selection.[6] Simple random sampling is the best-known and most widely used probability sampling method. With probability sampling, the researcher must closely adhere to precise selection procedures that avoid arbitrary or biased selection of sample elements. When these procedures are followed strictly, the laws of probability hold, allowing calculation of the extent to which a sample value can be expected to differ from a population value. This difference is referred to as *sampling error*. The debate continues regarding whether online panels produce probability samples.

→ **probability samples**
Samples in which every element of the population has a known, nonzero likelihood of selection.

Nonprobability samples are those in which specific elements from the population have been selected in a nonrandom manner. *Nonrandomness* results when population elements are selected on the basis of convenience—because they are easy or inexpensive to reach. *Purposeful nonrandomness* occurs when a sampling plan systematically excludes

→ **nonprobability samples**
Samples in which specific elements from the popu-lation have been selected in a nonrandom manner.

Exhibit 11.4

Classification of Sampling Methods

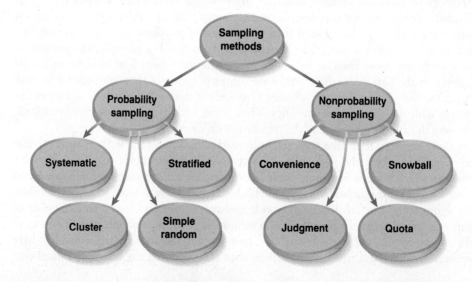

PRACTICING MARKETING RESEARCH

How to Achieve Nearly Full Coverage for Your Sample Using Address-Based Sampling[7]

Address-based sampling (ABS) offers potential benefits in comparison to a strictly telephone-based method of contact. Landlines offer access to only about 75 percent of U.S. households, and contacting people via wireless devices can be a complicated process. Market research firm Survey Sampling International (SSI), however, has found that using an ABS approach can almost completely fill that access gap.

SSI combines a telephone database with a mailing list—entries with a telephone number are contacted normally, while entries possessing only the address are sent a survey in the mail. Using the U.S. Postal Service's (USPS's) Delivery Sequence File (DSF) combined with other commercial databases offering more complete information on individual households, SSI has been able to achieve coverage of 95 percent of postal households and 85 percent of those addresses matched to a name. Between 55 and 65 percent are matched to a telephone number, and demographic data can be accessed as well when creating a sample.

The trend toward mobile is making telephone surveys more difficult. Twenty percent of U.S. households have no landline. This is especially true of people in their 20s. ABS, however, still offers access to households that use a cell phone as the primary or only mode of communication, but it also provides greater geodemographic information and selection options than would an approach based strictly on a wireless database.

While ABS does face certain challenges—mail surveys are generally more expensive and multimode designs can lead to variable response rates—there are methods that can be used to compensate. Selection criteria can be modified to maximize the delivery efficiency of mailers. Appended telephone numbers can be screened as well to improve accuracy and response rates. On the whole, ABS helps research achieve a more complete sample with greater response rates and also allows respondents an option of exercising their preferred response channel.

Questions

1. Can you think of any demographic segments that might be difficult to reach via ABS?

2. What are some ways researchers could use to mitigate the increased costs of mail surveys?

---

or overrepresents certain subsets of the population. For example, if a sample designed to solicit the opinions of all women over the age of 18 were based on a telephone survey conducted during the day on weekdays, it would systematically exclude working women. See the Practicing Marketing Research feature above.

Probability samples offer several advantages over nonprobability samples, including the following:

- The researcher can be sure of obtaining information from a representative cross section of the population of interest.

- Sampling error can be computed.

- The survey results can be projected to the total population. For example, if 5 percent of the individuals in a probability sample give a particular response, the researcher can project this percentage, plus or minus the sampling error, to the total population.

On the other hand, probability samples have a number of disadvantages, the most important of which is that they are usually more expensive than nonprobability samples of the same size. The rules for selection increase interviewing costs and professional time spent in designing and executing the sample design.[8]

Step 5: Determine Sample Size

→ **sample size**
The number of population elements chosen in the sample.

Once a sampling method has been chosen, the next step is to determine the appropriate **sample size**. (The issue of sample size determination is covered in detail in Chapter 12.) In the case of nonprobability samples, researchers tend to rely on such factors as available budget, rules of thumb, and number of subgroups to be analyzed in their determination of sample size. However, with probability samples, researchers use formulas to calculate the sample size required, given target levels of *acceptable error* (the difference between sample result and population value) and *levels of confidence* (the likelihood that the confidence interval—sample result plus or minus the acceptable error—will take in the true population value). As noted earlier, the ability to make statistical inferences about population values based on sample results is the major advantage of probability samples.

© Uschools University Images/iStockphoto

The population for a study must be defined. For example, a population for a study may be defined as those individuals who have spent 2 or more hours on the Internet in the past week.

Step 6: Develop Operational Procedures for Selecting Sample Elements

The operational procedures to be used in selecting sample elements in the data-collection phase of a project should be developed and specified, whether a probability or a nonprobability sample is being used.[9] However, the procedures are much more critical to the successful execution of a probability sample, in which case they should be detailed, clear, and unambiguous and should eliminate any interviewer discretion regarding the selection of specific sample elements. Failure to develop a proper operational plan for selecting sample elements can jeopardize the entire sampling process. Exhibit 11.5 provides an example of an operational sampling plan.

Step 7: Execute the Operational Sampling Plan

The final step in the sampling process is execution of the operational sampling plan. This step requires adequate checking to ensure that specified procedures are followed.

Sampling and Nonsampling Errors

→ **population parameter**
A value that accurately portrays or typifies a factor of a complete population, such as average age or income.

Consider a situation in which the goal is to determine the average gross income of the members of a particular population.[10] If the researcher could obtain accurate information about all members of the population, he or she could simply compute the population parameter average gross income. A **population parameter** is a value that defines a true characteristic of a total population. Assume that μ (the population parameter, average gross income) is $42,300. As already noted, it is almost always impossible to measure an entire population (take a census). Instead, the researcher selects a sample and makes inferences about population parameters from sample results. In this case, the researcher might take a sample of 400 from a population of 250,000. An estimate of the average age of the members of the population ($\overline{X}$) would be calculated from the sample values. Assume that the average gross income of the sample members is $41,100. A second random sample of 400 might be drawn from the same population, and the average again computed. In the second case, the average might be $43,400. Additional samples might

PRACTICING MARKETING RESEARCH

Can a Single Online Respondent Pool Offer a Truly Representative Sample?[11]

Online research programs can often benefit by building samples from multiple respondent pools. Achieving a truly representative sample is a difficult process for many reasons. When drawing from a single source, even if researchers were to use various verification methods, demographic quotas, and other strategies to create a presumably representative sample, the selection methods themselves create qualitative differences—or allow them to develop over time. The same is true of the parameters under which the online community or respondent pool was formed (subject matter mix, activities, interaction opportunities, etc.). Each online community content site is unique, and members and visitors choose to participate because of the individual experience their preferred site provides. As such, the differences between each site start to solidify as site members share more and more similar experiences and differences within the site's community decrease. (Think, birds of a feather flock together.)

As such, researchers cannot safely assume that any given online respondent pool offers an accurate probability sample of the adult U.S. or Internet population. Consequently, both intrinsic (personality traits, values, locus of control, etc.) and extrinsic (panel tenure, survey participation rates, etc.) differences will contribute variations to response-measure distribution across respondent pools. To control distribution of intrinsic characteristics in the sample while randomizing extrinsic characteristics as much as possible, researchers may need to use random selection from multiple respondent pools.

The GfK Research Center for Excellence in New York performed a study to see how the distribution of intrinsic and extrinsic individual differences varied between respondent pools. Respondents were drawn from five different online resource pools, each using a different method to obtain survey respondents. A latent class regression method separated the respondents into five underlying consumer classes according to their Internet-usage driver profiles.

Researchers then tested which of the intrinsic characteristics tended to appear within the different classes. No variable appeared in more than three classes. Furthermore, the concentration of each class varied considerably across the five respondent pools from which samples were drawn.

Within the classes themselves, variations appeared in their demographic distributions. One of the five experienced a significant skew based on gender, and two other classes exhibited variable age concentrations, with one skewed toward younger respondents and the other toward older ones.

Overall, GfK's study revealed numerous variations across different respondent resource pools. As their research continues, current findings suggest that researchers must be aware of these trends, especially in choosing their member acquisition and retention strategies and in determining which and how many respondent pools to draw from.

Questions

1. If one respondent pool is not sufficient, how many do you think you would have to draw from to get a truly representative sample? Why do you think that?

2. When creating a sample, how would you propose accounting for the types of extrinsic characteristics mentioned?

Exhibit 11.5

Example of Operational Sampling Plan

In the instructions that follow, reference is made to follow your route around a block. In cities, this will be a city block. In rural areas, a block is a segment of land surrounded by roads.

1. If you come to a dead end along your route, proceed down the opposite side of the street, road, or alley, traveling in the other direction. Continue making right turns, where possible, calling at every third occupied dwelling.

2. If you go all the way around a block and return to the starting address without completing four interviews in listed telephone homes, attempt an interview at the starting address. (This should seldom be necessary.)

3. If you work an entire block and do not complete the required interviews, proceed to the dwelling on the opposite side of the street (or rural route) that is *nearest* the starting address. Treat it as the next address on your Area Location Sheet and interview that house only if the address appears next to an "X" on your sheet. If it does not, continue your interviewing to the left of that address. Always follow the right turn rule.

4. If there are no dwellings on the street or road opposite the starting address for an area, circle the block opposite the starting address, following the right turn rule. (This means that you will circle the block following a clockwise direction.) Attempt interviews at every third dwelling along this route.

5. If, after circling the adjacent block opposite the starting address, you do not complete the necessary interviews, take the next block found, *following a clockwise direction*.

6. If the third block does not yield the dwellings necessary to complete your assignment, proceed to as many blocks as necessary to find the required dwellings; follow a clockwise path around the primary block.

Source: From "Belden Associates Interviewer Guide," Reprinted from interviewer guide by permission of Belden Associates, Dallas, Texas. The complete guide is over 30 pages long and contains maps and other aids for the interviewer.

be chosen, and a mean calculated for each sample. The researcher would find that the means computed for the various samples would be fairly close but not identical to the true population value in most cases. Issues for online panelists that can produce sampling and nonsampling errors are discussed in the Practicing Marketing Research feature on page 285.

The accuracy of sample results is affected by two general types of error: sampling error and nonsampling (measurement) error. The following formula represents the effects of these two types of error on estimating a population mean:

$$\overline{X} = \mu \pm \epsilon_s \pm \epsilon_{ns}$$

where
$\overline{X}$ = sample mean
μ = true population mean
ϵ_s = sampling error
ϵ_{ns} = nonsampling, or measurement, error

sampling error
Error that occurs because the sample selected is not perfectly representative of the population.

Sampling error results when the sample selected is not perfectly representative of the population. There are two types of sampling error: administrative and random. *Administrative error* relates to the problems in the execution of the sample—that is, flaws in the design or execution of the sample that cause it to be nonrepresentative of the population. These types of error can be avoided or minimized by careful attention to the design and execution of the sample. *Random sampling error* is due to chance and cannot be avoided. This type of error can be reduced, but never totally eliminated, by increasing the sample size. **Nonsampling**, or measurement **error**, includes all factors other than sampling error that may cause inaccuracy and bias in the survey results.

nonsampling error
All error other than sampling error; also called *measurement error*.

Probability Sampling Methods

As discussed earlier, every element of the population has a known and equal likelihood of being selected for a probability sample. There are four types of probability sampling methods: simple random sampling, systematic sampling, stratified sampling, and cluster sampling.

Simple Random Sampling

Simple random sampling is the purest form of probability sampling. For a simple random sample, the known and equal probability is computed as follows:

$$\text{Probability of selection} = \frac{\text{Sample size}}{\text{Population size}}$$

For example, if the population size is 10,000 and the sample size is 400, the probability of selection is 4 percent:

$$.04 = \frac{400}{10,000}$$

If a sampling frame (listing of all the elements of the population) is available, the researcher can select a **simple random sample** as follows:

1. Assign a number to each element of the population. A population of 10,000 elements would be numbered from 1 to 10,000.

2. Using a table of random numbers, begin at some arbitrary point and move up, down, or across until 400 (sample size) five-digit numbers between 1 and 10,000 have been chosen. The numbers selected from the table identify specific population elements to be included in the sample.

Simple random sampling is appealing because it seems easy and meets all the necessary requirements of a probability sample. It guarantees that every member of the population has a known and equal chance of being selected for the sample. Simple random sampling begins with a current and complete listing of the population. Such listings, however, are extremely difficult, if not impossible, to obtain. Simple random samples can be obtained in telephone surveys through the use of random digit dialing. They can also be generated from computer files such as customer lists; software programs are available or can be readily written to select random samples that meet all necessary requirements.

> **simple random sample**
> A probability sample selected by assigning a number to every element of the population and then using a table of random numbers to select specific elements for inclusion in the sample.

Systematic Sampling

Because of its simplicity, **systematic sampling** is often used as a substitute for simple random sampling. It produces samples that are almost identical to those generated via simple random sampling.

To obtain a systematic sample, the researcher first numbers the entire population, as in simple random sampling. Then the researcher determines a *skip interval* and selects names based on this interval. The skip interval can be computed very simply through use of the following formula:

> **systematic sampling**
> Probability sampling in which the entire population is numbered and elements are selected using a skip interval.

$$\text{Skip interval} = \frac{\text{Population size}}{\text{Sample size}}$$

For example, if you were using a local telephone directory and had computed a skip interval of 100, every 100th name would be selected for the sample. The use of this formula would ensure that the entire list is covered.

A random starting point should be used in systematic sampling. For example, if you were using a telephone directory, you would need to draw a random number to determine the page on which to start—say, page 53. You would draw another random number to determine the column to use on that page—for example, the third column. You would draw a final random number to determine the actual starting element in that column—say, the 17th name. From that beginning point, you would employ the skip interval until the desired sample size had been reached.

The main advantage of systematic sampling over simple random sampling is economy. Systematic sampling is often simpler, less time-consuming, and less expensive to use than simple random sampling. The greatest danger lies in the possibility that hidden patterns within the population list may inadvertently be pulled into the sample. However, this danger is remote when alphabetical listings are used.

Stratified Sampling

→ **stratified sample**
A probability sample that is forced to be more representative through simple random sampling of mutually exclusive and exhaustive subsets.

Stratified samples are probability samples that are distinguished by the following procedural steps:

1. The original, or parent, population is divided into two or more mutually exclusive and exhaustive subsets (for example, male and female).

2. Simple random samples of elements from the two or more subsets are chosen independently of each other.

Although the requirements for a stratified sample do not specify the basis on which the original or parent population should be separated into subsets, common sense dictates that the population be divided on the basis of factors related to the characteristic of interest in the population. For example, if you are conducting a political poll to predict the outcome of an election and can show that there is a significant difference in the way men and women are likely to vote, then gender is an appropriate basis for stratification. If you do not do stratified sampling in this manner, then you do not get the benefits of stratification, and you have expended additional time, effort, and resources for no benefit. With gender as the basis for stratification, one stratum, then, would be made up of men and one of women. These strata are mutually exclusive and exhaustive in that every population element can be assigned to one and only one (male or female) and no population elements are unassignable. The second stage in the selection of a stratified sample involves drawing simple random samples independently from each stratum.

Researchers prefer stratified samples to simple random samples because of their potential for greater statistical efficiency.[12] That is, if two samples are drawn from the same population—one a properly stratified sample and the other a simple random sample—the stratified sample will have a smaller sampling error. Also, reduction of a sampling error to a certain target level can be achieved with a smaller stratified sample. Stratified samples are statistically more efficient because one source of variation has been eliminated.

If stratified samples are statistically more efficient, why are they not used all the time? There are two reasons. First, the information necessary to properly stratify the sample frequently may not be available. For example, little may be known about the demographic characteristics of consumers of a particular product. To properly stratify the sample and to get the benefits of stratification, the researcher must choose bases for stratification that yield significant differences between the strata in regard to the measurement of interest. When such differences are not identifiable, the sample cannot be properly stratified. Second, even if the necessary information is available, the potential value of the information may not warrant the time and costs associated with stratification.

In the case of a simple random sample, the researcher depends entirely on the laws of probability to generate a representative sample of the population. With stratified sampling, the researcher, to some degree, forces the sample to be representative by making sure that important dimensions of the population are represented in the sample in their true population proportions. For example, the researcher may know that although men and women are equally likely to be users of a particular product, women are much more likely to be heavy users. In a study designed to analyze consumption patterns of the product, failure to properly represent women in the sample would result in a biased view of consumption patterns. Assume that women make up 60 percent of the population of interest and men account for 40 percent. Because of sampling fluctuations, a properly executed simple random sampling procedure might produce a sample made up of 55 percent women and 45 percent men. This is the same kind of error you would obtain if you flipped a coin 10 times. The ideal result of 10 coin tosses would be five heads and five tails, but more than half the time you would get a different result. In similar fashion, a properly drawn and executed simple random sample from a population made up of 60 percent women and 40 percent men is not likely to consist of exactly 60 percent women and 40 percent men. However, the researcher can force a stratified sample to have 60 percent women and 40 percent men.

Three steps are involved in implementing a properly stratified sample:

1. *Identify salient (important) demographic or classification factors.* Factors that are correlated with the behavior of interest. For example, there may be reason to believe that men and women have different average consumption rates of a particular product. To use gender as a basis for meaningful stratification, the researcher must be able to show with actual data that there are significant differences in the consumption levels of men and women. In this manner, various salient factors are identified. Research indicates that, as a general rule, after the six most important factors have been identified, the identification of additional salient factors adds little in the way of increased sampling efficiency.[13]

2. *Determine what proportions of the population fall into the various subgroups under each stratum* (for example, if gender has been determined to be a salient factor, determine what proportion of the population is male and what proportion is female). Using these proportions, the researcher can determine how many respondents are required from each subgroup. However, before a final determination is made, a decision must be made as to whether to use proportional allocation or disproportional, or optimal, allocation.

   Under **proportional allocation**, the number of elements selected from a stratum is directly proportional to the size of the stratum in relation to the size of the population. With proportional allocation, the proportion of elements to be taken from each stratum is given by the formula n/N, where n = the size of the stratum and N = the size of the population.

> **proportional allocation** Sampling in which the number of elements selected from a stratum is directly proportional to the size of the stratum relative to the size of the population.

→ **disproportional, or optimal, allocation**
Sampling in which the number of elements taken from a given stratum is proportional to the relative size of the stratum and the standard deviation of the characteristic under consideration.

Disproportional, or **optimal**, **allocation** produces the most efficient samples and provides the most precise or reliable estimates for a given sample size. This approach requires a double weighting scheme. Under this scheme, the number of sample elements to be taken from a given stratum is proportional to the relative size of the stratum and the standard deviation of the distribution of the characteristic under consideration for all elements in the stratum. This scheme is used for two reasons. First, the size of a stratum is important because those strata with greater numbers of elements are more important in determining the population mean. Therefore, such strata should have more weight in deriving estimates of population parameters. Second, it makes sense that relatively more elements should be drawn from those strata having larger standard deviations (more variation) and relatively fewer elements should be drawn from those strata having smaller standard deviations. Allocating relatively more of the sample to those strata where the potential for sampling error is greatest (largest standard deviation) is cost-effective and improves the overall accuracy of the estimates. There is no difference between proportional allocation and disproportional allocation if the distributions of the characteristic under consideration have the same standard deviation from stratum to stratum.[14]

3. *Select separate simple random samples from each stratum.* This process is implemented somewhat differently than traditional simple random sampling. Assume that the stratified sampling plan requires that 240 women and 160 men be interviewed. The researcher will sample from the total population and keep track of the number of men and women interviewed. At some point in the process, when 240 women and 127 men have been interviewed, the researcher will interview only men until the target of 160 men is reached. In this manner, the process generates a sample in which the proportion of men and women conforms to the allocation scheme derived in step 2.

Stratified samples are not used as often as one might expect in marketing research. The reason is that the information necessary to properly stratify the sample is usually not available in advance. Stratification cannot be based on guesses or hunches but must be based on hard data regarding the characteristics of the population and the relationship between these characteristics and the behavior under investigation. Stratified samples are frequently used in political polling and media audience research. In those areas, the researcher is more likely to have the information necessary to implement the stratification process.

Cluster Sampling

→ **cluster sample**
A probability sample in which the sampling units are selected from a number of small geographic areas to reduce data collection costs.

The types of samples discussed so far have all been single unit samples, in which each sampling unit is selected separately. In the case of **cluster samples**, the sampling units are selected in groups.[15] There are two basic steps in cluster sampling:

1. The population of interest is divided into mutually exclusive and exhaustive subsets.

2. A random sample of the subsets is selected.

If the sample consists of all the elements in the selected subsets, it is called a *one-stage cluster sample.* However, if the sample of elements is chosen in some probabilistic manner from the selected subsets, the sample is a *two-stage cluster sample.*

Both stratified and cluster sampling involve dividing the population into mutually exclusive and exhaustive subgroups. However, in stratified samples the researcher selects a sample of elements from each subgroup, while in cluster samples, the researcher selects a sample of subgroups and then collects data either from all the elements in the subgroup (one-stage cluster sample) or from a sample of the elements (two-stage cluster sample).

All the probability sampling methods discussed to this point require sampling frames that list or provide some organized breakdown of all the elements in the target population. Under cluster sampling, the researcher develops sampling frames that specify groups or clusters of elements of the population without actually listing individual elements. Sampling is then executed by taking a sample of the clusters in the frame and generating lists or other breakdowns for only those clusters that have been selected for the sample. Finally, a sample is chosen from the elements of the selected clusters.

The most popular type of cluster sample is the area sample in which the clusters are units of geography (for example, city blocks). Cluster sampling is considered to be a probability sampling technique because of the random selection of clusters and the random selection of elements within the selected clusters.

Cluster sampling assumes that the elements in a cluster are as heterogeneous as those in the total population. If the characteristics of the elements in a cluster are very similar, then that assumption is violated and the researcher has a problem. In the city-block sampling just described, there may be little heterogeneity within clusters because the residents of a cluster are very similar to each other and different from those of other clusters. Typically, this potential problem is dealt with in the sample design by selecting a large number of clusters and sampling a relatively small number of elements from each cluster.

Another possibility is multistage area sampling, or multistage area probability sampling, which involves three or more steps. Samples of this type are used for national surveys or surveys that cover large regional areas. Here, the researcher randomly selects geographic areas in progressively smaller units.

From the standpoint of statistical efficiency, cluster samples are generally less efficient than other types of probability samples. In other words, a cluster sample of a certain size will have a larger sampling error than a simple random sample or a stratified sample

Photo by Harry Lynch/Raleigh News & Observer/MCT via Getty Images/ Getty Images, Inc.

A stratified sample may be appropriate in certain cases. For example, if a political poll is being conducted to predict who will win an election, a difference in the way men and women are likely to vote would make gender an appropriate basis for stratification.

of the same size. To see the greater cost efficiency and lower statistical efficiency of a cluster sample, consider the following example. A researcher needs to select a sample of 200 households in a particular city for in-home interviews. If she selects these 200 households via simple random sampling, they will be scattered across the city. Cluster sampling might be implemented in this situation by selecting 20 residential blocks in the city and randomly choosing 10 households on each block to interview. It is easy to see that interviewing costs will be dramatically reduced under the cluster sampling approach. Interviewers do not have to spend as much time traveling, and their mileage is dramatically reduced. In regard to sampling error, however, you can see that simple random sampling has the advantage. Interviewing 200 households scattered across the city increases the chance of getting a representative cross section of respondents. If all interviewing is conducted in 20 randomly selected blocks within the city, certain ethnic, social, or economic groups might be missed or over- or underrepresented.

As noted previously, cluster samples are, in nearly all cases, statistically less efficient than simple random samples. It is possible to view a simple random sample as a special type of cluster sample, in which the number of clusters is equal to the total sample size, with one sample element selected per cluster. At this point, the statistical efficiency of the cluster sample and that of the simple random sample are equal. From this point on, as

The most popular type of cluster sample is the area sample, in which the clusters are units of geography (for example, city blocks). A researcher, conducting a door-to-door survey in a particular metropolitan area, might randomly choose a sample of city blocks from the metropolitan area, select a sample of clusters, and then interview a sample of consumers from each cluster. All interviews would be conducted in the clusters selected, dramatically reducing interviewers' travel time and expenses. Cluster sampling is considered to be a probability sampling technique because of the random selection of clusters and the random selection of elements within the selected clusters.

© LHB Photo/Alamy

the researcher decreases the number of clusters and increases the number of sample elements per cluster, the statistical efficiency of the cluster sample declines. At the other extreme, the researcher might choose a single cluster and select all the sample elements from that cluster. For example, he or she might select one relatively small geographic area in the city where you live and interview 200 people from that area. How comfortable would you be that a sample selected in this manner would be representative of the entire metropolitan area where you live?

Nonprobability Sampling Methods

In a general sense, any sample that does not meet the requirements of a probability sample is, by definition, a nonprobability sample. We have already noted that a major disadvantage of nonprobability samples is the inability to calculate sampling error for them. This suggests the even greater difficulty of evaluating the overall quality of nonprobability samples. How far do they deviate from the standard required of probability samples? The user of data from a nonprobability sample must make this assessment, which should be based on a careful evaluation of the methodology used to generate the nonprobability sample. Is it likely that the methodology employed will generate a cross section of individuals from the target population? Or is the sample hopelessly biased in some particular direction? These are the questions that must be answered. Four types of nonprobability samples are frequently used: convenience, judgment, quota, and snowball samples.

Convenience Samples

→ **convenience samples**
Nonprobability samples based on using people who are easily accessible.

Convenience samples are primarily used, as their name implies, for reasons of convenience. Companies such as Frito-Lay often use their own employees for preliminary tests of new product formulations developed by their R&D departments. At first, this may seem to be a highly biased approach. However, these companies are not asking employees to evaluate existing products or to compare their products with a competitor's products. They are asking employees only to provide gross sensory evaluations of new product formulations (for example, saltiness, crispness, greasiness). In such situations, convenience sampling may represent an efficient and effective means of obtaining the required information. This is particularly true in an exploratory situation, where there is a pressing need to get an inexpensive approximation of true value.

Some believe that the use of convenience sampling is growing at a faster rate than the growth in the use of probability sampling.[16] The reason, as suggested is the growing availability of databases of consumers in low-incidence and hard-to-find categories. For example, suppose a company has developed a new athlete's foot remedy and needs to conduct a survey among those who suffer from the malady. Because these individuals make up only 4 percent of the population, researchers conducting a telephone survey would have to talk with 25 people to find 1 individual who suffered from the problem. Purchasing a list of individuals known to suffer from the problem can dramatically reduce the cost of the survey and the time necessary to complete it. Although such a list might be made up of individuals who used coupons when purchasing the product or sent in for manufacturers' rebates, companies are increasingly willing to make the trade-off of lower cost and faster turnaround for a lower-quality sample.

Judgment Samples

The term **judgment sample** is applied to any sample in which the selection criteria are based on the researcher's judgment about what constitutes a representative sample. Most test markets and many product tests conducted in shopping malls are essentially judgment sampling. In the case of test markets, one or a few markets are selected based on the judgment that they are representative of the population as a whole. Malls are selected for product taste tests based on the researcher's judgment that the particular malls attract a reasonable cross section of consumers who fall into the target group for the product being tested.

> ➤ **judgment samples**
> Nonprobability samples in which the selection criteria are based on the researcher's judgment about representativeness of the population under study.

Quota Samples

Quota samples are typically selected in such a way that demographic characteristics of interest to the researcher are represented in the sample in target proportions. Thus, many people confuse quota samples and stratified samples. There are, however, two key differences between a quota sample and a stratified sample. First, respondents for a quota sample are not selected randomly, as they must be for a stratified sample. Second, the classification factors used for a stratified sample are selected based on the existence of a correlation between the factor and the behavior of interest. There is no such requirement in the case of a quota sample. The demographic or classification factors of interest in a quota sample are selected on the basis of researcher judgment.

> ➤ **quota samples**
> Nonprobability samples in which quotas, based on demographic or classification factors selected by the researcher, are established for population subgroups.

Snowball Samples

In **snowball samples**, sampling procedures are used to select additional respondents on the basis of referrals from initial respondents. This procedure is used to sample from low-incidence or rare populations—that is, populations that make up a very small percentage of the total population.[17] The costs of finding members of these rare populations may be so great that the researcher is forced to use a technique such as snowball sampling. For example, suppose an insurance company needed to obtain a national sample of individuals who have switched from the indemnity form of healthcare coverage to a health maintenance organization in the past 6 months. It would be necessary to sample a very large number of consumers to identify 1,000 that fall into this population. It would be

> ➤ **snowball samples**
> Nonprobability samples in which additional respondents are selected based on referrals from initial respondents.

far more economical to obtain an initial sample of 200 people from the population of interest and have each of them provide the names of an average of four other people to complete the sample of 1,000.

The main advantage of snowball sampling is a dramatic reduction in search costs. However, this advantage comes at the expense of sample quality. The total sample is likely to be biased because the individuals whose names were obtained from those sampled in the initial phase are likely to be very similar to those initially sampled. As a result, the sample may not be a good cross section of the total population. There is general agreement that some limits should be placed on the number of respondents obtained through referrals, although there are no specific rules regarding what these limits should be. This approach may also be hampered by the fact that respondents may be reluctant to give referrals.

Internet Sampling

The advantages of Internet interviewing are compelling:

- *Target respondents can complete the survey at their convenience.* It can be completed late at night, over the weekend, and at any other convenient time.

- *Data collection is relatively inexpensive.* Once basic overhead and other fixed costs are covered, interviewing is essentially volume-insensitive. Thousands of interviews can be conducted at an actual data-collection cost of less than $1 per survey. This low cost may, to some extent, be offset by the need to use incentives to encourage responses. By comparison, a 10-minute telephone interview targeting people who make up 50 percent of the population may cost $15 or more per survey. Data entry and data processing costs are dramatically reduced because respondents essentially do the data entry for the researcher.

- *The interview can be administered under software control.* This allows the survey to follow skip patterns and do other "smart" things.

- *The survey can be completed quickly.* Hundreds or thousands of surveys can be completed in a day or less.[18]

Unfortunately, there is no large body of scientific research regarding the representativeness of Internet samples, as there is for other data-collection approaches. Those who have carefully evaluated Internet surveying are most concerned that the pool of people available in cyberspace does not correctly represent the general population. The group of Internet respondents tend to be richer, whiter, more male, and more tech savvy.[19] The biases are becoming less pronounced over time as the percentage of the population connected to the Internet increases.[20] However, the nonrepresentativeness of Internet respondents will exist for some time into the future. This general problem is compounded by the fact that no comprehensive and reliable source of e-mail addresses exists.

Finally, research firms such as survey sampling and research now and tout the fact that they have developed large panels of individuals who have responded to their solicitations and have agreed to accept and complete online surveys.[21]

There are cases where Internet surveys, with all their other inherent advantages, may produce excellent samples. Those cases involve situations in which the client organization or the researcher has e-mail addresses for all members of a particular population. For example, high-technology firms such as Texas Instruments may have lists of essentially all individuals who make decisions regarding the purchase of their products for incorporation in other products. These industrial buyers are probably fairly heavy users of the Internet, both at home and at work. Selecting a true random sample of all members of such a population is relatively easy. At minimal cost, all the individuals can be sent invitations to participate and reminders to complete the survey. Response rates in excess of

PRACTICING MARKETING RESEARCH

How Building a Blended Sample Can Help Improve Research Results[22]

Most researchers prefer building a sample from a single source. In many cases, however, getting a truly representative sample from a single source is becoming more difficult. Survey Sampling International (SSI) has used a blended sample approach of panels, Web traffic, and aligned interest groups, and has found the resulting quality of the data is higher than with a single source sample.

Using a blended sample source creates two benefits: (1) It helps capture the opinions of people who would not otherwise join panels, and (2) it increases heterogeneity. As the breadth of sources increases, however, it is important to identify the unique biases of each of those sources and control for it in order to ensure high sample quality. The only way to achieve this balance is to understand where the bias is coming from. By using a panel exclusively, for example, you might eliminate individuals with valuable opinions who just aren't willing to commit to joining the panel.

Researchers should also make sure their samples are consistent and predictable. Studies indicate that controlling just for demographics and other traditional balancing factors does not always account for the variations created by the distinct characteristics of different sample sources. Demographic quotas may work, but only if the selected stratification relates directly to the questionnaire topic. Comparing sources to external benchmarks can improve consistency as well, but often those benchmarks are not readily available.

SSI's research on variance between data sources indicates that psychographic and neurographic variables have a greater capacity to influence variance between diverse sources than traditional demographic variables have. Even still, these variables do not account for all the possible variance, so researchers must continue testing in order to ensure consistency within the blended sampling method.

SSI offers the following suggestions for creating a blended sample:

- *Consider including calibration questions.* Look for existing external benchmarks for your survey topic.
- *Understand the sample blending techniques used to create your sample.* Tell your sample provider what kind of source smoothing and quality control methods are being used.
- *Know your sources.* Ask your sample provider how source quality is being maintained.
- *Plan ahead.* Incorporate blending into the sample plan from the start.
- *Ensure that respondents are satisfied with the research experience.* Be aware that significantly high nonresponse and noncompletion rates can introduce bias.

Questions

1. Beyond the variables discussed, can you think of any others that might be relevant when creating a blended sample?

2. Do you think a blended sample would be useful, and if so would you be inclined to try it? Are there any situations in which you would think a single-source sample would be more effective? Why?

70 percent are not uncommon for surveys of this type, especially if incentives are offered to encourage responses. Internet surveys are an emerging form of data collection that will probably become dominant at some point in the future. Their advantages are numerous and compelling. However, until the sampling issues discussed in this chapter can be resolved, the results of Internet surveys will be suspect because of lack of survey representativeness. Increasingly, researchers are blending data from online panels with data generated from telephone, mail, and other data-collection techniques to deal with the limitations of online panels. Issues in this type of sample blending are covered in the Practicing Marketing Research feature on page 295.

SUMMARY

A population, or universe, is a total group of people in whose opinions one is interested. A census involves collecting desired information from every member of the population of interest. A sample is simply a subset of a population. The steps in developing a sampling plan are as follows: define the population of interest, choose the data-collection method, identify the sampling frame, select the sampling method, determine sample size, develop and specify an operational plan for selecting sampling elements, and execute the operational sampling plan. The sampling frame is a list of the elements of the population from which the sample will be drawn or a specified procedure for generating the list.

In probability sampling methods, samples are selected in such a way that every element of the population has a known, nonzero likelihood of selection. Nonprobability sampling methods select specific elements from the population in a nonrandom manner. Probability samples have several advantages over nonprobability samples, including reasonable certainty that information will be obtained from a representative cross section of the population, a sampling error that can be computed, and survey results that can be projected to the total population. However, probability samples are more expensive than nonprobability samples and usually take more time to design and execute.

The accuracy of sample results is determined by both sampling and nonsampling error. Sampling error occurs because the sample selected is not perfectly representative of the population. There are two types of sampling error: random sampling error and administrative error. Random sampling error is due to chance and cannot be avoided; it can only be reduced by increasing sample size.

Probability samples include simple random samples, systematic samples, stratified samples, and cluster samples. Nonprobability samples include convenience samples, judgment samples, quota samples, and snowball samples. At the present time, Internet samples tend to be convenience samples. That may change in the future as better e-mail sampling frames become available.

KEY TERMS & DEFINITIONS

sampling The process of obtaining information from a subset of a larger group.

population An entire group of people about whom information is needed; also called *universe* or *population of interest*.

census A collection of data obtained from or about every member of the population of interest.

sample A subset of all the members of a population of interest.

sampling frame A list of population elements from which units to be sampled can be selected or a specified procedure for generating such a list.

random-digit dialing A method of generating lists of telephone numbers at random.

probability samples Samples in which every element of the population has a known, nonzero likelihood of selection.

nonprobability samples Samples in which specific elements from the population have been selected in a nonrandom manner.

sample size The number of population elements chosen in the sample.

population parameter A value that accurately portrays or typifies a factor of a complete population, such as average age or income.

sampling error Error that occurs because the sample selected is not perfectly representative of the population.

nonsampling error All error other than sampling error; also called *measurement error*.

simple random sample A probability sample selected by assigning a number to every element of the population and then using a table of random numbers to select specific elements for inclusion in the sample.

systematic sampling Probability sampling in which the entire population is numbered and elements are selected using a skip interval.

stratified sample A probability sample that is forced to be more representative though simple random sampling of mutually exclusive and exhaustive subsets.

proportional allocation Sampling in which the number of elements selected from a stratum is directly proportional to the size of the stratum relative to the size of the population.

disproportional, or optimal, allocation Sampling in which the number of elements taken from a given stratum is proportional to the relative size of the stratum and the standard deviation of the characteristic under consideration.

cluster sample A probability sample in which the sampling units are selected from a number of small geographic areas to reduce data-collection costs.

convenience samples Nonprobability samples based on using people who are easily accessible.

judgment samples Nonprobability samples in which the selection criteria are based on the researcher's personal judgment about representativeness of the population under study.

quota samples Nonprobability samples in which quotas, based on demographic or classification factors selected by the researcher, are established for population subgroups.

snowball samples Nonprobability samples in which additional respondents are selected based on referrals from initial respondents.

QUESTIONS FOR REVIEW & CRITICAL THINKING

1. What are some situations in which a census would be better than a sample? Why are samples usually employed rather than censuses?

2. Develop a sampling plan for examining undergraduate business students' attitudes toward Internet advertising.

3. Give an example of a perfect sampling frame. Why is a telephone directory usually not an acceptable sampling frame?

4. Distinguish between probability and nonprobability samples. What are the advantages and disadvantages of each? Why are nonprobability samples so popular in marketing research?

5. Distinguish among a systematic sample, a cluster sample, and a stratified sample. Give examples of each.

6. What is the difference between a stratified sample and a quota sample?

7. American National Bank has 1,000 customers. The manager wishes to draw a sample of 100 customers. How could this be done using systematic sampling? What would be the impact on the technique, if any, if the list were ordered by average size of deposit?

8. Do you see any problem with drawing a systematic sample from a telephone book, assuming that the telephone book is an acceptable sample frame for the study in question?

9. Describe snowball sampling. Give an example of a situation in which you might use this type of sample. What are the dangers associated with this type of sample?

10. Name some possible sampling frames for the following:
    a. Patrons of sushi bars
    b. Smokers of high-priced cigars
    c. Snowboarders
    d. Owners of DVD players
    e. People who have visited one or more countries in Europe in the past year
    f. People who emigrated to the United States within the past 2 years
    g. People with allergies

11. Identify the following sample designs:
    a. The names of 200 patrons of a casino are drawn from a list of visitors for the past month, and a questionnaire is administered to them.
    b. A radio talk show host invites listeners to call in and vote yes or no on whether handguns should be banned.
    c. A dog food manufacturer wants to test a new dog food. It decides to select 100 dog owners who feed their dogs canned food, 100 who feed their dogs dry food, and 100 who feed their dogs semimoist food.
    d. A poll surveys men who play golf to predict the outcome of a presidential election.

WORKING THE NET

1. Toluna offers *QuickSurveys*, a self-service tool that enables you to conduct market research quickly, easily and cost effectively. You can:

   - Create a survey of up to five questions.
   - Select up to 2,000 nationally representative respondents.
   - Pay online using a credit card or PayPal.

- Immediately follow the results live online and complete within 24 hours. (Speed of completion may vary by country.)

With this system, once your survey has been created it will automatically appear live on targeted specific areas of Toluna—a global community site that provides a forum where more than 4 million members interact and poll each other on a broad range of topics. Visit *www.toluna-group.com* to view a *QuickSurveys* Flash demo.

2. Throughout 2008, Knowledge Networks worked in conjunction with Associated Press and Yahoo! to repeatedly poll 2,230 people (from random telephone sampling) about likely election results and political preferences. Visit *www.knowledge networks.com* and evaluate the methodology and ultimate accuracy (or inaccuracy) on this topic.

REAL-LIFE RESEARCH • 11.1

New Mexico National Bank

New Mexico National Bank (NMNB) operates branches in 23 cities and towns throughout the state of New Mexico. The bank offers a complete range of financial services, including Visa and MasterCard credit cards. NMNB has 53,400 people in the state using its credit cards. Based on their original applications, the bank has certain information about these individuals, including name, address, zip code, telephone number, income, education, and assets. NMNB is interesting in determining whether a relationship exists between the volume of purchases charged on credit cards and the demographic characteristics of the individual cardholders. For example, are individuals in certain parts of the state more or less likely to be heavy users of the card? Is there a relationship between a person's income and his or her level of card usage? Is there a relationship between the person's level of education and card usage? The data can be used to more effectively target offering sent through the mail if significant relationships are found. Paul Bruney, research director for NMNB, is in the process of developing a design for the research. If you were Paul Bruney, how would you answer the following questions?

Questions

1. How would you define the population of interest for the study?
2. What sampling frame(s) might you use for the project?
3. What procedure would you use to select a simple random sample from the sampling frame you chose above?
4. Would it make sense to use a stratified sample in the situation? Why or why not? How would you approach the process of developing a stratified sample from the sampling frame you chose?
5. Could you use the sampling frame to draw a cluster sample? How would you go about it? Would it make any sense to do this?
6. Which of the three probability sampling methods just mentioned would you choose for this study? Why would you choose that option?

© Aerial Archives/Alamy

CHAPTER 12

Sample Size Determination

LEARNING OBJECTIVES

→ **1.** To learn the financial and statistical issues in the determination of sample size.

→ **2.** To discover methods for determining sample size.

→ **3.** To gain an appreciation of a normal distribution.

→ **4.** To understand population, sample, and sampling distributions.

→ **5.** To distinguish between point and interval estimates.

→ **6.** To recognize problems involving sampling means and proportions.

Determining Sample Size for Probability Samples

The process of determining sample size for probability samples involves financial, statistical, and managerial issues. As a general rule, the larger the sample is, the smaller the sampling error. However, larger samples cost more money, and the resources available for a project are always limited. Although the cost of increasing sample size tends to rise on a linear basis (double the sample size, almost double the cost), sampling error decreases at a rate equal to the square root of the relative increase in sample size. If sample size is quadrupled, data collection cost is almost quadrupled, but the level of sampling error is reduced by only 50 percent.

Managerial issues must be reflected in sample size calculations. How accurate do estimates need to be, and how confident must managers be that true population values are included in the chosen confidence interval? Some cases require high levels of precision (small sampling error) and confidence that population values fall in the small range of sampling error (the confidence interval). Other cases may not require the same level of precision or confidence.

Budget Available

The sample size for a project is often determined, at least indirectly, by the budget available. Thus, it is frequently the last project factor determined. A brand manager may have $50,000 available in the budget for a new product test. After deduction of other project costs (for example, research design, questionnaire development, data processing), the amount remaining determines the size of the sample that can be surveyed. Of course, if the dollars available will not produce an adequate sample size, then management must make a decision: either additional funds must be found, or the project should be canceled.

Although this approach may seem highly unscientific and arbitrary, it is a fact of life in a corporate environment. Financial constraints challenge the researcher to develop research designs that will generate data of adequate quality for decision-making purposes at low cost. This "budget available" approach forces the researcher to explore alternative data-collection approaches and to carefully consider the value of information in relation to its cost.

Rule of Thumb

Potential clients may specify in the RFP (request for proposal) that they want a sample of 200, 400, 500, or some other size. Sometimes, this number is based on desired sampling error. In other cases, it is based on nothing more than past experience. The justification for the specified sample size may boil down to a "gut feeling" that a particular sample size is necessary or appropriate.

If the researcher determines that the sample size requested is not adequate to support the objectives of the proposed research, then she or he has a professional responsibility to present arguments for a larger sample size to the client and let the client make the final decision. If the client rejects arguments for a larger sample size, then the researcher may decline to submit a proposal based on the belief that an inadequate sample size will produce results with so much error that they may be misleading.[1]

Number of Subgroups Analyzed

In any sample size determination problem, consideration must be given to the number and anticipated size of various subgroups of the total sample that must be analyzed and about which statistical inferences must be made. For example, a researcher might decide that a sample of 400 is quite adequate overall. However, if male and female respondents must be analyzed separately and the sample is expected to be 50 percent male and 50 percent female, then the expected sample size for each subgroup is only 200. Is this number adequate for making the desired statistical inferences about the characteristics of the two groups? If the results are to be analyzed by both sex and age, the problem gets even more complicated.

Assume that it is important to analyze four subgroups of the total sample: men under 35, men 35 and over, women under 35, and women 35 and over. If each group is expected to make up about 25 percent of the total sample, a sample of 400 will include only 100 respondents in each subgroup. The problem is that as sample size gets smaller, sampling error gets larger, and it becomes more difficult to tell whether an observed difference between two groups is a real difference or simply a reflection of sampling error.

Other things being equal, the larger the number of subgroups to be analyzed, the larger the required total sample size. It has been suggested that a sample should provide, at a minimum, 100 or more respondents in each major subgroup and 20 to 50 respondents in each of the less important subgroups.[2]

Traditional Statistical Methods

You probably have been exposed in other classes to traditional approaches for determining sample size for simple random samples. These approaches are reviewed in this chapter. Three pieces of information are required to make the necessary calculations for a sample result:

- An estimate of the population standard deviation
- The acceptable level of sampling error
- The desired level of confidence that the sample result will fall within a certain range (result ± sampling error) of true population values

With these three pieces of information, the researcher can calculate the size of the simple random sample required.[3]

The Normal Distribution

General Properties

The normal distribution is crucial to classical statistical inference. There are several reasons for its importance. First, many variables encountered by marketers have probability distributions that are close to the normal distribution. Examples include the number of cans, bottles, or glasses of soft drink consumed by soft drink users, the number of times that people who eat at fast-food restaurants go to such restaurants in an average month, and the average hours per week spent viewing television. Second, the normal distribution is useful for a number of theoretical reasons; one of the more important of these relates to the central limit theorem. According to the **central limit theorem**, for any population, regardless of its distribution, the distribution of sample means or sample proportions approaches a normal distribution as sample size increases. The importance of this tendency will become clear later in the chapter. Third, the normal distribution is a useful approximation of many other discrete probability distributions. If, for example, a researcher measured the heights of a large sample of men in the United States and plotted those values on a graph, a distribution similar to the one shown in Exhibit 12.1

→ **central limit theorem**
The idea that a distribution of a large number of sample means or sample proportions will approximate a normal distribution, regardless of the distribution of the population from which they were drawn.

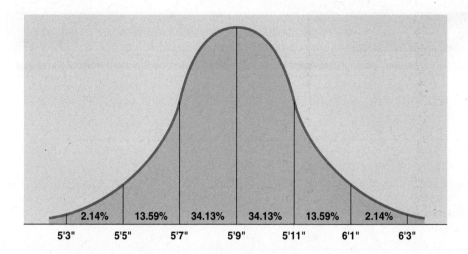

Exhibit 12.1

Normal Distribution for Heights of Men

would result. This distribution is a **normal distribution**, and it has a number of important characteristics, including the following:

1. The normal distribution is bell shaped and has only one mode. The mode is a measure of central tendency and is the particular value that occurs most frequently. (A bimodal, or two-mode, distribution would have two peaks or humps.)

2. The normal distribution is symmetric about its mean. This is another way of saying that it is not skewed and that the three measures of central tendency (mean, median, and mode) are all equal.

3. A particular normal distribution is uniquely defined by its mean and standard deviation.

4. The total area under a normal curve is equal to one, meaning that it takes in all observations.

5. The area of a region under the normal distribution curve between any two values of a variable equals the probability of observing a value in that range when an observation is randomly selected from the distribution. For example, on a single draw, there is a 34.13 percent chance of selecting from the distribution shown in Exhibit 12.1 a man between 5'7" and 5'9" in height.

6. The area between the mean and a given number of standard deviations from the mean is the same for all normal distributions. The area between the mean and plus or minus one standard deviation takes in 68.26 percent of the area under the curve, or 68.26 percent of the observations. This **proportional property of the normal distribution** provides the basis for the statistical inferences we will discuss in this chapter.

Standard Normal Distribution

Any normal distribution can be transformed into what is known as a standard normal distribution. The **standard normal distribution** has the same features as any normal distribution. However, the mean of the standard normal distribution is always equal to zero, and the standard deviation is always equal to one. A simple transformation formula, based on the proportional property of the normal distribution, is used to transform any value X from any normal distribution to its equivalent value Z from a standard normal distribution:

$$Z = \frac{\text{Value of the variable} - \text{Mean of the variable}}{\text{Standard deviation of the variable}}$$

normal distribution
A continuous distribution that is bell shaped and symmetric about the mean; the mean, median, and mode are equal.

proportional property of the normal distribution
A feature that the number of observations falling between the mean and a given number of standard deviations from the mean is the same for all normal distributions.

standard normal distribution
A normal distribution with a mean of zero and a standard deviation of one.

EXHIBIT 12.2	Area under the Standard Normal Curve for Z Values (Standard Deviations) of 1, 2, and 3
Z Values (standard deviation)	**Area under the Standard Normal Curve (%)**
1	68.26
2	95.44
3	99.74

Exhibit 12.3

Standard Normal Distribution

Note: The term Pr(Z) is read "the probability of Z."

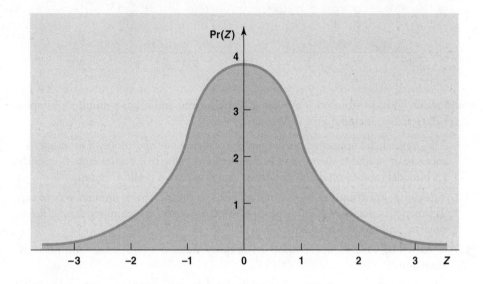

standard deviation
A measure of dispersion calculated by subtracting the mean of the series from each value in a series, squaring each result, summing the results, dividing the sum by the number of items minus 1, and taking the square root of this value.

Symbolically, the formula can be stated as follows:

$$Z = \frac{X - \mu}{\sigma}$$

where X = value of the variable
μ = mean of the variable
σ = standard deviation of the variable

The areas under a standard normal distribution (reflecting the percent of all observations) for various Z values (**standard deviations**) are shown in Exhibit 12.2. The standard normal distribution is shown in Exhibit 12.3.

Population and Sample Distributions

The purpose of conducting a survey based on a sample is to make inferences about the population, not to describe the sample. The population, as defined earlier, includes all possible individuals or objects from whom or about which information is needed to meet the objectives of the research. A sample is a subset of the total population.

A **population distribution** is a frequency distribution of all the elements of the population. It has a mean, usually represented by the Greek letter μ; and a standard deviation, usually represented by the Greek letter σ.

A **sample distribution** is a frequency distribution of all the elements of an individual (single) sample. In a sample distribution, the mean is usually represented by X and the standard deviation is usually represented by S.

> → **population distribution**
> A frequency distribution of all the elements of a population.

> → **sample distribution**
> A frequency distribution of all the elements of an individual sample.

The Sampling Distribution of the Mean

At this point, it is necessary to introduce a third distribution, the sampling distribution of the sample mean. Understanding this distribution is crucial to understanding the basis for our ability to compute sampling error for simple random samples. The **sampling distribution of the mean** is a conceptual and theoretical probability distribution of the means of all possible samples of a given size drawn from a given population. Although this distribution is seldom calculated, its known properties have tremendous practical significance. Actually, deriving a distribution of sample means involves drawing a large number of simple random samples (for example, 25,000) of a certain size from a particular population. Then, the means for the samples are computed and arranged in a frequency distribution. Because each sample is composed of a different subset of sample elements, all the sample means will not be exactly the same. If the samples are sufficiently large and random, then the resulting distribution of sample means will approximate a normal distribution. This assertion is based on the central limit theorem, which states that as sample size increases, the distribution of the means of a large number of random samples taken from virtually any population approaches a normal distribution with a mean equal to μ and a standard deviation (referred to as *standard error*) $S_{\bar{x}}$, where n = sample size and

> → **sampling distribution of the mean**
> A theoretical frequency distribution of the means of all possible samples of a given size drawn from a particular population; it is normally distributed.

$$S_{\bar{x}} = \frac{\sigma}{\sqrt{n}}$$

The **standard error of the mean** ($S\bar{x}$) is computed in this way because the variance, or dispersion, within a particular distribution of sample means will be smaller if it is based on larger samples. Common sense tells us that with larger samples individual sample means will, on the average, be closer to the population mean.

> → **standard error of the mean**
> The standard deviation of a distribution of sample means.

It is important to note that the central limit theorem holds regardless of the shape of the population distribution from which the samples are selected. This means that, regardless of the population distribution, the sample means selected from the population distribution will tend to be normally distributed.

The notation ordinarily used to refer to the means and standard deviations of population and sample distributions and sampling distribution of the mean is summarized in Exhibit 12.4. The relationships among the population distribution, sample distribution, and sampling distribution of the mean are shown graphically in Exhibit 12.5.

EXHIBIT 12.4	Notation for Means and Standard Deviations of Various Distributions	
Distribution	**Mean**	**Standard Deviation**
Population	μ	σ
Sample	X	S
Sampling	$\mu_{\bar{x}} = \mu$	$S_{\bar{x}}$

© marko turk/Age Fotostock America, Inc.

The results of a simple random sample of fast-food restaurant patrons could be used to compute the mean number of visits for the period of 1 month for 1,000 samples.

Basic Concepts

Consider a case in which a researcher takes 1,000 simple random samples of size 200 from the population of all consumers who have eaten at a fast-food restaurant at least once in the past 30 days. The purpose is to estimate the average number of times these individuals eat at a fast-food restaurant in an average month.

If the researcher computes the mean number of visits for each of the 1,000 samples and sorts them into intervals based on their relative values, the frequency distribution shown in Exhibit 12.6 might result. Exhibit 12.7 graphically illustrates these frequencies in a histogram, on which a normal curve has been superimposed. As you can see, the histogram closely approximates the shape of a normal curve. If the researcher draws a large enough number of samples of size 200, computes the mean of each sample, and plots these means, the resulting distribution will be a normal distribution. The normal curve shown in Exhibit 12.7 is the sampling distribution of the mean for this particular problem. The sampling distribution of the mean for simple random samples that are large (30 or more observations) has the following characteristics:

- The distribution is a normal distribution.
- The distribution has a mean equal to the population mean.

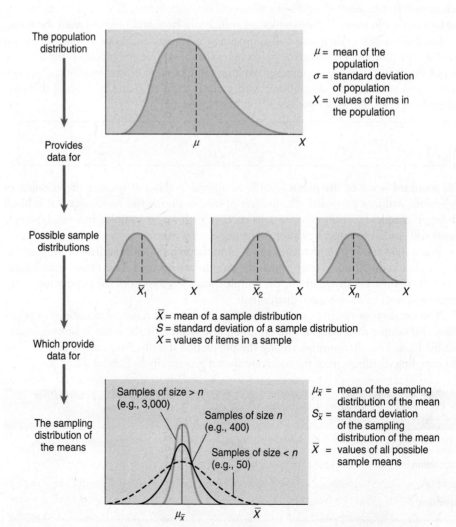

Exhibit 12.5

Relationships of the Three Basic Types of Distribution

Source: Adapted from *Statistics, A Fresh Approach,* 4th ed., by D. H. Sanders et al. © 1990 McGraw-Hill, Inc. Reprinted with permission of the McGraw-Hill Companies.

EXHIBIT 12.6	Frequency Distribution of 1,000 Sample Means: Average Number of Times Respondent Ate at a Fast-Food Restaurant in the Past 30 Days

Number of Times	Frequency of Occurrence
2.6–3.5	8
3.6–4.5	15
4.6–5.5	29
5.6–6.5	44
6.6–7.5	64
7.6–8.5	79
8.6–9.5	89
9.6–10.5	108
10.6–11.5	115
11.6–12.5	110
12.6–13.5	90
13.6–14.5	81
14.6–15.5	66
15.6–16.5	45
16.6–17.5	32
17.6–18.5	16
18.6–19.5	9
Total	1,000

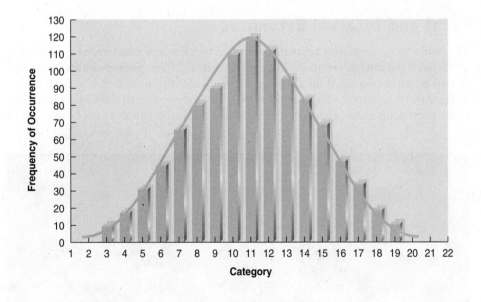

Exhibit 12.7

Actual Sampling Distribution of Means for Number of Times Respondent Ate at Fast-Food Restaurant in the Past 30 Days

■ The distribution has a standard deviation (the standard error of the mean) equal to the population standard deviation divided by the square root of the sample size:

$$\sigma_{\bar{x}} = \frac{\sigma}{\sqrt{n}}$$

This statistic is referred to as the standard error of the mean (instead of the standard deviation) to indicate that it applies to a distribution of sample means rather than to the standard deviation of a sample or a population. Keep in mind that this calculation applies *only* to a simple random sample. Other types of probability samples (for example, stratified samples and cluster samples) require more complex formulas for computing standard error. Note that this formula does not account for any type of bias, including nonresponse bias.

Making Inferences on the Basis of a Single Sample

In practice, there is no call for taking all possible random samples from a particular population and generating a frequency distribution and histogram like those shown in Exhibits 12.6 and 12.7. Instead, the researcher wants to take one simple random sample and make statistical inferences about the population from which it was drawn. The question is, what is the probability that any one simple random sample of a particular size will produce an estimate of the population mean that is within one standard error (plus or minus) of the true population mean? The answer, based on the information provided in Exhibit 12.2, is that there is a 68.26 percent probability that any one sample from a particular population will produce an estimate of the population mean that is within plus or minus one standard error of the true value, because 68.26 percent of all sample means fall in this range. There is a 95.44 percent probability that any one simple random sample of a particular size from a given population will produce a value that is within plus or minus two standard errors of the true population mean, and a 99.74 percent probability that such a sample will produce an estimate of the mean that is within plus or minus three standard errors of the population mean.

Point and Interval Estimates

The results of a sample can be used to generate two kinds of estimates of a population mean: point and interval estimates. The sample mean is the best **point estimate** of the population mean. Inspection of the sampling distribution of the mean shown in Exhibit 12.7 suggests that a particular sample result is likely to produce a mean that is relatively close to the population mean. However, the mean of a particular sample could be any one of

➜ **point estimate**
A particular estimate of a population value.

The sampling distribution of the proportion is used to estimate the percentage of the population that watches a particular television program.

OJO Images/Robert Daly/Getty Images, Inc.

the sample means shown in the distribution. A small percentage of these sample means are a considerable distance from the true population mean. The distance between the sample mean and the true population mean is the sampling error.

Given that point estimates based on sample results are exactly correct in only a small percentage of all possible cases, interval estimates generally are preferred. An **interval estimate** is a particular interval or range of values within which the true population value is estimated to fall. In addition to stating the size of the interval, the researcher usually states the probability that the interval will include the true value of the population mean. This probability is referred to as the **confidence level**, and the interval is called the **confidence interval**.

Interval estimates of the mean are derived by first drawing a random sample of a given size from the population of interest and calculating the mean of that sample. This sample mean is known to lie somewhere within the sampling distribution of all possible sample means, but exactly where this particular mean falls in that distribution is not known. There is a 68.26 percent probability that this particular sample mean lies within one standard error (plus or minus) of the true population mean. Based on this information, the researcher states that he or she is 68.26 percent confident that the true population value is equal to the sample value plus or minus one standard error. This statement can be shown symbolically, as follows:

$$\bar{X} - 1\sigma_{\bar{x}} \leq \mu \leq \bar{X} + 1$$

By the same logic, the researcher can be 95.44 percent confident that the true population value is equal to the sample estimate ± 2 (technically 1.96) standard errors, and 99.74 percent confident that the true population value falls within the interval defined by the sample value ± 3 standard errors.

These statements assume that the standard deviation of the population is known. However, in most situations, this is not the case. If the standard deviation of the population were known, by definition the mean of the population would also be known, and there would be no need to take a sample in the first place. Because information on the standard deviation of the population is lacking, its value is estimated based on the standard deviation of the sample.

Sampling Distribution of the Proportion

Marketing researchers frequently are interested in estimating proportions or percentages rather than or in addition to estimating means. Common examples include estimating the following:

- The percentage of the population that is aware of a particular ad.
- The percentage of the population that accesses the Internet one or more times in an average week.
- The percentage of the population that has visited a fast-food restaurant four or more times in the past 30 days.
- The percentage of the population that watches a particular television program.

In situations in which a population proportion or percentage is of interest, the sampling distribution of the proportion is used. The **sampling distribution of the proportion** is a relative frequency distribution of the sample proportions of a large number of random samples of a given size drawn from a particular population. The sampling distribution of a proportion has the following characteristics:

- It approximates a normal distribution.
- The mean proportion for all possible samples is equal to the population proportion.

---

interval estimate
The interval or range of values within which the true population value is estimated to fall.

confidence level
The probability that a particular interval will include true population value; also called *confidence coefficient*.

confidence interval
The interval that, at the specified confidence level, includes the true population value.

sampling distribution of the proportion
The relative frequency distribution of the sample proportions of many random samples of a given size drawn from a particular population; it is normally distributed.

■ The standard error of a sampling distribution of the proportion can be computed with the following formula:

$$S_p = \sqrt{\frac{P(1 - P)}{n}}$$

where S_p = standard error of sampling distribution of proportion

P = estimate of population proportion

n = sample size

Consider the task of estimating the percentage of all adults who have purchased something over the Internet in the past 90 days. As in generating a sampling distribution of the mean, the researcher might select 1,000 random samples of size 200 from the population of all adults and compute the proportion of all adults who have purchased something over the Internet in the past 90 days for all 1,000 samples. These values could then be plotted in a frequency distribution and this frequency distribution would approximate a normal distribution. The estimated standard error of the proportion for this distribution can be computed using the formula provided earlier.

For reasons that will be clear to you after you read the next section, marketing researchers have a tendency to prefer dealing with sample size problems as problems of estimating proportions rather than means.

Determining Sample Size

Problems Involving Means

Consider once again the task of estimating how many times the average fast-food restaurant user visits a fast-food restaurant in an average month. Management needs an estimate of the average number of visits to make a decision regarding a new promotional campaign that is being developed. To make this estimate, the marketing research manager for the organization intends to survey a simple random sample of all fast-food users. The question is, what information is necessary to determine the appropriate sample size for the project? The formula for calculating the required sample size for problems that involve the estimation of a mean is as follows:[4]

$$n = \frac{Z^2 \sigma^2}{E^2}$$

where Z = level of confidence expressed in standard errors

σ = population standard deviation

E = acceptable amount of sampling error

Three pieces of information are needed to compute the sample size required:

1. The acceptable or allowable level of sampling error E.
2. The acceptable level of confidence Z. In other words, how confident does the researcher want to be that the specified confidence interval includes the population mean?
3. An estimate of the population standard deviation σ.

The level of confidence Z and **allowable sampling error** E for this calculation must be set by the researcher in consultation with his or her client. As noted earlier, the level of confidence and the amount of error are based not only on statistical criteria but also on financial and managerial criteria. In an ideal world, the level of confidence would always be very high and the amount of error very low. However, because this is a business decision, cost must be considered. An acceptable trade-off among accuracy, level of confidence, and cost must be developed. High levels of precision and confidence may be less important in some situations than in others. For example, in an exploratory study, you may be interested in developing a basic sense of whether attitudes toward your product are generally positive or negative. Precision may not be critical. However, in a product concept test, you would need a much more precise estimate of sales for a new product before making the potentially costly and risky decision to introduce that product in the marketplace.

> **allowable sampling error**
> The amount of sampling error a researcher is willing to accept.

Making an estimate of the **population standard deviation** presents a more serious problem. As noted earlier, if the population standard deviation were known, the population mean also would be known (the population mean is needed to compute the population standard deviation), and there would be no need to draw a sample. How can the researcher estimate the population standard deviation before selecting the sample? One or some combination of the following four methods might be used to deal with this problem:

> **population standard deviation**
> The standard deviation of a variable for an entire population.

1. *Use results from a prior survey.* In many cases, the firm may have conducted a prior survey dealing with the same or a similar issue. In this situation, a possible solution to the problem is to use the results of the prior survey as an estimate of the population standard deviation.

2. *Conduct a pilot survey.* If this is to be a large-scale project, it may be possible to devote some time and some resources to a small-scale pilot survey of the population. The results of this pilot survey can be used to develop an estimate of the population standard deviation that can be used in the sample size determination formula.

3. *Use secondary data.* In some cases, secondary data can be used to develop an estimate of the population standard deviation.

4. *Use judgment.* If all else fails, an estimate of the population standard deviation can be developed based solely on judgment. Judgments might be sought from a variety of managers in a position to make educated guesses about the required population parameters.

It should be noted that after the survey has been conducted and the sample mean and sample standard deviation have been calculated, the researcher can assess the accuracy of the estimate of the population standard deviation used to calculate the required sample size. At this time, if appropriate, adjustments can be made in the initial estimates of sampling error.[5]

Let's return to the problem of estimating the average number of fast-food visits made in an average month by users of fast-food restaurants:

▦ After consultation with managers in the company, the marketing research manager determines that an estimate is needed of the average number of times that fast-food consumers visit fast-food restaurants. She further determines that managers believe that a high degree of accuracy is needed, which she takes to mean that the estimate should be within .10 (one-tenth) of a visit of the true population value. This value (.10) should be substituted into the formula for the value of E.

▦ In addition, the marketing research manager decides that, all things considered, she needs to be 95.44 percent confident that the true population mean falls in the interval defined by the sample mean plus or minus E (as just defined). Two (technically, 1.96) standard errors are required to take in 95.44 percent of the area under a normal curve. Therefore, a value of 2 should be substituted into the equation for Z.

▦ Finally, there is the question of what value to insert into the formula for σ. Fortunately, the company conducted a similar study one year ago. The standard deviation in that study for the variable—the average number of times a fast-food restaurant was visited in the past 30 days—was 1.39. This is the best estimate of σ available. Therefore, a value of 1.39 should be substituted into the formula for the value of σ. The calculation follows:

$$n = \frac{Z^2 \sigma^2}{E^2}$$
$$= \frac{2^2(1.39)^2}{(.10)^2}$$
$$= \frac{4(1.93)}{.01}$$
$$= \frac{7.72}{.01}$$
$$= 772$$

Based on this calculation, a simple random sample of 772 is necessary to meet the requirements outlined.

Problems Involving Proportions

Now let's consider the problem of estimating the proportion or percentage of all adults who have purchased something via the Internet in the past 90 days. The goal is to take a simple random sample from the population of all adults to estimate this proportion.[6]

▪ As in the problem involving fast-food users, the first task in estimating the population mean on the basis of sample results is to decide on an acceptable value for E. If, for example, an error level of 34 percent is acceptable, a value of .04 should be substituted into the formula for E.

▪ Next, assume that the researcher has determined a need to be 95.44 percent confident that the sample estimate is within 34 percent of the true population proportion. As in the previous example, a value of 2 should be substituted into the equation for Z.

▪ Finally, in a study of the same issue conducted one year ago, 5 percent of all respondents indicated they had purchased something over the Internet in the past 90 days. Thus, a value of .05 should be substituted into the equation for P.

The resulting calculations are as follows:

$$n = \frac{Z^2[P(1 - P)]}{E^2}$$
$$= \frac{2^2[.05(1 - .05)]}{.04^2}$$
$$= \frac{4(.0475)}{.0016}$$
$$= \frac{.19}{.0016}$$
$$= 119$$

Given the requirements, a random sample of 119 respondents is required. It should be noted that, in one respect, the process of determining the sample size necessary to estimate a proportion is easier than the process of determining the sample size necessary to estimate a mean: If there is no basis for estimating P, the researcher can make what is sometimes referred to as the most pessimistic, or worst-case, assumption regarding the value of P. Given the values of Z and E, what value of P will require the largest possible sample? A value of .50 will make the value of the expression $P(1 - P)$ larger than any possible value of P. There is no corresponding most pessimistic assumption that the researcher can make regarding the value of σ in problems that involve determining the sample size necessary to estimate a mean with given levels of Z and E.

Determining Sample Size for Stratified and Cluster Samples

The formulas for sample size determination presented in this chapter apply only to simple random samples. There also are formulas for determining required sample size and sampling error for other types of probability samples such as stratified and cluster samples. Although many of the general concepts presented in this chapter apply to these other types of probability samples, the specific formulas are much more complicated.[7] In addition, these formulas require information that frequently is not available or is difficult to obtain. For these reasons, sample size determination for other types of probability samples is beyond the scope of this introductory text.

Sample Size for Qualitative Research

The issue of sample size for qualitative research often comes up when making decisions about the number of traditional focus groups, individual depth interviews or online bulletin board focus groups to conduct. Given the relatively small sample sizes we intentionally use in qualitative research, the types of sample size calculation discussed in this chapter are never going to help us answer this question. Experts have discussed a rule based on experience and some analysis suggests that after we have talked to 20–30 people in a qualitative setting the general pattern of responses begins to stabilize.

Population Size and Sample Size

You may have noticed that none of the formulas for determining sample size takes into account the size of the population in any way. Students (and managers) frequently find this troubling. It seems to make sense that one should take a larger sample from a larger population. But this is not the case. Normally, there is no direct relationship between the size of the population and the size of the sample required to estimate a particular population parameter with a particular level of error and a particular level of confidence. In fact, the size of the population may have an effect only in those situations where the size of the sample is large in relation to the size of the population. One rule of thumb is that an adjustment should be made in the sample size if the sample size is more than 5 percent of the size of the total population. The normal presumption is that sample elements are drawn independently of one another (**independence assumption**). This assumption is justified when the sample is small relative to the population. However, it is not appropriate when the sample is a relatively large (5 percent or more) proportion of the population. As a result, the researcher must adjust the results obtained with the standard formulas. For example, the formula for the standard error of the mean, presented earlier, is as follows:

> **independence assumption**
> The assumption that sample elements are drawn independently.

$$\sigma_{\bar{x}} = \frac{\sigma}{\sqrt{n}}$$

For a sample that is 5 percent or more of the population, the independence assumption is dropped, producing the following formula:

$$\frac{\sigma}{\sqrt{n}} \sqrt{\frac{N-n}{N-1}}$$

→ finite population correction factor (FPC)
An adjustment to the required sample size that is made in cases where the sample is expected to be equal to 5 percent or more of the total population.

The factor $(N - n)/(N - 1)$ is referred to as the **finite population correction factor (FPC)**.

In those situations in which the sample is large (5 percent or more) in relation to the population, the researcher can appropriately reduce the required sample size using the FPC. This calculation is made using the following formula:

$$\frac{nN}{N + n - 1}$$

where n' = revised sample size
       n = original sample size
       N = population size

If the population has 2,000 elements and the original sample size is 400, then

$$n' = \frac{400(2000)}{2000 + 400 - 1} = \frac{800,000}{2399}$$
$$= 333$$

With the FPC adjustment, a sample of only 333 is needed, rather than the original 400.

The key is not the size of the sample in relation to the size of the population, but whether the sample selected is truly representative of the population. Empirical evidence shows that relatively small but carefully chosen samples can quite accurately reflect characteristics of the population. Many well-known national surveys and opinion polls, such as the Gallup Poll and the Harris Poll, are based on samples of fewer than 2,000. These polls have shown that the behavior of tens of millions of people can be predicted quite accurately using samples that are minuscule in relation to the size of the population.

Determining How Many Sample Units Are Needed

Regardless of how the target sample size is determined, the researcher is confronted with the practical problem of figuring out how many sampling units (telephone numbers, addresses, and so on) will be required to complete the assignment. For example, if the target final sample size is 400, then obviously more than 400 telephone numbers will be needed to complete a telephone survey.

PRACTICING MARKETING RESEARCH

Estimating with Precision How Many Phone Numbers Are Needed

Calculating how many phone numbers are needed for a project may seem like a difficult task, but following a few basic rules can make it simple. The formula used by Survey Sampling International (SSI) to calculate sample size involves four factors: (1) the number of completed interviews needed, (2) the working phone (or "reachable") rate, (3) the incidence rate, and (4) the contact/completion rate.

Completed Interviews

The number of completed interviews is based on the sample size calculation formula for simple random samples. It is the final sample size you want to achieve.

Working Phone Rate

The working phone rate varies with the sampling methodology used. An SSI RDD (Random Digit Dialing) sample yields a 60 percent working phone rate. That is a good number to use in the formula for estimation purposes.

Incidence Rate

The incidence rate is the percentage of contacts that will qualify for the interview. Or, put another way, what percentage of people who answer the phone (or reply to your mail questionnaire) will pass your screening questions? Accurate incidence data are critical to determining proper sample size. An incidence figure that is too high will leave you short of sample once your study is in the field.

Contact/Completion Rate

The last factor is the contact/completion rate. SSI defines this rate as the percentage of people who, once they qualify for your study, will agree to cooperate by completing the interview. There are several important elements you should consider when trying to reasonably estimate the completion rate:

- Contact rate
- Length of interview
- Sensitivity of topic
- Time of year
- Number of attempts/callbacks
- Length of time in the field

Provided that the interview is short (less than 10 minutes) and nonsensitive in nature, sufficient callbacks are scheduled, and the study will be in the field for an adequate period of time, SSI estimates a 30 percent completion rate. The completion rate should be adjusted according to the specifications of each study. If the subject matter is sensitive or the interview is long, the completion rate should be reduced. If the length of time in the field is less than one week, SSI recommends increasing the sample size by at least 20 percent.

An Example

Suppose you wish to complete 300 interviews in the United Kingdom. Using a random-digit sample, you can expect a working phone rate of 60 percent. Start by dividing the number of completed interviews you need (300) by the working phone rate (.60), to yield 500. You need to reach heavy soft drink users (17 percent of adults), and you estimate that 30 percent of the people contacted will complete the interview. Divide 500 by the incidence rate for the group under study (.17) and then by the completion rate (.30). This calculation shows you need 9,804 phone numbers to complete this survey.[8]

If you wish to complete 300 interviews in the United Kingdom, you need to determine the contact/completion rate in order to figure out how many calls will actually have to be made to complete the survey.

Lou Jones/ZUMA Press/NewsCom

Some of the numbers on the list will be disconnected, some people will not qualify for the survey because they do not meet the requirements for inclusion in the population, and some will refuse to complete the survey. These factors affect the final estimate of the number of phone numbers, which may be used to place an order with a sample provider, such as Survey Sampling International, or to ask the client for customer names and phone numbers for a satisfaction survey. This estimate must be reasonably accurate because the researcher wants to avoid paying for more numbers than are needed; on the other hand, the researcher doesn't want to run out of numbers during the survey and have to wait for more.

Estimating the number of sample units needed for a telephone sample is covered in the feature on page 315.

Statistical Power

Although it is standard practice in marketing research to use the formulas presented in this chapter to calculate sample size, these formulas all focus on *type I error*, or the error of concluding that there is a difference when there is not a difference. They do not explicitly deal with *type II error*, or the error of saying that there is no difference when there is a difference. The probability of not making a type II error is called **statistical power**.[9] The standard formulas for calculating sample size implicitly assume a power of 50 percent. For example, suppose a researcher is trying to determine which of two product concepts has stronger appeal to target customers and wants to be able to detect a 5 percent difference in the percentages of target customers who say that they are very likely to buy the products. The standard sample size formulas indicate that a sample size of approximately 400 is needed for each product test. By using this calculation, the researcher implicitly accepts the fact that there is a 50 percent chance of incorrectly concluding that the two products have equal appeal.

Exhibit 12.8 shows the sample sizes required, at an alpha (probability of incorrectly rejecting the null hypothesis) of 0.25, for specific levels of power and specific levels of

statistical power
The probability of not making a type II error.

EXHIBIT 12.8	Sample Size Required to Detect Differences between Proportions from Independent Samples at Different Levels of Power and an Alpha of 0.25					
Difference	Power					
to Detect	50%	60%	70%	75%	80%	90%
0.01	19,205	24,491	30,857	34,697	39,239	52,530
0.05	766	977	1,231	1,384	1,568	2,094
0.10	190	242	305	343	389	518
0.15	83	106	133	150	169	226

differences between two independent proportions. Formulas are available to permit power calculations for any level of confidence; however, they are somewhat complex and will not help you understand the basic concept of power. Programs available on the Internet can be used to make these calculations. To reproduce the numbers in Exhibit 12.8, go to http://www.dssresearch.com/KnowledgeCenter/toolkitcalculators/statistical powercalculators.aspx.

■ Click on the Two-Sample Using Percentage Values option under Sample Size.

■ Enter the Sample 1 Percentage and the Sample 2 Percentage in the boxes so that the figures entered reflect the differences you want to be able to detect and the values are in the expected range. These figures are set at the 50 percent level (value of p in the standard sample size formula).

■ Below those boxes, enter the Alpha and Beta Error Levels. Alpha is the value you would use for E in the standard sample size formula, and Beta is the probability of incorrectly failing to reject the null hypothesis of no difference when a real difference exists. Power is equal to 1 – beta.

■ Click on the Calculate Sample Size button at the bottom of the screen for the answer.

SUMMARY

Determining sample size for probability samples involves financial, statistical, and managerial considerations. Other things being equal, the larger the sample is, the smaller the sampling error. In turn, the cost of the research grows with the size of the sample.

There are several methods for determining sample size. One is to base the decision on the funds available. In essence, sample size is determined by the budget. Although seemingly unscientific, this approach is often a very realistic one in the world of corporate marketing research. The second technique is the so-called rule of thumb approach, which essentially involves determining the sample size based on a gut feeling or common practice. Samples of 300, 400, or 500 are often listed by the client in a request for proposal. A third technique for determining sample size is based on the number of subgroups to be analyzed. Generally speaking, the more subgroups that need to be analyzed, the larger is the required total sample size.

In addition to these methods, there are a number of traditional statistical techniques for determining sample size. Three pieces of data are required to make sample size calculations: an estimate of the population standard deviation, the level of sampling error that the researcher or client is willing to accept, and the desired level of confidence that the sample result will fall within a certain range of the true population value.

Crucial to statistical sampling theory is the concept of the normal distribution. The normal distribution is bell shaped and has only one mode. It also is symmetric about its mean. The standard normal distribution has the features of a normal distribution; however, the mean of the standard normal distribution is always equal to zero, and the standard deviation is always equal to one. The transformation formula is used to transform any value X from any normal distribution to its equivalent value Z from a standard normal distribution. The central limit theorem states that the distribution of the means of a large number of random samples taken from virtually any population approaches a normal distribution with a mean equal to μ and a standard deviation equal to $S_{\bar{x}}$, where

$$S_{\bar{x}} = \frac{\sigma}{\sqrt{n}}$$

The standard deviation of a distribution of sample means is called the standard error of the mean.

When the results of a sample are used to estimate a population mean, two kinds of estimates can be generated: point and interval estimates. The sample mean is the best point estimate of the population mean. An interval estimate is a certain interval or range of values within which the true population value is estimated to fall. Along with the magnitude of the interval, the researcher usually states the probability that the interval will include the true value of the population mean—that is, the confidence level. The interval is called the confidence interval.

The researcher who is interested in estimating proportions or percentages rather than or in addition to means uses the sampling distribution of the proportion. The sampling distribution of the proportion is a relative frequency distribution of the sample proportions of a large number of random samples of a given size drawn from a particular population. The standard error of a sampling distribution of proportion is computed as follows:

$$S_p = \sqrt{\frac{P(1 - P)}{n}}$$

The following are required to calculate sample size: the acceptable level of sampling error E, the acceptable level of confidence Z, and an estimate of the population standard deviation 3. The formula for calculating the required sample size for situations that involve the estimation of a mean is as follows:

$$n = \frac{Z^2 \sigma^2}{E^2}$$

The following formula is used to calculate the required sample size for problems involving proportions:

$$n = \frac{Z^2[P(1 - P)]}{E^2}$$

Finally, statistical power is the probability of not making a type II error. A type II error is the mistake of saying that there is not a difference when there is a difference. The standard sample size formula implicitly assumes a power of 50 percent. It may be important to use different levels of power depending on the nature of the decision in question.

KEY TERMS & DEFINITIONS

central limit theorem The idea that a distribution of a large number of sample means or sample proportions will approximate a normal distribution, regardless of the distribution of the population from which they were drawn.

normal distribution A continuous distribution that is bell shaped and symmetric about the mean; the mean, median, and mode are equal.

proportional property of the normal distribution A feature that the number of observations falling between the mean and a given number of standard deviations from the mean is the same for all normal distributions.

standard normal distribution A normal distribution with a mean of zero and a standard deviation of one.

standard deviation A measure of dispersion calculated by subtracting the mean of the series from each value in a series, squaring each result, summing the results, dividing the sum by the number of items minus 1, and taking the square root of this value.

population distribution A frequency distribution of all the elements of a population.

sample distribution A frequency distribution of all the elements of an individual sample.

sampling distribution of the mean A theoretical frequency distribution of the means of all possible samples of a given size drawn from a particular population; it is normally distributed.

standard error of the mean The standard deviation of a distribution of sample means.

point estimate A particular estimate of a population value.

interval estimate The interval or range of values within which the true population value is estimated to fall.

confidence level The probability that a particular interval will include the true population value; also called *confidence coefficient.*

confidence interval The interval that, at the specified confidence level, includes the true population value.

sampling distribution of the proportion The relative frequency distribution of the sample proportions of many random samples of a given size drawn from a particular population; it is normally distributed.

allowable sampling error The amount of sampling error a researcher is willing to accept.

population standard deviation The standard deviation of a variable for an entire population.

independence assumption The assumption that sample elements are drawn independently.

finite population correction factor (FPC) An adjustment to the required sample size that is made in cases where the sample is expected to be equal to 5 percent or more of the total population.

statistical power The probability of not making a type II error.

QUESTIONS FOR REVIEW & CRITICAL THINKING

1. Explain how the determination of sample size is a financial, statistical, and managerial issue.

2. Discuss and give examples of three methods that are used in marketing research for determining sample size.

3. A marketing researcher analyzing the fast-food industry noticed the following: The average amount spent at a fast-food restaurant in California was $3.30, with a standard deviation of $0.40. Yet in Georgia, the average amount spent at a fast-food restaurant was $3.25, with a standard deviation of $0.10. What do these statistics tell you about fast-food consumption patterns in these two states?

4. Distinguish among population, sample, and sampling distributions. Why is it important to distinguish among these concepts?

5. What is the finite population correction factor? Why is it used? When should it be used?

6. Assume that previous fast-food research has shown that 80 percent of the consumers like curly french fries. The researcher wishes to have a standard error of 6 percent or less and be 95 percent confident of an estimate to be made about curly french fry consumption from a survey. What sample size should be used for a simple random sample?

7. You are in charge of planning a chili cook-off. You must make sure that there are plenty of samples for the patrons of the cook-off. The following standards have been set: a confidence level of 99 percent and an error of less than 4 ounces per cooking team. Last year's cook-off had a standard deviation in amount of chili cooked of 3 ounces. What is the necessary sample size?

8. Based on a client's requirements of a confidence interval of 99.74 percent and acceptable sampling error of 2 percent, a sample size of 500 is calculated. The cost is estimated at $20,000. The client replies that the budget for this project is $17,000. What are the alternatives?

9. A marketing researcher must determine how many telephone numbers she needs order from a sample provider to complete a survey of ATM users. The goal is to complete 400 interviews with ATM users. From past experience, she estimates that 60 percent of the phone numbers provided will be working phone numbers. The estimated incidence rate (percentage of people contacted who are ATM users) is 43 percent. Finally, she estimates from previous surveys that 35 percent of the people contacted will agree to complete the survey. How many telephone numbers should she order?

WORKING THE NET

1. Go to *http://research-advisors.com/documents/SampleSize-web.xls* to get a download of an Excel spreadsheet for a sample size table. The spreadsheet enables users to change the margin of error, confidence level, and population size. Experiment with different combinations.

2. For an online statistical power calculator, go to: ***www.dssresearch.com/toolkit/spcalc/power.asp*** Estimate the statistical power (type II error or beta error) for existing survey projects.

3. Use the sample size calculator online at ***www.dssresearch.com/toolkit/sscalc/size.asp*** to work out these problems. What size samples are needed for a statistical power of 70 percent in detecting a difference of 5 percent between the estimated percentages of recent CD buyers in two independent samples? Assume an expected percentage in the range of 50 percent and an alpha error of 5 percent.

REAL-LIFE RESEARCH • 12.1

HealthLife

HealthLife is a leading provider of employee wellness programs to Fortune 500 companies. Its programs are designed to improve employee health and wellness with the goal of developing a healthier, happier, more productive workforce. In addition, it has shown that its programs reduce medical claims for its clients. This is an important consideration given that nearly all of its clients are self-insured in regard to medical benefits. The company offers an array of programs and can tailor programs to the needs of individual clients. HealthLife is about to start the second year of a brand image campaign.

The company is planning to spend $3.5 million to promote awareness and a positive image of its services among Fortune 500 companies and their employees. It is pursuing this strategy because the market for its services is becoming more competitive as interest in employee wellness has grown and as more competitors have entered the market in recent years.

In the first year of the brand image campaign, HealthLife spent $3 million pursuing the same goals of increasing awareness and building its image. In order to see if the campaign was successful, the company conducted tracking research by telephone. It conducted a pretest before the campaign began and a posttest on its conclusion. The surveys were designed to measure awareness of HealthLife and the image of HealthLife among decision makers in Fortune 500 companies. Healthlife estimates an average of 20 executives were involved in the decision-making process for the purchase of its services per company, or a total target audience of around 10,000. Changes in either measure from the pretest to the posttest were to be attributed to the effects of the ad campaign. No other elements of this marketing strategy were changed during the course of the campaign.

Unaided or top-of-mind awareness (what companies come to mind when you think of companies that provide group health care coverage?) increased from 21 percent in the pretest to 25 percent in the posttest. In the pretest, 42 percent reported having a positive image of HealthLife. This figure increased to 44 percent in the posttest. Though both key measures increased, the sample sizes for the two tests were relatively small. Random samples of 100 decision makers were used for both tests. Sampling error for the measure of awareness at 95 percent confidence is ±8.7 percent. The comparable figure for the image measure is ±9.9 percent. The value used for p in the formula is the posttest result. With these relatively large sampling errors and the relatively small changes in awareness and image, HealthLife could only say with 95 percent confidence that awareness in the posttest was 25 percent ±8.7 percent, or in the range of 16.3 percent to 33.7 percent.

In regard to the image measure, it could only say with 95 percent confidence that the percent of targeted decision makers with a positive image of HealthLife in the posttest was 44 percent ±9.9 percent, or in the range of 34.1 percent to 53.9 percent. Based on the relatively small changes in awareness and positive image and the relatively large errors associated with these measures, HealthLife could not conclude with any confidence that either measure had actually changed.

The CEO of HealthLife is concerned about the amount of money being spent on advertising and wants to know whether the advertising is achieving what it is supposed to achieve. She wants a more sensitive test so that a definitive conclusion regarding the effect of the advertising can be reached.

Questions

1. Show how the sampling error calculations for the posttest measures were calculated.

2. If the CEO wanted to be sure that the estimates of awareness and positive image are within ±2 percent of the true value at 95 percent confidence, what is the required sample size?

3. Using all the same information used in question 2, what is the required sample size if the CEO wants to be 99.5 percent confident?

4. If the current budget for conducting the telephone interviews is $20,000 and the cost per interview is $19, can HealthLife reach the goal specified in question 3? What error levels can it reach for both measures with the $20,000 budget? What is the required budget to reach the goal set in question 3?

 • **SPSS JUMP START FOR CHI-SQUARE TEST**

Exercise 1: Sample Size Determination Using the Sample Means Method SPSS-H1

1. Go to the Wiley Web site, at **www.wiley.com/college/mcdaniel,** and download the *Segmenting the College Student Market for Movie Attendance* database to SPSS windows. Using the *Segmenting the College Student Market for Movie Attendance* database, assume that the most important items in the survey are in question 5, which has nine movie items in which respondents rate their relative importance (download a copy of the *Segmenting the College Student Market for Movie Attendance* questionnaire). Notice the computer coding for each of the variables, which is the same as that in the *variable view* option on the SPSS Data Editor.

2. The sample means method of sample size determination consists of:
   i. required confidence level (z)
   ii. level of tolerable error (e)
   iii. estimated population variance (σ)
   iv. estimated sample size (n)
   v. *Formula: $n = (z^2 * \sigma^2)/e^2$*

3. Of the various methods of deriving sample size, estimated population standard deviation can be estimated based on prior studies, expert judgment, or by conducting a pilot sample. For this problem, we are going to estimate population standard deviation using a *pilot sample.* To do this you will use only the first 200 cases in the *Segmenting the College Student Market for Movie Attendance* database. Invoke the *data/select cases* sequence to select the first 200 cases in the database. We are assuming that these are responses to a pilot sample and we will use them to estimate the needed sample size.

4. Use the *analyze/descriptive statistics/descriptive* sequence to compute the standard deviation for variables Q5a–Q5i. We are assuming that each of the nine variables is equally important with respect to the research objective.

5. From your knowledge of sample size determination, you should know that the variable to select for sample size determination is the one with the largest standard deviation. Select that variable.

Answer the following questions:

1. Which of the nine movie theater items had the largest standard deviation?

   _____

2. Invoke the sample means method of sample size determination to make the necessary computations for each of the following:

   a. Compute sample size given the following:

      i. Required confidence level (Z) is 95.44%.

      ii. Tolerable error (e) is .1 or 1/10 of a response point.

      iii. Standard deviation (σ) = _____

      iv. Sample size (n) = _____

   b. Compute sample size given the following:

      i. Required confidence level (Z) is 99.72%.

      ii. Tolerable level (e) is .1 or 1/10 of a response point.

      iii. Standard deviation (σ) = _____

      iv. Sample size (n) = _____

3. How do your computed sample sizes in the problems above compare to the total number of cases in the *Segmenting the College Student Market for Movie Attendance* database?

   _____

4. We are going to assume that the objective of our research concerning students' attendance at movies can be expressed as a dichotomy (greater or lesser, etc.); for example, it doesn't matter how much one group attends movies over another group, but just *who* attends the most. To accomplish this we can use the much less complicated *sample proportions* formula. We are going to assume that we have no prior studies, hence, in the sample proportions formula $P = .5$ and $(1 - P) = .5$. *You will not need SPSS to assist you with this computation.*

   a. Compute sample size given the following:

      i. Required confidence level (Z) is 95.44%.

      ii. Tolerable error (e) is .05 or accuracy within 5% of the true population mean.

      iii. Standard deviation $P = .5$ and $(1 - P) = .5$

      iv. Sample size (n) = _____

c. Compute sample size given the following:

    i.   Required confidence level (Z) is 99.72%.

    ii. Tolerable error (e) is .03 or accuracy within 3% of the true population mean.

    iii. Standard deviation $P = .5$ and $(1 - P) = .5$

    iv. Sample size (n) = _____

Exercise 2: Determining the Reliability/Confidence of Sample Results

1.   In the subsequent exercise, the objective will not be to determine the needed sample size, but to evaluate the confidence level of results derived from the entire *Segmenting the College Student Market for Movie Attendance* database. To evaluate this type of confidence, using the sample means formula, solve for Z instead of n. Hence, use the formula $Z^2 = n * e^2/\sigma^2$. Then take the square root of Z^2. Go to the normal distribution table in the appendix of your text to determine the confidence level associated with the database. For the sample proportions formula, solve for Z using the formula $Z^2 = (n * e^2)/[P(1 - P)]$, then take the square root of Z^2.

2.   For this problem again assume that question #5 has the most important questions in the questionnaire, with respect to the research objectives. Using the *analyze/ descriptive statistics/descriptives* sequence, compute the standard deviation for variables Q5a–Q5i. We are assuming that each of the nine variables are equally important with respect to the research objective. **Again, choose the variable with the largest standard deviation** to input into the analysis.

3.   Given the preceding, compute the confidence level associated with the *Segmenting the College Student Market for Movie Attendance* database, given the following:

    1. a. Tolerable error is .1 or 1/10 of a response point

       b. Sample size = 500

       c. Standard deviation _____

    2. Confidence Level = _____ %

    3. How do the results in 2, above compare to the results in 2 of the sample size determination problem?

    _____

    4. **Sample Proportions Formula:** Given the following information, compute the confidence level associated with the *Segmenting the College Student Marketing for Movie Attendance* database. ***You will not need SPSS to make this computation.***

       a. Tolerable error is .05 or 5%.

       b. Sample size = 500

       c. Standard deviation $P = .5$ and $(1 - P) = .5$

       Confidence Level = _____ %

       How do the results in this problem compare to the confidence level in #2 of (3)?

       _____

Justin Horricks/Stockphoto

Data Processing, Data Analysis, and Statistical Testing

CHAPTER 13

LEARNING OBJECTIVES

→ 1. To develop an understanding of the importance and nature of quality control checks.

→ 2. To understand the data entry process and data entry alternatives.

→ 3. To learn how surveys are tabulated and cross tabulated.

→ 4. To understand the concept of hypothesis development and how to test hypotheses.

Overview of the Data Analysis Procedure

Once data collection has been completed and questionnaires have been returned, the researcher may be facing anywhere from a few hundred to several thousand interviews, each ranging from a few pages to 20 or more pages. We recently completed a study involving 1,300 questionnaires of 10 pages each. The 13,000 pages amounted to a stack of paper nearly 3 feet high. How should a researcher transform all the information contained on 13,000 pages of completed questionnaires into a format that will permit the summarization necessary for detailed analysis? At one extreme, the researcher could read all the interviews, make notes while reading them, and draw some conclusions from this review of the questionnaires. The folly of this approach is fairly obvious. Instead of this haphazard and inefficient approach, professional researchers follow a five-step procedure for data analysis:

Step 1:   Validation and editing (quality control)
Step 2:   Coding
Step 3:   Data entry
Step 4:   Logical cleaning of data
Step 5:   Tabulation and statistical analysis

Step 1: Validation and Editing

The purpose of the first step is twofold. The researcher wants to make sure that all the interviews actually were conducted as specified (validation) and that the questionnaires have been filled out properly and completely (editing).

Validation

First, the researcher must determine, to the extent possible, that each of the questionnaires to be processed represents a valid interview. Here, we are using the term *valid* in a different sense than in Chapter 9. In Chapter 9, *validity* was defined as the extent to which what was being measured was actually measured. In this chapter, **validation** is defined as the process of ascertaining that interviews were conducted as specified. In this context, no assessment is made regarding the validity of the measurement. The goal of validation is solely to detect interviewer fraud or failure to follow key instructions. You may have noticed that the various questionnaires presented throughout the text almost always have a place to record the respondent's name, address, and telephone number. This information is seldom used in any way in the analysis of the data; it is collected only to provide a basis for validation.

➤ **validation**
The process of ascertaining that interviews actually were conducted as specified.

Professional researchers know that interviewer cheating does happen. Various studies have documented the existence and prevalence of interviewer falsification of several types. For this reason, validation is an integral and necessary step in the data processing stage of a marketing research project.

After all the interviews have been completed, the research firm recontacts a certain percentage of the respondents surveyed by each interviewer. Typically, this percentage ranges from 10 to 20 percent. If a particular interviewer surveyed 50 people and the research firm normally validates at a 10 percent rate, 5 respondents surveyed by that interviewer would be recontacted by telephone. Telephone validation typically answers four questions:

1. Was the person actually interviewed?
2. Did the person who was interviewed qualify to be interviewed according to the screening questions on the survey?

3. Was the interview conducted in the required manner? For example, a mall survey should have been conducted in the designated mall. Was this particular respondent interviewed in the mall, or was she or he interviewed at some other place, such as a restaurant or someone's home?

4. Did the interviewer cover the entire survey? Sometimes interviewers recognize that a potential respondent is in a hurry and may not have time to complete the entire survey.

The purpose of the validation process, as noted earlier, is to ensure that interviews were administered properly and completely. Researchers must be sure that the research results on which they are basing their recommendations reflect the legitimate responses of target individuals.

Editing

Whereas validation involves checking for interviewer cheating and failure to follow instructions, **editing** involves checking for interviewer and respondent mistakes. The editing process for paper surveys involves manual checking for a number of problems, including the following:

1. *Whether the interviewer failed to ask certain questions or record answers for certain questions*—In the questionnaire shown in Exhibit 13.1, no answer was recorded for question 19. According to the structure of the questionnaire, this question should have been asked of all respondents. Also, the respondent's name does not give a clear indication of gender. The purpose of the first edit—the field edit—is to identify these types of problems when there is still time to recontact the respondent and determine the appropriate answer to questions that were not asked. This may also be done at the second edit (by the marketing research firm), but in many instances there is not time to recontact the respondent and the interview has to be discarded.

2. *Whether skip patterns were followed*—According to the **skip pattern** in question 2 in Exhibit 13.1 if the answer to this question is "Very unlikely" or "Don't know," the interviewer should skip to question 16. The editor needs to make sure that the interviewer followed instructions. Sometimes, particularly during the first few interviews in a particular study, interviewers get mixed up and skip when they should not or fail to skip when they should.

3. *Whether the interviewer paraphrased respondents' answers to open-ended questions*—Marketing researchers and their clients usually are very interested in the responses to open-ended questions. The quality of the responses, or at least what was recorded, is an excellent indicator of the competence of the interviewer who recorded them. Interviewers are trained to record responses verbatim and not to paraphrase or insert their own language.

The person doing the editing must make judgment calls in regard to substandard responses to open-ended questions. She or he must decide at what point particular answers are so limited as to be useless and whether respondents should be recontacted.

The editing process is extremely tedious and time-consuming. (Imagine for a moment reading through 13,000 pages of interviews!) However, it is a very important step in the processing of survey responses.

PhotoDisc, Inc./Getty Images

A mall survey should be conducted in the designated mall. An important part of data analysis is validating that the data were gathered as specified.

→ **editing**
The process of ascertaining that questionnaires were filled out properly and completely.

→ **skip pattern**
A sequence in which later questions are asked based on a respondent's answer to an earlier question or questions.

EXHIBIT 13.1 | **Sample Questionnaire**

Consumer Survey
Mobile Telephone Survey Questionnaire

Long Branch—Asbury, N.J.

Date ____1-05-09_____   (01-03) _001_

Respondent Telephone Number _____201-555-2322_____

Hello. My name is ___Sally___ with POST Research. May I please speak with the male or female head of the household?

(IF INDIVIDUAL NOT AVAILABLE, RECORD NAME AND CALLBACK INFORMATION ON SAMPLING FORM.)

(WHEN MALE/FEMALE HEAD OF HOUSEHOLD COMES TO PHONE): Hello, my name is _____,
with POST Research. Your number was randomly selected, and I am not trying to sell you anything. I simply want to ask you a few
questions about a new type of telephone service.

1. First, how many telephone calls do you make during a typical day?

(04)

0–2	1
3–5	2
6–10	③
11–15	4
16–20	5
More than 20	6
Don't know	7

Now, let me tell you about a new service called cellular mobile telephone service, which is completely wireless. You can get either a
portable model that may be carried in your coat pocket or a model mounted in any vehicle. You will be able to receive calls and make
calls, no matter where you are. Although cellular phones are wireless, the voice quality is similar to your present phone service. This is
expected to be a time-saving convenience for household use.

This new cellular mobile phone service may soon be widely available in your area.

2. Now, let me explain to you the cost of this wireless service. Calls will cost 26 cents a minute plus normal toll charges. In addition, the
monthly minimum charge for using the service will be $7.50 and rental of a cellular phone will be about $40. Of course, you can buy the
equipment instead of leasing it. At this price, do you think you would be very likely, somewhat likely, somewhat unlikely, or very unlikely
to subscribe to the new phone service?

(05)

Very likely	1
Somewhat likely	②
Somewhat unlikely	3
Very unlikely . . . .(GO TO QUESTION 16)	4
Don't know . . . .(GO TO QUESTION 16)	5

INTERVIEWER—IF "VERY UNLIKELY" OR "DON'T KNOW," GO TO QUESTION 16.

3. Do you think it is likely that your employer would furnish you with one of these phones for your job?

(06)

No . . . .(GO TO QUESTION 5)	1
Don't know . . . .(GO TO QUESTION 5)	2
Yes . . . .(CONTINUE)	③

INTERVIEWER—IF "NO" OR "DON'T KNOW," GO TO QUESTION 5; OTHERWISE CONTINUE.

4. If your employer did furnish you with a wireless phone, would you also purchase one for household use?

(07)

Yes . . . .(CONTINUE)	①
No . . . .(GO TO QUESTION 16)	2
Don't know . . . .(GO TO QUESTION 16)	3

5. Please give me your best estimate of the number of mobile phones your household would use (write in "DK" for "Don't know").

Number of Units _____01_____ (08–09)

6. Given that cellular calls made or received will cost 26 cents a minute plus normal toll charges during weekdays, how many calls on the average would you expect to make in a typical weekday?

RECORD NUMBER _____ 06 _____ (10–11)

7. About how many minutes would your average cellular call last during the week?

RECORD NUMBER _____ 05 _____ (12–13)

8. Weekend cellular calls made or received will cost 8 cents per minute plus normal toll charges. Given this, about how many cellular calls on the average would you expect to make in a typical Saturday or Sunday?

RECORD NUMBER _____ 00 _____ (14–15)

9. About how many minutes would your average cellular call last on Saturday or Sunday?

RECORD NUMBER _____ (16–17)

10. You may recall from my previous description that two types of cellular phone units will be available. The vehicle phone may be installed in any vehicle. The portable phone will be totally portable—it can be carried in a briefcase, purse, or coat pocket. The totally portable phones may cost about 25 percent more and may have a more limited transmitting range in some areas than the vehicle phone. Do you think you would prefer portable or vehicle phones if you were able to subscribe to this service?

(18)

Portable 1
Vehicle . . . . .②
Both 3
Don't know 4

11. Would you please tell me whether you, on the average, would use a mobile phone about once a week, less than once a week, or more than once a week from the following geographic locations.

	Less Than Once a Week	Once a Week	More Than Once a Week	Never	
Monmouth County	1	2	③	4	(19)
(IF "NEVER," SKIP TO QUESTION 16)					
Sandy Hook	1	2	3	④	(20)
Keansburg	1	2	3	④	(21)
Atlantic Highlands	1	2	③	4	(22)
Matawan-Middletown	①	2	3	4	(23)
Red Bank	①	2	3	4	(24)
Holmdel	1	2	③	4	(25)
Eatontown	1	②	3	4	(26)
Long Branch	1	2	3	④	(27)
Freehold	1	2	3	④	(28)
Manalapan	1	2	3	④	(29)
Cream Ridge	1	2	3	④	(30)
Belmar	1	2	3	④	(31)
Point Pleasant	1	2	③	4	(32)

I'm going to describe to you a list of possible extra features of the proposed cellular service. Each option I'm going to describe will cost not more than $3.00 a month per phone. Would you please tell me if you would be very interested, interested, or uninterested in each feature:

	Very Interested	Interested	Uninterested
12. Call forwarding (the ability to transfer any call coming in to your mobile phone to any other phone).	①	2	3 (33)
13. No answer transfer (service that redirects calls to another number if your phone is unanswered).	1	2	③ (34)

(continued)

| **EXHIBIT 13.1** | **Sample Questionnaire (Continued)** |

	Very Interested	Interested	Uninterested
14. Call waiting (a signal that another person is trying to call you while you are using your phone).	1	②	3 (35)
15. Voice mailbox (a recording machine that will take the caller's message and relay it to you at a later time. This service will be provided at $5.00 per month).	1	2	③ (36)

16. What is your age group? (READ BELOW)

(37)

Under 25 1
25–44 ....②
45–64 3
65 and over 4
Refused, no answer, or don't know 5

17. What is your occupation?

(38)

Manager, official, or proprietor ....①
Professional (doctors, lawyers, etc.) 2
Technical (engineers, computer programmers, draftsmen, etc.) 3
Office worker/clerical 4
Sales 5
Skilled worker or foreman 6
Unskilled worker 7
Teacher 8
Homemaker, student, retired 9
Not now employed X
Refused ....Y

18. Into which category did your total family income fall in 2008? (READ BELOW)

(39)

Under $15,000 1
$15,000-$24,999 2
$25,000-$49,999 3
$50,000-$74,999 4
$75,000 and over ....⑤
Refused, no answer, don't know 6

19. (INTERVIEWER—RECORD SEX OF RESPONDENT):

(40)

Male 1
Female 2

20. May I have your name? My office calls about 10 percent of the people I talk with to verify that I have conducted the interview.
Gave name ....①
Refused 2

_____ Jordan Beasley
Name

Thank you for your time. Have a good day.

Step 2: Coding

Coding refers to the process of grouping and assigning numeric codes to the various responses to a particular question. Most questions on surveys are closed-ended and precoded, meaning that numeric codes have been assigned to the various responses on the questionnaire. All answers to closed-ended questions should be precoded, as they are in question 1 in Exhibit 13.1. Note that each answer has a numeric code to its right; the answer "0–2" has the code 1, the answer "3–5" has the code 2, and so on. The interviewer can record the response by circling the numeric code next to the answer given by the respondent. In this case, the respondent's answer was seven calls per day. The code 3 next to the category "6–10" (calls per day) is circled.

Open-ended questions create a coding dilemma. They were phrased in an open-ended manner because the researcher either had no idea what answers to expect or wanted a richer response than is possible with a closed-ended question.

→ **coding**
The process of grouping and assigning numeric codes to the various responses to a question.

The Coding Process

The process of coding responses to open-ended questions includes the following steps:

1. *List responses.* Coders at the research firm prepare lists of the actual responses given to each open-ended question on a particular survey. In studies of a few hundred respondents, all responses may be listed. With larger samples, responses given by a sample of respondents are listed.

2. *Consolidate responses.* A sample list of responses to an open-ended question is provided in Exhibit 13.2. Examination of this list indicates that a number of the responses can be interpreted to mean essentially the same thing; therefore, they can be appropriately consolidated into a single category. This process of consolidation might yield the list shown in Exhibit 13.3.

EXHIBIT 13.2	Sample of Responses to Open-Ended Question

Question: Why do you drink that brand of beer? (BRAND MENTIONED IN ANSWER TO PREVIOUS QUESTION)

Sample responses:
1. Because it tastes better.
2. It has the best taste.
3. I like the way it tastes.
4. I don't like the heavy taste of other beers.
5. It is the cheapest.
6. I buy whatever beer is on sale. It is on sale most of the time.
7. It doesn't upset my stomach the way other brands do.
8. Other brands give me headaches. This one doesn't.
9. It has always been my brand.
10. I have been drinking it for over 20 years.
11. It is the brand that most of the guys at work drink.
12. All my friends drink it.
13. It is the brand my wife buys at the grocery store.
14. It is my wife's/husband's favorite brand.
15. I have no idea.
16. Don't know.
17. No particular reason.

EXHIBIT 13.3	Consolidated Response Categories and Codes for Open-Ended Responses from Beer Study	
Response Category Descriptor	**Response Items from Exhibit 13.3 included**	**Assigned Numeric Code**
Tastes better/like taste/tastes better than others	1, 2, 3, 4	1
Low/lower price	5, 6	2
Does not cause headache, stomach problems	7, 8	3
Long-term use, habit	9, 10	4
Friends drink it/influence of friends	11, 12	5
Wife/husband drinks/buys it	13, 14	6

EXHIBIT 13.4	Example Questionnaire Setup for Open-Ended Questions

37. Why do you drink that brand of beer? (BRAND MENTIONED IN PREVIOUS QUESTION)?

(48) __2__

Because it's cheaper. (P) Nothing. (AE) Nothing.

3. *Set codes.* A numeric code is assigned to each of the categories on the final consolidated list of responses. Code assignments for the sample beer study question are shown in Exhibit 13.3.

4. *Enter codes.* After responses have been listed and consolidated and codes set, the last step is the actual entry of codes. This involves several substeps:

   a. Read responses to individual open-ended questions on questionnaires.
   b. Match individual responses with the consolidated list of response categories, and determine the appropriate numeric code for each response.
   c. Write the numeric code in the appropriate place on the questionnaire for the response to the particular question (see Exhibit 13.4) or enter the appropriate code in the database electronically.[1]

Automated Coding Systems

With CATI and Internet surveys, data entry and coding are completely eliminated for closed-ended questions. However, when the text of open-ended questions is electronically captured, a coding process is still required. A number of developments are making it likely that the tedious coding process for open-ended questions will soon be replaced with computer-based systems requiring limited high-level human intervention and decision making.[2]

The TextSmart module of SPSS is one example of the automated coding systems. Algorithms based on semiotics are at the heart of these systems and show great promise for speeding up the coding process, reducing its cost, and increasing its objectivity. Basically, these algorithms use the power of computers to search for patterns in open-ended responses and in group responses, based on certain keywords and phrases.

Step 3: Data Entry

Once the questionnaires have been validated, edited, and coded, it's time for the next step in the process—data entry. We use the term **data entry** here to refer to the process of converting information to a form that can be read by a computer. This process requires a data entry device, such as a PC, and a storage medium, such as a hard (magnetic) disk.

> ➤ **data entry**
> The process of converting information to an electronic format.

Intelligent Entry Systems

Most data entry is done by means of **intelligent entry** systems. Intelligent entry systems can be programmed to avoid certain types of errors at the point of data entry, such as invalid or wild codes and violation of skip patterns.

> ➤ **intelligent entry**
> A form of data entry in which the information being entered into the data entry device is checked for internal logic.

Consider question 2 on the questionnaire in Exhibit 13.1. The five valid answers have the associated numeric codes 1 through 5. An intelligent data entry system programmed for valid codes would permit the data entry operator to enter only one of these codes in the field reserved for the response to this question. If the operator attempts to enter a code other than those defined as valid, the device will inform the data entry operator in some manner that there is a problem. The data entry device, for example, might beep and display a message on the screen that the entered code is invalid. It will not advance to the next appropriate field until the code has been corrected. Of course, it is still possible to incorrectly enter a 3 rather than the correct answer 2. Referring again to question 2, note that if the answer to the question is "Very unlikely" or "Don't know," then the data entry operator should skip to question 16. An intelligent data entry device will make this skip automatically.

The Data Entry Process for Paper Surveys

The validated, edited, and coded questionnaires have been given to a data entry operator seated in front of a personal computer. The data entry software system has been programmed for intelligent entry. The actual data entry process is ready to begin. Usually, the data are entered directly from the questionnaires, because experience has shown that a large number of errors are introduced when questionnaire data are transposed manually to coding sheets. Going directly from the questionnaire to the data entry device and associated storage medium is much more accurate and efficient. To better understand the mechanics of the process, look again at Exhibit 13.1:

▪ In the upper-right corner of the questionnaire, the number 001 is written. This number uniquely identifies the particular questionnaire, which should be the first questionnaire in the stack that the data entry operator is preparing to enter. This number is an important point of reference because it permits the data entry staff to refer back to the original document if any errors are identified in connection with the data input.

▪ To the left of the handwritten number 001 is (01–03). This tells the data entry operator that 001 should be entered into fields 01–03 of the data record. Throughout the questionnaire, the numbers in parentheses indicate the proper location on the data record for the circled code for the answer to each question. Question 1 has (04) associated with the codes for the answers to the question. Thus, the answer to this question would be entered in field 04 of the data record. Now, take a look at the open-ended question in Exhibit 13.4. As with closed-ended questions, the number in parentheses refers to the field on the data record where the code or codes for the response to this question should be entered. Note the number 2 written in to the right of (48); a 2 should be entered in field 48 of the data record associated with this questionnaire.

Exhibit 13.1 clearly illustrates the relationship between the layout of the questionnaire, in terms of codes (numbers associated with different answers to questions) and fields (places on the data record where the code is entered), and the layout of the data record.

Scanning

As all students know, the scanning of documents (test scoring sheets) has been around for decades. It has been widely used in schools and universities as an efficient way to capture and score responses to multiple-choice questions. However, until more recently, its use in marketing research has been limited. This limited use can be attributed to two factors: setup costs and the need to record all responses with a no. 2 pencil. Setup costs include the cost of special paper, special ink in the printing process, and very precise placement of the bubbles for recording responses. The break-even point, at which the savings in data entry costs exceeded the setup costs, was in the 10,000 to 12,000 survey range. Therefore, for most surveys, scanning was not feasible.

However, changes in **scanning technology** and the advent of personal computers have changed this equation. Today, questionnaires prepared with any one of a number of Windows word-processing software packages and printed on a laser printer or by a standard printing process can be readily scanned, using the appropriate software and a scanner attached to a personal computer. In addition, the latest technology permits respondents to fill out the survey using almost any type of writing implement (any type of pencil, ballpoint pen, or ink pen). This eliminates the need to provide respondents with a no. 2 pencil and greatly simplifies the process of mailing surveys. Finally, the latest technology does not require respondents to carefully shade the entire circle or square next to their response choices; they can put shading, a check mark, an X, or any other type of mark in the circle or square provided for the response choice.[3]

As a result of these developments, the use of scannable surveys is growing dramatically. An analyst who expects more than 400 to 500 surveys to be completed will find scannable surveys to be cost-effective.

Though no reliable volume figures are available, it is an accepted fact that the amount of survey data being captured electronically is increasing. For example, electronic data capture is used in computer-assisted telephone interviewing, Internet surveys, and touchscreen kiosk surveys.

Step 4: Logical Cleaning of Data

At this point, the data from all questionnaires have been entered and stored in the computer that will be used to process them. It is time to do final error checking before proceeding to the tabulation and statistical analysis of the survey results. Many colleges have one or more statistical software packages available for the tabulation and statistical analysis of data, including SAS (Statistical Analysis System) and SPSS (Statistical Package for the Social Sciences), which have proven to be the most popular statistical packages. Most colleges have personal computer versions of SPSS and SAS, in addition to other PC statistical packages. The number of other PC packages is large and growing with new packages such as Q offering innovative features (see the Practicing Marketing Research feature on page 335).

Regardless of which computer package is used, it is important to do a final computerized error check of the data, or what is sometimes referred to as **logical cleaning of data**. This may be done through error checking routines and/or marginal reports.

→ **scanning technology**
A form of data entry in which responses on questionnaires are read in automatically by a data entry device.

→ **logical cleaning of data**
Final computerized error checking of data.

PRACTICING MARKETING RESEARCH

Q Data Analysis Software a Very Functional Choice[4]

The Australian software design firm Numbers International recently released a new data analysis program called Q. Q offers researchers a wide range of advanced statistical testing and modeling tools, packaged in a way that allows even those not specializing in statistical analysis to get meaningful results when studying survey data of almost any question format.

Although some of its features may require some familiarization to fully grasp, Q is supported by numerous tools to help researchers get started. A 60-page quick-start guide provides an overview of tables, functions, and modeling tools, and an instant-start guide summarizes them into a one-page reference sheet. The software also comes with help functions, tutorials, and online training tools.

Unlike many analytical software packages, Q provides researchers with easy and direct access to the basic data, and it keeps them engaged with the data throughout the analytical process. Erik Heller, general manager of the Sydney office for market research firm Sweeney Research, has adopted Q with great success. He comments, "Where Q differentiates itself from other tools like SPSS is the extent to which it is intuitive and easy for people to immerse themselves in the data."

Most analytical functions are accessible through drop-down menus and toolbars and allow users to manipulate the data from the main view. Q's tools also allow for significant analytical depth. For those who just need basic reports of the data, Q offers straight cross tabs but also provides advance multivariate analysis to help identify deeper, more complex trends. When venturing into these more involved multivariate methods, however, Q always starts the researcher at the same level of the basic data and builds the analytical process up from there. The research stays grounded in progressively verifiable results. As the researcher proceeds, Q helps organize tables and data sets and can package them for delivery once the analysis is done. Heller adds, "It is very easy for someone who is not that involved in the data analysis to go into the data and run some additional cross tabs." Q offers free Reader software, which allows recipients to easily view and access these reports even if its analytical functions are limited.

One slight weakness in the software is its limited range of output functions. With no support for Excel or PowerPoint and limited chart and graph options, the final reports that Q is able to produce may be less dynamic than those of some other data analysis programs. The current version of Q is also not the ideal choice for time-series analysis and multiwave research projects. Ultimately, its biggest weaknesses may be attributed to merely an overemphasis of function over style.

Question

1. Are you at all familiar with any other analytical software packages that can be used to study market research? If so, how does Q compare?

Some computer programs permit the user to write **error checking routines**. These routines include a number of statements to check for various conditions. For example, if a particular field on the data records for a study should be coded with only a 1 or a 2, a logical statement can be written to check for the presence of any other code in that field. Some of the more sophisticated packages generate reports indicating how many times

→ **error checking routines** Computer programs that accept instructions from the user to check for logical errors in the data.

a particular condition was violated and the data records on which it was violated. With this list, the user can refer to the original questionnaires and determine the appropriate values.

This is the final error check in the process. When this step is completed, the computer data file should be ready for tabulation and statistical analysis.

Step 5: Tabulation and Statistical Analysis

When the survey results have been stored in a computer file and are free of logical data entry and interviewer recording errors, the next step is to tabulate the survey results.

One-Way Frequency Tables

→ **one-way frequency table**
A table showing the number of respondents choosing each answer to a survey question.

The most basic tabulation is the **one-way frequency table**, which shows the number of respondents who gave each possible answer to each question. An example of this type of table appears in Exhibit 13.5. This table shows that 144 consumers (48 percent) said they would choose a hospital in St. Paul, 146 (48.7 percent) said they would choose a hospital in Minneapolis, and 10 (3.3 percent) said they didn't know which location they would choose. A printout is generated with a one-way frequency table for every question on the survey. In most instances, a one-way frequency table is the first summary of survey results seen by the research analyst. In addition to frequencies, these tables typically indicate the percentage of those responding who gave each possible response to a question.

An issue that must be dealt with when one-way frequency tables are generated is what base to use for the percentages for each table. There are three options for a base:

1. *Total respondents*—If 300 people are interviewed in a particular study and the decision is to use total respondents as the base for calculating percentages, then the percentages in each one-way frequency table will be based on 300 respondents.

2. *Number of people asked the particular question*—Because most questionnaires have skip patterns, not all respondents are asked all questions. For example, suppose question 4 on a particular survey asked whether the person owned any dogs and 200 respondents indicated they were dog owners. Since questions 5 and 6 on the same survey were to be asked only of those individuals who owned a dog, questions 5 and 6 should have been asked of only 200 respondents. In most instances, it would be appropriate to use 200 as the base for percentages associated with the one-way frequency tables for questions 5 and 6.

EXHIBIT 13.5	One-Way Frequency Table

Q.30 If you or a member of your family were to require hospitalization in the future, and the procedure could be performed in Minneapolis or St. Paul, where would you choose to go?

	Total
Total	300
	100%
To a hospital in St. Paul	144
	48.0%
To a hospital in Minneapolis	146
	48.7%
Don't know/no response	10
	3.3%

3. *Number of people answering the question*—Another alternative base for computing percentages in one-way frequency tables is the number of people who actually answered a particular question. Under this approach, if 300 people were asked a particular question but 28 indicated "Don't know" or gave no response, then the base for the percentages would be 272.

Ordinarily, the number of people who were asked a particular question is used as the base for all percentages throughout the tabulations, but there may be special cases in which other bases are judged appropriate Exhibit 13.6 is a one-way frequency table in which three different bases are used for calculating percentages.

Some questions, by their nature, solicit more than one response from respondents. For example, consumers might be asked to name all brands of vacuum cleaners that come to mind. Most people will be able to name more than one brand. Therefore, when these answers are tabulated, there will be more responses than respondents. If 200 consumers are surveyed and the average consumer names three brands, then there will be 200 respondents and 600 answers. The question is, should percentages in frequency tables showing the results for these questions be based on the number of respondents or the number of responses? Exhibit 13.7 shows percentages calculated using both bases. Most commonly, marketing researchers compute percentages for multiple-response questions on the basis of the number of respondents, reasoning that the client is primarily interested in the proportion of people who gave a particular answer.

Cross Tabulations

Cross tabulations are likely to be the next step in analysis. They represent a simple-to-understand, yet powerful, analytical tool. Many marketing research studies go no further than cross tabulations in terms of analysis. The idea is to look at the responses to

➤ **cross tabulation**
Examination of the responses to one question relative to the responses to one or more other questions.

EXHIBIT 13.6	One-Way Frequency Table Using Three Different Bases for Calculating Percentages

Q.35 Why would you not consider going to St. Paul for hospitalization?

	Total[a] Respondents	Total Asked	Total Answering
Total	300	64	56
	100%	100%	100%
They aren't good/service poor	18	18	18
	6%	28%	32%
St. Paul doesn't have the services/ equipment that Minneapolis does	17	17	17
	6%	27%	30%
St. Paul is too small	6	6	6
	2%	9%	11%
Bad publicity	4	4	4
	1%	6%	7%
Other	11	11	11
	4%	17%	20%
Don't know/no response	8	8	
	3%	13%	

[a]A total of 300 respondents were surveyed. Only 64 were asked this question because in the previous question those respondents said they would not consider going to St. Paul for hospitalization. Only 56 respondents gave an answer other than "Don't know."

The base for each percentage must be determined before one-way frequency tables are run. If a survey question asks whether the person has a dog and 200 respondents indicate that they do, further questions designated for dog owners should have only 200 respondents.

Corbis Digital Stock

EXHIBIT 13.7	Percentages for a Multiple-Response Question Calculated on the Basis of Total Respondents and Total Responses

Q.34 To which of the following towns and cities would you consider going for hospitalization?

	Total Respondents	Total Responses
Total	300	818
	100%	100%
Minneapolis	265	265
	88.3%	32.4%
St. Paul	240	240
	80.0%	29.3%
Bloomington	112	112
	37.3%	13.7%
Rochester	92	92
	30.7%	11.2%
Minnetonka	63	63
	21.0%	7.7%
Eagan	46	46
	15.3%	5.6%

one question in relation to the responses to one or more other questions. Exhibit 13.8 shows a simple cross tabulation that examines the relationship between cities consumers are willing to consider for hospitalization and their age. This cross tabulation includes frequencies and percentages, with the percentages based on column totals. This table shows an interesting relationship between age and likelihood of choosing Minneapolis or St. Paul for hospitalization. Consumers in successively older age groups are increasingly likely to choose St. Paul and increasingly less likely to choose Minneapolis.

EXHIBIT 13.8	Sample Cross Tabulation

Q.30 If you or a member of your family were to require hospitalization in the future, and the procedure could be performed in Minneapolis or St. Paul, where would you choose to go?

			Age		
	Total	18–34	35–54	55–64	65 or Over
Total	300	65	83	51	100
	100%	100%	100%	100%	100%
To a hospital in St. Paul	144	21	40	25	57
	48.0%	32.3%	48.2%	49.0%	57.0%
To a hospital in Minneapolis	146	43	40	23	40
	48.7%	66.2%	48.2%	45.1%	40.0%
Don't know/no response	10	1	3	3	3
	3.3%	1.5%	3.6%	5.9%	3.0%

EXHIBIT 13.9	Cross Tabulation Table with Column, Row, and Total Percentages[a]

Q.34 To which of the following towns and cities would you consider going for hospitalization?

	Total	Male	Female
Total	300	67	233
	100.0%	100.0%	100.0%
	100.0%	22.3%	77.7%
	100.0%	22.3%	77.7%
St. Paul	265	63	202
	88.3%	94.0%	86.7%
	100.0%	23.6%	76.2%
	88.3%	21.0%	67.3%
Minneapolis	240	53	187
	80.0%	79.1%	80.3%
	100.0%	22.1%	77.9%
	80.0%	17.7%	62.3%
Bloomington	112	22	90
	37.3%	32.8%	38.6%
	100.0%	19.6%	80.4%
	37.3%	7.3%	30.0%

[a]Percentages listed are column, row, and total percentages, respectively.

Following are a number of considerations regarding the setup of cross tabulation tables and the determination of percentages within them:

■ The previous discussion regarding the selection of the appropriate base for percentages applies to cross tabulation tables as well.

■ Three different percentages may be calculated for each cell in a cross tabulation table: column, row, and total percentages. Column percentages are based on the column total, row percentages are based on the row total, and total percentages are based on the table total. Exhibit 13.9 shows a cross tabulation table in which the frequency and all three of the percentages are shown for each cell in the table.

■ A common way of setting up cross tabulation tables is to use columns to represent factors such as demographics and lifestyle characteristics, which are expected to be predictors of the state of mind, behavior, or intentions data shown as rows of the table. In such tables, percentages usually are calculated on the basis of column totals. This approach permits easy comparisons of the relationship between, say, lifestyle characteristics and expected predictors such as sex or age. For example, in Exhibit 13.8 this approach facilitates examination of how people in different age groups differ in regard to the particular factor under examination.

Cross tabulations provide a powerful and easily understood approach to the summarization and analysis of survey research results. However, it is easy to become swamped by the sheer volume of computer printouts if a careful tabulation plan has not been developed. The cross tabulation plan should be created with the research objectives and hypotheses in mind.

Graphic Representations of Data

You have probably heard the saying "A picture is worth a thousand words." Graphic representations of data use pictures rather than tables to present research results. Results—particularly key results—can be presented most powerfully and efficiently through graphs.

Marketing researchers have always known that important findings identified by cross tabulation and statistical analysis could be best presented graphically. However, in the early years of marketing research, the preparation of graphs was tedious, difficult, and time-consuming. The advent of personal computers, coupled with graphics software and laser printers, has changed all of this. Spreadsheet programs such as Excel have extensive graphics capabilities, particularly in their Windows versions. In addition, programs designed for creating presentations, such as PowerPoint, permit the user to generate a wide variety of high-quality graphics with ease. With these programs, it is possible to do the following:

■ Quickly produce graphs
■ Display those graphs on the computer screen
■ Make desired changes and redisplay
■ Print final copies on a laser or inkjet printer

All of the graphs shown in this section were produced using a personal computer, a laser printer, and a graphics software package.

Line Charts

Line charts are perhaps the simplest form of graphs. They are particularly useful for presenting a given measurement taken at several points over time. Exhibit 13.10 shows monthly sales data for Just Add Water, a retailer of women's swimwear. The results reveal similar sales patterns for 2001 and 2002, with peaks in June and generally low sales in January through March and September through December. Just Add Water is evaluating the sales data to identify product lines that it might add to improve sales during those periods.

Pie Charts

Pie charts are another type of graph that is frequently used. They are appropriate for displaying marketing research results in a wide range of situations. Exhibit 13.11 shows

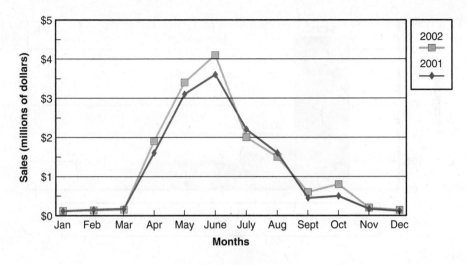

Exhibit 13.10

Line Chart for Sales of Women's Swimwear

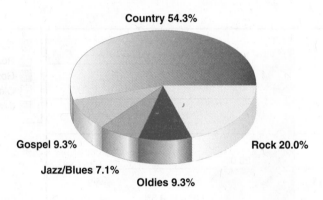

radio music preferences gleaned from a survey of residents of several Gulf Coast metropolitan areas in Louisiana, Mississippi, and Alabama. Note the three-dimensional effect produced by the software.

Bar Charts

Bar charts may be the most flexible of the three types of graphs discussed in this section. Anything that can be shown in a line graph or a pie chart also can be shown in a bar chart. In addition, many things that cannot be shown—or effectively shown—in other types of graphs can be readily illustrated in bar charts. Four types of bar charts are discussed here.

1. *Bar chart*—The same information displayed in the pie chart in Exhibit 13.11 is shown in the bar chart in Exhibit 13.12. Draw your own conclusions regarding whether the pie chart or the bar chart is the more effective way to present this information. Exhibit 13.12 is a traditional two-dimensional chart. Many of the software packages available today can take the same information and present it with a three-dimensional effect, as shown in Exhibit 13.13. In addition, you can create clustered, stacked, and other types of bar charts. Again, decide for yourself which approach is visually more appealing and interesting.

2. *Multiple-row, three-dimensional bar chart*—This type of bar chart (Exhibit 13.14) provides what we believe to be the most visually appealing way of presenting cross tabulation information.

Exhibit 13.12

Simple Two-Dimensional Bar Chart for Types of Music Listened to Most Often

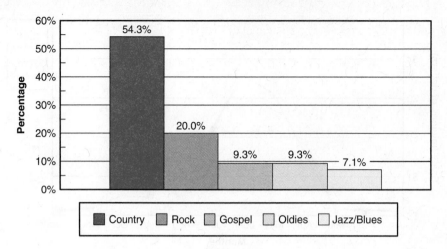

Exhibit 13.13

Simple Three-Dimensional Bar Chart for Types of Music Listened to Most Often

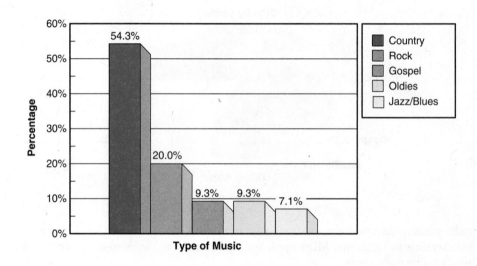

Exhibit 13.14

Multiple-Row, Three-Dimensional Bar Chart for Types of Music Listened to Most Often by Age

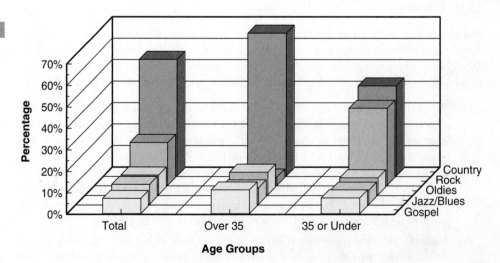

Descriptive Statistics

Using descriptive statistics is the most efficient way of summarizing the characteristics of large sets of data. In a statistical analysis, the analyst calculates one number or a few numbers that reveal something about the characteristics of large sets of data.

Measures of Central Tendency

Before beginning this section, you should review the types of data scales presented in Chapter 8. Recall that there are four basic types of measurement scales: nominal, ordinal, interval, and ratio. Nominal and ordinal scales are sometimes referred to as nonmetric scales, whereas interval and ratio scales are called metric scales. Many of the statistical procedures discussed in this section and in following sections require metric scales, whereas others are designed for nonmetric scales.

The three measures of central tendency are the arithmetic mean, median, and mode. The **mean** is properly computed only from interval or ratio (metric) data. It is computed by adding the values for all observations for a particular variable, such as age, and dividing the resulting sum by the number of observations. With survey data, the exact value of the variable may not be known; it may be known only that a particular case falls in a particular category. For example, an age category on a survey might be 18 to 34 years of age. If a person falls into this category, the person's exact age is known to be somewhere between 18 and 34. With grouped data, the midpoint of each category is multiplied by the number of observations in that category, the resulting totals are summed, and the total is then divided by the total number of observations. This process is summarized in the following formula:

> **mean**
> The sum of the values for all observations of a variable divided by the number of observations.

$$\overline{X} = \frac{\sum_{i=1}^{h} f_i X_i}{n}$$

where f_i = frequency of the i th class
X_i = midpoint of that class
h = number of classes
n = total number of observations

The **median** can be computed for all types of data except nominal data. It is calculated by finding the value below which 50 percent of the observations fall. If all the values for a particular variable were put in an array in either ascending or descending order, the median would be the middle value in that array. The median is often used to summarize variables such as income when the researcher is concerned that the arithmetic mean will be affected by a small number of extreme values and, therefore, will not accurately reflect the predominant central tendency of that variable for that group.

> **median**
> The value below which 50 percent of the observations fall.

The **mode** can be computed for any type of data (nominal, ordinal, interval, or ratio). It is determined by finding the value that occurs most frequently. In a frequency distribution, the mode is the value that has the highest frequency. One problem with using the mode is that a particular data set may have more than one mode. If three different values occur with the same level of frequency and that frequency is higher than the frequency for any other value, then the data set has three modes. The mean, median, and mode for sample data on beer consumption are shown in Exhibit 13.15.

> **mode**
> The value that occurs most frequently.

| EXHIBIT 13.15 | Mean, Median, and Mode for Beer Consumption Data |

A total of 10 beer drinkers (drink one or more cans, bottles, or glasses of beer per day on the average) were interviewed in a mall-intercept study. They were asked how many cans, bottles, or glasses of beer they drink in an average day.

Respondent	Number of Cans/Bottles/Glasses per Day
1	2
2	2
3	3
4	2
5	5
6	1
7	2
8	2
9	10
10	1

Mode = 2 cans/bottles/glasses
Median = 2 cans/bottles/glasses
Mean = 3 cans/bottles/glasses

Measures of Dispersion

Frequently used measures of dispersion include standard deviation, variance, and range. Whereas measures of central tendency indicate typical values for a particular variable, measures of dispersion indicate how spread out the data are. The dangers associated with relying only on measures of central tendency are suggested by the example shown in Exhibit 13.16. Note that average beer consumption is the same in both markets—3 cans/bottles/glasses. However, the standard deviation is greater in market two, indicating more dispersion in the data. Whereas the mean suggests that the two markets are the same, the added information provided by the standard deviation indicates that they are different.

The formula for computing the standard deviation for a sample of observations is as follows:

$$S = \sqrt{\frac{\sum_{i=1}^{n} (X_i - \bar{X})^2}{n - 1}}$$

where
S = sample standard deviation
X_i = value of the i th observation
$\bar{X}$ = sample mean
n = sample size

The variance is calculated by using the formula for standard deviation with the square root sign removed. That is, the sum of the squared deviations from the mean is divided by the number of observations minus 1. Finally, the range is equal to the maximum value for a particular variable minus the minimum value for that variable.

EXHIBIT 13.16	Measures of Dispersion and Measures of Central Tendency

Consider the beer consumption data presented in Exhibit 13.15. Assume that interviewing was conducted in two markets. The results for both markets are shown.

Respondent	Number of Cans/ Bottles/Glasses Market One	Number of Cans/ Bottles/Glasses Market Two
1	2	1
2	2	1
3	3	1
4	2	1
5	5	1
6	1	1
7	2	1
8	2	3
9	10	10
10	1	10
Mean	3	3
Standard deviation	2.7	3.7

Percentages and Statistical Tests

In performing basic data analysis, the research analyst is faced with the decision of whether to use measures of central tendency (mean, median, mode) or percentages (one-way frequency tables, cross tabulations). Responses to questions either are categorical or take the form of continuous variables. Categorical variables such as "Occupation" (coded 1 for professional/managerial, 2 for clerical, etc.) limit the analyst to reporting the frequency and relative percentage with which each category was encountered. Variables such as age can be continuous or categorical, depending on how the information was obtained. For example, an interviewer can ask people their actual age or ask them which category (under 35, 35 or older) includes their age. If actual age data are available, mean age can be readily computed. If categories are used, one-way frequency tables and cross tabulations are the most obvious choices for analysis. However, continuous data can be put into categories, and means can be estimated for categorical data by using the formula for computing a mean for grouped data (presented earlier).

Finally, statistical tests are available that can indicate whether two means—for example, average expenditures by men and average expenditures by women at fast-food restaurants—or two percentages differ to a greater extent than would be expected by chance (sampling error) or whether there is a significant relationship between two variables in a cross tabulation table.

Occupation is an example of a categorical variable. The only results that can be reported for a variable of this type are the frequency and the relative percentage with which each category was encountered.

Evaluating Differences and Changes

The issue of whether certain measurements are different from one another is central to many questions of critical interest to marketing managers. Some specific examples of managers' questions follow:

■ Our posttest measure of top-of-mind awareness is slightly higher than the level recorded in the pretest. Did top-of-mind awareness really increase, or is there some other explanation for the increase? Should we fire or commend our agency?

© Shaun Lowe/iStockphoto

■ Our overall customer satisfaction score increased from 92 percent three months ago to 93.5 percent today. Did customer satisfaction really increase? Should we celebrate?

■ Satisfaction with the customer service provided by our cable TV system in Dallas is, on average, 1.2 points higher on a 10-point scale than is satisfaction with the customer service provided by our cable TV system in Cincinnati. Are customers in Dallas really more satisfied? Should the customer service manager in Cincinnati be replaced? Should the Dallas manager be rewarded?

■ In a recent product concept test, 19.8 percent of those surveyed said they were very likely to buy the new product they evaluated. Is this good? Is it better than the results we got last year for a similar product? What do these results suggest in terms of whether to introduce the new product?

■ A segmentation study shows that those with incomes of more than $30,000 per year frequent fast-food restaurants 6.2 times per month on average. Those with incomes of $30,000 or less go an average of 6.7 times. Is this difference real—is it meaningful?

■ In an awareness test, 28.3 percent of those surveyed have heard of our product on an unaided basis. Is this a good result?

These are the eternal questions in marketing and marketing research. Although considered boring by some, statistical hypothesis testing is important because it helps researchers get closer to the ultimate answers to these questions. We say "closer" because certainty is never achieved in answering these questions in marketing research.

Statistical Significance

The basic motive for making statistical inferences is to generalize from sample results to population characteristics. A fundamental tenet of statistical inference is that it is possible for numbers to be different in a mathematical sense but not significantly different in a statistical sense. For example, suppose cola drinkers are asked to try two cola drinks in a blind taste test and indicate which they prefer; the results show that 51 percent prefer one test product and 49 percent prefer the other. There is a mathematical difference in the results, but the difference would appear to be minor and unimportant. The difference probably is well within the range of accuracy of researchers' ability to measure taste preference and thus probably is not significant in a statistical sense. Three different concepts can be applied to the notion of differences when we are talking about results from samples:

■ *Mathematical differences*—By definition, if numbers are not exactly the same, they are different. This does not, however, mean that the difference is either important or statistically significant.

■ *Statistical significance*—If a particular difference is large enough to be unlikely to have occurred because of chance or sampling error, then the difference is statistically significant.

■ *Managerially important differences*—One can argue that a difference is important from a managerial perspective only if results or numbers are sufficiently different. For example, the difference in consumer responses to two different packages in a test market might be statistically significant but yet so small as to have little practical or managerial significance.[5]

This chapter covers different approaches to testing whether results are statistically significant, but, keep in mind that statistical precision is not everything, as discussed in the Practicing Marketing Research feature on page 347.

PRACTICING MARKETING RESEARCH

Does Statistical Precision Validate Results?[7]

The presence of statistical significance in marketing research analysis can be deceptive. *Statistical* significance does not necessarily mean that the difference has any *practical* significance. In addition to large sample sizes, there are many potential sources of error that can create problems for researchers when identifying statistically significant differences.

Generally, two kinds of error affect the validity of statistical measurements. *Random error* introduces error variance, but as it occurs randomly across respondents, it does not add statistical bias to the data. *Systematic error* is consistent across respondents, creating a bias within the data that may or may not be known. Typically, the causes for these kinds of error fall into two categories: sampling error, arising in the process of building a respondent pool; and measurement error, arising from the way the questionnaire is constructed.

Sampling Error

Three major sources of sampling error are under-coverage, nonresponse, and self-selection:

1. *Under-coverage*—Under-coverage occurs when a certain segment of the population is not adequately represented.
2. *Nonresponse*—Nonresponse error is a result of portions of the population being unwilling to participate in research projects.
3. *Self-selection*—Self-selection can result from respondents having control over survey completion. For instance, participants in an online survey panel might get bored and opt out before the survey is over.

Measurement Error

The following six types of measurement error can result in random or systematic error:

1. *Question interpretation*—Respondents may interpret vague or ambiguously worded questions differently.
2. *Respondent assumptions*—Regardless of the way a question is worded, respondents still bring personal assumptions to the table, including any number of varying external factors influencing their understanding of the question.
3. *Question order*—Respondents might answer a question differently depending on where it falls in the survey, as their opinions might be influenced by their thoughts on surrounding questions.
4. *Method variance*—Researchers must be aware of potential errors introduced by the method used to deliver the survey.
5. *Attribute wording*—The way in which survey attributes are described may elicit different answers from respondents.
6. *Omitting important questions*—Systematic error most commonly results from inadequate coverage of critical variables within the question battery. Absent variables can significantly affect the results of data analysis.

Managerial Significance

Researchers must be careful to differentiate between resultant random and systematic errors. Furthermore, they must also realize that statistical precision does not necessarily validate results. Rather than focusing on statistical significance in and of itself, researchers need to identify results that have managerial significance—results that are relevant to the decision-making process. Given a large enough sample, any null hypothesis can be discounted, and any two means can be shown to be statistically different. An absence of statistical significance may be just as relevant as any demonstrated statistical significance. As such, statistical testing should be used as a tool to discover practical insights, not to define them.

Questions

1. Of the potential causes for error described above, which do you think would be easiest to identify? Hardest? Explain your reasoning.

2. Can you think of any ways that could help researchers determine whether occurrences of statistical significance in their results have managerial significance?

Hypothesis Testing

→ **hypothesis**
An assumption or a theory that a researcher or manager makes about some characteristics of the population under study.

A **hypothesis** is an assumption or guess that a researcher or manager makes about some characteristic of the population being investigated. The marketing researcher is often faced with the question of whether research results are different enough from the norm that some element of the firm's marketing strategy should be changed. Consider the following situations:

- The results of a tracking survey show that awareness of a product is lower than it was in a similar survey conducted six months ago. Are the results significantly lower? Are the results sufficiently low enough to call for a change in advertising strategy?

- A product manager believes that the average purchaser of his product is 35 years of age. A survey is conducted to test this hypothesis, and the survey shows that the average purchaser of the product is 38.5 years of age. Is the survey result different enough from the product manager's belief to cause him to conclude that his belief is incorrect?

- The marketing director of a fast-food chain believes that 60 percent of her customers are female and 40 percent are male. She does a survey to test this hypothesis and finds that, according to the survey, 55 percent are female and 45 percent are male. Is this result sufficiently different enough from her original theory to permit her to conclude that her original theory was incorrect?

All of these questions can be evaluated with some kind of statistical test. In hypothesis testing, the researcher determines whether a hypothesis concerning some characteristic of the population is likely to be true, given the evidence. A statistical hypothesis test allows us to calculate the probability of observing a particular result if the stated hypothesis is actually true.[6]

There are two basic explanations for an observed difference between a hypothesized value and a particular research result. Either the hypothesis is true and the observed difference is likely due to sampling error, or the hypothesis is false and the true value is some other value.

Steps in Hypothesis Testing

Five steps are involved in testing a hypothesis. First, the hypothesis is specified. Second, an appropriate statistical technique is selected to test the hypothesis. Third, a decision rule is specified as the basis for determining whether to reject or fail to reject (FTR) the null hypothesis H_0. Please note that we did not say "reject H_0 or accept H_0." Although a seemingly small distinction, it is an important one. The distinction will be discussed in greater detail later on.

Fourth, the value of the test statistic is calculated and the test is performed. Fifth, the conclusion is stated from the perspective of the original research problem or question.

Step One: Stating the Hypothesis

Hypotheses are stated using two basic forms: the null hypothesis H_0 and the alternative hypothesis H_a. The null hypothesis H_0 (sometimes called the *hypothesis of the status quo*) is the hypothesis that is tested against its complement, the alternative hypothesis H_a (sometimes called the *research hypothesis of interest*). Suppose the manager of Burger City believes that his operational procedures will guarantee that the average customer will wait two minutes in the drive-in window line. He conducts research, based on the observation of 1,000 customers at randomly selected stores at randomly selected times. The average customer observed in this study spends 2.4 minutes in the drive-in window line. The null hypothesis and the alternative hypothesis might be stated as follows:

- Null hypothesis H_0: Mean waiting time $\neq$ 2 minutes
- Alternative hypothesis H_a: Mean waiting time $=$ 2 minutes

It should be noted that the null hypothesis and the alternative hypothesis must be stated in such a way that both cannot be true. The idea is to use the available evidence to ascertain which hypothesis is more likely to be true.

Step Two: Choosing the Appropriate Test Statistic

As you will see in the following sections of this chapter, the analyst must choose the appropriate statistical test, given the characteristics of the situation under investigation. A number of different statistical tests, along with the situations where they are appropriate, are discussed in this chapter. Exhibit 13.17 provides a guide to selecting the appropriate test for various situations. Most of the tests in this table are covered in detail later in this chapter.

Step Three: Developing a Decision Rule

Based on our previous discussions of distributions of sample means, you may recognize that one is very unlikely to get a sample result that is exactly equal to the value of the population parameter. The problem is determining whether the difference, or deviation, between the actual value of the sample mean and its expected value based on the hypothesis could have occurred by chance (5 times out of 100, for example) if the statistical hypothesis is true. A decision rule, or standard, is needed to determine whether to reject or fail to reject the null hypothesis. Statisticians state such decision rules in terms of significance levels.

The significance level (α) is critical in the process of choosing between the null and alternative hypotheses. The level of significance—.10, .05, or .01, for example—is the probability that is considered too low to justify acceptance of the null hypothesis.

Consider a situation in which the researcher has decided that she wants to test a hypothesis at the .05 level of significance. This means that she will reject the null hypothesis if the test indicates that the probability of occurrence of the observed result (for example, the difference between the sample mean and its expected value) because of chance or sampling error is less than 5 percent. Rejection of the null hypothesis is equivalent to supporting the alternative hypothesis.

Step Four: Calculating the Value of the Test Statistic

In this step, the researcher does the following:

- Uses the appropriate formula to calculate the value of the statistic for the test chosen
- Compares the value just calculated to the critical value of the statistic (from the appropriate table), based on the decision rule chosen
- Based on the comparison, determines to either reject or fail to reject the null hypothesis, H_0

EXHIBIT 13.17 | **Statistical Tests and Their Users**

Area of Application	Subgroups or Samples	Level Scaling	Test	Special Requirements	Example
Hypotheses about frequency distribution	One	Nominal	χ^2	Random sample	Are observed differences in the numbers of people responding to three different promotions likely/not likely due to chance?
	Two or more	Nominal	χ^2	Random sample, independent samples	Are differences in the numbers of men and women responding to a promotion likely/not likely due to chance?
Hypotheses about means	One (large sample)	Metric (interval or ratio)	Z test for one mean	Random sample, $n \geq 30$	Is the observed difference between a sample estimate of the mean and some set standard or expected value of the mean likely/not likely due to chance?
	One (small sample)	Metric (interval or ratio)	t test for one mean	Random sample, $n < 30$	Same as for small sample above
	Two (large sample)	Metric (interval or ratio)	Z test for one mean	Random sample, $n \geq 30$	Is the observed difference between the means for two subgroups (mean income for men and women) likely/not likely due to chance?
	Three or more	Metric (interval or ratio)	One-way ANOVA	Random sample	Is the observed variation between means for three or more subgroups (mean expenditures on entertainment for high-, moderate-, and low-income people) likely/not likely due to chance?
Hypotheses about proportions	One (large sample)	Metric (interval or ratio)	Z test for one proportion	Random sample, $n \geq 30$	Is the observed difference between a sample estimate of proportion (percentage who say they will buy) and some set standard or expected value likely/not likely due to chance?
	Two (large sample)	Metric (interval or ratio)	Z test for two proportions	Random sample, $n \geq 30$	Is the observed difference between estimated percentages for two subgroups (percentage of men and women who have college degrees) likely/not likely due to chance?

Step Five: Stating the Conclusion The conclusion summarizes the results of the test. It should be stated from the perspective of the original research question.

Types of Errors in Hypothesis Testing

→ **type I error (α error)** Rejection of the null hypothesis when, in fact, it is true.

Hypothesis tests are subject to two general types of errors, typically referred to as type I error and type II error. A **type I error** involves rejecting the null hypothesis when it is, in fact, true. The researcher may reach this incorrect conclusion because the observed difference between the sample and population values is due to sampling error.

EXHIBIT 13.18	Type I and Type II Errors	
Actual State of the Null Hypothesis	**Fail to Reject H_0**	**Reject H_0**
H_0 is true	Correct $(1-\alpha)$	Type I error (α)
H_0 is false	Type II error (β)	Correct $(1-\beta)$

The researcher must decide how willing she or he is to commit a type I error. The probability of committing a type I error is referred to as the *alpha* (α) *level*. Conversely, $1-\alpha$ is the probability of making a correct decision by not rejecting the null hypothesis when, in fact, it is true.

A **type II error** involves failing to reject the null hypothesis when it actually is false. A type II error is referred to as a *beta* (β) *error*. The value $1-\beta$ reflects the probability of making a correct decision in rejecting the null hypothesis when, in fact, it is false. The four possibilities are summarized in Exhibit 13.18.

➤ **type II error (β error)** Failure to reject the null hypothesis when, in fact, it is false.

As we consider the various types of hypothesis tests, keep in mind that when a researcher rejects or fails to reject the null hypothesis, this decision is never made with 100 percent certainty. There is a probability that the decision is correct and there is a probability that the decision is not correct. The level of α is set by the researcher, after consulting with his or her client, considering the resources available for the project, and considering the implications of making type I and type II errors. However, the estimation of β is more complicated and is beyond the scope of our discussion. Note that type I and type II errors are not complementary; that is, $\alpha + \beta \neq 1$.

Accepting H_0 versus Failing to Reject (FTR) H_0

Researchers often fail to make a distinction between accepting H_0 and failing to reject H_0. However, as noted earlier, there is an important distinction between these two decisions. When a hypothesis is tested, H_0 is presumed to be true until it is demonstrated to be likely to be false. In any hypothesis testing situation, the only other hypothesis that can be accepted is the alternative hypothesis H_a. Either there is sufficient evidence to support H_a (reject H_0) or there is not (fail to reject H_0). The real question is whether there is enough evidence in the data to conclude that H_a is correct. If we fail to reject H_0, we are saying that the data do not provide sufficient support of the claim made in H_a—not that we accept the statement made in H_0.

One-Tailed versus Two-Tailed Test

Tests are either one-tailed or two-tailed. The decision as to which to use depends on the nature of the situation and what the researcher is trying to demonstrate. For example, when the quality control department of a fast-food organization receives a shipment of chicken breasts from one of its vendors and needs to determine whether the product meets specifications in regard to fat content, a one-tailed test is appropriate. The shipment will be rejected if it does not meet minimum specifications. On the other hand, the managers of the meat company that supplies the product should run two-tailed tests to determine two factors. First, they must make sure that the product meets the minimum specifications of their customer before they ship it. Second, they want to determine whether the product exceeds specifications because this can be costly to them. If they are consistently providing a product that exceeds the level of quality they have contracted to provide, their costs may be unnecessarily high.

The classic example of a situation requiring a two-tailed test is the testing of electric fuses. A fuse must trip, or break contact, when it reaches a preset temperature or a fire may result. On the other hand, you do not want the fuse to break contact before it reaches the specified temperature or it will shut off the electricity unnecessarily. The test used in the quality control process for testing fuses must, therefore, be two-tailed.

Independent versus Related Samples

In some cases, one needs to test the hypothesis that the value of a variable in one population is equal to the value of that same variable in another population. Selection of the appropriate test statistic requires the researcher to consider whether the samples are independent or related. **Independent samples** are samples in which measurement of the variable of interest in one sample has no effect on measurement of the variable in the other sample. It is not necessary that there be two different surveys, only that the measurement of the variable in one population has no effect on the measurement of the variable in the other population. In the case of **related samples**, measurement of the variable of interest in one sample may influence measurement of the variable in another sample.

If, for example, men and women were interviewed in a particular survey regarding their frequency of eating out, there is no way that a man's response could affect or change the way a woman would respond to a question in the survey. Thus, this would be an example of independent samples. On the other hand, consider a situation in which the researcher needed to determine the effect of a new advertising campaign on consumer awareness of a particular brand. To do this, the researcher might survey a random sample of consumers before introducing the new campaign and then survey the same sample of consumers 90 days after the new campaign was introduced. These samples are not independent. The measurement of awareness 90 days after the start of the campaign may be affected by the first measurement.

➤ **independent samples**
Samples in which measurement of a variable in one population has no effect on measurement of the variable in the other.

➤ **related samples**
Samples in which measurement of a variable in one population may influence measurement of the variable in the other.

p Values and Significance Testing

For the various tests discussed in this chapter, a standard—a level of significance and associated critical value of the statistics—is established, and then the value of the statistic is calculated to see whether it beats that standard. If the calculated value of the statistic exceeds the critical value, then the result being tested is said to be statistically significant at that level.

However, this approach does not give the exact probability of getting a computed test statistic that is largely due to chance. The calculations to compute this probability, commonly referred to as the ***p*** **value**, are tedious to perform by hand. Fortunately, they are easy for computers. The *p* value is the most demanding level of statistical (not managerial) significance that can be met, based on the calculated value of the statistic. Computer statistical packages usually use one of the following labels to identify the probability that the distance between the hypothesized population parameter and the observed test statistic could have occurred due to chance:

➤ **p value**
The exact probability of getting a computed test statistic that is due to chance. The smaller the *p* value, the smaller the probability that the observed result occurred by chance.

■ *p* value
■ ≤ PROB
■ PROB =

The smaller the *p* value, the smaller is the probability that the observed result occurred by chance (sampling error).

SUMMARY

Once questionnaires have been returned from the field, a five-step process takes place. These steps are (1) validation and editing, which are quality control checks, (2) coding, (3) data entry, (4) logical cleaning of data, and (5) tabulation and statistical analysis. The first step in the process, making sure that the data have integrity, is critical. Otherwise, the age-old adage is true: "Garbage in, garbage out." Validation involves determining with as much certainty as possible that each questionnaire is, in fact, a valid interview. A valid interview in this sense is one that was conducted in an appropriate manner. The objective of validation is to detect interviewer fraud or failure to follow key instructions. Validation is accomplished by recontacting a certain percentage of the respondents surveyed by each interviewer. Any surveys found to be fraudulent are eliminated. After the validation process is completed, editing begins. Editing involves checking for interviewer and respondent mistakes—making certain that all required questions were answered, that skip patterns were followed properly, and that responses to open-ended questions were accurately recorded.

Upon completion of the editing, the next step is to code any open-ended questions. Most questions on surveys are closed ended and precoded, which means that numeric codes already have been assigned to the various responses on the questionnaire. With open-ended questions, the researcher has no idea in advance what the responses will be. Therefore, the coder must establish numeric codes for response categories by listing actual responses to open-ended questions and then consolidating those responses and assigning numeric codes to the consolidated categories. Once a coding sheet has been created, all questionnaires are coded using the coding sheet categories.

The next step is data entry. Today, most data entry is done by means of intelligent entry systems that check the internal logic of the data. The data typically are entered directly from the questionnaires. New developments in scanning technology have made a more automated approach to data entry cost-effective for smaller projects.

Logical cleaning of data is the final, computerized error check, performed through the use of error checking routines and/or marginal reports. Error checking routines indicate whether or not certain conditions have been met.

The final step in this process is tabulation of the data. The most basic tabulation involves one-way frequency tables, which show the number of respondents who gave each answer to each question.

Statistical measures provide an even more powerful way to analyze data. The most commonly used statistical measures are those of central tendency: the arithmetic mean, median, and mode. The arithmetic mean is computed only from interval or ratio data by adding the values for all observations of a particular variable and dividing the resulting sum by the number of observations. The median can be computed for all types of data except nominal data by finding the value below which 50 percent of the observations fall. The mode can be computed for any type of data by simply finding the value that occurs most frequently. The arithmetic mean is, by far, the most commonly used measure of central tendency.

In addition to central tendency, researchers often want to have an indication of the dispersion of the data. Measures of dispersion include standard deviation, variance, and range.

The purpose of making statistical inferences is to generalize from sample results to population characteristics. Three important concepts applied to the notion of differences are mathematical differences, managerially important differences, and statistical significance.

A hypothesis is an assumption or theory that a researcher or manager makes about some characteristic of the population being investigated. By testing, the researcher determines whether a hypothesis concerning some characteristic of the population is valid.

A statistical hypothesis test permits the researcher to calculate the probability of observing the particular result if the stated hypothesis actually were true. In hypothesis testing, the first step is to specify the hypothesis. Next, an appropriate statistical technique should be selected to test the hypothesis. Then, a decision rule must be specified as the basis for determining whether to reject or fail to reject the hypothesis. Hypothesis tests are subject to two types of errors called type I (α error) and type II (β error). A type I error involves rejecting the null hypothesis when it is, in fact, true. A type II error involves failing to reject the null hypothesis when the alternative hypothesis actually is true. Finally, the value of the test statistic is calculated, and a conclusion is stated that summarizes the results of the test.

KEY TERMS & DEFINITIONS

validation The process of ascertaining that interviews actually were conducted as specified.

editing The process of ascertaining that questionnaires were filled out properly and completely.

skip pattern A sequence in which later questions are asked based on a respondent's answer to an earlier question.

coding The process of grouping and assigning numeric codes to the various responses to a question.

data entry The process of converting information to an electronic format.

intelligent entry A form of data entry in which the information being entered into the data entry device is checked for internal logic.

scanning technology A form of data entry in which responses on questionnaires are read in automatically by a data entry device.

logical cleaning of data Final computerized error checking of data.

error checking routines Computer programs that accept instructions from the user to check for logical errors in the data.

one-way frequency table A table showing the number of respondents choosing each answer to a survey question.

cross tabulation Examination of the responses to one question relative to the responses to one or more other questions.

mean The sum of the values for all observations of a variable divided by the number of observations.

median The value below which 50 percent of the observations fall.

mode The value that occurs most frequently.

hypothesis An assumption or a theory that a researcher or manager makes about some characteristics of the population under study.

type I error (α error) Rejection of the null hypothesis when, in fact, it is true.

type II error (β error) Failure to reject the null hypothesis when, in fact, it is false.

independent samples Samples in which measurement of a variable in one population has no effect on measurement of the variable in the other.

related samples Samples in which measurement of a variable in one population may influence measurement of the variable in the other.

_p_ value The exact probability of getting a computed test statistic that is due to chance. The smaller the _p_ value, the smaller the probability that the observed result occurred by chance.

QUESTIONS FOR REVIEW & CRITICAL THINKING

1. What is the difference between measurement validity and interview validation?

2. Assume that Sally Smith, an interviewer, completed 50 questionnaires. Ten of the questionnaires were validated by calling the respondents and asking them one opinion question and two demographic questions over again. One respondent claimed that his age category was 30–40, when the age category marked on the questionnaire was 20–30. On another questionnaire, in response to the question "What is the most important problem facing our city government?" the interviewer had written, "The city council is too eager to raise taxes." When the interview was validated, the respondent said, "The city tax rate is too high." As a validator, would you assume that these were honest mistakes and accept the entire lot of 50 interviews as valid? If not, what would you do?

3. What is meant by the editing process? Should editors be allowed to fill in what they think a respondent meant in response to open-ended questions if the information seems incomplete? Why or why not?

4. Give an example of a skip pattern on a questionnaire. Why is it important to always follow the skip patterns correctly?

5. It has been said that, to some degree, coding of open-ended questions is an art. Would you agree or disagree? Why? Suppose that, after coding a large number of questionnaires, the researcher notices that many responses have ended up in the "Other" category. What might this imply? What could be done to correct this problem?

6. What is the purpose of logical cleaning data? Give some examples of how data can be logically cleaned. Do you think that logical cleaning is an expensive and unnecessary step in the data tabulation process? Why or why not?

7. It has been said that a cross tabulation of two variables offers the researcher more insightful information than does a one-way frequency table. Why might this be true? Give an example.

8. Illustrate the various alternatives for using percentages in one-way frequency tables. Explain the logic of choosing one alternative method over another.

9. Explain the differences among the mean, median, and mode. Give an example in which the researcher might be interested in each of these measures of central tendency.

10. Explain the notions of mathematical differences, managerially important differences, and statistical significance. Can results be statistically significant and yet lack managerial importance? Explain your answer.

11. Describe the steps in the procedure for testing hypotheses. Discuss the difference between a null hypothesis and an alternative hypothesis.

12. Distinguish between a type I error and a type II error. What is the relationship between the two?

WORKING THE NET

1. Go to *www.ats.ucla.edu/stat/mult_pkg/whatstat/default.htm* for a guide to choosing the correct statistical test for particular problems in various statistical packages.

2. Many statistical procedures can be done in Microsoft Excel. See *http://pages stern.nyu.edu/~jsimonof/classes/1305/pdf/excelreg.pdf* for a number of good examples. Use one of these examples on data you have, data from the book, or data you make up to see how it can work for a particular problem.

REAL-LIFE RESEARCH • 13.1

PrimeCare

PrimeCare is a group of 12 emergency medical treatment clinics in the Columbus and Toledo, Ohio, markets. The management group for PrimeCare is considering a communications campaign that will rely mainly on radio ads to boost its awareness and quality image in the market. The ad agency of Dodd and Beck has been chosen to develop the campaign. Currently, the plan is to focus on PrimeCare's experienced, front-line health professionals.

Two themes for the ad campaign are now being considered. One theme ("We are ready!") focuses primarily on the special training given to PrimeCare's staff, and the second theme ("All the experts—all the time") focuses primarily on PrimeCare's commitment to having the best, trained professionals available at each PrimeCare facility 24/7. Dodd and Beck's research team has conducted a survey of consumers to gauge the appeal of the two campaigns. Overall results and results broken down by gender and by location are shown in the table:

		Gender		Location	
	Total	Male	Female	Columbus	Toledo
Total	400	198	202	256	144
	100%	100.0%	100.0%	100.0%	100.0%
Prefer "Ready"	150	93	57	124	26
Campaign	37.5%	47.0%	28.2%	48.4%	18.1%
Prefer "All the	250	105	145	132	118
Time" campaign	62.5%	53.0%	71.8%	51.6%	81.9%

Questions

1. Which theme appears to have more appeal overall? Justify your answer.

2. How does the appeal of the campaigns differ between men and women? What is your basis for that conclusion?

3. Are the campaign themes equally attractive to residents of Columbus and Toledo? Why do you say that?

SPSS EXERCISES FOR CHAPTER 13

Exercise #1: Logical Cleaning of Data

1. Go to the Wiley Web site at **www.wiley.com/college/mcdaniel** and download the "*Segmenting the College Student Market for Movie Attendance*" database to SPSS Windows. This database will have several errors for you to correct. In the SPSS Data Editor, go to the *variable view* option and notice the **computer coding** for each variable.

2. Also from the Wiley Web site, download a copy of the "*Segmenting the College Student Market for Movie Attendance*" questionnaire. Notice the computer coding for each of the variables; which is the same as that in the *variable view* option on the SPSS Data Editor. This information will be important in finding errors in the database.

3. In the SPSS Data Editor, invoke the *analyze/descriptive statistics/frequencies* sequence to obtain frequencies for all of the variables in the database.

4. From the SPSS Viewer *output screen*, determine which variables have input errors. Summarize the errors using the template below as a guide.

Questionnaire Number	Variable Containing Error	Incorrect Value	Correct Value

Going back to the *data view* screen of the *SPSS Data Editor*.

5. Another possible source of errors is in question 8. Notice that in this question the sum of the answers should be 100 percent. Create a summated variable for question 8 (Q8a+Q8b+Q8c+Q8d) to check for errors by invoking the *transform/compute* sequence. Now, compute a frequency distribution for Q8sum. The values that are not "100" indicate an input error. (Such an error could be the result of the respondent not totaling percentages to 100, but for this logical cleaning exercise, the assumption is that it is an input error.) Summarize the errors using the template above.

6. Once you have completed summarizing the variables containing errors, go back to the *data view* screen of the *SPSS Data Editor*. Position the cursor on each of the variables containing errors. Use the *ctrl-f* function to find the questionnaire numbers where the errors occurred. At this point, you will need the corrected database, or the database with no errors. Your professor has access to this database with no errors. After getting the corrected database, finish filling in the table in part 4 above with the correct values. Then make the changes in your database, so that you have a database with no errors. Be sure to resave your database after correcting it for errors.

7. After logically cleaning your data, rerun the *analyze/descriptive statistics/frequencies* sequence to obtain frequencies for your corrected database.

8. You will use the results of this exercise to answer the questions in Exercises #2 and #4.

Exercise #2: Analysis of Data with Frequency Distributions

If you did not complete Exercise #1, you will need the corrected database from your professor. After getting the corrected database, use the *analyze/descriptive statistics/frequencies* sequence to obtain frequency distributions for all of the variables in your database except the questionnaire number (QNO).

If you completed Exercise #1, you will have a corrected database, which consists of frequency distributions for each of the variables in the database.

Answer the following questions.

1. What percentage of all respondents attended at least one movie in the past year? _____%

2. What percentage of all respondents *never buy food items* at a movie? _____%

3. Produce a table indicating the percentage of all respondents that consider each of the movie theater items in question 5 of the questionnaire *very important*. List the top five movie items in descending order (start with the movie items that have the highest percentage of *very important* responses).

For Example:

Movie Item	Percentage of Respondents
Movie item with the highest percentage	75.0%
Movie item with the 2nd highest percentage, etc.	39.2%

4. What percentage of respondents consider the "newspaper" a *very important* source of information about movies playing at movie theaters? _____%

5. What percentage of respondents consider the "Internet" a *very unimportant* source of information about movies playing at movie theaters? _____%

6. By observing the distribution of responses for Q8a, Q8b, Q8c, and Q8d, which is the most popular *purchase option* for movie theater tickets? _____

7. Produce a table listing in descending order the percentage of respondents that consider each of the movie theater information sources (Q7) *very important*.

For Example:

Movie Theater Information Sources	Percentage of Respondents Indicating Very Important
Internet	55%
Newspaper	31%

surveysolutions XP

Exercise #3: Analysis of Data with Descriptive Statistics

If you did not complete Exercises #1 or #2, you will need the corrected database from your professor. The objective of this exercise is to analyze data using measures of central tendency and measures of dispersion. To analyze means and standard deviations, use the *analyze/descriptive statistics/descriptives* sequences. To analyze medians and modes, use the *analyze/descriptive statistics/frequencies* sequence, and select *statistics*. You will see the box with all three measures of central tendency (mean, median and mode).

On the questionnaire, question 5 utilizes a four-point itemized rating scale (illustrated below). This scale is balanced and can be assumed to yield interval scale/metric data. Given the preceding, invoke SPSS to calculate the mean and standard deviation for all of the variables in question 5 (Q5a–Q5i).

Very Unimportant	Somewhat Unimportant	Somewhat Important	Very Important
1	2	3	4

Answer the following questions.

1. Using only the **mean** for each of the variables, which of the movie theater items was considered "most important"? _____

2. Using only the **standard deviation** for each of the variables, for which question was there the greatest amount of agreement? _____ Hint: Least amount of dispersion regarding the response to the movie item.

3. Questions 4 and 6 utilize multiple choice questions which yield nonmetric data, but which is ordinal scale. The appropriate measures of central tendency for nonmetric data are the median and the mode.

   a. What is the *median* response for question 4, concerning the amount a person spends on food/drink items at a movie? _____

Never Buy Food Items at Movies (0)	Up to $7.49 (1)	$7.50 to $14.99 (2)	$15.00 or More (3)

   b. Concerning question 6, the distance a person would drive to see a movie on a "big screen," what is the *mode* of that distribution of responses?

Zero (0)	1 to 9 Miles (1)	11 to 24 Miles (2)	25 to 49 Miles (3)	50+ Miles (4)

4. In this question the objective will be to compare the results of median and mean responses for Q3.
    a. Mean response: _____
    b. Median response: _____
    c. Standard deviation: _____
    d. Minimum response: _____
    e. Maximum response: _____

5. When the responses to a question contain extreme values, the mean response can lie in the upper or lower quartile of the response distribution. In such a case, the median value would be a better indicator of an average response than the mean value. Given the information you obtained from answering item 4 above, is the mean or median a better representative of the "average" response to Q3?

    _____
    _____
    _____

Exercise #4: Analysis of Demographic Characteristics Using Charts

If you completed Exercise #1 and/or Exercise #2 you will have the information to complete this exercise.

   If you did not complete either Exercise #1 or #2, you will need to get a corrected soft drink database from your professor. After getting the database, use the *analyze/descriptive statistics/frequencies* sequence to obtain frequency distributions for the demographic questions (questions 11–14).

Answer the following questions.

1. Display the demographic data for each of the four demographic variables in tables.
2. For each demographic variable, illustrate the table results using some type of graphic representation of the data (pie charts, line charts, or bar charts).

Note: Some students who are proficient in Excel may want to paste their databases into an Excel spreadsheet for the geographical depiction of the demographic variables.

Exercise #5: Analyzing Data Using Cross Tabulation Analysis

Note: If you did not complete any of the SPSS exercises in Chapter 13 thus far, you will need a corrected database from your professor.

Use the *analyze/descriptive statistics/crosstab* sequence to obtain cross tabulated results. In addition, click on the "cell" icon and make sure the *observed, expected, total, row,* and *column* boxes are checked. Then, click on the "statistics" icon and check the *chi-square* box. Once you run the analysis, on the output for the chi–square analysis, you will only need the *Pearson chi-square statistic* to assess whether or nor the results of the cross tab are statistically significant.

In this exercise we are assessing whether or not persons who attend movies at movie theaters are demographically different from those who do not. Invoke the cross tab analysis for the following pairs of variables:

    a. Q1 & Q11
    b. Q1 & Q12
    c. Q1 & Q13
    d. Q1 & Q14

Answer questions 1–6 <u>using only the sample data. Do not consider</u> the results of the *chi-square test*.

1. What % of males do not attend movies at movie theaters?   _____%

2. What % of all respondents are African American and do not attend movies at movie theaters?   _____%

3. What % of respondents not attending movies at movie theaters are in the 19–20 age category?   _____%

4. Which classification group is most likely to attend movies at movie theaters?   _____

5. Which age category is least likely to attend movies at a movie theater?   _____

6. Are Caucasians less likely to attend movie theaters than African Americans?   _____

For question 7, the objective is to determine whether the people who go to and don't go to movies are significantly different in a statistical sense in their demographic characteristics. We do this by using the results of the *chi-square test for independent samples*.

7. Evaluate the chi-square statistic in each of your cross tab tables. Construct a table to summarize the results. For example:

Variables	Pearson Chi-Square	Degrees of Freedom	Asymp sig.	Explanation
Q1 (attend or not attend movies at movie theaters & Q12 (gender))	2.71	1	.10	We can be 90% confident that based on our sample results, males differ significantly from females in their tendency to attend or not attend movies at movie theaters.

Exercise #6: T/Z Test for Independent Samples

Use the *analyze/compare means/independent samples t-test* sequence to complete this exercise. This exercise compares males and females regarding the information sources they utilize to search for information about movies at movie theaters. SPSS calls the variable in which the means are being computed the *test variable,* and the variable in which we are grouping responses the *grouping variable.*

surveysolutions XP

Note: In statistics, if a sample has less than 30 observations or cases, then we invoke a *t* test. If there are 30 or more cases, we invoke a *z* test, as *the t test values and z test values are virtually the same, hence SPSS refers only to a t test.*

Answer the following questions.

The result of the *t* test generates a table of **group statistics**, which is based only on the **sample** data. The other output table generated by the *t* test has statistical data from which we can determine whether or not the sample results can be generalized to the population from which the sample data was drawn. If the *t* test is significant, then we can use the group statistics to determine the specifics of the computed results. For example, a significant *t* test may tell us that males differ from females regarding the importance they place on the newspaper as an information source, but the group statistics tell us "who" considers it most important.

From our *sample data*, can we generalize our results to the population by saying that males differ from females regarding the importance they place on various information sources to get information about movies at movie theaters by:

1. the newspaper (Q7a)?
2. the Internet (Q7b)?
3. phoning in to the movie theater for information (Q7c)?
4. the television (Q7d)?
5. friends or family (Q7e)?

You may want to use the template below to summarize your *t* test results. For example:

Variables	Variance Prob. of Sig. Diff.	Means Prob. of Sig. Diff.	Interpretation of Results
Q12 (gender) & Q7a (newspaper)	.000	.035	96.5% confident that based on our sample results, males differ significantly from females concerning the importance they place on the newspaper as an information source about movies at movie theaters (**means test**). 100% confident that males and females were significantly different regarding to the variance of response within each gender (**variance test**).

Exercise #7: ANOVA Test for Independent Samples

Invoke the *analyze/compare means/One-Way ANOVA* sequence to invoke the ANOVA test to complete this exercise. This exercise compares the responses of freshman, sophomores, juniors, seniors, and graduate students to test for significant differences in the importance placed on several movie theater items. For the ANOVA test, SPSS calls the variable in which means are being computed the *independent variable* and the variable in which we are grouping responses the *factor variable*. Be sure to click the *options* icon and check *descriptives* so that the output will produce the mean responses by student classification for the sample data.

As with the *t* test, the ANOVA test produces a table of *descriptives* based on sample data. If our ANOVA test is significant, the *descriptives* can be used to determine, for example, which student classification places the most importance on comfortable seats.

Answer the following questions.

From our sample data, can we generalize our results to the population by saying that there are significant differences across the <u>classification of students</u> by the importance they place on the following movie theater items?

1. video arcade at the movie theater (Q5a)
2. soft drinks and food items (Q5b)
3. plentiful restrooms (Q5c)
4. comfortable chairs (Q5d)
5. auditorium-type seating (Q5e)
6. size of the movie theater screens (Q5f)
7. quality of the sound system (Q5g)
8. number of screens at a movie theater (Q5h)
9. clean restroom (Q5i)
10. Using only the *descriptive statistics*, which classification group (Q13) places the least amount of importance on clean restrooms (Q5i)? _____
11. Using only the *descriptive statistics*, which classification group (Q13) places the greatest amount of importance on quality of sound system (Q5i)? _____

Summarize the results of your ANOVA analysis using a table similar to the one below.

Variables	Degrees of Freedom	F-Value	Probability of Insignificance	Interpretation of Results
Q5a (importance of a video arcade) & Q13 (student classification)	4.461	12.43	.001	99.9% confident that based on the sample results, students differ significantly by classification concerning the importance placed on there being a video arcade at the movie theater.

surveysolutions XP

Robert Stainforth/Alamy

CHAPTER 14

More Powerful Statistical Methods

LEARNING OBJECTIVES

→ **1.** To comprehend the nature of more powerful statistical methods.

→ **2.** To understand appropriate applications for the procedures presented.

→ **3.** To become aware of the potential pitfalls of each procedure.

→ **4.** To understand how to interpret results from each method.

Advances in computer hardware and software have provided the basis for remarkable developments in the use of powerful statistical procedures to analyze large amounts of complex data with relative ease. The powerful procedures covered in this chapter have been extremely significant in this data analysis revolution. The hot job market for people with skills in this area is discussed in the following Practicing Marketing Research feature.

PRACTICING MARKETING RESEARCH

Statistician: The Hot Job of the Future[1]

With the dramatic proliferation of digital data over the last several years, professionals in the fields of statistics and data analysis are becoming hot commodities. At top companies like Google and IBM, new recruits holding a PhD in a statistics field can land jobs with starting salaries as high as $125,000. In a world where almost anything can be monitored or measured, the applications created through advanced data analysis are opening up a wealth of opportunities.

The key is the statisticians. All the raw data in the world, in and of itself, is not very useful until its significance can be determined. That's why companies are calling on the statisticians to turn these treasure troves of raw data into applicable and actionable information. Google, for example, employs statisticians to continuously find new ways to improve its search algorithms. Statistical analysts have been upgrading Google's crawler software, which is used to update its search index. Analytical improvements are helping the software better identify Web sites that are more frequently updated over Web sites that have gone dormant. Because of the scale of Google's operations (running the same operations billions and trillions of times), even incremental improvements can have a dramatic effect.

IBM is looking to take advantage of opportunities in the field as well, with the introduction of its Business Analytics and Optimization Services Department, by providing data mining and analysis services to other firms. The unit originally comprised 200 of IBM's top mathematicians, statisticians, and researchers, but the company plans to expand through training and new hiring to tap the expertise of over 4,000 staff members.

As many statisticians point out, however, the use of statistics is not without its challenges. If not carefully analyzed, the massive amount of data available can overwhelm statistical models, and even strong statistical correlations in the data do not necessarily indicate a causal relationship. Still, as the explosion of available data continues, the ability to identify mathematically abnormal relationships in the data creates a wealth of opportunities. Organizations need to be able to properly explain these abnormalities though, and that's why they need the best analysts and statisticians. These skill sets are quickly becoming the kind you can take to the bank!

Questions

1. Where have you recently seen the use of statistics and data analysis where you might not have expected it? How was it being used?

2. Top companies are finding that many talented analysts and statisticians actually have backgrounds in other disciplines such as economics, mathematics, and computer sciences. How do you think these disciplines relate to and inform the approach to data analysis?

In this chapter, we will consider five statistical procedures:

- Correlation analysis
- Regression analysis
- Cluster analysis
- Factor analysis
- Conjoint analysis

You may have been exposed to regression analysis in introductory statistics courses. The remaining procedures are newer, less widely studied, or both. Summary descriptions of the techniques are provided in Exhibit 14.1.

Although awareness of these techniques is far from universal, they have been around for decades and have been widely used for a variety of commercial purposes. Fair Isaac & Co. has built a very large business around the commercial use of these techniques.[2] The firm and its clients have found that they can predict with surprising accuracy who will pay their bills on time, who will pay late, and who will not pay at all. The federal government uses secret formulas, based on the firm's analyses, to identify tax evaders. Fair Isaac has also shown that results from its analyses help in identifying the best sales prospects.

Statistical Software

The computational requirements for the various procedures discussed in this chapter are substantial. As a practical matter, running the various types of analyses presented requires a computer and appropriate software. Until the late 1980s, most types of analyses discussed in this chapter were done on mainframe or minicomputers because personal computers were limited in power, memory, storage capacity, and range of software available. Those limitations are in the past. Personal computers have the power to handle just about any problem that a marketing researcher might encounter. Most problems can be solved in a matter of seconds, and a wide variety of outstanding Windows software is available for advanced statistical analysis. SPSS for Windows is the most widely used by professional marketing researchers.

SPSS includes a full range of software modules for integrated database creation and management, data transformation and manipulation, graphing, descriptive statistics, and multivariate procedures. It has an easy-to-use, graphical interface. Additional information on the SPSS product line can be found at *www.spss.com/software/statistics* and *www.spss.com/software/modeler.*

EXHIBIT 14.1	**Brief Descriptions of Statistical Procedures Covered**
Correlation analysis	Measures the degree to which changes in one variable are associated with changes in another variable.
Regression analysis	Enables the researcher to predict the level of magnitude of a dependent variable based on the levels of more than one independent variable.
Cluster analysis	Is a procedure for identifying subgroups of individuals or items that are homogeneous within subgroups and different from other subgroups.
Factor analysis	Permits the analyst to reduce a set of variables to a smaller set of factors or composite variables by identifying underlying dimensions in the data.
Conjoint analysis	Provides a basis for estimating the utility that consumers associate with different product features or attributes.

Correlation Analysis

Correlation for Metric Data: Pearson's Product–Moment Correlation

Correlation is the degree to which changes in one variable (the dependent variable) are associated with changes in another. When the relationship is between two variables, the analysis is called simple, or bivariate, **correlation analysis**. With metric data, **Pearson's product–moment correlation** may be used.

In our example of bivariate regression, we used the coefficient of determination R^2 as a measure of the strength of the linear relationship between X and Y. Another descriptive measure, called the *coefficient of correlation R*, describes the degree of association between X and Y. It is the square root of the coefficient of determination with the appropriate sign (+ or –). The value of R can range from –1 (perfect negative correlation) to +1 (perfect positive correlation). The closer R is to ±1, the stronger the degree of association between X and Y. If R is equal to zero, then there is no association between X and Y.

> ➔ **correlation analysis**
> Analysis of the degree to which changes in one variable are associated with changes in another.

> ➔ **Pearson's product–moment correlation**
> A correlation analysis technique for use with metric data.

Example of Correlation Analysis

Stop 'N Go recently conducted a research effort designed to measure the effect of vehicular traffic past a particular store location on annual sales at that location. To control for other factors, researchers identified 20 stores that were virtually identical on all other variables known to have a significant effect on store sales (for example, square footage, amount of parking, demographics of the surrounding neighborhood). This particular analysis is part of an overall effort by Stop 'N Go to identify and quantify the effects of various factors that affect store sales. The ultimate goal is to develop a model that can be used to screen potential sites for store locations and select, for actual purchase and store construction, the ones that will produce the highest level of sales.

After identifying the 20 sites, Stop 'N Go took a daily traffic count for each site over a 30-day period. In addition, from internal records, the company obtained total sales data for each of the 20 test stores for the preceding 12 months (see Exhibit 14.2).

Doug Meszler / SplashNews/NewsCom

Bivariate regression analysis can help answer such questions as "How does advertising affect sales?"

EXHIBIT 14.2	Annual Sales and Average Daily Vehicular Traffic	
Store Number (i)	Average Daily Vehicular Count in Thousands (X_i)	Annual Sales in Thousands of Dollars (Y_i)
1	62	1,121
2	35	766
3	36	701
4	72	1,304
5	41	832
6	39	782
7	49	977
8	25	503
9	41	773
10	39	839
11	35	893
12	27	588
13	55	957
14	38	703
15	24	497
16	28	657
17	53	1,209
18	55	997
19	33	844
20	29	883

In this case, the correlation of .896 indicates a positive correlation between the average daily vehicular traffic and annual sales. In other words, successively higher levels of sales are associated with successively higher levels of traffic.

Regression Analysis

Researchers use regression analysis when their goal is to examine the relationship between two or more metric predictor (independent) variables and one metric dependent (criterion) variable.[3] Under certain circumstances, described later in this section, nominal predictor variables can be used if they are recoded as binary variables.

regression analysis
A procedure for predicting the level or magnitude of a (metric) dependent variable based on the levels of multiple independent variables.

Regression analysis is an extension of bivariate regression. Instead of fitting a straight line to observations in a two-dimensional space, multiple regression analysis fits a plane to observations in a multidimensional space. The output obtained and the interpretation are essentially the same as for bivariate regression. The general equation for regression is as follows:

$$Y = a + b_1X_1 + b_2X_2 + b_3X_3 + \cdots + b_nX_n$$

where Y = dependent or criterion variable

a = estimated constant

$b_1 - b_n$ = coefficients associated with the predictor variables so that a change of one unit in X will cause a change of b_1 units in Y; values for the coefficients are estimated from the regression analysis

$X_1 - X_n$ = predictor (independent) variables that influence the dependent variable

surveysolutions XP

Steps that you need to go through to do the correlation problem shown in the book are provided below along with the output produced. Use the data set **Correx**, which you can download from the Web site for the text.

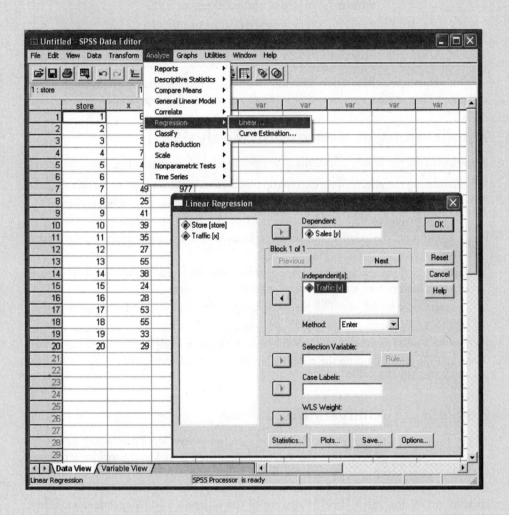

Steps in SPSS

1. Select *Analyze →Regression →Linear*.
2. Move **y** to Dependent.

For example, consider the following regression equation (in which values for a, b_1, and b_2 have been estimated by means of regression analysis):

$$\hat{Y} = 200 + 17X_1 + 22X_2$$

where
$\hat{Y}$ = estimated sales in units
X_1 = advertising expenditures
X_2 = number of salespersons

This equation indicates that sales increase by 17 units for every \$1 increase in advertising and 22 units for every one-unit increase in number of salespersons.

Applications of Regression Analysis

There are many possible applications of regression analysis in marketing research:

- Estimating the effects of various marketing mix variables on sales or market share
- Estimating the relationship between various demographic or psychographic factors and the frequency with which certain service businesses are visited
- Determining the relative influence of individual satisfaction elements on overall satisfaction
- Quantifying the relationship between various classification variables, such as age and income, and overall attitude toward a product or service
- Determining which variables are predictive of sales of a particular product or service

Regression analysis can serve one or a combination of two basic purposes: (1) predicting the level of the dependent variable, based on given levels of the independent variables, and (2) understanding the relationship between the independent variables and the dependent variable.

Regression Analysis Measures

> **coefficient of determination**
> A measure of the percentage of the variation in the dependent variable explained by variations in the independent variables.

A statistic referred to as the **coefficient of determination**, or R^2, is a key output of regression analysis. This statistic can assume values from 0 to 1 and provides a measure of the percentage of the variation in the dependent variable that is explained by variation in the independent variables. For example, if R^2 in a given regression analysis is calculated to be .75, this means that 75 percent of the variation in the dependent variable is explained by variation in the independent variables. The analyst would always like to have a calculated R^2 close to 1. Frequently, variables are added to a regression model to see what effect they have on the R^2 value.

> **regression coefficients**
> Estimates of the effect of individual independent variables on the dependent variable.

The b values, or **regression coefficients**, are estimates of the effect of individual independent variables on the dependent variable. It is appropriate to determine the likelihood that each individual b value is the result of chance. This calculation is part of the output provided by virtually all statistical software packages. Typically, these packages compute the probability of incorrectly rejecting the null hypothesis of $b_n = 0$.

Dummy Variables

> **dummy variables**
> In regression analysis, a way of representing two-group or dichotomous, nominally scaled independent variables by coding one group as 0 and the other as 1.

In some situations, the analyst needs to include nominally scaled independent variables such as gender, marital status, occupation, and race in a multiple regression analysis. **Dummy variables** can be created for this purpose. Dichotomous nominally scaled independent variables can be transformed into dummy variables by coding one value (for example, female) as 0 and the other (for example, male) as 1. For nominally

© Brian McEntire/iStockphoto

Regression analysis can be used to estimate the relationship between various demographic or psychographic factors and the frequency with which a service business is hired.

scaled independent variables that can assume more than two values, a slightly different approach is required. Consider a question regarding racial group with three possible answers: African American, Hispanic, or Caucasian. Binary or dummy variable coding of responses requires the use of two dummy variables, X_1 and X_2, which might be coded as follows:

	X_1	X_2
If person is African American	1	0
If person is Hispanic	0	1
If person is Caucasian	0	0

Potential Use and Interpretation Problems

The analyst must be sensitive to certain problems that may be encountered in the use and interpretation of regression analysis results. These problems are summarized in the following sections.

Collinearity   One of the key assumptions of regression analysis is that the independent variables are not correlated (collinear) with each other.[4] If they are correlated, the predicted Y value is unbiased, and the estimated B values (regression coefficients) will have inflated standard errors and will be inaccurate and unstable. Larger than expected coefficients for some b values are compensated for by smaller than expected coefficients for others. This is why you still produce reliable estimates of Y and why you can get sign reversals and wide variations in b values with **collinearity**, but still produce reliable estimates of Y.

The simplest way to check for collinearity is to examine the matrix showing the correlations between each variable in the analysis. One rule of thumb is to look for

→ **collinearity**
The correlation of independent variables with each other, which can bias estimates of regression coefficients.

correlations between independent variables of .30 or greater. If correlations of this magnitude exist, then the analyst should check for distortions of the b values. One way to do this is to run regressions with the two or more collinear variables included and then run regressions again with the individual variables. The b values in the regression with all variables in the equation should be similar to the b values computed for the variables run separately.

A number of strategies can be used to deal with collinearity. Two of the most commonly used strategies are (1) to drop one of the variables from the analysis if two variables are heavily correlated with each other and (2) to combine the correlated variables in some fashion (for example, an index) to form a new composite independent variable, which can be used in subsequent regression analyses.

Causation   Although regression analysis can show that variables are associated or correlated with each other, it cannot prove **causation**. Causal relationships can be confirmed only by other means (see Chapter 8). A strong logical or theoretical basis must be developed to support the idea that a causal relationship exists between the independent variables and the dependent variable. However, even a strong logical base and supporting statistical results demonstrating correlation are only *indicators* of causation.

➤ **causation**
Inference that a change in one variable is responsible for (caused) an observed change in another variable.

➤ **scaling of coefficients**
A method of directly comparing the magnitudes of the regression coefficients of independent variables by scaling them in the same units or by standardizing the data.

Scaling of Coefficients   The magnitudes of the regression coefficients associated with the various independent variables can be compared directly only if they are **scaled** in the same units or if the data have been standardized. Consider the following example:

$$\hat{Y} = 50 + 20X_1 + 20X_2$$

where $\hat{Y}$ = estimated sales volume
X_1 = advertising expenditures in thousands of dollars
X_2 = number of salespersons

At first glance, it appears that an additional dollar spent on advertising and another salesperson added to the salesforce have equal effects on sales. However, this is not true because X_1 and X_2 are measured in different kinds of units. Direct comparison of regression coefficients requires that all independent variables be measured in the same units (for example, dollars or thousands of dollars) or that the data be standardized. *Standardization* is achieved by taking each number in a series, subtracting the mean of the series from the number, and dividing the result by the standard deviation of the series. This process converts any set of numbers to a new set with a mean of 0 and a standard deviation of 1. The formula for the standardization process is as follows:

$$\frac{X_i - \bar{X}}{\sigma}$$

where X_i = individual number from a series of numbers
$\bar{X}$ = mean of the series
σ = standard deviation of the series

Sample Size   The value of R^2 is influenced by the number of predictor variables relative to sample size.[5] Several different rules of thumb have been proposed; they suggest

Steps that you need to go through to do a regression analysis are provided below along with the output produced. Use the data set **Mulregex**, which you can download from the Web site for the text.

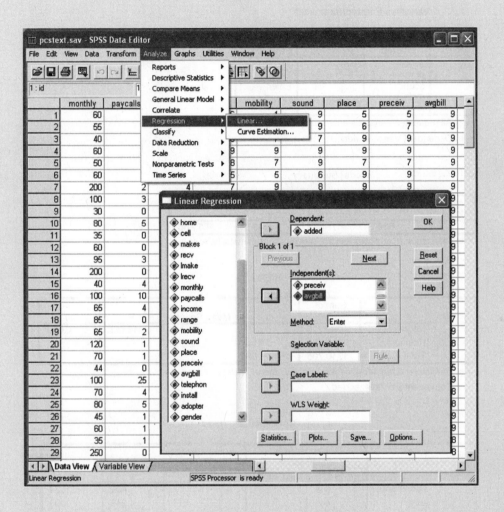

Steps in SPSS

1. Select *Analyze → Regression → Linear*.
2. Move **added** to Dependent.
3. Move **range, mobility, sound, preceiv**, and **avgbill** to Independent(s).
4. Click OK.

surveysolutions XP

SPSS Output for Regression Analysis

Regression

Variables Entered/Removed[b]

Model	Variables Entered	Variables Removed	Method
1	avgbill, preceiv, sound, mobility, range	.	Enter

a. All requested variables entered.

b. Dependent Variable: added

Model Summary

Model	R	R Square	Adjusted R Square	Std. Error of the Estimate
1	.866[a]	.749	.743	1.486

a. Predictors: (Constant), avgbill, preceiv, sound, mobility, range

ANOVA[b]

Model		Sum of Squares	df	Mean Square	F	Sig.
1	Regression	1282.226	5	256.445	116.085	.000[a]
	Residual	428.569	194	2.209		
	Total	1710.795	199			

a. Predictors: (Constant), avgbill, preceiv, sound, mobility, range

b. Dependent Variable: added

Coefficients[a]

Model		Unstandardized Coefficients		Standardized Coefficients		
		B	Std. Error	Beta	t	Sig.
1	(Constant)	.819	1.667		.491	.624
	range	.441	.104	.211	4.249	.000
	mobility	.687	.065	.522	10.541	.000
	sound	.209	.125	.067	1.667	.097
	preceiv	.449	.123	.206	3.645	.000
	avgbill	1.444	.173	.321	8.329	.000

a. Dependent Variable: added

that the number of observations should be equal to at least 10 to 15 times the number of predictor variables. For the preceding example (sales volume as a function of advertising expenditures and number of salespersons) with two predictor variables, a minimum of 20 to 30 observations would be required.

■ The adjusted R^2 value is .743, indicating that 74.3 percent of the variation in the amount consumers are willing to pay for wireless service is explained by the variation in the five independent, or predictor, variables.

Cluster Analysis

The term **cluster analysis** generally refers to statistical procedures used to identify objects or people that are similar in regard to certain variables or measurements. The purpose of cluster analysis is to classify objects or people into some number of mutually exclusive and exhaustive groups so that those within a group are as similar as possible to one another.[6] In other words, clusters should be homogeneous internally (within cluster) and heterogeneous externally (between clusters).

→ **cluster analysis**
A general term for statistical procedures that classify objects or people into some number of mutually exclusive and exhaustive groups on the basis of two or more classification variables.

Procedures for Clustering

A number of different procedures (based on somewhat different mathematical and computer routines) are available for clustering people or objects. However, the general approach underlying all of these procedures involves measuring the similarities among people or objects in regard to their values on the variables used for clustering.[7] Similarities among the people or objects being clustered are normally determined on the basis of some type of distance measure. This approach is best illustrated graphically. Suppose an analyst wants to group, or cluster, consumers on the basis of two variables: monthly frequency of eating out and monthly frequency of eating at fast-food restaurants. Observations on the two variables are plotted in a two-dimensional graph in Exhibit 14.3. Each dot indicates the position of one consumer in regard to the two variables. The distance between any pair of points is positively related to how similar the corresponding individuals are when the two variables are considered together. (The closer the dots, the more similar the individuals.) In Exhibit 14.3, consumer X is more like consumer Y than like either Z or W.

Inspection of Exhibit 14.3 suggests that three distinct clusters emerge on the basis of simultaneously considering frequency of eating out and frequency of eating at fast-food restaurants:

- Cluster 1 includes those people who do not frequently eat out or frequently eat at fast-food restaurants.
- Cluster 2 includes consumers who frequently eat out but seldom eat at fast-food restaurants.
- Cluster 3 includes people who frequently eat out and also frequently eat at fast-food restaurants.

The fast-food company can see that its customers are to be found among those who, in general, eat out frequently. To provide more insight for the client, the analyst should develop demographic, psychographic, and behavioral profiles of consumers in cluster 3.

As shown in Exhibit 14.3, clusters can be developed from scatterplots. However, this time-consuming, trial-and-error procedure becomes more tedious as the number of variables used to develop the clusters or the number of objects or persons being clustered increases. You can readily visualize a problem with two variables and fewer than 100 objects. Once the number of variables increases to three and the number of observations increases to 500 or more, visualization becomes impossible. Fortunately, computer algorithms are available to perform this more complex type of cluster analysis. The mechanics of these algorithms are complicated and beyond the scope of this discussion. The basic idea behind most of them is to start with some arbitrary cluster boundaries and modify the boundaries until a point is reached where the average interpoint distances within clusters are as small as possible relative to average distances between clusters.

Cluster Analysis Based on Two Variables

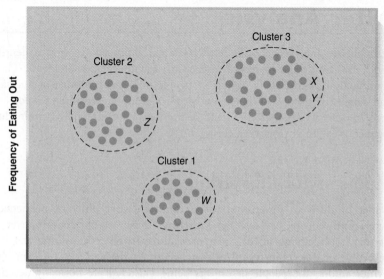

Burke/Triolo Productions/Getty Images, Inc.

Clustering people according to how frequently and where they eat out is a way of identifying a particular consumer base. An upscale restaurant can see that its customers fall into cluster 2 and possibly cluster 3 in Exhibit 14.3.

Factor Analysis

→ **factor analysis**
A procedure for simplifying data by reducing a large set of variables to a smaller set of factors or composite variables by identifying underlying dimensions of the data.

The purpose of **factor analysis** is data simplification.[8] The objective is to summarize the information contained in a large number of metric measures (for example, rating scales) with a smaller number of summary measures, called *factors*. As with cluster analysis, there is no dependent variable.

Many phenomena of interest to marketing researchers are actually composites, or combinations, of a number of measures. These concepts are often measured by means of rating questions. For instance, in assessing consumer response to a new automobile, a general concept such as "luxury" might be measured by asking respondents to rate different cars on attributes such as "quiet ride," "smooth ride," or "plush carpeting." The product designer wants to produce an automobile that is perceived as luxurious but knows that a variety of features probably contribute to this general perception. Each attribute rated should measure a slightly different facet of luxury. The set of measures should provide a better representation of the concept than a single global rating of "luxury."

Several measures of a concept can be added together to develop a composite score or to compute an average score on the concept. Exhibit 14.4 shows data on six consumers who each rated an automobile on four characteristics. You can see that those respondents who gave higher ratings on "smooth ride" also tended to give higher ratings on "quiet ride." A similar pattern is evident in the ratings of "acceleration" and "handling." These four measures can be combined into two summary measures by averaging the pairs of ratings. The resulting summary measures might be called "luxury" and "performance" (see Exhibit 14.5).

Factor Scores

Factor analysis produces one or more factors, or composite variables, when applied to a number of variables. A **factor**, technically defined, is a linear combination of variables. It is a weighted summary score of a set of related variables, similar to the composite derived by averaging the measures. However, in factor analysis, each measure is first weighted according to how much it contributes to the variation of each factor.

In factor analysis, a factor score is calculated on each factor for each subject in the data set. For example, in a factor analysis with two factors, the following equations might be used to determine factor scores:

> **factor**
> A linear combination of variables that are correlated with each other.

$$F_1 = .40A_1 + .30A_2 + .02A_3 + .05A_4$$
$$F_2 = .01A_1 + .04A_2 + .45A_3 + .37A_4$$

where $F_1 - F_n$ = factor scores
$A_1 - A_n$ = attribute ratings

EXHIBIT 14.4	Importance Ratings of Luxury Automobile Features			
Respondent	Smooth Ride	Quiet Ride	Acceleration	Handling
Bob	5	4	2	1
Roy	4	3	2	1
Hank	4	3	3	2
Janet	5	5	2	2
Jane	4	3	2	1
Ann	5	5	3	2
Average	4.50	3.83	2.33	1.50

EXHIBIT 14.5	Average Ratings of Two Factors	
Respondent	Luxury	Performance
Bob	4.5	1.5
Roy	3.5	1.5
Hank	3.5	2.5
Janet	5.0	2.0
Jane	3.5	1.5
Ann	5.0	2.5
Average	4.25	1.92

With these formulas, two factor scores can be calculated for each respondent by substituting the ratings she or he gave on variables A_1 through A_4 into each equation. The coefficients in the equations are the factor scoring coefficients to be applied to each respondent's ratings. For example, Bob's factor scores (see Exhibit 14.5) are computed as follows:

$$F_1 = .40(5) + .30(4) + .02(2) + .05(1) = 3.29$$
$$F_2 = .01(5) + .04(4) + .45(2) + .37(1) = 2.38$$

In the first equation, the factor scoring coefficients, or weights, for A_1 and A_2 (.40 and .30) are large, whereas the weights for A_3 and A_4 are small. The small weights on A_3 and A_4 indicate that these variables contribute little to score variations on factor 1 (F_1). Regardless of the ratings a respondent gives to A_3 and A_4, they have little effect on his or her score on F_1. However, variables A_3 and A_4 make a large contribution to the second factor score (F_2), whereas A_1 and A_2 have little effect. These two equations show that variables A_1 and A_2 are relatively independent of A_3 and A_4 because each variable takes on large values in only one scoring equation.

The relative sizes of the scoring coefficients are also of interest. Variable A_1 (with a weight of .40) is a more important contributor to factor 1 variation than is A_2 (with a smaller weight of .30). This finding may be very important to the product designer when evaluating the implications of various design changes. For example, the product manager might want to improve the perceived luxury of the car through product redesign or advertising. The product manager may know, based on other research, that a certain expenditure on redesign will result in an improvement of the average rating on "smooth ride" from 4.3 to 4.8. This research may also show that the same expenditure will produce a half-point improvement in ratings on "quiet ride." The factor analysis shows that perceived luxury will be enhanced to a greater extent by increasing ratings on "smooth ride" than by increasing ratings on "quiet ride" by the same amount.

Factor Loadings

factor loading
Correlation between factor scores and the original variables.

The nature of the factors derived can be determined by examining the **factor loadings**. Using the scoring equations presented earlier, a pair of factor scores (F_1 and F_2) are calculated for each respondent. Factor loadings are determined by calculating the correlation (from 31 to 31) between each factor (F_1 and F_2) score and each of the original ratings variables. Each correlation coefficient represents the loading of the associated variable on the particular factor. If A_1 is closely associated with factor 1, the loading or correlation will be high, as shown for the sample problem in Exhibit 14.6. Because the loadings are correlation coefficients, values near 31 or 31 indicate a close positive or negative association. Variables A_1 and A_2 are closely associated (highly correlated) with scores on factor 1, and variables A_3 and A_4 are closely associated with scores on factor 2.

EXHIBIT 14.6	Factor Loadings for Two Factors	
	Correlation with	
Variable	**Factor 1**	**Factor 2**
A_1	.85	.10
A_2	.76	.06
A_3	.06	.89
A_4	.04	.79

Stated another way, variables A_1 and A_2 have high loadings on factor 1 and serve to define the factor; variables A_3 and A_4 have high loadings on and define factor 2.

Naming Factors

Once each factor's defining variables have been identified, the next step is to name the factors. This is a somewhat subjective step, combining intuition and knowledge of the variables with an inspection of the variables that have high loadings on each factor. Usually, a certain consistency exists among the variables that load highly on a given factor. For instance, it is not surprising to see that the ratings on "smooth ride" and "quiet ride" both load on the same factor. Although we have chosen to name this factor "luxury," another analyst, looking at the same result, might decide to name the factor "prestige."

Number of Factors to Retain

In factor analysis, the analyst is confronted with a decision regarding how many factors to retain. The final result can include from one factor to as many factors as there are variables. The decision is often made by looking at the percentage of the variation in the original data that is explained by each factor.

There are many different decision rules for choosing the number of factors to retain. Probably the most appropriate decision rule is to stop factoring when additional factors no longer make sense. The first factors extracted are likely to exhibit logical consistency; later factors are usually harder to interpret, for they are more likely to contain a large amount of random variation.

Conjoint Analysis

Conjoint analysis is a popular procedure used by marketers to help determine what features a new product or service should have and how it should be priced. It can be argued that conjoint analysis has become popular because it is a more powerful, more flexible, and often less expensive way to address these important issues than is the traditional concept testing approach.[9]

Conjoint analysis is not a completely standardized procedure.[10] A typical conjoint analysis application involves a series of steps covering a variety of procedures; it is not a single procedure as is, for example, regression analysis. Fortunately, conjoint analysis is not difficult to understand, as we demonstrate in the following example concerning the attributes of golf balls.

➤ **conjoint analysis**
A procedure used to quantify the value that consumers associate with different levels of product/service attributes or features.

An Example of Conjoint Analysis

Put yourself in the position of a product manager for Titleist, a major manufacturer of golf balls. From focus groups recently conducted, past research studies of various types, and your own personal experience as a golfer, you know that golfers tend to evaluate golf balls in terms of three important features or attributes: average driving distance, average ball life, and price.

You also recognize a range of feasible possibilities for each of these features or attributes, as follows:

1. Average driving distance
   - 10 yards more than the golfer's average
   - Same as the golfer's average
   - 10 yards less than the golfer's average

2. Average ball life
   - 54 holes
   - 36 holes
   - 18 holes
3. Price per ball
   - $2.00
   - $2.50
   - $3.00

From the perspective of potential purchasers, the ideal golf ball would have the following characteristics:

- Average driving distance—10 yards above average
- Average ball life—54 holes
- Price—$2.00

From the manufacturer's perspective, which is based on manufacturing cost, the ideal golf ball would probably have these characteristics:

- Average driving distance—10 yards below average
- Average ball life—18 holes
- Price—$3.00

This golf ball profile is based on the fact that it costs less to produce a ball that travels a shorter distance and has a shorter life. The company confronts the eternal marketing dilemma: the company would sell a lot of golf balls but would go broke if it produced and sold the ideal ball from the golfer's perspective. However, the company would sell very few balls if it produced and sold the ideal ball from the manufacturer's perspective. As always, the "best" golf ball from a business perspective lies somewhere between the two extremes.

A traditional approach to this problem might produce information of the type displayed in Exhibit 14.7. As you can see, this information does not provide new insights regarding which ball should be produced. The preferred driving distance is 10 yards above average and the preferred average ball life is 54 holes. These results are obvious without any additional research.

Considering Features Conjointly In conjoint analysis, rather than having respondents evaluate features individually, the analyst asks them to evaluate features conjointly or in combination. The results of asking two different golfers to rank different combinations of "average driving distance" and "average ball life" conjointly are shown in Exhibits 14.8 and 14.9.

As expected, both golfers agree on the most and least preferred balls. However, analysis of their second through eighth rankings makes it clear that the first golfer is willing to trade off ball life for distance (accept a shorter ball life for longer distance), while the second golfer is willing to trade off distance for longer ball life (accept shorter distance for a longer ball life).

This type of information is the essence of the special insight offered by conjoint analysis. The technique permits marketers to see which product attribute or feature potential customers are willing to

Conjoint analysis could be used by a manufacturer of golf balls to determine the three most important features of a golf ball and to see which ball meets the most needs of both consumer and manufacturer.

© Justin Horrocks/iStockphoto

EXHIBIT 14.7	Traditional Nonconjoint Rankings of Distance and Ball Life Attributes		
Average Driving Distance		**Average Ball Life**	
Rank	Level	Rank	Level
1	275 yards	1	54 holes
2	250 yards	2	36 holes
3	225 yards	3	18 holes

EXHIBIT 14.8	Conjoint Rankings of Combinations of Distance and Ball Life for Golfer 1		
	Ball Life		
Distance	54 holes	36 holes	18 holes
275 yards	1	2	4
250 yards	3	5	7
225 yards	6	8	9

EXHIBIT 14.9	Conjoint Rankings of Combinations of Distance and Ball Life for Golfer 2		
	Ball Life		
Distance	54 holes	36 holes	18 holes
275 yards	1	3	6
250 yards	3	5	8
225 yards	4	7	9

trade off (accept less of) to obtain more of another attribute or feature. People make these kinds of purchasing decisions every day (for example, they may choose to pay a higher price for a product at a local market for the convenience of shopping there).

Estimating Utilities The next step is to calculate a set of values, or **utilities**, for the three levels of price, the three levels of driving distance, and the three levels of ball life in such a way that, when they are combined in a particular mix of price, ball life, and driving distance, they predict a particular golfer's rank order for that particular combination. Estimated utilities for golfer 1 are shown in Exhibit 14.10. As you can readily see, this set of numbers perfectly predicts the original rankings. The relationship among these numbers or utilities is fixed, though there is some arbitrariness in their magnitude. In other words, the utilities shown in Exhibit 14.10 can be multiplied or divided by any constant and the same relative results will be obtained. The exact procedures for estimating these utilities are beyond the scope of this discussion. They are normally calculated by using procedures related to regression, analysis of variance, or linear programming.

The trade-offs that golfer 1 is willing to make between "ball life" and "price" are shown in Exhibit 14.11. This information can be used to estimate a set of utilities for "price" that can be added to those for "ball life" to predict the rankings for golfer 1, as shown in Exhibit 14.12.

This step produces a complete set of utilities for all levels of the three features or attributes that successfully capture golfer 1's trade-offs. These utilities are shown in Exhibit 14.13.

> **utilities**
> The relative value of attribute levels determined through conjoint analysis.

EXHIBIT 14.10	Ranks (in parentheses) and Combined Metric Utilities for Golfer 1—Distance and Ball Life		
	Ball Life		
Distance	**54 holes** **50**	**36 holes** **25**	**18 holes** **0**
275 yards	(1) 150	(2) 125	(4) 100
250 yards	(3) 110	(5) 85	(7) 60
225 yards	(6) 50	(8) 25	(9) 0

EXHIBIT 14.11	Conjoint Rankings of Combinations of Price and Ball Life for Golfer 1		
	Ball Life		
Price	**54 holes**	**36 holes**	**18 holes**
$2.00	1	2	4
$2.50	3	5	7
$3.00	6	8	9

EXHIBIT 14.12	Ranks (in parentheses) and Combined Metric Utilities for Golfer 1—Price and Ball Life		
	Ball Life		
Price	**54 holes** **50**	**36 holes** **25**	**18 holes** **0**
$2.00	(1) 70	(2) 45	(4) 20
$2.50	(3) 55	(5) 30	(7) 5
$3.00	(6) 50	(8) 25	(9) 0

EXHIBIT 14.13	Complete Set of Estimated Utilities for Golfer 1				
Distance		**Ball Life**		**Price**	
Level	**Utility**	**Level**	**Utility**	**Level**	**Utility**
275 yards	100	54 holes	50	$1.25	20
250 yards	60	36 holes	25	$1.50	5
225 yards	0	18 holes	0	$1.75	0

Simulating Buyer Choice For various reasons, the firm might be in a position to produce only 2 of the 27 golf balls that are possible with each of the three levels of the three attributes. The possibilities are shown in Exhibit 14.14. If the calculated utilities for golfer 1 are applied to the 2 golf balls the firm is able to make, then the results are the total utilities shown in Exhibit 14.15. These results indicate that golfer 1 will prefer the ball with the longer life over the one with the greater distance because it has a higher

EXHIBIT 14.14	Ball Profiles for Simulation	
Attribute	Distance Ball	Long-Life Ball
Distance	275	250
Life	18	54
Price	$2.50	$3.00

EXHIBIT 14.15	Estimated Total Utilities for the Two Sample Profiles			
	Distance Ball		Price	
Attribute	Level	Utility	Level	Utility
Distance	275	100	250	60
Life	18	0	54	50
Price	$2.50	5	$3.00	0
Total utility	105	110		

total utility. The analyst need only repeat this process for a representative sample of golfers to estimate potential market shares for the 2 balls. In addition, the analysis can be extended to cover other golf ball combinations.

The three steps discussed here—collecting trade-off data, using the data to estimate buyer preference structures, and predicting choice—are the basis of any conjoint analysis application. Although the trade-off matrix approach is simple, useful for explaining conjoint analysis, and effective for problems with small numbers of attributes, it is currently not widely used. An easier and less time-consuming way to collect conjoint data is to have respondents rank or rate product descriptions on a paper questionnaire or to use computer-based interviewing software that applies certain rules to determine what questions and product profiles to present to each respondent based on his or her previous answers.

As suggested earlier, there is much more to conjoint analysis than has been discussed in this section. However, if you understand this simple example, then you understand the basic concepts that underlie conjoint analysis.

Data Mining[11]

Data mining is a relatively new field that draws upon statistics (including all of the tools discussed in this chapter), artificial intelligence, database management, and computer science to identify patterns in market data sets. It is an increasingly important tool for business to transform the exponentially growing quantities of digital data into business intelligence as firms seek informational advantages to improve efficiency and effectiveness. It is applied in a wide range of areas, but we are particularly interested in its applications to marketing problems. Extending our earlier comments, the primary reason for using data mining in marketing is to analyze large collections of observational, survey, or experimental data regarding buyer behavior.

Data Mining Process

Pre-processing Before we can apply data mining tools, we must assemble a target data set relevant to the problem of interest. Data mining can only uncover patterns and relationships in the data we feed into them. Typically, the data set we are using must be large enough to include all the patterns that exist in the real world, though not so large as to make the assembly too costly or too time-consuming. Once assembled, the data set must be cleaned in a process where we remove those observations that contain excessive noise or error and missing data.

The actual data mining process typically involves four classes of tasks:[12]

- *Clustering*—This is a task of discovering groups and structures in the data that are similar on certain, selected sets of variables. These are groupings that are not obvious and are not based on a single set of variables or just a few of them. We normally evaluate a number of solutions to decide which one to use. Cluster analysis is commonly used to address as the tool for this type of analysis.

- *Classification*—Here, we apply the structure we identified with cluster analysis or some other technique to another subset of the same data. For example, we might apply customer segments identified in the clustering process using a subset of data or data from a survey to an entire customer database. If the results are similar to what we achieved in the first step then we move ahead. Otherwise, we need to go back and reanalyze.

- *Modeling*—Here, we use regression or a similar technique to model the relationship or predict subgroup membership when we mask the membership identified as described above. We are looking for high predictive accuracy, and if we don't get it then we need to repeat the previous steps.

- *Application*—If we have successfully completed the first three steps, then we are ready to put what we have learned to work to improve the efficiency and effectiveness of our marketing efforts. For example, if we get a sales inquiry, we might get enough information from the inquirer to classify them into a market segment and then provide information on the version of our product or service known to be most preferred by members of that segment, stress the sales points known to be most likely to resonate with members of that segment, and so on.

Results Validation

A final step of knowledge discovery from the target data and modeling is to attempt to verify the patterns produced by the data mining algorithms in the wider data set. Not every pattern and relationship we identify in the previous steps turns out to be valid in the real world. In the evaluation process, we use a test data set that was not used to develop the data mining algorithm. The patterns that we identified or learned are applied to the test data, and the resulting output is compared to the desired output. For example, a data mining algorithm developed to predict those most likely to respond to a mail offer would be developed or trained on certain past mail offers. Once developed or trained, the algorithm developed from the test mailings would be applied to either other mailings not used in the development of the algorithm or to actual results from a mailing recently completed. If the data mining algorithm does not meet the desired accuracy standards, then it is necessary to go through the previous steps again in order to develop an algorithm or model with the desired level of accuracy.

Privacy Concerns and Ethics

Most believe that data mining itself is ethically neutral. However, the ways in which data mining can be used raise ethical questions regarding privacy, legality, and ethics. For example, data mining data sets for national security or law enforcement purposes has raised privacy concerns.

Commercial Data Mining Software and Applications

There are an increasing number of highly integrated packages for data mining, including:

- SAS Enterprise Miner
- SPSS Modeler
- *STATISTICA* Data Miner

SUMMARY

Regression analysis enables a researcher to predict the magnitude of a dependent variable based on the levels of more than one independent variable. Regression analysis fits a plane to observations in a multidimensional space. One statistic that results from regression analysis is called the coefficient of determination, or R^2. The value of this statistic ranges from 0 to 1. It provides a measure of the percentage of the variation in the dependent variable that is explained by variation in the independent variables. The b values, or regression coefficients, indicate the effect of the individual independent variables on the dependent variable.

Cluster analysis enables a researcher to identify subgroups of individuals or objects that are homogeneous within the subgroup, yet different from other subgroups. Cluster analysis requires that all independent variables be metric, but there is no specification of a dependent variable. Cluster analysis is an excellent means for operationalizing the concept of market segmentation.

The purpose of factor analysis is to simplify massive amounts of data. The objective is to summarize the information contained in a large number of metric measures such as rating scales with a smaller number of summary measures called factors. As in cluster analysis, there is no dependent variable in factor analysis. Factor analysis produces factors, each of which is a weighted composite of a set of related variables. Each measure is weighted according to how much it contributes to the variation of each factor. Factor loadings are determined by calculating the correlation coefficient between factor scores and the original input variables. By examining which variables load heavily on a given factor, the researcher can subjectively name that factor.

Perceptual maps can be produced by means of factor analysis, multidimensional scaling, discriminant analysis, or correspondence analysis. The maps provide a visual representation of how brands, products, companies, and other objects are perceived relative to each other on key features such as quality and value. All the approaches require, as input, consumer evaluations or ratings of the objects in question on some set of key characteristics.

Conjoint analysis is a technique that can be used to measure the trade-offs potential buyers make on the basis of the features of each product or service available to them. The technique permits the researcher to determine the relative value of each level of each feature. These estimated values are called utilities and can be used as a basis for simulating consumer choice.

Data mining draws on statistics, artificial intelligence, and computer science to identify patterns in market data sets. It is becoming increasingly important as the amount of data available grows exponentially.

KEY TERMS & DEFINITIONS

correlation analysis Analysis of the degree to which changes in one variable are associated with changes in another.

Pearson's product–moment correlation A correlation analysis technique for use with metric data.

coefficient of determination A measure of the percentage of the variation in the dependent variable explained by variations in the independent variables.

regression coefficients Estimates of the effect of individual independent variables on the dependent variable.

regression analysis A procedure for predicting the level or magnitude of a (metric) dependent variable based on the levels of multiple independent variables.

coefficient of determination A measure of the percentage of the variation in the dependent variable explained by variations in the independent variables.

regression coefficients Estimates of the effect of individual independent variables on the dependent variable.

dummy variables In regression analysis, a way of representing two-group or dichotomous, nominally scaled independent variables by coding one group as 0 and the other as 1.

collinearity The correlation of independent variables with each other, which can bias estimates of regression coefficients.

causation Inference that a change in one variable is responsible for (caused) an observed change in another variable.

scaling of coefficients A method of directly comparing the magnitudes of the regression coefficients of independent variables by scaling them in the same units or by standardizing the data.

cluster analysis A general term for statistical procedures that classify objects or people into some number of mutually exclusive and exhaustive groups on the basis of two or more classification variables.

factor analysis A procedure for simplifying data by reducing a large set of variables to a smaller set of factors or composite variables by identifying underlying dimensions of the data.

factor A linear combination of variables that are correlated with each other.

factor loading Correlation between factor scores and the original variables.

conjoint analysis A procedure used to quantify the value that consumers associate with different levels of product/service attributes or features.

utilities The relative value of attribute levels determined through conjoint analysis.

QUESTIONS FOR REVIEW & CRITICAL THINKING

1. What purpose does regression analysis serve? Give an example of how it might be used in marketing research. How is the strength of regression measures of association determined?

2. What is a dummy variable? Give an example using a dummy variable.

3. Describe the potential problem of collinearity in multiple regression. How might a researcher test for collinearity? If collinearity is a problem, what should the researcher do?

4. A sales manager examined age data, education level, a personality factor that indicated level of introvertedness/extrovertedness, and level of sales attained by the company's 120-person salesforce. The technique used was regression analysis. After analyzing the data, the sales manager said, "It is apparent to me that the higher the level of education and the greater the degree of extrovertedness a salesperson has, the higher will be an individual's level of sales. In other words, a good education and being extroverted cause a person to sell more." Would you agree or disagree with the sales manager's conclusions? Why?

5. The factors produced and the results of the factor loadings from factor analysis are mathematical constructs. It is the task of the researcher to make sense out of these factors. The following table lists four factors produced from a study of cable TV viewers. What label would you put on each of these four factors? Why?

		Factor Loading
Factor 1	I don't like the way cable TV movie channels repeat the movies over and over.	.79
	The movie channels on cable need to spread their movies out (longer times between repeats).	.75
	I think the cable movie channels just run the same things over and over and over.	.73
	After a while, you've seen all the pay movies, so why keep cable service.	.53
Factor 2	I love to watch love stories.	.76
	I like a TV show that is sensitive and emotional.	.73
	Sometimes I cry when I watch movies on TV.	.65
	I like to watch "made for TV" movies.	.54
Factor 3	I like the religious programs on TV (negative correlation).	−.76
	I don't think TV evangelism is good.	.75
	I do not like religious programs.	.61
Factor 4	I would rather watch movies at home than go to the movies.	.63
	I like cable because you don't have to go out to see the movies.	.55
	I prefer cable TV movies because movie theaters are too expensive.	.46

6. The following table shows regression coefficients for two dependent variables. The first dependent variable is willingness to spend money for cable TV. The independent variables are responses to attitudinal statements. The second dependent variable is stated desire never to allow cable TV in their homes. By examining the regression coefficients, what can you say about persons willing to spend money for cable TV and those who will not allow cable TV in their homes?

	Regression Coefficients
Willing to Spend Money for Cable TV	
Easygoing on cable repairs	−3.04
Cable movie watcher	2.81
Comedy watcher	2.73
Early to bed	−2.62

(Continued)

Breakdown complainer	2.25
Lovelorn	2.18
Burned out on repeats	−2.06
Never Allow Cable TV in Home	
Antisports	0.37
Object to sex	0.47
Too many choices	0.88

WORKING THE NET

1. For a demonstration of TwoStep cluster analysis using a scalable cluster analysis algorithm, visit *www.spss.com/spss/data_analysis.htm.*
2. For some easy-to-digest and comprehensive information on multivariate analysis, visit *http://core.ecu.edu/psyc/wuenschk/spss/SPSS-MV.htm.*

REAL-LIFE RESEARCH • 14.1

Custom Car Wash Systems

Custom Car Wash Systems offers car wash franchises throughout the United States. Currently, 872 car washes franchised by Custom are in operation. As part of its service to franchisees, Custom runs a national marketing and advertising program.

Carl Bahn is the senior vice president in charge of marketing for Custom. He is currently in the process of designing the marketing and advertising campaigns for the upcoming year. Bahn believes that it is time for Custom to take a more careful look at user segments in the market. Based on other analyses, he and his associates at Custom have decided that the upcoming campaign should target the heavy user market. Through other research, Custom has defined "heavy car wash users" as those individuals who have their cars washed at a car wash facility three or more times per month on average. "Light users" are defined as those who use such a facility less than three times a month but at least four times a year. "Nonusers" are defined as those who use such a facility less than four times per year.

Bahn and his associates are currently in the process of attempting to identify those factors that discriminate between heavy and light users. In the first stage of this analysis, Custom conducted interviews with 50 customers at 100 of its locations for a total of 5,000 interviews. Cross tabulation of the classification variables with frequency of use suggests that four variables may be predictive of usage heaviness: vehicle owner age, annual income of vehicle owner, age of vehicle, and socioeconomic status of vehicle owner (based on an index of socioeconomic variables).

Custom retained a marketing research firm called Marketing Metrics to do further analysis for the company. Marketing Metrics evaluated the situation and decided to use multiple discriminant analysis to further analyze the survey results and identify the relative importance of each of the four variables in determining whether a particular individual is a heavy or light user. The firm obtained the following results:

$$Z = .18X_1 + .53X_2 - .49X_3 + .93X_4$$

where
X_1 = age of vehicle owner
X_2 = annual income of vehicle owner
X_3 = age of vehicle
X_4 = socioeconomic status of owner (as measured by an index in which a higher score means higher status)

Questions

1. What would you tell Bahn about the importance of each predictor variable?
2. What recommendations would you make to him about the type of people Custom should target, based on its interest in communicating with heavy users?

SPSS EXERCISES FOR CHAPTER 14

Exercise 1: Regression Analysis

This exercise uses regression analysis to explain and predict how many movies a respondent attends in a month.

1. Go to the Web site for the text and download the Movie database.
2. Open the database in SPSS and view the variables under Variable View. We will be using the independent variables Q2 Q4 Q6 Q8a Q8b Q8c Q8d Q9 Q10 Q12 and Q13 to predict the dependent variable Q3.
   We are including the variables Q4 and Q6 as is. Strictly speaking, is this proper? What might you want to do instead and why? Why might you decide to leave a variable in bins instead? Would it ever be proper to use a variable like Q11 as is?

3. Go to Analyze → Descriptive Statistics → Descriptives and move Q3 Q2 Q4 Q6 Q8a Q8b Q8c Q8d Q9 Q10 Q12 and Q13 to the Variable(s) box and click OK. Regression analysis requires that every variable have a legitimate value. If a respondent did not answer every question, then the analyst must either ignore the observation entirely or impute estimates for the missing values. The default for statistical software is to ignore those observations automatically. We will not do imputation for this exercise.

a. Is this sample size large enough for regression analysis?

b. What would some possible problems be if the sample size were not large enough?

c. Are the minimum and maximum values for each variable within the proper range? A value that is out of range would indicate either a data input error or a user-defined missing value like "Refused" or "Don't Know." Data input errors should be corrected or deleted. User-defined missing values should be declared in SPSS.

d. Are all the variables within the proper range?

4. Go to Analyze → Regression → Linear.
   Move Q3 to Dependent.
   Move Q2 Q4 Q6 Q8a Q8b Q8c Q8d Q9 Q10 Q12 Q13 to Independent(s).
   Change Method to Stepwise.
   Click OK.

   a. Which independent variables did the stepwise regression select? Why not the rest?

   b. Is each variable chosen significant?

   c. Are the variables that have not been chosen necessarily insignificant?

   d. Is the model significant?

   e. Does this method guarantee that you get the "best" model?

5. Go to Analyze → Descriptive Statistics → Descriptives and remove Q6 Q8a Q8b Q8c Q8d Q9 Q10 and Q12 from the Variable(s) box, so that only Q3 Q2 Q4 and Q13 remain in the box and then click OK.
   What is the sample size now?

6. Go to Analyze → Regression → Linear.
   Move Q3 to Dependent.
   Remove Q6 Q8a Q8b Q8c Q8d Q9 Q10 and Q12 from Independent(s) so that only Q2 Q4 and Q13 remain.
   Change Method to Enter.
   Click OK.

   a. How and why does this model differ from the model based on stepwise regression?

   b. Which model is better?

Interpretation

1. How does stated importance affect the number of times one attends movies?

2. How does spending money on snacks affect the number of times one attends movies?

3. How does student classification affect the number of times one attends movies?

4. If a sophomore thought that going to the movies was somewhat important and typically spent $12 on snacks, how many times per month would he or she attend movies based on this model?

5. Do any of the variables, according to the results, appear to have an effect on the number of times one attends movies, or does it seem that other factors not covered in this survey are driving movie attendance?

Exercise 2: Factor Analysis

This exercise uses factor analysis to explore how survey respondents consider various aspects of a theater visit.

1. Go to the Web site for the text and download the Movie database.

2. Open the database in SPSS and view the variables under Variable View. Notice that question 5 has 9 importance rating items.

3. Go to Analyze → Descriptive Statistics → Descriptives and move Q5a through Q5i to the Variable(s) box and click OK.

   a. Which item is the most important?
   b. Which item is the least important?

   Factor analysis requires that every variable have a legitimate value. If a respondent did not answer every question, then the analyst must either ignore the observation entirely or impute estimates for the missing values. The default for statistical software is to ignore those observations automatically. We will not get involved with imputation for this exercise.

   a. Is this sample size large enough for factor analysis?
   b. What would some possible problems be if the sample size were not large enough?
   c. It is a good idea to check that the minimum and maximum values for each variable are within the proper range. A value that is out of range indicates either a data input error or a user-defined missing value such as "Refused" or "Don't Know." Data input errors should be corrected or deleted. User-defined missing values should be declared in SPSS.
   d. Are all the variables within the proper range?

4. Go to Analyze → Descriptive Statistics → Descriptives and move Q5a through Q5i to the Variables box and click OK.

   Examine the resulting correlations matrix.

   a. Other than the 1's down the main diagonal of the matrix, what is the highest correlation in absolute value?
   b. Does any variable "just not fit" with the others?
   c. Does multicollinearity appear to exist among some of the items?

5. Go to Analyze → Data Reduction → Factor.

   Move Q5a through Q5i to the Variables box.
   Click the Rotation button, place a check in front of "Varimax," and click Continue.
   Click the Options button.
   Place a check in front of "Sorted by size."
   Place a check in front of "Suppress absolute values less than" and set the value after it to .25.
   Click Continue.
   Click OK.
   SPSS produces a lot of output Factor Analysis. It is possible to create much more output than we have generated here by setting various subcommands and options.

   a. How many factors did SPSS create?
   b. Why did it stop at that number?
   c. How could you change the defaults to create a different number of factors?

surveysolutions XP

d. Go to the output entitled Total Variance Explained. How much variance was explained in this Factor Analysis?

e. Go to the output entitled Rotated Component Matrix. Why are some elements in this matrix blank?

f. Do the components or factors make sense?

g. Can you identify a common theme for each component or factor?

Interpretation

1. Is this a good factor solution? Why do you say that?

2. How might you create a better factor solution?

3. What understanding has this analysis helped you gain about how moviegoers perceive their movie-going experience?

4. What recommendations would you give a manager of a movie house based on this analysis?

© It Stock Free/Age Fotostock America, Inc.

Communicating Results and Managing Marketing Research

CHAPTER 15

→ **8.** To gain insights into the unique management issues of managing a corporate marketing research department.

→ **9.** To see what marketing research departments are doing to gain a more strategic role in the corporation.

→ **10.** To examine how corporations are measuring the contribution of marketing research to the organization.

Here's a common scenario troubling many excellent researchers: Your research group is too successful. You've been head of your research department for more than a year and are worried. Things have been going very well since you took over—maybe too well. While research was sometimes an afterthought under your predecessor, you have worked hard to make your research indispensable. By having in-depth project planning conversations and using project approval forms, you have made sure that each research design fits client needs and objectives. By using state-of-the-art research methodologies and best-in-class suppliers, you have made sure that your methodologies and analyses are the best possible. By coaching your staff and hiring experienced people with a range of skills, you have several senior people in your department who think and act like consultants. And they are able to work with your clients to plan the research objectives, as well as the actions to be taken when the research is completed.

More and more clients have noticed the improvements, and they are asking for more and more research. In fact, your research volume has nearly doubled in the last year. You are being invited to participate in top management meetings, as well as in the firm's strategic planning.

So what's the problem? There's too much work, and too few resources are available. Your staff is rapidly burning out. They are starting to skip staff meetings and are too busy to build relationships among themselves or with clients between projects. When you manage to break away to attend conferences, you and your staff find yourselves working your BlackBerrys—instead of building your skills and connections. You have streamlined your basic research processes by simplifying project sign-offs, using preferred suppliers, creating report and presentation templates, and blueprinting work flow—but there is no more "fat" in your work that you can cut.

Clients keep asking you for more work. And when you politely say you are working at capacity right now, they respond by saying that they are willing to pay for the projects they want. You are simply drowning and are afraid that your work quality will soon suffer if you don't do something quickly.[1]

The above scenario, described by two marketing research consultants, cries out for better management. In this chapter we will explore how to effectively manage marketing research. This process begins with effectively communicating the research results. We will cover this important topic first. We will then examine research management from the perspective of both the research supplier and the corporate research department.

The Research Report

A good researcher is anticipating the report almost from the time she writes the proposal for a project, before she even has the business. The genesis of the report and the researcher's thinking are the objectives provided by the client in the request for proposal (RFP). Along with any background information provided with the RFP or developed as part of the process of preparing the proposal, the objectives give the researcher insight into the client's thinking and needs. What problem/opportunity is the client organization facing? What resources and competencies can it bring to bear on the problem or opportunity? What decisions is the client facing, and what information is it going to need to make those decisions in the most effective manner? If the researcher does not get a handle on these issues, then that failure will be reflected in the resulting proposal, and she probably will not get the job to begin with.

Given that we are about to write the report, we have to assume that the researcher did understand the client's needs and wrote a proposal, including a detailed methodology, that resonated with the client to the extent that she was chosen to do the work over the other competitors.

The research objectives, the decisions to be made based on the research, and a vision of the analysis and the report to be written should have guided the researcher through the design and execution of the research. For a survey-based project, the development of the questionnaire, in particular, should have been based on continuous reference to the research objectives. Now, we have the data, it has been cross-tabulated, statistical testing has been performed, extensive statistical analysis has been conducted, and the researcher and her team have spent time sifting through all of this information and relating it back to the original objectives and the decisions associated with those objectives. This process could go on and on, but deadlines in the schedule push the process to a conclusion, often faster than we would like.

The researcher has a tremendous amount of information—piles of crosstabs, reams of statistical analyses, tons of notes, and an assortment of other pieces of information. The challenge is: How to package all of this in a coherent report that efficiently and effectively communicates the key findings and the decision implications of those findings? We like to think of this process as one of trying to figure out how to tell a story. Before you can tell a story, you have to have a pretty good idea of where the story is going to end up. All the analysis brings one to that conclusion. Once you know or have ascertained the key points that you want to make, it becomes much easier to map out what you need to get across to your readers to bring them to that same conclusion.

It is important that a research firm have a consistent style for reporting. This puts all analysts on the same page so that even a glance at a report will tell clients it was produced by a certain research firm. Having said all this, we must admit that when a client has a different internal standard for reporting, it is sometimes necessary to follow a different approach than the one recommended above. In some cases, the client may even dictate that the research supplier produce the report on the client's PowerPoint template according to the client's style rules.

Organizing the Report

The traditional research report follows an outline like the following one:

1. *Title page*—The title page should be dominated by the name of the project. Other elements that should be included are the name of the client organization, name of the research firm, and date of the report.

2. *Table of contents*—This should not exceed one page and should list the major sections of the report along with the page numbers on which they start. It is a convenience for the reader and, often, the researcher in that it permits quick reference for finding specific information in the report.

3. *Executive summary*—This is perhaps the most difficult part of the report to write because it must succinctly cover the key findings and any recommendations that flow from those findings. Not all reports include recommendations. Whether they include recommendations depends on the nature of the research, what is expected

from the research firm, and what the research found. However, all research reports should include key findings. What makes it tough to do the executive summary is that it should be short (two to four pages at a maximum), and many researchers find it very difficult to summarize the massive amount of information available to them in just two to four pages. It is easy to be long winded, but it is difficult to be compact in your summarization. The executive summary should not summarize every single finding but should focus on those findings that are important and relevant to the goals of the research.

4. *Background*—The background sets the context for the research and addresses such things as the overall goal of the research, the decisions that need to be made, the company's strength and weaknesses regarding the issue in question, and other similar information. It should not be more than one or two pages. Again, it is often difficult to compress a lot of information down to its essentials.

5. *Methodology*—Here we should discuss how the research was done and why it was done that way. Issues that need to be addressed include who was interviewed, why did we interview those people, how were they interviewed (for example, telephone survey, mail survey, Internet survey, or some hybrid of these methods), why were they interviewed in that manner, how were people selected, what type of sampling methodology did we use, whether the sample is a representative sample, how many people did we interview, how were the completed surveys processed, what special statistical procedures were used and why did we use those procedures, and so forth. It is not necessary that this section be long—one to two pages is appropriate. If it is necessary to address some technical elements of the methodology in a more extensive manner, then more detailed information on, for example, statistical procedures used should be provided in an appendix.

6. *Findings*—This is typically the longest section of the report and should summarize results for almost every question on the survey.

7. *Appendixes*—This final section of the report provides a number of supporting items such as a copy of the questionnaire, a set of cross tabulations for every question on the survey (client can look up specific issues not addressed in the findings), and other supporting material such as detailed technical information on special research procedures and techniques.

Interpreting the Findings

The most difficult task for individuals preparing reports for the first time is interpreting the findings to arrive at conclusions and then using these conclusions to formulate recommendations. The **executive summary** is the portion of the report that explains what the research found, what the data mean, and what action, if any, should be taken, based on the research. The difficulties of this process are completely understandable, given that the marketing researcher is often inundated with piles of computer printouts, stacks of questionnaires, hundreds of pages of cross tabulations, the results of hundreds of statistical tests, pages and pages of statistical analysis printouts, and a scratch pad full of notes on the project. There is, however, a systematic method that the researcher can follow to draw conclusions.

The research objectives and background stated early in the marketing research process should serve as the primary guide for interpreting findings and drawing conclusions. These objectives should have been stated as specifically as possible, perhaps even with an explicit priority rank for each objective. Although the questionnaire should have been designed to touch on all facets of the objectives, specific bits of information about any one objective may be spread across the questionnaire. Computer printouts often contain

> ➤ **executive summary**
> The portion of a research report that explains why the research was done, what was found, what those findings mean, and what action, if any, management should undertake.

information in statistical order rather than in the order in which managers will use the data. Consequently, the researcher's first task is to pull together all the printouts and results that pertain to each of the various objectives. A system will evolve as the researcher focuses attention on the objectives one at a time.

For example, assume that Burger King is reconsidering its breakfast menu. An objective of its breakfast research study is "to determine the feasibility of adding (1) bagels and cream cheese, (2) a western omelette, or (3) French toast." All cross tabulations and one-dimensional tables referring to these food items should be brought together. Generally, the researcher first examines the one-dimensional tables to get the overall picture—that is, understand which of the three breakfast items was most preferred. Next, cross tabulations are analyzed to obtain a better understanding of the overall data—that is, to get a clear view of which age group is most likely to prefer French toast.

Conclusions are generalizations that answer the questions raised by the research objectives or otherwise satisfy the objectives. These conclusions are derived through the process of *induction,* or generalizing from small pieces of information. The researcher should try to merge the information and then paraphrase it in a few descriptive statements that generalize the results. In short, the conclusion of a research report should be a statement or series of statements that communicate the results of the study to the reader but would not necessarily include any of the data derived from the statistical analysis. Some of the challenges in communicating results to clients are covered in the Practicing Marketing Research feature on page 398.

> **conclusions**
> Generalizations that answer the questions raised by the research objectives or otherwise satisfy the objectives.

Format of the Report

The format and preparation of marketing research reports have changed dramatically over the past 15 years. The pressure to find more efficient and effective ways to communicate research results has pushed researchers toward a heavy reliance on presentation software to tell their stories. Microsoft's PowerPoint dominates the market today.

A typical marketing research report tells its story with pictures or graphics. This is what clients expect the researcher to deliver. It is not unusual for clients to specify that they want graphics-based reports in their RFPs. Research reports that might have included 50 or more pages of text and a handful of graphs in the past are now presented in a limited amount of text, perhaps just a few pages if it were all strung together, and 20 or 30 pages of graphs and tables. This approach enables time-pressed executives to quickly grasp the story and the key findings and move ahead to conclusions and recommendations.

Graphics, text boxes, bulleted lists, and the like are used to interpret the meaning of various graphs. Examples of pages from a report prepared using presentation software are provided in Exhibits 15.1 through 15.9.

Formulating Recommendations

Recommendations are gained from the process of deduction. The analyst applies the conclusions to specific areas in order to make suggestions for marketing strategies or tactics. A recommendation usually focuses on how the client can gain a differential advantage. A *differential advantage* is a true benefit offered by a potential marketing mix that the target market cannot obtain anywhere else (for example, American Airlines having exclusive U.S. carrier landing rights at a foreign airport).

In some cases, a marketing researcher must refrain from making specific recommendations and instead fall back on more general ones. For example, the marketing researcher might not have sufficient information about the resources and experience base of the company or about the decision maker to whom the report is being directed. Or the researcher may have

> **recommendations**
> Conclusions applied to marketing strategies or tactics that focus on a client's achievement of differential advantage.

PRACTICING MARKETING RESEARCH

Lost in Translation: Challenges Researchers Face in Communicating Their Results to Clients[2]

For anyone in a specialized field like market research, there comes a point at which the specialist must figure out how to communicate this expertise to those who do not have that kind of expertise. For market researchers, even long-standing clients at some point will want an explanation of the researcher's methodology—but these methodologies are often complex. Communicating this information accurately, however, can be critical for clients as they make strategic decisions.

Market researchers generally face two major challenges to producing compelling research for clients. First, they must use their research to convey a practical view of the world. Second, they must apply the appropriate level of analytics.

Researchers often make mistakes facing the first challenge when they view their analysis in a vacuum or reduce it to a one- or two-dimensional view. Researchers must discipline themselves to analyze research data based on multiple dimensions. Because of the great diversity of the market, researchers who view trends from a single dimension are likely to miss particular opportunities. A segmentation approach can help researchers produce a more complete picture of the groups of people the client wishes to identify.

The primary difficulty in confronting the second challenge—determining the appropriate level of analytics to apply—is that the necessary level of analytics varies directly with the ease of understanding the data. So as the analytics uncover more granular details, it becomes increasingly more difficult to see the broader picture. Researchers may be tempted to oversimplify things in an effort to make them more accessible to their clients, but this only results in thin, unreliable analysis. And complex and jargon-filled reports ultimately offer clients no insight at all. It is not easy to balance these extremes, so understanding the client's needs and what they are willing to pay for is a solid place to start. Once the client's expectations are known, the strategies for making deeper analysis more accessible will become more apparent.

Researchers should not hesitate to exercise their capabilities. By addressing the challenges of producing research that reflects real-life situations and analysis that is both clear and sufficiently deep, researchers can greatly help clients improve their profitability.

Questions

1. Which of these two challenges do you think is the more difficult to address? Why?

2. How would you go about clarifying the client's needs and expectations? What kinds of issues would you look for, and what kinds of questions would you ask?

been notified that the recommendations will be determined by the decision maker. Under these circumstances, the researcher offers conclusions and stops at that point.

The final report represents the culmination of the research effort. The quality of the report and its recommendations often determine whether a client will return to a supplier. Within a corporation, an internal report prepared by a research department may have less impact, but a history of preparing excellent reports may lead to merit salary increases and, ultimately, promotion for a research staff member.

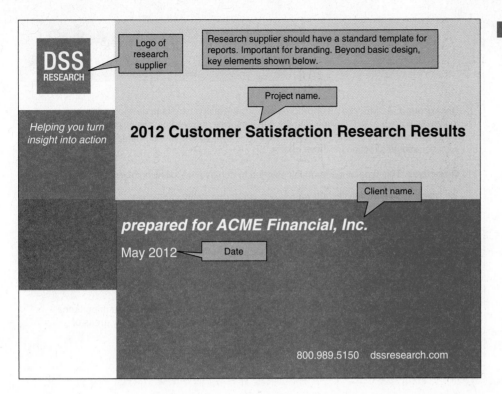

Exhibit 15.1

Sample Title Slide

DSS
RESEARCH

Helping you turn
insight into action

Logo of
research
supplier

Research supplier should have a standard template for
reports. Important for branding. Beyond basic design,
key elements shown below.

Project name.

2012 Customer Satisfaction Research Results

Client name.

prepared for ACME Financial, Inc.

May 2012   Date

800.989.5150   dssresearch.com

Exhibit 15.2

**Sample Table
of Contents**

Table of Contents

Not more than a page. Helps user refer to specific areas
of interest. Lists major sections.

Exhibit 15.3

Sample Background and Objective

Keep it concise. Put key objectives in bulleted list.

Background and Objectives

Background. ACME, like other progressive organizations, wants to develop a program to assess customer satisfaction with the services they receive from the organization. This information will be used in ACME's quality improvement efforts. The goal is to provide rational direction for those efforts.

Objectives. This type of research is designed to achieve the following objectives:

- Measure overall satisfaction with ACME compared to the competition.
- Measure customer satisfaction with ACME's new Web site where all transactions with ACME can be handled.
- Measure satisfaction with specific elements of all other programs and services provided to customers by ACME.
- Identify major reasons for satisfaction/dissatisfaction.
- Evaluate and classify program and service elements on the basis of their importance to customers and ACME's perceived performance of ACME (i.e., identify areas of strength and opportunities for improvement).

2012 Customer Satisfaction Research | ACME Financial | May 2012   2   DSS Research

Exhibit 15.4

Sample First Page of Executive Summary

Focus on key findings, not just reiteration of detailed results.

Executive Summary

The majority are loyal, but satisfaction declined.

- Four out of five customers see their relationship with ACME continuing on a long-term basis. Over half are categorized as secure or favorable and can be considered loyal to ACME.
- Two-thirds report they are satisfied with ACME in 2010. However, this is a significant decline from 80.1% in 2010.
- ACME overall satisfaction and loyalty measures are significantly lower than the National Average.

Heavy Users are highly satisfied; Light Users less so.

- Heavy users report significantly higher satisfaction than light users and are more likely to see their relationship with ACME continuing on a long-term basis.
- Although only a small percentage of customers is categorized as alienated, Light Users make up a higher proportion of this group.

ACME processes are primary areas of strength.

- Both the customer service and application processes are identified through key driver analysis as areas of strength for ACME.
- Satisfaction with the billing process continues an upward trend. Ratings are on par with the National Average and significantly higher than 2011.

Staff ratings remain strong, with knowledge a key asset.

- The majority of customers are satisfied with all aspects relatedto ACME staff. About four out of five are satisfied with staff knowledge, the area of highest satisfaction across all staff levels.
- Although still high, relatively lower staff ratings are associated with accessibility related measures. Key driver analysis identifies ease of reaching staff as an opportunity forimprovement.

2012 Customer Satisfaction Research | ACME Financial | May 2012   3   DSS Research

Exhibit 15.5

Sample Methodology Slide

Explain what was done in a simple, straightforward manner.	Methodology

Questionnaire. DSS was responsible for developing the survey instrument. ACME approved the final draft of the questionnaire. A copy of the mail survey instrument used is provided in Appendix B.

Methodology employed. Eligible respondents included a list of customers provided by ACME. The sample design is as follows:

	2012			2011			2010		
	Heavy Users	Light Users	Overall	Heavy Users	Light Users	Overall	Heavy Users	Light Users	Overall
Completed surveys	52	60	112	101	71	172	87	71	158
Mailed Surveys	200	200	400	200	200	400	200	200	400
Returned undeliverable surveys	NA	NA	4	NA	NA	8	NA	NA	14
Response rate	26.0%	30.0%	28.0%	50.5%	35.5%	43.0%	43.5%	35.5%	39.5%
Adjusted response rate**	NA	NA	28.3%	NA	NA	43.9%	NA	NA	40.9%
Sample error*	NA	NA	±7.9%	NA	NA	±5.6%	NA	NA	±6.1%
Initial survey mailed	February 28, 2012			March 7, 2011			February 28, 2010		
Second survey mailed	March 21, 2012			March 28, 2011			March 21, 2010		
Last day to accept surveys	April 27, 2012			May 2, 2011			April 25, 2010		

Data collection. All data were collected by DSS Research.

Data processing and analysis. DSS processed all completed surveys and analyzed the results. A complete set of survey tabulations is provided in Appendix C of this report.

* At 95% confidence, using the most pessimistic assumption regarding variance (p=0.5).
** Excludes undeliverables.

2012 Customer Satisfaction Research | ACME Financial | May 2012   4   DSS Research

---

Exhibit 15.6

Graphics Make Communication More Efficient

Slide takeaways summarize key points. Plan loyalty	Over half of customers are categorized as secure or favorable and can be considered loyal to ACME. Another one in four is at risk though not necessarily dissatisfied. Only a small percentage is categorized as alienated; however specialists make up a greater proportion of this group.

Loyalty Analysis

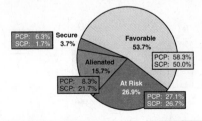

National Average	
Secure:	11.8%
Favorable:	61.1%
At risk:	21.4%
Alienated:	5.6%

Secure 3.7% — PCP: 6.3% SCP: 1.7%
Favorable 53.7% — PCP: 58.3% SCP: 50.0%
Alienated 15.7% — PCP: 8.3% SCP: 21.7%
At Risk 26.9% — PCP: 27.1% SCP: 26.7%

Questions used to determine "loyalty":

- Q13 - Overall, how satisfied are you with ACME? *Very satisfied, satisfied, dissatisfied, very dissatisfied*
- Q15 - Would you recommend ACME to your patients who asked your advice about which managed care plan to join? *Definitely yes, probably yes, probably not, definitely not*
- Q16 - Would you recommend ACME to a physician who was interested in contracting with a managed care plan? *Definitely yes, probably yes, probably not, definitely not*
- Q17 - I see my relationship with ACME continuing on a long-term basis. *Strongly agree, agree, disagree, strongly disagree*

Definitions of groups:

- **Secure** –Top box answer on all four questions. Very satisfied and loyal to ACME.
- **Favorable** –Top-two-box answer on all four questions (but not top box on all four). Satisfied and fairly loyal to ACME.
- **At Risk**–Bottom-two-box answer on one, two or three (but not all) of the four questions. Not necessarily satisfied and has questionable loyalty to ACME.
- **Alienated**–Bottom-two-box answer on all four questions. Dissatisfied and likely to leave ACME.

2012 Customer Satisfaction Research | ACME Financial | May 2012   5   DSS Research

Exhibit 15.7

Multiple Graphics Provide Summary on a Topic

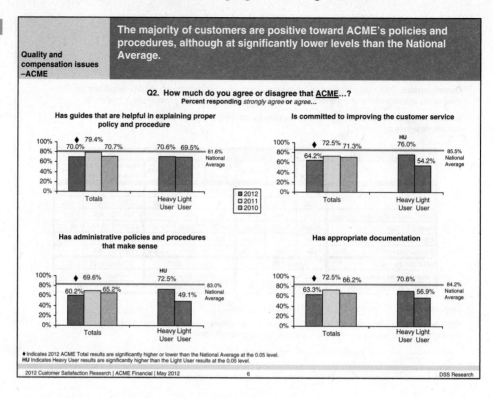

Exhibit 15.8

Graphic and Table Work Together

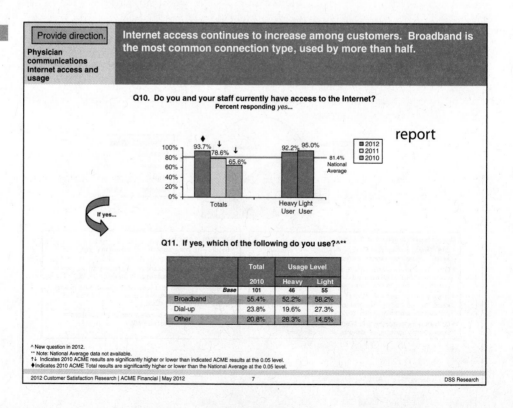

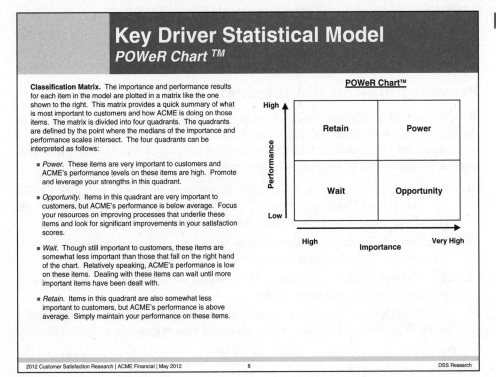

Exhibit 15.9

Graphic and Text Tell How to Interpret Statistical Results

Key Driver Statistical Model
POWeR Chart ™

Classification Matrix. The importance and performance results for each item in the model are plotted in a matrix like the one shown to the right. This matrix provides a quick summary of what is most important to customers and how ACME is doing on those items. The matrix is divided into four quadrants. The quadrants are defined by the point where the medians of the importance and performance scales intersect. The four quadrants can be interpreted as follows:

- *Power.* These items are very important to customers and ACME's performance levels on these items are high. Promote and leverage your strengths in this quadrant.

- *Opportunity.* Items in this quadrant are very important to customers, but ACME's performance is below average. Focus your resources on improving processes that underlie these items and look for significant improvements in your satisfaction scores.

- *Wait.* Though still important to customers, these items are somewhat less important than those that fall on the right hand of the chart. Relatively speaking, ACME's performance is low on these items. Dealing with these items can wait until more important items have been dealt with.

- *Retain.* Items in this quadrant are also somewhat less important to customers, but ACME's performance is above average. Simply maintain your performance on these items.

POWeR Chart™

(Chart: Performance (Low–High) vs. Importance (High–Very High), with four quadrants: Retain, Power, Wait, Opportunity)

2012 Customer Satisfaction Research | ACME Financial | May 2012   8   DSS Research

The Presentation

Clients may expect a presentation of the research results. A presentation serves many purposes. It requires that the interested parties assemble and become reacquainted with the research objectives and methodology. It also brings to light any unexpected events or findings and highlights the research conclusions. In fact, for some decision makers in the company, the presentation will be their *only* exposure to the findings; they will never read the report. Other managers may only skim the written report, using it as a memory-recall trigger for points made in the presentation. In short, effective communication in the presentation is absolutely critical.

Making a Presentation

An effective presentation is tailored to the audience. It takes into account the receivers' frame of reference, attitudes, prejudices, educational background, and time constraints. The speaker must select words, concepts, and illustrative figures to which the audience can relate. A good presentation allows time for questions and discussion.

One reason presentations are sometimes inadequate is that the speaker lacks an understanding of the barriers to effective communication. A second factor is that the speaker fails to recognize or admit that the purpose of many research reports is persuasion. *Persuasion* does not imply stretching or bending the truth, but rather using research findings to reinforce conclusions and recommendations. In preparing a presentation, the researcher should keep the following questions in mind:

- What do the data really mean?
- What impact do they have?
- What have we learned from the data?

- What do we need to do, given the information we now have?
- How can future studies of this nature be enhanced?
- What could make this information more useful?

Presentations on the Internet

With PowerPoint, publishing presentations to the Web is easier than ever. Publication to the Web enables individuals to access the presentation, regardless of where they are or when they need to access it. In addition, researchers can present results at multiple locations on the Internet. The steps are very simple:

1. Open your presentation in PowerPoint. To see what your slides will look like on the Web, choose "Web Page Preview" from the "File" menu. After you have made any edits, choose "Save as Web Page" from the same menu.

2. The "Save As" dialog box allows you to change the title of your presentation to whatever you want displayed in the title bar of your visitor's browser.

3. The "Publish" button takes you to the "Publish as Web Page" dialog box, where you can customize your presentation.

4. The "Web Options" dialog box lets you specify the way your published file will be stored on the Web server and whether to update internal links to these files automatically.

We now turn our attention from making effective presentations to managing the marketing research function.

Managing Research Suppliers

What Do Clients Want?

Managing a marketing research supplier organization involves understanding what clients want and expect, maintaining good communications with the client, effectively managing the research process, and good time management, cost management, and client profitability management. If a marketing research department in a large organization is conducting its own research, then it will also face these same managerial issues. If it farms out its research, then good management requires selecting the right vendor. A research department must also try to become less of an "order taker" and play a greater role in the marketing decision-making process within the organization.

Market Directions, a marketing research firm in Kansas City, Missouri, asked marketing research clients across the United States to rate the importance of several statements about research companies and research departments. Replies from a wide range of industries are summarized in the following top-10 list:

1. Maintains client confidentiality
2. Is honest
3. Is punctual
4. Is flexible
5. Delivers against project specifications
6. Provides high-quality output
7. Is responsive to the client's needs
8. Has high quality-control standards

9. Is customer oriented in interactions with client

10. Keeps the client informed throughout a project.[3]

The two most important factors, confidentiality and honesty, are ethical issues, which were covered earlier in the text. The remaining issues relate to managing the research function and maintaining good communication.

Communication

The key to good supplier–client relations is excellent communication. Every project should have a liaison who serves as a communication link between the supplier and the client. In large firms, this individual may be an account executive or project manager, while in small firms, he or she may be an owner or a partner. But, whatever the job title, the liaison must communicate accurately, honestly, and frequently with the client.

Before a project begins, the communication liaison should go over the project objectives, methodology, and timing with the client to make certain that there are no misunderstandings. The client should then sign off on the questionnaire, thereby agreeing that the questionnaire is sufficient to gather the raw data needed to accomplish the research objectives.

John Colias, vice-president of M/A/R/C Research, says the following about communication between a research supplier and its client:

When a company hires a market research firm to design a study, the supplier must operate as part of the team of researchers and marketers. To be an effective member of the team, the supplier must also intimately understand the marketing questions. This understanding results from interactive dialogue among the researcher, marketer, and the supplier about the marketing questions and business decisions. Such a dialogue crystallizes the research objectives into concrete deliverables that directly influence business decisions.[4]

The liaison must ascertain how often the client wants progress reports. At a minimum, these reports should be issued weekly. The report should cover the status of the project, unusual problems encountered, and, if it is a cost-plus project, expenses incurred to date. *Cost-plus* refers to actual costs plus an additional markup to cover overhead. Cost-plus projects are typically found in situations where a research department of a large corporation, such as General Foods, conducts a project for another department.

Managing the Research Process

Research management has seven important goals beyond excellent communication: building an effective organization, assurance of data quality, adherence to time schedules, cost control, client profitability management, and staff management and development.

> **research management**
> Overseeing the development of excellent communication systems, data quality, time schedules, cost controls, client profitability, and staff development.

Organizing the Supplier Firm   Traditionally, most marketing research firms were organized around functions. Large suppliers, for example, may have separate departments for sampling, questionnaire programming, field, coding, tabulation, statistics, and sales. Even the client service staff may be separate from those who manage projects and write questionnaires and reports. Each of these departments has a head who is expert in the functions of that department and manages work assignments within the department. Projects flow from department to department.

A functional form of organization allows technical people to perform backroom tasks such as programming and data analysis and the "people people" to handle project management and client contact. It provides for knowledgeable supervision, so that, for example, beginners in sample design are working under the direction of veteran experts. It permits the development of good work processes and quality standards, so that tasks are performed consistently. It lets the difficulty of a given project be matched with the skill of the person doing it, so that routine work is given to junior staff and the most complex tasks are reserved for the expert. This matching of work and skill levels leads to happier staff and lower project costs.

Yet functional organizations are not without their problems. Department staff can become focused on the execution of their task, to the detriment of the whole process and the client. Departmental standards and scheduling policies may take on lives of their own, optimizing the efficiency and quality of a department's work but making timely completion of the whole project difficult. By becoming removed from client contact, departments can become inwardly oriented, viewing clients as problems rather than the source of their livelihood. Interdepartmental communication and scheduling can become time-consuming and flawed, as project managers or operations schedulers negotiate each project's schedule with a series of independent department heads. Each department may feel that it is performing perfectly, yet the whole process viewed from the outside can seem rigid, bureaucratic, and ineffective.

In response to problems like these, some companies are organizing by teams. They are breaking up functional departments and organizing their staff into units based around client groups or research types. These teams include people with all or most of the skills necessary to complete a study from beginning to end. A typical team might include several client service/project management people, a field director, a questionnaire programmer, and a tab specwriter. Staff are frequently cross-trained in multiple functions. The team is almost always headed by a senior staff member with a client service or project management background.

There are many variations on this theme. Within the teams, work may remain specialized (the specwriter does the tables), or there can be extensive cross-training (everyone does tables). Highly specialized functions (such as statistical analysis) that are carried out by one or two experts may remain as functional departments, available to all. A hybrid approach is also possible, where some functions are moved within the teams, while others (such as field management) remain as separate departments.

Because each client group controls its own resources, scheduling and communication are easier. With no department heads or central scheduling to go through, the group head directly prioritizes the work of everyone working on his or her projects.

PhotoDisc, Inc./Getty Images

Effective time management is becoming increasingly important in all aspects of professional life. One requirement of research management is to keep a project on the schedule specified by the client.

Technical and operations personnel become closer to clients and more aligned with their needs. By reducing the organizational distance between the client and these staff members, it is easier for them to appreciate the client's situation and focus on serving his or her needs.

Staff may develop more flexibility and broader skills. Cross-training and cross-assignment of work are easier when all the people involved report to the same person.[5]

Data Quality Management   Perhaps the most important objective of research management is to ensure the quality or integrity of the data produced by the research process. You have probably heard announcers on television say, "The poll had a margin of error of 3 percent." Some problems and implicit assumptions are associated with this statement. First, you learned in the discussion of sampling error in Chapter 13 that this statement is missing an associated level of confidence. In other words, how confident are the pollsters that the poll has a margin of error of 3 percent? Are they 68.26 percent confident, 95.44 percent confident, 99.74 percent confident, or confident at some other level? Second, this statement does not make clear that the margin of error applies only to *random sampling error*. The implicit, or unstated, assumption is that there are no other sources of error, that all other sources of error have been effectively dealt with by the research design and procedures, or that all other sources of error have been effectively randomized by taking summary measures across the entire sample. By definition, error is random when there are just as many errors in one direction as in the other direction, leaving overall measures, such as averages, unaffected. Marketing research managers can help assure high-quality data by having policies and procedures in place to minimize sources of error (see Chapter 4).

Time Management A second goal of research management is to keep the project on schedule. Time management is important in marketing research because clients often have a specified time schedule that they must meet. For example, it may be imperative that the research results be available on March 1 so that they can be presented at the quarterly meeting of the new product committee. The findings will affect whether the test product will receive additional funding for development.

Two problems that can play havoc with time schedules are inaccuracies in estimates of the incidence rate and the interview length. A lower-than-expected incidence rate will require more interviewing resources than originally planned to get the job done on time. If the research manager does not have idle resources to devote to the project, then it will take longer to complete. The same is true for a longer-than-anticipated interview.

Recall that the *incidence rate* is the percentage of persons or households out of the general population that fit the qualifications to be interviewed in a particular study. Often, estimates of incidence rate are based not on hard-and-fast data but on data that are incomplete, known to be relatively inaccurate, or dated. Incidence rate problems cannot only increase the amount of time required to complete the sample for the project but also negatively affect the costs of the data-collection phase of the research.

The project manager must have early information regarding whether or not a project can be completed on time. If a problem exists, the manager must first determine whether anything can be done to speed up the process. Perhaps training additional interviewers would help expedite completion of the survey. Second, the researcher must inform the client that the project is going to take longer than expected. The researcher can then explore with the client whether a time extension is possible or what changes the client might be willing to make to get the project completed on the original time schedule. For example, the client might be willing to reduce the total sample size or shorten the length of the interview by eliminating questions that are judged to be less critical. Thus, it is very important that the system be structured so that both the researcher and the client are alerted to potential problems within the first few days of the project.

Time management, like cost control, requires that systems be put in place to inform management as to whether or not the project is on schedule. Policies and procedures must be established to efficiently and quickly solve schedule problems and promptly notify the client about the problem and potential solutions.

Tips for doing high-quality work in a timely manner are provided in the Practicing Marketing Research feature on page 408.

Cost Management In comparison to data quality and time management, cost management is straightforward. All it requires is adherence to good business practices, such as procedures for cost tracking and control. In particular, good procedures for cost control include the following elements:

- Systems that accurately capture data collection and other costs associated with the project on a daily basis.

PRACTICING MARKETING RESEARCH

Doing High-Quality Work—On Time[6]

Here are seven tips on time management for marketing management project research directors.

Manage expectations. Most job descriptions for project directors mention writing skills, facility with mathematics, organizational ability, and experience with presentations, but managing expectations may be the most critical skill to master. If you're pretty sure that the work will be done by Thursday, don't say you're "shooting for Wednesday." You're better off promising Friday and giving yourself a chance to be a hero.

Think about priorities. When the client has a crisis, sometimes you just have to drop everything and help out. Clients are, after all, the ones paying our salaries. Even without a crisis, however, it doesn't hurt to think about your priorities. The time-management books suggest concentrating on the most important tasks only and ignoring the others until they too join the "most important" list. If you don't mind a messy desk, this is pretty good advice.

Think about leverage. What if the client is not in crisis mode, but you still have 10 things to do? Concentrate first on the tasks that require contributions from others. If the interviewers are waiting for your briefing or the data processing people are waiting for your codes, then everyone's work is backing up.

Provide regular updates. It is amazing how many games of voice-mail tag can be avoided by filling out a simple form. Set up a form that you can fax or e-mail every day explaining how many interviews have been finished, where the incidence is coming out, how you are doing on interview length, and whatever other facts your client requires. If you are working with 10 field services on a study, get them to fill out update forms too—this saves you another 10 calls a day.

Be on the lookout for problems. A statistician I worked with used to say, "All lists are bad." Actually, he used a stronger term—"the trick is to find out why this particular list is bad."

Project directing is problem solving. Incidence estimates will be off, questionnaires will be too long, respondents will be uncooperative, and lists will be, uh, bad. Spending a little extra time on instructions, briefings, and safety checks today will save a lot of extra work tomorrow.

When you discover a problem, let the client know quickly. You can stick a problem in a folder for a day or two, but it's not likely to solve itself. The sooner the client hears about the problem, the sooner he or she can adjust schedules or budgets. In my experience, you can almost always go back to a client—once—to discuss changes in specifications, schedules, and budgets. But you need to bring these issues up early, when your client still has some flexibility. Surprises at the 11th hour are both painful and time-consuming for everyone.

If you need to bring up a problem, don't be afraid to suggest some solutions as well. Suggesting solutions will help to solve the issue quickly and efficiently. As a general rule, the range of possible solutions is not hard to come up with. The following should cover about 80 percent of all possible problems:

- Order more sample.
- Change the screening criteria.
- Raise the incentives.
- Rebrief the interviewers.
- Reschedule the focus groups.
- Reduce the number of interviews.
- Lengthen the interviewing schedule.
- Increase the budget.

The challenge is in getting beyond the issue of who is to blame and determining which solution will work best this time.

Questions

1. Would you like to be a project manager? Why or why not?

2. What do you think are the most important characteristics of a good project manager?

■ Daily reporting of costs to the communication liaison. Ideally, reports should show actual costs in relation to budget.

■ Policies and practices in the research organization that require the liaison to communicate the budget picture to clients and to senior managers at the research company.

■ Policies and practices that quickly identify over-budget situations and then find causes and seek solutions.

If the project is over budget because the client provided information that proved to be erroneous (for example, incidence rate, interview length), then it is imperative that the client be offered options early in the process: a higher cost, smaller sample size, shorter interview, or some combination of these. If the firm waits until the project is complete to communicate this problem to the client, the client is likely to say, "You should have told me sooner; there is nothing I can do now." In this situation, the firm will probably have to swallow the cost overrun.

Outsourcing   One way that research firms are cutting costs is outsourcing. The term **outsourcing** as used in this text is having personnel in another country perform some, or all, of the functions involved in a marketing research project. When a research firm sets up a wholly-owned foreign subsidiary, it is called **captive outsourcing**. Simple outsourcing is where a domestic research company enters into a relationship with a foreign company that provides a variety of marketing research functions. For example, Cross-Tab Services of Mumbai, India, offers online survey programming, data processing, data analysis, and other services. Other services that are beginning to be outsourced are data management and panel management. A number of issues need to be considered when one is outsourcing, as shown in Exhibit 15.10.

India is most likely the world leader in marketing research outsourcing firms. Over 110 marketing research outsourcing firms in India (noncaptive) employ over 9,000 people.[7] The country's revenues from marketing research outsourcing are expected to reach $800 million by 2012.[8]

> **outsourcing**
> Having personnel in another country perform some or all of the functions involved in a marketing research project.

> **captive outsourcing**
> A research firm's creating a wholly owned foreign facility for outsourcing.

Client Profitability Management   While marketing research departments may be able to focus on doing "on-demand" projects for internal clients, marketing research suppliers have to think about profitability. The old adage that 20 percent of the clients generate 80 percent of the profits is often true.

Custom Research Incorporated (CRI), of Minneapolis, realized a few years back that it had too many clients—or too few good ones.[9] The company divided its clients into four categories based on the client's perceived value to CRI's bottom line (see Exhibit 15.11). Only 10 of CRI's 157 customers fell into the most desirable category (generating a high dollar volume and a high profit margin). Another 101 customers contributed very little to the top or bottom line. In short, CRI was spending too much time and too many valuable employee resources on too many unprofitable customers.

In assessing which customers to keep, CRI calculated the profit for each one by subtracting all direct costs and selling expenses from the total revenues brought into CRI by that customer for the year. That is, CRI asked, "What costs would we not incur if this customer went away?" The cutoff points for high and low scores were purely subjective; they corresponded to CRI's goals for profit volume and profit margin. CRI management decided that it had to systematically drop a large number of old customers and carefully screen potential new customers. CRI's screening questions for new customers are shown in Exhibit 15.12.

Using the customer's analysis, CRI went from 157 customers and $11 million in revenue to 78 customers and $30 million in revenue. Most importantly, profits more than doubled.

EXHIBIT 15.10	Outsourcing Issues
Issues	**Management Strategies**
Confidentiality	Proper confidentiality and data security agreements need to be signed with third-party providers and senior personnel of captive centers. Frequent audits are also recommended to ensure compliance.
Infrastructure	It is important that the destination country and the city selected within the country have access to required infrastructure such as power, bandwidth, good connectivity through airports, hotel facilities for visits by customer's team, and of course talented workers.
Quality of deliverables	Careful documentation is important for processes executed in any location, but they are doubly important in the case of offshore outsourcing. Also, proper systems and protocols must be laid down for communication between teams in the client country and in the vendor country.
Domain knowledge	It is important to ensure that the senior members of the team in the offshore location have a strong domain understanding of market research and do not have just an IT or data processing background.
Cultural issues	It is necessary to understand the culture of the offshore location and the sensitivities of the people. Cultural misunderstandings can cause misgivings and can affect the quality of work.
Job losses in the client country and associated negative publicity for the agency	Good people can be retained and be provided jobs in other roles in the same agency in order to fuel the growth that will result from the cost savings realized. It is important to have a proper PR initiative to explain the benefits of offshoring to the economy of the client country. (Economic studies have shown that in the long term offshoring leads to greater benefits for the economy of the client country and actually creates more jobs.)
Employee liability	This risk is not an issue if one outsources to third-party providers. If one is going the captive route, then it is important to carefully study the employment laws of the destination country to ensure no legal conflicts.

Source: Ashwin Mittal and Kedar Sohoni, "A Brief Guide to Oursourcing," *Quirk's Marketing Research Review*, November 2005, p. 70.

Exhibit 15.11

CRI's Client Profitability Analysis

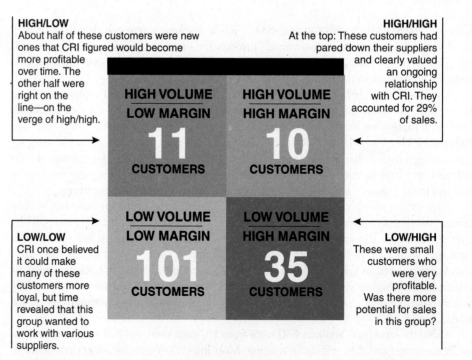

HIGH/LOW
About half of these customers were new ones that CRI figured would become more profitable over time. The other half were right on the line—on the verge of high/high.

HIGH/HIGH
At the top: These customers had pared down their suppliers and clearly valued an ongoing relationship with CRI. They accounted for 29% of sales.

HIGH VOLUME
LOW MARGIN
11
CUSTOMERS

HIGH VOLUME
HIGH MARGIN
10
CUSTOMERS

LOW VOLUME
LOW MARGIN
101
CUSTOMERS

LOW VOLUME
HIGH MARGIN
35
CUSTOMERS

LOW/LOW
CRI once believed it could make many of these customers more loyal, but time revealed that this group wanted to work with various suppliers.

LOW/HIGH
These were small customers who were very profitable. Was there more potential for sales in this group?

EXHIBIT 15.12	Screening Questions Used by CRI and the Rationale for Each Question

Quesion	Rationale
How did you hear about us?	A bad answer: "I found you in the Yellow Pages." Unlike many companies, CRI doesn't ask this question so that it can decide how to divvy up the marketing dollars. "If someone finds us in the Yellow Pages, they have no reason to use us over anyone else," CRI cofounder Judy Corson explains. A good answer: "A colleague of mine worked with you at another company."
What kind of work is it (in terms of industry or scope)?	More than anything, the answer reveals whether the caller is trying to price a quick, one-time project or one that's totally outside CRI's realm. If so, the caller is referred to an indirect competitor.
What's your budget?	That's akin to asking someone how much money he or she makes, but the prospect's response to a ballpark guess on the cost of the project helps CRI ascertain what the client has in mind.
What are your decision criteria?	CRI knows that it doesn't fare well in blind bidding or in drawn-out, committee-style decisions, so it's interested in dealing with callers who have some level of decision-making power—and assiduously avoids getting involved in anything that smells like a bidding war.
Whom are we competing against for your business?	CRI likes to hear the names of its chief rivals, a half-dozen large companies, including the M/A/R/C Group, Market Facts, and Burke Marketing Research.
Why are you thinking of switching?	"There's a two-edged sword here," explains cofounder Jeff Pope. "Clients that are hard to break into are better because they don't switch too easily. But you need a way to get in—so a legitimate need for a new supplier is OK." Each month only 2 or 3 of 20 to 30 callers answer enough questions correctly to warrant more attention. So why spend time with the rest? "Do unto others. . . . You never know where people will go."

Source: Susan Greco, "Choose or Lose," *INC.*, December 1998, pp. 57–59, 62–66.

Managers had calculated they'd need to reap about 20 to 30 percent more business from some two dozen companies to help make up for the roughly 100 customers they planned to "let go" within two years. This was accomplished by building a close personal relationship with the clients that remained. The process involved CRI's researching the industry, the client company, and its research personnel to fully understand the client's needs. For each client, CRI created a Surprise and Delight plan to deliver a "value-added" bonus to the client. For example, Dow Brands received some complimentary software that CRI knew the company needed. This one-on-one relationship marketing has been the key to CRI's success.

Staff Management and Development The primary asset of any marketing research firm is its people. Proprietary techniques and models can help differentiate a marketing research company, but eventually its success depends on the professional nature of its staff and their determination to deliver a quality product. Consequently, recruiting and retaining a competent, enthusiastic staff are crucial and constant management challenges.

Kathleen Knight is president and CEO of BAIGlobal, Incorporated, a Tarrytown, New York, marketing research firm. She offers several suggestions for staff development in a research firm:

1. *Create an environment that encourages risk taking, experimentation, and responsibility.* The benefits to the research firm, such as new service development, new techniques, and business growth, outweigh any potential risks. However, employees need to feel that they will be supported in taking risks. New ideas and different business approaches need to be treated with respect and given room to develop.

2. *Foster recognition and accountability.* Recognize good effort and reward it. One of the best forms of reward is visibility within the company. Make sure that everyone knows when an outstanding job was done and that excellence matters.

3. *Provide job autonomy within a certain structure.* Marketing research is a technical science, and the numbers have to add up. But it also is a business, and projects have to generate money to pay the bills. Within these boundaries, there are many different ways to get the job done. Let employees put their personal stamp on a project and they will feel like true partners in their work.

4. *Attract and support people with entrepreneurial attitudes.* Set business goals and management parameters; then let the staff determine the path to take to get the job done. This allows each person to leverage his or her own abilities and achieve the highest level of success.

5. *Connect rewards to a business result.* Providing open financial data to researchers seems to create a business consciousness that is exciting for all. Often, very talented researchers know little about the financial dynamics of the industry. They welcome the chance to learn and thus become more accountable for bottom-line results.

6. *Open your financial books.* Research firms can provide senior employees with full financial information to let them know how well they are doing across the months and years. The bottom line is the best aggregate measure of performance—individually, as a group, and as a firm. Opening the books establishes a common mission and goal across the organization.

7. *Offer diversity within your organization.* It's fun and exciting to learn new products, serve new clients, and work with a new research team. A chance at a new position is often the spark someone needs to really do well within a firm. And the possibility of this kind of job change seems to add to the satisfaction that employees feel. If you pay attention to individuals and create a career path across disciplines within your organization, it's more likely that talented researchers will stay.

8. *Provide clear promotional paths.* Employees like to know how they can advance and want to feel some control over their careers. Clear criteria and expectations go a long way toward helping researchers feel comfortable. In the marketing research business, the best training is as an apprentice, working with senior researchers doing interesting work. Talented people will grow and prosper where the expectations are that senior managers will be mentors, that junior staff will learn, and that excellent work produced together will lead to everyone's career advancement.[10]

Managing a Marketing Research Department

A manager of a marketing research department within a corporation faces a different set of issues from a research supplier. Among these issues are effective spending of the research budget, prioritizing projects for the corporation, retaining skilled staff, selecting the right research suppliers, moving the marketing research function to a more strategic role in the firm, and measuring return on investment for marketing research.

Allocating the Research Department Budget[11]

No matter who controls the research project budget, it's important to spend money and (most importantly) research staff time wisely. That is especially important when the clients (new product development managers or brand managers) fund each project and cannot understand why the marketing research department doesn't have the staff time to do whatever they want. In that case, many research heads are learning how to prioritize projects. There are several effective ways to accomplish that.

A research study found that only about 20 percent of research projects are focused on strategically important issues. The other 80 percent of projects are focused on tactical issues, such as setting prices, advertising, distributing products, or adding new features to existing products. Researchers and clients agree that they would prefer to spend more time on the strategic issues, such as identifying promising new markets or developing new products and services.[12]

For example, one research group took it upon itself to improve its firm's new product development process by bringing together experts from marketing research, marketing, research and development, manufacturing, and sales to design a new process.

Another research group head learned to facilitate strategic planning (an ad hoc effort in her firm), so that she could help her executive team plan when cross-functional action was needed.

Several research heads said that they try to meet with their clients annually before budgeting season begins to talk about what research issues will be most important to clients in the coming year. Both parties then agree on the vital projects for the coming year and on how much time or money to allocate to them. While everyone admits that unforeseen circumstances almost always force the plans to be altered, having an annual plan enables a manager to adapt quickly and be flexible.

Many department heads say that they believe it's important for the research group to have a discretionary budget for important projects. That is considered especially important if research projects are usually funded by the clients. One new director of research used the discretionary budget to study why demand for his organization's main product appeared to be dropping in the face of a changing industry. Another researcher paid for a project on store designs because he felt that the designs were probably holding back sales—and he was right. Still another group paid to learn scenario planning and used it to help clients pick options for new-product testing.

Prioritize Projects

Estimating the financial return from a research project is a great way to rationalize spending across projects because it provides a quantitative methodology that helps clients identify "must-have" versus "nice-to-have" projects. It is not only an effective way of turning away less important work; it also helps strengthen relations with clients because it shows that researchers are thinking about their bottom line, too.

Retaining Skilled Staff

When researchers are feeling overworked and finding it difficult to meet client needs without sacrificing their personal time needs, they begin to burn out and think about working elsewhere. Losing a skilled staff member can damage a research group: It means more work for the remaining staff members, and it can leave a hole in valuable client relationships. It is especially important to recognize and reward hard-working staff members. How can this be done? Research shows that staff members of marketing research departments value doing interesting and fulfilling work, getting recognition for a job well done, and earning adequate pay.[13]

A few techniques for retaining key research staff are as follows:

1. Conduct regular performance reviews that give continuing feedback on a job well done—or offer ways to improve. Many staff members think their bosses play

favorites during performance reviews. So department heads try to use clear performance criteria for each position and offer objective appraisals for everyone.

2. Offer public recognition for great work. Some groups mention great work during staff meetings; post client comments on a "wall of fame" in the department; have bosses send personal letters to staff members at home, praising their work; hold pizza parties for teams that have performed "above and beyond"; or simply have the head of the department stop by a staff member's office to offer congratulations and thanks.

3. Give differential pay raises that recognize superior performance. While across-the-board, uniform pay increases are often used (because they are the easiest to administer), they do not recognize the high performers—and they allow the lower performers to believe they are doing adequate work.

4. Vary the work. In order to keep everyone interested, some research groups identify one-off projects and then allow staff members to volunteer for them. Examples of special projects could include a project that will feed into the firm's strategic plans, formation of a high-visibility cross-functional team, or a project that uses a new technique or addresses an unusually interesting topic.[14]

Selecting the Right Marketing Research Suppliers

Once the nature, scope, and objectives of the project have been determined, the next step is to assess the capabilities of alternative suppliers. Some research vendors have a particular area of specialization. Some firms specialize in advertising or customer satisfaction research, while others are devoted to a particular technique (for example, conjoint analysis or market segmentation) or data-collection method (for example, mall intercepts, mail surveys, or Internet panels).

A research department manager should beware of firms committed to a particular technique and/or data-collection method, as they are more likely to "force" the department's research project into their particular model, rather than tailor the research to fit the specific needs of the research department's project.

Research department managers must consider the size of the firms in their decision. The size of the vendor is an extremely important decision criterion. It is important not to overwhelm a small firm with an enormous project, and, conversely, a small project may not get the proper attention at a large firm.

The general rule is to favor the smallest firm consistent with the scope of the project. However, any project that is 30 percent or more of a marketing research supplier's annual revenues may be too large for that firm to handle effectively.

The research department manager should establish, up front, the individual who will be managing the project. It should be determined in advance who would be responsible for the day-to-day management of the project; that is, will it be the person who "sold" the project or a project director hundreds of miles away? If the contact becomes unavailable, will competent support staff be available?

The research department manager needs to become acquainted with the backgrounds of the potential vendors. There are some general questions that every potential vendor should be asked to determine the stability of the company and its qualifications to complete the project in a satisfactory manner. These questions would include:

▪ How long has the vendor been in business?

▪ For what other companies has the vendor conducted research projects? Remember it is imperative to request references and check them for each firm.

▪ What are the academic backgrounds and experience of those persons who will be working on the project, that is, the project director, field director, data processing manager, and so forth? Does the composition of the project team strike the right balance between top-level management and technical researchers and analysts?

■ Does the success of the project depend on the capabilities of a subcontractor? If the marketing research supplier will be subcontracting any elements of the project, it is important that the subcontractor and his or her qualifications be identified.

Also, the research manager should review the quality control standards of each potential vendor. The validity of the results of any research project is dependent on the quality control measures practiced by the vendor. For example, on telephone studies, what are the procedures with respect to callbacks, monitoring, and validation? It is prudent to avoid firms that do not practice generally accepted practices in their operations.

The reputations of the firms must be considered in the decision. Reputation is important, but a department should not pay a larger premium for it. However, some situations may require the services of a prestigious research firm because a company plans to publicize the results, or use them in advertisements, so having the best reputation available may actually be a good investment. For example, Dell touts its standings in J.D. Power Customer Satisfaction surveys.

Finally, a manager should avoid letting price be the sole determining factor in the selection. When reviewing proposals, price should be the last item to be considered.[15]

Moving Marketing Research into a Decision-Making Role

A more strategic managerial question regarding the marketing research department is the role and importance of marketing research in the managerial decision-making process. The researchers' challenge is to shed their long-held traditional role as a support function, one that reacts to requests from project and new product development managers and then focuses on producing the numbers but not on their meaning to the business.

"There's a gap between what research believes it's capable of providing and what top management perceives it can get from research," says Larry Stanek, senior associate of the Hartman Group, located in Bellevue, Washington. "Researchers believe they have answers critical to decision making, while management views research as having the data but maybe not the insight to drive business."[16]

Experts agree that, to earn the ear of senior management, researchers must move beyond the task of simply crunching numbers and churning out results; they need to understand the underlying business issues at stake and adjust the information they gather and how they analyze it. They also must reach out to other departments, building relationships and a better understanding of the issues companywide. "We need to evolve just from doing research to doing insights," says Peter Daboll, chief of insights for Sunnyvale, California-based Yahoo! Inc. "If you want to be at the table you have to be senior. [To be senior means to] go from collecting, collating and presenting to anticipating, reconciling and recommending. . . . [Executives] want the freaking answer, not the tool to give them the answer."[17]

Experts also suggest that researchers should spend more time discussing the decisions that need to be made with the results before designing and conducting a study—to avoid a that's-nice-to-know-but-I-really-need-this-*other*-information response from management. And when it comes to reporting results, researchers must translate the numbers into specific recommendations and even link the findings to other data that management typically uses to make decisions. Not surprisingly, researchers agree that securing a seat at the table not only demands strong analytical abilities, but also so-called softer skills in persuasion, communication, and presentation.

"I strongly emphasize that while [the research managers and associates] may be in my official marketing research department—it's my insistence that they view themselves as members of the business team" first and foremost, says Daryl Papp, Lilly's director of U.S. market research. He adds that about half of his department comprises professionals who come from areas of marketing other than research for a several-year "broadening assignment" to learn about the company's businesses. Papp believes that having marketing researchers sit side by side with other colleagues who aspire to high-level management helps contribute to the business-oriented mentality in his department.[18]

Most firms rely on marketing research departments to provide data to the brand marketing and sales teams so that successes can be achieved in many areas, including new product launches, brand management and stewardship, the efficiency of marketing operations, and advertising effectiveness. In this context, the marketing researcher participates on a team charged with accomplishing an objective for the firm. The great majority of a firm's marketing research activities fall into this category. At this stage, the question of whether the objective or initiative has merit is already decided. The marketing researcher helps the team make decisions about the most efficient and effective ways to spend its limited marketing funds to achieve the greatest result. This is not limited to new product initiatives. These activities include tracking studies, usage and attitude studies, copy testing and advertising research, sales promotion evaluation, sales analysis, strategic positioning studies, and many more.[19]

In order to influence senior management, the marketing researcher needs to move beyond fulfilling research assignments designed to avoid failure or enable success. When marketing researchers look beyond already-generated ideas and already-created products, services, ads, or distribution channels, their strategic value increases. And this begins to attract management's attention. Management places high value on this activity because companies need growth, which has become exceedingly hard to achieve. At its best, marketing research redefines business strategy by using data in novel ways to create a sustainable competitive advantage.[20]

To keep management's attention during strategic presentations, Barry Jennings, marketing research manager for Dell Computer, offers an excellent tip. Jennings says that researchers can best sell their data to executives when they explicitly present their research as relaying the voice of the customer. "So often we use words like 'respondent' or 'participant,' but they are all customers. (When you say) 'customers say' this or that—then the C-level listens because they can then put a dollar value on them. . . . Putting it in their language makes a huge, huge difference," he says. "The customer needs a seat at the table."[21]

SUMMARY

The six primary sections of a contemporary marketing research report are, in order, the table of contents, background and objectives, executive summary, methodology, findings, and appendixes with supporting information.

The primary objectives of the marketing research report are to state the specific research objectives, explain why and how the research was done, present the findings of the research, and provide conclusions and recommendations. Most of these elements are contained in the executive summary. The conclusions do not necessarily contain statistical numbers derived from the research but rather generalize the results in relation to the stated objectives. Nor do conclusions suggest a course of action. This is left to the recommendations, which direct the conclusions to specific marketing strategies or tactics that would place the client in the most positive position in the market.

The marketing research report of today makes heavy use of graphics to present key findings. For most researchers, PowerPoint is the software of choice for creating research reports. In terms of mechanics, reports minimize the use of words, feed information to clients in "minibites," and make extensive use of bulleted charts and graphics. In addition to the written report which is often nothing more than a copy of the PowerPoint presentation, a presentation of research results is often required. It is common for research reports to be published on the Internet by the client or by the researcher at the client's request. This has the advantage of making the results available to individuals worldwide in the client's organization. The Internet can also be used to support simultaneous presentation of the research results in multiple locations.

Supplier research marketing management has six important goals beyond excellent communication: creation of an effective organization, assurance of data quality, adherence to time schedules, cost control, client profitability management, and staff management and development. Many research firms are transitioning to a team-based organization from the traditional functional organizational structure. Marketing research managers can help assure high-quality data by attempting to minimize sources of error. Researchers should also strive for better client and audience understanding of the margin of error concept. Time management requires a system to notify management of potential problems and policies to solve behind-schedule problems both efficiently and quickly. Cost management demands good cost-tracking and cost control processes. Client profitability management requires that the marketing research supplier determine how much each client contributes to the researcher's overall profitability. Unprofitable clients should be dropped; marginally profitable clients should be developed into high-profit clients or dropped. The supplier should use relationship marketing to build a solid, increasingly profitable long-term relationship with clients identified as high-profit contributors. Finally, staff management and development requires that employees be encouraged to take risks and assume responsibility, be recognized for a job well done, and be offered job autonomy, financial rewards tied to business results, new challenges, and a clear career path.

A trend embraced by both research suppliers and departments is marketing research outsourcing. Outsourcing can be a source of cost reduction and also often save time. Most outsourcing by American firms is to India. Outsource firms offer programming, data processing, data analysis, data management, and panel management. Some important issues when considering outsourcing are confidentiality, infrastructure, quality of deliverables, domain, knowledge, culture considerations, potential negative publicity from job losses, and employee liability.

A manager of a marketing research department within a corporation faces a different set of issues than from a research supplier. Among these are effective spending of the research budget, prioritizing projects for the corporation, retaining skilled staff, selecting the right research suppliers, moving the marketing research function to a more strategic role in the firm, and measuring return on investment for marketing research.

One technique for prioritizing projects is to focus first on strategic projects and then the tactical. This is also true for allocating the corporate research budget. Also, projects should be funded that have the highest potential ROI. Ways to retain key staff are to offer interesting and fulfilling work, recognizing someone for a job well done, and offering competitive pay.

A manager of a corporate research department must develop methodologies and skills for selecting the right research suppliers. This includes assessing competing supplier capabilities and reviewing the quality controls of each supplier.

KEY TERMS & DEFINITIONS

executive summary The portion of a research report that explains why the research was done, what was found, what those findings mean, and what action, if any, management should undertake.

conclusions Generalizations that answer the questions raised by the research objectives or otherwise satisfy the objectives.

recommendations Conclusions applied to marketing strategies or tactics that focus on a client's achievement of differential advantage.

research management Overseeing the development of excellent communication systems, data quality, time schedules, cost controls, client profitability, and staff development.

outsourcing Having personnel in another country perform some, or all, of the functions involved in a marketing research project.

captive outsourcing A research firm's creating a wholly owned foreign facility for outsourcing.

QUESTIONS FOR REVIEW & CRITICAL THINKING

1. Why is it so hard to summarize results and their implications in a few pages?
   What consideratons should guide these process?
   What are the roles of the research report?
2. Why should research reports contain executive summaries? What should be contained in an executive summary?
3. Describe four different ways a manager can help ensure high data quality.

WORKING THE NET

1. Go to *www.gallup.com* and examine some of the special reports on American opinions, such as those found under "Social Issues and Policy." Do these reports meet the criteria discussed in the text for good marketing research reports? Why or why not?
2. Go to *www.presentations.com.* Describe the different ways this organization can help an individual become a more effective speaker.

REAL-LIFE RESEARCH • 15.1

The United Way

The United Way was concerned about the attitudes of nondonors toward the organization with the theory that their reasons for not donating are tied to their perceptions of United

Way. They are also interested in getting a sense of what factors might convert nondonors to donors. The executive summary from the research report is provided below. Each heading and the text that follows were provided on PowerPoint slides in the report, and the presentation was provided by the research firm that conducted the study of these issues.

Executive Summary Objectives and Methodology

- The general purposes of this study were to determine the attitudes of nondonors toward the United Way, to assess the reasons for not donating, and to ascertain factors that may influence nondonors to contribute in the future.
- The study relied on primary data gathered through online surveys.
- The study employed a probability sample.
- Responses were obtained from 726 respondents.

Findings

- The percentage with positive perceptions of the United Way was greater than the percentage having negative perceptions. However, the majority had no opinions about United Way.
- Only 5.2 percent rated United Way fair or poor in providing benefits to those in need.
- United Way actually spends 9 to 10 percent of contributions on administrative costs, although 80.6 percent believed that the United Way used more than 10 percent of its contributions on administrative costs.
- Primary reasons for not contributing were contribution to other charities or religious organizations, personal financial circumstances, lack of knowledge of how donated funds are used, personal beliefs, absence of favorite charities, pressure to contribute, and preference to donate time rather than money.
- Of those who were asked to contribute, pressure seemed somewhat important in influencing their decision not to contribute.
- Of those who indicated that personal financial reasons influenced their decision not to give, 35.6 percent indicated they would give to United Way if asked.
- Other charities and religious denominations are clearly in competition with United Way for donations.
- Many respondents indicated that they would contribute if they could specify the charity to receive their contributions, had more knowledge about the United Way and the charities it supports, were asked to give, had less pressure to give, could use payroll deduction, and had the option of spreading contributions over time.
- Of those whose place of employment participated in the United Way campaign, 49.6 percent had been asked to give but did not.
- Workplace campaigns reach a large number of executives and professional and administrative personnel in the higher-income brackets but do not reach a significant number of service personnel or lower-income households.

Conclusions

- Negative perceptions do not appear to be a major factor affecting reasons for not contributing. However, a positive perception does not necessarily translate into a contribution.
- Noncontributors lack sufficient information regarding the United Way to form an accurate perception of the organization.

- There is a lack of knowledge concerning the United Way and the organizations to which it allocates contributions.
- Respondents believe that the United Way uses more for administrative costs than it actually does.
- The United Way is in competition for a limited number of charity dollars.

Recommendations

- Conduct additional research to determine noncontributor's level of knowledge of the United Way and the purpose that the United Way serves.
- Increase education for potential contributors regarding the United Way's purpose, the organizations it supports, and the United Way's reasonable administrative costs.
- Expand the frequency of campaigns in the workplace and develop ways to increase awareness of the methods of contributing.
- Develop appropriate competitive marketing strategy to address the United Way's competitors.

Questions

1. Do you think that the executive summary provides guidance for decision-making information?
2. Are all of the elements present that should be included in an executive summary as discussed in this chapter?
3. Do the findings, conclusions, and recommendations logically follow from the objectives? Why or why not?

ENDNOTES

Chapter 1

1. *www.marketingpower.com* accessed October 25, 2010

2. "Women Take No-Muss, No Fuss, Approach to Beauty Products," *Quirk's Marketing Research Review*, July 2010, p. 74.3.

3. "Understanding Discontinuous Opportunities," *Marketing Research,* Fall 1999, p. 9.

4. Stephen E. Brown, Anders Gustafsson and Lars Witell, "Beyond Products," *Wall Street Journal*, June 22, 1009, p. R7.

5. "Satisfaction Not Guaranteed," *Business Week*, June 19, 2006, p. 33.

6. "Why Some Customers Are More Equal Than Others," *Fortune*, September 19, 1994, pp. 215–224; and William Wright, "Determinants of Customer Loyalty and Financial Performance," *Journal of Management Accounting Research,* January 2009, pp. 1–12.

7. Sunil Gupta, Donald Lehmann, and Jennifer Ames Stuart, "Valuing Customers," *Journal of Marketing Research*, February 2004, pp. 7–18.

8. "How Current Are Your Beliefs about Social Media?" *Marketing Research,* Fall 2010, p. 26.

9. "Compulsively Connected? Millennials Can't Not Social Network," *Quirk's Marketing Research Review,* July 2010, p. 6.

10. "Basic Research Loses Some Allure," *Wall Street Journal,* October 7, 2009, p. A3.

11. "Retailers and Consumers Reach Symbiosis through Couponing," *Quirk's Marketing Research Review,* October 2010, p. 8.

Appendix 1-B

1. These ethical theories are from Catherine Rainbow, "Descriptions of Ethical Theories and Principles," *www.bio.davidson.edu/people/Kabernd/Indep/carainbow .htm*, June 22, 2005.

2. David Haynes, "Respondent Goodwill Is a Cooperative Activity," *Quirk's Marketing Research Review*, February 2005, pp. 30–32.

3. "New York State Sues Survey Firm for Allegedly Tricking Students," *Wall Street Journal*, August 30, 2002, p. B4.

4. Shelby Hunt, Lawrence Chonko, and James Wilcox, "Ethical Problems of Marketing Researchers," *Journal of Marketing Research*, August 1984, p. 314. Reprinted by permission of the American Marketing Association.

5. Terry Grapentine, "You Can't Take the Human Nature out of Black Boxes," *Marketing Research*, Winter 2004, pp. 20–22.

6. "The Code of Marketing Research Standards," *www.mra-net.org/pdf/expanded_ code.pdf*, June 29, 2005.

7. Diane Bowers, "New Requirement for Research: Privacy Assurance and Professional Accountability," *CASRO Journal*, 2002, pp. 115–116.

8. "Professional Researcher Certification," *http://www.mra-net.org*, June 29, 2005.

Chapter 2

1. Terry H. Grapentine and Dianne Weaver, "Business Goals Are Key to Proper Marketing Research," *Marketing News*, September 15, 2006, pp. 28–31.

2. Ted Grenager, "A Revolution in a Box," *Brandweek*, October 25, 2010, p. 17.

3. Ibid.

4. Diane Schmalensee and Dawn Lesh, "How to Make Research More Actionable," *Marketing Research*, Winter 1998/Spring 1999, pp. 23–26. Reprinted with permission from *Marketing Research,* published by the American Marketing Association.

5. Todd Wasserman, "K-C Tries Seeing Things from Consumer's POV," *Brandweek*, September 5, 2005, p. 6.

6. "Request for Proposal: Write It Well and You Will Be on Your Way," *Marketing News,* February 15, 2008, p. 8.

7. Joseph Rydholm, "What Do Clients Want from a Research Firm?" *Marketing Research Review,* October 1995, p. 82.

8. Fred Luthans and Janet K. Larsen, "How Managers Really Communicate," *Human Relations*, 1986, pp. 161–178; and Harry E. Penley and Brian Hawkins, "Studying Interpersonal Communication in Organizations: A Leadership Application," *Academy of Management Journal*, 1985, pp. 309–326.

9. Rohit Deshpande and Scott Jeffries, "Attitude Affecting the Use of Marketing Research in Decision Making: An Empirical Investigation," in *Educators' Conference Proceedings*, Series 47, edited by Kenneth L. Bernhardt et al. (Chicago: American Marketing Association, 1981), pp. 1–4.

10. Rohit Deshpande and Gerald Zaltman, "Factors Affecting the Use of Market Information: A Path Analysis," *Journal of Marketing Research*, February 1982, pp. 14–31; Rohit Deshpande, "A Comparison of Factors Affecting Researcher and Manager Perceptions of Market Research Use," *Journal of Marketing Research*, February 1989, pp. 32–38; Hanjoon Lee, Frank Acito, and Ralph Day, "Evaluation and Use of Marketing Research by Decision Makers: A Behavioral Simulation," *Journal of Marketing Research*, May 1987, pp. 187–196; Michael Hu, "An Experimental Study of Managers' and Researchers' Use of Consumer Market Research," *Journal of the Academy of Marketing Science,* Fall 1986, pp. 44–51; and Rohit Deshpande and Gerald Zaltman, "A Comparison of Factors Affecting Use of Marketing Information in Consumer and Industrial Firms," *Journal of Marketing Research*, February 1987, pp. 114–118.

Chapter 3

1. John Goodman and David Beinhacker. "By the Numbers," *Quirk's Marketing Research Review*, October 2003, pp. 18, 82.

2. "Survey Says: BtoB Database Marketers Are All Grown Up," *BtoB*, October 8, 2007, p. 26.

3. "A Potent New Tool for Selling Database Marketing," *BusinessWeek*, September 5, 1994, pp. 56–62.

4. Joan Raymond, "Home Field Advantage," *American Demographics*, April 2001, pp. 34–36.

5. "What've You Done for Us Lately?" *BusinessWeek*, April 23, 1999, pp. 24–34.

6. Gordon Plutsky, "Behavioral Targeting: Does It Make Sense for a Company?" *www.cmo.com*, accessed June 17, 2010.

7. "Exploring Ways to Build a Better Consumer Profile," *Wall Street Journal*, March 15, 2010, p. B4.

8. "Connect the Thoughts," *Adweek Media*, June 29, 2009, pp. 10–11.

9. Ibid.

10. "Behave," *Marketing News*, September 15, 2008, pp. 13–15.

11. "Sites Feed Personal Details to New Tracking Industry," *http://online.wsj.com*, July 31, 2010.

12. Ibid.

13. "Tracking Is an Assault on Liberty, with Real Dangers," *Wall Street Journal*, August 7–8, 2010, pp. W1–W2.

14. "Scrapers Dig Deep for Data on Web," *Wall Street Journal*, October 12, 2010, pp. A1, A18.

15. Ibid.

16. Ibid.

17. "To Stem Privacy Abuses, Industry Groups Will Track Web Trackers," *Wall Street Journal*, June 24, 2010, pp. B1–B2.

18. *www.privacy.org*, February 13, 2001.

19. "The Great Data Heist," *Fortune*, May 16, 2005, pp. 66–75.

20. "Choice Point to Exit Non-FCRA, Consumer-Sensitive Data Markets," *www.choicepoint.com*, March 4, 2005.

21. "Hackers Aren't Only Threat to Privacy," *Wall Street Journal*, June 23, 2010, p. B5.

22. Ibid.

23. "On My Mind: The Privacy Hoax: Consumers Say They Care about Internet Privacy but Don't Act That Way. Let the Market Rule," *Forbes*, October 14, 2002, pp. 42–44.

24. Joseph Rydholm, "Report shows the Changing Face of Motherhood," *Quirk's Marketing Research Review*, June 2010, pp. 76–77.

Chapter 4

1. Projections by the authors, October 2010.

2. "Second Half of '09 Could Set Research in Motion," *Quirk's Marketing Research Review*, July 2009, p. 80. Forecast updated by the authors.

3. Marilyn Rausch, "Qualities of a Beginning Moderator," *Quirk's Marketing Research Review*, December 1996, p. 24. Reprinted by permission of *Quirk's Marketing Research Review*; also see Tom Neveril, "Ten Qualities for Qualitative Researchers," *Quirk's Marketing Research Review*, June 2004, pp. 18–21.

4. Dennis Rook, "Out of Focus Groups," *Marketing Research*, Summer 2003, pp. 10–15.

5. "Selecting a Moderator," *Quirk's Marketing Research Review*, May 2010, p. 68.

6. "How to Make Sure Your Moderator Does Great Groups," *Quirk's Marketing Research Review*, March 2009, pp. 16–18.

7. Jacob Brown, "For Best Results, Plan Ahead," *Quirk's Marketing Research Review*, November 2005, pp. 44–47.

8. "In My Professional Opinion," *Quirk's Marketing Research Review*, May 2009, pp. 52–55.

9. "Dealing with the Digresser," *Quirk's Marketing Research Review*, December 2008, pp. 32–35.

10. Gerald Berstell and Denise Nitterhouse, "Asking All the Right Questions," *Marketing Research,* Fall 2001, pp. 15–20.

11. "One-on-Ones Put the Quality in Qualitative," *Quirk's Marketing Research Review*, November 2006, pp. 16–18.

12. Jennifer Haid, "Understand the Mind of the Market," *Quirk's Marketing Research Review*, December 2004, pp. 26–31.

13. Carla Penel and Will Leskin, "Mixing Art and Science," *Quirk's Marketing Research Review*, May 2006, pp. 48–50.

14. "Toward a Broader Definition," *Quirk's Marketing Research Review*, May 2006, p. 64.

15. The material on analogies is from Andrew Cutler, "What's the Real Story?" *Quirk's Marketing Research Review*, December 2006, pp. 38–45.

16. The material on personification is from Andrew Cutler, "What's the Real Story?" *Quirk's Marketing Research Review*, December 2006, pp. 38–45.

17. Ronald Lieber, "Storytelling: A New Way to Get Closer to Your Customer," *Fortune*, February 3, 1997, pp. 102–110; see also "Marketers Seek the Naked Truth in Consumers' Psyches," *Wall Street Journal*, May 30, 1997, pp. B1, B13; for details on Zaltman's technique, see Gwendolyn Catchings-Castello, "The ZMET Alternative," *Marketing Research,* Summer 2000, pp. 6–12.

18. Tom Neveril, "I'll Always Go Back to That Hotel," *Quirk's Marketing Research Review*, December 2009, p. 42.

19. Joseph Rydholm, "Steering In the Right Direction," *Quirk's Marketing Research Review*, May 2010, pp. 26–32.

Chapter 5

1. "Research Department As Bellwether?" *Quirk's Marketing Research Review*, June 2005, p. 8; and "Industry Study Finds Researchers Struggling, Adapting," *Quirk's Marketing Research Review*, December 2009, pp. 160–161.

2. The Respondent Cooperation and Industry Image Survey (New York: Council for Marketing and Opinion Research, 2003), p. 2; also see Joseph Rydholm, "A Cooperative Effort on Cooperation," *Quirk's Marketing Research Review*, November 2006, pp. 137–138; Chezy Ofir, Itamar Simonson, and Song-Oh Yoon, "The Robustness of the Effects of Consumers' Participation in Marketing Research: The Case of Service Quality Evaluation," *Journal of Marketing Research*, November 2009, pp. 105–114; and Bert Weijters, Niels Schillewaert, and Maggie Geuens, "Assessing Response, Styles across Modes of Data Collection," *Journal of The Academy of Marketing Science,* Fall 2008, pp. 409–422.

3. "SPSS Debuts Advancement in Predictive Dealing," *Quirk's Marketing Research Review*, January 2009, p. 12.

4. S.J. Blumberg and J.V. Luke, "Wireless Substitution: Early Release of Estimates from the National Health Interview Survey, July–December 2009." National Center for Health Statistics, May 2010. Available online: *www.cdc.gov/nchs/data/nhis/earlyrelease/wireless201005.htm.*

5. "Cellphone Numbers Just Don't Add Much to Political Polling," *Wall Street Journal*, February 1, 2008, p. 131; and "Be Mindful of Cellphone Interviews," *Marketing Management,* Summer 2009, p. 4.

6. "Calling Cell Phones—The FCC Makes a Bad Regulation Worse," *Quirk's Marketing Research Review*, July 2010, pp. 18–20.

7. For a high-tech variation of the self-administered questionnaire, see John Weisberg, "The MCAPI Primer," *Quirk's Marketing Research Review*, February 2003, pp. 24–34; see also Karl Feld and Steven Wygant, "Einterviewers Add Human Touch to Web-Based Research," *Quirk's Marketing Research Review*, July–August 2000, pp. 36–41.

8. "Mail Surveys—The Right Alternative," *Quirk's Marketing Research Review*, July–August 2005, p. 18.

9. SurveySpot Panel, April 2004.

10. Amanda Lenhart, Rich Ling, Scott Campbell, and Kristen Purcell, "Teens and Mobile Phones," Pew Research Center, April 20, 2010.

Chapter 6

1. "Internet Usage Statistics: The Internet Big Picture—World Internet Users and Population Stats," *www.internetworldstats.com/stat.htm*.

2. Kira Signer and Andy Korman, "One Billion and Growing," *Quirk's Marketing Research Review*, July/August 2006, pp. 62–67.

3. Ibid.

4. Conversation with Craig Stevens, EVP of Research Now Market Research, based on company research, November 2, 2007; also see "Market Research," *Marketing News*, September 15, 2007, p. 16.

5. Ibid.

6. Tim Macer and Sheila Wilson, "Online Makes More Inroads," *Quirk's Marketing Research Review*, February 2007, pp. 50–58.

7. "Blog Analysis as Market Research," by Jeffrey Henning, *http://blog.vovici.com/blog/bid/21872/Blog-Analysis-as-Market-Research*, September 23, 2009.

8. This section is from *www.lib.berkeley.edu/TeachingLib/Guides/Internet/Strategies.html*.

9. This section is adapted from Nick Wingfield, "A Marketer's Dream," *Wall Street Journal*, December 7, 1998, p. R20.

10. Kate Maddox, "Virtual Panels Add Real Insight for Marketers," *Advertising Age*, June 29, 1998, pp. 34, 40; and "Turning the Focus Online," *Marketing News*, February 28, 2000, p. 15; see also "The Hows, Whys, Whens and Wheres of Online Focus Groups," *MRA Alert*, December 1999, p. 21, and "Online Group Messaging," *Marketing News*, September 1, 2007, p. 24.

11. "How to Use Online Focus Groups," *www.focusgrouptips.com/online-focus-groups.html*.

12. Hy Mariampolski and Pat Sabena, "Qualitative Research Develops in China," *Quirk's Marketing Research Review*, December 2002, pp. 44–49.

13. Vauhini Vara, "Researchers Mine Web for Focus Groups," *Wall Street Journal*, November 17, 2007, p. B3E.

14. Gregory S. Heist, "Beyond Brand Building," *Quirk's Marketing Research Review*, July/August 2007, pp. 62–67.

15. Ibid.

16. Ibid.

17. "Online Depth Interviews," *www.focusgrouproom.com/depth.php.*

18. "Internet-Adapted Qualitative Techniques: Time Extended Online Dept Interviews," *www.decisionanalyst.com/Services/OnlineQualitative.dai.*

19. Amy Savin, "Liven Up Your Qualitative with These Online Solutions," *Quirk's Marketing Research Review,* December 2009, p. 24.

20. Chris Yalonis, "The Revolution in e-Research," *CASRO Marketing Research Journal,* 1999, pp. 131–133; "The Power of On-line Research," *Quirk's Marketing Research Review,* April 2000, pp. 46–48; Bill MacElroy, "The Need for Speed," *Quirk's Marketing Research Review,* July–August 2002, pp. 22–27; Cristina Mititelu, "Internet Surveys: Limits and Beyond Limits," *Quirk's Marketing Research Review,* January 2003, pp. 30–33; Nina Ray, "Cybersurveys Come of Age," *Marketing Research,* Spring 2003, pp. 32–37; "Online Market Research Booming, According to Survey," *Quirk's Marketing Research Review,* January 2005; Roger Gates, "Internet Data Collection So Far," speech given to Kaiser Permanente, May 2005; and Gabe Gelb, "Online Options Change Biz a Little—And a Lot," *Marketing News,* November 1, 2006, pp. 23–24.

21. Misha Neverov and Robert Schieffer, "Tips on Conducting Research in Russia: From an Old Order, a New Frontier," *Quirk's Marketing Research Review,* November 2009, p. 42.

22. Gates, "Internet Data Collection So Far."

23. Lee Smith, "Online Research's Time Has Come as a Proven Methodology," *CASRO Journal,* 2002, pp. 45–50.

24. Bill MacElroy, "International Growth of Web Survey Activity," *Quirk's Marketing Research Review,* November 2000, pp. 48–51.

25. "Tips Offer Better Response Rates, Engaging Surveys," *Marketing News,* April 1, 2007, p. 28.

26. *www.comscore.com/custom-research/sample.asp.* Also referenced by Mary Beth Weber, Sigma Validation at AMA 2005 Marketing Research Conference, Boston, September 25–28, 2005, "Why Validate Internet Research?"

27. "US Mobile Web Usage Grew 110 Percent Last Year," *http://techcrunch .com/2010/01/05quantcast-mobile-web-apple-android/.*

28. Tim Snaith, "Mobile Research—The Fifth Methodology? Like the Early Days of Online Research, Opportunities Exist as Questions Persist," *Quirk's Marketing Research Review,* August 2009, p. 26.

29. Birgi Martin, "Research-to-Go," *Quirk's Marketing Research Review,* November 2007, pp. 68–72.

30. Ibid.

31. "Good Things Come to Brands That Give," *Brandweek,* March 19, 2007, p. 6.

Chapter 7

1. "Loose Change, Lotion, and Expired Coupons," *Quirk's Marketing Research Review,* February 2008, p. 20.

2. Author's estimate.

3. "The Chocolate War," *Marketing Research,* Winter 2005, p. 4.

4. "Paying More to Get More," *Quirk's Marketing Research Review,* December 2008, p. 44.

5. "Business Ethnography and the Discipline of Anthropology," *Quirk's Marketing Research Review*, February 2009, pp. 20–27; also see "Watch Me As I Buy," *Quirk's Marketing Research Review*, February 2010, pp. 32–35.

6. "The Science of Desire," *BusinessWeek*, June 5, 2006, p. 104.

7. "Trendy Method or Essential Tool?" *Quirk's Marketing Research Review*, February 2009, pp. 34–37.

8. Jerry Thomas, "Worth a Thousand Words," *Decision Analyst Flyer*, 2006.

9. "Mystery Shopper," *Smart Money*, December 2005, p. 98.

10. Randall Brandt, "Improve the Customer Experience," *Quirk's Marketing Research Review*, January 2006, p. 68.

11. Newl Templin, "Undercover with a Hotel Spy," *Wall Street Journal*, May 12, 1999, pp. B1, B12; permission conveyed through Copyright Clearance Center, Inc., and Celina Abernathy, Sonic Drive-In. Republished with permission of the *Wall Street Journal*.

12. Rebecca Gardyn, "What's on Your Mind?" *American Demographics*, April 2000, pp. 31–33.

13. "Brain Scanning Surprises Researchers in Sunscreen Study," *Quirk's Marketing Research Review*, October 2010, p. 6; also see "This Is Your Brain on Advertising," *Quirk's Marketing Research Review*, August 2009, pp. 32–35.

14. John Cacioppo and Richard Petty, "Physiological Responses and Advertising Effects," *Psychology and Marketing*, Summer 1985, pp. 115–126; and Jack Shimell, "Testing Ads Using Galvanic Skin Response Measurements," *Quirk's Marketing Research Review*, March 2002, pp. 46–55.

15. "Check Your Head," *Marketing News*, March 30, 2009, p. 22.

16. "Tobii Glasses Aim to Make Eye-Tracking More Mobile," *Quirk's Marketing Research Review*, October 2010, p. 14.

17. "The Proof Is in the Pupil," *Quirk's Marketing Research Review*, April 2009, pp. 38–42.

18. Andy Rasking, "A Face Any Business Can Trust," *Business 2.0*, December 2003, pp. 58–60.

19. Ibid; also see Dan Hill, "What Lies Beneath," *Quirk's Marketing Research Review*, October 2006, pp. 68–74.

20. "Billboards That Can See You," *Wall Street Journal*, September 3, 2010, p. B5; and "Ad Displays Track Age," *Wall Street Journal*, February 3, 2010, p. B5.

21. *www.pretesting.com/print.html*, November 8, 2010.

22. "Cracking the Code," *AdWeek Media*, August 17, 2009, pp. 1–4.

23. "Nielsen Lands Data Deal," *Wall Street Journal*, December 2, 2008, p. B7.

24. "Media Measurement on the Move," *Brandweek*, February 10, 2010, p. M4.

25. *www.symphonyiri.com*, accessed November 8, 2010.

26. "Cookies Cause Bitter Backlash," *Wall Street Journal*, September 20, 2010, pp. B1–B2.

27. "Target-Marketing Becomes More Communal," *Wall Street Journal*, November 5, 2009, p. B10

28. "The Web's New Gold Mine: Your Secrets," *Wall Street Journal*, July 31–August 1, 2010, pp. W1–W2.

29. "A Web Pioneer Profiles Users by Name," *Wall Street Journal*, October 25, 2010, pp. A1, A16.

30. *www.comscore.com*, accessed November 8, 2010.

31. "Everyone Hates comScore," *Fortune*, September 29, 2008, pp. 60–62.

32. "By the Numbers: Social Networks," *Fortune*, September 6, 2010, p. 34.

33. Ibid.

34. "Does UGC Make You Say Ugh?" *Quirk's Marketing Research Review*, August 2010, pp. 24–28.

35. "Making Sense of the Chatter," *Quirk's Marketing Research Review*, August 2010, pp. 48–51.

36. "Does UGC Make . . ."

37. Raymond R. Burke, "Virtual Shopping: Breakthrough in Marketing Research," *Harvard Business Review*, March/April 1996, pp. 120–131.

38. Ellen Byron, "A Virtual View of the Store Aisle," *Wall Street Journal*, October 3, 2007, pp. B1, B12.

39. Ibid.

40. Ibid.; also see "Virtual Shopping, Real Results, *Brandweek*, April 16, 2009, pp. 16–18.

41. Maren Elwood, "Of Stoves and Laptops," *Quirk's Marketing Research Review*, May 2010, pp. 42–45.

Chapter 8

1. Thomas D. Cook and Donald T. Campbell, *Experimentation: Design Analysis Issues for Field Settings* (Chicago: Rand McNally, 1979).

2. See Claire Selltiz et al., *Research in Social Relations*, rev. ed. (New York: Holt, Rinehart & Winston, 1959), pp. 80–82.

3. A good example of a laboratory experiment is described in Caroll Mohn, "Simulated-Purchase 'Chip' Testing vs. Trade-Off Conjoint Analysis—Coca-Cola's Experience," *Marketing Research,* March 1990, pp. 49–54.

4. A. G. Sawyer, "Demand Artifacts in Laboratory: Experiments in Consumer Research," *Journal of Consumer Research*, March 1975, pp. 181–201; and N. Giges, "No Miracle in Small Miracle: Story Behind Failure," *Advertising Age*, August 1989, p. 76.

5. Natasha Singer, "The Fountain of Old Age," *The New York Times* February 6, 2011. Available at *www.nytimes.com/2011/02/06/business/06aging.html*, accessed March 3, 2011.

6. John G. Lynch, "On the External Validity of Experiments in Consumer Research," *Journal of Consumer Research*, December 1982, pp. 225–239.

7. For a more detailed discussion of this and other experimental issues, see Thomas D. Cook and Donald T. Campbell, "The Design and Conduct of Quasi-Experiments and True Experiments in Field Settings," in M. Dunnette, ed., *Handbook of Industrial and Organizational Psychology* (Skokie, IL: Rand McNally, 1978).

8. Ibid.

9. Bob Gertsley, "Data Use: The Insidious Top-Box and Its Effects on Measuring Line Share," *Quirk's Marketing Research Review*, August 2008, p. 20.

10. For further discussion of the characteristics of various types of experimental designs, see Donald T. Campbell and Julian C. Stanley, *Experimental and Quasi-Experimental Design for Research* (Chicago: Rand McNally, 1966); see also Richard Bagozzi and Youjar Ti, "On the Use of Structural Equation Models in Experimental Design," *Journal of Marketing Research*, August 1989, pp. 225–270.

11. Thomas D. Cook and Donald T. Campbell, *Quasi-Experimentation: Design and Analysis Issues for Field Settings* (Boston: Houghton Mifflin, 1979), p. 56.

12. T. Karger, "Test Marketing as Dress Rehearsals," *Journal of Consumer Marketing*, Fall 1985, pp. 49–55; Tim Harris, "Marketing Research Passes Toy Marketer Test," *Advertising Age*, August 24, 1987, pp. 1, 8; John L. Carefoot, "Marketing and Experimental Designs in Marketing Research: Uses and Misuses," *Marketing News*, June 7, 1993, p. 21; and Jim Miller and Sheila Lundy, "Test Marketing Plugs into the Internet," *Consumer Insights*, Spring 2002, p. 23.

13. Norma Ramage, "Testing, Testing 1–2–3," *Marketing Magazine*, July 18, 2005.

14. Gilbert A. Churchill, Jr., *Basic Marketing Research*, 4th ed. (Fort Worth, TX: Dryden Press, 2001), pp. 144–145.

15. Prince, Melvin "Choosing Simulated Test Marketing Systems," *Marketing Research*, September 1992, pp. 14–16.

16. Ibid.

17. Joseph Rydholm, "To Test or Not to Test," *Quirk's Marketing Research Review*, February 1992, pp. 61–62.

18. "Test Marketing Is Valuable, but It's Often Abused," *Marketing News*, January 2, 1987, p. 40.

19. Deborah L. Vence, "Proper Message, Design in Global Markets Require Tests," *Marketing News*, September 1, 2006, pp. 18–25.

20. "Miller to Test Market Low-Cal Craft Beers in Minneapolis," *Minneapolis–St. Paul Business Journal*, December 14, 2007.

21. Roger Fillion, "Denver Test Market for Beer Ads," *Rocky Mountain News*, July 4, 2006.

22. Jeremiah McWilliams, "Anheuser-Busch Test Markets New Vodka Brand," *St. Louis Post–Dispatch*, November 27, 2007.

23. Dina Berta, "Utah City Turns Out to be Best Test Market for Brazilian Concept," *Nation's Restaurant News*, September 22, 2003.

Chapter 9

1. Adapted from Brian Toyne and Peter G.P. Walters, *Global Marketing Management: A Strategic Perspective* (Boston: Allyn & Bacon, 1989), p. 201. Used with permission of Allyn & Bacon.

2. F. N. Kerlinger, *Foundations of Behavioral Research*, 3rd ed. (New York: Rinehart and Winston, 1986), p. 403; see also Mel Crask and R. J. Fox, "An Exploration of the Internal Properties of Three Commonly Used Research Scales," *Journal of Marketing Research Society*, October 1987, pp. 317–319.

3. Adapted from Claire Selltiz, Laurence Wrightsman, and Stuart Cook, *Research Methods in Social Relations*, 3rd ed. (New York: Holt Rinehart and Winston, 1976), pp. 164–168.

4. Bill MacElroy, "The Anonymity Gradient," *Quirk's Marketing Research Review*, October 1997, pp. 34–35.

5. See Edward McQuarrie, "Integration of Construct and External Validity by Means of Proximal Similarity: Implications for Laboratory Experiments in Marketing," *Journal of Business Research,* February 2004, pp. 142–153.

6. Adapted from William Trochim, *Research Methods Knowledge Base, www.atomicdog. com/trochim,* October 20, 2006.

7. Gerald Albaum, Catherine Roster, Julie H. Yu, and Robert D. Rogers, "Simple Rating Scale Formats: Exploring Extreme Response," *International Journal of Market Research, 49,* no. 5, 2007, pp. 633–649.

8. For an excellent discussion of the semantic differential, see Charles E. Osgood, George Suci, and Percy Tannenbaum, *The Measurement of Meaning* (Urbana: University of Illinois Press, 1957). Also see Karin Braunsberger and Roger Gates, "Developing Inventories for Satisfaction and Likert Scales in a Service Environment," *Journal of Services Marketing, 23,* no. 4, 2009, pp. 219–225.

9. Ibid., pp. 140–153, 192, 193; see also William D. Barclay, "The Semantic Differential as an Index of Brand Attitude," *Journal of Advertising Research,* March 1964, pp. 30–33.

10. Theodore Clevenger, Jr., and Gilbert A. Lazier, "Measurement of Corporate Images by the Semantic Differential," *Journal of Marketing Research,* February 1965, pp. 80–82.

11. Michael J. Etzel, Terrell G. Williams, John C. Rogers, and Douglas J. Lincoln, "The Comparability of Three Stapel Forms in a Marketing Setting," in Ronald F. Bush and Shelby D. Hunt, eds., *Marketing Theory: Philosophy of Science Perspectives* (Chicago: American Marketing Association, 1982), pp. 303–306.

12. An excellent article on purchase intent is Pierre Chandon, Vicki Morwitz, and Werner Reinartz, "Do Intentions Really Predict Behavior? Self-Generated Validity Effects in Survey Research," *Journal of Marketing,* April 2005, pp. 1–14.

13. Albert Bemmaor, "Predicting Behavior from Intention-to-Buy Measures: The Parametric Case," *Journal of Marketing Research,* May 1995, pp. 176–191.

14. We use a more conservative set of weights than those recommended by Linda Jamieson and Frank Bass, "Adjusting Stated Intention Measures to Predict Trial Purchase of New Products: A Comparison of Models and Methods," *Journal of Marketing Research,* August 1989, pp. 336–345.

15. William O. and Richard G. Netemeyer, *Handbook of Marketing Scales,* 2nd ed. (Newbury Park, CA: Sage Publications, 1999), pp. 1–9.

16. Brian Engelland, Bruce Alford, and Ron Taylor, "Cautions and Precautions on the Use of Borrowed Scales in Marketing Research," *Proceedings: Society for Marketing Advances,* November 2001.

17. J. A. Krosnick and L. R. Fabrigar, "Designing Rating Scales for Effective Measurement in Surveys," in L. Lybert, M. Collins, L. Decker, E. Deleeuw, C. Dippo, N. Schwarz, and D. Trewing, eds., *Survey Measurement and Process Quality* (New York: Wiley-Interscience, 1997). Also see Madhubalan Viswanathan, Seymore Sudman, and Michael Johnson, "Maximum Versus Meaningful Discrimination in Scale Response: Implications for Validity Measurement of Consumer Perceptions about Products," *Journal of Business Review,* February 2004, pp. 108–124.

18. Tim Jastrzembski and Barbara Leable, "Unearthing the Truth," *Quirks Marketing Research Review,* November 2002, pp. 20–21, 78–80.

Chapter 10

1. Neil Kalt, "Address Objectives without Objections," *Quirk's Marketing Research Review*, May 2009, pp. 58–64.

2. Matt Schroder, "Laddering Showed Infiniti How Drivers Views Its Around-View Monitor Technology" *Quirk's Marketing Research Review*, October 2009, p. 26.

3. This section is adapted from Naomi Henderson, "The Power of Probing," Marketing Research, Winter 2007, pp. 38–39.

4. Ibid.

5. "Intelligent Survey Design," *Quirk's Marketing Research Review*, July 2010, pp. 42–46.

6. "Ask and You Shall Receive," *Quirk's Marketing Research Review*, October 2010, pp. 66–68.

7. *www.CMOR.org,* June 15, 2005; also see "A Playbook for Creating Survey Introductions for Online Panels," *Quirk's Marketing Research Review*, March 24, 2009.

8. Lynn Newmann, "That's a Good Question," *American Demographics*, June 1995, pp. 10–15. *Reprinted from American Demographics* with permission. Copyright © 1995, Cowles business Media, Ithaca, New York.

9. *www.sawtooth.com,* November 15, 2010.

10. "Could Researchers Get Answers from Facebook Questions?" *Quirk's Marketing Research Review*, November 2010, p. 6.

11. Internal company documents supplied to the authors by M/A/R/C, Inc.

12. Internal company documents supplied to the authors by M/A/R/C, Inc.

13. Joseph Rydhol, "New Product Survey Plumbs Consumer Mind–Sets," *Quirk's Marketing Research Review*, March 2010, pp. 68–69.

Chapter 11

1. For excellent discussions of sampling, see Seymour Sudman, *Applied Sampling* (New York: Academic Press, 1976), and L. J. Kish, *Survey Sampling* (New York: John Wiley & Sons, 1965).

2. "Report of the President's Blue Ribbon Panel on the Census," *American Statistical Association,* 2003; and Brad Edmondson, "The Cliffhanger Census," *American Demographics,* January 1998, p. 2.

3. Sudman, *Applied Sampling*, pp. 63–67.

4. G. J. Glasser and G. D. Metzger, "Random-Digit Dialing as a Method of Telephone Sampling," *Journal of Marketing Research,* February 1972, pp. 59–64; and S. Roslow and L. Roslow, "Unlisted Phone Subscribers Are Different," *Journal of Advertising,* August 1972, pp. 59–64.

5. Charles D. Cowan, "Using Multiple Sample Frames to Improve Survey Coverage, Quality, and Costs," *Marketing Research,* December 1991, pp. 66–69.

6. James McClove and P. George Benson, *Statistics for Business and Economics* (San Francisco: Dellen Publishing, 1988), pp. 184–185; and "Probability Sampling in the Real World," *CATI NEWS* (Summer 1993), pp. 1, 4–6; and Susie Sangren, "Survey and Sampling in an Imperfect World," *Quirk's Marketing Research Review,* April 2000, pp. 16, 66–69.

7. Survey Sampling International.

8. Richard M. Jaeger, *Sampling in Education and the Social Sciences* (New York: Longman, 1984), pp. 28–35.

9. Lewis C. Winters, "What's New in Telephone Sampling Technology?" *Marketing Research,* March 1990, pp. 80–82; and *A Survey Researcher's Handbook of Industry Terminology and Definitions* (Fairfield, CT: Survey Sampling, 1992), pp. 3–20.

10. For discussions of related issues, see John E. Swan, Stephen J. O'Connor, and Seug Doug Lee, "A Framework for Testing Sampling Bias and Methods of Bias Reduction in a Telephone Survey," *Marketing Research,* December 1991, pp. 23–34; Charles D. Cowan, "Coverage Issues in Sample Surveys: A Component of Measurement Error," *Marketing Research,* June 1991, pp. 65–68; and Susie Sangren, "Survey and Sampling in an Imperfect World," *Quirk's Marketing Research Review,* April 2000, pp. 16, 66–69.

11. Michael A. Fallig and Derek Allen, "An Examination of Strategies for Panel-Blending," *Quirk's Marketing Research Review,* July 2009, p. 50.

12. For an excellent discussion of stratified sampling, see William G. Cochran, *Sampling Techniques*, 2nd ed. (New York: John Wiley & Sons, 1963); and Sangren, "Survey and Sampling in an Imperfect World," pp. 16, 66–69.

13. Sudman, *Applied Sampling*, pp. 110–121.

14. Ibid.

15. Earl R. Babbie, *The Practice of Social Research*, 2nd ed. (Belmont, CA: Wadsworth Publishing, 1979), p. 167.

16. "Convenience Sampling Outpacing Probability Sampling" (Fairfield, CT: Survey Sampling, March 1994), p. 4.

17. Leo A. Goodman, "Snowball Sampling," *Annuals of Mathematical Statistics, 32,* 1961, pp. 148–170.

18. Douglas Rivers, "Fulfilling the Promise of the Web," *Quirk's Marketing Research Review,* February 2000, pp. 34–41.

19. Roger Gates and Michael Foytik, "Implementing an HRA on the Internet: Lessons Learned," *Society of Prospective Medicine,* October 1998.

20. Beth Clarkson, "Research and the Internet: A Winning Combination," *Quirk's Marketing Research Review,* July 1999, pp. 46–51.

21. Gates and Foytik, "Implementing an HRA on the Internet."

22. "New Research from Survey Sampling International Suggests Sample Blending Results in Better Data Quality," *Market Research Bulletin,* April 26, 2010. Available at *http://marketresearchbulletin.com/?p5537* (accessed March 9, 2011).

Chapter 12

1. Tom McGoldrick, David Hyatt, and Lori Laffin., "How Big Is Big Enough?" *Marketing Tools,* May 1998, pp. 54–58.

2. McGoldrick et al., "How Big Is Big Enough?" pp. 54–58.

3. Lafayette Jones, "A Case for Ethnic Sampling," *Promo,* October 1, 2000, p. 12.

4. Gang Xu, "Estimating Sample Size for a Descriptive Study in Quantitative Research," *Quirk's Marketing Research Review,* June 1999, pp. 14, 52–53.

5. Susie Sangren, "A Simple Solution to Nagging Questions about survey sample size and validity," *Quirk's Marketing Research Review,* January 1999, pp. 18, 53.

6. Xu, "Estimating Sample Size for a Descriptive Study in Quantitative Research."

7. For discussions of these techniques, see Bill Williams, *A Sampler on Sampling* (New York: John Wiley & Sons, 1978); and Richard Jaeger, *Sampling in Education and the Social Sciences* (New York: Longman, 1984).

8. Survey Sampling International, "Estimate Sample Size with Precision," *The Frame,* January 1999, p. 1.

9. David Anderson, Dennis Sweeney, and Thomas Williams, *Statistics for Business and Economics*, 4th ed. (St. Paul, MN: West Publishing, 1990), pp. 355–357.

Chapter 13

1. Raymond Raud and Michael A. Fallig, "Automating the Coding Process with Neural Networks," *Quirk's Marketing Research Review*, May 1993, pp. 14–16, 40–47.

2. For information on semiotics, see Paul Cobley, Litza Jansz, and Richard Appignanesi, *Introducing Semiotics* (Melbourne Australia Totem Books, 1997); Marcel Danesi, *Of Cigarettes, High Heels and Other Interesting Things: An Introduction to Semiotics* (New York: St. Martin's Press, 1998); and Umberto Eco, *Semiotics and the Philosophy of Languages* (Bloomington: Indiana University Press, 1986).

3. Joseph Rydholm, "Scanning the Seas: Scannable Questionnaires Give Princess Cruises Accuracy and Quick Turnaround," *Quirk's Marketing Research Review,* May 1993, pp. 38–42.

4. Tim Macer, "Software Review: Q Data Analysis Software," *Quirk's Marketing Research Review,* August 2010, p. 20.

5. Hank Zucker, "What Is Significance?" *Quirk's Marketing Research Review*, March 1994, pp. 12, 14; Gordon A. Wyner, "How High is Up?" *Marketing Research,* Fall 1993, pp. 42–43; Gordon A. Wyner, "The Significance of Marketing Research," *Marketing Research,* Fall 1993, pp. 43–45; and Patrick M. Baldasare and Vikas Mittel, "The Use, Misuse and Abuse of Significance," *Quirk's Marketing Research Review,* November 1994, pp. 16, 32.

6. Thomas T. Semon, "Probability a Perennial Problem for Gamblers—and Also for Researchers." *Marketing News*, January 1999, p. 11

7. Terry H. Grapentine, "Statistical Significance Revisited," *Quirk's Marketing Research Review,* April 2011 pp. 18–23.

Chapter 14

1. Steve Lohr, "For Today's Graduate, Just One Word—Statistics," *The New York Times,* August 5, 2009. Available at *www.nytimes.com/2009/08/06/technology/06stats .html?_r=2&scp=1&sq=for+today%27s+graduate%2C+just+one+word%3A+statistics &st=nyt* (accessed April 12, 2011).

2. Joseph R. Garber, "Deadbeat Repellant," *Forbes,* February 14, 1994, p. 164.

3. For a thorough discussion of regression analysis, see Schroeder, Larry D., Sjoquist, David L., & Stephan, Paula E. (1986). *Understanding regression analysis: An introductory guide* (Sage Univesity Paper series on Quantitative Applications in the Social Sciences, series no. 07-057). Newbury Park, CA: Sage.

4. Charlotte H. Mason and William D. Perreault, Jr., "Collinear Power and Interpretation of Multiple Regression Analysis," *Journal of Marketing Research,* August 1991, pp. 268–280; Doug Grisaffe, "Appropriate Use of Regression in Customer Satisfaction Analyses: A Response to William McLauchlan," *Quirk's Marketing Review,* February 1993, pp. 10–17; and Terry Clark, "Managing Outliers: Qualitative Issues in the Handling of Extreme Observations in Market Research," *Marketing Research,* June 1989, pp. 31–45.

5. Joseph F. Hair, William C. Black, Barry J. Babin, and Rolph E. Anderson *Multivariate Data Analysis*, 7th ed. (New York: Prentice Hall, 2009).

6. See Girish Punj and David Stewart, "Cluster Analysis in Marketing Research: Review and Suggestions for Application," *Journal of Market Research,* May 1983, pp. 134–138; and G. Ray Funkhouser, Anindya Chatterjee, and Richard Parker, "Segmenting Samples," *Marketing Research,* Winter 1994, pp. 40–46.

7. Susie Sangren, "A Survey of Multivariate Methods Useful for Market Research," *Quirk's Marketing Research Review,* May 1999, pp. 16, 63–69.

8. This section is based on material prepared by Glen Jarboe; see also Paul Green, Donald Tull, and Gerald Albaum, *Research for Marketing Decision,* 5th ed. (Englewood Cliffs, NJ: Prentice Hall, 1998), pp. 553–573.

9. Dick Wittink and Phillipe Cattin, "Commercial Use of Conjoint Analysis: An Update," *Journal of Marketing,* July 1989, pp. 91–96; see also Rajeev Kohli, "Assessing Attribute Significance in Conjoint Analysis: Nonparametric Tests and Empirical Validation," *Journal of Marketing Research,* May 1988, pp. 123–133.

10. Examples of current issues and applications are provided in Richard Smallwood, "Using Conjoint Analysis for Price Optimization," *Quirk's Marketing Research Review,* October 1991, pp. 10–13; Paul E. Green, Abba M. Krieger, and Manoj K. Agarwal, "Adaptive Conjoint Analysis: Some Caveats and Suggestions," *Journal of Marketing Research,* May 1991, pp. 215–222; Paul E. Green and V. Srinivasan, "Conjoint Analysis in Marketing: New Developments with Implications for Research and Practice," *Journal of Marketing Research Review,* October 1990, pp. 3–19; Joseph Curry, "Determining Product Feature Price Sensitivities," *Quirk's Marketing Research Review,* November 1990, pp. 14–17; Gordon A. Wyner, "Customer-Based Pricing Research," *Marketing Research,* Spring 1993, pp. 50–52; Steven Struhl, "Discrete Choice Modeling Comes to the PC," *Quirk's Marketing Research Review,* May 1993, pp. 12–15, 36–41: Steven Struhl, "Discrete Choice: Understanding a Better Conjoint . . . ," *Quirk's Marketing Research Review,* June/July 1994, pp. 12–15, 36–39; Bashir A. Datoo, "Measuring Price Elasticity," *Marketing Research,* Spring 1994, pp. 30–34; Gordon A. Wyner, "Uses and Limitations of Conjoint Analysis—Part 1," *Marketing Research,* June 1992, pp. 12–44; Gordon A. Wyner, "Uses and Limitations of Conjoint Analysis—Part II," *Marketing Research,* September 1992, pp. 46–47; Yilian Yuan and Gang Xu, "Conjoint Analysis in Pharmaceutical Marketing Research," *Quirk's Marketing Research Review,* June 2001, pp. 18, 54–61; and Bryan Orme, "Assessing the Monetary Value of Attribute Levels with Conjoint Analysis: Warnings and Suggestions," *Quirk's Marketing Research Review,* May 2001, pp. 16, 44–47.

11. Mehmed Kantardzic, *Data Mining: Concepts, Models, Methods, and Algorithms,* ISBN 0471228524, Wiley-IEEE Press, 2002; and Peng, Y., Kou, G., Shi, Y., and Chen, Z., "A Descriptive Framework for the Field of Data Mining and Knowledge Discovery", *International Journal of Information Technology and Decision Making,* Vol. 7, Issue: 4, Page 639–682, 2008 (SCI, SSCI) http://dx.doi.org/10.1142/S0219622008003204

12. *www.thearling.com/text/dmwhite/dmwhite.htm.*

Chapter 15

1. Diane Schmalensee and A. Dawn Lesh, "Creating Win–Win Relationships," *Marketing Research,* Winter 2007, pp. 16–21.

2. Luke Williams and Timothy L. Keiningham, "How Deep Do You Go? When Presenting Research Results, Use Your Skill Set to Find Right Mix-of Detail and Perspective," *Quirk's Marketing Research Review,* May 2008, p. 76.

3. Joseph Rydholm, "What Do Clients Want from a Research Firm?" *Quirk's Marketing Research Review,* October 1996, p. 80.

4. John Walters and John Colias, "The Simple Secret to Effective Market Research," *CASRO Journal,* 2002, pp. 65–66.

5. The material on organizing a supplier firm is from Michael Mitrano, "Supplier Side: Organizing Your Company—Are Project Teams the Answer?" *Quirk's Marketing Research Review* (April 2002), pp. 20, 68.

6. Joshua Libresco, reprinted with permission from *Marketing News,* published by American Marketing Association, from "Advice for the Juggler", January 4, 1999, pp. 13, 23.

7. "Market Research Outsourcing—The India Growth Story," February 19, 2008, bporesearch@valuenotes.blz.

8. Ibid.

9. Susan Greco, "Choose or Lose." Reprinted with permission from *Inc.* magazine, February 2001. Copyright 1998 by Gruner & Jahr USA Publishing.

10. Kathleen Knight, "Finding and Retaining Research Staff: A Perspective," *Quirk's Marketing Research Review,* February 1998, pp. 18, 54. Reprinted by permission.

11. The sections on allocating the research budget, prioritizing projects, and retaining skilled staff are from Schmalensee and Lesh, "Creating Win–Win Relationships."

12. Ibid.

13. Ibid.

14. Ibid.

15. This section is adapted from Richard Snyder, *Quirk's Marketing Research Review,* November 2002, pp. 62–65.

16. Dana James, "Establish Your Place at the Table," *Marketing News,* September 16, 2002, pp. 1, 19–20; Keith Malo, "Raising Research's Profile," *Quirk's Marketing Research Review,* October 2007, pp. 76–85; and Michael Carlon, "Moving from Validation to Inspiration," *Quirk's Marketing Research Review,* October 2007, pp. 80–81.

17. Allison Enright, "Give 'em What They Need," *Marketing News,* February 1, 2008, p. 30.

18. Ibid.; also see Natalie Jobity and Jeff Scott, "Practices Make Perfect—Improving Research and Consulting Through Collaboration," *CASRO Journal,* 2002, pp. 19–24.

19. John Huppertz, "Passion vs. Dispassion," *Marketing Research,* Summer 2003, pp. 17–21.

20. Ibid.

21. Enright, "Give 'em What They Need."

INDEX